CONSTRUCTING ARCHITECTURE

ANDREA DEPLAZES (ED.)

CONSTRUCTING ARCHITECTURE
MATERIALS PROCESSES STRUCTURES
A HANDBOOK

THIRD, EXTENDED EDITION

Birkhäuser
Basel

Credits

Swiss Federal Institute of Technology, Zurich
Faculty of Architecture
Chair of Architecture and Technology III/IV
Prof. Andrea Deplazes
www.deplazes.arch.ethz.ch

Editing, concept and layout
Prof. Andrea Deplazes, Christoph Elsener, Sascha Roesler, Cordula Seger, Tobias Siegrist

Picture editors
Julia Buse, Janet Schacke

Cover design
Muriel Comby

Cover photo
Ruckstuhl AG Teppichfabrik
St. Urbanstrasse 21
CH-4901 Langenthal
www.ruckstuhl.com

Typesetting
Typink Srl., Bucharest
Third, extended edition 2013: Sven Schrape, Berlin

Collaborators since 1997
Stephan Achermann, Felix Ackerknecht, Patric Allemann, Oya Atalay Franck, Ozlem Ayan, Stefan Baumberger, Marcel Baumgartner, Martin Bischofberger, Dawit Benti, Ivana Bertolo-Kordic, Nik Biedermann, Matthias Blass, Tamara Bonzi, Sian Brehler, Gisela Brüllmann Roth, Kamenko Bucher, Ramun Capaul, Maud Châtelet, Zegeye Cherenet, Franca Comalini, Katja Dambacher, Nicole Deiss, Natalina Di Iorio, Alois Diethelm, Fabio Don, Christoph Elsener, Christine Enzmann, Serge Fayet Hemmi, Lukas Felder, Fabio Felippi, Eva Geering, Lorenzo Giuliani, Jasmin Grego, Céline Guibat, Daniel Gut, Kornelia Gysel, Martina Hauser, Dominik Herzog, Christian Hönger, Simone Hübscher, Marius Hug, Pascal Hunkeler, Tibor Joanelly, Dimitri Kaden, Thomas Käppeli, Roger Kästle, Sergej Klammer, Andreas Kohne, Rafael Kräutler, Zwi Kutner, David Leuthold, Robert Lüder, Michele Mambourg, Jan Meier, Thomas Melliger, Urs Meister, Maria Mohl Rodriguez, Peter Moor, Susanne Müller, Claudia Nussbaumer, Mauro Pausa, Thea Rauch, Sascha Roesler, Wolfgang Rossbauer, Martin Saarinen, Margarita Salmerón Espinosa, Maya Scheibler, Thomas Schwendener, Cordula Seger, Tobias Siegrist, Patrik Seiler, Roman Singer, Susanne Stacher, Katharina Stehrenberger, Mark van Kleef, Christa Vogt, Christoph Wieser, Barbara Wiskemann, Stephania Zgraggen, Raphael Zuber

Assistants since 1997
Thomas Allemann, Hanna Åkerstrom, Christof Ansorge, Stefan Bischof, Tamara Bonzi, Bettina Baumberger, Céline Bessire, Stefan Bischof, Michael Bösch, Martin Bucher, Andreas Buschmann, Julia Buse, Corina Cadisch, Ursina Caprez, Bori Csicsely, Johannes Dachsel, Ueli Degen, Christoph Heinrich Deiters, Angela Deuber, Martin-Ken Dubach, Cem Dutoit, Jonas Epper, Christiane Felber, Adrienne Fonyo, Simon Frommenwiler, Silvan Furger, Jean Lucien Gay, Jörg Grabfelder, Safia Hachemi, Pedja Hadzimanovic, Steffen Hägele, Steven Hänsler, Dominique Hasler, Philip Haspra, Valerie Heider, Theres Hollenstein, Ulrike Horn, Nadja Hutter, Harris Iliadis, Steffen Jürgensen, Thomas Kissling, Natalie Koerner, Lutz Kögler, Ariane Komeda, Katja Lässer, Phillipp Lehmann, Matthias Lehner, Andrea Linke, Mikael Ljunggren, Carmelia Maissen, David Mathyl, Sebastian Müller, Lisa Nestler, Mischa Obrecht, Anastasia Paschou, Ana Prikic, Jonas Ringli, Gian Salis, Janet Schacke, Hannes Schärer, Florian Schätz, Sara Schibler, Julian Schramek, Manuela Schubert, Cindy Schwenke, Eckart Schwerdtfeger, Katharina Schwiete, Matthias Stark, Martina Vogel, Christa Vogt, Claudia Vosti, Karen Wassung, Corinne Weber, Thomas Wirz, Helen Wyss

Translation into English:
Gerd H. Söffker, Philip Thrift (assistants: Carola Loth, Eva Rühle)
English copy editing of new texts of the third edition: Monica Buckland

This book is also available in a German (ISBN 978-3-03821-456-4, Hardcover; ISBN 978-3-03821-455-7, Softcover) and a French (ISBN 978-3-03821-453-3) language edition.

A CIP catalogue record for this book is available from the Library of Congress, Washington D.C., USA.

Bibliographic information published by the German National Library
The German National Library lists this publication in the Deutsche Nationalbibliografie; detailed bibliographic data are available on the Internet at http://dnb.dnb.de.

Third, extended edition 2013
© 2005 Birkhäuser Verlag GmbH, Basel
P.O. Box 44, CH-4009 Basel, Switzerland
Part of De Gruyter

Added to the third, extended edition is the folder "Archetypal forms of construction", a comparative overview of the content of this handbook.

Printed on acid-free paper produced from chlorine-free pulp. TCF ∞
Printed in Germany
ISBN 978-3-03821-451-9 (Hardcover)
ISBN 978-3-03821-452-6 (Softcover)

9 8 7 6 5 4 3 2 1   www.birkhauser.com

Contents

Contents

Floor

Roof

Stairs, lifts

STRUCTURES

Forms of construction

Contents

Preface

Andrea Deplazes, Christoph Elsener

"Constructing Architecture" describes that architectural position of architects which makes it possible for them to forge links between the planning of a project and its realisation, the competence to create coherence regarding content and subject. During the planning of a project this is reflected in the clarification and development of a design objective, and in the physical implementation becoming increasingly more clearly defined. When, for example, a literary work is translated into another language the use of the correct grammar or syntax is merely a technical prerequisite – a *conditio sine qua non*. The important thing is to reflect coherently the sense and the atmosphere of the original text, which in certain circumstances may itself have a specific influence on grammar and syntax. Architecture is similar: although it is not a language consisting of sounds, words or texts, it has a material vocabulary (modules), a constructive grammar (elements) and a structural syntax (structures). They are the fundamental prerequisites, a kind of "mechanics of architecture". This also includes the technical and structural basics which establish a set of rules and regulations of construction principles and know-how that can be learned and which are wholly independent of any particular design or construction project. Although these tools are logical in themselves they remain fragmentary, unrelated and therefore "senseless" until they are incorporated into a project.

Only in conjunction with a concept does a vigorous design process ensue in which the initially isolated technical and structural fragments are at once arranged to fill a consummate, architectural body. The fragments and the whole complement and influence each other. This is the step from construction to architecture, from assembly to tectonics.

Factors influencing the architectural form

All material has a shape, regardless of the existence of a forming will. An artefact raises the question: how did it gain its shape? We may distinguish between two approaches to answer this question. First, which external influences affect the development of a shape? This question suggests a number of factors, e.g. geographical and cultural aspects, as well as factors that are connected to the mentality and the history of a certain people, that unintentionally influence the shape. Second, which criteria determine the shape? This question focuses on the intent, on a range of criteria carefully chosen by the designer.

After all, the shape is the result of a complex interaction of different factors. Only this interaction of factors allows a sensible composition. Composition is not an inevitable result. Within the bounds of a logical solution there always exist different options.

Kenneth Frampton describes three important influencing factors: "Thus we may claim that the built invariably comes into existence out of the constantly evolving interplay of three converging vectors, the *topos*, the *typos*, and the *tectonic*." The term "tectonics" alone covers a broad range, encompassing the construction process from the materials up to the finished building. This book concentrates primarily on this range. However, the historico-cultural approach, as represented in some articles in this book, reminds us that the transitions between topos, typos and tectonics are fluid.

Structure of this book

The structure of the book, divided into the chapters "Materials – modules", "Elements" and "Structures", reflects the development process of architecture: starting with a single raw material via the joining of different building parts up to the finished building. This also points to a main objective of the book: it aims to show how much architectural expression depends on its constructional composition. In line with this goal the present work pays special attention to constructional aspects which create "sense", and in this aspect it differs from the albeit relevant but exclusively technology-focused literature. Technical requirements of raw materials and components are constantly checked with regard to their architectural effect. This approach leads to a chapter structure in which the reader will find sober detail drawings next to essay-like reflections, basic construction concepts next to specific

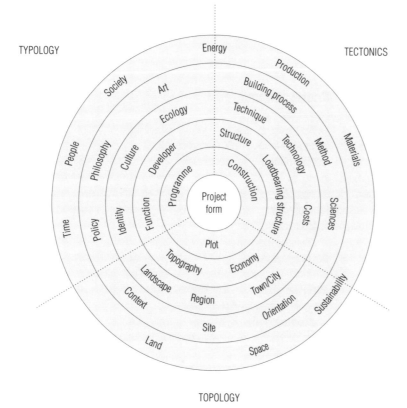

Fig. 1: Form-finding or form-developing processes

descriptions of construction processes, theoretical considerations next to practical ones. For reasons of clarity, however, the "holistic" view of the design processes advocated here has been arranged in a way that allows easy referencing. Besides the introductory essay thematic focal points occur repeatedly in the chapters, which help the reader to find his way around the book and make it possible to compare building materials and construction elements.

The term "properties of materials" covers descriptions of manufacturing methods, assembly and product ranges of the most important modern building materials: clay bricks, concrete, timber, steel, glass and insulating materials. The distinction between "concepts", "processes" and "system" points to the interaction of intellectual conception, construction process and building structure, which considerably influences the development of a constructional solution. "Concepts" describes analysis and interpretation procedures which have proved especially helpful during the development of construction systems. Under the heading "Processes" the reader will find descriptions of preparatory measures prior to starting work on site plus specific site assembly processes. "Systems" describes possible methods for joining modules and components to form coherent, structurally viable assemblies. The construction systems shown here are linked more closely to problems of architectural expression in the section titled "Systems in architecture". Reflections on particular buildings or special types of construction are united under the heading "Examples" and offer additional visual aids describing how construction-oriented thinking finally manifests itself in architecture.

The section entitled "Building performance issues" presents insights into the relationships between the construction and the performance of the building envelope.

The appendix contains a series of drawings, scale 1:20, which illustrate the complex build-up of layers in contemporary building envelopes. Plinths, wall and floor junctions, openings (doors and windows), as well as the roof, are still core areas in the realm of architectural construction. The construction forms presented are bound by a certain architectural concept and may not be generalised without prior examination.

A word for the autodidact

Subjects vary here as to the amount of material each is afforded. This is not implying any particular value, but reflects a working method focused on teaching. Furthermore, this book does not replace the subject material of lectures. It is rather a collection of diverse basic principles which were worked out at the Professorial Chair of Architecture and Construction at the ETH Zurich. Liability claims or claims of any other kind whatsoever cannot be entertained under any circumstances.

The best thing a university can hope to achieve is to turn the student into an autodidact. This includes acquiring the basics unaided, posing probing questions, intensive research, the formulation of hypotheses and the preparation of syntheses. Many topics in the foundation course are theses that are true not simply because they are printed in this book. It is rather that this book should be seen as a provisional collection of known and current architectural and technological issues – a platform for contemplating the complex business of architecture.

The sequence of architectural construction as an additive chain from small to large

Fig. 2: Earth
Mixing with cob and sand

Fig. 3: Clay bricks
Production, natural drying (in the air),
Pakistan

Fig. 4: Wall
Rediscovered remains of a house,
Lebanon

Fig. 5: Structural shell
Masonry building, under construction

Fig. 6: Structure
Hans Kollhoff, KNSM-Eiland housing
development, Amsterdam

1. Raw materials

According to Gottfried Semper the raw materials available as potential building materials prior to the first stage of processing can be classified into the following four categories according to their properties:

1. Flexible, tough, resistant to fracture, high absolute strength
2. Soft, plastic, capable of hardening, easy to join and retaining their given form in the hardened state
3. Linear forms, elastic, primarily *relatively* high resistance, i.e., to forces acting perpendicular to their length
4. Solid, dense, resistant to crushing and buckling, suitable for processing and for assembling to form solid systems

Owing to their properties, each of these four materials categories belongs, according to Semper, to a certain technical skill or category: textile art, ceramic art, tectonics (carpentry) or stereotomy (masonry).

This is based on the idea of "every technique has, so to speak, its own certain principal material which offers the most convenient means of producing the forms belonging to its original domains".

The raw material, however, remains "meaningless" in the architectural sense as long as it is "unreflected", i.e. its potential for cognition remains concealed.

The "selection" process itself (e.g. from undressed stones) in the form of a collection of modules, but also the preparatory work prior to building already form a planned stage of the work and consequently part of the first stage of production ("preparation").

2. Modules

The "building blocks" or "workpieces" form the smallest basic components intended for the construction. They are the result of a finishing process – a more or less complex and time-consuming production process:

– Dressed masonry units (blocks, slabs, squared and rough-hewn stones) are produced from irregular stones.
– Moulded and "cast" earths (clay bricks, ceramic tiles, air-dried, fired) or processed earths (cement, concrete) are produced from earths, sands and gravels (e.g. cob, clay).
– Prepared timber members (debarked logs, squared members, joists, boards, battens) are produced from linear, form-stable or elastic modules consisting of organic fibres (e.g. tree trunks, rods, branches).

All these modules exhibit their own inherent "tectonics", their own inherent jointing principles which are present in the second production stage: layering, interlocking, weaving, plastic formation ("modelling"), moulding, etc.

3. Elements

"Components" consisting of modules represent in a certain way the semi-finished goods of the second production stage (masonry walls and plates; walls; vaults and shells; floors and roofs).

Stability problems become evident during production and also during the ongoing assembly of the elements; these problems can be solved with the following measures:
– horizontal developments such as folds, corrugations, ribs
– vertical gradations with increasing height/depth
– formation of frames through the provision of stiffeners (diagonal stiffeners, supports as auxiliary constructions, corner stiffeners)

4. Structures

The third stage of production forms a "component fabric" whose subcomponents can be described as follows:

A. Loadbearing structure:
Precondition for the building structure. Only the elements necessary for the loadbearing functions (supporting, stabilising) are considered.
B. Building structure:
This is the interaction of all the elements required for the structure (supporting, separating for the purpose of creating spaces), sometimes also called "structural shell".
C. Interior layout structure:
This contains the realisation of a more or less complex sequence of internal spaces. The relationship between loadbearing structure, building structure and interior layout structure allows us to derive a "tectonics model". Tectonics in this sense is the physically visible part of this "higher bonding", the fabric of the architectural concept for the purpose of creating internal spaces.
D. Infrastructure:
All the permanently installed supply and disposal facilities necessary in a building. The relationship between the infrastructure and the building structure frequently results in conflicts.
E. Access structure:
Horizontal and vertical circulation routes and spaces. These include stairs and ramps plus the entrances to a building.

5. The structure

The structure is generated by:
Structure and process

Building – spaces – loadbearing structure
– tectonics
– "material fabric"
– loadbearing structure
– finishings and fittings
– infrastructure

Plan
– conception ("idea")
– draft design
– interpretation (significance)
– building documentation
– exchange of information (notation)
– chronology of actions

and

Production
– chronology of production stages
– logistics
– operative sequence
– jointing principles

Further reading
- Kenneth Frampton: *Studies in Tectonic Culture*, Cambridge (MA), 2001.
- Fritz Neumeyer: *Nachdenken über Architektur, Quellentexte zur Architekturtheorie*, Munich, 2002.
- Gottfried Semper: *Der Stil in den technischen und tektonischen Künsten oder praktische Ästhetik*, vol. I, Frankfurt a.M., Munich, 1860/1863 – English translation: *Style: Style in the Technical and Tectonic Arts; Practical Aesthetics*, Harry Francis Mallgrave (ed.), Los Angeles, 2004.

Solid and filigree construction

Christoph Wieser, Andrea Deplazes

On the occasion of a lecture on the "morphology of the architectural" at the ETH Zurich architecture theorist Kenneth Frampton drew on the works of Eugène Viollet-le-Duc and Gottfried Semper, who together pioneered the theory of architecture, to distinguish between the development of architectural forms from their origins as "earthworks" and "roofworks", or with the terms stereotomy (solid construction) and tectonics (filigree construction) that are used in architecture theory. While the term "earthwork" includes all the building techniques of solid wall construction (cob, pisé and adobe, clay-and-stone masonry, etc. and their stereotomic forms such as walls, arches, vaults and domes), the open "roofwork" encompasses all structures with linear and rodlike members – textile-like woven structures which span open spaces as "covers", forming the "roof", the overhead boundary to the space below. Timber engineering, with its layered, interwoven assembly, belongs to this category, as does industrialised steelwork from about 1800 onwards.

The principles of the structural formation in filigree construction were not new. They were known to us through anonymous and traditional timber buildings: conical and spherical domes made from straight and curved individual linear members, vertical solid timber construction, two- and three-dimensional frameworks (timber frames, timber studding), horizontal joist floors and roofs, and roof constructions (purlin and couple roofs, trussed frames) were the carpenter's daily bread. They were used principally wherever wood was readily available and a lightweight building material for medium spans was required. It was accepted that wood, in contrast to solid construction, was organic and hence not everlasting (fungal attack, rot, fire). For these reasons timber engineering has never seriously rivalled stereotomic solid construction nor superseded it.

Only after industrialised steel building technology was well established were questions raised about the hitherto undisputed tectonic principles of Western architecture. While in the case of solid construction the massiveness of the earth material finds its architectural expression in the archaic, and occasionally monumental character of stereotomy, the almost complete resolving of mass and massiveness (so-called sublimation) into the barely tangible skeleton or lattice framework of an ethereal phantom volume – the abstract Cartesian grid of a filigree construction – is drawn in space.[1]

The building and cultural revolution

In 1964 Sigfried Giedion was still maintaining that the issue of the origin of architecture was "very complex", as he writes in his book *The Eternal Present. A Contribution to Constancy and Change*. This is why – despite the tempting title – he does not explore this matter in detail.[2]

Instead, he confines himself to presenting the principal evolution, the content of which is backed up by later research. This evolution, in essence, extends from the simplest round or oval huts to rectangular shelters. According to Giedion, "this regular rectangular house which has remained even to this day the standard form for a dwelling, had evolved only after centuries of experimentation with innumerable variants." His underlying weighting of this can be plainly heard.[3] The rejection of round buildings in the course of the evolution of civilisation may well have been for primarily practical reasons – rectangular buildings can be more readily, i.e., more economically, subdivided and extended, and are easier to group together into settlements. The triumph of the rectangular building coincides with the onset of the establishment of permanent settlements; compact settlement forms are, at best, of only minor importance to nomadic peoples.

At the dawn of history, whether a building was rounded or angular was not only a question of practical needs but also an expression of spiritual ideals. According to Norberg-Schulz in the earliest cultures it is impossible "to distinguish between the practical and the religious (magical)".[4] The architectural forms and elements at this stage have both practical and symbolic significance – an interpretation that lives on in the tepees of the North American Indians and the yurts of nomadic Asian tribes. For their occupants these portable one-room homes symbolise the entire cosmos and their interior layout follows ancient rules that prescribe a certain place for every object and every occupant.

Construction archetypes

At this point, however, it is not the evolution of human shelters that we wish to place in the foreground but rather the characterisation of the two archetypal forms of construction – filigree construction[5] and solid construction. But here, too, the transition from a nomadic to a sedentary lifestyle played a crucial role. If we assume that the early, ephemeral shelters were filigree constructions, i.e., lightweight, framelike constructions, then the Mesopotamian courtyard house of c. 2500 BC is the first pioneering example of a shelter in solid construction. The historical development is reflected in the terminology: only with the development of permanent settlements do we first speak of architecture.[6] The Greek word *tekton* (carpenter) – whom we shall take as representing filigree construction – later led to the word *architekton*, our master builder, the architect.[7] Nevertheless, filigree construction should not be regarded merely as the forerunner of solid construction, as having lost its justification in the meantime. For in the end the construction systems depend on which natural resources are available locally and what importance is granted to the durability of a structure. Accordingly, the two archetypal construction systems are embodied differently yet equally in filigree construction and solid construction.

Filigree construction

The first filigree constructions were variations on lightweight, initially wall-less shelters. In terms of their construction these consisted of a framework of branches, rods or bones covered with a protective roof of leaves, animal skins or woven mats. According to Hans Soeder we can distinguish between three different types of house: "Round domed structures (like those of Euro-African hunter cultures), the round tepee-type houses or conical tents of the Arctic and Antarctic regions, and – in regions with a hot or temperate climate – rectangular, inclined windbreaks".[8] Besides the climatic conditions, the first shelters were characterised by the local availability of organic or animal-based materials. This is an assumption because, naturally, no corresponding remains have been found. Gradually, inorganic materials started to be employed for housebuilding as well – in a sense the first optimisation attempts. They were more durable, could withstand the weather better and presupposed a high level of cultural development. One such optimisation is, for example, the covering of a framework of rods with cob.

The term "filigree construction" refers directly to the way in which these forms of construction are put together. Since the 17th century the noun "filigree" (alternative spelling "filagree") has denoted an ornamental work of fine (usually gold or silver) wire, twisted, plaited and soldered into a delicate openwork design. This word is a variation on "filigreen", itself a variation of "filigrane", derived from the Latin words *filum* (thread) and *granum* (seed),[9] from which we can infer the roughness of the metal surfaces. A filigree construction is thus a structure of slender members, a weave of straight or rodlike elements assembled to form a planar or spatial lattice in which the loadbearing and separating functions are fulfilled by different elements. But this static framework contains many "voids", and to create an architecturally defined space we need to carry out one further step – to close this open framework or – according to Semper – to "clothe" it. The relationship between the interior and exterior of a building is thus achieved via secondary elements and not by the loadbearing structure itself. Openings appropriate to the system are consequently structural openings, the size of which is matched to the divisibility of the framework. The reference to Semper is therefore also interesting because in his book *Der Stil*, he designates textile art as an "original art", the earliest of the four "original techniques" from which he derives his four elements of architecture. He therefore describes the tectonic principle of filigree construction

– weaving, knotting and braiding – as the earliest of mankind's skills.[10]

Solid construction

Prime features of solid construction are, as the term suggests, heaviness and compactness, in contrast to filigree construction. Its primary element is a massive, three-dimensional wall made up of layers of stones or modular prefabricated materials, or by casting in a mould a material that solidifies upon drying. The jointing principle of solid construction could be described then by means of the techniques of casting and layering. The latter also results from the importance of the architectural theory equivalent of solid construction – stereotomy, the art of cutting stone into measured forms such that in the ideal case the simple layering of dressed stones and the pull of gravity are sufficient for the stability of the building, without the use of any additional media such as mortar etc. It becomes clear from this that solid constructions can only accommodate compressive forces and – unlike filigree constructions – cannot handle tensile forces. One example of the principle of "dry walling", loaded exclusively in compression, is provided by the all-stone buildings of the "Village des Bories" (borie = dry-stone hut) in the French town of Gordes, with their self-supporting pyramidal roofs.[11]

In solid construction the erection of walls creates interior spaces directly because the loadbearing and enclosing functions are identical. Consequently, the extent of the structural shell often corresponds to that of the final construction, with secondary elements being, in principle, superfluous. The sizes of openings in the walls are limited because these weaken the loadbearing behaviour of the wall. This type of construction is founded on the individual cell and groups of rooms are created by adding cells together or subdividing individual cells. As in the simplest case all walls have loadbearing and separating functions, there is no structural hierarchy. All parts tend to be of equal importance.

Hybrid forms

This pair of concepts – solid construction (stereotomy) and filigree construction (tectonics) – designates the two archetypal construction systems. All the subsequent forms of construction can be derived from these two, even though their origins are still considerably blurred. Today, the array of architectural design forms is less clearly defined than ever before. Everything is feasible, everything is available. From a technical viewpoint at least there seem to be no boundaries anymore. The often new and surprising utilisation of high-tech materials and complex system components leads to an ever greater blurring of the original boundaries between construction systems. Solid and filigree construction in their true character have long since been unable to do justice to new demands and new options; composite forms prevail.

The distinction between solid and filigree construction as pure constructions is interesting insofar as they illustrate the "how" and "why" of building. They provide a means of analysis which permits comparisons between contemporary systems and also renders their historical evolution legible. This whets our appetite for the specific and simultaneously creates their boundaries.

Notes

1   For example, the structures of the World Expositions of the 19th century, like the Crystal Palace in London or the Eiffel Tower in Paris. For details of the latter, see Roland Barthes, *The Eiffel Tower, and Other Mythologies,* transl. Richard Howard, New York, c 1979.
2   Sigfried Giedion: *The Eternal Present. A Contribution to Constancy and Change.* The National Gallery of Art, Washington, 1964, p. 177.
3   ibid, p. 177.
4   Christian Norberg-Schulz: *Logik der Baukunst (Bauwelt Fundamente 15),* Gütersloh, Berlin, Munich, 1968, p. 109.
5   Of all the known terms, filigree construction appears to be the most precise and most comprehensive in order to study the essence of the construction tectonics principle. In contrast to this, the term skeleton (or frame) construction, frequently regarded as a synonym, seems to draw unavoidable parallels with plant or animal structures and hence a reference to an "organic" architectural interpretation, which as such has nothing to do with the form of construction. The term lightweight construction is similarly restrictive because not only does it – unreasonably – tend to reduce filigree construction to a form of building "light in weight" but also – indirectly – tends to favour certain materials at the expense of others.
6   Markus Dröge, Raimund Holubek: "Der rechte Winkel. Das Einsetzen des rektangulären Bauprinzips"; in: Andreas Brandt: *Elementare Bauten. Zur Theorie des Archetypus, Urformen weltweiten, elementaren Bauens in einer Zusammenschau,* Darmstadt, 1997, pp. 499–508, p. 501.
7   Kenneth Frampton: *Studies in Tectonic Culture,* Cambridge, 1995, p. 3.
8   Hans Soeder: *Urformen der abendländischen Baukunst in Italien und dem Alpenraum* (Du-Mont Documents), Cologne, 1964, p. 19.
9   Oxford English Dictionary.
10 cf. Gottfried Semper: *Der Stil in den technischen und tektonischen Künsten oder praktische Ästhetik;* vol. 1: *Die textile Kunst,* Frankfurt a. M., 1860, p. 13.
11 Werner Blaser: *Elementare Bauformen,* Düsseldorf, 1982, pp. 31–43.

Comparing the relationship between structure
and space solid construction – filigree
construction

Solid construction	Filigree construction

Body
made from *walls* (vertical)
– solid, homogeneous
– plastic, solid bodies

Primacy of the space
– directly enclosed interior space
– distinct separation between interior and exterior
– plan layout concept

Principle of forming enclosed spaces
a) *Cells*
– additive, starting from the smallest room unit
– divisive, by subdividing a large initial volume (internal subdivision)
b) *Walls*
– hierarchical, parallel loadbearing walls, clear directional structure (open-end facades)
– resolution of the walls: parallel rows of columns (a form of filigree construction, cf. colonnade mosque)

Loadbearing principle
– horizontal: arches; shells (vault, dome); form-active loadbearing structures (stressed skins)
– for long spans: additional strengthening with ribs (e.g. Gothic) and downstand beams (T-beams)
– directional systems (truss designs) or non-directional systems (waffle designs)

Openings as wall perforations
– the structural disruption in the wall
– mediation between interior and exterior
– the hole: dependent on the wall–opening proportions

Lattice
made from *linear members* (horizontal and vertical)
– open framework (2D, 3D) reduced to the essentials

Primacy of the structure
– no direct architectural interior space creation
– no separation between interior and exterior
– the construction of the framework dominates: linear members as lattice elements, infill panels

Principle of forming enclosed spaces
Gradual *sequence of spaces*, from "very open" to "very enclosed", depending on the degree of closure of the infill panels
c) *Skeleton construction*
– partial closure of horizontal and vertical panels between lattice elements: floor/roof or wall as infill structure
d) *Column-and-slab construction*
– solid slab as floor/roof construction in reinforced concrete
– walls as infill between columns or user-defined wall developments (non-loadbearing)

Loadbearing principle
– horizontal beams (primary), possibly more closely spaced transverse members (secondary)
– eccentric nodes; directional hierarchy; layered; primarily timber engineering
– axial nodes; directional and non-directional; primarily structural steelwork
– for long spans: increased structural depth of primary elements
– trusses, plane frames (2D), space frames (3D)

Panel as structurally inherent opening principle
– the structural opening as a variation of the panel between lattice elements
– infill panels: solid; horizontal; vertical
– non-loadbearing curtain wall, horizontal ribbon windows

	Modules	Masonry	Concrete	Timber	Steel	Insulation	Glass or plastic
Introduction	The importance of the material	The pathos of masonry	On the metaphysics of exposed concrete	Wood: indifferent, synthetic, abstract – plastic	Why steel?	The "invisible" building material	Glass – crystalline, amorphous Plastic
Properties of materials	The perception of architectural space The longevity of materials	The materials	The materials The concreting process 10 rules for the production of concrete Exposed concrete surfaces	The materials Wood-based products: Overview Wood-based products: Layered products Wood-based products: Particleboards Wood-based products: Fibreboards Important panel and prefabricated systems: Overview Panel construction: Current developments	Sections – forms and applications Fire protection Potential applications for structural steelwork	Transparent thermal insulation Thermal insulation materials and their applications	Glass, the opaque building material Plastic on the threshold of architecture
Systems		Masonry terminology Design and construction Masonry bonds Tying and reinforcing double-leaf masonry walls	Floor supports, exposed concrete with internal insulation The fixing of heavy external cladding (concrete) The fixing of heavy external cladding (stone) Chart for establishing preliminary size of reinforced concrete slabs	Timber construction systems: Overview Platform frame construction: Construction principle Chart for establishing preliminary size of timber beams	Connections: A selection Structures – frame with cantilevering beams Structures – frame with continuous columns Structures – two-way frame Chart for establishing preliminary size of steel beams	Thermal insulation systems – Overview	
Systems in architecture		The skill of masonry construction Types of construction Prefabrication	Linear structural members Systems with linear members Planar structural members Systems with planar structural members		Folding and bending Frames Girder, lattice beam and facade Space frames Diamonds and diagonals Canopy structures		
Examples				Conversion of a trunk in traditional Japanese timber building culture The threads of the net			

The importance of the material

Andrea Deplazes

For me, designing and constructing is the same thing. I like the idea that form is the result of construction; and material, well, that's something finite. Nevertheless, confining myself to this formula would be a mechanistic reduction because the shape of the form, deliberate or not, bears – beyond its material or constructional component – information, an intent. Yes, even the absence of intent is information (which has been sufficiently well demonstrated by functionalism). Consequently, the separation between designing and constructing made by the teachers is a didactic strategy to create thematic focal points, which can be explained beautifully by the metaphor of the potter and his wheel. The potter models a vessel with both hands by applying force from outside with one hand and from inside with the other hand (in opposite directions) in order to reshape the mass of clay into a hollow space. A "vessel that holds space" is produced. At best these forces complement each other, or at least affect each other, as a result of which the didactics sometimes becomes the methodology of the work and, moreover, becomes the design process as such. This process advances from both directions: from outside in the classical way from the urbane to the architectural project, and from inside by means of the spatial and constructional fabric, the tectonics – and both lead from the abstract to the concrete.

Between them lies the architectural matter. It stands as the boundary and transition zone between the inside and the outside and unites in itself all architectural, cultural and atmospheric factors, which are broadcast into the space. This is the paradox of architecture: although "space" is its first and highest objective, architecture occupies itself with "non-space", with the material limiting the space, which influences the space outwards as well as inwards. Architecture obtains its *memoria*, its spatial power and its character from this material. As Martin Heidegger expresses it, "The boundary is not the point where something ends but, as the Greeks recognised, the point at which something begins its existence." From this point of view architects are metaphysicists who would not exist without the physicists (technicians, engineers, designers), or even more like Janus with his two faces on one head: the presence of space (antimatter) and the presence of matter are mutually interlinked and influence each other unceasingly.

Conceiving and designing space or space complexes in advance or reconstructing it/them subsequently are only possible when I know the conditions of realisation and can master them as well.

Consequently, the architect is a "professional dilettante", a kind of alchemist who tries to generate a complex whole, a synthesis from most diverse conditions and requirements of dissimilar priority which have to be appraised specifically every single time.

The character of the architectural space therefore depends on *how* things are done and for that reason it is determined by the technical realisation and by the structural composition of the substances and building materials used. In this respect a remark by Manfred Sack is very instructive: "Again and again there is the sensuality of the material – how it feels, what it looks like: does it look dull, does it shimmer or sparkle? Its smell. Is it hard or soft, flexible, cold or warm, smooth or rough? What colour is it and which structures does it reveal on its surface?"

Sack observes that architectural space is perceptible first and foremost in a physical-sensual way. By striding through it and hearing the echo of my steps I estimate and sound out its dimensions in advance. Later, these dimensions are confirmed by the duration of my striding and the tone of the echo gives me a feeling of the haptic properties of the boundaries to the space, which can be decoded by touching the surfaces of the walls and, perhaps, by the smell of the room too, originating from different things. So only by means of these sensual experiences do I realise what I later believe I can comprehend with one single glance. Vision is obviously something like a pictorial memory of earlier physical-sensual experiences which responds to surface stimuli. I also like the idea of "which structures does it reveal on its surface?" Under the surface lies a hidden secret, which means the surface depends on a concealed structure which existed before the surface, which created the surface, and in a certain way the surface is a plane imprint of this structure. In architecture the line and the two-dimensional area do not exist – they are mathematical abstractions. Architecture is always three-dimensional – even in a micro-thin layer of paint – and thus plastic and material. As an example we can consider the distinction between colour as colouring material and colour as a certain shade of colour, keeping in mind that the latter may be used to generate the impression of two-dimensional areas. This notion makes it easy for me to understand construction not only as a question of technique or technology, but as *tekhne* (Greek: art, craft), as the urge to create, which needs the presence of an artistic or creative, human expression of will or intent, which is the starting point for the creation of every artefact. "Understanding" construction means to grasp it intellectually after grasping it materially, with all our senses.

Excerpt from introductory lecture, ETH Zurich, 15 January 1999

The perception of architectural space

Tectonics ——— Form ——— Space

Physics of the space			Physiology of the perception		

Material	Mass		**Sight**	Light	
	Massiveness			Colour	
	Heaviness			Materiality	
	Lightness			– abstract	
	Hardness			– concrete	
	Softness				
	Filigreeness		**Touch**	Texture	
	Compactness			– rough	
	Transparency			– fine, smooth	
				– fibrous	
Boundaries	Opaque				
	Transparent		**Feeling**	Moist	
	Translucent			Dry	
	Surface			Hot	
	– flat			Cold	
	– sculpted				
			Odorous	Smell	
Structure	Tectonic, divided			Agreeable	
	Non-tectonic, homogeneous			"neutral"	
	– amorphous, "without form"				
	– monolithic – layered		**Sense of time**	Movement	
	– hierarchical – chaotic			Permanence	
	– non-directional – directional			Scale effect (feeling)	
				– "broadness"	
Figuration	Euclidian			– "narrowness"	
	Mathematical – rational			– "depth"	
	Geometrical				
	– abstract		**Hearing**	Noise	
	– concrete			Resonance, reverberation	
	Organic			Echo	
	– biomorphic			Muffled	
	– intuitive			Harsh	
Dimension	Scale				
	– broadness				
	– narrowness				
	– tallness				
	– depth				

↓

Thinking
Interpreting
Synthesising

The longevity of materials

Usage	Years
1. Floor coverings	
1.1 Textile floor coverings (needle felt + carpeting)	
Price category 1, medium quality, laid	10
Price category 2, hard-wearing quality, laid	12
Natural fibre carpet (sisal-coconut), laid	10
1.2 Ceramic floor coverings	
Plain clay tiles	30
Ceramic tiles	40
Hard-fired bricks, unglazed	50
Reconstituted stone flags	40
Slate flags	30
Granite flags	40
1.3 Other floor coverings	
Seamless cushioned vinyl	20
Plastic floor coverings (inlaid, PVC)	20
Linoleum	20
Cork	15
Parquet flooring	40
2. Plastering, painting and wallpapering	
Plastic grit, Chloster-style plaster	10
Dispersion paint, matt paint Blanc fixe, whitened	8
Woodwork (windows, doors) painted with oil-based or synthetic paint	20
Radiators, painted with synthetic paint	20
Wallpaper, hard-wearing, very good quality	15
3. Wood and plastic materials	
Wood panelling, glazed	20
Wood panelling, untreated	30
Skirting boards, plastic	15
Skirting boards, beech or oak	25
4. Ceramic and stone tiles	
Ceramic tiles in wet areas	30
Stone tiles in wet areas	40
5. Kitchen fittings	
Electric hob, conventional	12
Ceramic hob	15
Cooker, stove and oven, incl. baking sheet	20
Microwave	15
Refrigerator	10
Freezer (upright or chest)	15
Dishwasher	15
Extractor, fan	15

Usage	Years
6. Sanitary fittings	
Bath, shower tray, cast, steel	35
Bath, shower tray, enamel	20
Bath, shower tray, acrylic	25
Shower tray, ceramic	35
Lavatory, pan without cistern, bidet	35
"Closomat" (shower-toilet)	20
Mirror cabinet, plastic	10
Mirror cabinet, aluminium	10
Fittings for kitchen, bath, shower or WC	20
Washing machine and tumble drier in tenant's flat	15
Hot-water boiler in tenant's flat	15
7. Heating, flue, heat recovery system	
Thermostat radiator valves	20
Standard radiator valves	20
Electronic heat and flow counter	15
Plant for hot-air flue/heat recovery	20
Fan for smoke extraction	20
Log-burning stove (with flue)	25
8. Sunshading	
Sunblind, synthetic fabric	12
Louvres, plastic	15
Louvres, metal	25
Plastic roller shutter	20
Wooden roller shutter	25
Metal roller shutter	30
Operating cords for sunblinds and roller shutters	8
9. Locks	
Automatic door locking system	20
Lock to apartment door	30
Lock to internal door	30
10. Reduction in longevity for commercial use	
Manufacturing	25%
Retail	25%
Restaurants	50%
Offices	20%

Source
Schweizerische Vereinigung kantonaler Grundstückbewertungsexperten
(Swiss Association of Cantonal Real Estate Valuation Experts) SVKG+SEK/SVIT:
"*Schätzerhandbuch, Bewertung von Immobilien*", 2007.

The pathos of masonry

Ákos Moravánszky

Fig. 1: The intermeshing of nature and the built environment in the image of ruined masonry
Mario Ricci: "Capriccio" style with ancient ruins, pyramid and decoration

Layers

Pathos is "in" – despite its bad reputation for being "hollow", a reputation that, shadowlike, accompanies every emotional expression. Region, identity, space – terms that formerly were used with care – now take on an excessive force, probably in order to become points of reference in a rather uninteresting situation, or just to cause a sensation. And in architecture what could be more emotional than masonry? Where masonry is concerned we think of a figure with characteristics that tie the masonry to a certain place; characteristics like material, colour, weight, permanence. It is the artistic characteristic of masonry that provides the ethical and aesthetic resonance that legitimises many things. A wall with a coat of plaster or render is not necessarily masonry, regardless of how well it is built and coated. Masonry is "a structure that remains visible in its surface and works through it"[1] – regardless of the material used: natural stone or man-made bricks or blocks.

The relationship between nature and the built environment, as it was represented in the ruined masonry of the late Renaissance "Capriccio" genre, was intended to demonstrate the vanity of building and the corrupting power of death. In the end nature is waiting to take revenge for its violation "as if the artistic shaping was only an act of violence of the spirit".[2]

But the connection between masonry and nature can also be looked at from a less melancholy standpoint. Rudolf Schwarz described in his book *Von der Bebauung der Erde* (Of the Development of the Earth), published in 1949, the material structure of the Earth as masonry built layer by layer, starting with the seam "made from wafer-thin membranes of the universal material", from precipitation and sedimentation.[3]

Viewed by an unprejudiced onlooker the masonry *itself* should appear as a rather commonplace product when compared with the complex structures of high-tech industry. However, we sense the pathos quite clearly when masonry becomes the symbol for the building of the Earth, for the creation – or for homeliness as a contrast to modernisation. Brick-effect wallpaper, which decorates many basement night-clubs and discotheques, shows the sentimental meaning that attaches to masonry.

There are at least two debates about masonry: one about its surface as a medium for meaning and a boundary, the other about its mass as a product of manual work. Although both debates overlap constantly, I shall deal with them separately here.

The lightness: the wall, the art

No other theoretical study has formulated more new ideas regarding the double identity of masonry (and inspired a lot more) than the two volumes of Gottfried Semper's *Style in the Technical and Tectonic Arts: or, Practical Aesthetics*. The basis of Semper's system is the typology of human production methods: weaving, pottery, tectonics (construction in timber) and stereotomy (construction in stone). These four types of production correspond to the four original elements of architecture: wall, stove, roof and substructure (earth fill, terrace). What is important here is the ontological dimension of this breakdown: those four elements are not formally defined, but rather are aspects of human existence. It is remarkable to witness the flexibility that the seemingly rigid breakdown of architectural techniques allows with regard to the determination of its components. Even a mere sketch would be beyond the scope of this article. At this point it is important to establish that masonry artefacts could be products of the two "original techniques" – weaving and stereotomy. Tectonics, "the art of joining rigid, linear parts"[4] (an example of this is the roof framework), is alien to masonry.

Semper's observations were influenced by the remains of walls discovered during excavations in the Assyrian capital Nineveh, which he saw in 1849 when he visited the Louvre. In his opinion these masonry fragments confirmed his clothing theory: the wall as boundary is the primary element, the wall as a load-carrying element in the construction is of secondary importance. The stones forming the surface of the Assyrian masonry (the remains at least) were assembled horizontally on the ground, painted, enamelled, baked and only then erected. In his manuscript *Vergleichende Baulehre* (Comparative Building Method) Semper wrote: "It is obvious that clay brick building, although already well established in

Fig. 2: The wall as a boundary element is the primary function, the masonry as loadbearing element the secondary function.
Nineveh, excavations of town walls between 1899 and 1917

Fig. 4: Stereotomy and marble-clad masonry
Otto Wagner: Steinhof Church, Vienna (A), 1907

Fig. 3: Lightweight rendered facade over heavyweight masonry
Jože Plečnik: Sacred Heart of Jesus Church, Prague (CZ), 1939

Assyrian times, was not focused on construction. Its ornamentation was not a product of its construction but was borrowed from other materials."[5] This theory still provokes – and inspires – us today because of its apparent reversal of cause and effect. It is the appearance of the masonry, its wickerwork-like surface, that determined the technique, and not vice versa. Semper states that the knot is "the oldest technical symbol and ... the expression of the earliest cosmogonic ideas",[6] i.e. the prime motif of human *tekhne*, because a structural necessity (the connection of two elements) becomes an aesthetic, meaningful image. The effect of an oriental carpet is based on the rhythmic repetition of its knots; the whole surface is processed uniformly. Art is always a kind of wickerwork: a painter – no matter if he or she is a landscape painter of the 19th century or an "action painter" like Jackson Pollock working in the 1950s – works uniformly over the whole of the canvas, instead of placing coloured details onto a white surface. Only this calligraphy allows us to experience masonry. "The mesh of joints that covers everything, lends ... the surface not only colour and life in a general way but stamps a sharply defined scale onto it and thereby connects it directly with the imagination of human beings", wrote Fritz Schumacher in 1920.[7]

Although Semper's theory regarding the textile origin of the wall has it roots in historicism and has been misunderstood and criticised by many representatives of the modern theory of material authenticity, it still influenced the aesthetics of masonry in the 20th century. Naturally, this fact cannot always be attributed to the direct influence of Semper's theory. But in the architecture of Vienna the acceptance of Semper's ideas is unmistakable and even today architects like Boris Podrecca still feel bound by this tradition. Above all, it was the group led by Otto Wagner who interpreted Semper's theses early on in an innovative way. The facades of the Steinhof Church (1905–07) and the Post Office Savings Bank (1904–06) in Vienna are structured according to Semper's distinction between lower, stereotomic and upper, textile bays.

A pupil of Wagner, the Slovene Jože Plečnik interpreted these themes in a new way, as can be seen in his works in Vienna, Prague, and Ljubljana. "New" here means that he integrated his knowledge about ancient forms with virtuoso competence: distortions, alienations, borrowed and invented elements balance each other. The facade of the Sacred Heart of Jesus Church in Prague, built (1932–39) according to Plečnik's plans, is clearly divided into lower, brick-faced and upper, white-rendered zones with granite blocks projecting from the dark brick facing. The facade of the library of the university of Ljubljana (1936–41) is also a membrane of stone and brick. In this case the combination probably symbolises Slovenia's twofold bond with Germanic and Mediterranean building cultures.

Fig. 5: A weave of natural stone and clay bricks
Jože Plečnik: University Library, Ljubljana (SLO), 1941

Louis Henry Sullivan compared the effect of facades built with bricks made from coarse-grained clay to the soft sheen of old Anatolian carpets: "a texture giving innumerable highlights and shadows, and a mosslike appearance".[8]

As its name alone indicates, Frank Lloyd Wright's invention, "textile block" construction, tries to achieve the fabric-like effect of precast blocks made of lightweight concrete. In 1932 he wrote an article in which – distancing himself from the sculptor-architects – he called himself a "weaver" when describing the facades of his buildings in California, e.g. La Miniatura or Storer Residence (1923): "The blocks began to reach the sunlight and to crawl up

Fig. 6: Decorated brickwork
Louis Henry Sullivan: National Farmers' Bank, Owatonna (USA), 1908

between the eucalyptus trees. The 'weaver' dreamed of their impression. They became visions of a new architecture for a new life… The standardisation indeed was the soul of the machine and here the architect used it as a principle and 'knitted' with it. Yes, he crocheted a free wall fabric that bore a great variety of architectural beauty… Palladio! Bramante! Sansovino! Sculptors, all of them! But there was I – the 'weaver'."[9]

Ancient and Byzantine masonry and the religious architecture of the Balkans show in many different

Fig. 7: Wright's second "textile block" house in Los Angeles
Frank Lloyd Wright: Storer Residence, Hollywood (USA), 1923

examples how the surface of the masonry becomes a robe when decorations are used instead of a structural configuration with pilaster or column orders, e.g. by inserting

glazed ceramic pins or small stones into the mortar joints. These buildings manage without a facade formulated with the aid of openings and sculptural embellishments and instead favour the homogeneous impression of the masonry fabric. In the late 1950s the Greek architect Dimitris Pikionis designed the external works to a small Byzantine church on Philopappos hill, near the Acropolis in Athens. His plans included a footpath, an entrance gate and other small structures. Here, Dimitris worked, even more than Wright, as a "weaver", knitting together landscape, existing and new elements to form a colourful story.

Carlo Scarpa created a similar work with historic wall fragments and new layers at the Castelvecchio in Verona. Dominikus Böhm, Rudolf Schwarz and Heinz Bienefeld also used decorative masonry "clothing", often with inclined courses, brick-on-edge courses and lintels in order to illustrate that the shell is independent of the foundation. The facades to the Markus Church in Björkhagen (1956–60) designed by Sigurd Lewerentz demonstrate yet another strategy: the horizontal bed joints are as high as the masonry courses themselves. For this reason the brick wall exudes a "calm" expression, as if it was made of a completely different material to that used for the

Fig. 8: The interweaving of the structure and its surroundings
Dimitris Pikionis: Landscaping and refurbishment of St Dimitris Lumbardiaris Church, Philopappos hill, Athens (GR), 1957

construction of, for example, the Monadnock Building in Chicago – an ancient skyscraper which, in the era of frame construction, was built in brickwork at the request of the building owner. In this building the enormous compressive load could be visually expressed.

The textile skin corresponds to the idea of the "decorated shed" propagated by the American architect Robert Venturi. The Venturi practice, an imaginative workshop of Post-Modernism, strives for a rational (according to American billboard culture) separation between the building and the medium conveying the meaning. The facades of many buildings designed by this practice employee large-format panels covered with a floral pattern that leave a naive, ironical impression. The decorative brick facades of the Texan architectural practice of Cesar Pelli

Fig. 9: Historical wall fragments, new layers
Carlo Scarpa: Reconstruction of the Castelvecchio, Verona (I), 1958–74

Fig. 10: Bed joint widths approaching the height of an individual brick
Sigurd Lewerentz: Markus Church, Björkhagen near Stockholm (S), 1960

Fig. 11: The world's tallest self-supporting brick facade
Burnham & Root: Monadnock Building, Chicago (USA), 1884–91, extension: Holabird and Roche, 1893

also underline that the outer skin is a shell – like almost all masonry, at least since the oil crisis, when the new thermal insulation regulations made solid masonry quite uneconomic.

In the works of SITE, the architecture and environmental arts organisation led by James Wines, masonry as a kind of shell becomes a symbol for the consumer society; its character as a false, glued-on decorative layer peeling away from the substrate was featured in several department store projects. Such preparatory work was obviously necessary in order to pave the way for dropping all moralising about clothing as an illusion, about masonry as a mask. In today's architecture the material authenticity of masonry is often perceived as a myth – in keeping with SITE ideals, just a bit less pithy. The Swisscom headquarters in Winterthur (1999) by Urs Burkard and Adrian Meyer asks whether a facade system, a product of industrial technology and consisting of prefabricated masonry panels, still needs the pathos of manual skills, or – perhaps on closer inspection and thanks to the unusual precision and the joints between the panels – whether it comes closer to the modern ideal of brick as a material that has freed itself from manufacture (according to Ernst Neufert). The loadbearing structure of the apartment block in Baden designed by Urs Burkard and Adrian Meyer (2000) consists of the masonry of the facades,

Fig. 12: Brick wall as peel-off skin!
SITE: Peeling Project (Best department store),
Richmond, Virginia (USA), 1971–72

Fig. 13: Prefabricated brickwork panels
Burkard Meyer Architekten: Swisscom
headquarters, Winterthur (CH), 1999

Fig. 14: Colossal masonry wall
Giovanni Battista Piranesi: Masonry foundation to
the Marcellus Theatre in Rome

the concrete service tower and the in situ concrete floors. The distinctive floor edges allow for the stacking of the individual storeys, which is done by displacing the plain masonry panels and large window openings in successive storeys.

Solidity: the wall, the craft

In Semper's system of original techniques stereotomy is an ancient element. The weighty earth embankments and terraces do not have the anthropomorphic, organic traits of the other components of the building, but rather an inanimate, mineral quality that is, at best, rhythmically subdivided. Stereotomy works with materials "that, owing to their solid, dense, and homogenous state, render strong resistance to crushing and buckling, i.e. are of important retroactive consistency, and which through the removal of pieces from the bulk and working them into any form and bonding such regular pieces form a solid system, whereby the retroactive consistency is the most important principle of the construction."[10] The ancient function of stereotomy is the representation of the "solid ashlar masonry of the Earth", an artificial elevation that serves as a place of consecration where we can erect an altar. The symbol of stereotomic masonry is the "most primitive and simplest construction", the "grass-covered and, as such, fortified mound".[11] It is about hollow bodies, "cell structures" – Semper emphasises that the root of the word construct, *struere*, implies the filling in of hollow spaces.[12] Giovanni Battista Piranesi dedicated the four volumes of his *Antichità Romane* to the overwhelming effect of the colossal masonry walls of his "Carceri d'invenzione". Since then masonry architecture has been associated with the underground atmosphere of dungeons. This also correlates with the method of construction of the fortress. Masonry construction was in that sense originally the filling of the fortress walls; in contrast to wattling walls it meant heavy, physical labour that was definitely intended for strong male labourers, as opposed to the art of weaving and wattling.

In his book *Das Wesen des Neuzeitlichen Backsteinbaues* Fritz Schumacher actually speaks about two worlds of masonry, a Western and an Eastern model of masonry: "The main difference therein is that in contrast to our structural way of formation the superficial ornamentation is the focal point and depicts the brilliant achievement of the Islamic masonry culture. In the light of the carpet design fantasies of Eastern artists, this is no surprise".[13]

Correspondingly, in "structural", massive masonry the joints, the "weakest" element in the masonry, are also interpreted differently. In Semper's concept the network of joints is the image of the rhythmic rows of the knots of the carpets or wattling. Rudolf Schwarz, in his book quoted above, associates the joints with the cosmic process of

the Earth's creation: "A superstructure has horizontal layers and continuous joints and vertical fibres. The joints form the layers and together they provide the structure. The joint is the spaceless place where one layer abutting another starts a third".[14]

The pathos of masonry as a consequence of honest craftsmanship in the service of a national ideology cries

Fig. 15: Rubble stone wall
Ancient Temple of Apollo, Delphi

out of every line of the book *Mauerwerk* (Masonry) by Werner Linde and Friedrich Tamms. "We have learned to master nature's powers but have lost our reverence for it," the authors claim in order to formulate their aims clearly; "The development of the masonry trade shows the way the entire culture will travel".[15] An aesthetic claim is not intended here but rather an indispensable cultivation of attitude. "When such an attitude is awoken again and fortified even in the humblest tradesman it will fill him with the true joy of labour; then the labourer and his work will be one again. And that is needed!"[16] Lindner and Tamms begin their narrative with the retaining walls of terraced vineyards along the Rhine to show the beginnings of "a power of form that advanced to the ultimate consummation" – which then collapsed in the 19th century. The "desire to return to the fundamentals of all good design" makes it important to compare good and bad examples of masonry with the proven "home defence" pattern of Paul Schultze-Naumburg's cultural works.

We can follow these arguments back to the idea of material truth. John Ruskin compounded in his various writings the demand for morality with aesthetic expression. In the American architecture of the late 19th century bulky masonry arose out of granite and brick as the first results of the search for a national building style that could be called "American", expressing traits of originality, raw power, or a bond with nature. The first influential examples in this direction in the United States are the buildings of Henry Hobson Richardson such as Ames Gate House, North Easton (1880–81), and Allegheny County Courthouse, Pittsburgh (1883–88).

The modern conception of the true identity of material, the determining character of masonry, has increasingly suppressed Semper's clothing aesthetic. The question of why a brick facing is celebrated as material truth, but render is rejected as a deception, has not been put forward. One problem, however, was quickly recognised: the industrial mass production of bricks eliminated every individual irregularity of the masonry that had always been a characteristic of "honest" handiwork. Architects contemplated (as Ruskin did earlier) "the quest for exactness" as "the source of evil", as the cause behind monotony and tediousness in masonry architecture at the turn of the century. Justice and honesty vis-à-vis the material were nothing more than the code-words of those who intended to conceal nostalgia.

"Brick boredom" was recognised around the turn of the century as a consequence of technical perfection, the quest for purity. Many architects proposed the subsequent manual working of masonry. The advantage of this method according to Walter Curt Behrendt is that the "original workmanship" would be preserved which would guarantee the finished building a certain freshness. According to Behrendt the brickwork gains an artistic expressiveness when its surface is processed afterwards. The production of brick profiles on site – a proposal that suggests sculptors on scaffolding chiselling ornamentation into the facade – means that the building process should not be rationalised and industrialised but rather should remain an individual, creative act. In this sense the brick facades of the Ledigenheim in Munich (1925–27) by Theodor Fischer were "individualised" with sculptured figures.

Fritz Schumacher, on the other hand, expected the answer to come from the material itself: for him the brick was an individual, a teacher who – unlike rendered and plastered forms that willingly accommodate "all lustful instincts of inability and arrogance" – does not allow immature whims to be given shape. "It is not very easy to get it [brick] to do just what you want it to, its earnest countenance is averse to prostitution, and so it has an inherent natural barrier against the effervescence of misconstrued or hackneyed entrepreneurial fantasies."[17]

Schumacher's buildings are today being investigated primarily from the perspective of the of the turn-of-the-

Fig. 17: The search for a national building style for the USA
Henry Hobson Richardson: Ames Gate House, North Easton (USA), 1881

Fig. 18: Rusticated ashlar masonry as a symbol of the power of the state
Henry Hobson Richardson: Courthouse and prison, Allegheny County, Pittsburgh (USA), 1888

century reform movement, and that is the reason why his early decorative brick facades especially are reproduced, although his school buildings constructed between 1928 and 1930 (Wendenstrasse School, Hamburg-Hammerbrook, 1928–29) are outstanding examples of modern brickwork. Stone and brick masonry were the stepchildren of Modernism; too many courses, which linked the pure surface with country, region, time or work, have contaminated the purity of the International Style. Time is not to be understood here as a stylistic epoch. It is present in the form of sediments and pollution which could enrich the surface of traditional masonry or destroy the purism of classical Modernism.

And yet architects of classical Modernism such as Hugo Häring, Ludwig Mies van der Rohe or Alvar Aalto have also constructed buildings of brick or stone

Fig. 16: Masonry in Berlin (1937)
A comparison of masonry by Werner Lindner and Friedrich Tamms

Fig. 19: Decoration cut into brickwork after erection
Theodor Fischer: Ledigenheim, Munich (D), 1927

masonry. The brick masonry walls of Mies van der Rohe, e.g. those illustrated in the well-known publications of Werner Blaser, are suitable for conveying precision as a sublime quality, even as drawings. In the case of Aalto it is another issue entirely. As he had pursued the idea of "flexible standards", which, like the cells of a living organism, allows a variety of forms, he found brick to be a common denominator, comprising not only the values of mass production and industrialisation but also the warmth and identification, signs for a "new humanism".

The new humanism of the postwar period was also sought by Louis Kahn and Eero Saarinen. Kahn's library for the Philips Academy in Exeter, New Hampshire (1965–72) is a compromise. Originally, he visualised massive brick walls with arched openings; however, a concrete core with brick facing was implemented. The government buildings in Dhaka (1973-76) deliberately sought the connection to a Piranesian style for ancient engineering structures. In an interview Kahn emphasised the sought-after contrast between the coarseness of "viaduct architecture" and the fineness of the structures of human institutions.[18] This aesthetic and at the same time social vision was also a theme in many American student accommodation projects of the postwar period. Eero Saarinen wanted to suggest the atmosphere of a fortified city on the campus of Yale University; the buildings of Ezra Stiles College and Morse College (1960) are concrete walls with large natural pieces of stone "floating" in the aggregate. Saarinen reckoned that one of the reasons why modern

architecture does not use masonry is the anachronism of the manual implementation: "...we found a new techno-logical method for making these walls: these are 'mod-ern' masonry walls made without masons."[19]

In comparison with concrete or even stone, brickwork is not a suitable material for roofing over interior spaces. The small format of the brick makes either the use of brick vaulting or additional strengthening in the form of metal ties or concrete ribs essential. According to his convic-tion that it is precisely the weaknesses that challenge the performance, Schumacher is of the opinion that from an aesthetics standpoint the art of envelope design is surely "the pinnacle of all possibilities" possessed by masonry construction.[20] Without doubt the works of the Uruguayan architect Eladio Dieste, whose design concepts follow in the footsteps of Antoni Gaudí's, belongs to the zenith of the envelope design. Dieste used freestanding brick walls with conoid surfaces in double curvature (church in Atlántida, 1960). He developed a vocabulary of structural forms of masonry that was rational but likewise highly expressive like Gaudí's designs. He thus challenged the prevailing attitude of the large firms where rationalisation and ef-ficiency meant nothing more than routine, bureaucracy and the inflexible application of predictable solutions.

Fig. 20: Example of a modern building using facing masonry
Fritz Schumacher: Wendenstrasse School, Hamburg-Hammerbrock (D), 1929

According to Dieste it is accumulation of capital and not efficiency that drives such organisations. This is why he chose the other way, and used an ancient material with constructive intelligence instead of the newest devel-opments from materials research as a thin covering, a "veneer".

The restrained resistance of masonry

The purely decorative use of brick walls can always be defended with historical associations. For an artist like Per Kirkeby, who builds masonry objects as works of art, it is even more difficult – the work must exist in itself, even as a fragment it must be convincing and self-reliant. The brickwork in its double entity of structural purity and craftlike stigma opens up vast historical perspectives. An artist like Per Kirkeby finds his identity precisely through this: "The brick and its rules, in other words the bond and whatever else belongs to this thousand-year-old handicraft, form a pure structure corresponding to everything one could call conceptual vision. And on the other hand brickwork was full of associations and clues to the great historical architecture with its ruins and other set pieces, the wafts of mist and the moonlight. And for me full of childhood connotations in the shadow of overpowering boulders of Gothic brickwork".[21]

Fig. 24: Curving brickwork shells
Eladio Dieste: Church in Atlántida (Uruguay), 1960

Fig. 21: Maximum openness...
Louis I. Kahn: Library of the Philips Academy, Exeter (USA), 1972

Fig. 22: ...versus the "bricked-up" appearance of a fortification
Louis I. Kahn: Government buildings in Dhaka (Bangladesh), 1976

An early attempt to link the idea of standardisation with an intensified material presence was Baker House, the student accommodation by Alvar Aalto on the campus of the Massachusetts Institute of Technology (1946–49). Aalto pointed out that standardisation is evident even in nature "in the smallest units, the cells". According to Aalto: "This results in millions of elastic joints in which no type of formalism is to be found. This also results in the wealth of and never-ending change among organically

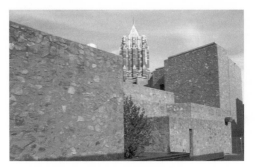

Fig. 23: Unconventional masonry
Eero Saarinen: Ezra Stiles College and Morse College, Yale University (USA), 1960

growing forms. This is the very same path that architectural standardisation must follow."[22]

How can a brick possibly have the same "elastic soul" as an amoeba? Aalto's decision to use distorted, scorched bricks is rather a metaphorical statement of the problem than a solution. He uses this as a reference to ancient forms of brick architecture, to massive walls constructed from amorphous, air-dried clay lumps. The bricks of Baker House – in his words, the "lousiest bricks in the world" – are elements of this alchemistic process, with the vulgar and worthless playing a crucial role in the longed-for harmony. Aalto avoided an either-or approach for the newest or most ancient; architecture joins the two and is neither of them. A crucial aspect is that his work did not remain an individual protest. Siegfried Giedion reacted immediately in his historiography of Modernism by adding "irrationalism" to his vocabulary.[23] The materiality of the facade exercises a restrained resistance in the face of the threat to resolve architecture into the all-embracing spatial grid proposed by Ernst Neufert. This resistance of the material made it possible for Aalto to conceive his idea of standardisation as opposition to the complete availability of architecture in the service of technicised demands.

At first glance Baker House, with the powerful effect of the material of its facade, appears to be related to modern struggles to create a setting for materiality. On the other hand we sense that the aura of the sacred, these days frequently the outcome of semantic cleansing attempts, does not surround Aalto's student accommodation. The "lousiest bricks in the world" give the masonry bond so much local earth that every dream of retreat to a pure state must remain an illusion.

Another, serious alternative today is the change in the situation that came about with the new thermal insulation

Fig. 25: Organic form making use of the identical, smallest "cell"
Alvar Aalto: Baker House, Massachusetts Institute of Technology, Cambridge (USA), 1954

References
1 Werner Lindner, Friedrich Tamms: *Masonry*
Berlin, 1937, p. 8.
2 Georg Simmel: "Die Ruine", idem.,
Philosophische Kultur, Berlin, 1998, p. 119.
3 Rudolf Schwarz: *Von der Bebauung der Erde,*
Heidelberg, 1949, pp. 22–23.
4 Gottfried Semper: *Der Stil in den technischen
und tektonischen Künsten oder praktische
Ästhetik (...)*, vol. II, p. 209.
– English translation: Gottfried Semper: *Style
in the Technical and Tectonic Arts: or, Practical
Aesthetics*, vol. II.
5 Gottfried Semper: Vergleichende Baulehre, in:
Wolfgang Herrmann: *Gottfried Semper – Theo-
retischer Nachlass an der ETH Zurich. Katalog
und Kommentare*, Basel, 1981, p. 199, ref.
6 Gottfried Semper: *Der Stil*, vol. I, p. 180.
– English translation: Gottfried Semper: *Style
in the Technical and Tectonic Arts: or, Practical
Aesthetics*, vol. I.
7 Fritz Schumacher: *Das Wesen des
neuzeitlichen Backsteinbaues*, Munich, 1920,
p. 19.
8 Louis Henry Sullivan: "Artistic Brick", in: Robert
Twombly (ed.), *Louis Sullivan, The Public
Papers*, Chicago and London, 1988, p. 202.
9 Frank Loyd Wright: "La Miniatura", idem.:
Schriften und Bauten, Munich/Vienna, 1963,
p. 164.
10 Semper: *Der Stil*, vol. II, p. 351.
– English translation: Semper: *Style in the
Technical and Tectonic Arts: or, Practical
Aesthetics*, vol. II.
11 Ibid., p. 378.
12 Ibid., p. 381, ref.
13 Schumacher: ibid., p. 116.
14 Schwarz: ibid., p. 24.
15 Lindner/Tamms: ibid., p. 8.
16 Lindner/Tamms: ibid., p. 8.
17 Schumacher: ibid., p. 46.
18 "...contrast of the toughness of the viaduct
archi-tecture and the gossamer delicacy of the
buildings of the institutions of man", in John
Peter: *The Oral History of Modern Architecture*,
New York/Abrams, 1994, p. 220.
19 *Eero Saarinen on his Work*, New Haven/London,
1962, p. 84.
20 Schumacher: ibid. p. 105.
21 Per Kirkeby: Backsteinskulpturen, idem.:
Kristallgesicht, Bern/Berlin, 1990, p. 180.
22 Alvar Aalto: "Die Entwicklung von Konstruktion
und Material...", idem., *Synopsis: Painting,
Architecture, Sculpture*, Basel/Boston, Stuttgart,
1980, p. 29.
23 Sigfried Giedion: *Raum, Zeit, Architektur. Die
Entstehung einer neuen Tradition*, 4th ed.
Zurich, München 1989, p. 376 f.
– English translation: Sigfried Giedion: *Space,
Time and Architecture: The Growth of a New
Tradition*, 4th ed., Zurich/Munich, 1989.

standards introduced after the oil crisis. The use of solid masonry walls with a high heat capacity, combined with appropriate heating systems that exploit precisely this property of masonry, can make solid masonry walls useful again. The Art Gallery in Marktdorf, Bavaria (Bearth & Deplazes, 2001) consists of – just like the systems of medieval dungeons and city walls – hall-type rooms and peripheral rooms. The latter are stairs and intermediate spaces located on the periphery of the building which Kahn used to achieve his longed-for separation of "servant" and "served".

So the pathos of masonry must not lead inevitability to the reinstatement of metaphorical qualities such as craftsmanship, regionalism, or heaviness – the latter understood as an answer to the increasing media compatibility of architecture. The accurate and correct questions address the use and fabrication from the perspective of rationality, not romanticism. If convenient conventions do not form a barrier to our thinking, then from a metaphorical presentation of the questions, masonry will be the right answer.

Fig. 26: The presence of the material is strengthened by using distorted, "reject" bricks.
Alvar Aalto: Baker House, Massachusetts Institute of Technology, Cambridge (USA), 1954

The materials

Fig. 27: Clay brick production
Extrusion

Fig. 28: Clay brick production
Automatic cutting to size

Fig. 29: Clay brick production
"Green bricks" on traversers prior to drying
and firing

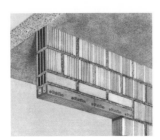

Fig. 30: Solid lintel element ("Stahlton")
Prestressed shallow lintel with make-up units to
maintain the masonry courses

Masonry units

The building blocks of masonry are essentially:
– stone
– clay
– calcium silicate
– cement
– clay units with special properties

Stone

Natural stone is available with the most diverse range of properties and qualities. Its weather and fading resistance depend not only on the type of stone and place of origin but also on its position in the quarry.

Clay

Fired clay masonry units are available in a wide range of forms (facing bricks, hard-fired bricks etc.). The raw materials for their production are natural loams and clays. The properties of the loams and clays vary depending on the content of clay minerals, lime, and iron oxide, and these in turn influence the colour and structure of the finished product.

After extraction, the loam is mixed, crushed, and sent for intermediate storage. The action of water and steam turns the loam into a kneadable, plastic mass which is then extruded to form a ribbon with a suitable cross-section (solid/voids). The ribbon is cut into bricks or blocks, which are then dried and finally fired at temperatures around 1000 °C. This temperature is just below the melting point of the most important components and brings about a sintering of the grains and hence solidification. Depending on the raw material used the colour of clay masonry units varies from yellow (due to the lime content) to dark red (owing to the iron oxide content).

Besides the sizes of any voids, the firing temperature, too, has a decisive influence on the properties of the final clay masonry unit. The higher the firing temperature, the more pronounced is the sintering action. During sintering the pores close up. This reduction in the air inclusions within the masonry unit decreases the thermal storage capacity but increases the compressive strength and the resistance to moisture and frost.

Facing bricks

Facing bricks are masonry units specially produced for masonry that is to remain exposed. Their colours and surface textures vary depending on the supplier. The surface finish of facing bricks can be smooth, granular or rough.

Facing bricks with three good faces (one stretcher and two headers) or even four good faces (two stretchers and two headers) can also be supplied. The facing side makes the brick frost resistant and hence suitable for exposure

to the weather. We can deduce from this that standard bricks are less suitable for exposed situations.

Calcium silicate

Calcium silicate masonry units are produced from lime and quartz sand and are hardened autoclaves. Compared to the fired masonry units, calcium silicate units exhibit excellent dimensional accuracy and are therefore ideal for use in facing masonry applications. Their standard colour is grey but they can be produced in a whole assortment of colours. In facing masonry made from calcium silicate units, special attention must be given to the quality of the edges.

Cement

Cement masonry units are made from cement with a sand aggregate and exhibit a somewhat higher strength. They are significantly more resistant to aggressive water than calcium silicate units and are used primarily in civil engineering works (e.g. cable ducts).

Clay units with special properties

Besides the customary masonry units there are also units with properties achieved through special methods of manufacture and/or shaping. These special masonry units include:
– thermal insulation units
– sound insulation units
– high-strength units
– facing bricks

Components

There are many products that can be added to masonry elements where this is necessary for structural or building performance reasons. Such products include, for example, hollow and solid lintels for spanning openings, thermally insulated masonry base elements, clay insulating tiles etc.

The "SwissModul" brick

"SwissModul" is a system of standards used by the Swiss brickmaking industry. Such bricks have modular or sub-modular dimensions and are designed for masonry which is to be plastered/rendered later. The bricks are grooved to provide a good key for the plaster/render and may be used without plaster/render only after consultation with the supplier. Masonry units with a rough or granular surface finish can be supplied by the brick manufacturers for facing masonry applications.

The brick manufacturers may introduce defined, small differences in the form of the brick or block, e.g. in the arrangement of the perforations. The various products from the individual plants are optimised depending on local raw materials and production methods. The product ranges available can change rapidly.

Masonry terminology

Fig. 31: Irregular or rustic bond

Definitions

excerpted from *Wasmuths Lexikon der Baukunst*, with borrowings from the *Penguin Dictionary of Building* and *British Standard 6100*.

Clay masonry unit. A brick or block made from loam or clay and hardened by means of firing. Available in various forms and sizes. See "Clay brick" below for more information.

Clay brick, clay block. A man-made building component made from clay, loam or clayey substances – sometimes with the addition of sand, quartz fragments, dried clay dust or fired clay – dried in the air or fired in a kiln. If they are fired, we obtain the familiar clay brick commonly used in building. They are generally prismatic in shape but there are regional variations in the dimensions which have also changed over the course of time.

Hard-fired bricks. Clay bricks fired up to the point of sintering, and with a surface which is already lightly vitrified. Such bricks are used for facing masonry applications. One stretcher and one header face are fired to "facing quality".

Bed joint. A horizontal mortar joint in brickwork or blockwork. In arches and vaulting the bed joints run between the arching/vaulting courses.

Perpend. The vertical mortar joint (1 cm wide on average) between bricks or blocks in the same course of brickwork or blockwork, which shows as an upright face joint. In arches and vaulting the perpends are the joints between the masonry units of one and the same course.

Stretcher. A brick, block or stone laid lengthwise in a wall to form part of a bond.

Header. A brick or block laid across a wall to bond together its two sides.

Course. A parallel layer of bricks or blocks, usually in a horizontal row of uniform format, including any mortar laid with them. Depending on the arrangement of the masonry units we distinguish between various types of course (see fig. 33).

Bonding dimension. In a masonry bond this is the dimension by which the masonry units in one course overlap those of the course below.

Bond. A regular arrangement of masonry units so that the vertical joints of one course do not coincide with those of the courses immediately above and below. To create a proper masonry bond, the length of a masonry unit must be equal to twice its width plus one perpend.

Masonry. A construction of stones, bricks or blocks.

Wall. Generally, a building component constructed using stones, bricks, blocks or other materials with or without a bonding agent. Walls in which there is no mortar in the joints, merely moss, felt, lead, or similar, are known as dry walls.

Depending on height and function, we distinguish between foundation, plinth, storey and dwarf walls. These expressions are self-explanatory, as are the distinctions between enclosing or external walls, and internal walls or partitions. If walls support the loads of joists, beams etc., they are known as loadbearing walls. If they have to withstand lateral pressures, they are known as retaining walls.

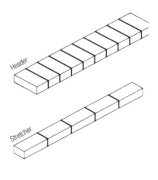

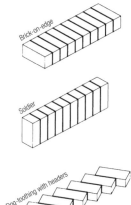

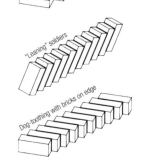

Fig. 32: Different types of course

Further reading
- *Wasmuths Lexikon der Baukunst*, Berlin, 1931.
- Günter Pfeifer, Rolf Ramcke et al.: *Masonry Construction Manual*, Basel/Boston/Berlin, 2001.
- Fritz Schumacher: *Das Wesen des neuzeitlichen Backsteinbaues*, Munich, 1985.
- Fleischinger/Becker: *Die Mauer-Verbände*, Hanover, 1993.
- Ludwig Debo: *Lehrbuch der Mauerwerks-Konstruktionen*, Hanover, 1901.
- Heinz Ronner: *Wand + Mauer*, Basel, 1991.
- Plumridge/Meulenkamp: *Ziegel in der Architektur*, Stuttgart, 1996.

Design and construction

Masonry components

Masonry components comprise masonry units joined with mortar. The complete assembly then exhibits certain properties, which are discussed below.

Masonry bonds

Half- and one-brick walls

The thickness of the wall is equal to either the width of the masonry unit (half-brick wall) or its length (one-brick wall). The following terms describe the arrangement of the masonry units:

- stretcher bond – a half-brick wall with the masonry units laid lengthwise along the wall
- header bond – a one-brick wall with the masonry units laid across the wall
- header bond with brick-on-edge courses

Bonded masonry

The width of the thickness of the wall is greater than the length of one masonry unit. A great variety of masonry bonds can be produced through different combinations of stretcher and header courses. The dimension of such bonds are the result of the particular sizes of the masonry units and the joints. Building with masonry units involves working with a relatively small-format, industrially produced building material – the bricks and blocks – in conjunction with mortar to form a bonded, larger construction element. The masonry bond is characteristic of masonry construction, and critical to its strength. In order to create interlocking corners, intersections, and junctions, the bond must continue uninterrupted at such details. To achieve this, the ratio of length to width of the units was originally an even number. The length of a standard-format masonry unit is therefore twice its width.

Apart from decorative walls with no loadbearing functions, the courses are always built with their vertical joints offset so that successive courses overlap. This overlapping should be equal to about one-third of the height of the masonry unit. It is recommended to take the following bonding dimensions as an absolute minimum:

- Half- and one-brick walls: min. 1/5 x length of unit (= 6 cm) in the longitudinal direction
- Bonded masonry: min. 6 cm in the longitudinal direction, min. 4 cm transverse (theoretical)
- For reasons of stability, single-leaf walls consisting of one vertical layer must be ≥ 12 cm thick, but ≥ 15 cm when using aerated concrete units. The load-carrying capacity of single-leaf walls, especially slender walls, is primarily limited by the risk of buckling.

Double-leaf walls consist of an inner and outer leaf, with possibly a layer of thermal insulation and/or air cavity in between. The inner, loadbearing leaf should be 12–15 cm thick, whereas the outer, weatherproof leaf should be ≥ 12 cm thick.

Joints

We distinguish between bed joints and perpends – the horizontal and vertical layers of mortar that bind together the individual masonry units. Masonry can be regarded as a composite building material consisting of mortar and bricks, blocks, or stones. From the structural viewpoint, the perpends are much less significant than the bed joints because they do not contribute to resisting tension and compression stresses. In terms of strength and movements, the mortar joints behave somewhat differently to the masonry units and this leads to shear stresses developing between the units and the mortar. It is generally true to say that the joints (the mortar component) should be kept as thin or as small as possible. On the other hand, a certain joint thickness is necessary in order to compensate for the tolerances of the units themselves. Therefore, bed joints with normal mortar should be 8–12 mm thick.

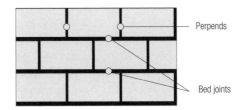

Perpends

Bed joints

Fig. 34: Joint definitions

As the wall is built, the mortar bulges out on both sides of the joints (especially the bed joints). This excess material is normally struck off, which, however, is not always possible on the side facing away from the bricklayer when building a double-leaf wall. This can lead to the (already) narrow air cavity between the two leaves of masonry becoming obstructed or blocked altogether. To be on the safe side, bulging of 2–3 cm should be allowed for.

Depending on the desired appearance of the structure, the joints can be finished in different ways: flush, recessed etc. (see fig. 34). In masonry that has to satisfy a demanding specification, e.g. special acoustic, seismic or architectural requirements, the mortar in the perpends is crucial to achieving the desired properties. On the other hand, masonry that does not have to satisfy any special demands can even be constructed with brick-to-brick perpends (i.e. no mortar in the vertical joints).

Dimensional coordination

Every structure, facing masonry in particular, should take account of dimensional coordination in order to rationalise the design and construction. This is understood to be a system of principal dimensions that can be combined to derive the individual dimensions of building components. The application of dimensional coordination results in components (walls, doors, windows etc.) that are

Fig. 33: Examples of jointing
a) Bucket handle
b) Flush
c) Weathered
(non-facing side of masonry partially exposed to weather)
d) Recessed
(non-facing side of masonry partially exposed to weather)
e) Protruding
(joint material severely exposed to weather)

harmonised with each other in such a way that they can be assembled without having to cut the masonry units. The nominal dimensions are even multiples of the basic module. They represent the coordinating dimensions for the design. Manufacturers subtract the joint dimension from these to arrive at a work size for each component.

The design team must specify whether the masonry concerned is normal masonry left exposed (e.g. in a basement), a faced external wall, or internal facing masonry. The requirements placed on the surface finish of the bricks or blocks, the jointing, and the quality of workmanship increase accordingly.

Thickness of wall
The thickness of the masonry in a half- or one-brick wall corresponds to the width or length of the unit respectively, and thicker walls depend on the bricks/blocks used and the bond chosen.

Length of wall
A wall may be any length. Any necessary adjustments and sufficient interlocking within the masonry bond are achieved by cutting/sawing the bricks or blocks. Short sections of wall, columns, and piers should preferably be of such a size that whole bricks or blocks can be used. In facing masonry the dimensions must be chosen to suit the desired appearance of the masonry bond.

Factory-produced cut bricks (called bats) for adjusting wall lengths are available for facing masonry only. As a rule, the bricks or blocks are cut/sawn on site when the masonry is to be plastered or rendered subsequently, or to suit non-standard dimensions.

Height of wall
Clay bricks and blocks should not be cut within their height. Coordination between the courses and the overall height of the wall is therefore essential. Various make-up units (called tiles) are available, and by combining these any desired overall height can be achieved. However, it is advantageous to choose the height such that make-up units are reduced to a minimum, if possible to just one size. A change in the normal bed joint thickness should normally be reserved for compensating for unevenness and tolerances.

Nominal dimensions
Single-leaf loadbearing walls must be ≥ 12 cm thick, but ≥ 15 cm when using aerated concrete units. In double-leaf walls the inner, loadbearing leaf should be 12–15 cm thick, whereas the outer, non-loadbearing leaf should be ≥ 12 cm thick for reasons of stability. The stability of slender walls is primarily limited by the risk of buckling, i.e. transverse tensile stresses can no longer be resisted without a large compression load.

Masonry bonds

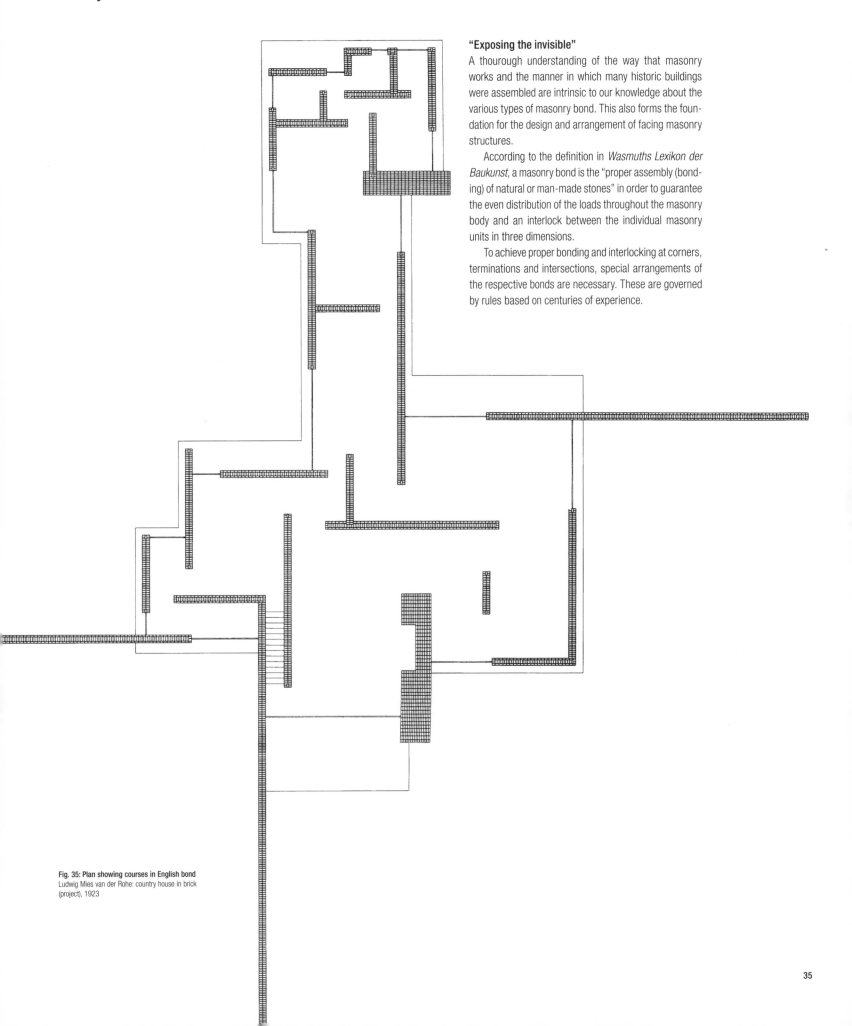

"Exposing the invisible"

A thourough understanding of the way that masonry works and the manner in which many historic buildings were assembled are intrinsic to our knowledge about the various types of masonry bond. This also forms the foundation for the design and arrangement of facing masonry structures.

According to the definition in *Wasmuths Lexikon der Baukunst*, a masonry bond is the "proper assembly (bonding) of natural or man-made stones" in order to guarantee the even distribution of the loads throughout the masonry body and an interlock between the individual masonry units in three dimensions.

To achieve proper bonding and interlocking at corners, terminations and intersections, special arrangements of the respective bonds are necessary. These are governed by rules based on centuries of experience.

Fig. 35: Plan showing courses in English bond
Ludwig Mies van der Rohe: country house in brick
(project), 1923

The principles of masonry bonds

using English bond as an example

This applies only to a bond consisting of man-made masonry units (i.e. clay, calcium silicate, concrete bricks, or blocks).

1. Exactly horizontal courses of masonry units are the prerequisite for a proper masonry bond.
2. Stretcher and header courses should alternate regularly on elevation.
3. There should be as many headers as possible in the core of every course.

4. There should be as many whole bricks or blocks as possible and only as many bats as necessary to produce the bond (3/4 bats at corners and ends to avoid continuous vertical joints).
5. As far as possible, the perpends in each course should continue straight through the full thickness of the masonry.
6. The perpends of two successive courses should be offset by 1/4 to 1/2 of the length of a masonry unit and should never coincide.
7. At the corners, intersections, and butt joints of masonry components the stretcher courses should always continue through uninterrupted, whereas the header courses can form a straight joint.
8. At an internal corner the perpends in successive courses must be offset.

Numerous variations can be produced according to the principles of masonry bonds, indeed as interesting

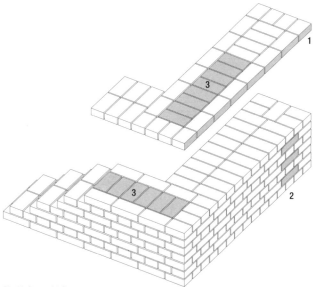

$$L = 2W + joint$$

derivations based on the following logic: the length of a masonry unit is equal to twice its width plus one perpend (e.g. 29 = 14 + 14 + 1).

Fig. 36: Corner detail

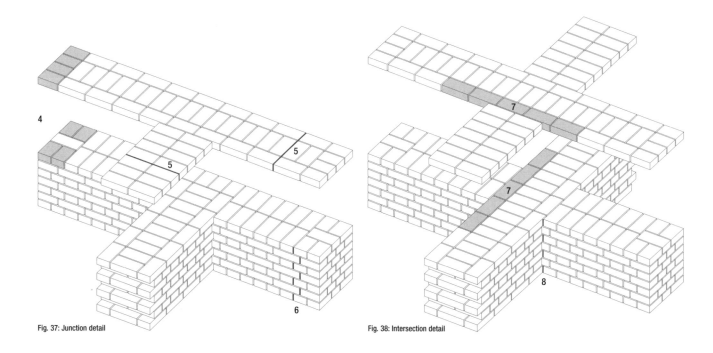

Fig. 37: Junction detail

Fig. 38: Intersection detail

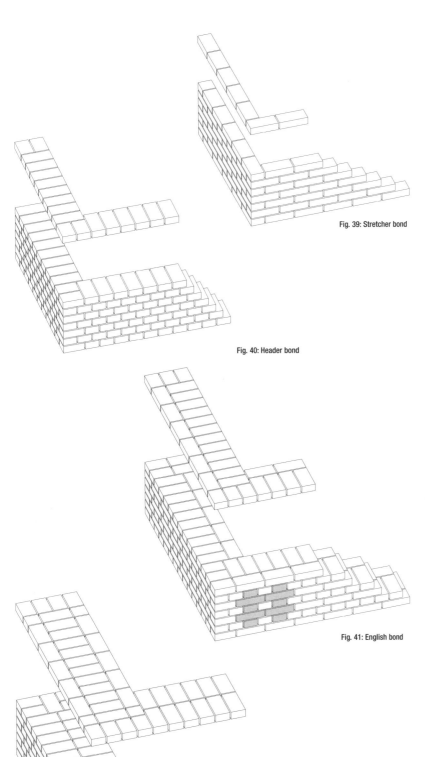

Fig. 39: Stretcher bond

Fig. 40: Header bond

Fig. 41: English bond

Fig. 42: English cross bond

The principal or trainee bonds

We distinguish between half-, one-brick, and bonded masonry. In half- and one-brick walls the width of the courses is limited to one half or the whole length of a masonry unit respectively, whereas in bonded masonry the bond can extend over more than one brick or block within the depth of the wall.

Half- and one-brick walls

Stretcher bond (common bond)

All courses consist exclusively of stretchers. Owing to the bonding dimension, which is normally half the length of a masonry unit, this bond results in masonry with good tensile and compressive strength. Stretcher bond is suitable for half-brick walls only. It is therefore employed for internal partitions, facing leaves and walls made from insulating bricks/blocks. The bonding dimension can vary, but must be at least 1/4 x length of masonry unit.

Header bond

As all courses consist exclusively of headers, this bond is primarily suited to one-brick walls. Successive courses are offset by 1/4 x length of masonry unit. This is a bond with a very high compressive strength which in the past was frequently used for foundations, too. Owing to the short bonding dimension, however, header bond is susceptible to diagonal cracking following the line of the joints.

Fig. 43: Stretcher bond   Fig. 44: Header bond

Bonded masonry

English bond

This bond, with its alternating courses of headers and stretchers, is very widespread. The perpends of all header courses line up, likewise those of all stretcher courses.

English cross bond (St Andrew's bond)

In contrast to English bond, in English cross bond every second stretcher course is offset by half the length of a brick, which on elevation results in innumerable interlaced "crosses". This produces a regular stepwise sequence of joints which improves the bond and therefore improves the strength over English bond.

Fig. 45: English bond   Fig. 46: English cross bond

Fig. 47: Flemish bond

Fig. 48: Monk bond

Fig. 49: Dutch bond

Variations on English bond

Flemish bond

In Flemish bond stretchers and headers alternate in every course. The headers are always positioned centrally above the stretchers in the course below. It is also possible, in one-brick walls only, to omit the headers and thus create a honeycomb wall. Flemish bond has often been used for faced walls, i.e. walls with the core filled with various masonry units grouted solid with mortar, because the alternating headers in every course guarantee a good interlock with the filling.

Fig. 50: Flemish bond   Fig. 51: Flemish bond, filled

Monk bond (flying bond, Yorkshire bond)

Similar to Flemish bond, in monk bond there are two stretchers between each header, and the headers in successive courses are offset by the length of one brick.

Variation on English cross bond

Dutch bond

This bond is distinguished from English cross bond by the fact that it alternates between courses of headers and courses of alternating headers and stretchers. But as in English cross bond the stretchers line up.

Fig. 52: Monk bond   Fig. 53: Dutch bond

Tying and reinforcing double-leaf masonry walls

Fig. 54: Installation sequence, wall tie in mortar joint
– Spread mortar.
– Place wall tie in mortar and lay masonry unit on top.
– Push insulation over wall tie, cast tie into bed joint of second (facing) leaf.

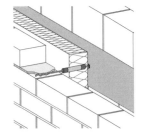

Fig. 55: Installation sequence, wall tie in concrete
– Drill hole in concrete and insert metal anchor.
– Screw in wall tie.
– Push insulation over wall tie, cast tie into bed joint of second (facing) leaf.

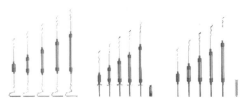

Fig. 56: Wall ties
for bed joints, for concrete and masonry

Wall ties and reinforcement

The wall ties of stainless steel or plastic must be able to transfer tensile and compressive forces perpendicular to the plane of the masonry. The behaviour of the two leaves varies. Owing to the fluctuating temperature effects, the outer leaf moves mainly within its plane. But the inner floor and wall constructions behave differently – deforming due to loads, shrinkage, and creep. Wall ties must be able to track these different movements elastically. For practical reasons the wall ties are fixed in horizontal rows, generally two or three rows per storey, at a spacing of 80–100 cm. It is fair to assume roughly one wall tie per square metre.

As each row of wall ties effectively creates a horizontal loadbearing strip, it is recommended to include bed joint reinforcement, either in the bed joint above or below the row of wall ties, or in both of these bed joints.

Reinforced masonry for controlling cracking

Most cracks are caused by restricting load-related movements, e.g. shinkage, and/or temperature stresses. Such cracks can be prevented, or at least minimised, through the skilful inclusion of reinforcement. The number of pieces or layers are calculated in conjunction with the bricks/blocks supplier or the structural engineer depending on the stresses anticipated and the complexity of the external wall.

Furthermore, it should be remembered that expansion (movement) joints must be provided at corners and in sections of wall exceeding 12 m in length.

Other measures

In order to avoid stress cracking in masonry, other measures may be necessary at eaves, lintels, transfer structures etc., e.g. cast-in rails with dovetail anchors, support brackets, expansion joints etc.

Fig. 57: Building up the outer leaf
View from the side (left) and from above (right)

The skill of masonry construction

Katja Dambacher, Christoph Elsener, David Leuthold

Fig. 58: Masonry units

Fig. 59: Masonry wall

Morphology

"Masonry is a building component made from bricks and blocks that are joined by mortar and therefore function as a coherent unit."[1] Well, that's the definition – which could hardly be briefer – by the Swiss standards authority. But from this constrained condition a whole host of applications have developed.

We understand masonry to be a single- or multi-layer component assembled from natural or man-made stones that interlock with each other and are completed with mortar as the adhesive or filler.

Masonry components can be constructed from quarry or river-bed stones, dressed stones, man-made moulded, fired or unfired bricks and blocks, a mixture of the aforementioned (e.g. in a faced wall), or cast and compacted masses such as cob, concrete, or reinforced concrete.

We distinguish masonry according to the method of construction and whether it is solid or contains voids.[2]

Art history aspects

In cultural terms masonry represents a constant value – neither its functions nor its significance have changed substantially over the course of time. Acknowledged as a craft tradition in all cultures of the world, it is always based on the same principle despite the huge number of different architectural forms. And owing to its strength, its massiveness, and its stability it presumably represents the same values of safety, security, durability, and continuity – in other words tradition – as well as discipline and simplicity always and everywhere. Distinct levels of importance are achieved through choice of material and surface finish. For instance, structures of dressed stones exude monumentality and durability (e.g. the pyramids of Egypt). Contrasting with this, the clay brick is an inexpensive, ordinary building material which is used primarily for housebuilding and utility structures (e.g. for Roman aqueducts, as the cheap industrial material of the 19th century).

Masonry has undergone continuous change due to technical progress. Throughout the history of architecture the response to mass-produced industrial articles has always given rise to different strategies. The Expressionist buildings of Germany were using hard-fired bricks in the sense of a pointed continuation of the northern tradition of facing masonry at the same time as most of the brickwork of white Modernism was being coated with plaster and render to diminish the differentiation.

Facing masonry

What masonry shows us is the materials, the building technology and the process-related quality of the jointing and coursing. Various elements determine the architectural expression of a wall of facing bricks. "First, the unit surface – its colours created by fire, shine, cinder holes, blisters, tears, and grooves; next, the joint – its colour, surface and relief; and finally the bond – its horizontal, vertical and diagonal relationships and interactions as visible reminders of invisible deeds."[3]

If we speak of solid facing masonry, it seems sensible to differentiate between facing and core. The hidden core of the wall can be filled with (relatively) unworked, inexpensive stones or bricks in such a way that it forms an effective bond with the facing. The design of the facing, the surface of the wall with its structural, plastic, material, coloured and haptic properties, embodies the relationship and link with the masonry body.

Module

"Like all simple devices or tools, the masonry unit is an ingenious element of everyday life."[4]

The shape and size of the individual masonry unit are part of a system of governing dimensions; the part – frequently designated the first standardised building element – is a substantial part of the whole. The individual masonry unit determines the laws of masonry building, i.e. the bonding, the bond for its part enables the regular distribution of the joints. As soon as we choose our individual brick or block, with its defined ratio of length to width to height, we establish an inevitable, prevailing system of dimensional coordination for every design, which leads to a prevailing relationship among the parts. Masonry thickness, length, height, right up to positions and dimensions of openings are defined as a consequence of multiples of the basic module.

Format

Masonry units are usually in the form of rectangular prisms, although the actual dimensions have varied from region to region over time. However, their production has remained virtually identical throughout history. And history shows us that the fired masonry unit has seldom exceeded a length and width of 35 cm or a height of 11 cm in order to guarantee proper firing of the units and prevent excessive distortion during firing. The construction of a complex masonry bond (see "Masonry bonds") generally requires a masonry unit whose length is equal to twice its width plus one joint. However, many different dimensions are available today because many walls are now executed in stretcher bond to satisfy building performance requirements and structural principles dictate other dimensions (e.g. half- and one-brick walls).

In addition, masonry units must be (relatively) easy to handle so that the bricklayer can lift and lay a unit with one hand. Apart from a few exceptions, this rule still applies today. The factory production of bricks has led a standard size of approx. 25 x 12 x 6.5 cm becoming established for facing bricks, although different specifications as well as regional differences among the raw materials and production techniques still guarantee a wealth of different masonry units with diverse shapes, sizes, colours, surface textures, and properties. The various – larger and smaller – formats render a subtle, individual approach to the desired appearance or character of a structure possible. However, besides aesthetic necessities there are also practical reasons behind the various masonry unit formats. It is precisely the small formats that lead to greater freedom in the design of relatively small surfaces, thereby making it easier to overcome the rigidity inherent in the, initially, fixed form of the brick or block. The choice of a particular masonry unit, its format and appearance, therefore proves to be a very fundamental decision.

Colours and surface finishes

The colours of bricks and blocks are influenced by the chemical composition of the raw material (clay) plus the firing temperature and firing process. These conditions lead to a wide range of colours and lend the masonry a direct vividness and very specific quality. To use the words of Fritz Schumacher, every brick is highly individual thanks to its "corporeal" as opposed to its "non-corporeal" colour. "For in the actual material the colour is not merely a shade, but rather this shade has its own life. We feel that it exudes from inside the material, is not adhering to the outside like a skin, and that gives it extra strength."[5] The term "colour" differentiates between colour as material and colour as a shade.

So no brick is exactly like any other. And it is precisely this lack of an absolutely perfect, smooth, sharp-edged, right-angled, dimensionally accurate and identically coloured brick, whose standard size, form and quality are merely approximate, that gives masonry its overwhelming fascination. The objective modularity of an individual masonry unit is balanced by the subjective composition within the masonry structure.

One traditional form of surface treatment and improvement for bricks and blocks is glazing, which can be applied when firing the unit itself or in a second firing process.

Bond

The erection of a wall is carried out according to a basic conception intrinsic to masonry: the bond. The bond is a system of rules with which a "readable, but largely invisible composition"[6] is produced. The heart of this process is "exposing the invisible".[7]

The art of facing masonry lies in combining relatively small units by means of a solid, mass-forming but also artistic interlocking arrangement to form a structure such that the vertical joints of successive courses do not coincide. Every brick or block must be linked to its neighbours above and below in order to achieve masonry with

maximum stability and consistency. This applies, above all, to the "core" of the wall which is later hidden. The masonry units interlock, carrying each other.

The arrangements of stretchers and headers create patterns stretching over several courses (rapport), and their repetition becomes a crucial design element, determining the character of the resulting surface. And the "weave" of the masonry units in every course determines whether this regular repetition takes place after two or three or, at the latest, after four courses, thus creating our stretcher bond, header bond, English bond, English cross bond, Flemish bond etc. (see "Masonry bonds").

Strength through the bond

Masonry is a composite material – bricks/blocks plus mortar – with high compressive and low tensile strength. The load-carrying capacity is due to the bond which interlocks the wall in three dimensions. When applying a compression load to a masonry body held at top and bottom it is the bond in conjunction with regular mortar joints that ensures an even distribution of the compressive stresses. The mortar cannot resist any tensile stresses. This therefore restricts the load-carrying capacity of masonry and hence the height of masonry structures. The highest masonry building constructed to date, the Monadnock Building in Chicago, has merely 16 storeys and measures 60 m in height. (Prior to that the tallest masonry structures had just 10 storeys.) Correspondingly, the ground floor walls of this "ancient skyscraper" (Á. Moravánsky) are two metres thick.

Fig. 60: Various formats, colours and surface textures
Alvar Aalto: experimental house, Muuratsalo (FIN), 1954

Ornamentation

The effects of the various masonry bonds vary in their character. The choice of bond together with the material's character and the surface characteristics complement each other and determine the appearance of the facing masonry – but to differing degrees, depending on the observer's distance from the wall.

The brick itself creates the scale for the size of the ornamentation, and the pattern can be developed out of the module itself. The ornamentation created by the rapport is the outcome and also the expression of the production and jointing process; it is, as it were, itself inherent in the principle of the masonry wall.

Fritz Schumacher, for example, relies in his designs exclusively on the effect of attractive hard-fired materials in skilfully constructed walls. His ornamentation is purely superficial, the result of the alternating positions and interweaving of the bricks. However, ornamentation can also take on the form of subtly protruding individual bricks or courses, or make use of special forms such as brick-on-edge topmost courses.

Fritz Höger, the architect behind the famous Chile House in Hamburg, regards brickwork as a material with which he can achieve outstanding large-scale ornamentation by allowing individual bricks to protrude over whole surfaces to achieve extraordinary plays of light and shadow. His masonry surfaces employ relief, are even sculpted.

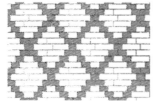

Fig. 61: Ornamentation through the bond
after Fritz Schumacher

Joint

In facing masonry the significance of the joint is frequently underestimated. The joint reveals the connection, "the bond", as the true concept of the masonry. Mortar and bricks are the materials of a wall; but joint and bond determine their nature. The joints cover the surface like a dense network and give it scale. According to Gottfried Semper's "clothing theory" it is the appearance of masonry that determines its technology, and not the other way round (see "The pathos of masonry").

Without joints, masonry would be inconceivable. The joint and the masonry material enjoy a fundamental but variable relationship with each other, each influencing the other. The network of joints can be designed in terms of dimensions, colouring, and form; the relationship between joints and masonry units determines the strength of a masonry construction and also its architectural expression. But the strength of masonry depends essentially on the thickness of the joints; the masonry units are generally more efficient than the mortar, meaning that wide joints, in principle, can reduce the overall strength of a masonry construction.

Emphasising the joints to a greater or lesser degree gives us the opportunity to harmonise the effect of the surface in terms of colouring and vividness. Identical

bricks can look totally different with the joints in a different colour. Furthermore, the variable position of the joint surface with respect to the visible surface of the brick, i.e. whether the joints are finished flush, recessed or projecting, has a critical influence on the appearance of a masonry surface. Joints struck off flush in a wall of bricks with irregular edges, for example, can conceal the irregularities and make the pattern of the joints even more conspicuous. One special way of emphasising the joints is to recess them to create regular, delicate lines of shadow.

Summing up, we can say that the joint pattern is a significant component in the masonry surface and its three-dimensional quality, either highlighting the structure of the masonry bond or giving it a homogeneous effect.

The opening

The solid and protective shell of a masonry wall initially forms a hard boundary separating interior from exterior. Mediation takes place via perforations punched through the fabric of the wall. Their form, size, and positioning is directly related to the individual module and is consequently embedded in the strict, geometrical, modular whole. Every opening must fit into the scale prescribed by the masonry shell, and requires a careful consideration of the surfaces within the depth of the wall (head, reveals, sill, threshold); in other words, the opening is a hole in a fabric which must be "bordered". Wall and opening

Fig. 62: Ornamentation through relief (bricks offset within depth of wall)
Hild & K: Wolf House, Aggstall (D), 2000

Fig. 63: Expressively sculpted facade
Fritz Höger: *Hannoverscher Anzeiger* newspaper
building, Hanover (D), 1928

form an indivisible, interrelated pair in which the former must express its inner consistency and corporeality by – of all things – an "empty space" within the masonry structure, whereas the dimensions of the opening, primarily height and depth, but also the width, will always be bound by the modularity of the masonry bond. On the other hand, the opening represents a disruption in the masonry, and the wider it is, the more permanent it seems to be. Although the opening itself is dimensionless, it is still subject to the laws of gravity because it has to be bridged by a loadbearing structure spanning its width.

Openings in masonry for windows, doors or other large apertures are spanned by lintels or arches.

Openings of up to about 1.5 m can be achieved without any additional means of support, simply by wedging the smallest units against inclined abutments. This produces an extremely shallow, cambered arch.

Horizontal lintels can be provided in the form of small beams of clay or concrete, with either prestressed or conventional reinforcement. Clay lintels enable openings to be spanned with little extra work and in the same material as the rest of the wall.

The arch, on the other hand, is without doubt *the* typical solution for solid and masonry construction when it is necessary to span larger openings or topographical features. The phenomenon of the mass and weight of the building material plus the physical principle of gravity are superimposed here to generate strength and stability

Fig. 64: Joint and bond used to create an autonomous image
Sigurd Lewerentz: St Peter's Church, Klippan (S), 1966

at the macro-level (building element "arch"); the arch is a structure purely in compression. At the micro-level the inherent strength, as already mentioned, is achieved through interlocking and hence the frictional resistance between brick and mortar ("adhesion effect").

Horizontal lintels over larger openings are built exclusively with steel or reinforced concrete beams. In his brick houses Mies van der Rohe was using concealed steel beams with a cladding of, as it were, "levitating bricks" as early as the 1920s in order to achieve window openings

of maximum width and with minimum disruption to the horizontal coursing of the masonry units.

The position of the window within the depth of the wall represents another important element in the overall effect of a masonry structure. Whether the theme of the "wall" or that of the "masonry" becomes noticeable at the design stage depends essentially on the extreme positions of windows fitted flush with the inside or outside face, indeed depends on any of the intermediate positions and possibilities within the depth of the opening. Basically, a "neutral statement" on this theme is impossible.

Layers

"Monolithic masonry"

"If walls are not to express any of their own weight, if we cannot see their mass, if mass only suggests stability, then those are not walls for me. One cannot ignore the powerful impression of the loadbearing force."[8] That was the view once expressed by German architect Heinz Bienefeld. (Note: He means "masonry", the term "walls" is misleading here.)

Solid brick walls are fascinating not only in the sense of being building elements with a homogeneous structure in which the bricks are interlocked with each other in three dimensions, but also because they can take on all the functions of separating, supporting, insulating, and protecting, even storing thermal energy. The mighty masonry wall regulates the humidity in the interior and achieves a balanced internal climate. Compared with the ongoing breakdown of the double-leaf wall construction into highly specialised but monofunctional components, this multiple functionality proves to be particularly topical and up to date. This enables the development of new design strategies that look beyond the technical, constructional, and building performance issues.

The impressive, homogeneous masonry wall guarantees an imposing separating element between interior and exterior spaces. Windows positioned deep within the openings and powerful reveals divulge the massiveness of the material, which provides opportunities for plastic modulation but also the inclusion of spaces.

The insulation standards for the building envelope that have been demanded since the late 1970s have made traditional, solid, facing masonry practically impossible, and so this form has almost disappeared. The problem of thermal insulation is solved with pragmatic systems, e.g. half- and one-brick walls composed of perforated masonry units built up in a synthetic, polyfunctional layer that favours exclusively the aspect of good insulation. This is at the expense of the visual quality of the masonry bond: for reasons of vapour diffusion and weather protection, half- and one-brick walls must always be rendered outside and plastered inside, and the maximum size of opening is restricted, too.

Fig. 65: Lintels

Double-leaf masonry walls

Building performance requirements simply put an end to the facade as we knew it and divided our monolithic masonry into layers. In the course of the European oil crisis of the 1970s and the subsequent demands for masonry constructions with a better thermal insulation performance double-leaf masonry walls, which were originally devised to protect against driving rain, experienced a growth in popularity. Double-leaf masonry walls have several distinct layers separated strictly according to function and this optimises the performance of individual aspects, e.g. improved insulation and sealing, more slender leaves and better economy. Both leaves, inner and outer, are generally half or one brick thick. The originally homogenous building component, the external wall, with its inherent laws stemming from the material properties and methods of working, has been resolved into discrete parts. The outer, visible leaf has been relieved of loadbearing functions and has assumed the role of a protective cladding for the insulating and loadbearing layers. Consequently, the double-leaf system has a structure that comprises mutually complementary, monofunctional layers: loadbearing, insulating, and protective.

That results in new material- and construction-related design options. In particular, the thin, outer masonry leaf with its exclusively cladding function can be featured architecturally. Expansion joints separate the wall divided into bays, whereas the lack of columns is a direct indication that the outer leaf has been relieved of heavy building loads. The original interwoven whole has been resolved into its parts.

Double-leaf constructions can be especially interesting when the independent development of the slender masonry leaves gives rise to new spaces with specific architectural qualities. In climatic terms such included spaces form intermediate zones which, quite naturally, can assume the function of a heat buffer.

Pragmatic optimisation has brought about "external insulation". The external leaf of masonry is omitted and replaced by a layer of render.

Bonds for double-leaf masonry walls

A wall split into two, usually thin, leaves for economic reasons is unsuitable for many masonry bonds; the half-brick-thick facing leaf is built in stretcher bond – the simplest and most obvious solution. What that means for modern multi-storey buildings with facing masonry is that they can no longer have a solid, continuous, loadbearing external wall. On the other hand, solid, bonded masonry (see fig. 63, house by Hild & K) is still possible for single-storey buildings (internal insulation). And there is the option of building the external leaf not in a masonry bond – which is always three-dimensional – but emulating this

Fig. 66: Whitewashed masonry
Heinz Bienefeld: Schütte House, Cologne (D), 1980

and hence forming a reference to the idea of a solid wall (see fig. 69).

Facing masonry and modern energy economy standards

The characteristics of solid masonry can be resolved into layers only to a limited extent. Expansion joints divide the non-loadbearing external leaf into segments and the deception of the solid outer wall (which is non-loadbearing) is usually unsatisfactory. In recent years we have therefore seen the development of new strategies to build solid facing masonry.

One approach is to combine the characteristics of facing, bonded masonry with the advantages of thermally optimised half- and one-brick walls (see "Buildings – Selected projects" – "Apartment blocks, Martinsbergstrasse, Baden; Burkard Meyer Architekten"). This approach is currently very labour-intensive because two different brick formats have to be combined in one bond and adjusted to suit.

Another strategy exploits the solid masonry wall as a heat storage element and integrates the heating pipes directly into the base of the walls. This enables the construction of uninsulated facing masonry (see "Buildings – Selected projects" – "Gallery for Contemporary Art, Marktoberdorf; Bearth + Deplazes").

Design potential and design strategy

Both the office-based design team and the site-based construction team must exercise great care when handling

Fig. 67: Solid masonry without additional layer of insulation
Bearth & Deplazes: Gallery for Contemporary Art, Marktoberdorf (D), 2001

facing brickwork. Every whim, every irregularity is betrayed with ruthless transparency and cannot be disguised. Designing and constructing with facing bricks therefore calls for a precise architectural concept in which the artistic and constructional possibilities of the material plus its sound, craft-like workmanship form a substantial part of the design process from the very beginning.

Initially, it would seem that the means available are limited, but the major design potential lies in the patient clarification of the interrelationships of the parts within a structured, inseparable whole. The brick module as a generator implies a obligatory logic and leads to a governing dimensional relationship between the parts.

The work does not evolve from the mass but rather assembles this mass in the sense of an "additive building process" from the small units of the adjacent, stacked modules. A great richness can therefore be developed on the basis of a precise geometrical definition, a richness whose sensual quality is closely linked with the production and the traces of manual craftsmanship. Fritz Schumacher expressed this as follows: "The brick does not tolerate any abstract existence and is unceasing in its demand for appropriate consideration and action. Those involved with bricks will always have the feeling of being directly present on the building site."[9]

The effect of the material as a surface opens up many opportunities. Tranquil, coherent surfaces and masses help the relief of the masonry to achieve its full effect, an expression of heaviness, stability, massiveness, but also permanence and durability. By contrast, the network of joints conveys the image of a small-format ornamental structure, a fabric which certainly lends the masonry "textile qualities".

The part within the whole

Bricks and blocks can look back on a long tradition citing the virtues of self-discipline and thriftiness – and architecture of materiality and durability. The structure of facing masonry reveals a system of lucid and rational

rules based on a stable foundation of knowledge and experience.

The image of the brick wall is the image of its production and its direct link with the precise rhythm of brick and joints. The relatively small brick is a winner thanks to its universal functionality: it can assume not only a separating, supporting, or protective role, but also structuring and ornamentation. Facades come alive thanks to the age and ageing resistance of masonry materials, their manual working, and the relationship between the masonry body with its legitimate openings.

A wall of facing masonry is a work indicating structure, assembly, and fabric. The face of the architecture almost "speaks" with its own voice and enables us to decipher the logic and the animated, but also complex, interplay in the assembly of the fabric. It is precisely the limits of this material that embody its potential and hence the success of masonry over the millennia.

In conclusion, we would gladly echo here the confession Mies van der Rohe once made: "We can also learn from brick. How sensible is this small handy shape, so useful for every purpose! What logic in its bonding, pattern and texture! What richness in the simplest wall surface! But what discipline this material imposes!"[10]

Fig. 69: The plastic effect of the surface
Alejandro de la Sota: Casa Calle Doctor Arce, Madrid (E), 1955

Fig. 68: The pattern of English cross bond in double-leaf masonry
Hans Kollhoff and Helga Timmermann:
Kindergarten, Frankfurt-Ostend (D), 1994

Notes
[1] Swiss standard SIA V177, *Masonry*, 1995 ed., corresponds to new SIA 266:2003, 266/1:2003; see also: DIN V105 pt 1 & 2, 2002 ed., and DIN 105 pt 3-5, 1984 ed.
[2] *Wasmuths Lexikon der Baukunst*, Berlin, 1931.
[3] Rolf Ramcke: "Masonry in architecture", in: *Masonry Construction Manual*, Basel/Boston/Berlin, 2001.
[4] Ramcke, ibid.
[5] Fritz Schumacher: *Zeitfragen der Architektur*, Jena, 1929.
[6] Ramcke, ibid.
[7] Ramcke, ibid.
[8] Wolfgang Voigt: *Heinz Bienefeld 1926–1995*, Tübingen, 1999.
[9] Fritz Schumacher: *Das Wesen des neuzeitlichen Backsteinbaues*, Munich, 1985.
[10] Excerpt from his inaugural speech as Director of the Faculty of Architecture at the IIT Chicago.

Types of construction

Compartmentation

The building of compartments is a typical trait of masonry construction. By compartments we mean a system of interlinked, fully enclosed spaces whose connections with one another and to the outside consist only of individual openings (windows, doors). The outward appearance is, for a whole host of reasons, "compartment-like". However, at least this type of construction does present a self-contained building form with simple, cubelike outlines. The compartment system uses the possibilities of the masonry to the full. All the walls can be loaded equally and can stabilise each other, and hence their dimensions (insofar as they are derived from the loadbearing function) can be minimised. The plan layout options are, however, limited.

Fig. 70: Compartmentation as a principle: elevation (top) and plan of upper floor (right) Adolf Loos: Müller House, Vienna (A), 1928

Of the categories presented here, compartmentation is the oldest type of construction. Contraints were imposed naturally by the materials available – apart from the frame we are aware of coursed masonry and, for floors and roofs, timber joists as valid precepts up until the 19th century. Over centuries these constraints led to the development and establishment of this form of construction in the respective architectural context. In fact, in the past the possibilities of one-way-spanning floor systems (timber joist floors) were not fully exploited. Today, the reinforced concrete slab, which normally spans in two directions, presents us with optimum utilisation options.

The following criteria have considerable influence on the order and discipline of an architectural design:
- the need to limit the depth and orientation of the plans;
- and together with this the independence of horizontal loadbearing systems (timber joists span approx. 4.5 m) at least in one direction;
- and together with this the restriction on the covered areas principally to a few space relationships and layouts;
- openings in loadbearing walls are positioned not at random but rather limited and arranged to suit the loadbearing structure.

Although today we are not necessarily restricted in our choice of materials (because sheer unlimited constructional possibilities are available), economic considerations frequently force similar decisions.

But as long as the range of conditions for compartmentation are related to the construction itself, the buildings are distinguished by a remarkable clarity in their internal organisation and outward appearance. Looked at positively, if we regard the provisional end of compact compartment construction as being in the 1930s (ignoring developments since 1945), it is possible to find good examples, primarily among the residential buildings of that time. After the war, developments led to variations on this theme. The compartmentation principle was solved three-dimensionally and is, in combination with small and mini forms, quite suitable for masonry; through experimentation, however, it would eventually become alienated into a hybrid form, mixed with other types of construction.

Box frame construction

This is the provision of several or many loadbearing walls in a parallel arrangement enclosing a large number of boxlike spaces subject to identical conditions. The intention behind this form of construction might be, for instance, to create repetitive spaces or buildings facing in

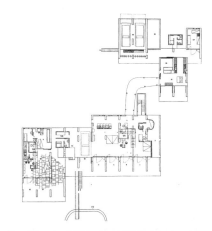

Fig. 71: Box frames as a governing design principle Le Corbusier: private house (Sarabhai), Ahmedabad (India), 1955

a principal direction for reasons of sunlight or the view, or simply the growing need for buildings – linked with the attempt to reach an aesthetic but likewise economical and technically simple basic form. In fact, box frame construction does present an appearance of conformity. After all, a row is without doubt an aesthetic principle which is acknowledged as such.

In terms of construction, a box frame is a series of loadbearing walls transverse to the longitudinal axis of a building, which are joined by the floors to longitudinal walls which stabilise the whole structure. To a certain extent, a true box frame is not possible owing to the need for stability in the longitudinal direction, which is laid down in numerous standards. Therefore, box frame construction is frequently used in conjunction with other categories (compartmentation and plates). The following criteria pre-ordain box frame construction for certain building tasks and restrict its degree of usefulness:

– Restrictions to width of rooms and building by spans that are prescribed in terms of materials, economy etc. (e.g. one-way-spanning floors).
– Heavy – because they are loadbearing – partitions with correspondingly good insulation properties ("screening" against the neighbours).
– External walls without restrictions on their construction, with maximum light admittance, option of deep plans and favourable facade–plan area ratios.

The first examples of true box frames originated on the drawing boards of architects who wanted to distance themselves from such primary arguments; the large residential estates of the 1920s designed by Taut, Wagner and May, influenced by industrial methods of manufacture.

Plates

In contrast to the parallel accumulation of boxes, we assume that plates enable an unrestricted positioning of walls beneath a horizontal loadbearing structure (floor or roof).

So, provided these plates do not surround spaces (too) completely – i.e. do not form compartments – we can create spaces that are demarcated partly by loadbearing

Fig. 72: **Uninterrupted space continuum**
Marcel Breuer: Robinson House, Williamstown (USA), 1948

walls (plates) and partly by non-loadbearing elements (e.g. glass partitions). This presupposes the availability of horizontal loadbearing elements which comply with these various conditions in the sense of load relief and transfer of horizontal forces.

We therefore have essentially two criteria:

– A type of spatial (fluid) connection and opening, the likes of which are not possible in the rigid box frame system, but especially in compartmentation.
– The technical restrictions with respect to the suitability of this arrangement for masonry materials; inevitably, the random positioning of walls leads to problems of bearing pressure at the ends of such wall plates or at individual points where concentrated loads from the horizontal elements have to be carried.

Only in special cases will it therefore be possible to create such an unrestricted system from homogeneous masonry (using the option of varying the thickness of the walls or columns).

Nevertheless, we wish to have the option of regarding buildings not as self-contained entities but rather as sequences of spaces and connections from inside and outside. As the wall is, in principle, unprejudiced with regard to functional conditions and design intentions, the various characteristics of the wall can be traced back to the beginnings of modern building.

The catalyst for this development was indubitably Frank Lloyd Wright, who with his "prairie houses", as he called the first examples, understood how to set standards. The interior spaces intersect, low and broad, and terraces and gardens merge into one.

Mies van der Rohe's design for a country house in brickwork (1923) is a good example (see "Masonry; Masonry bonds"). Here, he combines the flexible rules of composition with Frank Lloyd Wright's organic building principles, the fusion with the landscape.

The plan layout is derived exclusively from the functions. The rooms are bounded by plain, straight, and right-angled, intersecting walls, which are elevated to design elements and by extending far into the gardens link the house with its surroundings. Instead of the window apertures so typical of compartmentation, complete wall sections are omitted here to create the openings.

Richard Neutra and Marcel Breuer, representing the International Style, provide further typical examples. The sublimation of the wall to a planar, loadbearing element that completely fulfils an enclosing function as well is both modern and ancient.

We have to admit that pure forms, like those used by the protagonists of modern building, are on the decline. Combinations of systems are both normal and valid. A chamber can have a stiffening, stabilising effect in the sense of a compartment (this may well be functional if indeed not physical).

Fig. 73: **The openings lend structure to and result from the arrangement of the plates**
Marcel Breuer: Gane's Pavilion, Bristol (UK), 1936

The box frame can be employed to form identical interior spaces. And the straight or right-angled plate permits user-defined elements right up to intervention in the external spaces.

Schinkel's Academy of Architecture: an example of a grid layout

A close study of the plan layouts of the (no longer existent) Academy of Architecture in Berlin reveals how Schinkel was tied to the column grid when trying to realise the actual internal layout requirements. The possibility of creating interiors without intervening columns, as he had seen and marvelled at on his trip to England in 1826, was not available to him for reasons of cost. The factories in Prussia could not supply any construction systems that

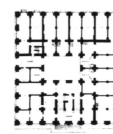
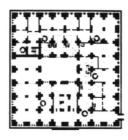

Fig. 74: Reduction of the structure
Karl Friedrich Schinkel: Academy of Architecture
(destroyed), Berlin (D), 1836

permitted multi-storey buildings with large-span floors. He therefore had to be content with a system of masonry piers and shallow vaults (jack arches).

The Academy of Architecture was based on a 5.50 x 5.50 m grid. The intersections of the grid lines were marked by masonry columns which, as was customary at the time, narrowed stepwise as they rose through the building, the steps being used to support the floors. Some of these columns were only as high as the vaulting on shallow transverse arches provided for reasons of fire protection. The continuity of the masonry columns was visible only on the external walls. This was a building without loadbearing walls. It would have been extremely enlightening to have been able to return this building to its structural elements just once. It must have had fantastic lines!

The building was braced by wrought iron ties and masonry transverse arches in all directions, joining the columns. A frame was certainly apparent but was not properly realised. At the same time, in his Academy of Architecture Schinkel exploited to the full the opportunities of building with bricks; for compared with modern frame construction, which can make use of mouldable, synthetic and tensile bending-resistant materials (reinforced concrete, steel, timber and wood-based products), the possibilities of masonry units are extremely limited. Schinkel managed to coax the utmost out of the traditional clay brickwork and accomplished an incredible clarity and unity on an architectural, spatial, and building technology level.

Owing to the faulted subsoil, the chosen form of construction led to major settlement problems because the columns had to carry different compression loads. Flaminius described the problems that occurred: "There are no long, continuous walls with small or even no openings on which the total load of the building can be supported and where the cohesion of the masonry transfers such a significant moment to balance the low horizontal thrust that every small opening generates; instead, the whole load is distributed over a system of columns which stand on a comparatively small plan area and at the various points within their height are subjected to a number of significant compression loads acting in the most diverse directions... Only after the columns collect the total vertical load they should carry and, with their maximum height, have been given a significant degree of strength should the windows with their arches, lintels and spandrel panels be gradually added and the entire finer cladding material for cornices and ornaments incorporated. Only in this way is it possible, if not to avoid totally the settlement of the building or individual parts of the same, but to at least divert it from those parts that suffer most from unequal compression and in which the effects of the same are most conspicuous."

Prefabrication

Kornelia Gysel,
Barbara Wiskemann

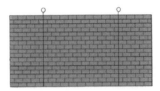

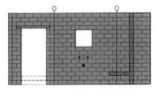

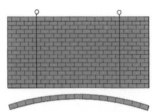

Fig. 75: Models of various masonry elements
Examples from a Swiss manufacturer: "preton"
element catalogue

Rationalisation in the craftsman-like tradition

Factory prefabrication in the brickmaking industry has in recent years been driven primarily by economic considerations. The aim is to ensure that the traditional, time-consuming method of masonry construction, which consists of labour-intensive manual work on the building site, remains competitive with other methods of building. In addition, the quality of a masonry element has always been heavily dependent on the quality of workmanship and the weather. There are companies that can supply industrially prefabricated, custom masonry walls to suit individual projects. Such elements include reinforcement to cope with the stresses of transport to the building site, and on-site handling by crane (e.g. "preton" elements), and can be ordered complete with all openings and slots for services etc.

This form of construction enables the accurate scheduling of building operations, reduces the cost of erection and speeds up progress (making the whole procedure less susceptible to the vagaries of the weather). In addition, the components can be delivered without any construction moisture. On the other hand, they call for very precise advance planning, and heavy lifting equipment on site. Another disadvantage is that there is little leeway for subsequent alterations, and none at all once the elements have arrived on site.

Such prefabricated masonry elements can be produced in different ways. One method is to construct them vertically from bricks and mortar (i.e. normally), but they can also be laid horizontally in a form, reinforced and given a concrete backing. Some bricks are produced with perforations for reinforcing bars. It is also possible to combine conventional, in-situ work with prefabricated elements, e.g. the reveal to a circular opening, or an arched lintel – factory prefabricated – can be inserted into a wall built in the conventional manner. On the whole it is reasonable to say that owing to the high cost of the detailed, manual jointing of masonry units to form a masonry bond, such work can be replaced by erecting large-format, heavy, prefabricated masonry elements. Of course, the aim is always to limit the variation between elements and to produce a great number of identical elements. Consequently, there is a high degree of standardisation. And a new problem arises: the horizontal and vertical joints between the prefabricated wall elements.

Fig. 76: Erection of a facade made from prefabricated "preton" elements
Burkard Meyer Architekten: Swisscom headquarters in Winterthur (CH), 1999

Fig. 77: Facade assembled from three different prefabricated elements
Burkard Meyer Architekten: Swisscom headquarters, Winterthur (CH), 1999

Two contemporary examples

Burkard Meyer Architekten: Swisscom headquarters, Winterthur

The entire facade of this building, completed in 1999, is a combination of three different standard elements, all of which were designed to match the building grid of 5.60 m. The three elements are a) horizontal strip window with spandrel panel, b) plain wall, and c) double window. Apart from the peripheral concrete floor slab edges, all plain parts of the facade are in masonry. The wall elements of hard-fired bricks are reinforced and have continuous vertical grooves at the sides. Inserting permanently elastic rubber gaskets into these grooves locks the individual wall panels together; this avoids the need for external silicone joints, which would be fully exposed to the weather. Each element is tied back to the loadbearing structure at the top, and fixed at the bottom to the concrete nib with pins. All joints are 2 cm wide, and the horizontal ones remain open to guarantee air circulation behind the elements.

The wall elements comprise clay bricks measuring 24.4 x 11.5 x 5.2 cm, which were specially produced for this project (optimum dimensions for corner details etc.). They were built manually in a jig at the factory. Besides the independence from weather conditions (construction time: 12 months indoors), the advantage of this for site management was the fact that a standard element could be defined and it was then the responsibility of the factory management to maintain the quality of workmanship.

Right from the outset of design, the architects planned as many parts of the building as possible based on pre-fabricated elements. They also included the loadbearing structure, which besides an in-situ concrete core consists of reinforced concrete columns, beams and slabs (described in more detail in "Steel – Frames"). This is not heavyweight prefabrication in the style of panel construction, where the external wall elements are erected complete with loadbearing leaf, thermal insulation and internal finishes, but rather an additive combination of finished parts on site, i.e. a complementary system. In terms of the facade, reducing the number of standard facade elements to three and using prefabrication to rationalise the construction process was advantageous for logistics, engineering and economics.

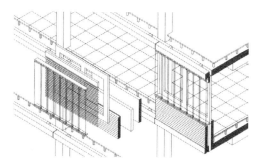

Fig. 79: Left: the various layers; right: element assembled and erected
Swisscom headquarters: exploded axonometric view of facade

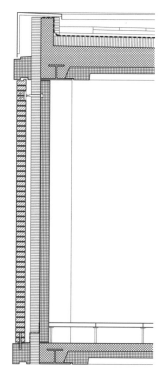

Fig. 78: Section through prefabricated facade element
Burkard Meyer Architekten: Swisscom headquarters, Winterthur (CH), 1999

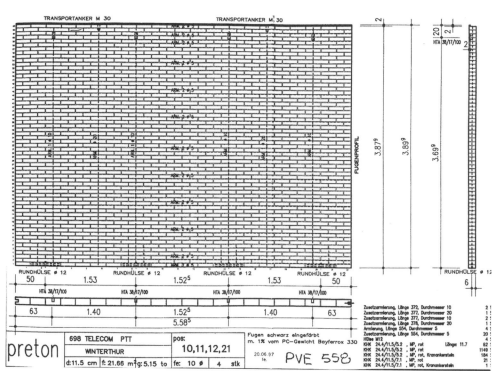

Fig. 80: Working (production) drawing for a prefabricated element
Burkard Meyer Architekten: Swisscom headquarters, Winterthur (CH), 1999

Fig. 81: West elevation, divided vertically into five segments: plinth, block, middle, tower, apex
Hans Kollhoff: high-rise block, Potsdamer Platz, Berlin (D), 1999

Hans Kollhoff: high-rise block, Potsdamer Platz, Berlin
The original plan was to construct a 100-m-high brick wall in Gothic bond. To do this, every bricklayer would have needed several stacks of bricks in various colours, plus specials, within reach on a 100-m-high scaffold. Owing to the load of the bricks, the hoists for the materials and the safety requirements, a very substantial, very expensive scaffold would have been needed for the entire duration of the project. In the light of the enormous size of the building and the complex logistics on the confined site in the centre of Berlin, the architects decided to use prefabricated components for the cladding. The industrially prefabricated facade elements were erected after the layer of insulation had been attached to the conventional loadbearing in situ concrete frame. The windows were installed last.

Individual parts such as spandrel panels, column cladding, lesenes and mullions make up the tectonic fabric of the facade. Their depth and (partial) profiling result in a massive, sculpted overall effect that evokes a masonry building. The principle of facade relief is employed elegantly here in the form of overlapping elements in order to conceal the unavoidable joints with their permanently elastic filling. As, on the one hand, the building does not have a rectangular footprint and, on the other, the facade is divided into five different sections (plinth, block, middle, tower and apex), there are very many different facade elements.

The production of the prefabricated elements was a complex process. Steel forms were used to minimise the tolerances. Rubber dies were laid in these with accurate three-dimensional joint layouts. This enabled the hard-fired bricks (the outermost layer of the element), cut lengthwise, to be laid precisely in the form. The next stage involved filling the joints with a concrete mix coloured with a dark pigment. The reinforcement was then placed on this external, still not fully stable facing and the form filled with normal-weight concrete. The porous surface of the hard-fired bricks resulted in an inseparable bond between the protective brick facing and the stabilising concrete backing. To create the (intended) impression of solid brickwork, specials were used at all edges and corners instead of the halved bricks.

The hard-fired bricks therefore assume no loadbearing functions and instead merely form a protective layer over the concrete. On the other hand, it is precisely the use of such bricks that promote the idea of the tower, i.e. humankind's presumption to want to build a skyscraper from thousands of tiny bricks. (Is that perhaps the reason behind the Gothic bond?) And in addition they paradoxically stand for the image of supporting and loading as well; in the plasticity of the facade they in no way appear to be merely "wallpaper".

As masonry materials have only a limited compressive strength, their use for high-rise loadbearing structures is limited – the tallest self-supporting clay brickwork building is the Monadnock Building in Chicago (18 storeys and external walls 2 m thick at ground-floor level!). Prefabricated facades therefore represent a satisfactory solution for high-rise buildings.

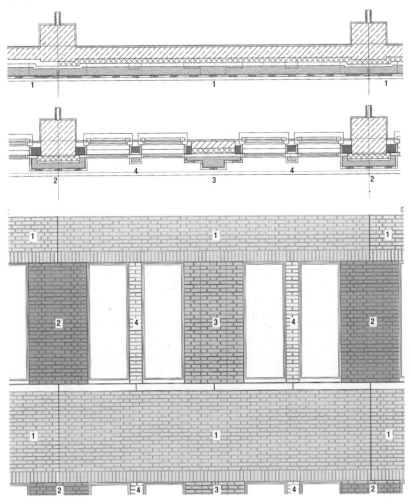

Fig. 82: Details of facade cladding to block: horizontal section through spandrel panel, horizontal section through windows, and elevation on windows and spandrel panel showing individual prefabricated parts and joints: 1 spandrel panel element, 2 column cladding, 3 lesene, 4 mullion
Hans Kollhoff: high-rise block, Potsdamer Platz, Berlin (D), 1999

Fig. 83: Digital prefabrication at the ETH Zurich
Wall elements for the Gantenbein vineyards in
Fläsch (CH), Bearth & Deplazes Architekten

**Fig. 84: Wall studies by students at the Chair of
Architecture & Digital Fabrication, ETH Zurich**
Robots with individual programs for defining the
position and orientation of every individual brick

Digital production

The logical consequence and climax of prefabrication in masonry construction is the complete mechanisation of the building process.

At the Chair of Architecture & Digital Fabrication at the ETH Zurich, Fabio Gramazio and Matthias Kohler have been experimenting with the mechanised fabrication of masonry elements since 2005. Within the scope of the scientific work, the fabrication workshops of the ETH have carried out pioneering trials and built prototypes of 100% digitally produced masonry elements. This means that a robot builds an element brick for brick – all at exactly the right angle and in the right position – according to a preset program. The controlled rotation of the bricks results in a configurable, "mouldable" surface, the precision, density and appearance of which far exceeds that of any traditional masonry bond.

It is a technology that achieves maximum results with minimum effort. By introducing this technological change to the laying of the bricks and by carrying out the work in the protected environs of a factory, the boundary conditions are altered. It is certainly conceivable that such robots will gain a foothold in the brickmaking industry. The consequence of this could be that the new technology will bring about major changes in the building materials industry as a whole because in the end the 1:1 worker–structure relationship no longer applies.

The aim of these developments is to combine the simplest, handed-down manual skills with the very latest technologies. This combination produces added value that has repercussions well beyond straightforward efficiency ideas. Digital production fulfils its purpose not only from the economic viewpoint, through savings in labour and time, but also in terms of its precision, which enables the ancient techniques of masonry construction to reach new heights. The complexity of the positioning of the bricks in the masonry construction can no longer be checked manually.

Furthermore, as the robot cannot handle mortar (at least so far), the courses of bricks must be joined with a special adhesive. From a technical viewpoint, this results in a better resistance to shear forces; and from the aesthetic viewpoint, the result is clean, precise lines. Of course, the joints remain the tectonic foundation of any masonry construction because they define the bricks. But by rotating the bricks, the empty perpends create a special type of perforation and in this way fulfil other building physics conditions. The joint without its mortar gains a new reason for its existence as a complementary, equal component in the function of a masonry wall. Besides the purely functional change, the visual effect is refreshingly different and lightweight. The joint now appears only in its extreme forms of "full" (bed joints) and "empty" (perpends), and therefore enables the drawing of digital images in a direct translation of the method of computer programming, which is based on sequences of ones and zeros only.

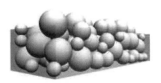

Fig. 85: From the sketch to the wall – steps in the design and production process
Bearth & Deplazes: Gantenbein vineyards, Fläsch (CH), 2006

Example of application

Bearth & Deplazes: Gantenbein vineyards, Fläsch

The basic requirements for wine production are low light levels and a constant temperature. Bearth & Deplazes Architekten therefore chose a design using perforated masonry for the Gantenbein vineyards in Fläsch.

The perforated wall is actually not a new invention, and besides contemporary examples can also be found in traditional forms of construction. Their history is as diverse as the techniques used. Karl Friedrich Schinkel's travel diary, written around 1826 during his journey through England, contains descriptions and sketches of the masonry walls of cloth factories, built in a "honeycomb" bond for ventilation purposes. Whereas in northern climates it is primarily ventilation requirements that

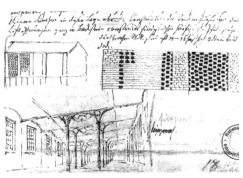

Fig. 86: Extract from the diary of Karl Friedrich Schinkel, written in England in 1826
"Construction of the drying houses [of cloth factories], where the ventilation openings are built entirely in bricks are common here. Piers between the perforated structure are often 14–16 feet high, 3 bricks wide, 2 bricks thick. Fireproof."

dictate a porous form of construction, in Arabic building traditions both climatic and cultural interests are important, in particular allowing women a view through the wall without attaining transparency. Individual, specially formed elements are integrated into the masonry bond and worked into arabesques. The origins of these can be found in the knitting and weaving of textiles.

For the application at the vineyard, after experimenting with various traditional facing masonry techniques, the architects decided to make use of the digital prefabrication above. In conjunction with Gramazio & Kohler, they developed a prototype in a real context.

The basic structure of the new production building consists of a concrete frame. The masonry elements prefabricated in the factory were then inserted as panels between the frame members. Each individual element rests on a prefabricated concrete lintel, which introduces a horizontal dividing element into the facade. Using a concrete frame means that the clay brick masonry does not have to carry any loads and that opens up further architectural options.

Fig. 87: View of facade: each brick looks like the pixel of a screen image.
Bearth & Deplazes: Gantenbein vineyards, Fläsch (CH), 2006

The use of a masonry robot and a skilfully structured program enabled the architects to achieve their artistic and constructional goals (light, ventilation, bracing of the structure) in an amazingly simple way and in a single, combined step. They accomplished these multiple demands by producing the individual panels with bricks positioned at different angles. This meant that in many instances two sides of a brick were visible. Besides the cross-ventilation and the play of light and shadow, this arrangement produces a surface that reinforces the sculpted effect of the facade.

In addition to the functional aspects, the appearance that this technology renders possible plays an important role. Characterised by the simple realisation of complex forms and enhanced by the absence of the mortar, the result is an extremely filigree effect from inside and a quasi-windowless solidity from outside. An image for the vineyard was developed step by step in the design process. The final outcome can be regarded as a media facade in its original sense.

Fig. 88: The light passing through the porous wall is reflected on the shiny floor and produces different images in the interior depending on the viewing angle.
Bearth & Deplazes: Gantenbein vineyards, Fläsch (CH), 2006

Fig. 89: Interior view
Rafael Moneo: Museo de Arte Romano, Mérida (E), 1986

Fig. 90: View during construction showing the "clay pipes"
Rafael Moneo: Museo de Arte Romano, Mérida (E), 1986

Composite construction and applications

As in all areas of building, there is an increased tendency towards hybrid systems in masonry as well, towards composite construction. Hardly any technique is still used "pure". Rather, materials and methods of working are combined and augmented, technologies adapted. In the case of masonry, this development is especially obvious because, although it points in a new direction, the actual technology of prefabrication is still based on the traditions practised for thousands of years. In a contemporary context, masonry that makes use of this handed-down knowledge is therefore even more exciting.

1. Prefabrication and *opus caementitium*
Rafael Moneo: Museo de Arte Romano, Mérida

The impressive building housing the Museum of Roman Art in Mérida, which is built on part of the largest Roman settlement in Spain, Augusta Emerita, consists of a series of massive arches and flying buttresses plus solid walls.

In the early 1980s during the construction of the museum the architect, Rafael Moneo, explained in a lecture at the ETH Zurich how he had managed to combine modern prefabrication and Roman building techniques in this project. The enormous arches, columns, and walls were prefabricated using an ingenious method allied to the Roman technique of *opus caementitium* (see "On the metaphysics of exposed concrete"). In the end, this represents a successful attempt to use an old method satisfactorily.

The concrete was poured between two slender leaves of hard-fired bricks with a very flat format; the finished wall thickness is equal to twice the brick (i.e. leaf) width plus the distance between the leaves. The concrete forms the core of the wall and binds the two leaves together. For their part, these leaves form the "attractive" surface and can be regarded as permanent formwork, which has to withstand the pressure of the wet concrete during casting and provide stability. But without the concrete core the masonry would be totally inadequate for the structural requirements of this building. In the Mérida project the clay bricks, which owing to their very flat format are reminiscent of Roman bricks, form the visible part of the loadbearing structure internally and externally. The concrete is used like a loose-fill material, which is why it is not reinforced. Together with the bricks it forms a compression-resistant element. The design of the loadbearing structure is such that all forces can be carried without the need for reinforcement. Masonry arches or exposed concrete lintels are incorporated over openings.

The prefabricated components, e.g. for walls and columns, were incorporated in the form of "clay pipes", which were assembled with a crane to form storey-high walls that were filled with concrete section by section. As the external walls are not insulated, the prefabricated units produced in this way needed only minimal butt joints, which are lost within the pattern of the brickwork. There are two options for the vertical joints: the hard-fired bricks can either be interlocked with each other (which would, however, mean high wastage), or the prefabricated units can be erected to leave a gap which is filled with masonry by hand ("zip" principle) and the concrete core cast later.

Fig. 91: Top: section through *opus caementitium* **wall;**
right: axonometric view of structure
Rafael Moneo: Museo de Arte Romano, Mérida (E), 1986

Fig. 92: Bamiyan, Afghanistan
Houses made from sun-dried loam bricks

Fig. 93: Building process: photos taken during construction
Rossbauer, Brnic, Graf: ETH House of Science, Bamiyan (Afghanistan), 2003–06

2. Low-tech, high-tech

Rossbauer, Brnic, Graf: ETH House of Science, Bamiyan
The ETH House of Science arose out of a competition entry and the diploma thesis written later by the students Ivica Brnic, Florian Graf and Wolfgang Rossbauer. The project is a model for knowledge transfer in the 21st century, i.e. always functioning in several directions.

Following an intensive investigation of the local circumstances and technologies, the form of construction chosen pays attention to local knowledge but at the same time introduces improvements. This basic idea is already part of the nature of building itself: modern technology and demanding architectural concepts are not ready-made products we can simply export to distant regions of the world. In order to implement them sensibly, according to the needs of other cultures, a careful, respectful adaptation to suit the local building culture and building technology conditions is needed. The interior layout and the typology were developed in close coordination with the local building culture and also to suit the existing facilities. The complex is therefore based on the courtyard typology. The entire structure – with the exception of the windows – is produced entirely from local building materials.

The extreme climatic situation with continental temperature fluctuations, the high level of solar radiation due to the high altitude, the strong winds and the increased risk of earthquakes were taken into account by designing a simple structure no more than two storeys high, and by using a composite system consisting of different types of masonry. All the masonry walls comprise several layers, with a core of reinforced concrete walls and columns to guarantee seismic resistance. Placed around them is a thick layer of straw-loam bricks serving as an insulating and heat storage layer, which is in turn protected from the weather by a facing of fired bricks.

These very thick masonry walls produce an essentially balanced temperature over the entire year. The heat stored in the bricks during the day is released slowly

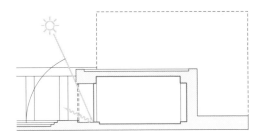

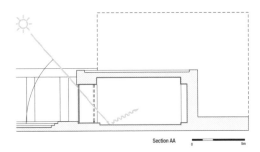

Section AA

Fig. 94: Regulating the climate by means of a double-leaf facade
Rossbauer, Brnic, Graf: ETH House of Science, Bamiyan (Afghanistan), 2003–06

at night. Besides the day–night rhythm, the seasonal changes are also taken into account. Whereas in summer, functioning sunshades are indispensable for preventing the heat from entering the building, in winter it is important to allow as much warm sunlight into the rooms as possible in order to heat the interior. Accordingly, the facade consists of a double layer of windows for summer and winter. During the summer the windows lie deep within the reveals, which shades them and protects them against direct sunlight. In the winter the panes of glass in the plane of the facade absorb the solar radiation and radiate the heat into the building.

Fig. 95: Complex masonry wall construction with seismic resistance
Rossbauer, Brnic, Graf: ETH House of Science, Bamiyan (Afghanistan), 2003–06

Fig. 96: The architects' vision realised: view of finished courtyard
Rossbauer, Brnic, Graf: ETH House of Science, Bamiyan (Afghanistan), 2003–06

On the metaphysics of exposed concrete

Andrea Deplazes

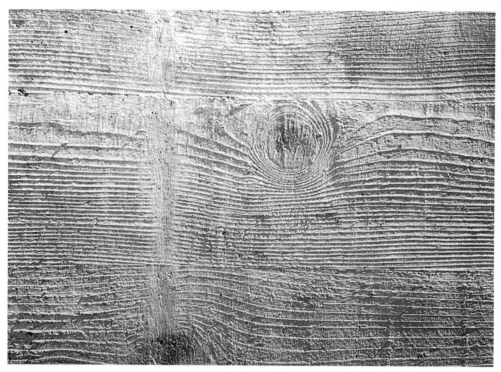

Fig. 1: Formwork "fingerprint"
Rough-sawn boards

Loadbearing structures made of reinforced concrete characterise everyday urban life. Whenever possible, the construction industry employs this material. It is relatively inexpensive in comparison with other building materials – as work on the building site progresses swiftly and (seemingly) no highly qualified specialists are required to install it. Reinforced concrete has simply become the 20th century's building material of choice – and the symbol of unbridled building activity. The "concreting of the environment" is a proverbial invective denouncing the destruction of landscape, nature and habitats.

However, the less visible reinforced concrete is – if it only serves as a "constructional means to an end" in the true sense of the word, i.e. for engineering purposes or the structural shell, and is later plastered or rendered – the more acceptable it seems to be (whether out of resignation or disinterest does not matter, as often there seems to be no competitive alternative to concrete). It's a completely different story with reinforced concrete designed to be openly visible, with so-called fair-face concrete. In order to recognise the characteristics of exposed concrete we have to distance ourselves from today's pragmatic approach. The term "exposed concrete" itself makes us sit up. If there is no invisible concrete, what is it that makes concrete become exposed? And if reinforced concrete is not used visibly, but as a "constructional means to an end", how does it influence the development and design of form?

Surface

With exposed concrete, what is visible is the concrete surface. This seemingly unspectacular observation becomes significant when we draw comparisons with facing masonry. Facing masonry demonstrates the order and logic of its bonded texture and jointing as well as the precision and the course of the building operations. The brickwork bond is therefore more than the sum of its parts, its structure is perceived as an aesthetic ornamentation, fixing or depicting a "true state of affairs". Louis Kahn argued that ornamentation – unlike decoration, which is applied, is a "foreign" addition – always develops from tectonic interfaces up to the point of independence (through the transformation of materials and the emancipation of originally constructional functions). Against the background of such a cultural view, aesthetics means: "Beauty is the splendour of the truth" (Mies van der Rohe's interpretation of St Augustine applied to modern building culture).

In contrast to this, exposed concrete – or rather the cement "skin" two or three millimetres thick – hides its internal composite nature. Exposed concrete does not disclose its inner workings, but instead hides its basic structure under an extremely thin outer layer. This surface layer formalises and withholds what our senses could perceive: an understanding of the concrete's composition and "how it works". And this is why concrete is not perceived as the natural building material it really is, but rather as an "artificial, contaminated conglomerate".

Formwork

But although no visible "powers of design" from inside the concrete conglomerate penetrate the thin outer layer, the surface still exhibits texture – traces of a structure that no longer exists: the formwork. All that can still be detected on exposed concrete are "fingerprints". The term "texture" stems from the same origin as "text" or "textile" – meaning fabric – and thus immediately hints at what earlier on has been dubbed "filigree construction". The formwork, made of timber or steel, belongs to this category of tectonics. Especially in the early stages of reinforced concrete technology, it was an autonomous, usually quite artful – albeit temporary – work of carpentry (e.g. Richard Coray's bridge centering). Formwork and concrete form a seemingly inseparable package.

As the concrete has to be poured into formwork in order to take on the desired form, three questions arise: Isn't every type of concrete in the end exposed concrete? (That is, how do we classify the quality of the concrete surface?) Which criteria apply to the design of the formwork? (That is, how do the materials and techniques of formwork construction influence the moulding of the concrete?) Isn't it odd that an ephemeral structure (filigree construction) is set up in order to generate another, monolithic one (solid construction)? (That is, what are the characteristics that tie concrete to its formwork?)

Incrustation

The Roman builders tried to counteract this metamorphic inconceivability by "exposing" the concrete's inner structure, while concealing its practical component – this unspectacular mixture of gravel, sand and cement. *Opus caementitium* is a composite of permanent stone or brick formwork with a "loose-fill" core of concrete. The concrete comprises the same materials as the "formwork" – in various grain sizes mixed with water and appropriate binding agents like hydrated lime or cement and worked into a pulp.

It's obvious that this – just like building with cob – is one of the most original creations of earthworks; the shapeless earthen pulp proves its worth in coursed masonry. This kind of exposed concrete construction has been preserved to this day, e.g. in the viaducts of the Rhätische railway line. It lends visible structure and expression to a mixture of materials that on its own has no quality of form, in the sense of a "reading" of the concrete sediment through the technique of incrustation: a kind of "permanent formwork" made of stone or brickwork, which at the same time forms a characterising crust on its visible surface.

Fig. 2: "Weightless" fair-face concrete
Tadao Ando: Koshino House, Ashiya (J), 1980

Transformation

The other line of development, the "strategy of formwork construction" mentioned above, leads through timber construction and carpentry, hence through tectonics, which has its own laws of construction and thus already influences the form-finding process of the concrete pour. Moreover, wood has a transitory and provisional character, which seems to predestine its use for formwork. It seems that within our image of the world, our ethical and religious understanding of nature and life, durability can only be achieved through transitoriness and constant renewal (optimisation).

This triggers – consciously or unconsciously – a process of transformation; for the transfer of timber to stone construction is another fundamental topic within the morphological development of Western architecture. Although – as with ancient temples – the laws of stone construction are applied, the original timber structures remain visible as ornamental, stylistic elements. In other words, technological immanence, advancing incessantly, stands face to face with recalcitrant cultural permanence.

It is the same with exposed concrete, where through the simple act of filling the formwork with concrete the underlying timber manifests itself, even though the concrete pulp, now hardened within the formwork, has nothing to do with timber and is anything but ephemeral.

Is this a clear contradiction to the plastic-cubic shape of a concrete block, which moreover has the appearance of being cast in stone?

Monolith

The monolithic appearance of exposed concrete makes a building look like a processed blank or sculpture, a workpiece created by removing material from a block. This is especially successful if the traces of the concreting work – the lifts, the pours – are suppressed or obscured by the thickly textured traces of the formwork. In reality, however, this character is the result of several cumulative operations!

The quality of the formwork, its make-up, plays a significant role in moulding a building's character. Sometimes it is coarse, lumpy, with leaking joints and honeycombing. As a result the conglomerate structure of a sedimentary rock and the metaphor of an archaic foundling can sometimes still be felt, e.g. in Rudolf Olgiati's Allemann House, set amid a precarious topography. At other times the formwork boasts skin-like smoothness, with formwork joints looking like the seams of a tent, which lends the exposed concrete a visual quality devoid of any "heaviness". This is the case with Koshino House by Tadao Ando. Here, the formwork is so smooth that, together with the concrete's tiny height differences, it lends the walls a textile materiality or even "ceramic fragility" when viewed with the light shining across its surface.

Fig. 3: "Archaic Foundling"
Rudolf Olgiati : House for Dr Allemann, Wildhaus
(CH), 1968

Hybrid

Having based our evaluations on pragmatic working methods, we find an unexpectedly complex result: the building as a heavy, monolithic edifice represents the dialectal pole of our observations by establishing the significant characteristics of exposed concrete's earthen component: mass, weight, plasticity, body, density, pressure. Consequently, we assume the other pole has to be derived from the filigree construction, which would allow one to deduce new form-finding criteria. The combination of concrete and steel basically creates a unique hybrid material, within which the concrete guarantees compressive strength. The steel, for its part, provides the tensile strength in the form of a reinforcing mesh, a tension net created from a minimum of material. Reinforced concrete is the only building material that possesses this perfect bi-polar quality. The term "hybrid", however, has to be defined more precisely: the two morphologic components exist and complement each other on different "levels of consciousness" – constantly interacting and shifting from one system to the other, from the consciously perceivable to the subconscious and vice versa. This is in contrast to structural steelwork, for example, where one and the same member can resist both compressive and tensile forces.) The outer form of the hardened concrete is physically perceptible (visually, sense of touch, acoustically etc.), and has completely shed the dull metaphysical quality it possessed in its original form, its embryonic state as an earthen pulp. Its Cartesian network of reinforcement, however, lies dormant within, although altogether invisible to the eye. On the outside, its existence manifests itself only indirectly. It can only be divined and "sensed", with the most delicate of all loadbearing structures in exposed concrete seemingly defying all the laws of physics. The formerly heavy, solid monolith loses its ground-based nature and is transformed into the opposite, e.g. a space frame of linear members, a leaf-like shell, a vertical stack of thin slabs and supporting rods, etc.

In his theory of architecture, Carl Bötticher defines these two "levels of consciousness" as an "art form" (external, possessing a cultural connotation, tectonics) and a "core form" (internal, function, Newtonian physics). As a design rule Bötticher required that both forms correspond logically in the best possible way, with the "core" – as "true fact", reflecting from inside to outside – merging into one with its artfully fashioned envelope or surface, pupating in it and thus taking on a visible form (iconography).

This theory and the circumstance that concrete depends on the rational availability of formwork correspond with the scientific, engineering view of the energy flow deep below the surface. This is actually – for technological reasons! – an intensification of formerly visible

Fig. 4: Outer form and inner life

tectonic form criteria (e.g. the visualisation of load and column present in the orders of ancient temple-building). It is an inversion of outer form and core, smoothing and thus formalising the outer form. (Example: the morphology of the column.) The formerly visible tectonic balance of power apparent in the outer form is now turned inside out like a glove and rationalised after the model of three-dimensional tension trajectories, a model which the accumulation and bundling of the reinforcement seeks to follow and correspond with as closely as possible.

Skeleton structures

Here lies the source of an agreement that engineers speaking on form-finding for loadbearing structures, e.g. for bridges or tunnels, like to refer to when they present the complex logic of energy flows as "the motor that powers form". More often than not, however, the outer form develops in accordance with the critical cross-section of a structural component and the most economic formwork material available. Over time this material has developed from a one-off to a reusable one. Through distinct stages of formwork construction, the building process has become more organised, and the construction itself now shows traces of the modularity of the formwork layout and the large sheet steel prefabricated formwork panels. The flow of forces, however, is organised according to the actual energy concentration through bundling and distributing the reinforcement deep inside the concrete, and this seldom influences the external form.

The delicate constructions resulting from this approach seem to originate from pure science, powered by the spirit of rationalism, operating with analysis, geometry, order and abstraction. Consequently, we try to rid the exposed concrete of all "worldly" traces, to achieve its transition from a primitive past as an "earthwork" to a smooth, seamless artefact, unsoiled by any working process.

Equally telling is the expression "skeleton structure", which I heard being used by several engineers explaining the character of their bridge designs. One described a complete, elementary de-emotionalisation "from inside to outside", which only manifested itself through utmost abstraction of form and a reduction to the naked loadbearing structure in the form of simple geometrical elements. Another described a biomorphic analogy with a skeleton. A natural skeleton structure, however, develops in a self-organised way along a network of tension trajectories. Its form is the immediate result of this network taking into account the position of its parts within the static and dynamic conditions of the skeleton as a whole. For the reasons mentioned earlier, such congruencies of cause and effect, energy and form are not feasible and seldom advisable.

Fig. 5: The skeletal frame

Liberated concrete

Another idiosyncrasy has to be discussed. Concrete, being a blend (amalgam), does not have any implicit form – it can be moulded into any shape imaginable. In the same way the steel mesh making up the reinforcement does not have any preconfigured limitations, no "boundary". This implies the possibility of a free, biomorphic workability of reinforced concrete – comparable to the process of modelling a lump of clay in the hand. In reality, however, the inflexibility of the formwork, its characteristic tectonic rigidity, must be overcome. This is possible with the help of the adhesives of modern timber engineering (moulded plywood) or synthetic fibres, but such solutions are difficult to justify economically. (Example: "Einstein Tower" Observatory by Erich Mendelsohn, planned in reinforced concrete but finally built in rendered brickwork). The only way out would be to release the concrete from its formwork – that tectonic, technological and iconographic corset! This can be done by using a flexible but relatively stable reinforcing mesh and sprayed concrete (e.g. Gunite, Shotcrete). So far, this technology in exposed concrete construction has left no noteworthy traces in architecture – except for the pitiful interior decoration found at some provincial dancehalls. Sadly, the liberated exposed concrete of such examples is only reduced to its primitive origins – the metaphor of a dull, platonic earthen cavern.

Conclusion

1. Despite the fact that exposed concrete is designed and developed according to rational and technical arguments, seemingly irrational construction processes abound.

2. Exposed concrete represents the outcome of various transformation processes and metamorphoses that have left their mark (a kind of "memory" of or former states).

3. A precarious congruency exists between outer form and "inner life". The thin surface layer of exposed concrete seldom plays the role of the iconographic mediator.

4. The quality of the concrete surface characterises the building as a whole within its architectural theme. It tends towards either the archaic or the abstract.

5. Form is defined as the pre-effected synthesis of various influencing factors, with technological immanence rarely correlating with cultural permanence.

6. The concrete form is relative to the internal flow of forces. This flow is interpreted either as a system in equilibrium based on constructional and spiritual factors, or as a stress model with foundations in natural science and reality.

7. Every kind of concrete shows a face.

Fig. 6: Planned on reinforced concrete, built in rendered brick work
Erich Mendelsohn: "Einstein Tower" Observatory, Potsdam (D), 1914

Further reading
- Carl Bötticher: *Die Tektonik der Hellenen*, Potsdam, 1852.
- Louis I. Kahn: *Die Architektur und die Stille. Gespräche und Feststellungen*, Basel, 1993.
- Fritz Neumeyer: *Ludwig Mies van der Rohe. Das Kunstlose Wort. Gedanken zur Baukunst*, Berlin, 1986.
- Werner Oechslin: *Stilhülse und Kern: Otto Wagner, Adolf Loos und der evolutionäre Weg zur modernen Architektur*, Zurich, 1994.
- Gottfried Semper: *Der Stil in den technischen und tektonischen Künsten ...* vol. I, Frankfurt a. M., 1860, vol. II, Munich, 1863.
  – English translation: Gottfried Semper: *Style, in the Technical and Tectonic Arts; or, Practical Aesthetics*, Los Angeles, 2004.
- Eugène Viollet-le-Duc: *Definitionen. Sieben Stichworte aus dem Dictionnaire raisonné de l'architecture*, Basel, 1993.
  – English translation: Eugène Viollet-le-Duc: *The Foundations of Architecture: Selections from the Dictionnaire raisonné*, Basel 1993.
- Urs Widmer: *5 Schweizer Brückenbauer: Othmar H. Ammann, Richard Coray, Guillaume-Henri Dufour, Hans Ulrich Grubenmann, Robert Maillart*, Zurich, 1985.
- Roland Barthes: *The Eiffel Tower and Other Mythologies*, transl. Richard Howard, New York, 1978.

The materials

Normal-weight concrete (density 2400–2550 kg/m³) is generally produced by mixing together cement, water, fine and coarse aggregates (sand and gravel respectively) in the following ratios:
- aggregates, grain size –32 mm   2000 kg/m³
- Portland cement   250–400 kg/m³
- water   150 kg/m³

Depending on the desired properties this ratio can be varied both during production and after hardening.

Wet concrete should exhibit the following properties:
- easy workability – good compactability
- plastic consistency – easy mouldability
- good cohesion – low segregation tendency
- good water-retention capacity – no tendency to "bleed" (water seeping from the wet concrete))

The requirements for hardened concrete are as follows:
- good strength
- homogeneous, dense and consistent concrete microstructure
- uniform surface structure without blowholes
- resistance to the weather and external influences

The wet concrete properties given above are closely related to the proportions of aggregates, ultra-fine particles, cement, water and cement paste. Changing any one of these variables can also change the properties of the wet and/or hardened concrete.

Composition of concrete

In terms of its weight and its volume, concrete consists primarily of aggregate. But the situation is somewhat different if we consider the internal surface area, i.e. the cumulative surface areas of all the constituents of the concrete. In this case the cement proportion is by far the largest. And because of its ability to react with water, the cement is also the sole constituent that causes the concrete to set.

Concrete mixes

When deciding on the composition of the concrete, the concrete mix, the prime aim is to optimise
- the workability of the concrete,
- its strength,
- its durability,
- the cost of its production.

Cement

Cement is a hydraulic binder, i.e. a substance which after mixing with water sets both in air and also underwater.

Cement production

The production of Portland cement involves preparing the raw material in terms of its grain size and composition, heating this until sintering takes place and finally crushing the heated product to form a fine, mixable and reactive cement powder. Basically, the production of cement involves four production stages:

1. Extraction and breaking-up of the raw material
One tonne of Portland cement requires 1.5 tonnes of raw material in the form of limestone and marl or clay because carbon dioxide and water are driven off during the heating process. The rocks are first broken down to fist size at the quarry.

2. Mixing and crushing the raw material to form a dust
At this stage the various raw materials are mixed together to achieve the correct chemical composition. The rocks are crushed in ball or roller mills and dried at the same time. They leave the mill as a fine dust which is thoroughly mixed in large homogenisation silos to achieve better consistency.

3. Heating the dust to produce clinker
The heating process (approx. 1450 °C) is a key operation in the production of cement. Before the dust is fed into the rotary kiln, it flows through the heat exchanger tower where it is preheated to nearly 1000 °C. After heating, the red-hot clinker leaves the kiln and is cooled quickly with air. Coal, oil, natural gas and, increasingly, alternatives such as scrap wood or dried sewage sludge are used as the fuel.

4. Grinding the clinker with gypsum and additives to form cement
In order to produce a reactive product from the clinker, it is ground in a ballmill together with a little gypsum as a setting regulator. Depending on the type of cement required, some of the clinker is mixed with mineral substances (limestone, silica dust, cinder sand [granulated blast furnace slag], pulverised fuel ash) during grinding, thereby producing other types of Portland-composite and blastfurnace cements.

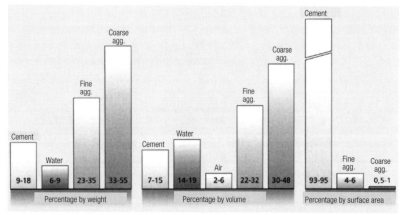

Fig. 7: Composition of concrete

Water

This is not just the potable water added during the mixing process but instead, the entire quantity of water contained in wet concrete; this total amount must be taken into account when determining the water/cement ratio. The water in the concrete is made up of:

- the water for mixing
- the surface moisture of the aggregates, if applicable, the water content of concrete additives and admixtures

The total water content has two concrete technology functions. First, to achieve hydration of the cement; second, to create a plastic, easily compacted concrete.

Mineral aggregates

The term mineral aggregates normally covers a mixture of (finer) sand and (coarser) gravel with a range of grain sizes. This blend of the individual grain-size fractions forms the framework for the concrete and should be assembled with a minimum of voids. A good-quality mineral aggregate has various advantages over the surrounding, binding, hydrated cement:

- normally a higher strength
- better durability
- no change in volume due to moisture, hence a reduction in the shrinkage mass of the concrete
- absorbs the heat of hydration and hence exercises an attenuating effect during the curing process

The most important properties of mineral aggregates are:

- density
- bulk density
- moisture content
- quality of stone, grain form and surface characteristics
- cleanliness
- granulometric composition

Grading

Porous and excessively soft materials impair the quality of the concrete. The grain form, but mainly its grading and the surface characteristics determine the compactability and water requirement.

Practical experience has shown that grading with exclusively angular grain-size fractions is acceptable. Angular mineral aggregates can improve the compressive strength, tensile strength and abrasion resistance of the concrete, but do impair its workability. Owing to the limited number of workable deposits of gravel still available in Switzerland, angular and recycled mineral aggregates will have to be employed more and more in future.

The water requirement, and hence one of the most important properties of a mineral aggregate, is governed by grading, the surface characteristics, the specific surface area and the form of the individual grains. The grading must guarantee a blend with minimum voids and optimum compactability (high density = good quality characteristics).

The grading of a mineral aggregate is determined by the ratios of the proportions of the individual grain sizes. Sieving the mixture with standardised mesh and square-hole sieves results in a certain amount being retained on every sieve. [These amounts are weighed separately and plotted (cumulatively) on a graph against the sieve size in percentage by weight of the mixture to produce the grading curve of the aggregate (see fig. 12).]

The absolute limits according to SN EN 12260 are shown in grey, tried-and-tested granulometric compositions are shown in dark grey.

Fig. 8: Natural/rounded grains   Fig. 9: Angular/squared grains

Fig. 10: Natural elongated grains   Fig. 11: Angular elongated grains

Concrete admixtures

Definition and classification

Concrete admixtures are solutions or suspensions of substances in water that are mixed into the concrete in order to change the properties of the wet and/or hardened concrete, e.g. workability, curing, hardening or frost resistance, by means of a chemical and/or physical action.

The modern building chemicals industry has developed a whole series of admixtures for influencing the properties of the concrete:

- Plasticisers: These achieve better workability, easier placing, etc. for the same water/cement ratio. So they enable the use of low water/cement ratios, which benefits the strength.

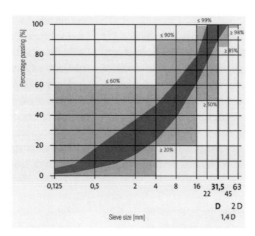

Fig. 12: Grading curve

In Switzerland the common concrete additives in use are:
– Inert additives (do not react with cement and water): inorganic pigments, used to colour concrete and mortar; fibrous materials, especially steel and synthetics, seldom glass fibres.
– Pozzolanic additives (react with substances released during hydration): contribute to developing strength and improving the density of the hydrated cement.

– Thickeners: These prevent premature segregation and improve the consistency. Particularly useful for fair-face concrete.
– Retarders: By delaying the reaction these products ensure that the wet concrete can still be compacted many hours after being placed. Construction joints can thus be avoided. They are primarily used for large mass concrete and waterproof concrete components.
– Accelerators: Through more rapid hydration these encourage faster setting. This may be desirable for timetable reasons (faster progress) or for special applications, e.g. sprayed concrete.
– Air entrainers: These create air-filled micropores (~0.3 mm). Such pores interrupt the capillaries and thus enhance the frost resistance.

The use of admixtures requires careful clarification and planning. Excessive amounts can lead to segregation, severe shrinkage, loss of strength etc.

There are economic and technical reasons for using concrete admixtures. They can lower the cost of labour and materials. Their application can save energy and simplify concreting operations. Indeed, certain properties of the wet and hardened concrete can be achieved only through the use of concrete admixtures.

Concrete additives

Concrete additives are fine minerals that influence certain properties of the concrete, primarily the workability of the wet concrete and the strength and density of the hardened concrete. In contrast to concrete admixtures, all the additives are generally added in such large quantities that their proportion must be taken into account in the volume calculations.

Source: Holcim (Schweiz AG): *Betonpraxis*, 2001/2003

The concreting process

Reinforcement

Reinforced concrete is a composite material consisting of concrete and steel. The interaction of these two materials – the reinforcement resisting the tensile stresses, the concrete resisting the compressive stresses – is not an additive process, but rather leads to a new loadbearing quality. The size of the reinforcement is determined in a structural analysis which takes into account the internal

Fig. 13: Profiles of reinforcing bars

forces. To simplify the process the main reinforcement is positioned at the most important sections to suit the maximum bending moments. Apart from the structural requirements, the arrangement and spacing of reinforcing bars and meshes also has to take account of optimum compaction; a poker vibrator must be able to pass through the cage of reinforcement.

Great attention must be paid to ensuring that the reinforcement has adequate concrete cover. Almost all damage to reinforced concrete structures can be attributed to insufficient concrete cover and not settlement or a lack of reinforcement. Sections with inadequate concrete cover are potential weak spots and invite corrosion of the reinforcing bars. The oxide crystals of the rust require more volume than the steel, and the ensuing bursting action results in the concrete cover cracking, thus allowing further corroding influences (moisture, air) even easier access to the steel, which can, in the end, impair the load-carrying capacity of the member. The concrete cover, i.e. the distance between the concrete surface (or the surface of the formwork) and the nearest reinforcing bars, depends on various factors but should not be less than 3 cm.

Fig. 14: Timber formwork with formwork ties

Fig. 15: Steelfixers at work

Formwork

In order to achieve the desired final form, concrete is cast in formwork.

Concrete cast in formwork on the building site is known as *in situ concrete*. The concrete cast in a factory, to produce *prefabricated components*, is known as *precast concrete*.

The building of formwork for concrete sometimes calls for excellent carpentry skills. The formwork material itself must be of sufficient strength and must represent a stable assembly propped and stiffened so that it remains dimensionally accurate (no distortion) during placing and compaction of the concrete.

All butt and construction joints must be sealed with appropriate materials, and the formwork must be leakproof on all sides to prevent cement paste from escaping during compaction.

Formwork for concrete surfaces that are to remain exposed in the finished building can make use of a number of materials depending on the type of surface required, e.g. timber boards, wood-based panels, sheet steel; even fibre-cement, corrugated sheet metal, glass, rubber or plastic inlays are used on occasions.

Timber formwork
Boards
In Switzerland the timber boards used for formwork are mainly indigenous species such as spruce or pine. The selection and assembly of the boards presumes a certain level of knowledge and experience. Boards of the same age having the same density and same resin content will exhibit similar absorption behaviour; boards with a high or low resin content can be seen to behave differently as soon as the release agent (oil, wax emulsion) is applied. Concrete surfaces cast against new, highly absorbent boards will have a lighter colour than those cast against old or reused boards.

Format: The dimensions are governed by the possibilities for solid timber. The boards should not distort when in contact with water or moisture. Max. width: approx. 30 cm; max. length: approx. 500–600 cm; customary width: 10–15 cm; customary length: up to 300 cm.

Panels
Compared with timber boards, formwork panels made from wood-based materials have considerable advantages. They are lighter in weight and can be assembled faster (50–70% of the erection costs can be saved when using panels instead of boards). In addition, they last longer because the synthetic resin lacquer which is normally used to coat such panels detaches more readily from the concrete when striking the formwork. Format: Formwork panels are available in the most

diverse sizes with the maximum dimensions depending on the conditions on site. In Switzerland the formats 50 x 200 cm and 50 x 250 cm, for example, are widely used.

Modular formwork, table forms, wall forms
Industry can now supply a highly varied range of formwork systems that enable large areas to be set up and taken down quickly: modular elements for walls, floor formwork with appropriate propping, self-supporting climbing and sliding formwork etc.

In order to combine the economic advantages of modular formwork with the aesthetic qualities of other types of formwork, modular formwork is these days often used merely to support "traditional" boards and panels.

Fig. 16: Table form for floor slab

Steel formwork
Forms made from sheet steel are used both for in situ and precast concrete. The higher capital cost of such formwork is usually offset by the high number of reuses possible.

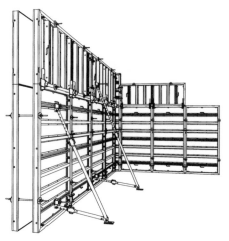

Fig. 17: Steel wall forms

Formwork surfaces
The formwork material (timber, wood-based panel, plywood, hardboard, fibre-cement, steel, plastic etc.) and its surface finish (rough, planed, smooth, plastic-coated etc.) determine the surface texture of the exposed concrete.

The smoothness or roughness of the formwork can influence the shade of the exposed concrete surface. For instance, completely smooth formwork results in an exposed concrete surface with a lighter colour than one produced with rough formwork.

Release agents
These are oil, wax, paste and emulsion products applied to the contact faces between the formwork material and the concrete to enable easier separation of formwork and concrete surface – without damage – when striking the forms. In addition, they help to create a consistent surface finish on the concrete and protect the formwork material, helping to ensure that it can be reused.

The suitability of a particular release agent depends on the material of the formwork (timber, plywood, hardboard, fibre-cement, steel, plastic etc.).

Placing and compacting the concrete

Good-quality exposed concrete surfaces call for a completely homogeneous, dense concrete structure. The wet concrete must be placed in the concrete without undergoing any changes, i.e. segregation, and then evenly compacted in situ.

Compacting
The purpose of compacting the concrete is not only to ensure that the formwork is completely filled, but rather to dissipate trapped pockets of air, distribute the cement paste evenly and ensure that the aggregates are densely packed without any voids. In addition, compaction guarantees that the concrete forms a dense boundary layer at the surface and thus fully surrounds the reinforcement.

Methods of compaction

Punning:	with rods or bars
Tapping forms:	for low formwork heights
Vibrating:	standard method on building sites
	immersion (poker) vibrators are immersed in the wet concrete
	external vibrators vibrate the formwork from outside
Tamping:	in the past the customary method of compaction

Fig. 18: Compacting the concrete

Vibrating

A poker vibrator should be quickly immersed to the necessary depth and then pulled out slowly so that the concrete flows together again behind the tip of the poker.

Vibrators should not be used to spread the concrete because this can lead to segregation. If segregation does occur during compaction, the result is clearly recognisable differences in the structure of the concrete, possibly even honeycombing on the surface.

The depth of concrete placed in one operation should be limited. The weight of the wet concrete can be so great that pockets of air cannot escape to the surface.

Curing

The hardening, or setting, of the concrete is not the result of it drying out. If we allow concrete to dry out too quickly, this leads to shrinkage cracks because the tensile strength is too low. And if we sprinkle the concrete with water, efflorescence (lime deposits on the surface) will almost certainly be the outcome. The answer is to allow the concrete to retain its own moisture for as long as possible, which is best achieved by covering it with waterproof sheeting. These must be positioned as close to the concrete surface as possible but without touching it because otherwise they may cause blemishes.

Such methods are labour-intensive but indispensable for exposed – especially fair-face – concrete surfaces.

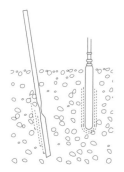

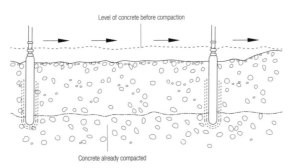

Level of concrete before compaction

Concrete already compacted

Figs 19 and 20: Compacting with a rod (punning) (left) and a poker vibrator (right)

Compaction procedure

Construction joints

When working with in situ concrete, joints between earlier and later pours are almost inevitable. The strength of the formwork required to resist the pressure of the wet concrete also places a limit on the quantity of concrete that can be economically placed in one operation. Concreting operations must therefore be planned in stages and separated by joints.

The location and form of these construction joints are determined by the architect and the structural engineer together. Given the fact that it is impossible to conceal such joints, it is advisable to plan them very carefully.

If new concrete is to be cast against a existing concrete surface (a construction joint), the concrete surface at the point of contact must be thoroughly roughened and cleaned, and prior to pouring the wet concrete wetted as well. And if such a construction joint must be watertight, it is advisable to use a richer mix at the junction with the existing concrete or to coat it first with a layer of cement mortar. It is also possible to add a retarder to the last section prior to the construction joint so that the concrete at the intended joint position does not set immediately and the following concrete can then be cast against this "still wet" concrete.

10 rules for the production of concrete

Fig. 21: Placing concrete by crane skip

1 Concrete is produced by mixing together cement, *coarse and fine aggregates* (gravel and sand respectively) and water. Normally, 1 m³ of concrete contains 300–350 kg cement, approx. 2000 kg aggregates and 130–200 l water. Depending on the intended use of the concrete, additives and/or admixtures can be mixed in (admixture: approx. 0.5–10 kg/m³; additive: approx. 5–50 kg/m³). After mixing, the concrete must be placed and compacted as soon as possible.

2 Together, the *cement* and the water form the paste which sets to form hydrated cement and binds together the aggregates. The cement is supplied as a powder and is therefore added to the fine/coarse aggregate blend based on weight.

Stored in the dry, cement can be kept for months. But as soon as it becomes moist, it forms lumps and is then unusable.

3 Aggregates must be washed clean. Contaminated, greasy and incrusted aggregates are unsuitable for use in concrete. Slate-like and marlaceous constituents or mica also impair the quality of concrete.

The aggregates must exhibit an appropriate *grading* that is as consistent as possible. The maximum grain size is usually 32 mm.

4 The water content has a crucial influence on the quality of the concrete: less water means fewer pores and hence a concrete with improved strength, density and durability.

The water content is specified by the *water/cement ratio* (w/c ratio). This ratio is calculated by dividing the weight of water (moisture in aggregate plus mixing water) by the weight of cement.

Good concrete requires a w/c ratio between 0.45 and 0.55; w/c ratios > 0.60 should be avoided. A concrete with a high sand content requires more water than one with coarser-grained aggregate. Good-quality concrete therefore contains more coarse than fine aggregate.

5 *Admixtures and/or additives* can be mixed into the concrete in order to modify certain properties of the wet and/or hardened concrete. The most important of these are:

– Plasticisers: to improve the workability of the concrete or enable the water content to be reduced and hence achieve a better quality concrete.

– Accelerators and retarders: to influence the onset and duration of the curing process.

– Air entrainers: to improve the frost resistance – essential when the concrete will be exposed to deicing salts, but micro hollow beads are often more advantageous for very stiff wet concrete.

– Additives: fillers and fly ash can replace ultra-fine particles – but not the cement – and improve the workability; hydraulic lime is also used as an additive; pigments can be added to produce coloured concrete.

6 The *formwork* should be thoroughly cleaned out prior to concreting. Water in the formwork, excessive release agent, sawdust and any form of soiling can impair the appearance of the concrete. The formwork should be leakproof. The distance between reinforcement and formwork must be correct and the reinforcement must be secured to prevent displacement.

7 Proper *mixing* of the concrete is vital for its quality and workability. The optimum mixing time is > 1 min. Prolonging the mixing time improves the workability and has a favourable effect on exposed surfaces. Insufficient mixing is not beneficial to the properties of the wet or hardened concrete.

8 When using ready-mixed concrete it must be ensured that the loss of water during transport is kept to a minimum. Concrete transported in open vehicles must be covered. During periods of hot weather the available working time on the *building site* can be severely shortened due to the effects of the heat during transport. Adding water on site to "dilute" the concrete impairs the quality of the concrete.

Ready-mixed concrete must be ordered in good time and specified in full.

9 Concrete should be *placed* in even, horizontal layers. The concrete should not be tipped in piles and then spread with a poker vibrator because this can result in segregation (honeycombing).

Every layer must be compacted immediately after being placed until all the air has escaped. The distance between successive immersion points for the poker vibrator is 25–70 cm depending on the diameter of the vibrator.

Excessive *vibration* causes segregation of the concrete because the large constituents sink to the bottom and the cement slurry and water rise to the top. On exposed concrete surfaces such segregation causes permanent blemishes. A stiff mix lowers the risk of segregation.

10 *Curing* is an essential part of concreting because it prevents premature drying-out of the concrete. Exposed concrete surfaces should be covered or continuously sprinkled with water for at least four days after being placed, especially if exposed to draughts or direct sunlight.

During cold weather, freshly placed concrete must be protected against freezing by covering it and, if necessary, by heating.

Source: *Cementbulletin*, April 1987

Exposed concrete surfaces

Fig. 22: Timber boards and honeycombing result in rough surfaces
Rudolf Olgiati: house for Dr G. Olgiati, Flims-Waldhaus (CH), 1964–65

Characteristics of concrete surfaces cast against formwork

The appearance of the struck concrete is determined mainly by the surface texture of the formwork material but also by the joints in the formwork and the formwork ties. This aspect calls for meticulous planning of all joints and ties plus subsequent rigorous inspections during the work on site, or a tolerant attitude towards the quality of the concrete surfaces.

Exposed concrete

Basically, we distinguish between two types of exposed concrete depending on whether the outermost, thin layer of cement directly adjacent to the surface of the formwork is retained or removed.

Cement "skin" retained

The pattern of the formwork and the formwork ties determine the appearance. Joints in the formwork can be dealt with in various ways – from the simple "butt joint" to the "open joint" to covering the joints with various strips and tapes.

The holes created by formwork ties are either filled with concrete subsequently, left open or plugged.

Cement "skin" removed

The outermost, thin layer of cement can be modified or completely removed by using various manual or technical treatments. The cement "skin", the surface layer, is worked or treated to reveal the aggregate.

Manual treatments
– Bossing
– Point tooling
– Bush hammering
– Comb chiselling

Technical treatments (exposing the grains of aggregate)
– Blasting (sand, steel shot, corundum, water/sand mixture)
– Flame cleaning
– Brushing and washing
– Acid etching

Mechanical treatments (surface only)
– Grinding
– Polishing

Characteristics of concrete surfaces not cast against formwork

These surfaces (floors and tops of walls) can also be worked with the above treatments once the concrete has hardened.

But before such surfaces have hardened, they can also be treated with a diverse range of tools.

Colour

The colour of the concrete is determined by the quality of the concrete mix (coarse aggregate and cement quality plus any pigments added) and the formwork (new or used formwork, also quality and quantity of release agent).

Fig. 23: Courtyard wall in in situ concrete, constructed with formwork panels the size of tatami mats (91 x 182 cm), courtyard floor finished with precast concrete flags
Tadao Ando: Vitra conference pavilion, Weil am Rhein (D), 1993

Surface characteristics of concrete cast against formwork

Type 1: Normal concrete surface
Surfaces without special requirements:
    with any surface texture
    without subsequent working of fins and differences in level

Type 2: Concrete surface with uniform texture
Surfaces with the following requirements:
    uniform surface texture
    board or panel size not specified
    subsequent working of fins and differences in level

Type 3: Exposed concrete surfaces with board texture
Surfaces that remain exposed with the following requirements:
– uniform surface texture without differences in level, fins and
  porous areas – a moderate number of blowholes caused by air
  pockets is permissible
– more or less even colouring
– constant board width, joints between boards not specified
– uniform board direction and parallel with larger dimension of
  surface
– smooth boards

Enhanced requirements are to be specified as follows
1. Sealed joints
2. Offset joints
3. Uniform board direction and perpendicular to larger dimension
   of surface
4. Pattern according to detailed drawing of surface
5. Use of rough-sawn boards

Type 4: Exposed concrete surfaces with panel texture
Surfaces that remain exposed with the following requirements:
– uniform surface texture without differences in level, fins and
  porous areas
– a moderate number of blowholes caused by air pockets is
  permissible
– more or less even colouring
– constant panel size, joints between panels not specified
– uniform panel direction and parallel with larger dimension of
  surface

Enhanced requirements are to be specified as follows
1. Sealed joints
2. Offset joints
3. Uniform panel direction and perpendicular to larger dimension
   of surface
4. Pattern according to detailed drawing of surface

Surface characteristics of concrete not cast against formwork

Treatments to not fully hardened concrete:

1	Roughly levelled	e.g. with timber board
2	Roughened	with brushes or rakes
3	Floated	without addition of mortar
4	Floated	with addition of mortar
5	Trowelled	smooth, flat surface without blowholes
6	Grooved	parallel grooves of equal width and depth
7	Brushed	rough surface with vertical, horizontal or herringbone pattern
8	Vacuum-dewatered	lowering of water/cement ratio in concrete already placed by means of special equipment

Treatments to hardened concrete:

1	Washing and brushing	washing out the fine particles in the surface layer to reveal the coarse aggregate
2	Sandblasting	mechanical roughening to produce a matt surface in the colour of the underlying material
3	Jetting	sprayed with compressed-air water jet
4	Acid etching	chemical treatment to remove the lime component and reveal the colour of the underlying material
4	Bush hammering	hammering the concrete surface with special, manual or power-driven tools to a depth of about 5 mm
6	Grinding	surface ground manually or by machine to remove all blowholes, subsequently treated with fluate, including wetting
7	Polishing	surface ground to achieve a high sheen, blowholes filled and reground
8	Sealing	colourless water-repellent seal applied to surface

Formwork qualities to Swiss standard SIA 118/262:2004
see also DIN 18217, 1981 ed., DIN 18331, 2002 ed., DIN 68791, 1979 ed.

Fig. 24: Horizontal timber boards
Formwork made from 3 cm thick Douglas fir boards, straight edges, butt joints between boards.

Fig. 25: Horizontal timber boards
Formwork made from 18 cm wide, 3 cm thick Douglas fir boards, chamfered edges, tight butt joints between boards. Characteristic, projecting concrete fins are the result.

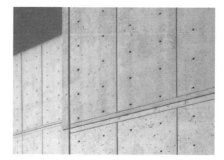

Fig. 26: Vertical panel formwork, panels coated with synthetic resin lacquer
Louis I. Kahn: Salk Institute, La Jolla (Cal, USA), 1959–65

Fig. 27: Concrete with exposed aggregate finish
Aggregate revealed by jetting

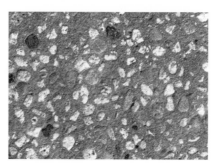

Fig. 28: Sandblasted surface
Aggregate revealed by blasting

Fig. 29: Point-tooled surface
Medium-coarse quality

Floor supports, exposed concrete with internal insulation

Causes of thermal bridges

The connection between wall and floor, or floor support, leads to a thermal bridge problem (heat losses) when using exposed concrete in conjunction with internal insulation. This problem can be solved properly only in single-storey, self-contained buildings where there are no intermediate or other floors to interrupt the layer of insulation. There are two potential solutions for all other cases, but both must be considered in conjunction with the structural concept.

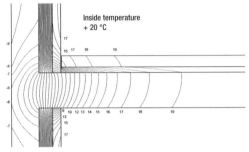

Outside temperature
- 10 °C

Inside temperature
+ 20 °C

Fig. 30: Isotherms diagram

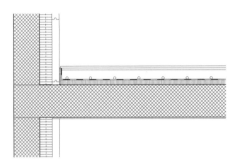

Fig. 31: Construction detail

Solution 1: Strip of insulation in soffit

The inclusion of insulation around the perimeter of the floor, at its junction with the external wall, maintains the structurally compact connection between wall and floor but does not solve the heat loss problem, the temperature drop at the surface of the concrete, entirely. Above all, it is the surface temperature at the base of the wall that remains critical. Furthermore, the layer of insulation disturbs the appearance of the soffit. If the soffit is plastered, it must be remembered that a crack could develop at the insulation–soffit interface.

Fig. 32: Insulation to the soffit along the perimeter concealed behind timber cladding
Bünzli & Courvoisier: Linde school, Niederhasli (CH), 2003

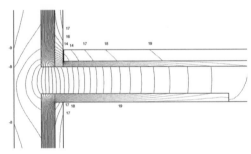

Fig. 33: Isotherms diagram

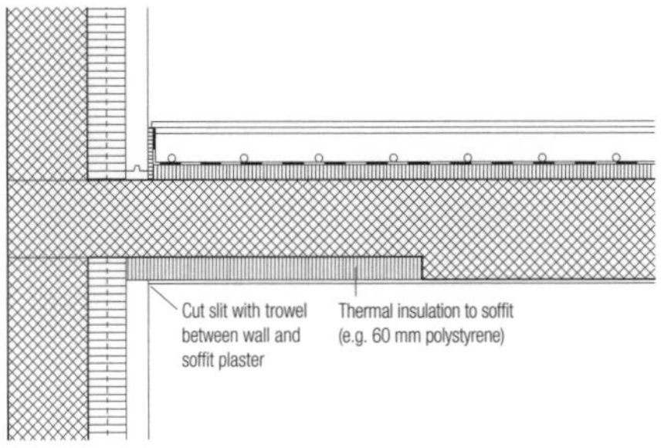

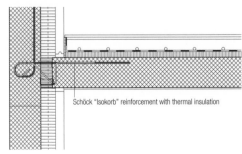

Cut slit with trowel between wall and soffit plaster

Thermal insulation to soffit (e.g. 60 mm polystyrene)

Fig. 34: Construction detail

Solution 2: Separation between floor and wall

The development of various special insulated reinforcement products mean that it is now possible to achieve "partial" separation between floor and wall. This has a detrimental effect on the compact connection between floor and wall. Additional expansion joints must be provided (at projecting and re-entrant corners). The temperature at the base of the wall is higher than that in solution 1.

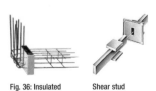

Fig. 35: Example of insulated reinforcement being installed

Insulated reinforcement and shear studs
Numerous variations on these two products are available. The shear studs can resist shear forces only, whereas the insulated reinforcement products can accommodate bending moments as well. The advantage of the shear studs over the insulated reinforcement is that they can accommodate a certain amount of movement (egg-shaped sleeve).

Fig. 36: Insulated reinforcement

Shear stud

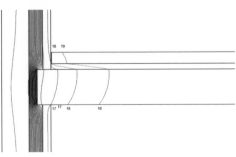

Fig. 37: Isotherms diagram

Schöck "Isokorb" reinforcement with thermal insulation

Fig. 38: Construction detail

The fixing of heavy external cladding (concrete)

Fig. 43: Heavy external cladding

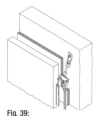

Fig. 39:
Top fixing
Main support at top of precast element

Dowels beneath element

Compression screw (spacer screw)

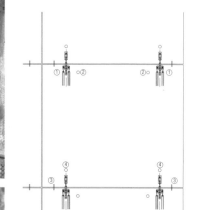

Fig. 40: Cladding panel fixing system: elevation (above) and section (right)

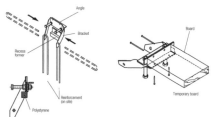

Fig. 41: A Installation work in the factory, temporary fittings in the form

Fig. 42: B Installation work on site

Fixing heavy cladding elements

The fixings for large, precast concrete cladding panels depend on the weight of the element. The high demands placed on fasteners mean that two fixings are usually necessary for storey-high panels. In order to accommodate tolerances, or to enable alignment of the elements, the fasteners must permit adjustment in three directions. Such fasteners represent discrete thermal bridges and this fact must be accepted. All fixings must be made of stainless steel (rustproof). The clearance between the in situ concrete structure and the precast elements can lie between 0 and 14 cm, and in special cases may even be greater. Wind pressure and wind suction effects must be taken into account.

Facade fixing systems consist of:

1 Top fastener (loadbearing fixing) with height-adjustable threaded bar
2 Spacer screw for adjusting position of cladding panel relative to structure
3 Dowels for locating the elements with respect to each other
4 If required, compression screws, depending on loading case (wind pressure or suction)

Facade fixings are installed at the same distance from the panel's centroidal axis. This ensures that every fixing carries half the self-weight of the facade element. The joints between individual facade elements should be sufficiently large (15 mm) to ensure that no additional loads (e.g. due to expansion) are placed on the elements.

Installation

A Place the top fastener (loadbearing fixing) in the formwork for the facade element at the precasting works and integrate it into the reinforcement. Place a polystyrene block (removed on site, see below) between bracket and angle. The timber board shown here serves only as an aid during casting (enabling fixing to facade element formwork).

B Positioning and attaching the supporting bracket on the structure
– Remove polystyrene.
– Insert perforated strip between bracket and angle.
– Secure perforated strip with screws.
– Apply "Loctite" or similar to the screw and fit finished component to supporting bracket.

The fixing of heavy external cladding (stone)

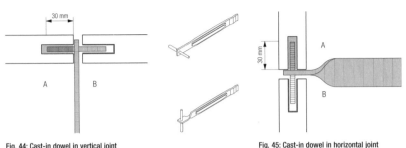

Fig. 44: Cast-in dowel in vertical joint
A Dowel cast in
B Dowel in plastic sleeve (to allow movement)

Fig. 45: Cast-in dowel in horizontal joint

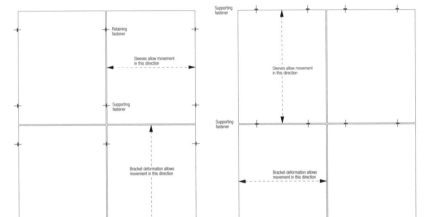

Fig. 46: Elevation on panels

Fixing stone cladding

Such cladding panels are usually suspended in front of the structure, and connected to it with various fasteners. These fasteners bridge the distance between the panel and the structure and hence create a space for thermal insulation and air circulation. Stone cladding panels are fixed with supporting and retaining fasteners located in the vertical and/or horizontal joints (four fixings are necessary). Besides carrying the self-weight of the panel, the fasteners must also resist wind pressure and wind suction forces. Many different fasteners are available on the market. And various loadbearing framing systems are available for the case of insufficient or even a total lack of suitable fixing options on the loadbearing structure. We distinguish between the following fastening systems:
– cast-in dowels
– bolts and brackets
– special brackets, metal subframes
The most popular form of support is the cast-in dowel shown here (figs 44 and 45).

Cast-in dowels

These must be of stainless steel. They penetrate approx. 30 mm into the hole drilled in the edge of the panel. The diameter of the hole should be approx. 3 mm larger than that of the dowel. The standard distance from corner of panel to centre of dowel hole should be 2.5 times the thickness of the panel. The minimum panel thickness is 30 mm.

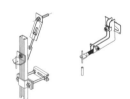

Fig. 47: Brackets for cast-in rail system

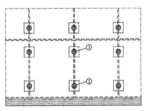

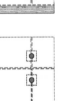 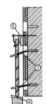

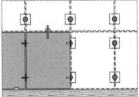

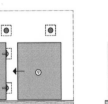 

Fig. 48: Installation of cast-in dowels
1 Align erection jig to exact height for bottom row of panels.
2 Cut out thermal insulation locally to facilitate drilling of holes.
3 Drill holes for anchors, ensuring that reinforcing bars are not drilled through; blow holes clean.
4 Set up stone panels to correct height.
5 Align top edge of panel and wedge at correct distance from structure.
6 Moisten holes for anchors, fill with grout and compact.
7 Insert anchors into grout and align; slide in dowel.
8 Compact grout again and strike off excess.
9 Replace thermal insulation around anchor, slide in next panel.

Fig. 49: Stone facade
Fixed with cast-in dowels

Installation of cast-in dowels

These must be fixed to a loadbearing substrate (concrete or masonry) with an adequate depth of penetration. The fixing to a loadbearing component should not weaken its cross-section excessively. The thermal insulation should be cut back prior to drilling the hole and should be replaced once the dowel has been fitted. The fastener is aligned as the mortar hardens (cures).

Chart for establishing preliminary size of reinforced concrete slabs
Initial size estimate at design stage

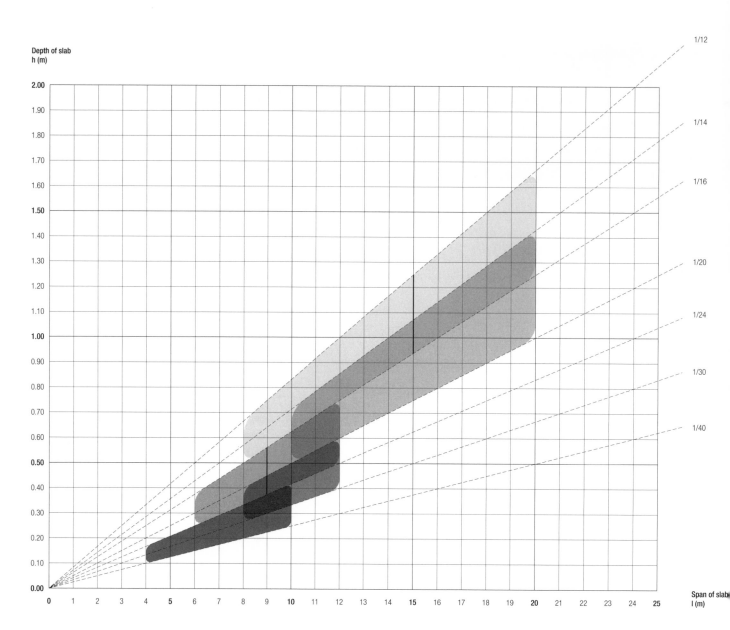

Element (loadbearing)	Span l (m)	h*/l
Slab on walls	– 10 m	1/24 – 1/40
Flat slab on columns, conventional reinforcement	6 – 12 m	1/16 – 1/24
Flat slab with flared column heads	8 – 12 m	1/20 – 1/30
Slab with downstand beams, conventional reinforcement	8 – 20 m	1/12 – 1/16
Waffle slab	10 – 20 m	1/14 – 1/20

Fig. 50: Notes for using this chart

With a high load (dead and imposed loads) use the maximum value for the slab depth as proposed by the chart – vice versa for a low load.

The sizes and relationships shown cannot be verified scientifically. The shaded areas are supposed to be slightly "indefinite". In the interest of the rational use of a loadbearing element, the "edges" of this chart should be avoided.

Source: M. Dietrich,
Burgdorf School of Engineering, 1990

*Prestressing can reduce the structural depth of the slab by up to about 30%.

Linear structural members

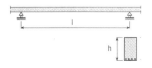

Fig. 51:
Dimensions of cross-sections for customary spacings and loads in buildings (approximation):

Beam depth h

simply supported beam	h/l = 1/11 to 1/13
simply supported T-beam	h/l = 1/13 to 1/15
continuous beam (end span)	h/l = 1/12 to 1/15
continuous beam (other spans)	h/l = 1/15 to 1/18

Beam width b

min. b	180 mm
min. b for l = 5 to 8 m	200 mm
min. b for l = 8 to 12 m	300 mm
min. b for l = 12 to 15 m	400 mm

Column length l
Buckling length l$_{cr}$

(1)   (2)

l$_{cr}$ l   l$_{cr}$ l

(1) pinned top and bottom   l$_{cr}$ = l
(2) fixed top and bottom   l$_{cr}$ = 0.5l

(3)   (4)

l$_{cr}$ l   l   l$_{cr}$

((3) pinned at top, fixed at bottom   l$_{cr}$ = 0.7l
(4) top free, bottom fixed   l$_{cr}$ = 2l

Column dimension b
b = smaller dimension of column cross-section

Rectangular cross-section   b = l$_{cr}$/14
(valid as approximation if buckling is not critical)

min. dimension for in situ concrete   b = >200 mm
min. dimension for precast concrete   b = >150 mm

Column dimension for multi-storey column
column grid 7.5 x 7.5 m, storey height 3.60 m
(normal loading, e.g. offices)

1 floor above column:	b = 250 mm
2 floors above column:	b = 350 mm
3 floors above column:	b = 400 mm
4 floors above column:	b = 450 mm

Beams

Beams are structural members primarily loaded in bending. The magnitude of the bending moments influences the dimensions (depth, slenderness, shape of cross-section) and the type of reinforcement (conventional or prestressed). Structural beams occur in various forms – with ends fixed, simply-supported, continuous, above the floor (upstand), below the floor (downstand) and in frames.

The conventional rectangular beam is rather rare in in situ concrete because it is frequently cast monolithically with a floor slab (T- or L-beam) and then functions together with this. If the compression zone in such a beam is wholly within the slab, the depth of the beam is less than that of a standard rectangular member.

Fig. 52: Precast concrete beams in a framed building
Angelo Mangiarotti: industrial building, Bussolengo Barese (I), 1982

Owing to the cost of formwork, adjusting the beam sizes to suit the loads exactly is only advisable in precasting works, where forms can be reused economically. For example, the depth of a beam can be designed to track the bending moment diagram, the width can be varied in line with the shear force diagram. On large spans the cross-section can therefore be optimised to save material

Fig. 53: Trussed beams
Factory building, Lustenau (A)

and hence weight and the beam constructed as a girder or trussed beam (trussing above or below).

Columns

The function of a column is to transfer the vertical loads to the foundation. Carrying horizontal loads simultaneously (shear forces due to wind, earthquakes) calls for correspondingly large cross-sections.

Thanks to the mouldability of concrete, the shape of the cross-section can be chosen virtually at will, but the cost of the formwork and the fixing of the reinforcement place practical limits on this. The "perfect" form is circular because the flexural strength is the same in all directions. However, in situ concrete columns are frequently square or rectangular to make the formwork easier and less costly. An in situ column must be at least 200 mm wide, a precast column 150 mm. The latter are cast horizontally, the surfaces are trowelled smooth or given subsequent treatment depending on the quality required. Spin-casting can be used for both square and round precast concrete columns. In this method the form is filled, closed and rotated to compact the concrete. This results in an absolutely smooth and consistent surface finish.

Slender columns loaded in compression are at risk of buckling; in other words, the more slender a column is, the lower is its permissible load (buckling load). The length of a column is therefore governed by its relationship to its smallest cross-section dimension. The buckling length depends on the type of support at each end, and maybe shorter (= high buckling load) or longer (= low buckling load) than the actual length of the column. Normally, however, columns with pinned ends are met with in superstructure works.

Fig. 54: Spun-concrete columns, connected to reinforced concrete roof via steel web plates. Axel Schultes: art gallery, Bonn (D), 1992

Systems with linear members

Fig. 55: Principle of a multi-storey framed building using precast concrete columns, beams and floor elements. The in situ concrete core stabilises the building by resisting the horizontal forces.

Arches

The arch is a curved linear member. Irrespective of the loading, the arch is subject to axial compression and bending. But if the arch has an accordingly favourable form, it can carry a uniformly distributed load exclusively by way of axial compression (no bending). The "perfect" form for an arch is the inverse of a spanned rope, which deforms only under the action of its own weight (catenary curve).

In reinforced concrete construction the arch is frequently used as the loadbearing element for long-span bridges. Whereas in times gone by – when the relationship between cost of labour and cost of materials was totally different – in situ concrete arches were also used in buildings for spanning over large areas (e.g. single-storey sheds), they are seldom met with today and then only in precast form.

Fig. 56: Fixed-based arch
Stuttgart Building Department (F. Fischle, F. Cloos): swimming pool, Heslach (D), 1929

Portal frames

Connecting horizontal and vertical linear members together rigidly produces a portal frame. The vertical members are sometimes known as legs, the horizontal ones as rafters. Owing to the bending moments at the corners it should be ensured that the cross-section of the legs is greater than that of conventional columns carrying concentric loads.

The portal frame represents a braced, stable system in the plane of the frame which can carry both vertical and horizontal loads and thus assume the function of a bracing "plate" in a building. Inherently stable portal frame systems are particularly economic in single- and two-storey buildings, but plates in the form of slabs and walls are the preferred form of bracing in multi-storey buildings.

Fig. 57: Fixed-based portal frame
Auguste + Gustave Perret: Ponthieu garage, Paris (F), 1906

Frames

Frames consist of prefabricated loadbearing elements such as columns, beams and floor slabs. In conjunction with fixed columns, such systems can form a rigid framework.

Horizontal forces are resisted by fixed columns (acting as vertical cantilevers) in single- and two-storey buildings, whereas in multi-storey structures the horizontal loads are transferred to the foundations by vertical wall plates (shear walls).

A frame provides maximum flexibility with respect to utilisation requirements because the loadbearing function is essentially separate from the other building functions.

Fig. 58: Use of precast concrete elements and glass
Hermann Hertzberger: extension to LinMij plant building, Amsterdam (NL), 1964

Planar structural members

Fig. 59: One-way-spanning continuous slab

Slab depth for one-way span:

cantilever slab:	$h/l = 1/12$
simply-supported slab:	$h/l = 1/25$
continuous slab (end span):	$h/l = 1/30$
continuous slab (other spans):	$h/l = 1/35$

Slab depth for two-way span:

simply-supported slab	$h/l = 1/30$
continuous slab (corner span):	$h/l = 1/40$
continuous slab (other spans):	$h/l = 1/45$
min. slab thickness (h)	180 to 200 mm
(fire protection and sound insulation)	

Economic spans:

one-way-span slabs:	$l < 6$ to 7 m
two-way-span slabs:	$l < 8$

Fig. 60: Ribbed slab

Structural depth of ribbed slabs:

overall depth (h)	$h = l/20$ to $l/35$
clear spacing of ribs (s)	$s = < 2h$
slab depth (h_o)	$h_o > 50–80$ mm
or 0.1 x rib spacing (centre-to-centre)	

Economic spans:

ribbed slab	$l = 7$ to 12 m
prefabricated, prestressed	$l =$ up to 18 m

Fig. 61: Flat slab

Structural depth of flat slabs:

rectangular slab (one-way span):	$h/l = 1/30$
square slab (two-way span):	$h/l = 1/35$
min. slab depth (h)	200 mm
(fire protection and sound insulation)	

Economic spans:

flat slab	$l \leq 8$ m

Slabs

Concrete slabs are loadbearing elements loaded perpendicular to their plane and primarily subjected to bending. We distinguish between one-way-spanning and two-way-spanning slabs. Examples of one-way-span slabs are cantilever slabs or those spanning between two walls placed opposite each other. The ideal two-way-span slab is square on plan and supported on all four sides. The loads are carried in (at least) two directions and the structural depth of the slab can be reduced accordingly. The ratio of slab depth to span depends on the form of support (cantilever, simply-supported, continuous).

On longer spans the slabs would be so heavy that they are resolved into lighter flooring systems. Flooring systems for buildings are divided into those with linear supports such as ribbed slabs (one-way span) and waffle slabs (two-way span), and those with discrete supports such as flat slabs (with or without column heads).

Compared with solid slabs, ribbed slabs and waffle slabs supported on walls or downstand beams have the advantage of being much lighter (reduction of material in tension zone), but their formwork is more elaborate (prefabricated formwork elements are essential).

Slabs supported on individual columns carry the loads entirely by means of the slab alone, without any beams or ribs. The high stresses around the columns calls for appropriate reinforcement or additional strengthening in the form of (flared) column heads. The structural depth

Fig. 62: Basement garage, c. 1960
Ribbed slab

of a flat slab is small compared to the resolved flooring systems. But concentrating the bending moments and shear forces around the columns does bring with it the risk of punching shear. Increasing the bearing area and the thickness of the slab at this point and including reinforcement or steel "studrails" to withstand the punching shear will guarantee the load-carrying capacity around the columns. Today, the flared column heads and columns are usually produced in precast concrete to optimise operations on site.

Fig. 63: Flared column heads transfer the loads from the upper floors into the columns.
Robert Maillart: warehouse, Giesshübelstrasse, Zurich (CH), 1910

Plates

Plates are used in buildings in the form of walls. They function as loadbearing and/or enclosing components. In contrast to a slab, which is primarily subjected to bending, a plate carries forces in its plane and therefore has to resist axial forces.

We distinguish between plates supported along their full length (linear supports), which can transfer the vertical loads directly, and those supported at individual points similar to beams, which transfer the loads to these supports (deep beams).

Owing to their high stiffness, plates are used for resisting horizontal forces (bracing) and as transfer structures.

Folded plates

If you place two pieces of paper on two supports, fold one concertina fashion and leave the other unfolded, you will notice that the unfolded sheet deforms under its own weight, but the folded piece remain stable. This is the principle of the folded plate.

Fig. 64: Model of loadbearing structure with shear walls offset or rotated through 90°
Morger & Degelo: Reinach community centre, Basel (CH), 1997–2000

Systems with planar structural members

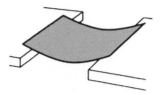

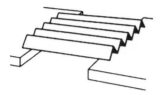

Fig. 65: Stiffening a piece of paper by folding it – the principle of the folded plate

Folded plates are inclined, flat surfaces with shear-resistant connections along the edges (the "folds"). The forces are carried by slab and plate action. Whereas slabs are loaded perpendicular to their plane and primarily in bending, the considerably stiffer plate with its higher load-carrying capacity can accommodate forces in its plane and transfer these to the supports.

Folded plates therefore enable large areas to be spanned without intermediate columns; they are used mainly for long-span roof structures.

Shells

Shells are three-dimensional, thin-wall structures. Owing to the mouldability of reinforced concrete and prestressed concrete, the majority of shells have been built in these materials.

The form not only governs the architectural appearance but also determines the loadbearing behaviour. Like with an arch there is also a "perfect" form for a shell structure. This is the case when, subject only to self-weight, the so-called membrane tension state is reached, i.e. exclusively axial and shear forces in the plane of the shell throughout. Consequently, a shell structure can have a slenderness ratio (ratio of span to depth) of 500 or more.

The structural engineer Heinz Isler developed three form-finding principles by means of various experiments:
– membrane form: subject to compression from inside
– suspended form: hanging fabric subject to self-weight (free forms)
– fluid form: escaping, solidified foam

The formwork requirements for a shell structure are relatively high. Three different methods of construction are available for reinforced concrete shells:
– concreting over centring
– the use of precast elements
– the use of pneumatic formwork

Of these three, centring is the one most widely used in practice.

Fig. 66: Forms with single curvature

Fig. 67: Forms with double curvature

Fig. 68: Folded plate roof supported on Y-columns
Hans Hofmann: waterworks, Birsfelden, Basel (CH), 1953/54

Fig. 69: Shell designed with perfect form (parabola), shell thickness approx. 6 cm. Robert Maillart: Cement Industry Pavilion for Swiss National Exhibition, 1939

Fig. 70: Shell designed as a fluid form
Heinz Isler (with P. Wirz, architect): Kilcher factory, Recherswil (CH), 1965

Fig. 71: Shell designed as membrane form, built over centering
Heinz Isler (with VSK and Frei Architekten): COOP warehouse, Olten (CH), 1960

Wood: indifferent, synthetic, abstract – plastic
Prefabrication technology in timber construction

Andrea Deplazes

Over the past ten years we have seen developments in systems and semi-finished products that have replaced everything that hitherto had been considered as standard practice for the tectonic fundamentals of timber construction. In fact, the "traditional platform frame construction of the 1990s", which promised the emergence of an "unconstrained", non-modular domain of prefabricated timber construction, is already an anachronism today.

It is surely no mere coincidence that the latest forms of timber construction have appeared in central Europe and Scandinavia, in other words in countries that rely on industry that promotes wood as a resource. To be able to overcome the stagnation in traditional timber building, such countries are dependent on innovations that can attract further market share away from the solid construction sector. Huge quantities of unused wood from storm-damaged trees in forests flattened by gusts of hurricane force exacerbate the situation and provoke a predatory battle in which timber construction for the first time starts to resemble solid construction.

Fundamental manual skills
A whole series of old carpentry techniques found favour again in the "traditional platform frame construction of the 1990s". For example, the jointing of squared sections to form plane frames with top and bottom members, or covering the frame with boards or planks to provide the stability and rigidity necessary for a construction element (wall or floor) to become a structurally effective plate. An opening in such an element always represents a disruption, which must be "trimmed" properly.

Complementary layers in platform frame construction
The tectonic goal appears to coincide with building performance objectives: the frame of squared sections carries the load, the inner sheathing provides the rigidity, and the outer sheathing closes off the frame, in which the thermal insulation is embedded, and thus holds the complete sandwich together. Finally, on the outside another layer (on battens to create a cavity for air circulation) protects the sandwich from the weather, and inside in similar fashion the visible wall surface is completed with the desired quality, concealing a void for the installation of services. The layer-type construction of such a facade element in platform frame construction is thus complementary, i.e. built up in such a way that the layers supplement each other, with each individual layer performing essentially just one function. The composition and the quality of the materials of the components in a platform frame system are largely defined by the supplier of the system. The architect no longer has to consider or draw the inner workings of such a package. He or she determines merely the aesthetic quality of the outer, visible surfaces.

Shaping deficit of new technologies
The growing interest in new timber construction technologies would seem to support the view that, for the first time in the history of architecture there would seem to be a trend away from solid to timber construction, which belongs to the category of filigree construction (tectonics). Gottfried Semper's "theory of metabolism" is a good example. It is less concerned with building technology itself and more concerned with consequences for architectural expression at the point of transition from tectonics to stereotomy, a sort of transfer of timber construction to solid construction. (I call this conflict "technological immanence versus cultural permanence".) We also have the first reinforced concrete structures of François Hennebique, which still adhered to the tectonic fabric of timber structures, with a hierarchical arrangement of posts, primary beams and secondary joists. And only after a certain period of acclimatisation did Robert Maillart manage to establish the intrinsic principles of reinforced concrete construction: columns with column heads that merge with flat slabs and in doing so create something like a hybrid plastic node at the column head in which the reinforcement – later no longer visible – is placed.

An inversion of the "art form" into the "core form" (Carl Bötticher) thus takes place, with the force indicated only through the concentration and grouping of the steel reinforcement before the concrete is poured. Through these observations we arrive at the following conclusion: the shaping criteria of the new technologies intrinsic to the system appear only after overcoming permanent cultural images (stereotypes).

The search for adequate structure and form
If traditional prefabricated platform frame construction with its studs internally and sheathing to both sides represents an interim form that is still clearly based on handed-down carpentry techniques and the strict, tectonic rules of timber construction, what structure and form can we expect to be inherent in and adequate for current timber construction technology?

To look for an answer to this question we must first study the way in which timber is processed these days. The operations involved in manufacturing the semi-finished products are characterised by a descending sequence. In a first operation sawn timber of high and medium quality, e.g. planks, squared sections and boards, are produced for traditional methods of working. Glued laminated timber (glulam) is one of the most important semi-finished products. The cuts become ever finer, the sections ever smaller. The second operation produces strips, battens and laminations, which are processed to form multiply

Fig. 1: Timber platform frame building during construction
Bearth & Deplazes: private house (Hirsbrunner), Scharans (CH), 1995

material. It is easy to imagine which options could emerge; in the production line from the architect's CAD system to the CAM and CNC roboting of the fabricator it is certainly realistic to order a "one-off" copy of a highly complicated carpentry joint, e.g. from a Japanese Shinto shrine, even for a relatively moderate price. That could be the beginning of a limited batch of architectural rarities (like in the world of fashion or cars), affordable for an eminent, selected clientele.

This fantasising leads us back to the starting point of a project, the design.

Today, planning with CAD software is standard practice in architectural design offices. The data line fits seamlessly into this so that the way in which the drawings are produced on the screen, irrespective of the traditional building technology, e.g. timber construction, must have a retroactive effect on the production and the tectonics of the structure. Non-modular, project-specific components are generated. Or in other words, the defined architectural project is broken down into manageable elements (plates, slabs and leaves), sent for production via the data line, and reassembled into a structure on the building site. This form of slab tectonics and the constructional fabric of layers of storeys, stacks of elements has long since become the norm in solid construction. But in timber construction it encourages new methods of design and construction. In addition, technological developments lead to ever stronger materials and, consequently, to ever thinner components.

Cardboard model on the scale of a structure

The "basic element" of modern timber construction is therefore the slab, and no longer the linear member. The slab consists of three or more layers (plies) of sawn timber, e.g. laminations or strips obtained from a relatively low-quality wood (formerly offcuts and waste), glued together with adjacent plies at right-angles to each other. This "cross-worked interweaving" produces a slab with high strength and good rigidity which can be used as a structural plate. Just like a textile, the length and width of our homogeneous slab without a recognisable internal hierarchy can be extended seemingly without limit (the only restrictions being the size of the presses and the road vehicles necessary to transport such elements), and in terms of thickness can be layered (specific slab thickness depending on loading case and stresses). Even the quality of the strips of softwood or hardwood or mixtures thereof – the "threads fabric" – can be optimised to suit the intended application. The direction of our slab is therefore irrelevant, our slab is isotropic, "indifferent" to the direction in which it has to span.

Theoretically, it can be produced as an endless band, but in practice the maximum dimensions are limited by transport. Both conditions have an effect on current

boards, solid timber panels, etc. The "waste" from these operations is cut into even finer pieces.

Sliced or peeled veneers are the outcome, e.g. for high-strength parallel strand lumber (PSL) or chipboard. Afterwards, the fine waste, e.g. sawdust, is used and in the final operation boiled to form a fibrous pulp: the wood is separated into its fibres and its own fluid (lignin) and pressed to form boards like hardboard, medium density fibreboard (MDF) and softboard to round off the whole spectrum of products.

Every stage in the sublimation process is the antithesis of the assembly, the re-formation, mainly in the form of slabs and plates. And gluing is the jointing, re-forming technology. This is the reason why the subsequent processing of the semi-finished products, the "refining" and the further processing towards prefabrication for building works, gives rise to an astounding suppleness in the material, allowing every shaping intervention – the CNC-controlled milling cutter, the robot machining – virtually without resistance. The term "modelling" is certainly apt here because not only complex patterns but also plastic shaping such as profiling and even three-dimensional workpieces are produced whose surface developments can be defined numerically before machining.

CAD – CAM – Roboting

Within this production method wood takes on the character of a readily modelled and hence indifferent raw timber construction. Slab tectonics and thin-wall plates (e.g. solid timber panels) behave, at full size, like cardboard packaging, as if a cardboard model the size of a real building had to be transported. This concerns not only the physical perception. It becomes more obvious when dealing with openings. Seemingly punched through or cut out of the plates at random, like cutting cardboard with a knife, the incredible resistance of slab tectonics becomes visible in the structure. A similar behaviour is

Fig. 2: Solid timber panel building during construction
Bearth & Deplazes: private house (Bearth-Candinas), Sumvitg (CH), 1998

evident in the American balloon frame, the assembly with the nailing gun in which it is easily possible to cut away a whole corner of a building after erection without the entire construction collapsing because the whole structure is well oversized. (Such an approach would be unthinkable in European platform frame construction!) However, compared with current European slab tectonics, the American balloon frame method seems old-fashioned, even "casual", with the need to replace insulation and sheathing again on site.

Forecast: compact systems
The state of European slab tectonics allows us to make the following predictions for its development. Only those systems with a compact solution for the loadbearing–building

performance–weather protection issue (sandwich facade elements, so-called compact systems) and simplified layering of the element, i.e. fewer layers, will prove worthwhile. I will call these complex synthetic systems consisting of multifunctional components. The total breakdown of the facade into countless layers began in the 1970s, as the building performance aspect started to accrue new significance due to the oil crisis. The construction was divided into individual functions which intelligent synthesis measures are now reassembling into fewer components. This also corresponds to a trend in solid construction in which new single-leaf loadbearing and insulating materials are being used as a reaction to the design-related complications and problematic guarantee pledges of the ever more complex specifications required by multi-layer, monofunctional complementary systems (double-leaf masonry etc.).

A synthetic facade element might then have the following make-up: a basic element consisting of a thin-wall ribbed slab, e.g. a solid timber panel 3.5 cm thick, with 20 cm deep transverse ribs in the same material glued on to provide buckling resistance, and the intervening spaces filled with thermal insulation. This basic element with its flat side on the inside functions as a loadbearing plate (supporting, stiffening, bracing), as a framework for the thermal insulation and as a vapour barrier (the adhesive within the solid timber panel guarantees this property). The homogeneous, internal wall surface can be subsequently worked simply and directly, e.g. painted or wallpapered. It is unnecessary to attach sheathing on the inside clear of the core element when there are no electric cables to be fitted (and hidden) on the internal face development. Simple timber boards fitted to the ribs on the outside close off the wall sandwich and function as a substrate for the external skin. In the house for Bearth-Candinas, which is described in more detail below, the larch shingles are nailed directly to the boarding without an air cavity in between.

The thin-wall ribbed panels represent a form of construction that is related to automobile and aircraft construction, where the thin loadbearing membrane of lightweight metal and plastic, stiffened with ribs, has to withstand very high stresses; optimum rigidity and stability coupled with minimum use of material. Whereas in aircraft design it is mainly the weight of the assembly that is critical, in the slab tectonics of current timber construction it is primarily the compactness of synthetic elements and, at the same time, their ability to perform several functions.

A comparison with the platform frame construction mentioned above illustrates the fine "revaluation" at once. Whereas the inner sheathing of the frame is merely the bracing and the vertical studs are clearly loadbearing posts, the ribbed slab, apparently similar in terms of

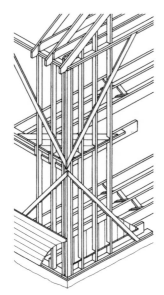

Fig. 3: Balloon frame method
Multistorey, continuous timber studding

architecture and engineering, is a reversal of this system. The thin slab – just 3.5 cm – is loadbearing, braced by fine transverse ribs. However, this analytical approach must be corrected immediately. The two components (slab and ribs) form an indispensable, compact, synthetic package (thanks to the structural adhesive) in which loadbearing structure (supporting, bracing) and building performance (vapour diffusion), constructional internal workings and visible surfaces are merged and every component assumes multiple functions in conjunction with all the other components. In current timber construction we therefore speak of compact systems.

In the vertical direction, as a succession of stacked facade elements, it is evident that the loadbearing and insulating layers continue without interruption because the floors are supported only on the 3.5 cm thick solid timber panel. The situation is different in platform frame construction with top and bottom members, where the facade construction is completely interrupted to support the floors; the only way of preventing this is to build in supports in the form of projecting steel angles (Z-sections). I shall explain this by means of an actual example:

Stretch pullover over slab tectonics

The house for Bearth-Candinas, a slim, four-storey "tower house", stands on the edge of the village of Sumvitg. The plan layout is a simple rectangle divided on the long side by a loadbearing central partition. That creates two elongated rooms per storey which could serve any type of function because they can be further subdivided depending on the needs of the occupants. As the quantity of run-off water on the slope is considerable, the house was built without a cellar. On entering the house we must first pass through a glazed hall (winter storage for plants and play area for the children) in order to reach the actual entrance door to the living quarters above. As all timber building systems have little heat storage capacity and therefore tend to adhere to the insulation concept of achieving a low thermal balance, the windows can be found in all facades, facing in every direction to ensure that there is no overheating in summer. In winter the solar radiation heats up the glazed entrance hall, and the heat rises and spreads through the living quarters and bedrooms above.

Without any finishes the surfaces of the solid timber wall panels would appear rather coarse, but – to return to our theme – they are painted white and lemon yellow so that the butt joints between facade elements and loadbearing walls are disguised and the interior appears homogeneous. The impression of a "wooden house" is relegated to the background in favour of a delicate, almost paper-like construction whose rooms appear to have been wallpapered. (A close inspection reveals thousands of fine, regularly spaced cracks in the walls, a

true "cultivation of the crack", which will never again give cause for clients to complain!) As the only shingle-maker in Grisons is based in the village, it seemed an excellent opportunity to clad the facade in wooden shingles. The shingles cover the building like a tight-fitting stretch pullover, lending it a uniform external appearance and concealing the slab tectonics. This building therefore benefits from a seamless interaction of industrial high-tech production and tried-and-tested craft skills plus expertise.

Abandoning the wooden paragons

If we continue to pursue slab tectonics and the option of a facade skin without a ventilation cavity, we inevitably discover that current timber construction is no longer bound to its "wooden paragons". This is due to two reasons:

First, these days a whole spectrum of non-wooden facade sheathing systems are available, e.g. sheet metal, glass, plastic panels, even plastic film, expanded metal for render, fibre-cement sheets and corrugated metal sheets. The latter characterise the architecture of Reykjavik, the capital of Iceland, in an extraordinary way. One result of the American–Icelandic economic development programme "sheep for sheets" (Iceland has no trees) is that the strip-like profiling of the colourfully painted facades turn out to be not timber boards with strips covering the joints – totally in keeping with Mr Semper's ideas. Or looked at in a more general sense: the modern timber buildings are hidden behind other, non-wooden materials whose advantages are lightness, thinness and large, sealed areas with few joints. Of course, the possibility of using the substrate for the protective sheathing as the protection itself in order to achieve the most compact facade element construction has been considered. However, the problem of the butt joints between elements and the network of joints then becomes more acute, as we know all too well from the heavyweight panel construction of the planned economies of the former Warsaw Pact countries.

The second tendency is, in my opinion, even more interesting. The slab tectonics of current timber construction are interpreted exclusively in structural and not material terms like conventional timber building. What was earlier described as cardboard packaging – as a technology-related process for working large panels of thin-wall ribbed slabs in solid timber, but also the thick-layer slabs – will have architectural consequences. Timber will be regarded as "synthetic" – above all when it is neutralised inside and outside with a coat of paint – and will take on a similar standing to monolithic concrete in solid construction, which in structural terms can take over all the tectonic elements of a building without ever allowing the material to express itself. (We sense, at best, that certain cantilevers, layouts and large spaces are only feasible thanks to the "invisible concrete".) In fact, the architectural theme of abstraction is enriched by the concept of cardboard packaging thanks to the phenomenon of "white blocks", which create maximum plasticity with thin-wall elements (comparable with the art works of Absalon). On the other hand, the simple method of fretsaw-like cutting of panels with openings sawn (almost) at random and the model-like assembly of the walls and floors promote do-it-yourself construction methods so typical of modern American balloon-frame architecture, and which, apart from that, are reflected in the building instructions of the Dutch artist Joep van Lieshout as a noble handicrafts workshop.

Professionalism in architecture

Owing to the growing interest in performance, ecological and biological issues in building, current timber construction will gain more significance. Only compact, multifunctional solutions will prove competitive, but the experts in the synthesis of the most diverse requirements will not restrict themselves to developing and mastering technological know-how. In the first place the experts will prove themselves in intelligent and competent architectural design strategies – the sole guarantor for professionalism and hence "sustainability" in architecture. It is therefore not the timber specialists, timber technologists, biologists or performance specialists who are being put to the test here, but instead, first and foremost, the architects.

Excerpt from: *werk, bauen + wohnen*, 1/2 (2001), pp. 10–17

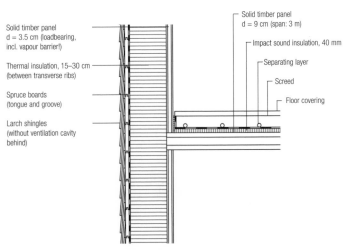

Fig. 4: Section through wall–floor junction
Bearth & Deplazes: private house (Bearth-Candinas), Sumvitg (CH), 1998

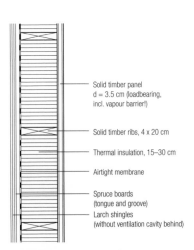

Fig. 5: Horizontal section through wall
Bearth & Deplazes: private house (Bearth-Candinas), Sumvitg (CH), 1998

The materials

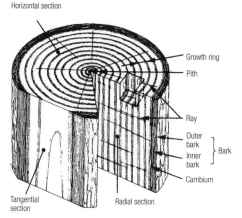

Horizontal section

Growth ring

Pith

Ray

Outer bark

Inner bark

} Bark

Cambium

Tangential section

Radial section

Fig. 6: Section through tree trunk

The structure of wood

The porous structure of wood is due to the cells and vessels which provide the tree with water and nutrients. Deciduous trees, in phylogenetic terms the younger variety, exhibit three different types of cells – for support, conduction and storage. Coniferous trees, however, have just one type of cell, which supports, conducts and stores all in one, and this fact increases the elasticity of this type of wood considerably.

At the very centre of the trunk we find the pith. This is the oldest part of the trunk around which the wood cells grow. The pith is usually dry and does not contribute to the provision of water and nutrients. A cross-section through the tree trunk reveals the radial rays. These, together with the colour and the growth rings, and in some species of wood the resin pockets as well, determine the characteristic appearance (figure) of the wood, and provide clues to age and diseases.

The structure of the growth rings is connected to varying phases of growth corresponding to the respective climate zones. In the temperate climate of Central Europe the growth phase begins in April/May and ends in August/September. In spring therefore we see a layer of large-pore, thin-wall early-wood cells which promote rapid transmission of water and nutrients, and in autumn the formation of the thick-wall late-wood cells that give the tree strength. The cambium is the layer below the bark; cell division here creates bark on the outside and wood cells on the inside.

Heartwood, sapwood and ripewood trees

The colouring of some species of wood is uniform, while the colour of others varies within the trunk cross-section. The inner, dark growth rings are surrounded by the sapwood (xylem) with its lighter colour. The sapwood contains the active, living wood cells, those in the heartwood are mostly dead. The heartwood starts to form once the tree reaches an age of between 20 and 40 years

(depending on the species), once sufficient sapwood is available to transmit water and nutrients. The inner heartwood then no longer needs to fulfil this function and its channels are blocked chemically. Deposits of tanning substances and pigments, resins and fats darken the middle of the trunk, the strength and resistance to pests increase.

Heartwood trees
Heartwood and sapwood exhibit different colouring pine, larch, oak, cherry, robinia, ash

Ripewood trees
Heartwood has lower water content than sapwood fir, spruce, copper beech

Sapwood trees
Heartwood dies after a delay or when tree has reached an advanced age
birch, alder, maple, poplar, hornbeam

Properties of wood

The main physical properties of wood depend on its density; this ranges from 0.1 to 1.2 g/cm³ depending on the species of wood and even fluctuates considerably within the trunk owing to the anisotropic nature of wood. Furthermore, the density also depends on the moisture content of the wood, which is why density figures must always be accompanied by the relevant moisture content.

Owing to its fine-pore structure, wood is a relatively good insulating material. The thermal conductivity of wood is around 0.13 W/mK for softwood and 0.20 W/mK for hardwood; this compares with figures of 0.44 W/mK for clay bricks and 1.80 W/mK for concrete. In comparison with steel or concrete the thermal expansion of wood is so small that it is irrelevant in building.

Parallel with the grain wood can carry tensile and compressive stresses with ease, but perpendicular to the grain it has a lower compressive strength. The main constituent of wood is cellulose (max. 40-50%), which is responsible for its tensile strength. Some max. 20–30% of the wood consists of hemicellulose, fillers and propolis which improve the compressive strength. Lignin or urea, which also have an influence on the compressive strength, make up another max. 20–30% of the wood. Further constituents are resins, fats and waxes, tanning substances and pigments, proteins, carbohydrates and mineral salts, which are responsible for giving the wood its colour and smell, and contribute to its resistance and strength. Softwood comes from fast-growing, hardwood from slow-growing trees.

In contrast to steel or concrete, wood remains unaffected by a wide range of pH values. Overall, working the material saves energy, partly because of its recyclability.

Fig. 7: Shrinkage and swelling of a trunk

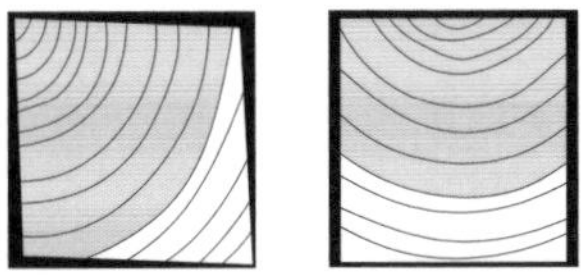

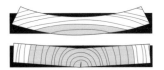

Fig. 8: Distortion of squared sections during drying

Fig. 9: Distortion of boards during drying

There are about 40 000 species of tree, some 600 of which are used commercially.

Moisture content of wood

Owing to its hygroscopic nature, the moisture content of wood changes depending on the level of moisture in the surrounding air. If moisture is absorbed, the wood swells (absorption), if moisture is released the wood shrinks (desorption). Freshly felled timber has a moisture content of about 60%. The fibre saturation point lies around 30%, and a further drop in the moisture content then leads to shrinkage.

In principle, timber for building work should be dry; a high moisture content reduces the strength and influences dimensional accuracy and form stability. Timber with a high moisture content is also at risk of being attacked by insects or fungi. And in order to prevent rot, the form of construction must ensure that the timber components remain well ventilated. Air-dried timber for external works should have a moisture content of 15–18%, for internal works 9–12%. Further drying-out leads to fissures and renders the timber unusable. Pieces of timber cut from the trunk cross-section may distort as they dry out. This is caused by the different moisture contents of the heartwood and sapwood. Fissures often form in round and sawn sections, and although such defects do not impair the loadbearing behaviour, the change in shape must be taken into account at joints and when accuracy is important.

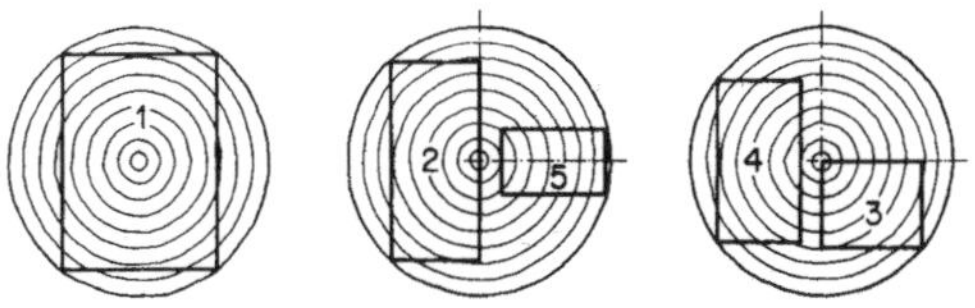

Round sections

These are essentially logs – tree trunks with all branches and bark removed – which are mostly used without needing any form of working, e.g. for scaffolds and bridges, piles, masts and propping. Round-section timber members exhibit a high strength because the natural course of the grain has not been disturbed.

Sawn timber

Generally, the method of sawing (converting) the tree trunk does not have a serious effect on the strength. However, it is important in the following instances:

Shrinkage and swelling: The distortion of the cross-sections as the moisture content changes depends on the position of the growth rings within the section.

Fissures that form as the wood dries: The shear strength can be impaired in sections containing the pith.

Compression perpendicular to the grain: The compressive strength perpendicular to the grain depends on the alignment of the growth rings within the section. However, this aspect is not normally relevant.

Biological resistance: Enhanced resistance can be achieved by using sections without sapwood.

Squared sections

The standard dimensions (in cm), in 2 cm gradations, at the time of conversion:

6 x 14...6 x 20, 8 x 12...8 x 24, 10 x 10...10 x 28, 12 x 12...12 x 28, 14 x 14...14 x 28, 16 x 16...16 x 28, 18 x 18...18 x 28

Battens

The standard dimensions (in mm), rough-sawn, air-dried:

24 x 30, 24 x 48, 27 x 35*, 27 x 40*, 27 x 50*, 27 x 60*, 30 x 48, 30 x 60, 50 x 50, 60 x 60, 60 x 80, 60 x 100, 60 x 120, 80 x 80, 80 x 100
*Western Switzerland

Boards

The standard thicknesses (in mm), rough-sawn, air-dried:

12, 15, 18, 21, 24, 27, 30, 33, 36, 40 ,42*, 45, 50, 55, 60, 65, 70, 80
*Western Switzerland

(to Swiss standards SIA 265:2003 and 265/1:2003)

1 Squared log (boxed heart)
2 Heart section (exposed pith on face)
3 Heart section (exposed pith on arris)
4 Side section
5 Centre section

Fig. 10: Conversion options for squared sections and battens
(to Swiss standard SIA 265/1 5.3.6.1: Timber construction – supplementary provisions)

 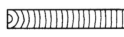 

Heart board (boxed heart)   Centre board   Side board

 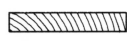 

Heart board
(exposed pith on face)   Heart board
                                 (exposed pith on edge)   Heart board
                                                                  (exposed pith on arris)

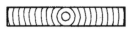  

Side board   Side boards   Slab (debarked)

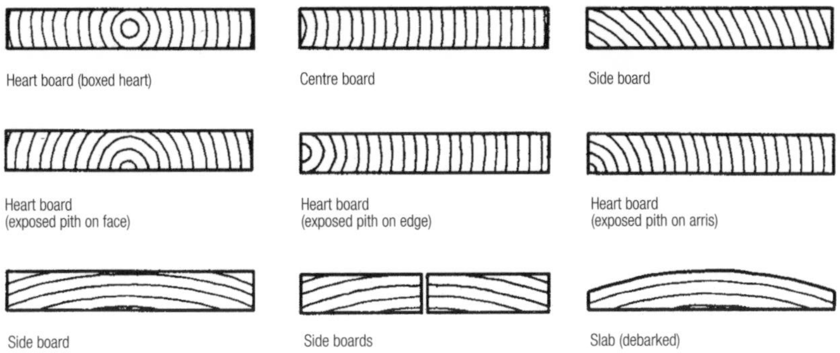

Fig. 11: Conversion options for boards
(to Swiss standard SIA 265/1 5.3.6.2: Timber construction – supplementary provisions)

Wood-based products
Overview

1

2

3

4

Fig. 12: Production of wood fibre boards
1 Timber from sawmill
2 Conveying the chips
3 Fibrous pulp on forming machine
4 Final processing

The question for the future is how to satisfy the increasing demand for timber in light of dwindling resources and poor quality (fast-growing wood). The answer is that wood-based products will increase in significance. The economic use of wood, or rather the use of the "waste" generated during its processing, has led to the development of numerous new wood-based products.

Wood-based products are manufactured by pressing together wood particles of various sizes, e.g. boards, strips, veneers, veneer strips, chips and fibres, with synthetic resin adhesives or mineral binders. In some cases wood's own binder (lignin) is activated. Besides larger pieces of wood, even residues and/or waste products from the processing of wood can be used. The manufacturing process clearly brings about a full exploitation of the raw material; and the process also homogenises the irregular properties of wood. Wood grows naturally and as a result contains unavoidable irregularities such as knots, fissures and interlocked grain, which can reduce the strength of the wood. However, these irregularities play only a minor role, if at all, in wood-based products because they are more or less neutralised by neighbouring particles. As a result, the structural properties of a wood-based product exhibit comparatively little scatter, which results in the very favourable 5% fractile to help establish the permissible stresses.

It is possible to influence the load-carrying capacity in a certain direction through the deliberate arrangement of the individual particles. Swelling and shrinkage of wood-based products is generally less than that of solid timber. Another advantage of slab-like wood-based products is the possibility of producing boards or beams in (theoretically) unlimited sizes, the only limits being those imposed by the machinery and transport. All wood-based products are available and/or produced with standard dimensions, a fact which is very useful for planning and stockpiling.

The range of products fulfils the demands of the most diverse applications. Furthermore, almost all products are easy to work with. As the range of wood-based products has in the meantime become very extensive and is undergoing continuous development, the following list cannot claim to be exhaustive, merely representative of the most common products currently available. These products are described in detail on the following pages.

Layered products
– Glued laminated timber (glulam)
– Plywood
– Veneer plywood
– Wood-based core plywood
– Multi-ply boards
– 3- and 5-ply core plywood
– Solid timber panels

Particleboards
– Chipboard
– Oriented strand board (OSB)
– Laminated strand lumber

Fibreboards
– Bitumen-impregnated wood fibre insulating board
– Medium density fibreboard (MDF)

Wood-based products with inorganic binders
Gypsum or cement can be used as a binder in the manufacture of wood-based products. The wood fibres embedded in the mass of gypsum or cement function as reinforcement. Such products are popular for thermal and sound insulation, fire protection, also for loadbearing and bracing applications. These products are not dealt with further in this book.

Wood-based products
Layered products

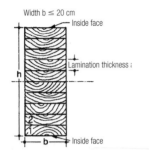

Width b ≤ 20 cm

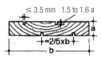

Width b > 20 cm

a) relieving grooves:

b) made from 2 parts

Fig. 13: Lay-up of glued laminated timber (glulam)

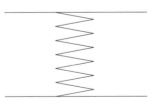

Fig. 14: Finger joint
wedged and glued joint

Glued laminated timber (glulam)

Structure and manufacture

Glued laminated timber consists of three or more individual boards, or laminations, stacked horizontally and glued together across their width. The thickness of the laminations should generally not exceed 30 mm, although in straight components this can be increased to 40 mm if drying and selection of the wood is carried out particularly carefully and the components are not exposed to any extreme climatic fluctuations in the finished building. As a rule, the planed laminations up to 20 cm wide are glued together in such a way that in each case only "outside" (i.e. furthest from pith) and "inside" (i.e. nearest to pith) faces are glued together but with only "inside" faces on the outer faces (see fig. 13) of the member. Such an arrangement (lay-up) is necessary in order to minimise any transverse tensile stresses in the adhesive joints and in the wood caused by changing climatic conditions. For widths exceeding 20 cm it is necessary to use at least two boards adjacent to each other in every lamination and to offset the joints in successive laminations by at least two times the thickness of the lamination (see fig. 13b). Individual boards exceeding 20 cm in width must include two continuous longitudinal relieving grooves on both sides of the board (see fig. 13a).

Glued laminated timber members can be manufactured in practically any length and depth. The length is limited only by the available space in the works, the gluing table and/or the transport possibilities, the depth by the working width of the planing machines available. However, dimensions exceeding those of such machines (approx. 2.00 to 2.30 m) have been achieved in the past by gluing together two part-sections. Generally, lengths of 30–35 m and depths of up to 2.20 m are possible.

Glued laminated timber members may only be manufactured by companies possessing the necessary equipment and fabrication facilities in which the humidity of the air remains more or less constant during the work and where the temperature favours the gluing process.

The glues used depend on the climatic conditions to which the finished component will be subjected. Filled synthetic resins based on urea or resorcinol are employed, spread by the gluing machinery on both sides of the planed and finger-jointed boards with a certain moisture content. The boards are assembled on the gluing table to form rectangular sections and pressed together with the prescribed pressure for the prescribed time. Once the glue has cured sufficiently, the section is planed on two or four sides and drilled or otherwise machined as required. The moisture content of the wood at the time of gluing is especially relevant to the resistance of the finished, glued assembly and its freedom from cracks.

Cross-sections and shaping

Glued laminated timber sections for columns, beams and frames are generally produced with a rectangular cross-sections. The depth-to-width of ratio for beams in bending usually lies between three and eight and should not exceed ten. In exceptional cases it is also possible to produce I- and box sections, which do save material but are more expensive to produce. However, this is often made up for by the better buckling and overturning resistance.

As wood is easily worked, members with straight sides can be produced in many forms. It is easy to discontinue certain laminations in order to vary the depth of the cross-section, but the slope must be relatively shallow in order to limit the transverse and axial stresses in the extreme fibres. Applying a gentle camber to the boards prior to gluing enables the production of curved glulam beams.

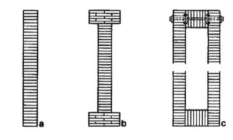

Fig. 15: Cross-sections in glued laminated timber
a Rectangular
b I-section
c Box section, dowelled or glued

Fig. 16: Surface (peeled) of plywood
The trunk is clamped in position and unrolled in order to produce veneers. This produces a relatively homogeneous surface with low contrast and irregular figure. In contrast to this, the production of sliced veneer involves cutting the trunk into thin slices.

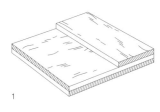

1

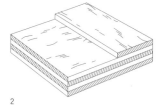

2

3

Fig. 17: Lay-up of plywood
1: 3-ply plywood
2: 5-ply plywood
3: Wood-based core plywood

Plywood

Plywood is made from at least three cross-banded plies (i.e. grain of adjacent plies at approx. 90° to each other). The plies are glued together with waterproof phenolic resin glue with the help of pressure and heat. After pressing, the edges are trimmed and the surface(s) sanded or otherwise processed. Plywood can also be moulded into virtually any shape by applying pressure, heat and moisture (moulded plywood).

Plywood is suitable for many applications. For example, it can be used as a bracing facade cladding, as roof decking, as wall sheathing or in interior fitting-out work.

Plywood absorbs moisture and swells in the plane of the board as well as in its thickness. If the material is left untreated, ultraviolet radiation and driving rain will turn it a grey colour, which can be very irregular on the side exposed to the weather in particular. A facade of plywood can be protected by a coat of diffusion-permeable, water-repellent paint. The edges especially must be sealed with a good-quality water-repellent paint.

Laminated veneer lumber

Laminated veneer lumber (LVL) is manufactured from several cross-banded veneer plies (i.e. thin sheets produced by a rotary cutting, slicing or sawing) pressed together. In comparison to other wood-based products, this material is ideal for loadbearing constructions because it's very high modulus of elasticity and high strength make it suitable for situations with high stresses.

Wood-based core plywood

This is a type of plywood with a central core of timber strips, known as blockboard, laminboard or battenboard depending on the width of the strips used.

Multi-ply boards

Plywood with at least five cross-banded plies and a ply thickness of 0.8–2.5 mm is often known as multi-ply board. Multi-ply boards can be used for external cladding, even in severe weather conditions, or internal linings. The high load-carrying capacity of such boards makes them suitable for loadbearing applications as well.

3- and 5-ply core plywood

A 3- or 5-ply core plywood consists of cross-banded plies with thicknesses between 4 and 50 mm. These boards

Fig. 18: Close-up of edges of multi-ply boards

are primarily used as loadbearing and bracing sheathing in timber buildings, and as formwork for concrete.

Solid timber panels

Three or more cross-banded layers of strips without any outer sheathing. These can be used as loadbearing plates, but must be protected from the weather.

Fig. 19: Surface (sliced) and edges of 3- and 5-ply core plywood

Wood-based products
Particleboards

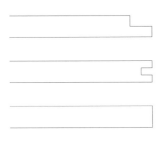

Fig. 20: Various edge profiles of chipboard

Chipboard

The residues from the forestry and woodworking industries form the raw material for the production of chipboard. The forest supplies deciduous and coniferous trees with diameters of about 8 cm and more in lengths from 1 to 6 m. The sawmills supply slabs and splinters, the so-called co-products resulting from the production of sawn goods, and the woodworking industry supplies offcuts, sawdust and shavings. Chipboard absorbs literally every last particle of the valuable resource wood. The particles of wood are mixed with organic binders and pressed together at high temperature to form the chipboard. However, particleboards can also be made by extrusion. In a pressed particleboard the chips lie essentially parallel with the plane of the board. They are produced with various particle arrangements within the thickness: single-layer (random distribution of particles) or multi-layer (three or more layers of particles of differing sizes), or as graded density chipboard in which the particles gradually decrease in size from the centre to the surfaces. Chipboard is usually supplied with its surfaces sanded but not further worked or finished. In extruded particleboard the chips lie mainly perpendicular to the plane of the board.

Chipboard is used for stiffening and covering floors and walls, for partitions and as sheathing. It is also suitable as a backing for veneers and coatings.

Chipboard generally exhibits a moderate strength. Its moisture resistance is lower than that of layered timber products and depends on the binder. However, special cement-bonded chipboards can be used in applications with a high moisture load or to meet demanding fire brigade stipulations.

Laminated strand lumber

This is a particleboard made from thin, flat, wide and long particles of poplar measuring about 0.8 x 25 x 300 mm glued together at high temperature. The size of the shavings results in a higher strength.

Oriented strand board (OSB)

This is a three-layered board in which the grain of the particles in each of the layers is aligned, the orientation in the centre layer being across the board, while the grain of the particles in the surface layers lies parallel to the long axis of the board. These particles measure approx. 0.6 x 35 x 75 mm. OSB is primarily employed in the form of loadbearing and bracing sheathing. Owing to its low glue content its behaviour in the biological degradation process is practically identical with that of solid timber.

Fig. 21: Surface and edge of a laminated strand lumber

Fig. 22: Surface and edge of oriented strand board (OSB)

Wood-based products
Fibreboards

Fibreboards

Fibreboards consist of a mixture of prepared long wood fibres (residues such as untreated sawmill waste and forestry thinnings, usually crushed softwood) and fillers that are pressed together with the help of water, pressure and heat without the need for any further binders. The structure of the wood is no longer recognisable. The strength of fibreboards varies from low to high depending on the degree of compaction.

The range of products on offer extends from soft insulating boards to medium-hard to hard boards. The latter are distinguished by their very hard surfaces and abrasion resistance; the soft insulating boards, on the other hand, exhibit high sorption and good heat storage capacity. Fibreboards are suitable for interior fitting-out works, roof decking, packaging, fillings and as sound and thermal insulation.

Fibreboards are produced using the wet method, which distinguishes them from a related type of board, the medium-density fibreboard (MDF). In the wet method the bonding forces inherent in the wood itself are used by employing a thermomechanical process to resolve the wood into its fibres; the resulting fibrous pulp is then bonded together under the action of pressure and heat. Therefore, no additional chemical binder is required.

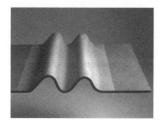

Fig. 23: Shaped MDF
MDF (medium density fibreboard) can be shaped with templates under the action of heat and moisture

Bitumen-impregnated wood fibre insulating board

A bitumen emulsion can be added during manufacture in order to make the board water-repellent. These boards are suitable for use as external insulation behind a ventilated timber leaf or facade, and also as impact sound insulation beneath floor finishes.

Medium density fibreboard (MDF)

MDF was first developed in the USA around 30 years ago. The dry method used for producing this type of board involves drying the fibres, spraying them with glue and subsequently pressing them together in a continuous process. Medium density fibreboards can be worked like solid timber. Three-dimensional profiling is possible with the thicker versions.

MDF is primarily used for furniture and fitting-out applications, also as a substrate for painting, veneer and coating work. Such boards are not stable at high moisture levels and should therefore not be used externally.

Fig. 24: Wood fibre insulating boards

Fig. 25: Medium density fibreboard (MDF)

Important panel and prefabricated systems in Switzerland
Overview

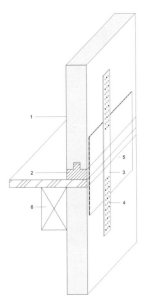

Fig. 26: Homogen80, detail of wall–floor junction
1) Homogen80 wall system
2) Timber sole plate
3) Nail plate
4) Annular-ringed shank nails
5) Seal in butt joint between panels
6) Edge beam

Homogen80

Structure

Homogen80 is an 80 mm thick softwood chipboard. The board is made up of several layers which therefore achieve an independent mechanical strength. The surface layers also form a good base for direct surface finishes. The boards are produced in sizes up to max. 537 x 203 cm and can be fitted (glued) together to form larger panels by means of tongue-and-groove joints.

Design process

The design is not bound by any production-related module. The project can be designed as required and subsequently divided into elements in conjunction with the manufacturer. The stability and homogeneity of the raw material leaves plenty of scope for cutting elements to almost any size, with openings of virtually any shape.

The system is very similar to traditional solid construction, or rather "heavyweight prefabrication", in respect of its structure, design options and building performance properties. The mass of the chipboard results in a heat storage capacity that creates similar interior climate conditions to a building of solid masonry or concrete.

Loadbearing behaviour: The direction of span is irrelevant.

Shaping: The material can be shaped during the production process.

Applications: The system must be combined with other systems at the floors and roof. The load-carrying capacity of the chipboard as a horizontal flooring element is inadequate over conventional spans.

Facade: It is possible to build a compact facade structure without adding a vapour barrier.

Insulation: The insulation is attached externally.

Surface finish: The surface of the chipboard is such that it can be rendered, plastered, wallpapered or tiled directly. The dimensionally accurate construction is beneficial to carrying out cutting work directly from the drawings.

Fig. 27: LenoTec
A) 3-ply, 81 mm
B) 5-ply, 135 mm
C) 7-ply, 216 mm

Leno solid panels

Structure

The LenoTec wood-based product is a solid cross-laminated timber panel made from between three and eleven spruce plies glued together cross-wise. The resulting homogeneous, dimensionally stable and rigid component can be produced in sizes up to 4.8 x 20 m. Thicknesses of 50–300 mm are available depending on the number of plies.

Design process

The design is not bound by any production-related module. Ready-to-install components ready to erect are manufactured at the works. The machine-based assembly enables individual panel formats and shapes to be cut as required, with openings, slots and holes for the joints and electrical services. Curved elements with a minimum radius of 7 m are also possible.

Loadbearing behaviour: The direction of span is irrelevant.

Shaping: Panels curved in one direction can be produced.

Applications: Walls, floors and roofs

Facade: It is possible to build a compact facade structure without adding a vapour barrier.

Insulation: The insulation is attached externally.

Surface finish: Available with industrial or fair-face finish. Facings with laminated veneer lumber (LVL) and special surface finishes are possible.

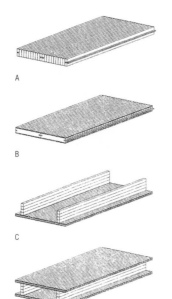

A

B

C

D

Fig. 28: Schuler solid timber panel
A) Single-ply panel
B) 3- and 5-ply panels
C) Ribbed panel
D) Box panel

Schuler solid timber ribbed panels

Structure
A solid timber panel of short, cross-banded plies of spruce and fir side boards with a lamination width of 20 or 26 mm forms the basis for the Schuler ribbed panel. Panels measuring 3.00 x 9.00 m can be produced with between one and five plies in different thicknesses. The buckling resistance of these solid timber panels is then improved by gluing on transverse ribs made from the same material. This method allows the production of large elements. Box beams can be produced by gluing panels to both sides of the ribs.

Design process
The design is not bound by any production-related module. The project can be designed as required and subsequently divided into elements in conjunction with the manufacturer. Openings can be cut virtually anywhere in the panels. The stiffening ribs can function as supports for planking and cladding.

Loadbearing behaviour: The direction of span is irrelevant.

Shaping: The elements cannot be shaped.

Applications: Walls, floors and roofs

Insulation: Insulating material can be laid between the ribs.

Facade: It is possible to build a compact facade structure without adding a vapour barrier.

Surface finish: Available with rough-sawn standard, industrial and fair-face finishes. Finishes with facing-quality boards or laminated veneer lumber (LVL) are possible.

Fig. 29: Bresta edge-fixed element

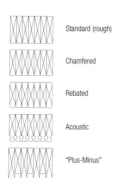

Standard (rough)

Chamfered

Rebated

Acoustic

"Plus-Minus"

Fig. 30: Bresta edge-fixed elements
Different types of section

Bresta edge-fixed elements

Structure
Side boards 30 mm thick, a cheap (waste) material readily available from any sawmill, form the basis for these elements. The boards are placed on edge and joined with continuous dowels in a fully automatic production plant. The hardwood dowels hold together the "stack" of boards through a clamping effect. Neither glue nor mechanical fasteners are used. This method can produce one-way-spanning elements in any width with thicknesses between 8 and 12 cm for walls, and between 18 and 26 cm for floors, depending on the span. The dowels perpendicular to the direction of the boards ensure that the transverse shrinkage and swelling movements are reduced virtually to zero.

Design process
The design is not bound by any production-related module. The project can be designed as required and subsequently divided into elements in conjunction with the manufacturer. Openings can be cut virtually anywhere in the panels.

In comparison with lightweight construction, the mass of an edge-fixed element results in a higher heat storage capacity. Such elements are ideal for timber-concrete composite floors. Narrow elements (27 cm) can be supplied for conversion work where space is limited.

Loadbearing behaviour: Element spans in one direction.
Shaping: The elements can be bent transverse to the boards (barrel-vault roofs are possible).

Applications: Walls, floors and roofs

Facade: A compact facade structure requires the addition of a vapour barrier. If the inner surface is not lined, the vapour barrier can be fitted between the element and the insulation.

Insulation: The insulation is attached externally.

Surface finish: Rough-sawn boards are dowelled together if the surface is to be clad afterwards. On exposed surfaces the boards are planed on four sides. The dimensions of the boards can be varied to suit aesthetic and acoustic requirements (see fig. 30).

Fig. 31: Lignotrend wall elements
A) Open both sides
B) Closed on both sides
C) Closed on one side

Lignotrend

Structure

Lignotrend consists of between three and seven cross-banded softwood plies, with gaps of several centimetres between the individual pieces of the inner plies. The raw material is exclusively side boards or low-strength wood. The wall elements are supplied in widths up to 62.5 cm and these elements can be joined together with timber plates and frames by woodworking firms to produce storey-high wall panels. Mechanical fasteners are used to join the individual elements together or to the floors above or below. The cross-banded arrangement of the plies results in very little shrinkage and swelling; movements are taken up in the joints.

Design process

There is a production module of 12.5 cm but the design is not necessarily bound by this. The project can be designed more or less as required and subsequently divided into elements in conjunction with the manufacturer. Openings can be cut virtually anywhere in the panels.

Floor and roof elements are available with a similar construction. Electric cables can be routed through the voids without having to cut or drill the panel itself.

Loadbearing behaviour: The direction of span is irrelevant.

Shaping: The elements cannot be shaped.

Applications: Walls, floors and roofs

Facade: A compact facade structure without an additional vapour barrier is possible, depending on the type of element chosen.

Insulation: The voids between the plies can be filled with insulating material. However, as this is very labour-intensive, corresponding tests have been cancelled.

Surface finish: A fair-face finish is available, depending on the type of element.

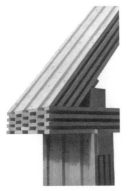

Fig. 32: Ligu timber element
for walls, floors, roofs

Ligu timber elements

Structure

Ligu timber elements consist of several offset layers of solid timber laminations – side boards in various softwoods – glued together and additionally secured with hardwood dowels in the overlaps. This results in air-filled chambers and a box-like glued loadbearing construction. Like a glued laminated timber beam, such elements can span long distances. The elements are produced in thicknesses from 140 to 240 mm, i.e. seven to twelve plies, and in widths of 62.5, 41.6 and 20.8 cm. Loose timber tongues are used to join single elements to form larger ones. It is necessary to include a timber stud in the corners.

Design process

It is advisable to adjust the design to suit the smallest element. Owing to the maximum element width of 62.5 cm, the openings should not lie within, but rather between the

elements. Joints between elements cannot accommodate any shear forces, which means that trimmers and lintels must be included.

Loadbearing behaviour: Element spans in one direction.

Shaping: The elements cannot be shaped.

Applications: Walls, floors and roofs

Facade: It is possible to build a compact facade structure without adding a vapour barrier.

Insulation: Depending on the thickness of the element, the enclosed air chambers (57% wood, 43% air) can provide adequate thermal resistance without the need for further insulation.

Surface finish: The elements must be clad.

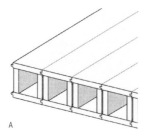

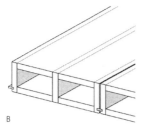

Fig. 33: Lignatur elements
A) Box element
B) Planar element

Fig. 34: Wellsteg hollow element

Lignatur box, panel and decking elements

Structure

Lignatur elements are hollow components produced industrially. They were developed for use as loadbearing floor and roof constructions. These modular elements are joined with double tongue-and-groove joints and can be pre-assembled in the works to form larger elements, the size of which is limited only by the restrictions imposed by transport. The box elements are produced with a cover width of 200 mm; the maximum length is generally 12 m, with longer lengths possible on request. The depth of the element can be chosen to suit the structural and building performance requirements.

Lignatur panels are produced in widths of 514 and 1000 mm as standard; the maximum length is 16 m. Lignatur decking elements are primarily intended for roofing applications.

Design process

The Lignatur elements are pre-assembled in the works to form larger elements. It is advantageous to base the design on the module given by the element width.

Loadbearing behaviour: Element spans in one direction.

Shaping: Individual Lignatur elements can be assembled to form curved roofs.

Applications: Floors and roofs

Facade: It is possible to build a compact facade structure without adding a vapour barrier.

Insulation: The voids in the elements can be filled with various insulating materials at the works.

Surface finish: Three surface finishes for the underside are available: industrial, normal and selected.

Wellsteg hollow elements

Structure

The primary component of the Wellsteg hollow element is the sine wave-web beam measuring 16.6 cm wide and 19–51 cm deep. This consists of two solid timber (spruce/fir) tongue-and-groove flanges plus a sine-wave (birch) plywood web. A curved groove to receive the web is milled in the flanges in a special production plant. The plywood web, splayed scarf joints within its length, is cut to fit the groove and glued in place. Afterwards the beam is pressed together. Individual beams can be joined together with transverse timber pieces (fitted inside) to form larger panels.

Design process

It is advantageous to base the design on the module given by the beam width. The elements can be prefabricated in any size up to a length of 15 m. Pipes and cables are installed in the works. It is easy to drill holes through the web to accommodate services in the transverse direction. Wellsteg hollow elements have a low self-weight and are particularly suitable for adding floors to existing buildings.

Compared with a reinforced concrete floor, the Wellsteg hollow element achieves a weight-saving of 7% for the same load, depth and span.

Loadbearing behaviour: Element essentially spans in one direction. However, the spacing between the flanges enables filler pieces to be inserted to enable the element to span in two directions. Openings can be cut in the floor at the works following the same principle.

Shaping: Sine wave-web beams can be assembled to form curved elements.

Applications: Walls, floors and roofs

Facade: A compact facade structure requires the addition of a vapour barrier.

Insulation: The voids in the elements can be filled with insulating material at the works.

Surface finish: Three surface finishes are available: industrial, fair-face and selected.

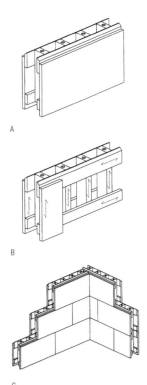

A

B

C

Fig. 35: Steko wall system
A) Steko basic module
B) Structure of module and direction of grain
C) Wall corner detail

Steko wall system

Structure

Steko is a modular system based on standardised, industrially produced solid timber modules. The individual modules are joined by means of a special clip-in arrangement which guarantees an optimum joint at corners and junctions with intermediate walls. Matching sill, lintel and jamb elements to suit the various openings round off the system. The compact modules consist of five plies of cross-banded solid timber. Used in a wall, the modules form a rigid, structural unit thanks to the clip-in connection.

Design process

The system is based on a primary module of 16 cm. The basic modular dimensions of 64/32/16 cm (length/height/thickness) also permit quarter, half and three-quarter formats within the 16 cm module. The depth module is 8 cm, which enables two finished depths of 32 and 24 cm to be achieved. Sole plates, head binders and lintel elements are coordinated with the modular dimensions. Hoses for services can be threaded through the modules.

The Steko wall system can be combined with standard windows and doors, also conventional floor and roof systems.

Loadbearing behaviour: Element spans in one direction.

Shaping: The modules cannot be shaped.

Applications: Walls

Facade: It is possible to build a compact facade structure without adding a vapour barrier.

Insulation: The voids in the modules can be filled with a suitable insulating material after erection. Additional insulation can be attached to the outside if the building performance specification calls for this.

Surface finish: the modules are available with a facing in fair-face quality, either a vertical single-ply board or, on request, horizontal 3-core plywood.

Panel construction
Current developments

Fig. 36: Erecting a panel construction element
LenoTec cross-laminated timber panel

Changes to design and building processes and hence the role of the architect have characterised recent developments in the construction industry. The diversity of the systems and materials on the market mean that the architect is increasingly reliant on the specific expertise of industry, which can offer ever more comprehensive end-to-end solutions. This is therefore focusing the specialist knowledge and guarantee clauses on the side of the manufacturer.

Looking at timber construction, we find that current developments and innovations are of a more fundamental nature. In this respect, the timber building sector has assumed a special status within the construction industry. Here again, however, high-tech skills are being delegated to the specialists employed by the manufacturers. This eases the architect's workload because he or she no longer has to consider the detailed inner workings of the construction. On the other hand, this skill will be lost over the long term from the architectural profession and the building trade.

Semi-finished products and the manufacture of wood-based products

In Central Europe and Scandinavia the movement in this sector was triggered by a crisis in the timber building industry. In order to regain market share from solid construction and to find a rapid use for wood from trees brought down in severe storms ("Vivian" in 1990 and "Lothar" in 1999), innovations were urgently required. Such innovations initially focused on semi-finished goods and the manufacture of wood-based products. Traditional woodworking processes require timber cross-sections with a fairly consistent quality. This means that when cutting planks, squared sections and boards, only healthy, straight trunks can be used, and therefore offcuts and side boards of lower quality abound. Nowadays, these sections are used, cut down into smaller strips, battens and laminations. Chips and sawdust are at the end of this processing chain.

The process of breaking down into ever smaller parts is accompanied by the inverse of this process – assembly. The smaller the constituents in the assembled products, the more homogeneous their physical properties are and the easier it is to influence these properties through the type of assembly and the choice of chemical binders or mechanical fasteners. When using chips or sawdust, synthetic materials such as adhesive or cement are used, depending on the intended application. Semi-finished products made from strips or laminations are usually glued together, which increases their structural qualities and opens up new options for construction.

The search for suitable connection options and their ratio to the proportion of wood paves the way for semi-finished products in which the boundary between

Fig. 37: Wood welding
Applying ultrasonic energy causes the plastic to bond with the wood at the macroporous level.

wood-based products and other materials, e.g. plastics, becomes indistinct as we try to achieve optimum properties. This is true of the current trials surrounding new connections, e.g. wood welding, where thermoplastic jointing materials are vibrated by ultrasonic energy and thus flow into the porous structure of the wood. Wood welding produces a stable connection that can be loaded immediately.

The – compared with natural wood – considerably more consistent physical properties, which are reaching hitherto unknown proportions, depending on the particular range of products, render new applications in timber engineering possible. It is therefore only a matter of time before the first timber building systems with completely new structural and building physics properties appear on the market.

Custom prefabrication

The shift from production on site to production in the factory, where controlled conditions and workflows make it possible to achieve greater accuracy, enables timber building contractors to keep control of the majority of the production process. Almost all current timber building systems are flexible enough to be able to react to individual designs. Trying to keep the design within a module suitable for timber engineering is now a thing of the past. Only the maximum possible spans still influence the plan layout. The traditional design process for a timber building constructed by carpenters has therefore been reversed: the structure can be designed with a relatively high degree of freedom, and broken down into suitable individual parts or elements in the next stage of the design (custom prefabrication). At best, the only restrictions imposed are those of transport.

Black box systems or sandwich systems

Today, it is possible to request quotations from suppliers of different systems based on tender drawings at a scale of 1:200. The days in which the architect drew the entire loadbearing timber construction in great detail are over. This work is carried out by the system supplier awarded the contract, who is also responsible for the detailed design of the system and compliance with the building physics criteria. The details specific to the project are solved in cooperation with the architect, possibly with repercussions for the loadbearing system. The closed black box elements – fulfilling all requirements – are delivered to the building site and erected, an inner lining and/or external cladding being added if required, depending on the system.

Isotropic panels

One characteristic that determines design in panel construction is whether the direction of the panels is relevant

Black box

Fig. 38: The ribbed solid timber panel as an example of a black box system
Finished sandwich elements are delivered to site with their internal structure no longer visible.

Fig. 39: The thin plate
Erection of panel elements

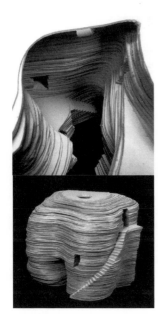

Fig. 40: The stack of horizontal boards
"Cardboard space piece", a project by first-year students at ETH Zurich

or irrelevant. Panels in which this aspect is irrelevant are those made from wood-based products whose structure within the plane of the panel is isotropic. As wood naturally has a directional – anisotropic – character, this distinction has only become possible thanks to progress in the manufacture of semi-finished and wood-based products, e.g. cross-banded plies of veneers or strips. Such panels exhibit high strength and rigidity. They achieve plate effects and can be cut and assembled almost like in modelmaking. This can be seen, for example, in the treatment of openings, which can be cut seemingly at random and do not even require trimming (lintel), provided there is enough material above the opening.

What shall we do with the board?

The semi-finished product in the form of a solid timber board is more or less a flat plate. If it were a shell, it would be curved in the plane of its surface in one or two directions, and therefore its plan shape would be independent.

What makes the board really interesting from the constructional viewpoint is its variable thickness, which ranges from very thin to very thick, theoretically to infinitely thick. The reason for this can be found in its own process-related formatting because it is produced from thin plies (battens or veneers), bonded mechanically or glued and pressed in parallel, diagonal or cross-banded layers.

Normal-thickness board

Using boards of normal thickness means that the constructional phenomena of solid construction come into play. The thickness of the board depends on the structural actions to be expected. We refer to board tectonics in the structural carcass.

The diagram of layers of the facade make-up reveals a complementary system of monofunctional layers with a strict breakdown into loadbearing layer (i.e. the board), insulating layer and protective layer (viewed from inside to outside). The protective layer has to be anchored back to the loadbearing layer by means of an appropriate, additional supporting construction (substrate). So in this sense we can speak of the completion of the facade. The constructional configuration of the protective layer visible externally is therefore relatively independent of the requirements of the structural boarding.

The situation is the same for the suspended floors, although here the board (loadbearing layer) must be sized to cope with bending as well, depending on the span. The rest of the floor make-up consists of the insulating layer (impact, structure-borne and airborne sound) and the protective layer, i.e. the floor finishes, again with the appropriate substrate.

Thin board

By itself, the thin board is not capable of carrying loads. Despite this, thin sections are used, and to prevent buckling, transverse ribs made from the same material as the board are attached at a regular pitch. If the ribbed board manufactured in this way is closed off by adding a second board layer to the underside of the ribs and the ensuing voids filled with an insulating material, we obtain an artificial facade system in which loadbearing layer, insulating layer and protective layer are not exactly fully combined, but at least substantially interlinked. In timber construction we therefore commonly speak of "sandwich construction", although these are in reality hollow-box elements.

The advantage of this form of production lies in the high degree of prefabrication, the disadvantage in finding a solution to the jointing problem. Such elements are very lightweight but nevertheless very strong, e.g. for resisting wind loads. In the form of hollow-box elements they are particularly useful for suspended floors, especially for longer spans. Horizontal pipes, cables and ducts can be integrated to a certain extent. The main problem here, though, is an acoustic one, which is why the right choice of floor finish is important.

When used as loadbearing internal walls, hollow-box elements provide an additional possibility: after installing the building services, they can be filled with a heavy, loose filling of sand, which not only improves the acoustics of the wall, but also provides a larger mass storage medium for improving the building's energy efficiency. Hollow-box elements therefore certainly offer the timber builder another range of architectural and constructional options related to traditional timber construction.

Very thick board

Boards can be stacked horizontally. Using pattern-cutting programs, similar to those used in the textiles industry, custom parts can be cut out of the boards and joined together, making optimum use of the material. Thanks to the computer-controlled cutting process, the cuts do not have to run perpendicular to the boards, but can be carried out at defined, even continuously changing angles. The cut surfaces of the stack of boards eventually form a continuous, three-dimensional surface development, which works directly as an enclosing form. Solid "space pieces", with an organic inner life, are the result. At this point timber building departs from all known forms of construction; the method owes more to sculpted than tectonic building forms. The notion of solid timber construction is given a completely new meaning.

Timber construction systems
Overview

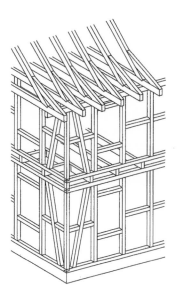

Fig. 41: Timber-frame construction

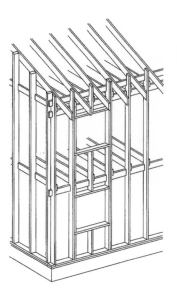

Fig. 42: Balloon frame construction, timber stud construction

Timber frame construction

This traditional method of building with timber, seldom used today, is based on a relatively small module with diagonal braces in the plane of the walls. We see the first signs of prefabrication in this form of construction. The loadbearing and separating functions are united in the same plane within the wall. Assembly of the individual pieces takes place on site storey by storey. The spacing between the individual vertical members depends on the loadbearing capacity of the timber sections which, prior to industrialisation, were cut to size with simple means (saws, axes). The individual connections are not highly stressed and can be in the form of true wood joints (e.g. tenons, halving joints, oblique dados). Vertical loads are transferred directly via the contact faces between the various timber members.

As the cross-sections of the members are often not derived from a structural analysis, in older timber-frame buildings they tend to be too large and hence uneconomic, or are an inevitable consequence of the usually consider-able weakening of the cross-section at the joints. Today, mechanical fasteners are therefore preferred in order to achieve a more economic sizing of the sections.

The infill panels of historical timber-frame buildings are usually of cob, wattle and daub or clay bricks, with masonry and render in later buildings. Today, the infilling is usually insulating materials with a weatherproof cladding.

Balloon frame construction, timber stud construction

The balloon frame system widespread in America con-sists of closely spaced squared sections of standard sizes based on a "2 x 8 inch" module (roughly 5 x 20 cm). When, as a result of a structural analysis, larger cross-sections are called for, these are made by simply nailing several smaller squared sections together. This timber stud construction is nailed together on site and usually extends over two or more storeys. Stability is assured by solid timber boarding or wood-based panels attached diagonally.

The simplicity of the system, in which additional mem-bers are often simply nailed to the main framework as required, enables rapid erection with unskilled labour, despite minimum prefabrication. The system is also char-acterised by a great degree of design freedom regarding plan layout, volume and positioning of openings. Indeed, openings can even be "cut out" subsequently because the construction is oversized. However, this oversizing is a disadvantage compared to newer systems because it leads to high material consumption.

In Europe, *timber stud construction* is the equivalent of the American balloon frame. Timber stud construction also uses closely spaced squared sections of standard sizes extending over two or more storeys. However, there is less standardisation and the connections are not limited to nailing as in the balloon frame – tenons and halving joints are also used. Another aim is a more economic use of material.

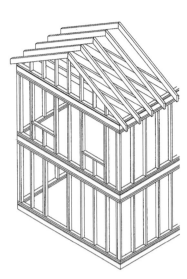

Fig. 43: Platform frame construction

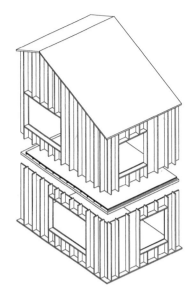

Fig. 44: Panel construction

Platform frame construction

Platform frame construction is a further development of timber stud construction. It is distinguished by a high degree of prefabrication and is therefore very popular these days. The loadbearing elements consist of storey-high pre-assembled frames of squared sections braced by flat cladding panels or diagonal boards. Platform frame construction is based on a small module, although the spacing can be varied as required, e.g. depending on the thermal insulation used (mats or loose fill). The individual loadbearing ribs are assembled in the works and transported to the building site as self-contained elements. On site they are merely erected and clad if necessary. The tectonic structure of platform frame construction is based on the principle of stacking storeys one upon the other.

The advantage of this form of construction is its versatility because it can respond to many different design specifications. Platform frame construction is straightforward and economic because it uses identical timber sections wherever possible, which thanks to their small size are easy and cheap to produce. The simple nailed and screwed connections are another advantage of this system.

Panel construction

The latest development in panel construction is leading to a reversal of the principle of platform frame construction. The loadbearing element is now a slab, no longer a linear member. This slab must exhibit high strength and rigidity in order to achieve a structural plate action. One answer to such requirements is the solid timber panel, which consists of cross-banded plies of sawn timber strips. The addition of transverse ribs made from the same material increases the buckling resistance of such panels. Insulation is placed between the ribs. The planar, non-directional nature of this loadbearing slab results in structural and architectural characteristics hitherto unknown in timber construction. The traditional grid or spacing of loadbearing elements is no longer necessary. Openings can be cut almost at random.

The construction principle results in a rationalisation of the layered assembly. Single components can play a multifunctional role, which reduces the number of layers and hence the additive character of the layered assembly. The loadbearing solid timber panel, for example, needs no further surface finish internally, apart from a coat of paint. If the building is to be clad with a uniform outer leaf, this can be attached directly to the sheathing of the wall element.

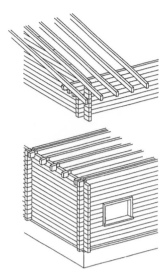

Fig. 45: Log construction

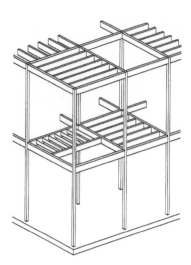

Fig. 46: Frame construction

Log construction

Traditional log construction is the only form of timber construction that also falls under the heading of "solid construction". The building envelope consists of a single leaf of timber members – stacked horizontally and joined by means of cogged joints – that performs the cladding, space-enclosing and loadbearing fractions simultaneously. Stability is achieved through the friction resistance in the bed joints, which leads to the solid timber wall acting as a plate, and through the cogged joints between the timber members at the corners. No mechanical fasteners are required. The possible spans depend on the timber members available, which do not usually exceed 4.5 m.

Log construction leads to substantial shrinkage and settlement movements because the timber members are loaded perpendicular to the grain. Settlement movements must be taken into account in the details, e.g. at window openings. The insulating value of a log building no longer meets modern requirements; contemporary log buildings must therefore be provided with extra insulation. This method of construction is only economic in places where the corresponding infrastructure (sawmill) and expertise (carpentry skills) are available.

Frame construction

This is the most delicate form of construction in timber. Vertical columns and horizontal joist floors ("tie beams") or "plates" form the loadbearing structure (similar to the column-and-slab principle of solid construction). The consistency of the materials used for the vertical and horizontal linear members (sawn timber or glued laminated timber) and the form of the joints determine the spans that can be achieved and the architectural appearance of the loadbearing construction. Besides solid timber, glued laminated timber and other glued structural elements are available these days. The joints usually employ mechanical fasteners such as gusset plates and dowels, the principle of which is similar to structural steelwork. True wood joints are hardly ever used in frame construction.

Stability is achieved through the inclusion of diagonal ties and struts, or wall plates, or solid cores that extend through all storeys.

Frame construction is distinguished from other forms of timber construction by the fact that the loadbearing structure functions completely independently of the enclosing elements such as partitions or facades (glazing is conceivable). This specialisation of the elements is not very economic in terms of material consumption, but does lead to good flexibility in the internal layout and design of the facade, and enables longer spans.

Platform frame construction
Construction principle

Fig. 47: Platform frame elements prior to erection
Bearth & Deplazes: private house (Willimann), Sevgein (CH), 1998

Fig. 49: Erection of platform frame elements with sheathing both sides
Bearth & Deplazes: private house (Willimann), Sevgein (CH), 1998

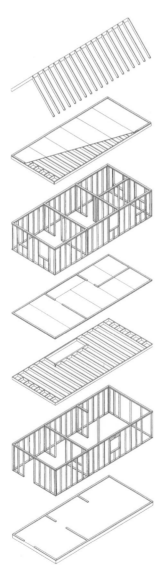

Fig. 48: In platform frame construction the elements are stacked storey by storey.

Platform frame construction is currently very popular in Switzerland. This is the outcome of marketing campaigns and engineering developments carried out by the timber building industry during the 1980s. The goal was to transform timber stud construction – which had been used widely since 1930 and itself had been inspired by the balloon frame system used in the USA and Canada – into a new building system. This new system had to exhibit a high degree of prefabrication and standardisation of the parts.

Consequently, platform frame construction is a further development of the tradition of improving timber buildings raised using traditional carpentry skills. The primary loadbearing system continues to rely on an arrangement of linear members which has been optimised and developed so that most of the work can be carried out in the factory. The degree of prefabrication has been gradually increased since the introduction of this system and has virtually reached the limits imposed by the system itself.

Thanks to its great flexibility and high degree of prefabrication, platform frame construction has been widely accepted by the building industry. However, it is itself now facing competition brought about by newly developed wood-based products which are tending to render the system of linear loadbearing members obsolete in favour of planar loadbearing elements (see "Panel construction – Current developments").

The system is based on a close grid of loadbearing linear members whose spacing can be varied depending on the given geometry, the format of the insulating material between the members, and the loads expected. Timber members with the same cross-section are used for the vertical studs as well as the horizontal head binders and bottom plates; their arrangement enables them to fulfil almost all structural requirements. The inner layer of sheathing stiffens the whole frame and leads to the whole providing a plate effect. All connections are generally nailed, but if necessary (tension-resistant) screws can also be used.

The use of standardised building materials is one of the prime advantages of platform frame construction. The majority of buildings employ timber members with cross-sections between 60 x 120 mm and 60 x 200 mm. These relatively small sizes result in little waste when being cut to size and are easy to store; they are ideal for kiln-drying and machine-grading.

It is advisable to fix sheathing to the prepared frames (so-called black box). To do this, battens, if necessary also counter battens, are fixed inside and outside and the sheathing attached to this, creating a "sandwich". The ensuing air cavities provide ventilation on the outside and space for services inside. The choice of material and surface finish is wide and only loosely dependent on the system.

Custom prefabrication

Unlike methods of construction that use batch prefabrication based on the use of standard basic elements (modular construction) or a fixed grid, timber platform frame construction is a method that allows custom prefabrication.

This means that, starting with a specific project which can be designed more or less as required (subject to the usual boundary conditions), a sensible breakdown into units can be achieved in conjunction with the manufacturer.

The individual elements of this "set of parts" are produced as self-contained "black box" assemblies in the factory and delivered to the building site as stable wall plates. These consist of a frame of linear timber members that is filled with insulating material and covered on both sides with suitable sheathing. The arrangement of the individual linear members within each element is chosen depending on the structural requirements and the geometry, taking into account any openings necessary in that section of wall.

The thickness and format of the insulating material chosen also influences on the spacing of the linear members and their sizes. The most common cross-sections in use lie between 60 x 120 mm and 60 x 200 mm because the thickness of insulation varies from 12 to 20 cm depending on the specification.

The assembly on the building site involves merely erecting these finished wall panels. The butt joints between the panels are either nailed or screwed depending on requirements. Normally, the elements are set up storey by storey, with the floors either being placed between successive wall panels or suspended from these inside.

Once completed, our assembled set of parts forms a stable, insulated building. To protect the building against

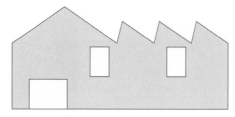

1 "Facade"

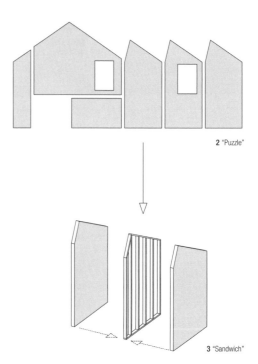

2 "Puzzle"

3 "Sandwich"

Fig. 51: Timber platform frame construction as a "building kit"
1 Individual project
2 Breakdown into sensible parts
3 Elements as self-contained "black box" assemblies (stable wall plates)

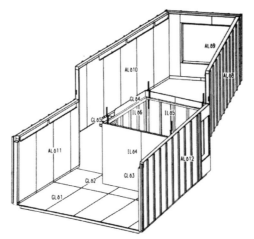

Fig. 50: Axonometric view of wall elements offset to accommodate split-level floor
Bearth & Deplazes: private house (Willimann), Sevgein (CH), 1998

the effects of the weather, it needs to be clad. There are hardly any limits to the type of cladding that can be chosen, but it must guarantee air circulation for the timber construction underneath. Timber platform frame buildings are mostly lined on the inside. This protects the inside sheathing to the black box (which, depending on the insulating material used, must provide a vapour barrier or vapour check) against mechanical damage and penetration. The lining permits individual interior design requirements to be met (plaster, wood panelling etc.) and also conceals any electric cables subsequently installed (these may not be routed through the insulation).

Fig. 52: Custom prefabrication:
The design and construction sequence in
timber platform frame construction

Schemes 1–4, plans

Schemes 1–4, sections

**Dividing a specific project into sensible
"building units" made up of wall and floor
elements**

Cooperation between architect, manufacturer and,
possibly, engineer

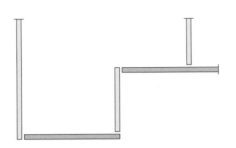

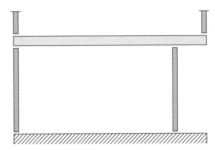

**Production of elements as self-contained
"black box" assemblies in the factory**

Arrangement of linear members based on
structural requirements and insulating material
format (50 x 100 mm or 60 x 120 mm)

Sizing of linear members depends on thickness of
integral thermal insulation (120–200 mm)

Joint design (butt joints with seals or overlapping
as shown here)

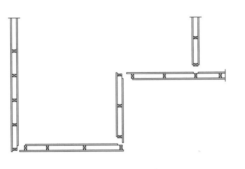

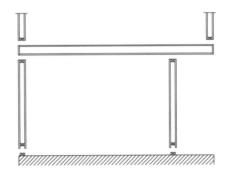

**Delivery of elements to building site and
erection**

Plan: vertical butt joints nailed (for compression
only) or screwed (also for tension)

Section: stacking the elements

In order to guarantee the continuity of the vapour
barrier, vertical and horizontal butt joints must be
sealed accordingly.

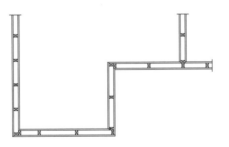

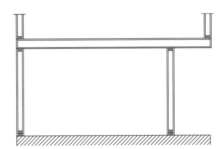

**Attaching the external cladding (and internal
lining)**

The external cladding must guarantee a circulation
of air for the underlying timber construction.

The internal lining may be chosen to suit interior
design requirements and can also conceal electric
cables. There are no services (electrics, water, gas,
waste water etc.) in the platform frame elements
themselves because otherwise they would have to
penetrate the vapour barrier.

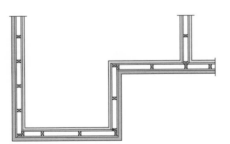

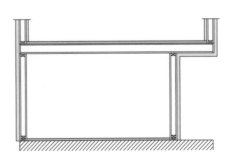

Fig. 53: Timber platform frame element, layers and sheathing

1 Internal lining, 12 mm
2 Vertical battens (services), 50 mm
3 Wood-based panel (vapour-tight), 12 mm
4 Frame: head binder, 60 x 150 mm to 60 x 300 mm
5 Frame: stud, 60 x 150 mm to 60 x 300 mm
6 Frame: bottom plate, 60 x 150 mm to 60 x 300 mm
7 Insulation, e.g. ISOFLOC, 150–300 mm
8 Bitumen-impregnated wood fibre insulating board, 18 mm (airtight)
9 Vertical battens, ventilation cavity, 40 mm
10 Horizontal sheathing, 24 mm
11 3-ply board with tongue and groove, impact sound insulation
12 LIGNATUR box element
13 Airtight membrane over butt joint
14 Counter battens, 40 mm (needed to guarantee vertical continuation of ventilation cavity)
15 Horizontal battens, 40 mm
16 Vertical sheathing, 24 mm

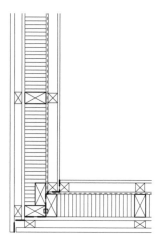

Horizontal section through corner joint
Horizontal sheathing

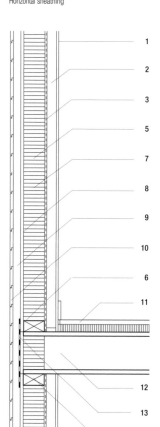

Section through wall–floor junction
Horizontal sheathing

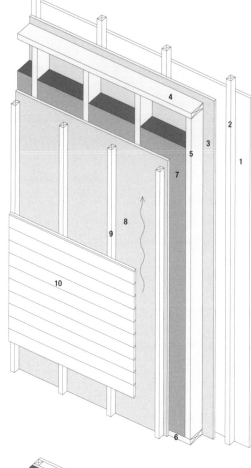

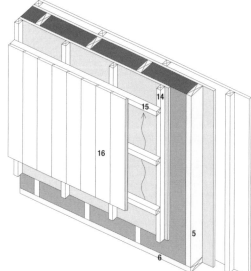

Axonometric view of layers
Horizontal sheathing (top) and vertical sheathing (bottom)

Chart for establishing preliminary size of timber beams
Initial size estimate at design stage

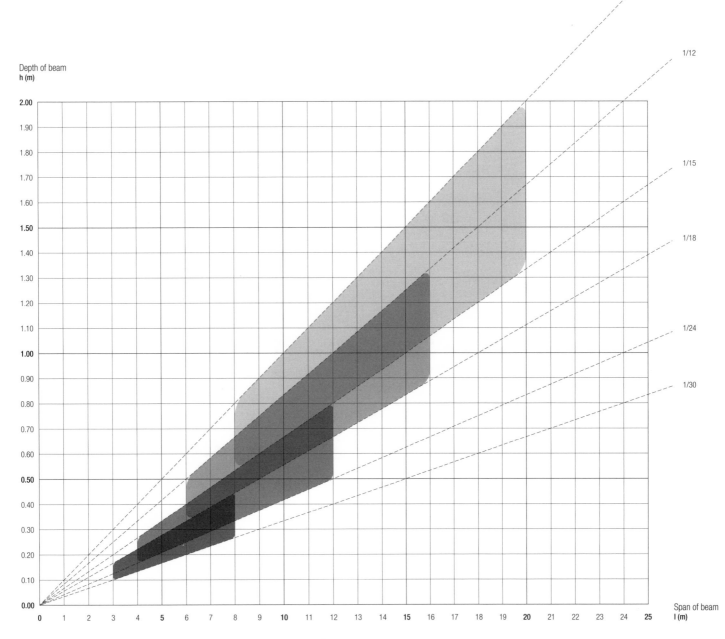

Depth of beam
h (m)

Span of beam
l (m)

Element	Span	h*/l
(loadbearing)	l (m)	
Rafter	– 8 m	1/18 – 1/30
Purlin, beam	4 – 12 m	1/15 – 1/24
Solid-web beam	6 – 16 m	1/12 – 1/18
Lattice beam	8 – 20 m	1/10 – 1/15

Fig. 54: Notes for using this chart
With a high load (dead and imposed loads) use the
maximum value for the member depth as proposed
by the chart – vice versa for a low load.
The sizes and relationships shown cannot be verified
scientifically. The shaded areas are supposed to be
slightly "indefinite". In the interest of the rational use
of a loadbearing element, the "edges" of this chart
should be avoided.

Source: M. Dietrich, Burgdorf School of
Engineering, 1990

*A beam cross-section (h/b = 2/1) can be used for the initial, rough sizing; Glulam beams are often more slender.

Conversion of a trunk in traditional Japanese timber building culture
The workshops at the Grand Shrine of Ise

Christoph Henrichsen

Thanks to the ritual of completely rebuilding the shrine every 20 years, a centuries-old tradition of conversion has been handed down to the present day in the workshops of the Grand Shrine of Ise. This bears witness to a profound knowledge of wood, and the procedures for cutting the wood illustrate the rules that must be observed when obtaining high-quality sawn timber sections from mature tree trunks in order to do justice to the individual characteristics of every trunk. Ise is certainly the only place in Japan where everything is in the hands of one master carpenter: forest husbandry, felling, conversion and final building work.

Fig. 56: The master carpenter at work
Marking the end of a trunk with a plumb line

Fig. 55: Secondary shrine of Ise
Contrast between old and new structures

sections, as a precaution the master carpenter attaches further lines. In this way he can be sure that even in the case of minimal crookedness the necessary sections can be cut from the trunk. The timber sections are marked out at the crown end. But here the master carpenter also includes all the information required to ensure that the sections end up at the right place in the building: building name, component name, component number, trunk number.

Fig. 57: Three tree trunks marked ready for cutting in the sawmill
Visible here are the marked-out sections plus additional information such as building name, component name, component number, and trunk number.

Felling and storing the trunks

The trees intended for the shrine – these days hiba trees (from Northern Japan) which have virtually replaced cypresses for economic reasons – are felled in the winter, between October and February. Upon arrival in the store an inventory number is stamped into the crown end. Prior to conversion, the trunks are stored for up to three years in ponds. This avoids cracks due to drying, but also, allegedly, removes certain substance from the wood, and this leads to quicker drying after conversion. The trunks are lifted out of the water with a winch and taken to the sawmill on small rail-mounted trolleys. If required, they are cut to length first. The master carpenter then turns them to inspect them for damage and flaws. He works the crown end of each trunk with electric and hand planes because it is easier to perform the marking-out work on a smooth surface. The marking-out of the trunks (Japanese: *kidori*, to divide up the wood) always begins with a line through the heart (*shinzumi*) at the crown end (*sue-koguchi*). To do this, the master carpenter uses a plumb bob and a carpenter's try-square. The central mark is subsequently transferred to the stump end (*moto-koguchi*), whose diameter is normally some 10 cm larger, with a line (*mizuito*). If required, a mark can therefore be drawn slightly off-centre in order to avoid, for example, damage in the trunk. Prior to marking out the

Marking-out

For marking-out the master carpenter uses a stick split from a piece of bamboo (*sumi-sashi*) one end of which is fanned out over a length of about 2 cm to form numerous narrow teeth, which he dips into the piece of cotton wool soaked in ink belonging to his snap line. The marking-out usually starts with the largest sections and the secondary parts are cut from the remainder of the trunk. The trunks are always marked out by the master carpenter of the workshop. He knows all the buildings and knows best which requirements will be placed on every single part. Besides the best possible use of the trunk, he must

Fig. 58: Boards stacked for weathering

also ensure that every component is cut from that part of the trunk most suitable for that component. For example, slightly crooked trunks are preferred for beams, which are then positioned so that the rounded side is on the top; trunks with a high resin content are turned into beams and purlins. The list of timber parts specifies quality grades for the components. The highest quality (*shihoake*), which is required for producing containers for storing holy objects and is used for only a few building components, must be absolutely free from flaws on all four sides. This quality grade is followed by parts which must be free from knots on two sides (*nihoake*). Sound knots up to a diameter of about 2 cm are permitted in the quality grade for secondary and concealed parts (*jokobushi*). The list of timber parts also includes details of whether the converted section is to be cut to length afterwards or whether the parts are to be assembled to form a larger cross-section.

will remain exposed in the finished building or if they are in the immediate vicinity of the effigies, wedge-shaped strips are cut, glue applied to one side (*sewari wo umeru*), and the strips fitted into the sections and finished flush. This elaborate treatment prevents the majority of uncontrolled drying cracks.

Fig. 60: Beams with heart cuts and wedges driven in

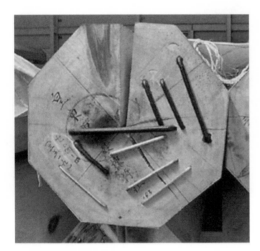

Fig. 59: End face of octagonal column
The end grain has been coated with a wax emulsion. Numerous cramps prevent uncontrolled cracking during drying. The sawcut down to the heart can be readily seen.

Conversion and storage

The trunks are cut on a large log bandsaw section by section and have to be turned many times during the process. The daily quota lies between five and fifteen trunks. Afterwards, they are loaded onto small rail-mounted trolleys which take them to one of the many storage sheds. Here, the end grain is painted with a wax emulsion. Cramps are also driven into the end grain to prevent cracks at the crown ends. The parts are sorted according to building and stacked for drying.

Dealing with sections containing heart

Sections containing heart (*shinmochi*), which are required for posts, beams and purlins, for example, are given a sawcut down to the heart after conversion (*sowari*). Wedges are driven in immediately afterwards and these are re-driven every few weeks. If the sections concerned

This text is an edited abridged version of an article entitled "The workshops at the Grand Shrine of Ise" by Christoph Henrichsen that appeared in *DETAIL* (10/2002).

The threads of the net

Urs Meister

Fig. 61: View from access road
Shin Takasuga: "Railway Sleeper House", house formerly belonging to the Seitogakushi School, Miyakejima (J), 1980

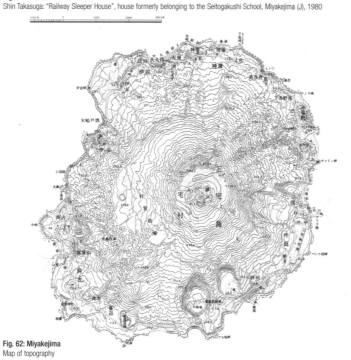

Fig. 62: Miyakejima
Map of topography

In the 1970s Japanese architects were searching for independence. One example of this search between centuries-old tradition and rigid, unbridled Modernism is Shin Takasuga's "Railway Sleeper House", which has a contemporary look but in many respects is linked with Japanese cultural heritage.

The house is situated amidst a forest on the small island of Miyakejima in the Pacific Ocean. It was planned in the 1970s by students of the New Left and members of the Peace Movement as a communal residential building and place of retreat. Financial constraints meant that the inhabitants had to build the house themselves. Shin Takasuga's decision to use old, wooden railway sleepers resulted in a five-year construction time. But it was not the use of sleepers that was novel, rather the universal utilisation of one single type of construction element for the whole structure – walls, floors, columns, roof structure, the built-in furniture too.

The three-storey building is situated on a slope, raised clear of the ground on a concrete substructure. A skilful arrangement of the rooms characterises the compact

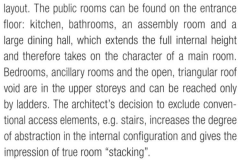

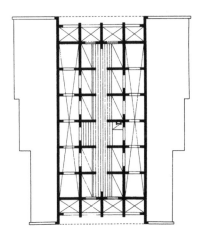

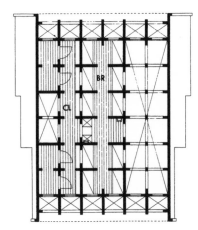

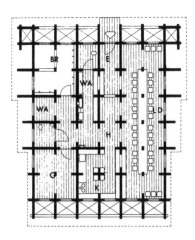

layout. The public rooms can be found on the entrance floor: kitchen, bathrooms, an assembly room and a large dining hall, which extends the full internal height and therefore takes on the character of a main room. Bedrooms, ancillary rooms and the open, triangular roof void are in the upper storeys and can be reached only by ladders. The architect's decision to exclude conventional access elements, e.g. stairs, increases the degree of abstraction in the internal configuration and gives the impression of true room "stacking".

In trying to find the roots of traditional Japanese housebuilding and its specific method of construction you will come across a simple dwelling, the *tateana*. Four timber stakes are driven into the soil to carry four beams. Together with a number of poles arranged in a circle and a covering made from leaves, grass or straw this produces a tent-like shelter. Two basic architectural themes are already evident in this archetypal form, both of which characterised housebuilding and temple architecture from that time onwards. Indeed, they proved legitimate up to the last century and exercised a decisive influence on Takasuga's work: the house as roof and as structure.

Fig. 63: Plans of roof void, upper floor and entrance floor
Shin Takasuga: "Railway Sleeper House", Miyakejima (J), 1980

Fig. 64: *Tateana,* the Japanese "prehistoric shelter"
Finished shelter (top), internal frame (bottom)

Fig. 65: Roof covering of wooden shingles
Shin Takasuga: "Railway Sleeper House", Miyakejima (J), 1980

The roof as a protective barrier

While Western architecture evolved on the basis of the wall and the facade[1], in traditional Japan the roof assumed this important role. The house is first and foremost a roof, which is constructed immediately after the erection of the supporting structure, even before any interior walls are built. Oversailing eaves and canopies protect against extreme weathers, and relegate the actual facade to the background. The significance of the roof as a protective barrier and the "compact darkness spreading beneath it" inspired the author Tanizaki Jun'ichiro to write about the aesthetics of shadow[2], and until the last century women in the traditional Japanese house did indeed still blacken their teeth in order to control the light–shade contrast! The roof as an autonomous sculpture-like configuration was described impressively by Bruno Taut in his summary of his visit to Japan[3] – in addition to his deductions based on technical and constructional conditions – as a basic cultural phenomenon of Japan.

Moving closer to Shin Takasuga's building, which today is overgrown, the first thing you notice is the bright, reflective roof. It appears as an abstract surface and its gable line gives the impression of having been drawn with a thick pencil right through the vegetation. What is underneath cannot be readily seen and only by approaching nearer does the house reveal itself to be a solid, heavily subdivided timber structure. The roof covering of wood shingles imparts a great lightness, only the line of the ridge and the verges are highlighted with sleepers – as if the thin roof surface has to be protected against the wind. The delicate covering seems to be reduced to a minimum in order to balance the heaviness of the structure below, the sleeper construction.

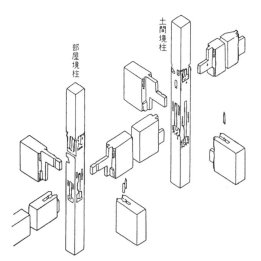

Fig. 66: Traditional Japanese house design
Column–beam wood joint

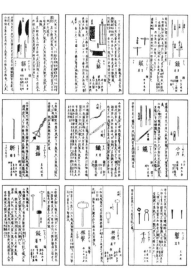

Fig. 67: Traditional Japanese carpentry tools
Pages from an encyclopaedia dating from 1712

Mass and elasticity

However, traditional Japanese houses often show a contradictory picture: the (usually) thick thatch coverings to their roofs contrast in a peculiar way with the delicate construction underneath them. The weight, raised clear of the ground on a fragile-looking arrangement of linear members, paradoxically guarantees the whole structure maximum elasticity – like a heavy table top resting on thin table legs. Due to the permanent danger of earthquakes in Japan elasticity is vital. The Western tradition of diagonal bracing is known to Japanese carpenters but does not correspond to their classical, aesthetic principles, and it would make the system more rigid and thus susceptible to seismic forces. In Japanese construction the stability of the connections, which is achieved through utmost jointing precision, guarantees the stability of the building as a whole, as well as the necessary freedom of movement for the structure.

Therefore, the sphere of activity of the carpenter in Japan is broader than that of his colleagues in Europe: he has to take on tasks normally performed by architects, along with cabinet-maker's jobs. Japanese carpenters are equipped with an incredible array of special tools and their work is distinguished by extreme intricacy and complexity, recognisable in the exploded views of timber joints. The carpenter's goal – to make the joint appear like a really simple connection – has resulted in a highly artistic technique of timber members intermeshing at a single point, often with a seemingly absurd sublimation of the cross-section. Despite maximum perforation of the members at the highly loaded joints, the connection itself gains stability due to the accurate fit and precise interlocking, and its characteristic elegance through elimination of all visible details.

Fig. 68: Detail of jointing at projecting stack of sleepers on the entrance facade
Shin Takasuga: "Railway Sleeper House", Miyakejima (J), 1980

Fig. 69: Treasure house of the Todai-ji in Nara
View of corner

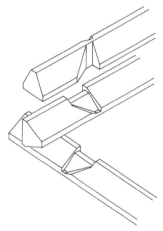

Fig. 70: Treasure house of the Todai-ji in Nara
Detail of log construction joint

Fig. 71: The dining hall extends the full internal height of the building
Shin Takasuga: "Railway Sleeper House", Miyakejima (J), 1980

In comparison with this, Japanese log construction – normally used only for storage buildings and treasure houses – contradicts the picture of the resulting timber constructions with their linear members. An impressive example of this is the treasure house of the Todai-ji in Nara, which stands out due to its mass, its self-contained nature and the elementary jointing technique. The unusual triangular shape of the logs, laid edgewise on top of each other, creates a three-dimensionally textured facade on the outside but a perfectly smooth wall surface on the inside. Although the edge-on-edge assembly of the joists does not seem sensible from the engineering point of view it has a certain purpose: in dry weather the wood shrinks and small gaps appear between the logs, allowing natural ventilation of the interior. In wet weather the wood swells and the gaps close, thus preventing moisture from entering the building.

The house as a structure

Log construction is characterised by intersecting corner joints that leave a short section of log projecting in both directions. By multiplying this corner detail Takasuga enhances the original planar character of this construction method, creating unsuspected spaciousness; and by letting the ends of the sleepers protrude at the gable facades he creates an abstract, three-dimensional composition. The stability of the protruding sleeper stacks is guaranteed with the aid of transverse sleepers, thus further balancing the horizontal–vertical arrangement of the entrance facade. In the large dining and communal room the same principle grows to nearly monumental proportions and the fragile equilibrium between the load-carrying and load-generating effects of the huge beams gives rise to an impressive three-dimensional sculpture.

The "cage-like" clarity of horizontal and vertical elements, of heavy beams and slender columns placed on them characterises the open roof structure inside the Japanese house and gives the impression of a pick-up-sticks game suspended in mid-air. The aesthetic preference for open, exposed timber structures is just a part of the

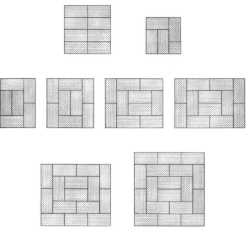

Fig. 72: Traditional *tatami* mat combinations
Four lines intersecting to form a cross is usually avoided – the combination of eight mats (top left) is reserved for special purposes. The arrangement with four mats (top right) is used in rooms where the tea ceremony is held.

Fig. 73: House in Takayama
Interior with exposed roof structure

Fig. 74: The concrete substructure beneath the log construction superstructure
Shin Takasuga: "Railway Sleeper House", Miyakejima (J), 1980

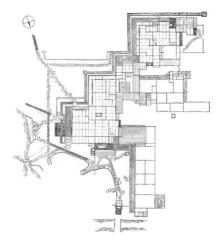

Fig. 75: The additive jointing principle of the rooms
Katsura Imperial Villa

Japanese tradition as is the specific treatment of the surfaces. The warm, dark tint of the treated sleepers used for Takasuga's house reflects the classical colouration of wood, which in earlier times was generated inside the houses by the open charcoal fires and the facade outside was then tinted by applying soot or by singeing. The surfaces of the sleepers, branded by their previous utilisation in the form of notches, cracks and damaged edges, give the wood a raw and rough appearance but at the same time it seems to be coated with a kind of patina, as if every single sleeper has been evenly worn away and polished.

A rigid system of dimensions based on the *tatami* mat on the floor and the *shoji*, the paper-covered door, determines the Japanese house and controls the complex network of relationships between the different elements. Both plan and section show characteristics of this modular principle, which led to a "structural grammar" and reached its architectural zenith in the 17th century in the construction of the Katsura Imperial Villa in Kyoto. Apart from the dimensions and proportions of the individual rooms, the relationships and transitions between them are strictly controlled and form an additive plan layout with an especially open character, which anticipated the flexible layout of Modernism in the Western world.

So the Japanese house is an open, additive configuration of individual rooms and in the "Railway Sleeper House" we can identify a subtractive design principle: the rooms seem to have been hacked out of a closed, cruciform stack with a rigid outer shape. In this context the paradoxical statement of Takasuga – that this house did not have to be designed but that the use of railway sleepers generated the actual structure itself – sounds like an echo of the Minimal Art concepts of the 1960s. The visual power of the succession of the same basic elements and the fascination of the brutal rawness of the timber members, laid on top of each other like in a children's game, reminds us of the disciplined tendencies of minimalist sculptures.

Fig. 76: Orderly rows forming a sculpture
Carl André: "Shiloh", 1980, 91 x 563 x 563 cm

Fig. 77: View of gable facade on valley side
Shin Takasuga: "Railway Sleeper House", Miyakejima (J), 1980

Far away from the sophisticated carpenter's techniques, Takasuga was able to create an ingenious work that by concentrating the means in many respects relies on Japanese traditions. At the fundamental figurative level – the house as a roof – as well as at the complex design level of space formation, the construction and the choice of materials – the house as a structure – in Takasuga's unique project the threads of the net[4] are woven in many different ways with Japanese architectural culture. However, the artistic radicalness of this project allows it to stand out from the conservative traditionalism that began to grow in Japan during the 1970s.

First published in *tec21*, No. 21, 25 May 2001

Notes
[1] Arthur Drexler: *The Architecture of Japan*, New York, 1955, p. 44.
[2] Tanizaki Jun'ichiro: *Lob des Schattens*, Zurich 1987 (1933).
   – English translation: Tanizaki Jun'ichiro: *In Praise of Shadows*, 1988.
[3] Bruno Taut: *Das japanische Haus und sein Leben*, Berlin 1998 (1937).
   – English translation: Bruno Taut: *The Japanese House,* 1998.
[4] This is the title of a chapter in Taut's book.

Fig. 78: Sleepers inserted into and cantilevering from the projecting stack provide stability
Shin Takasuga: "Railway Sleeper House", Miyakejima (J), 1980

Why steel?

Alois Diethelm

Steel has a problem. Once upon a time the product made from ore pointed the way to forms of architecture that had been inconceivable in the past, and during the 1920s it enjoyed the rank of a material preferred by the avant-garde. But the importance of steel in current architectural accomplishments leaves behind conflicting impressions. On the one hand, modern construction would hardly be conceivable without steel; on the other, the reasons for

Fig. 1: Probably half of all the pavilions were made of steel.
Ateliers Jean Nouvel: Swiss National Exhibition, Expo.02, Murten (CH), 2002

using steel – above all as the basis for a design – are not so obvious. The explanations for this might be that until a few years ago fire regulations specified that fire protection measures in multistorey steel structures could be achieved only by using cladding or thermal performance requirements that made it difficult to penetrate the climate boundary (facade) owing to the good thermal conductivity of metal. In addition, steel lacks attributes such as "natural", "ecological", or "homey" – attributes of, for example, timber building, which are so readily accepted by many groups of people. What is not widely known is that 90% of steel used in building work today is recycled from society's scrap metal (cars, refrigerators etc.).

Nevertheless, we saw at Expo.02 in Switzerland that presumably, half of all the exhibition pavilions were made of steel: from Jean Nouvel's Monolith in Murten, to the "Cloud" (or "Blur Building") by Diller & Scofidio in Yverdon, to the "Towers of Biel" by Coop Himmelb(l)au in Biel. And there is no stopping the flood of photographs of new airports from around the world, with their long-span roofs of steel lattice girders and steel columns reminiscent of trees. But the lion's share of steel in building is visible only for a short time, while the building is under construction – and I don't mean just the steel reinforcement in concrete.

Material transformations

It is interesting that although steel, as a child of the Industrial Revolution, was taken up simultaneously in the building of machines, vehicles, and ships, the interdisciplinary "cultivation" of the new material hardly led to technological transfers among these disciplines. Apart from structural engineering, whose influence cannot be overestimated, the best examples are to be found in so-called machine aesthetics, but less in the context of a certain material usage and rather as a method of design which is based – primarily in the context of new building – on the ideal of a engineering logic reduced to the essentials. As Le Corbusier wrote in his *Towards a New Architecture* (1923): "Engineers create the architecture because they apply the calculations dictated by nature, and their works make us feel nature's harmony."

One explanation for the minimal mutual stimulation is the fact that housebuilding is only very rarely based on batch production. Even if the advocates of "Neues Bauen" did predict the industrial production of houses, the aspect of assembly and dismantling was secondary (or it is only now that this has become an important ecological criterion) and buildings are not associated with dynamic stresses.

This exclusivity of a single material, which characterises the production of machines and means of transport (metal replaced wood astonishingly quickly in those situations where form was not reliant on the new material) is alien to the construction industry. Solid and filigree construction, which became established as mankind built its very first shelters in the form of – depending on region and culture – caves and tents, still represent opposite poles marking the limits of the building industry's playing field today. This traditional duality explains why new

Fig. 2: Steel frame concealed behind brick facade
Diener & Diener: Vogesen School, Basel (CH), 1994

Fig. 3: The relationship between steel and timber construction
Jules Saulnier: Menier chocolate factory, Noisiel-sur-Marne (F), 1872

materials never really unleash a genuine change, but instead lead to material transformations and hybrid forms. And steel was no different. In the same way that reinforced concrete first translated the principles of timber building (columns and beams) into concrete (cf. the Hennebique frame) before the flat slab appeared, Saunier's famous Menier chocolate factory (1871/72) was based on an iron truss whose only difference from a timber truss was its smaller cross-sections. And in Labrouste's Bibliothèque Nationale in Paris (1875) the ribs to the domes remind us of (Gothic) stone vaulting. In the tense span between solid and filigree construction, steel finally introduced a hybrid form in which the partner material was no longer "only" an infill without a structural function, as is the case with the infill panels to timber-frame buildings, but rather, in mutual dependency, becomes an integral component of the loadbearing construction. I am talking here about the combination of steel and concrete,

Fig. 4: Translation of a stone structure into cast iron
Henri Labrouste: Bibliothèque Nationale, Paris (F), 1875

of course, and that marriage in which steel continues to provide a frame of columns and beams but the stability is achieved only through composite action with the concrete. In this volatile relationship the two materials complement each other; for example, steel beams replace concrete downstand beams, and trapezoidal profile sheets function as permanent formwork and reinforcement for the floors. Good arguments in favour of composite construction, besides structural reasons, which in the case of the floors includes a more uniform distribution of the loads, involve building performance aspects (concrete introduces mass for good airborne sound insulation) and, above all, improved fire protection because the fire resistance of steel sections depends on the ratio of unprotected surface area (development) to cross-sectional area; accordingly, every steel surface in contact with concrete reduces the surface area exposed to the flames.

As a result of the above advantages and the rational form of building, steel–concrete composite construction

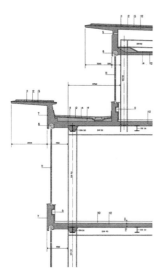

Fig. 5: Steel frame in conjunction with in situ concrete
Roland Rohn: BBC factory, Baden (CH), 1952

has become a popular, common option in today's building industry, primarily for multistorey office and commercial buildings, and highlights the spread of "impure" forms of construction. If we regard this hybrid approach as helpful, then that is a characteristic that designates a major strategy in the use of steel in architecture: the "hidden aid". Other categories are those structures that do not have to satisfy building performance measures (mostly temporary structures and small utility buildings) and engineering structures with large spans.

Large spans – substitute material

Even before the appearance of reinforced concrete, the outstanding structural properties of steel enabled the construction of larger buildings – buildings that, compared with those of stone or timber, could exceed previous building heights by, initially, a couple of storeys, later many storeys with the same or even fewer loadbearing components. Steel therefore created the foundation for a whole new type of building: the skyscraper, whose plan layout is characterised by the stairs and lifts needed to transport the larger number of users quickly to the corresponding floors. On the facade the use of steel meant larger spans and hence larger windows, a fact that was demonstrated impressively in Chicago in the late 19th century. Regardless of whether the steel frame was left exposed or concealed behind cladding, windows extending from floor to ceiling and from column to column indicated a structural steel frame. But there were also new buildings whose size alone pointed to the use of this new technology. Enclosed in a stone jacket perforated by small windows, the facades of these framed buildings were hardly distinguishable from those of solid construction. Coupled with a pragmatism fed by industrialisation, it was quickly realised that steel – particularly in high-rise buildings – could assume the role of a substitute structural material, as a replacement for stone and timber, whose load-carrying capacity above a certain height was no longer adequate, and, later, in some instances also as a replacement for concrete, with its intensive labour and material input and many separate operations (formwork, reinforcement, concrete). The fact that steel's significance as a substitute material has continued unabated is underscored by current developments in which steelwork and timber construction come into contact (again); for the transfer of the principles of timber platform frame construction (slender columns and stiffening sheathing) to structural steelwork is more widespread in those regions with minimal timber resources than elsewhere. In fact, systems with thin-wall sheet metal profiles exhibit unmistakable advantages over timber platform frame construction, e.g. no distortion, less weight. They are therefore predestined for adding floors to existing buildings, where saving weight is a prime criterion, but equally for new buildings. However, although the structural and tectonic logic of steelwork is identical with that of timber platform frame construction, the "steel platform frame" does not supply any of its own exclusive design criteria. It must therefore be considered as another partially synthetic system consisting of wall

Fig. 6: The opening–wall ratio points to a frame behind the facade.
Louis Henry Sullivan: Schlesinger & Mayer department store, Chicago (USA), 1904

plates that provide supporting and insulating functions simultaneously.

It almost seems as though the technology transfer takes place in one direction only, i.e. from timber to steel. However, a look at contemporary timber engineering projects reveals that the types of joints between linear members and the bolted connections customary today have derived directly from structural steelwork.

Steel still plays an outstanding, almost singular, role in large spans. Long-span roofs over single-storey sheds, like those of aircraft hangars and exhibition buildings, are built almost exclusively in steel. This is where the fine lines of the loadbearing structure become the dominating interior motif and therefore generate a vocabulary that is exclusive to structural steelwork. And as these are single-storey buildings, fire-resistant cladding (which usually hinders the choice of steel as a construction material and certainly impairs the appearance of the finished construction) is unnecessary.

Fig. 7: Erecting a "steel platform frame"
The similarity with timber building: sheet metal profiles instead of planks

Small sections – paving the way for glass buildings

Whereas in high-rise buildings the sizes of the steel columns and beams were important from the point of view that, compared with stone or timber, they could *carry*

considerably more or enable *longer spans*, the exponents of "Neues Bauen" saw in steel the means to create *more slender* constructions. Non-loadbearing lightweight panels were often used between the slender columns to save material and weight; these panels – and the columns too! – were then covered with render outside. Such buildings, often raised clear of the ground and with their windows fitted flush with the facade, appear as weightless, abstract objects. The steel frames to these "lightweight" buildings were seen, if at all, only at isolated points (where "lightweight" is to be understood both in physical – in the sense of optimisation of material – and visual terms). Steel was therefore regarded, on the one hand, as a means of achieving rationalisation in construction and, on the other, as a means of attaining a purist, essentially dematerialised architecture. The inherent relief of the steel sections with their webs and flanges and the principles of frame construction remained concealed behind the external cladding and the internal lining; the fact that this was a steel building was only divulged through the slenderness of the construction, a slenderness that, like the columns of Neutra's Lovell Health House (1927–29), was hardly differentiated from the window frames and rendered possible an opening–wall ratio (large expanses of glass and long horizontal windows) that was no longer dictated by the positioning of the structural members.

Joseph Paxton's Crystal Palace (1851) had already demonstrated that the combination with glass could become an outstanding feature of building with steel or iron. Backed up by knowledge gained in the building of palm houses and large greenhouses, the filigree beams resolved into girders and trusses and the panes of glass framed by the very thinnest of metal glazing bars resulted in a transparency that would have been unthinkable in a timber building. Now, 150 years later, the words "steel" and "glass" still conjure up images of interiors flooded with light (not only among the general public), which have become intrinsic to modern building. Indeed, the glass building, a category linked

Fig. 8: The steel columns are hardly distinguishable from the window frames.
Richard Neutra: Lovell Health House, Los Angeles (USA), 1927–29

with certain materials like virtually no other, challenged the architects of the 20th century again and again; and if we take a look at the latest projects designed by architects from the most diverse camps it would seem as though glass, at the start of the 21st century, has freed itself from the ideological trench warfare of the 1990s ("stony Berlin") and it no longer expresses a single architectural statement. Mies van der Rohe's design for a high-rise block on Friedrichstrasse in Berlin (1922) was just a vision, but not long afterwards the glass industry was already in the position to supply panes that could almost satisfy the desire for virtually dematerialised walls devoid of mullions or transoms. After the oil crisis of the 1970s and the growing environmental awareness of the 1980s, the view that the majority of glass buildings were only habitable in conjunction with costly air-conditioning and heating systems seemed to anticipate the demise of such buildings. But linked to alternative energy con-

Fig. 11: The glass house was a recurrent theme in the 20th century.
Ludwig Mies van der Rohe: Farnsworth House, Plano (USA), 1945–50

conductor of heat. However, it should not be forgotten that exposed steel sections in the facades of old industrialised buildings are frequently part of a secondary framework that carries the external cladding only, e.g. a facing leaf of clay brickwork. In this sense the outer divisions reflect the loadbearing structure behind only indirectly. The distinction between infilling and cladding is also vague where the size of the glass elements coincides with the structural grid and, as a result, columns and beams are concealed behind the frame of the element. This may even resemble parts of the structural frame and hence fulfil the expectation that the nature of the chosen form of construction – in this case a slender three-dimensional lattice – should be reflected in the appearance of the building.

Fig. 9: The loadbearing steel structure disappears behind the render.
Wassili and Hans Luckhardt: house on Rupenhorn, Berlin (D), 1928

Fig. 10: Steel frame during construction
Wassili and Hans Luckhardt: house on Rupenhorn, Berlin (D), 1928

cepts in which glass is used to gain, to "focus", solar heat energy, and the willingness of architects to add external sunshades, buildings of glass (incorporating new types of glass with U-values as low as 0.4 W/m^{2}K) are more topical than ever before. Insulating glass opened up new opportunities – opportunities we thought had already been abandoned: the steel frame exposed internally and externally. The insulating layer is now draped around the building like a transparent veil and comes close to what Mies van der Rohe called "skin and bones" architecture but never quite attains this level of authenticity – the smooth membrane – owing to technological limits.

The topic of infilling, in which windows or panels, to save space, are positioned between the exposed columns (and which characterises Le Corbusier's "Maison Clarté" in Geneva as much as it does many of the industrialised buildings erected in the first half of the 20th century) is no longer in vogue these days owing to the stricter thermal insulation requirements. This is because, unlike timber, which is a relatively good heat insulator, steel acts as a

Fig. 12: Windows positioned as panels between steel frame members
Le Corbusier & Pierre Jeanneret: Maison Clarté, Geneva (CH), 1932

Fig. 13: The exposed steel columns support the masonry only.
Ludwig Mies van der Rohe: Illinois Institute of Technology, Chicago (USA), 1940–50

Prefabrication and "anything goes"

More so than in timber construction, building with steel is characterised by prefabrication. The poor on-site welding conditions alone make this necessary, as well as the fact that adjustments during erection result in damage to the corrosion protection measures (zinc dust coating plus appropriate paint or hot-dip galvanising), which means that on-site connections are designed for bolting wherever possible. This form of construction also embodies simple dismantling, which may explain the widespread use of steel for exhibitions, like the aforementioned Expo.02 in Switzerland. However, the appearance of prefabrication affects both the loadbearing structure and the building envelope, which almost presupposes some form of prefabrication when using metal; for the potential of thin sheet metal is linked directly with the options of enhancing stability by way of folding and bending, a feature that can

Fig. 14: Industrial manufacture of facade
elements: single element
Jean Prouvé: CIMT, Paris (F), c. 1955

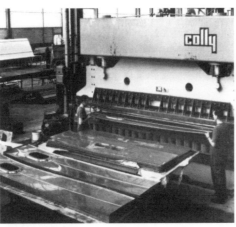

Fig. 15: Industrial manufacture of facade elements:
individual parts of element
Jean Prouvé: CIMT, Paris (F), c. 1955

be achieved with other materials only through introducing supplementary ribs or supporting frameworks. Whether the panels visible on the facade are (sandwich) units delivered to site ready for use, or whether they are first assembled on site in the sense of partial prefabrication (prefabrication of individual layers), is less important here. Also of secondary importance is the fact that prefabrication simplifies transport, speeds up the work on site and enables the production of large batches. Folding the sheet metal is quite simply a machine process coupled with the factory and at most – e.g. in the production of waffle forms – involves additional operations such as welding and surface treatments like stove-enamelling or anodising.

If we are talking about building with steel – or better, with metal – then we can speak of exclusive factory production. Metalworking based its attempts at standardisation on this fact from an early stage – whether serving a single project or a building system (e.g. USM factory by Fritz Haller). Whereas in the former case inexpensive

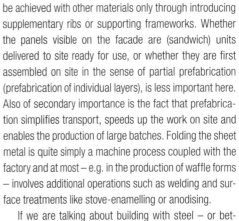

Fig. 16: MAXI building system by Fritz Haller
Fritz Haller: USM factory, Münsingen (CH), 1963–84 (extended in four phases)

production is linked with repetition, building systems render the interchangeability of individual elements and seamless expansion possible. Furthermore, building systems are not linked to any specific type of building.

Steelwork is usually based on a sequential, orthogonal assembly, but it can translate any other form by using groups of linear members. Just like a line drawing, sculpted objects like those of Frank Gehry can be resolved into straight members, where concave and convex deformations plus twists and tapers are reduced to the simplest economic formula. As the linear members, which emulate the polymorphic form, do not correlate with the flow of forces everywhere, further ties and struts are added that mingle with the balloon frame like a handicrafts workshop behind a veil of uniform cladding. When considering economic criteria this would hardly be possible in any other

Fig. 17: There is a steel frame lurking behind the sculpted outer skin.
Frank O. Gehry: Guggenheim Museum, Bilbao (E), 1997

Fig. 18: The dynamic forms were translated into linear lattice structures.
Frank O. Gehry: Guggenheim Museum, Bilbao (E), 1997

material; just imagine the elaborate, one-off formwork required for such a structure in concrete! So steel becomes the material that makes anything and everything possible.

Or must the negatively charged undertone of enthusiasm be softened because steel – with the assistance of CAD and CAM – obviously renders possible a form of architecture that nullifies or at least broadens our usual understanding of sculpture and gravitation? The computer has cancelled orthogonality as the overriding criterion for economic loadbearing structures. The "new" spaces are affordable. But will they provide useful containers for functions other than museums and concert halls?

Constructional ornamentation

In the light of a series of recent buildings and some still under construction we must add a third form to playful plasticity and Cartesian coordination: the diagonal, or the raking column. The time for the rediscovery of the diagonal would seem to be not just coincidental. Following the profound minimalism of the 1990s and, after a sudden deliverance, an opulence tending to randomness, nonorthogonal loadbearing structures seem to unite objectivity and a newly discovered enthusiasm for ornamentation. Whereas structural steelwork once sported decoration in the form of rivets – accepted even by the purists because they were an engineering necessity – structural steelwork and constructional ornamentation seem to have become bedfellows again at the start of the 21st century. The focus of our attention this time though is no longer the connec-

tions but rather the structures that deviate from the preeminence of the right angle and are fabricated principally from steel for structural, economic, and/or architectural reasons (slenderness of the construction). Such structures do not need to demonstrate an ornamental character as loadbearing elements, but instead can inspire a detailed working of the fitting-out parts. What I mean here is the appropriation of a structure-related form that is perceived as an ornament through scaling and multiple repetition. In doing so, it may be our knowledge of the vocabulary of artistic decoration or facetted precious stones that allows us to assign undeniably ornamental qualities to the repetition of non-right-angled surfaces (triangles, hexagons, trapeziums, or rhombuses), whereas in the case of rectangles we may need different colours, textures, or materials in order to be reminded of jewellery or decoration.

Two recently completed buildings provide good examples of this. Their facades have rhombus-shaped openings and raking loadbearing columns at acute angles. At first sight the close-mesh facades of these two buildings appear similar. But the facade of the Prada Epicenter Store coincides exactly with the loadbearing structure behind, whereas on the Swiss Re Tower it is a scaled image of the structure. And whereas in the former building each storey is equivalent to two rhombuses, in the latter it takes four storeys for the loadbearing structure to form even one rhombus. There are other differences, but what the two buildings do have in common is the fact that the facade lattice forms a rigid "corset",

Fig. 19: Loadbearing structure and glazing bars coincide.
Herzog & de Meuron: Prada Epicenter Store, Tokyo (J), 2003

Fig. 20: The rhombuses are bisected at the corners of the building.
Herzog & de Meuron: Prada Epicenter Store, Tokyo (J), 2003

which means that the service core no longer has to provide a bracing function, and that rhombuses are visible although triangles are formed. To do this, Norman Foster used black paint on his Swiss Re Tower in London (2004) in order to relegate the horizontal members to the background and by default highlight the white diagonals. Herzog & de Meuron, on the other hand, positioned the horizontal ties of their Prada Epicenter Store in Tokyo (2003) level with the floors. There is an attempt at disentanglement in both buildings – one using paint, the other careful positioning.

Rhombus and building form

Besides the loadbearing behaviour of diagonal structures, we must also raise the question of their importance for the volume of the building. If we stick with these two examples, it seems that only in the Swiss Re Tower is there a connection between structure and form. In the case of the Prada Epicenter Store it seems that by choosing a rhombus-shaped lattice, which extends over the entire surface of the building, the architects created tectonic and formal continuity between the cranked sides of this prismatic object. If an arris is not parallel with the facade grid, the deviation is hardly noticeable within this envelope dominated by slanting lines.

From the mathematical viewpoint the rhombus belongs to the family of quadrilaterals and its potential

lies in its formal transformation capability. Starting with a square standing on one of its corners, the proportions change almost unnoticeably through compressing and stretching the diagonals; other deformations lead to the parallelogram or the trapezium. In this category the right-angle is the exception and the acute angle the rule – a vocabulary that readily accepts even triangles – triangles that reproduce a structural function or have stereometric origins.

Rhombuses, even horizontal and/or vertical sequences, always form diagonal bands that make it difficult to assign a clear direction. This is totally different from the situation with orthogonal divisions, where the observer sees the fields in horizontal and vertical relationships only. The lattice structure of the Prada Epicenter Store therefore seems to have no hierarchy, to such an extent that it never enters into a conflict with the order of the building.

Irregular plasticity therefore does not necessarily need customised structures, which usually have structural frames that need some form of cladding.

Fig. 21: The size of the rhombuses matches the form of the building.
Foster & Partners: Swiss Re Tower, London (UK), 2000–04

Further reading
- Sigfried Giedion: *Bauen in Frankreich*, Berlin, 1928.
- Schweizer Stahlbauverband (ed.): *Bauen in Stahl*, Zurich, 1956.
- Kunstverein Solothurn (ed.): *Fritz Haller – Bauen und forschen*, Solothurn, 1988.
- Helmut C. Schulitz, Werner Sobek, Karl J. Habermann: *Steel Construction Manual*, Basel, Boston, Berlin, 2000.
- Laurence Allégret, Valérie Vaudou (ed.): *Jean Prouvé et Paris*, Paris, 2001.
- Friedrich Grimm: *Konstruieren mit Walzprofilen*, Berlin, 2003.

Sections – forms and applications

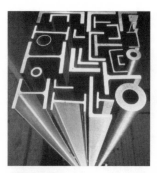

Fig. 22: Various sections

Designation	Smallest size (depth x width)			Largest size (depth x width)		
Wide-flange beams						
HEA light-duty series	HEA 100	(96 mm x 100 mm)	16.7 kg/m	HEA 1000	(990 mm x 300 mm)	272.0 kg/m
HEB standard series	HEB 100	(100 mm x 100 mm)	20.4 kg/m	HEB 1000	(1000 mm x 300 mm)	314.0 kg/m
HEM heavy-duty series	HEM 100	(120 mm x 106 mm)	41.8 kg/m	HEM 1000	(1008 mm x 302 mm)	349.0 kg/m
Standard sections						
INP	INP 80	(80 mm x 42 mm)	5.9 kg/m	INP 500	(500 mm x 200 mm)	166.0 kg/m
UNP	UNP 65	(65 mm x 42 mm)	7.1 kg/m	UNP 400	(400 mm x 110 mm)	71.8 kg/m
Sections with parallel flanges						
IPE	IPE 80	(80 mm x 46 mm)	6.0 kg/m	IPE 600	(600 mm x 220 mm)	122.0 kg/m
IPET	IPET 80	(40 mm x 46 mm)	3.0 kg/m	IPET 600	(300 mm x 220 mm)	61.2 kg/m
UPE	UPE 80	(80 mm x 50 mm)	7.9 kg/m	UPE 400	(400 mm x 115 mm)	72.2 kg/m
Structural hollow sections						
RRW / RRK square	RRW 40 x 40	(40 mm x 40 mm)	3.4 kg/m	RRW 400 x 400	(400 mm x 400 mm)	191.0 kg/m
RRW / RRK rectangular	RRW 50 x 30	(50 mm x 30 mm)	3.6 kg/m	RRW 400 x 200	(400 mm x 200 mm)	141.0 kg/m
ROR circular	ROR 21.3	(ø 21.3 mm)	0.9 kg/m	ROR 813	(ø 813 mm)	159.0 kg/m
Solid round and square sections						
RND	RND 10	(ø 10 mm)	0.6 kg/m	RND 500	(ø 500 mm)	1540.0 kg/m
VKT	VKT 10	(6 mm x 6 mm)	0.3 kg/m	VKT 200	(200 mm x 200 mm)	314.0 kg/m

For details of national structural steelwork associations and further ranges of sections go to www.steelconstruct.com.

Type of section

Applications, remarks

Fig. 23: Wide-flange beams
HEA, HEB and HEM

For heavy loads (columns and beams).

Their wide flanges make these sections suitable for inclined loads as well.

Note: Only in the HEB series does the section designation, e.g. HEB 200, correspond to the actual depth of the section.

Fig. 24: Standard sections
INP and UNP

Standard sections are the less costly alternative to sections with parallel flanges. They are best suited to welded constructions. Owing to their tapering inner flanges, they are seldom used for bolted constructions.

Fig. 25: Sections with parallel flanges
IPE, UPE and IPET

IPE sections are slender and therefore better suited to being used as beams (owing to the narrow flange they are less suitable as compression members).

UPE sections are frequently compounded in pairs because the asymmetric shape permits only low loads.

IPET sections (IPE sections halved by the fabricators) are used for trusses, girders and also as the glazing bars to glass roofs.

Fig. 26: Structural hollow sections
Square, rectangular or circular

Primarily used as columns and for trusses and girders, ideal for concentric loading.

Compared to HEA sections, structural hollow sections exhibit small surface development (less painting).

The outside diameter remains the same for different wall thicknesses ("invisible" combinations).

We distinguish between cold-rolled – RRK, lightweight and inexpensive – and hot-rolled – RRW, with good buckling resistance thanks to the upset corners.

Fig. 27: Solid round and square sections
RND and VKT

Primarily used as hangers and ties.

Larger cross-sections also suitable as compression members, e.g. in concrete-encased columns (for fire protection).

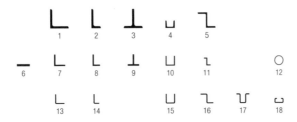

Fig. 28: Angle and small sections
Common sections for general metalworking projects (balustrades, canopies, simple doors and windows etc.)

1 Equal angle, rounded edges	7 Equal angle, sharp edges	13 Equal angle, cold-rolled
2 Unequal angle, rounded edges	8 Unequal angle, sharp edges	14 Unequal angle, cold-rolled
3 Long-stalk T-section, rounded edges	9 T-section, sharp edges	15 Channel, cold-rolled
4 Channel	10 Channel	16 Z-section, cold-rolled
5 Z-section, standard	11 Z-section, sharp edges	17 Lipped channel, cold-rolled
6 Flat	12 Handrail tube	18 C-section, cold-rolled

Fire protection

As in timber engineering, fire protection is also a key theme in structural steelwork; for although steel does not burn as such, the effects of heat change its microstructure and, consequently, its load-carrying ability. Therefore, if a loadbearing steel member has to withstand a fire for 60 minutes (F 60 fire resistance class), it must be suitably clad – a totally different situation to loadbearing structures of concrete or masonry. The question of which measures can be taken to reduce the technical fire protection requirements of the structure is more important in the design of steel structures than any other building material. The use of a building and the associated fire risk together with the occupancy, the type of space heating (open or enclosed) and the number of storeys form the heart of a specific project-related fire protection concept. For instance, minimal requirements will suffice for a single-storey industrial building because there are direct means of escape to the outside, the workers are familiar with their surroundings and, usually, will have taken part in a fire drill. The situation is totally different in a building to which the public has access, where the majority of the people using the building are not familiar with their surroundings. Furthermore, single-storey buildings and the topmost storey of multi-storey building are subject to less strict criteria because there are no rooms (or persons) above that can be endangered.

fire developing in the first place. An aircraft hangar is a prime example: the cost of the aircraft parked inside is many times the cost of the building.

If the *active* fire protection measures (i.e. technical systems such as fire alarms, sprinklers, etc.) are not sufficient or the cost of such measures is deemed to be too high, the properties of the loadbearing structure must be such that it will remain intact for 30, 60 or 90 minutes should a major fire develop (with temperatures up to 1000 °C). This is known as *passive* fire protection. The methods available for structural steelwork range from systems in which there is no change to the shape of the section (e.g. by "oversizing" the section or applying fire-resistant intumescent paint, which foams up during a fire), to applying cladding, which encloses the steel members directly or forms a void (e.g. for services) around them, to composite arrangements in which steel is partly or completely filled with or encased in concrete. This latter option also increases the load-carrying capacity of the member. In doing so, columns are frequently enclosed in a steel jacket that serves as permanent formwork for the concrete (see Swisscom headquarters by Burkard Meyer Architekten, 1999). The enclosing concrete protects the steel section inside against excessive temperature increases and can itself still assume a loadbearing function. In the reverse situation, i.e. filling a structural hollow section with concrete, a transfer of the load takes place during a fire, and the concrete core takes over the loadbearing function exclusively.

Fig. 29: Composite columns
a) Concrete-filled circular hollow section: during a fire the concrete core assumes the loadbearing function
b) Steel core encased in concrete with steel jacket: the concrete protects the core against high temperatures
c) Concrete-cased steel section without steel jacket

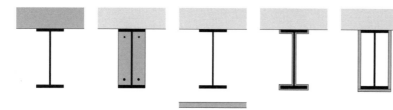

Fig. 30: Passive fire protection measures
a) Unclad section in conjunction with concrete floor slab for fire resistance class up to F 30
b) Section with concrete infill between the flanges
c) Fire-resistant suspended ceiling
d) Fire-resistant paint or plaster
e) Fire-resistant cladding

Means of escape – saving lives – together with the way the building and its contents are protected – saving property – are the two fundamental objectives of every fire protection concept. In terms of saving lives, it should not be forgotten that suffocation caused by the smoke and fumes given off during a fire – and not collapsing building components, for instance – is the most frequent cause of fire-related deaths. The option of allowing smoke and heat to escape to the outside quickly – in addition to avoiding the inclusion of materials that generate extreme quantities of smoke and fumes – should not be underestimated. The installation of preventive measures and the use of fire alarm systems plus sprinkler systems are not only helpful in saving lives and protecting valuable contents, but also obviate the need to clad the structural steelwork because there is little risk of a major

Further reading
- Eurofer Steel Promotion Committee (ed.): *Steel and Fire Safety – A Global Approach*, Brussels, 1993.
- Schweizerische Zentralstelle für Stahlbau (ed.): *Brandsichere Stahl-Beton-Verbundtragwerke*, Zurich, 1997.

Potential applications for structural steelwork

Steel exposed	Fire resistance class R30	Fire resistance class R60	Fire resistance class R90
Columns (1/2)	SZS/EKS N° 89 (U/A < 50 m^{-1}) (3) ■ ● min. RND/VKT 80 ▬ min. 60x120 ✚ min. 150x150 I min. HHD 320x300	SZS/EKS N° 89 (U/A < 14 m^{-1}) (3) ■ ● min. RND/VKT 280 ▬ min. 200x500 ▮ min. 400x400 ● min. 320x320	none
Beams supporting floor slabs (2)	SZS/EKS N° 89 min. HEM 300	SZS/EKS N° 89 solid steel min. FLB 150/300	none
Constructions with intumescent paint (4)	I T [□ all sections http://bsronline.vkf.ch	I T [□ all sections http://bsronline.vkf.ch	not permitted

Composite construction (steel/concrete)

Columns	SZS C2.3, SZS C2.4, EKS N° 32 min. HEA 160, RRK 140, ROR 139,7	SZS C2.3, SZS C2.4, EKS N° 32 min. HEA 200, RRK 160, ROR 159	SZS C2.3, SZS C2.4, EKS N° 32 min. HEA 240, RRK 180, ROR 177,8
Beams, with concrete infill between flanges, supporting floor slabs (≥ 120 mm)	SZS C2.4 min. HEA 100, IPE 120	SZS C2.4 min. HEA 100, IPE 200	SZS C2.4 min. HEA 180, IPE 300
Profiled metal sheets with concrete infill/topping Average slab depth h_{eff}	SZS C2.4, EKS N° 32 $h_{eff} \geq 60$ mm	SZS C2.4, EKS N° 32 $h_{eff} \geq 80$ mm	SZS C2.4, EKS N° 32 $h_{eff} \geq 100$ mm

Clad steel sections (5)

Box-type fire-resistant boards (e.g. columns)	SZS/EKS N° 89 all sections http://bsronline.vkf.ch typical board thickness: approx. 15 mm	SZS/EKS N° 89 all sections http://bsronline.vkf.ch typical board thickness: approx. 25 mm	SZS/EKS N° 89 all sections http://bsronline.vkf.ch typical board thickness: approx. 35 mm
Spray-on protective coating (e.g. beams)	SZS/EKS N° 89 alle Profile http://bsronline.vkf.ch typical coat thickness: approx. 20 mm	SZS/EKS N° 89 alle Profile http://bsronline.vkf.ch typical coat thickness: approx. 30 mm	SZS/EKS N° 89 alle Profile http://bsronline.vkf.ch typical coat thickness: approx. 40 mm

(1)   Figures apply exactly to continuous columns for 3 m storey height (to Euro-nomogram ECCS No. 89).
(2)   Smaller dimensions possible when not fully utilised structurallly (see Euro-nomogram ECCS No. 89).
(3)   Section factor U/A (or Am/V to Euro-nomogram).
(4)   Application must be approved for particular project by fire protection authorities (see VKF* fire protection memo 1008).
(5)   Concrete always reinforced, except hollow sections in class R30.
(6)   Cladding products to VKF* fire protection register, application and constructional boundary conditions as checked and approved (QS responsibility of site management).

*Association of Cantonal Fire Insurers

Fig. 31: Potential applications for structural steelwork
A design aid published by Stahlbau Zentrum Schweiz, *steeldoc*, March 2006

Connections
A selection

Column continuous

pinned connections   rigid connections   prefabricated nodes

Beam continuous

rigid connections

2-D (x, z)

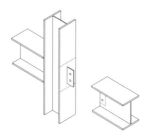

Bolted, cleat welded to column

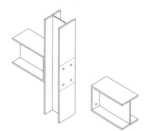

Bolted, end plate welded to beam

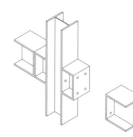

Bolted, end plates welded to column and beam

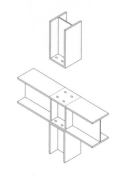

Bolted, stiffeners welded to beam
below column flanges

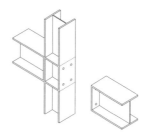

Bolted, stiffeners welded to column in line
with beam flanges

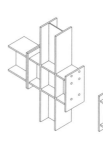

Bolted, with projecting end plates, stiffeners welded
to column in line with beam flanges

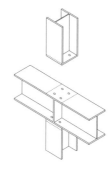

Bolted, stiffeners welded to beam
below column web

3-D (x, y, z)

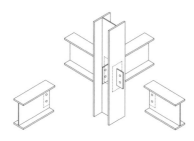

Bolted, cleats welded to column

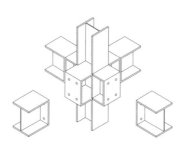

Bolted, end plates welded to column

Fig. 32: Steel connections, selection

Fig. 33: Erecting a steel column

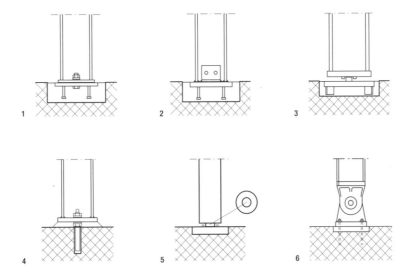

Base details for pinned-base columns

1 – 2 no tension
    3 for low tension, with lower base plate
       installed beforehand
    4 no tension, with hinge
    5 with threaded bars cast in beforehand
    6 with base plate installed beforehand,
       column welded to base plate on site

Base details for fixed-base columns

7 – 10 column in pocket to accommodate large
        bending moments

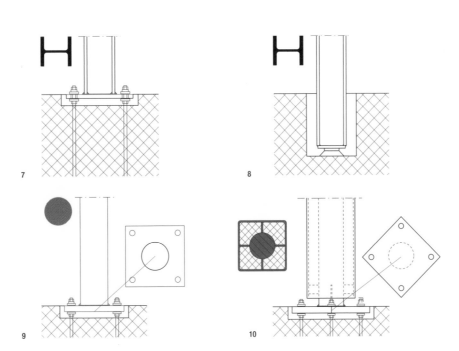

Fig. 34
Source: Swiss Central office for Structural Steelwork (SZS) (ed.): *steeldoc 01/06*, Zurich, 2006

Structures – frame with cantilevering beams

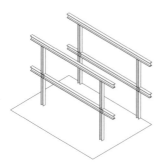

Fig. 35: Frame with cantilevering beams

The loadbearing structure consists of a series of frames with pairs of columns set back from the facade. As the columns are interrupted by the beams, stiffeners must be fitted between the beam flanges to transfer the vertical loads. The drawing below shows three variations for the floor, all of which share the feature of being positioned above the main beams.

D1 makes use of a secondary construction of small beams or joists placed on top of the main beams. In contrast to secondary beams at the same level as the main beams, this arrangement allows services to be easily routed transverse to the frames. Depending on requirements, the floor itself could be simple wooden floorboards. D2 and D3 do not use any secondary beams or joists and rely on the trapezoidal profile metal sheets to carry the floor – in D2 merely as a support for a dry floor covering, but in D3 as permanent formwork for a reinforced concrete slab.

Floor construction D1

Wooden floorboards	27 mm
Steel beams, IPE 160	160 mm
Total	*187 mm*

Floor construction D2

Flooring panels	27 mm
Rubber separating layer	20 mm
Trapezoidal profile metal sheets	160 mm
Total	*207 mm*

Floor construction D3

Reinforced concrete topping	120 mm
"Holorib" sheets	50 mm
Total	*170 mm*

Profiles
a) HEA 400, interrupted at every storey
b) HEA 400, continuous beam
c) Stiffeners below column flanges to carry vertical loads

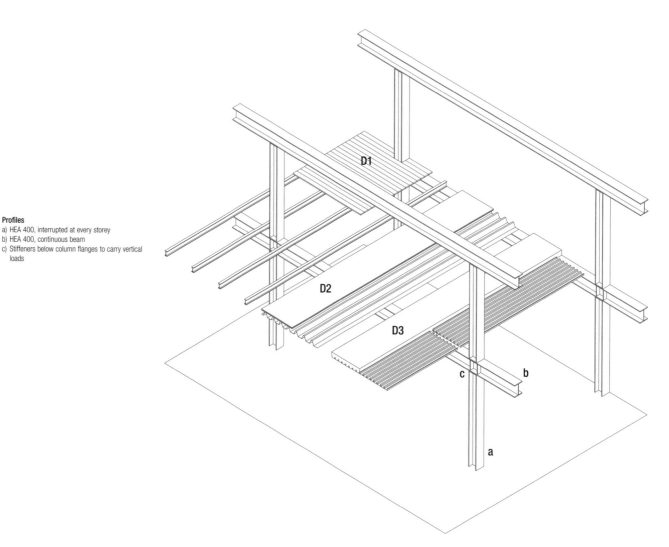

Fig. 36: Frame with continuous beams
Shown here with floor constructions above level of primary structure

Steel floors

Steel floors consist of profiled metal sheets, 0.80–1.75 mm thick, with a filling/topping of concrete. The cross-section of the profiling is usually trapezoidal, produced by rolling. Additional ribs and folds are sometimes included to enhance the stiffness. The sheets are available in widths of 0.30–0.90 m. Some forms are known as cellular floor decks.

The sheets can be supplied with or without galvanising (25–30 μm). Non-galvanised sheets are given a coat of paint on the underside to prevent corrosion.

Profiles
1 overview of common profiles:
1.1 and 1.2 single profiles
1.3 to 1.7 sheets
1.8 and 1.9 pre-assembled cellular floor decks

Advantages of floors with profiled metal sheeting:
· low weight,
· fast erection,
· no formwork required for concrete,
· floors can support loads immediately after erection, and
· workers below protected against objects falling from above.

Disadvantages of floors with profiled metal sheeting:
· steel serves either as permanent formwork only, or
· if required to be loadbearing, the underside needs special fire protection measures, and
· compared with completely dry construction, the in situ concrete introduces a wet trade into the construction.

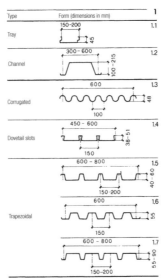

Erection of floors with profiled metal sheets
The metal sheets are cut to length, packaged together and delivered according to the plan layout so that erection on site can proceed quickly and smoothly, directly after erection of the structural steelwork. Cutting is usually carried out with special cutters to suit the particular profile. Oblique cuts are carried out manually.

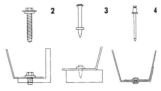

The connections
The profiled metal sheets can be connected to the steel beams by:
· welding, according to the instructions of the manufacturer,
· self-tapping screws (drawing 2),
· shot-fired pins (drawing 3).
The connections between the sheets themselves are by way of:
· blind rivets (drawing 4), which can be fitted from just one side without needing access to the other side, or
· punching and interlocking the edges with each other, according to the instructions of the manufacturer.

Composite floor slabs

 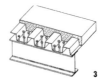

1   2   3

1 The profiled metal sheets are used only as permanent formwork to enable fast progress and immediate provision of floors. Reinforcement is in the form of round bars. The floor acts like a ribbed concrete slab. With sufficient concrete cover to the reinforcing bars, the floor slab is, however, fire resistant. The concrete slab acts as a horizontal plate resisting wind forces.

2 Composite action between sheet metal and concrete. The steel together with the concrete forms a composite cross-section. The sheet steel acts as the reinforcement for the concrete slab. Rolled spines or ribs in the sheet steel transfer the shear forces between concrete and steel. This floor slab requires fire protection to the soffit.

3 Composite action between concrete slab and steel beams. Studs are welded through the sheet steel to the top flange of each beam. In this case the concrete slab forms a composite cross-section with the steel beams. Only the concrete above the ribs is structurally effective. Very economic form of construction. The studs are welded on site according to special instructions.

4 "Holorib" is a steel sheet with rolled dovetail-shaped ribs. The concrete slab is self-supporting and must be reinforced accordingly. The sheet metal serves only as permanent formwork. Tests have shown that in this form of floor the adhesion between the sheet metal and the concrete is sufficient to generate a composite action between the metal and the concrete. The drawing shows shear studs, which create a composite effect between slab and steel beams. The dovetail-shaped ribs are useful for fixing suspended ceilings and services – very helpful in buildings with many services.

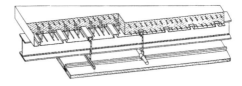

Fig. 37: Composite floor construction
Profiled metal sheeting prior to concreting

Fig. 38
Excerpt from Hart, Henn, Sontag: *Stahlbau Atlas* (1st ed.), Munich, 1982

Structures – frame with continuous columns

Fig. 39: Frame with continuous columns

The loadbearing structure consists of a series of frames with continuous columns. In this structure the columns are placed directly on the facade so they hardly intrude into the interior. If the plan area is the same as in the previous example, the beams must be larger because the span is greater.

The extra depth can be partly compensated for by positioning the secondary beams for the floor between the main beams. Floor D4, like D1, is based on a secondary construction of small beams or joists, but this time level with the top of the main beams. That means that holes will be required in the beams to accommodate services transverse to the frames. The services can be grouped together or distributed over the full length of the beam in the case of a castellated or cellular beam. Another advantage of such perforated beams is the saving in weight of up to 30%.

D5 is a ribbed slab comprising trapezoidal profile metal sheets suspended between the main beams plus

a concrete infill/topping. Studs welded to the beams beforehand guarantee the composite action between floor and primary structure. The metal sheets are supported on steel cleats (angles, 25 x 35 mm) welded to the beams at the steel fabrication works.

Floor construction D4

Glued laminated timber floor panels,	
e.g. bakelised	27 mm
Steel beams, IPE 160	160 mm
Total	*187 mm*

Floor construction D5

Reinforced concrete topping	120 mm
Trapezoidal profile metal sheets	200 mm
Total	*320 mm*

Profiles
a) HEA 200
b) IPE 600, partly shown as cellular beam

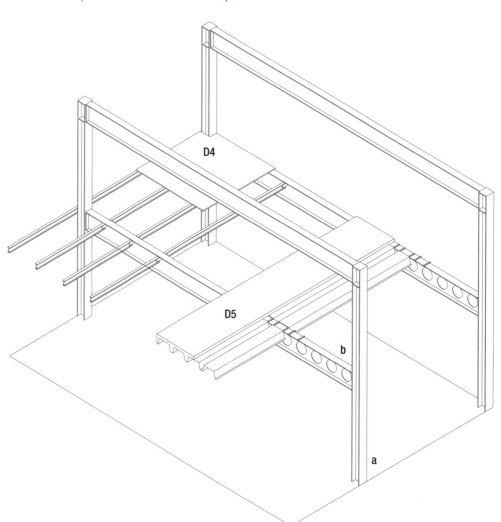

Fig. 40: Frame with continuous columns
Shown here with floor constructions shallower than the beams

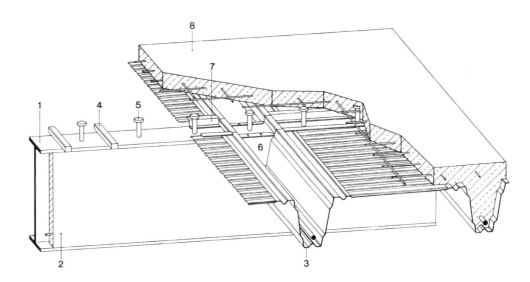

Fig. 41: Composite floor slab with deep trapezoidal sections

1   steel beam (acts compositely with slab)
2   concrete infill between flanges
3   steel trapezoidal section
4   steel cleat (25 x 35 mm)
5   shear stud
6   plastic profile filler
7   Z-section closer piece
8   reinforced concrete ribbed slab

Fig. 42: Cellular beams
showing holes being used for services

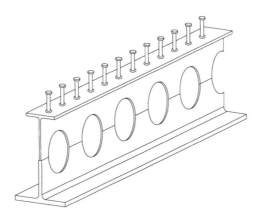

Fig. 44: Cellular beam
Example with different top and bottom flanges to save weight

Fig. 43: Castellated beams

Structures – two-way frame

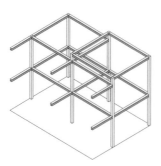

Fig. 45: Two-way frame

The loadbearing structure consists of a two-way frame with columns made from structural hollow sections which, in contrast to I-sections, present the same connection options on all sides. As the columns are continuous, beams can be connected at any height, which permits different ceiling heights in different bays. To ensure that all floor beams are loaded equally, the direction of span of the floors should change from bay to bay.

The flooring examples illustrate solutions in which the beams are the same depth as the floor ("Slimfloor", "Integrated Floor Beam – IFB" etc.). In both cases here a wider bottom flange plate is welded to the beams to support the floor. D6 is based on precast prestressed hollow-core floor planks which can span up to 12 m. The voids merely save weight; services must still be routed underneath the floor slabs. The great advantage is the dry form of construction. Like D5, D7 is a ribbed slab with, once again, trapezoidal profile metal sheets suspended between the main beams and a concrete infill/topping. Services can be routed between the ribs. When constructed as a composite slab, the floor serves as a horizontal plate bracing the structure.

Floor construction D6

Cement screed	80 mm
Impact sound insulation	20 mm
Prestressed hollow-core floor planks	220 mm
Total	*320 mm*

Floor construction D7

Reinforced concrete topping	120 mm
Trapezoidal profile metal sheets	200 mm
Total	*320 mm*

Structural members
a) columns: RRW 20 hollow sections, continuous (ROR also possible)
b) beams: HEB 200 sections with additional flange rate (type SFB), pinned connections

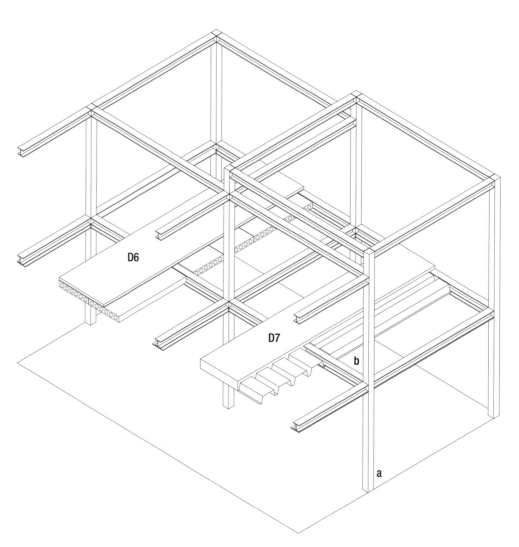

Fig. 46: Frame with continuous columns
shown here with floor constructions equal to the beam depth (e.g. Slimfloor)

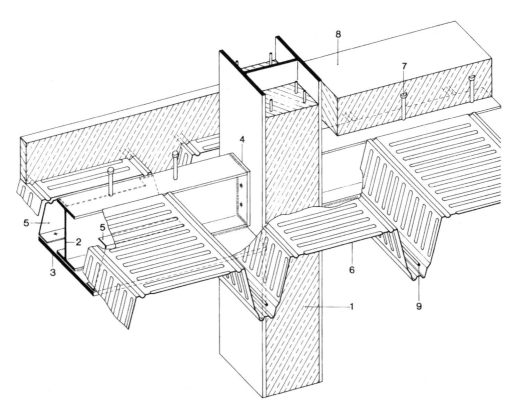

Fig. 47: Composite floor slab with deep trapezoidal sections

1   composite column (concrete infill between flanges)
2   steel beam
3   flange plate
4   end plate
5   closer plate
6   profiled sheet metal
7   shear studs
8   in situ concrete
9   longitudinal reinforcement in ribs

Fig. 48: Positioning a hollow-core floor plank

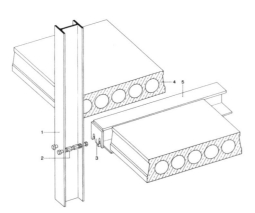

Fig. 50: Prestressed hollow-core planks
Steel beams have wider bottom flange to support floor planks

Fig. 49: Erecting a floor of hollow-core planks

131

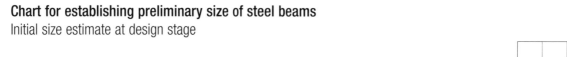

Chart for establishing preliminary size of steel beams

Initial size estimate at design stage

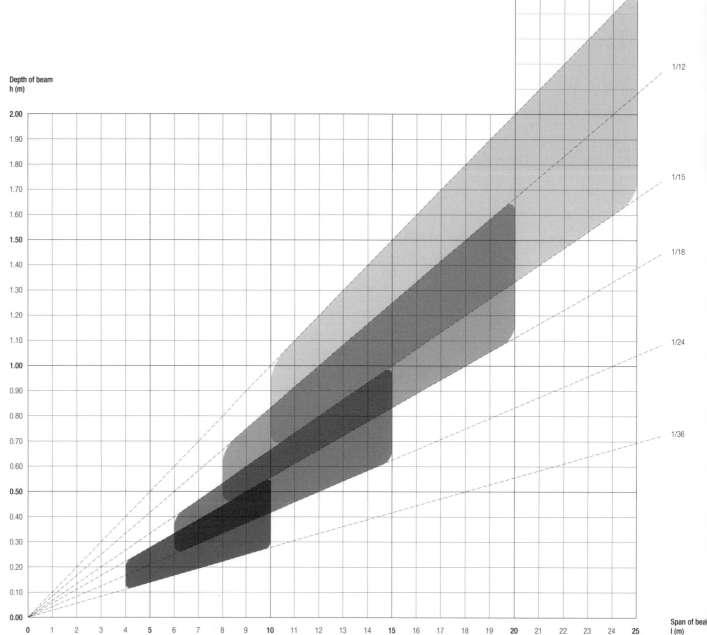

Fig. 51: Notes for using this chart
With a high load (dead and imposed loads) use the
maximum value for the member depth as proposed
by the chart – vice versa for a low load.
The sizes and relationships shown cannot be verified
scientifically. The shaded areas are supposed to be
slightly "indefinite". In the interest of the rational use
of a loadbearing element, the "edges" of this chart
should be avoided.

Source: M. Dietrich, *Burgdorf School of
Engineering*, 1990

Element (loadbearing)	Span l (m)	h*/l
Roof purlin (I)	– 10 m	1/18 – 1/36
Floor beam (I)	6 – 15 m	1/15 – 1/24
Castellated beam (I)	8 – 20 m	1/12 – 1/18
Lattice beam	10 – 25 m	1/10 – 1/15

*An HEA (h/w = 1/1 to 2/1) or an IPE (h/w = 2/1 to 3/1) can be used for the initial, rough sizing.

Folding and bending

Fig. 52: Bent sheet steel (d =12 mm) as a structural element (above); plan, scale approx. 1:140 (left)
Hild und K: bus shelter, Landshut (D), 1999

Folding is a fundamental metalworking technique and a whole industry has grown up around this process. Besides paper and cardboard, metal is the only material that allows this sort of deformation. The folding of spines and ribs enhances the stability of thin sheet metal, which enables large plates and sheets to be laid directly on the loadbearing structure without any further support. This is why corrugated sheet metal – and later trapezoidal profile sheets – has been so popular as a roofing material and also as a cladding for utility and industrial buildings since its invention in 1829.

The work of the French engineer Jean Prouvé (1901–84) went way beyond simply optimising the processes for cladding materials. Using his favourite material, aluminium, he devised entire loadbearing constructions based on folded sheet metal. His pavilion to celebrate the 100th anniversary of the industrial production of aluminium in 1954 is a good example. It demonstrated how aluminium could replace timber and steel, the traditional materials

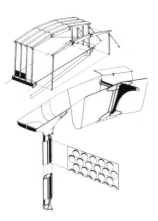

Fig. 53: Details of loadbearing construction
Jean Prouvé: Pavillon du centenaire de l'aluminium, Paris (F), 1954

for exhibition structures. This 152 m long structure is based on 15 m long beams at 1.34 m centres with sheet aluminium suspended between in such a way that the trough sections act as gutters. The beams themselves were made from three separate pieces first joined on site by means of cast connecting brackets. This is a clear reference to mechanical and automotive engineering.

While in the aluminium pavilion the loadbearing structure made use of linear members and its "column" and "beam" components obviously obeyed the principles of filigree construction, these elements were combined into self-supporting elements at Prouvé's observatory structure of 1951. The building has a parabolic cross-section formed by two half-shells that support each other. The

Fig. 56: The aluminium roof beams resemble a gutter in section.
Jean Prouvé: Pavillon du centenaire de l'aluminium, Paris (F), 1954

curved form here is due to the rigid connection between the inner and outer aluminium sheets.

Released from building performance stipulations, Hild und K managed to fabricate the walls to their bus shelters in Landshut from thick sheet metal without any further supporting framework. The exposed feet were milled out of the 12 mm thick Cor-Ten (weathering) steel plate just like the ornamentation. On plan the shelter consists of two L-shaped plates.

Fig. 54: Loadbearing structure and building envelope united in the form of semicircular, loadbearing sandwich elements, shown here almost complete.
Jean Prouvé: La Méridienne de l'observatoire, Paris (F), 1951

Fig. 55: Erecting the sandwich elements
Jean Prouvé: La Méridienne de l'observatoire, Paris (F), 1951

Frames

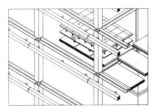

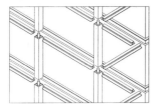

Fig. 57: Steel frame with prefabricated floor elements and concrete topping
Burkard Meyer Architekten: Swisscom headquarters, Winterthur (CH), 1999

Fig. 58: On the facade the floor slab edges are the only visible part of the loadbearing structure.
Burkard Meyer Architekten: Swisscom headquarters, Winterthur (CH), 1999

Apart from reinforcing bars in reinforced concrete, the majority of steel in buildings is to be found in the form of frames. The columns and beams form a framework of linear members with floors and non-loadbearing walls as the "infill" panels. Dry construction techniques can be used for the floors and walls, or the composite action of steel and concrete can be exploited. The steel frame is characterised by rational procedures.

Fig. 59: The square grid visible on the facade is only a covering to the loadbearing elements behind.
Georg Marterer: teahouse in Neustift am Walde, Vienna (A), 1998

The Swisscom headquarters in Winterthur by Burkard Meyer Architekten (1999) is a good example of a steel frame for a building of this size. Surrounding the solid, stiff core housing stairs, lifts and services are concrete-cased steel columns on a 5.6 x 5.6 m grid; these columns consist of a solid steel core and a sheet metal jacket (permanent formwork) filled with concrete. Precast concrete floor elements are supported on the widened bottom flanges of the steel beams. A concrete topping is added to this to form a solid composite structure. The loadbearing structure is enclosed by the facade in such a way that the floor edges are the only visible part of this assembly.

At first sight the teahouse in Neustift am Walde (1998) by Georg Marter seems to convey the impression that the grid outlines on the facade are the structural steel frame. But in reality these pieces are merely applied to cover the joints between the elements, although the visible grid does indeed correspond exactly with the loadbearing structure behind, on a square grid (2.46 x 2.46 m),

Fig. 60: Steel frame and profiled metal sheets left exposed internally
Lacaton & Vassal: holiday chalet, Lège Cap-Ferret (F), 1998

which carries the fixed glazing, sliding windows and plain infill panels.

Like the holiday chalet by Lacton & Vassal in Lège Cap-Ferret (1998), which was built around existing trees, the frame in the teahouse appears as sculpted relief in the interior.

Another similarity with the holiday chalet – and totally different to the Swisscom headquarters – is that this is a completely dry construction in which only the floor slab is made of concrete. The building's stability is guaranteed by the diagonal X-bracing positioned behind the elements.

For further examples of frames, please refer to the chapter entitled "Structures".

Girder, lattice beam and facade

Fig. 64: A house in the form of a bridge
Craig Ellwood: holiday chalet, San Luis Obispo (USA), 1967/68

Once the span exceeds a certain distance, off-the-shelf rolled steel sections are no longer adequate. To save material and weight we truss the beam with ties underneath, use a castellated or cellular section, or provide a lattice beam or girder. Up until the mid-20th century the construction of loadbearing structures assembled from the most delicate sections was a daily occurrence – if not the only option for long spans. The welding together of individual members (top and bottom chords, struts and ties) is, however, very labour-intensive, which leads to plate girders with solid webs and flanges still being used despite the considerably higher material consumption.

Although the resolution of the loadbearing structure into a framework of linear members involves higher labour costs, the advantages are savings in weight, easier routing of services and transparency. This latter feature

– the Ellwood design more so than the Herzog & de Meuron, where the steelwork is situated behind a semi-transparent veil. But the structural steelwork to the senior citizens' home in Amsterdam by MVRDV (1997) is totally concealed, where the enormous length of the two-storey cantilevers is the only clue to the fact that a weight-saving design in structural steelwork lies behind the facades.

Fig. 61: Two-part top and bottom chords enable posts and diagonals to be "clamped" between.
Craig Ellwood: holiday chalet, San Luis Obispo (USA), 1967/68

Fig. 62: The lantern lights (clad with patterned glass) span from wall to wall.
Herzog & de Meuron: locomotive depot "Auf dem Wolf", Basel (CH), 1995

Fig. 65: Aerial view of site, the longest locomotive shed is not yet finished.
Herzog & de Meuron: locomotive depot "Auf dem Wolf", Basel (CH), 1993

was exploited by Herzog & de Meuron in their locomotive depot "Auf dem Wolf" (1995), where the girders form lantern lights. The building comprises a concrete box frame with a steel roof construction. Supported on the concrete walls every 13 m are pairs of girders that form square tubes spanning distances of up to 40 m. Clad in patterned glass, these 3 m high tubes, from which the beams for the intermediate flat roofs are suspended, simultaneously act as lantern lights.

Whereas in the Herzog & de Meuron design the girders are used only on the roof, at Craig Ellwood's holiday chalet in San Luis Obispo (1967/68) they are the primary loadbearing structure and, as such, the longitudinal facades of the house. Like a bridge, they form a long tube that spans an 18 m wide canyon. Each of the girders comprises pairs of channel sections (as top and bottom chords) with square hollow sections as the ties and struts in between. Floor and roof are supported on steel beams spanning the two girders at the same spacing as the vertical members of the girder.

In the above examples the structural steelwork characterises the architectural appearance of the building

This supposition is probably helped by the openings, whose positioning and maximum size is determined by the posts and diagonals.

Fig. 63: The windows are located between the posts and the diagonals.
MVRDV: senior citizens' apartments, Amsterdam (NL), 1997

Fig. 66: Steel frame concealed behind timber cladding
MVRDV: senior citizens' apartments, Amsterdam (NL), 1997

Space frames

Space frames consist of delicate linear members often joined via ball-like nodes with up to 18 connection options. Besides Konrad Wachsmann and Buckminster Fuller, who devoted themselves enthusiastically to the development of such lightweight structures for long-span roofs, Max Mengeringhausen also played a significant role. It is his "Mero" node, a screwed connection invented in 1942, that is still used today. A space frame comprises top and bottom chord levels together with intermediate three-dimensional diagonals. Depending on whether the space frame is a combination of tetrahedra, octahedra and/or cuboctahedra, the upper and lower levels are either parallel with each other on plan or offset diagonally.

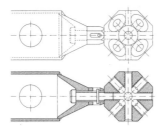

Fig. 67: "Mero" node with member attached
Elevation and section

Fig. 68: Exposed corner
Norman Foster: Sainsbury Centre for Visual Arts,
Norwich (UK), 1978

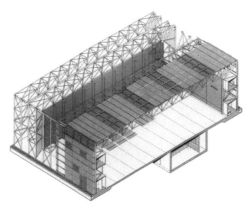

Fig. 69: Identical structure and building envelope for roof and walls,
axonometric view of loadbearing construction with and without cladding
Norman Foster: Sainsbury Centre for Visual Arts, Norwich (UK), 1978

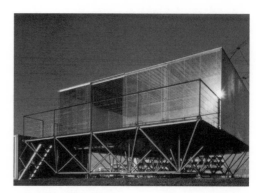

Fig. 70: The space frame distributes the loads of the building to four pad foundations.
Benthem Crouwel: private house, Almere (NL), 1984

Space frames are generally associated with roofs, or rather long-span roofs; a space frame with a depth of, for example, 4 m, can span up to 120 m. The private house in Almere (NL) by Benthem Crouwel (1984) should therefore be regarded as an extension of the application without ignoring the principles of this form of construction completely. Poor subsoil conditions and the fact that this was originally intended to be a temporary structure – it is still standing and was in fact extended in 1991! – inspired the use of an easily dismantled space frame which distributes the load of the house to four pad foundations, which should be regarded as stub columns. Raising the ground floor above the level of the site also helps to protect the building against moisture from the ground.

In Norman Foster's Sainsbury Centre for Visual Arts (1978) the space frame is resolved into individual triangular girders (each of which is itself a pair of two lattice beams with a common bottom chord). It is interesting to note that the roof and the walls utilise the same structure and same building envelope. In the walls Foster uses the girder depth of about 3 m not only to integrate services but also to access corridors within the loadbearing level. The nodes of the girders are welded; only the diagonals between the girders were bolted in place on site to suit the erection procedure.

Buckminster Fuller's USA Pavilion for the 1967 World Exposition in Montreal managed to disintegrate entirely the boundary between wall and roof. The truncated sphere – with a diameter of 110 m at the base and an impressive 167 m at the "equator", all achieved with steel tubes having a maximum size of just 9 cm – formed a container for the USA's exhibits. Contrary to Foster's design, the building envelope here – hexagonal acrylic panels – was attached to the inside of the frame. The hexagonal panels matched the framing of the lower level (bottom chord), while the upper level (top chord) consisted of a triangular grid.

Fig. 71: The truncated sphere has a base diameter of 110 m.
Buckminster Fuller: USA Pavilion, EXPO 67, Montreal (CAN), 1967

Diamonds and diagonals

The bracing diagonal is frequently an addition, an unavoidable solution inserted to complete the structural concept in those designs where bracing components such as rigid service cores and shear walls are lacking. But when used as a primary structural element they are very popular, as recent examples show – whether as a bundle of apparently random, raking columns ("pick-up-sticks" effect), or integrated into a regular lattice. In such cases the fascination is due to the fact that the vertical and horizontal loads can be accommodated with a single structure of linear members seemingly without any hierarchy, but equally because the network takes on an ornamental quality.

Fig. 74: Glazed barrel-vault roof based on triangular lattice
Norman Foster: Faculty of Law, Cambridge University (UK), 1995

Fig. 72a: The four corner columns with intersecting linear members function in a similar way to Suchov's mast.
Toyo Ito: Mediothek, Sendai (J), 2001

Fig. 72b: The corner columns house the stairs.
Toyo Ito: Mediothek, Sendai (J), 2001

Fig. 73: Rhombus-shaped loadbearing structure to facade
Herzog & de Meuron: Prada store, Tokyo (J), 2003

Early examples of non-orthogonal lattice structures are the towers of Vladimir Suchov, which originated out of a search for a form of water-tower construction that would save materials. A comparison between Suchov's radio mast in Moscow (1919–22) and the Eiffel Tower in Paris (1889) supplies impressive proof of the potential savings of a tower constructed exclusively of angle and channel sections. Whereas the Eiffel Tower is 305 m high and weighs 8850 tonnes, the radio mast is 350 m high and weighs just 2200 tonnes!

The hyperbolic form employed is based on two cylinders with straight members whose top and bottom rings are "rotated" in opposite directions to create a rhombus-shaped lattice structure. The intersections were riveted together and horizontal rings were attached inside to increase the stiffness, which resulted in the triangular look of the lattice.

A contemporary example that borrows the ideas of Suchov can be seen in Toyo Ito's Mediothek in Sendai (2001), where the four corner towers are constructed according to similar principles.

Whereas the loadbearing members in the structures of Suchov and Ito adhere to a clear hierarchy, the diagonal and horizontal members of the barrel-vault roof to Norman Foster's Faculty of Law in Cambridge (spanning nearly 40 m) appear to be equals. The construction employs circular hollow sections with a diameter of 160 mm, with alternate ones braced together in pairs. It is interesting to note that the glazing is positioned a few centimetres in front of the loadbearing structure. Was this done merely to enable Foster to feature this membrane, or was there a more practical reason – the fact that the circular sections are unsuitable for fixing the glazing directly?

There is no such separation at the Prada Store in Tokyo by Herzog & de Meuron (2003). In this building the glazing is fixed directly to the lattice structure, which together with the three internal cores carries the vertical loads. This is an impressive demonstration of the structural potential of welding (at the nodes of the horizontal rhombuses); for the loading is considerably higher than with vertical rhombuses and therefore calls for rigid corner joints.

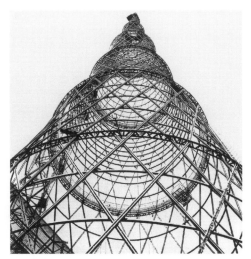

Fig. 75: Linear members consisting of two channels in a spiral form create a hyperbola.
Vladimir G. Suchov: Sabolovka radio mast, Moscow (RUS), 1919–22

Canopy structures

The majority of loadbearing structures are derived from basic units that can enclose spaces only through repetition. For example, a frame (two columns plus one beam) requires at least one other frame in order to generate an interior space. A canopy structure, on the other hand, can form an independent structure on its own, e.g. a petrol station forecourt, a bus shelter.

Fig. 76a: Canopies under construction
Pier Luigi Nervi: Hall of Labour, Turin (I), 1961

Fig. 76b: Canopies of concrete and steel, bay size 38 x 38 m
Pier Luigi Nervi: Hall of Labour, Turin (I), 1961

Fig. 77: "Trees" with 48 "branches"
von Gerkan, Marg & Partner: Stuttgart airport (D), 1990

The independence of the individual canopy enables it to be erected in isolation. A narrow separation allows daylight to enter, a wide separation enables the roof module to be incorporated again but without the column. A representative of the former category is Nervi's "Hall of Labour" (1961) in which 16 canopies spaced 40 m apart cover a square main area flanked by two-storey ancillary buildings on each side. Each 20 m high canopy is supported on a concrete tower, the cross-section of which gradually transforms from a cruciform at the base to a circle at the top. The roof itself is supported on a steel drum from which 20 identical cantilevering, tapering beams radiate, the outer ends of which are connected by a perimeter member. The taper of the beams and the angled underside of the drum clearly illustrate the flow of the forces. As the facade is flush with the edges of the outer canopies, the construction can be properly perceived from the inside only.

Fig. 79: Modular roof; a second element is suspended between the columns.
Norman Foster: Stansted airport, London (GB), 1991

Comparable with Nervi's design in every way is Atocha station in Madrid by Rafael Moneo (1984–92). He, too, uses concrete columns, but the roof beams follow a clear hierarchy: the underside is divided into four triangles containing beams perpendicular to the edges. Duo-pitch rooflights cover the slits between the canopies and therefore delineate the roof surface.

A totally different concept underlies the "tree" structures of Norman Foster's airport terminal at Stansted (1991). The canopies here are so far apart that another roof section with a side length of 18 m can be suspended between. There is also no difference between the materials of the roof and those of the supporting structure. Resolved into four circular hollow sections (d = 45 cm), the central column beneath each canopy itself encloses space which is used for accommodating infrastructure components. The raking compression members seem to instil a merger between roof and structure, forming a three-dimensional edifice.

The term "tree structure" is even more apt at the airport terminal in Stuttgart (Gerkan, Marg & Partner, 1990). Starting from four circular hollow sections each 40 cm in diameter, the "trees" each divide into 48 "branches", the thinnest of which has a diameter of 16 cm.

Fig. 78: The table-like construction lends texture to the trainshed roof.
Rafael Moneo: Atocha station, Madrid (E), 1984–92

Fig. 80: The structure is legible both internally and externally.
Rafael Moneo: Atocha station, Madrid (E), 1984–92

The "invisible" building material

Eva Geering, Andrea Deplazes

Of concealment and exposure

The "multi-layer wall construction", designed to satisfy the thermal performance requirements of a building, grew out of the oil crisis of the 1970s and the subsequent realisation that we must reduce our consumption of energy. The outermost layer in our wall – now resolved into layers – serves to protect the (usually) unstable insulation from the weather. The insulation in turn (usually) encloses the loadbearing structure for the whole building, to which it is fixed, like a wool coat. This technically obvious development raised new questions related to the architecture: What does an insulated wall look like? Could or should its form correspond to that of a monolithic wall? One obvious solution to this dilemma is to build the outer protective layer in the form of a self-supporting leaf of masonry or concrete. That enables our multi-layer wall to appear like a solid wall, almost as if there had never been an oil crisis. Even if the insulation is protected only by a thin layer of render in order to reduce the amount of work, our wall still appears to be a solid structure. At least so long as we do not actually touch it… Systems with ventilation cavities avoid these pretences and convey a more lightweight yet protective appearance, with a cladding of wood, sheet metal or slates. This arrangement also covers the inevitable layer of insulation and uses it only indirectly as a reason for altering the architecture. It is hardly surprising that in the 1970s, in contrast to the dogmas of Modernism, architecture again became a medium with meaning, and the clothing theory of Gottfried Semper again became topical.

In their Suva Building in Basel, Herzog & de Meuron pursued a strategy contrary to the concealment theory. As the insulation is protected by a transparent, glass skin, we get to see materials that were not actually intended to be visible. Although during the age of Modernism all decoration was renounced and the "truth of construction" proclaimed, revealing the insulation material in this instance is not concerned with a didactic derivation of constructional details. Instead, what we have here is the breaking of a taboo and the fascination with "ugly" materials. In particular, the use of unconventional materials raises probing questions of cultural conventions and reveals the beauty of their shabbiness. The tension between meaning and effect results in a poetry of the material: "How is poetry revealed? It is revealed by the fact that a word is recognised as a word and not as a mere substitute for something it designates." (Roman Jakobson, *Questions de poétique*)

Heat losses versus heat gains

Insulation protects against heat losses from the inside, but also against an excess of heat entering from the outside. One or the other of these effects is relevant depending on the climate; in the temperate climate of continental Europe preserving heat *and* gaining heat are desirable, depending on the season. One attempt to deal with this paradox that is intrinsic to materials is the development of transparent thermal insulation. This type of insulation, comprising several components, does not block out the light and hence heat but rather allows it to penetrate and heat up a wall capable of storing this energy. Transparent thermal insulation is not only permeable to light and heat but is also transparent to visible light. This is especially obvious in the direct gain system in which the transparent thermal insulation is employed as an enclosing element without any wall behind it. The use of transparent thermal insulation in this way is similar to the use of a not completely transparent window. Not only the outer protective layer of this wall construction is transparent, as we can see on the Suva Building, the insulation itself is virtually invisible. It is, so to speak, non-existent and permits the illusion of being reckless with the building performance parameters (see "Transparent thermal insulation", p. 145).

Synthetic building materials

Whether visible or invisible, the forms of thermal insulation mentioned above are part of an elaborate system of complementary and interdependent layers.

Synthetic building materials such as masonry or concrete with insulating properties satisfy the desire for simple buildability. In the meantime, industry can offer

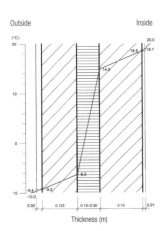

Outside / Inside

Fig. 1: Multi-layer wall construction
Temperature gradient within the layers

Thickness (m)

Fig. 2: Existing and new buildings linked by insulating glass facade;
top: straight on the road side; bottom: diagonally in the inner courtyard
Herzog & de Meuron: Suva combined residential and commercial development, Basel (CH), 1988–93

a wide variety of building materials that provide both loadbearing and insulating functions. The key physical and structural issue is to be found in this duality. The loadbearing material is so permeated with air-filled pores that it just exhibits sufficient load-carrying capacity, while the air captured in the pores, with its poor conduction, provides an insulating effect. So the insulating function always weakens the loadbearing material, with the ratio of strength to insulation needing to be determined in each case. The blurred dividing line between a loadbearing material with insulating properties and a loadbearing insulation material characterises such materials. Synthetic building materials, especially porous and brittle insulating masonry units, call for careful workmanship on site and must always be protected against moisture. In order to guarantee the required protection from the weather, synthetic building materials must be rendered or treated with a water repellent.

Polyurethane as a loadbearing shell

Another strategy comes to the fore in the example described below. The insulation is no longer applied to the loadbearing layer, nor does it imply it; instead, the layer of insulation *is* the loadbearing layer.

Rigid insulating materials with a good compressive strength have been developed for insulating components subjected to compression loads, e.g. flat roofs or parking decks for heavy-goods vehicles. Philip Johnson exploited this technical development for the architecture of Gate House in New Canaan (Massachusetts, USA).

Gate House (a visitors' pavilion for Johnson's "Glass House") was erected using a complementary method with the help of conventional materials: insulation, concrete, reinforcement. However, their interaction is not easy to decipher. The components do not simply complement each other in the finished building nor are they completely

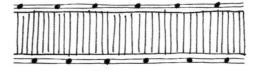

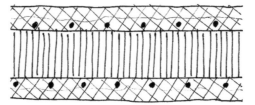

Fig. 3: Sketches of wall construction (horizontal sections)
Top: the rigid PUR foam insulation between two layers of reinforcing mesh serves as permanent formwork. Bottom: rigid PUR foam insulation panel covered with two coats of sprayed concrete both sides
Philip Johnson: Gate House, New Canaan (USA), 1995

fused. The reinforced layer of insulation functions as permanent formwork for a thin strengthening and protective layer of concrete. The method of construction used at Gate House is based on an Italian patent which Johnson's structural engineer, Ysrael A. Seinuk, brought to his attention. Normally, this method of construction – in the form of panels made from two parallel layers of reinforcing mesh and an intervening layer of insulation (rigid polyurethane foam), the whole covered with a thin layer of sprayed concrete – is used to construct cheap housing. Unlike conventional concreting no formwork is required. In order to erect the complex shapes required at Gate House the horizontal sections through the building were built as wooden templates and positioned with the help of a scaffold.

Using these as a guide, similar to the construction lines on a drawing, the building was assembled from the prefabricated rigid foam panels. The partly flat, partly convex, partly concave parts were joined together on site like the pieces of a puzzle. At this point the shape of the building could still be changed, a fact that Johnson made full use of; the opening for the door was cut out, the surfaces and edges given the correct form. The first layer of sprayed concrete stiffened the assembly of panels and enabled most of the templates and the scaffold to be removed. The second layer of concrete gave the wall the necessary thickness and provided the necessary cover to the reinforcement. The outcome of this reversal, in which the formwork is suddenly on the inside, is an apparently monolithic, thin-wall concrete shell. This method of construction in which the design can be manipulated during the building process renders possible the dream of plastically deformable, insulated concrete.

Walls of straw

Straw is a pure insulating material. However, if you compress it, it can become a loadbearing material. Here again, it is the enclosed pockets of air, not the straw itself, that create the insulating effect. The development of straw bale presses began around 1800 in the USA. In those regions in which grains and cereals were cultivated the fields were literally covered in "oversized roofing tiles" following the harvest. It didn't take much fantasy to turn these elements into temporary shelters.

It transpired that these temporary buildings outlived their planned period of usefulness completely unscathed, indeed even thwarted the extreme summer and winter conditions of Nebraska, and that a comfortable climate prevailed inside throughout the year.

Today, this old strategy is gaining favour again, albeit in the guise of sustainable building, e.g. Tscheppa House in Disentis (Grisons) by Werner Schmidt. In order to prevent moisture problems, a concrete foundation is cast on which the bales of straw and the timber reveals to the

1   Horizontal wooden templates positioned and fixed with the help of a scaffold

2   Rigid foam panels already erected on the left

3   Finished assembly of rigid foam panels

4   Cut-out for large entrance opening (note the difference between this and photo 3).
     Edges reinforced with additional bars.

5   Building coated with the first layer of sprayed concrete

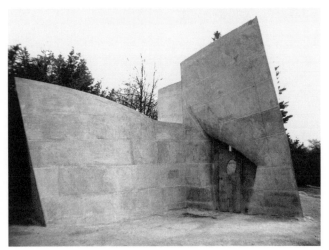

6   Gate House cleaned and prepared ready for painting

Fig. 4: Progress on site
Philip Johnson: Gate House, New Canaan (USA), 1995

1 Reveals to openings mounted on concrete foundation; first course of straw bales in position

2 Building up the wall with straw bales in a "masonry bond"

3 Positioning the intermediate timber layer to act as a bearing for the floor and reveals of the upper storey; the vertical strapping is readily visible here

4 Structural shell almost complete, only the protective layer of render has yet to be applied

Fig. 5: Progress on site
Werner Schmidt: Tscheppa House, Disentis (CH), 2002

Fig. 6: Built from bales of straw
Simonton House in Purdum, Nebraska (USA), 1908

openings are built. The bales of straw are assembled in a brick-like bond. Vertical straps, which have to be retightened several times during the brief period of erection, draw the straw bales tightly together and hence consolidate the walls to such an extent that even two-storey buildings are quite possible. Intermediate timber boards serve as bearings for the joists, beams and reveals of the upper storey. Once the straw house has finally settled, it can be rendered and hence protected from the ravages of the weather. Therefore, the inevitable form of construction results in a building with metre-thick, sculpted walls. The straw wall seems, quite by chance, to solve the dilemma sparked by the oil crisis. What initially began as an ecological experiment, could lead to a new architectural style of "Baroque plasticity". The game has begun.

Further reading
- Gottfried Semper: *Style: Style in the Technical and Tectonic Arts; Or, Practical Aesthetics*, Harry Francis Mallgrave (ed.), Los Angeles, 2004.
- Martin Steinmann: *Die Unterwäsche von Madonna*, lecture, 1996, published within the scope of the Alcopor Award 2000.
- Roman Jakobson: *Questions de poétique*, Paris, 1973. English translation: Roman Jakobsen: *On Language*, Harvard, 1995.
- Jeffrey Kipnis, Philip Johnson: *Architectural Monographs No. 44*, London, 1996.
- Herbert Gruber and Astrid Gruber: *Bauen mit Stroh*, Staufen, 2000.
- *Die Südostschweiz*, "Im Stroh schlafen", 27. 11. 2002, p. 19.

Transparent thermal insulation

Fig. 7: Shimmering building envelope:
Dietrich Schwarz: house in Domat/Ems (CH), 1996

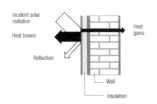

Conventional insulation

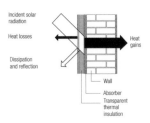

Fig. 8: Transparent thermal insulation

Fig. 9: Wall construction with transparent thermal insulation

Definition

Transparent thermal insulation functions only in conjunction with glass, which protects the insulation from the weather and, thanks to its transparency, admits daylight and especially solar radiation. Inside the building the light is converted into heat and contributes to the space heating requirement. In addition, transparent thermal insulation reduces heat losses from inside to outside and therefore functions as a thermal insulation. In contrast to the majority of customary insulating products, this material also very frequently remains visible from the outside behind a pane of glass. Transparent thermal insulation elements are also permeable to wavelengths of the solar spectrum other than visible light.

Construction (from outside to inside):
– Protective layer of glass
– Layer of insulation comprising transparent thermal insulation elements (dense, honeycomb-like capillary structure of transparent plastic)
– Protective layer of glass or solid loadbearing layer, or rather absorber

How transparent thermal insulation works

Three principal forms gradually appeared in the evolution of applications for transparent thermal insulation. These can be distinguished according to the way in which the solar energy is used.

Direct gain system

The transparent thermal insulation is employed as an enclosing element without any wall behind. It is therefore similar to a light-permeable but not transparent window element or glass facade. The solar radiation passes through the transparent thermal insulation directly into the interior and is converted into heat at the various surfaces within the interior. The interior temperature changes almost simultaneously with the temperature of the surfaces. Therefore, in summer fixed or movable sunshades must be provided in order to prevent overheating in the interior.

Solar wall

In the solar wall system the incident solar radiation is converted into heat on the outside face of a solid external wall. Controlled by the insulating effect of the transparent thermal insulation material, the heat energy flows through the wall to the inside face and is then radiated into the interior. Fluctuations in the outside temperature are tracked internally but with a delay. This delay can be influenced by the material and thickness of the wall.

Thermally decoupled system

In the thermally decoupled system the incident solar radiation is converted into heat at an absorber surface isolated from the interior. The heat is fed either directly into the interior via a system of ducts, or into a heat storage medium, which can be part of the building itself (e.g. hollow floor slab or double-leaf wall), or part of the building services (e.g. pebble bed or water tank). With thermally isolated storage media the release of heat into the interior can be controlled irrespective of the absorber or storage temperature.

Fig. 10: Direct gain system

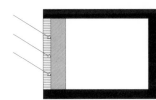

Fig. 11: Solar wall

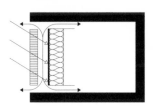

Fig. 12: Thermally decoupled system

Thermal insulation materials...

Fig. 13: Glass wool

Fig. 14: Cellular glass (foam glass)

Fig. 15: Extruded polystyrene (XPS)

Fig. 16: Wood fibres

Fig. 17: Rockwool

Fig. 18: Expanded polystyrene (EPS)

Fig. 19: Rigid foam

Fig. 20: Cellulose fibres

	Insulating material	Name of typical product	Physical appearance	Diffusion resistance index [–] (*bonded joints)	Thermal conductance [W/mK] 0.06 0.09 0.12
Inorganic, synthetic raw materials	**Mineral fibre glass wool**	Isover	Yellow boards	Open to diffusion ($\mu = 1$)	▬
	Mineral fibre rockwool	Flumroc, Rockwool	Green-grey boards	Open to diffusion ($\mu = 1$–2)	▬
	Cellular glass	Foamglas	Black, hard boards	Vapourtight * ($\mu = \infty$)	▪
Inorganic, natural raw materials	**Expanded clay**	Leca	Brown granulate		▬▬
Organic, synthetic raw materials	**Expanded polystyrene (EPS)**	Styropor (BASF)	White, grainy boards	Vapourtight* ($\mu = 40$–100)	▪
	Extruded polystyrene (XPS)	Styrofoam	Light blue boards	Vapourtight* ($\mu = 80$–250)	▪
	Rigid polyurethane foam	Swisspor	White-yellow boards	Vapourtight* ($\mu = 60$–80)	▪
	In situ polyurethane foam		Yellow foam		▪
Organic, natural raw materials	**Wood fibres**	Pavatex	Medium brown, fibrous boards	Open to diffusion ($\mu = 5$)	▬
	Cement-bonded wood-wool	Heraklith, Schichtex	"Spaghetti boards"	Open to diffusion ($\mu = 2$–7)	▬▬▬
	Cellulose fibres	Isofloc	Usually newspaper flakes	Open to diffusion ($\mu = 1$–2)	▪
	Sheep's wool	doscha, isolena	Mats, fleece, felt, loose fill	Open to diffusion ($\mu = 1$–2)	▬▬
	Flax, hemp	Flachshaus	Boards, mats, loose fill	Open to diffusion ($\mu = 1$)	▬▬
	Cork		Brown, coarse-grained boards	Open to diffusion ($\mu = 2$–8)	▬

Fig. 21: Various insulating materials

Properties of materials

...and their applications

Price category	Remarks	Thermal insulation material, not subject to compression, e.g. for walls, floors and ventilated roofs	Thermal insulation material, not subject to compression, e.g. for insulation between rafters and joists	Thermal insulation material, subject to compression, e.g. for casting against concrete as permanent formwork, for general use in floors and roofs	Thermal insulation material with defined compressive strength for use beneath floors distributing compression loads, e.g. industrial floors	Thermal insulation material with enhanced compressive strength for use beneath floors distributing compression loads, e.g. parking decks for heavy goods vehicles	Thermal insulation material able to withstand bending moments, e.g. for cladding timber-frame constructions subject to wind loads	Thermal insulation material able to withstand pull-off loads, e.g. for facades with mineral render	Impact sound insulation material	Impact sound insulation material, also suitable for use with defined low compressibility
inexpensive	The smallest fibres can be inhaled	■	■	■				■	■	
inexpensive	The smallest fibres can be inhaled	■	■	■				■	■	
expensive	Can be reused as road sub-base, raw material: scrap glass	■		■	■	■				■
	Incombustible insulating material	Loose fill								
inexpensive	Does not rot, ultraviolet radiation causes embrittlement, can be worked mechanically	■		■			■	■	■	■
moderate exp.	Does not rot, ultraviolet radiation causes embrittlement, can be worked mechanically	■		■						
moderate exp.	Dust must not be inhaled, not resistant to ultraviolet radiation	■		■	■				■	■
		■		■	■				■	■
moderate	Fine dust during sawing, sheets can be reused	■	■	■				■	■	■
moderate	Fixed with nails, wall anchors, tile adhesive, suitable as substrate for plaster/render, ceramic products, plasterboard	■		■			■	■		
inexpensive	Loose fill (tipped or blown)	■	■							
moderate exp.	Formaldehyde catalyst, hence recommended for air hygiene aspects, easily reused	■	■						■	
inexpensive exp.	Easily reused (except facade panels), facade insulation panels readily available	■	■						■	
inexpensive exp.	Smell of material must be considered when used indoors	■			■	■			■	

Source: Reyer, Schild, Völkner: *Kompendium der Dämmstoffe*, Stuttgart, 2000

Thermal insulation systems
Overview

Complementary systems

The feature of the complementary system is its hierarchical functional breakdown into monofunctional components. The building envelope is divided into layers providing loadbearing, insulating and protection functions, whereby the development of the individual layers must be continuous. Drawing a diagram of the layers helps to analyse a structure and determine the key details.

Based on the position of the structural elements in relation to the layer of insulation, we distinguish between two different complementary systems:

Loadbearing layer inside
– Double-leaf construction in masonry and/or concrete (1)
– Ventilated construction with lightweight or heavyweight cladding (2)
– Rendered external insulation (3)

Synthetic systems

In a synthetic system a single non-hierarchical element provides multiple functions, e.g. loadbearing and insulating, or insulating and protecting. The building envelope is either essentially homogeneous (e.g. single-leaf masonry) or in the form of a "black box" whose components form an inseparable composite (e.g. timber panel construction). Synthetic systems are often supplemented by complementary systems because certain details are otherwise impossible to solve properly (e.g. plinth and wall–roof junction in single-leaf masonry). It is therefore not helpful to draw a diagram of the layers.

Synthetic systems can be divided into two types:

Compact systems
– Single-leaf masonry with/without insulating render (5)
– Concrete with insulating properties

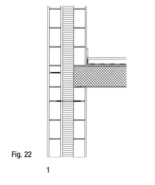

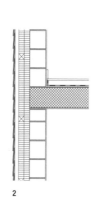

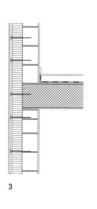

Fig. 22

1   2   3   5

Loadbearing layer outside
– Exposed concrete with monolithic or isolated floor junction (4)
– Facing masonry externally
– Solid timber construction with internal insulation

Sandwich systems
– Timber platform frame construction (6)
– Timber panel construction (7)

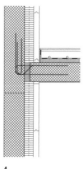

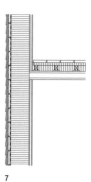

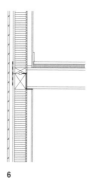

Fig. 23

4   6   7

Glass – crystalline, amorphous

Tibor Joanelly

Glass is transparent, hard and precious. These properties clutter our view of a material that, on closer inspection, defies a clear physical and phenomenological description. And it is precisely in this obviously unfocused definition that glass reveals its own fascination.

The fact that we can see through glass sets it apart from other materials, makes it unusual and valuable. When we speak of glass we usually mean industrially manufactured glass in the form of vessels or windows. We forget that, for example, cellular glass loses its transparency and hence its "glassiness" during the foaming process. However, it remains a form of glass still produced – or better, recycled – in large quantities. Or glass fibres – this thread-like material developed to transmit light and data does not comply with our general idea of glass either.

Specific technical requirements have led to a huge variety of glass products. So the word glass more rightly describes a physical state rather than a clearly defined molecular material. However, in this chapter we shall speak of glass mainly in terms of the common understanding of this material and how this can be interesting for architecture.

Compared with its almost 5000-year history, the use of glass as a building material is a relatively recent development. The technology required to use glass in the building envelope in the form of small panes joined together was not available until the blowing iron was invented by the Romans. However, since that time glass has been available in two basic forms. The sheet glass we produce these days is based on the principle of drawing out a ribbon of molten glass. In both the ancient technique of blowing and turning the blowing iron, and today's method of levelling the glass on a bath of molten tin, the force of gravity makes a major contribution to giving the glass its form. The glass is drawn out like dough and then given its shape.

These technologies contrast with the ancient production of glass. Over many thousands of years the soft glass mass, only available in small amounts, was pressed into moulds. In order to produce hollow vessels, sand was placed in the mould and then, after the glass had solidified, scraped out again. Even today, glass objects are formed by pressing, or by pouring the molten material into moulds; the majority of glass vessels and – important for the development of modern architecture – glass bricks and blocks are produced in this way.

Astonishingly, the production of such a variety of different glass products is actually due to the structure of the material itself. In physical terms glass is in a solid state, but its structure is amorphous, not crystalline. We speak of a *liquid in a solid state*. At the molecular level a coherent crystal lattice is not evident; instead alternating groups of crystalline and non-crystalline molecules are seen. If we had to define the nature of glass, we would have to say

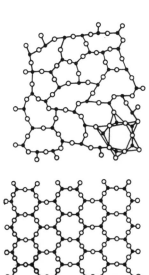

Fig. 1: Glass as a liquid in a solid state
2D presentations of $[SiO_4]^4$ tetrahedra in quartz glass (top) and rock crystal (bottom)

Fig. 2: Crystalline, amorphous – the microscopic structure of glass

that glass represents a dilemma. Accordingly, its use in our built environment is also Janus-like.

Out of the earth into the fire

Glass in an amorphous state is the best way of looking at its origins. The essential components of glass are quartz sand, lime and potash or soda. The natural deposits of quartz sand appear to make the discovery by mankind as almost inevitable; but coincidence *must* have led to a mixture of the basic constituents in a fire which produced this valuable phenomena. Glass was born out of the earth through fire.

Helmut Federle, together with Gerold Wiederin, created a work in the form of the Pilgrim Chapel in Locherboden that, besides its religious significance, symbolises the origin of glass. In their monograph on this chapel, Jaques Herzog and Pierre de Meuron describe the seemingly raw glass fragments in the alcove in the rear wall as glass *in its original state*: "The pieces of glass light up in all colours: orange, green, violet, white and blue. Every fragment works as an individual lighting element. There are heavy pieces lying on top of one another, and small, delicate slivers like in diaphanous Gothic wall constructions with their intangible appearance. The light generated here is leaden and dark, light from the earth's core so to speak, from a cave, an underground gallery. Light, a blazing light, but one that is restrained with great vigour..."

The Expressionists of the early 20th century, who celebrated this new building material euphorically, promised us an all-embracing architecture with their pictorial reference to the rock crystal, an image that itself had been derived from the Gothic cathedral. Glass, the ancient primeval material, was able to give substance to the light of the new age that was dawning.

The image of the Gothic cathedral is one of rising upwards from the earth towards God in Heaven, and

Fig. 3: Coloured glass fragments as glass "in its original state"
Gerold Wiederin, Helmut Federle: Pilgrim Chapel, Locherboden (A), 1996

Fig. 5: Architectural use of glass
Pierre de Montreuil (attributed): Sainte-Chapelle, Paris (F), consecrated in 1246

Fig. 4: Expressionism
Bruno Taut: glass pavilion, Werkbund Exhibition, Cologne (D), 1914

the *architectural* use of glass is clearly visible here. The vertical sandstone structures are reduced to a minimum and the glazing gives the impression of a finer, crystallised image of the tracery framing it. We seem to be able to reach out and touch the light that penetrates the small panes of coloured glass, whereas the pointed arches of the stone structure almost crumble into the backlighting.

Glazed lattice, reflections

As described above, the use of glass in a church with Gothic tracery also represented an immense technological advance. Glass was being produced in huge quantities never envisaged before, and with the aid of a new technique, leaded lights, it could be made useful in the form of coherent panes. For the first time this valuable material, which so far had mainly been used as ornamentation, could establish itself as a veritable building material. The huge church windows also showed glass to be a *complementary building material* that gives the impression of a material counterweight to the massive wall. This led to the assumption that glass, like other building materials, is subject to the laws of *tectonics*. However, the tectonic relationship between the internal flow of forces and the external form, which is typical of most materials, cannot be proved to be similar in glass; for glass shows its inner workings *a priori*, or, in

the words of Carl Bötticher: "The artificial shape is the core shape. This means nothing more than that glass generally adopts each shape given to it and this shape cannot be incompatible with its nature. For this reason every attempt to describe glass in tectonic terms remains metaphorical."

On a microscopic level the surface of glass is finely notched. Glass is therefore a very brittle material and can accommodate hardly any tension and due to this fact it was only used for closing openings until the advent of toughened glass after the First World War. Exceptions were the glasshouses of the 19th century, which were designed in such a way that the glass in connection with the steel structure had a *fake*, stiffening effect. Due to the fact that in the 20th century it became possible to produce larger and larger panes of glass (at first in the form of industrially produced plate glass and from the 1950s onwards float glass) the demand for large-format panes grew as well. Glass was used quasi-structurally, mainly to form huge facade areas. As a result of the increasing use of glass, the massive, architectural object started to break up and more and more its core could be enclosed by a thin, transparent skin. Architecture presented itself in a new way, in a play of sparkling surfaces.

Very soon even the bracing elements of the glass facade were also made from glass. Italy, first and foremost, is famous for the huge expanses of glass that have become a popular means of expression in modern architecture. The architectural language that evolved incidentally made use of tectonic metaphors. Giuseppe Terragni's draft for the Danteum in Rome established the – up to now still unfulfilled – ideal of a sublimated architecture: the columns of this paradise are made of glass and carry a lattice of glass downstand beams which reflect only the sky…

One characteristic becomes obvious here, the one that distinguishes glass from all other building materials. In addition to the fact that we can see through glass, the glass surface also reflects our world. Or the surface steps back from its own body and the material – despite its transparency – awakens the impression of mysterious depth. These two phenomena seem to make glass a material without characteristics.

Science Fiction

Today, Terragni's ideal – a house made completely of glass – is conceivable from the technical point of view. Glass is no longer just for windows; it now can be produced and encoded according to specific requirements. It is quite probable that soon glass will become able to carry greater loads – through reinforcement with films or related technologies like ceramising – such that primary structural parts of buildings will become transparent. Since the 1950s this has been formulated and

Fig. 6: Synthetic building envelope
Palm house, Bicton Gardens, Budleigh Salterton (UK), c. 1843

Fig. 7: Prismatic form and the play of reflections
Ludwig Mies van der Rohe: project for a high-rise building, Friedrichstrasse, Berlin (D), 1919

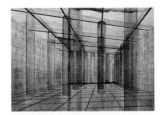

Fig. 8: Dematerialised lattice
Giuseppe Terragni: Danteum project, Rome (I), 1938–40

Fig. 9: Just a pavilion!
Glasbau Hahn: Frankfurt (D), 1951

implemented on the scale of the pavilion. Taking into consideration the fact that facade technology has already formulated similar objectives, there is no obstacle to stop the construction of the "all-glass" house. The sublimation of the building envelope will then be nearly complete. In this futuristic scenario it will be possible to realise every imaginable function of the facade with the aid of a sequence of different film layers. As glass can also direct light it might be possible to transform the building itself into an information medium, leading to a complete blurring of the boundaries between the virtual or media world and our physical world.

The total-media-experience glass building could transmit moods *unnoticed* through the optic nerve. But there is a problem: as in the movie "The Matrix" (1999) we would exist in a virtual space in which our needs would be seemingly satisfied while our physical environment could be truly miserable. If the "all-glass" building could be made *habitable*, e.g. by using carpets (which would be a real challenge for us architects), the futuristic scenario of total-media-experience architecture described above would itself become perverted because it would mark the end of architecture; we would be left solely with mood design, with synthetic films as information media. I can imagine a self-polymerising layer of synthetic material with corresponding optoelectronic characteristics which could be applied to any background in the form of a spray.

The near future

Maybe there will be a new chance for the glass brick. Nowadays, glass is widely used as an insulating material in the form of glass wool or cellular (foam) glass. Thanks to modern production processes it is possible to manufacture complex building elements in several operations at acceptable prices – if architectural added-value can be marketed. So why should – from the technical point of view – a structural, insulating, shaped composite brick not be feasible?

Further reading
- *Archithese* 6/96 "In Glas", Zurich, 1996.
- Sophia Behling (ed.): *Glas, Konstruktion und Technologie in der Architektur*, Munich, 2000.
- Jan Hamm (dissertation): *Tragverhalten von Holz und Holzwerkstoffen im statischen Verbund mit Glass*, EPFL, Lausanne, 2000.
- Ulrich Knaack: *Konstruktiver Glasbau*, Cologne, 1998.
- Thomas Kretschmer, Jürgen Kohlhoff (ed.): *Neue Werkstoffe*, Berlin, 1995.
- Elena Re: *Transparenza al limite*, Florence, 1997.
- Siegmar Spauszus, Dieter Schnapp: *Glas allgemeinverständlich*, Leipzig, 1977.
- Christian Schittich et al.: *Glass Construction Manual*, Basel, Boston, Berlin, 1999.
- Nicola Stattmann, Dieter Kretschmann (ed.): *Handbuch Material Technologie*, Ludwigsburg, 2000.
- Otto Völckers: *Bauen mit Glas*, Stuttgart, 1948.
- Gerold Wiederin, Helmut Federle, Kunsthaus Bregenz (pub.): *Nachtwallfahrtskapelle Locherboden*, Stuttgart, 1997.
- Michael Wigginton: *Glas in der Architektur*, Stuttgart, 1996. – English translation: Michael Wigginton: *Glass in Architecture*, London, 2002.

Plastic

Roland Barthes

Although the names of some plastics (polystyrene, poly-vinyl, polyethylene) might remind us more of a one-eyed Greek shepherd, plastic is essentially an alchemistic substance. Recently, there was an exhibition dedicated to the whole gamut of plastic products. At the entrance the visitors waited patiently in a long queue to view the magic process *par excellence*, the remodelling of matter. An ultimate machine, an elongated arrangement with a large number of tubes (an ideal form to bear witness to the mysteriousness of a long journey), easily turned out glossy, fluted bowls from a pile of greenish crystals. On one side the tellurium material – on the other side the perfect artefact. And between the two extremes: nothing. Nothing but a journey, supervised by an employee wearing a peaked cap – half god, half robot.

Plastic is not so much a substance as the notion of infinite remodelling. It is, like its ordinary name indicates, the omnipresence that has been rendered visible. And that is exactly why it is a truly miraculous substance – the miracle being a sudden conversion of nature every time. And plastic is infused with this astonishment: it is not so much an item as the trace of a movement.

Since this movement here is almost infinite and converts the original crystals into a quantity of ever more surprising objects, plastic is basically a spectacle that has to be deciphered: the spectacle of its final products. Looking at all the different final shapes (a suitcase, a brush, a car body, a toy, fabrics, tubes, bowls or plastic film), the matter presents itself unceasingly as a picture puzzle in the mind of the observer. This is due to the total versatility of plastic: we can use it to form buckets as well as pieces of jewellery. That's why we are constantly astonished by and are constantly dreaming of the proliferation of the material, in view of the connections we are amazed to discover between the single source and the multiplicity of its effects. It is a happy astonishment since mankind measures its power by the range of possible conversions, and plastic bestows on us the euphoria of an enchanting glide through nature.

But there is a price to be paid for this, and that is that plastic, sublimated as a movement, hardly exists as a substance. Its constitution is negative: it is neither hard nor deep. In spite of its usefulness it has to be content with a neutral quality of substance: resistance – a condition that demands infallibility. It is not fully accepted within the order of the "big" substances: lost between the elasticity of rubber and the hardness of metal it does not attain one of the true products of the mineral order: foam, fibre, plates. It is a congealed substance. Regardless of its particular state it keeps its flaky appearance, something vague, creamy and solidified – an inability to attain the triumphant smoothness of nature. But above all it gives itself away by the noise it makes, that hollow, weak tone. Its sound destroys it; just like its colours, for it seems only

to be able to retain the markedly chemical ones: yellow, red, green, and it keeps only the aggressive side of them. It uses them just like a name which is only in the position to show shades of colours.

The popularity of plastic bears witness to a development regarding the myth of imitation. As is well known, imitations are – from the historical point of view – a middle-class tradition (the first clothing imitations date from the early years of capitalism). Up to now, however, imitation was always pretentious, was part of the world of simulation, not application. Imitation aims to reproduce cheaply the most precious substances: precious stones, silk, feathers, fur, silver – all the world's luxurious glory. Plastic does without this, it is a household substance. It is the first magic matter that is ready for ordinariness, and it is ready because it is precisely this ordinariness that is its triumphant reason for existence. For the first time the artificial aims at the ordinary, not the extraordinary. At the same time the ancient function of nature has been modified: nature is no longer the idea, the pure substance that has to be rediscovered or has to be imitated; an artificial substance, more abundant than all the world's deposits of raw materials, plastic replaces them all, even determines the invention of shapes. A luxury item is always linked with the earth and always reminds us in an especially precious way of its mineral or animal origin, of the natural subject of which it is only a topical image. Plastic exists for being used. Only in very rare cases are items invented just for the pleasure of using plastic. The hierarchy of substances has been destroyed – a single one replaces them all. The whole world could be plasticised and even living matter itself – for it seems that plastic aortas are already being produced.

"Plastic" (1957)
Excerpt from: Roland Barthes: *Mythologies*, Paris, 1957

Glass, the opaque building material
On the contradictions in glass

Christoph Elsener

Of all the materials used in building, glass is the most contradictory. It is, on the one hand, a solid and durable material, but on the other, it is extremely fragile and breakable; glass can be as secure as an armoured tank, but sometimes all it needs is a snowball to break it. Glass is available in so many different qualities and products that an overview is barely possible. Just what is glass? What do we see when we look at it, or through it? Is glass the material without properties, only taking on a character through the materials opposite it?

The myth of transparency

Glass is the promise of our modern society. It is clear and pure, stands for cleanliness and transparency, and for the dissolution of the massive, dark walls of the pre-industrial age. Light and transparency are the glass-related aspects of a healthy society in which we can review and collaborate in the political processes, in which the members of that society can watch each other's lives through the glass display windows of the department stores and the glass screen of the television. Glass has become the symbol of the open society and its transparency thus a synonym for democracy. But glass is anything but transparent, and when we take a closer look, the symbolism of transparency all too quickly associated with glass is in fact deceptive, a fundamental mistake with serious consequences.

Glass is not transparent

In the majority of cases in which we meet glass in architecture, it is not simply transparent, but rather a shiny, reflective surface which also usually appears dark. The glass of the windows in their openings in our masonry urban settings are blind surfaces with a lighter or darker reflection of the sky. The glass facades of the post-war modern age are highly polished mirrors that reproduce their surroundings and are in no way those highly transparent, highly praised, invisible enclosing elements their architects probably really thought them to be. Nevertheless, under certain conditions glass is indeed transparent.

Our perception of glass

When we look at glass, we perceive either that which is in front of or behind the glass; surprisingly, the glass itself generally plays no role. Glass is therefore what its surface reflects or what we see through it. Reflection and depth are the two poles of the perception spectrum of glass. It is transparent to the same extent as the space behind the glass is light. If the glass appears transparent with a backlight, its opacity increases as the space behind the glass grows darker, and the smooth surface of opaque glass reflects the light in front of it like a mirror.

Fig. 10: The glass of the windows appears dark

Fig. 11: Two levels of images mingle on the surfaces of the glass
Richard Estes: "Teleflorist", 1974, oil on canvas, 91 x 132 cm

Reflections

Glass is therefore primarily a reflective material and transparency is only a secondary feature. Two levels of images are mixed on the surface of the glass: the image of the space visible behind the glass and the image of the reflection of the space in front of it. These two images – in each case existing on the inner and the outer surfaces of the glass – become superimposed to form one single image in which one of the images dominates, depending on the relationship between the light levels on either side of the glass. Our eyes are able to perceive the two images separately, but the superimposition blurs the spaces in front of and behind the glass – we get a single impression of a constantly moving space. Let us briefly consider the modern movement: does not this impermeable, environs-distorting, space-dissolving feature of the glass correspond to the image of a complex modern movement as the ideal of a pure, transparent and therefore democratic society? Is therefore the reflection and not the transparency the symbol of the modern movement? Is its true identity the space lost in the reflection and its resolution?

Reflection studies

Ludwig Mies van der Rohe studied the expressive forms of glass using models for his "glass tower project", and recorded them in photographs. A relatively horizontal line of sight allows us to see through the storeys to the light-coloured model facades of its neighbourhood; the glass facades are transparent and light. If we allow our viewing point to wander downwards, our view is interrupted by the suspended floors in shadow, the glass tower becomes dark and its enclosing envelope is only transparent at those points where the sky can be seen between the ends of the floor slabs. In the beautiful outline study and the famous perspective views of the "Friedrichstrasse glass tower project", glass – the "transparent" material – is ironically represented by black outlines in charcoal and pencil.

So glass generally appears opaque and dark when it is used as the facade material for buildings deep on plan. In open-plan buildings such as Philip Johnson's Glass House or Mies's Farnsworth House, the glass remains transparent only because the depth of the building and the undivided interior space permit a view through the building even when viewed at an angle. However, we cannot conclude that narrow, glazed open-plan layouts automatically generate transparent buildings; for there are other factors, like the quality of the glass itself, the nature of the facade construction or the sunshades that have a major effect on the appearance of glass buildings.

Fig. 12: Transparent under certain conditions
Ludwig Mies van der Rohe: glass tower, project, unknown location, photo of model, 1922

Fig. 13: Dark body with transparent corners
Ludwig Mies van der Rohe: study of reflections for the glass tower, around 1922

Fig. 14: The transparent glass tower illustrated with opaque charcoal
Ludwig Mies van der Rohe: outline study for a glass tower
Charcoal, Conté pencil and pencil on paper, mounted on card, 138.5 x 83.2 cm

Opaque glass buildings

Having realised that glass buildings are not automatically transparent, we can now discover further fascinating, "aesthetic" properties of glass. From the 1950s to the 1970s, the colour of glass and its reflective properties expressed the architecture of business to such an extent that the observer could be forgiven for thinking it was necessary to compensate for the non-transparent glass buildings of the pre-war years. That prime model for the glass post-war modern movement that encircled the globe, Lever House by Skidmore Owings & Merrill, is a greenish, shimmering block reflecting the neighbouring buildings

Fig. 15: Transparent space
Philip Johnson: Glass House, New Canaan, Connecticut (USA), 1949 (Ezra Stoller © Esto)

Fig. 16: Glass is at first glance reflective and only sometimes transparent after taking a second look.
Walter Gropius: Bauhaus Dessau (D), 1925–26

Fig. 17: Grid-like glass facade
Skidmore Owings & Merrill: Lever House, New York (USA), 1952

with plain spandrel panels clad in opaque, coloured glass. The icon of glass grid facade architecture, which Lever House is regarded to be, has little in common with the transparent tower model of Mies van der Rohe.

Shine and value

The extremely smooth surface of glass, any depressions in which are smaller than the wavelength of visible light, is what gives glass its shine. The fascination for reflective materials is found in countless things: in the sparkling of traditional jewellery, the intense shimmer of polished natural stone, also in the desire for high-gloss finishes on modern motor cars. But we are also happily blinded by the reflected light: glass is not the expensive natural product it seems to be – glass is an industrial substitute and, like the glass pearls of the conquistadors or the synthetic crystals in the displays of jewellers' shops, it is a relatively inexpensive substitute. If the shine is also real, then as in every reflection there is still a degree of pretence.

Nevertheless, glass facades are comparatively to very expensive components; in the end the industrially produced glass pane is only one small part of an elaborate glass facade construction system. In modern investment architecture, "shining" is what the use of glass promises – a never-fading radiance of elegance and nobility.

Views by day and night

If glass buildings are essentially opaque during the day, their internal workings become fully visible during the hours of darkness, at least when the interior lighting is on. Night-time views, which in recent years have become increasingly popular certainly because of our disappointment with the reflective glass of the daytime, compensate for the invisible during the day and unreservedly turn such glass buildings virtually inside-out. So the myth of the transparent glass building "functions" after all, even if

the sign has to be reversed. The principle responsible for the property that glass becomes transparent only when the space behind it is lit, and, consequently, reflective when the space behind the glass is dark, of course also applies to the interiors at night; their glazed openings become mirrors and prevent a view of the night-time world outside. As we switch off our artificial lights, more and more of our surroundings gradually become visible in the dark.

Living under glass, glass from inside

In the dark, glass facades can provoke a feeling in occupants of "being on display", which calls for control measures to ensure some degree of privacy. Another advantage of this is that the night-time reflections are hidden, which have an increasingly dominant effect on the character of the interior as the size of the window increases. The unpleasant recognition that the reflections make it impossible to establish whether someone is watching from outside is similar to an interrogation situation in a room fitted with one-way mirrors. Curtains and shutters therefore

Fig. 18: View by day
Norman Foster Associates: offices of Willis Faber & Dumas, Ipswich (UK), 1971–75

Fig. 19: View by night
Norman Foster Associates: offices of Willis Faber & Dumas, Ipswich (UK), 1971–75

Fig. 20: Night-time reflection of the interior, film scene
Sophia Coppola: "Lost in Translation", 2003

came about through the desire to prevent a view of the interior from the outside as well as to cut out the night-time reflective effect; their function as sunshades and thermal insulators (which can be fulfilled only to a limited extent on the inside of the glass) was probably less important originally.

The radicality of the completely transparent house contradicts the human need to be able to withdraw – be it at work or at home, even if some changes in this respect are evident in the age of television, exhibitionism and totally glazed detached houses. Even Mies van der Rohe's design for Edith Farnsworth's weekend retreat did not include curtains on the inside of the glass and used wooden fittings in the kitchen and bathroom to create areas with different degrees of openness.

Glass must be protected
against the properties of glass

Glass can be used successfully in architecture only when it is combined with accompanying measures. The fact that such measures in turn jeopardise the motivation for using glass in the first place is yet another fundamental contradiction of this material: glass must be protected against the properties of glass. Apart from the hard-to-control transparency phenomena, the use of glass also involves energy gains, which without suitable measures would make living under it impossible. Such measures concern the quality of the glass itself (low E glass, solar-control glass, patterned glass) as well as features of the building envelope (fixed and movable sunshades) and, of course, the building services (ventilation and air-conditioning systems). These measures compensate for the energy consequences that go hand in hand with the use of glass, sometimes at great expense, and

also have a crucial influence on the architecture of glass buildings.

Another "natural" disadvantage of glass is its fragility. Glass can break as a result of external circumstances but also through inherent, unseen stresses. In order to reduce the fragility of glass and ensure that, when it does break, there are no sharp splinters, various processes and subsequent test procedures are necessary. Glass is hardened, prestressed and/or bonded to plastic sheets to form a composite material, which again can affect its aesthetic properties. Similar processes can be used to make glass fire-resistant. These processes improve the quality of the glass and in many cases its use in building is only possible thanks to them. However, each of these measures affects the price, which means that a glass facade tailored to the specific needs of a project by way of several treatment methods becomes the most expensive form of facade construction.

The cleaning of glass is also a cost factor that is underestimated and hence becomes another disadvantage of glass. In order to preserve the effect of glass both optically and aesthetically, it must be cleaned regularly. Although properly cleaned glass is an inexpensive material in the long term because of its almost limitless durability, the short-term costs for facade cradles and building maintenance are often the decisive criteria. Self-cleaning glasses originally developed to improve the safety of car windscreens promise cheap convenience here.

The durability of glass is sometimes severely limited by the various treatment and refining processes. The more the characteristics of this durable material are determined by "foreign" substances, the more these substances govern the service life of glass. Coatings can become cloudy or matt, or the gas filling can escape from insulating units

Fig. 21: Exploiting the advantages, avoiding the disadvantages
Glass with sunshades of timber battens

Fig. 22: What colour is glass?
Vehicle windows with black borders

because of an edge seal that has become permeable over the years.

The colour of glass

In order to do justice to the myth of the invisible transparency, glass should actually be clear and colourless. However, the production of such "extra-clear" glass is expensive, which is why modern glass – after the period of experimentation with reddish, yellowish and bronze shades – generally has a greenish, bluish, greyish tint. The reason is that these colours exhibit a lower light permeability, and for reasons of cost the glass industry prefers to limit itself to a few, more effective colours. As the float glass method became established, the production of glass became much more expensive compared to the hitherto widely used drawing, casting and rolling methods.

In addition to the reflective effect, which makes glass visible in the first place, colour is another factor we can use to make glass visible. The allegedly invisible glass can be perceived via its shade of colour, which has a major influence on the expression of its application. The colouring is influenced by coatings and plastic sheets, which increase the reflections and expand the range of colours, and by the modern practice of double and triple glazing, which intensify and darken the colouring.

So what is the colour of glass? Is it green like the majority of glass products? Is it colourless, or rather "extra-clear", as promised by the myth? Or is it kaleidoscopic because its reflective properties allow it to reflect the changing colours of the day and the seasons? Is not the sum of all colours, the average of all the colours of glass, black? At least black is the colour used most commonly when the aim is to simulate or provide a substitute for glass: black preformed gaskets seal, inconspicuously, the gap between edge of glass and frame, black silk-screen printing laminates and protects the adhesives used on stepped glass or car windows and suggests, discreetly, on the outside the optical enlargement of what is effectively perceived internally as a smaller glass component.

Coatings, the reflective glass as a mirror

In the course of unceasing efforts to improve the physical and building physics properties of glass, i.e. its permeability to light and heat radiation plus its hardness and durability, and following optimisation of the production process and hence the glass itself, attention has also been given to the treatment and refinement processes that extend the spectrum of glass types. In addition to colouring the glass itself, coatings have been applied to the surface of the glass so that the relationship between transmission values and degrees of reflection can be better regulated. Modern surface coatings extend from almost invisible, ultra-thin vapour-deposited single

coatings to combinations of several coatings and plastic sheets in order to achieve the desired performance for a glass or glazing unit. Depending on their quality and thickness, coatings can alter the transparency and reflectiveness of the inner and outer glass surfaces from a material permeable to light and heat in both directions to a one-sided "polished glass".

As the degree of reflection on a glass building increases, so the view of the interior decreases, the interior and hence the internal image plane of the facade becomes less and less visible. In terms of the complexity of its expression, the facade is reduced by one layer and the effect of depth is lessened (at least during the day). This makes it appear thinner and the volume it encloses harder, more withdrawn and hence perhaps also more solid.

Adding reflective coatings to glass that is reflective anyway may sound like whiter-than-white washing powder. But in fact the reflective coating increases the reflective effect exponentially, although not to the extent that the glass becomes a type of "super mirror", but rather by excluding all further transparency effects that compete with the reflections. The climax of this reflectivity is architecture dissolved into its environment because all it does is reflect its surroundings; architecture without properties made from a material without properties.

Coatings and plastic sheets now determine the properties of glass to such an extent that the original glass seems to be turning into a mere backing material for these treatments; untreated glass is not used in building, at least not to the extent we would expect. How long can we go on talking about glass when the properties responsible for its choice are generated by some other

Fig. 23: Reflections, glass, grid – the architecture of the 20th century?
Arne Jacobsen: offices for Jespersen & Son, Copenhagen (DK), 1953–55, and neighbouring buildings

Fig. 24: Reflections of the surroundings cause the building itself to disappear
Johnson/Burgee: Garden Grove Community Church, Los Angeles (USA), 1978–80

material? For how long will we still go on using glass as a substrate?

The glass system

Although at the start of its manufacture glass is a fluid material, it is nevertheless impossible to mould on the building site. The production of glass for building work calls for an elaborate industrial process without which glass in its present form would be unthinkable. Glass is part of an extensive, interrelated system of production, post-production, transport and erection, and, partly determined by this system, a classic product of prefabrication. The series and the right angle were the determining factors up to the introduction of computer-controlled machines, the grid facade of international business architecture the synonym for its expression. In addition, the glass system depends on other systems – the development of window and metalworking technology always keeps pace with the technical developments in glass and offers the market those components and accessories without which it would be impossible to use glass in and on buildings.

Completely untreated single panes of glass are used today at best as a replacement for broken windows in old buildings or in interior fitting-out works. The vast majority of all glass applications now involve bonded laminated glasses or gas-filled insulating glasses with two or more pretreated or vapour-deposition coated glass panes. Silver, reflective glass webs hold these in place and black compounds or gaskets seal the units. Advantageously, all these components have been coordinated with each other during the development stage. This is what makes the system sensible; but on the other hand, it shows that the planners are themselves a part of this system and not vice versa. The glass facade system has meanwhile become so complex that facade consultants now act as mediators between architects and contractors.

Limited choice of glass despite technical progress

The technical developments in glass have resulted in an apparently infinite diversity of glass qualities. However, this choice is severely limited when we become involved with the specific task of using glass on a facade. As some glass qualities, including some from the late 20th century, are already out of date, the range of glasses is sometimes reduced even further to a very modest selection (with hardly any differences between the various types) once the specific safety and energy regulations are known. This restriction has to be made compatible with the remaining options of the proportions and formats of the panes and the configuration of the metal or timber assemblies that are always necessary in one form or another, with the "customisation" through printing, lighting or by introducing the third dimension into the two-dimensional facade.

Fig. 25: Shimmering kaleidoscope
Barkow Leibinger: Trutec Building, Seoul (ROK), 2006

Barkow and Leibinger achieved a shimmering, kaleidoscopic effect on the facade of the Trutec Building in Seoul by arranging two different glass qualities within a simple principle consisting of two modules. One flat element and another that projects 200 mm, each with transparent and translucent polished glass, create a complex play of exasperating reflections through regular variation, alternating with a 180° rotation.

Deceptive material

The desire to be able to master the technical potential and the forms of expression of glass permanently, including beyond the production process, would seem to be possible with switchable glass, which is being developed for the automotive industry and at some stage will become available for buildings. Controlled automatically by a computer program or manually "at the touch of a button", an electric current can be applied to the glass to change its colour from light to dark and thus influence its permeability to light and energy; such technology could eventually make the sunshades necessary today redundant. Another system allows the degree of transparency to be altered from transparent to opaque by applying an electric current to an opaque liquid-crystal film embedded between two PET membranes with an electrically conductive coating and two panes of glass. Increasingly, glass seems to be becoming an all-rounder, but as we play around with its abilities individually, the more difficult it becomes to exercise control in the design process – difficult at the best of times.

Fig. 26: Flat glass placed at an angle
Barkow Leibinger: Trutec Building, Seoul (ROK), 2006

Fig. 27: Already common in the cinema: switchable glass, transparent or opaque
AIDS sufferer Andrew Beckett (Tom Hanks) appears before the board, a scene from "Philadelphia", 1993

Glass dissolved

The inherent tendency of glass to dissolve its surroundings does not stop at the glass itself. Just how far can we go with the tireless advance in the physical dissolution of the space-enclosing masonry wall into the thin glass wall? Just how thin can an enclosing envelope be? Just how thin and how unreflective can glass be before it disappears? Plastic sheets seem to be leading glass down a path, the end of which marks its dissolution and an (almost) dematerialised state, which has apparently accompanied the dream of glass since time immemorial. In building greenhouses for plants, where a less demanding relationship between light and heat gains is permitted (and desired) than in housing and office projects, plastic membranes and membrane cushions are already being widely used. It is to be expected that plastic membrane products with cavities filled with specific gases will soon take over further tasks where, currently, glass products are the only solution. After glass has dissolved the interior space, it itself dissolves into space.

Extremely heavy lightweight glass

Glass is lighter than aluminium. However, as it breaks easily, it must be employed in adequate thicknesses, which for large expanses of glass or in the form of double and triple glazing produces a surprisingly heavyweight assembly. Even small glass formats can weigh so much that the work required for the surrounding components is considerable and, for example, the window frames of conventional windows with two opening lights are quite chunky and have to be fitted with the most efficient hardware. Owing to the weight of the glass, and of course its format, the erection of glass facade components calls for considerable logistics efforts and expense because each element has to be lifted into place with a crane between the scaffolding and the structural carcass before being adjusted, fixed and sealed simultaneously by several workers.

Such non-loadbearing glazing units attached to the edges of the suspended floors are known as "suspended facades", or more usually "curtain walls", which tends to

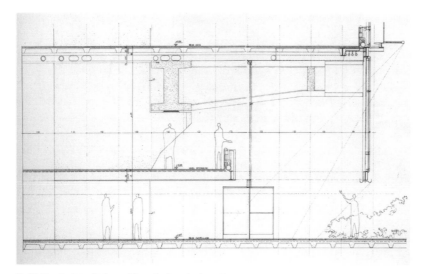

Fig. 28: Megastructure with glass curtain: section through entrance foyer
Francisco Javier Sáenz de Oiza: Banco de Bilbao, Madrid (E), 1971–78

Fig. 30: Horizontal bands of metal and glass forming a striped enclosure with off-centre seam
Francisco Javier Sáenz de Oiza: Banco de Bilbao, Madrid (E), 1971–78

Fig. 29: The weight hanging here is immense: the lightweight-looking "hem" of the facade cladding
Francisco Javier Sáenz de Oiza: Banco de Bilbao, Madrid (E), 1971–78

make us think of a lightweight, enclosing fabric rather than a bulky, heavyweight, brittle material. This further apparent contradiction linked with glass forces architects repeatedly to take up a new position in the field of tension between building structure and glass cladding. In his design for the Banco de Bilbao in Madrid, Francisco Javier Sáenz de Oiza has tried to represent a textile, soft, movable, suspended fabric in the facade design. He wraps the glass together with the cleaning walkways around the powerful concrete structure, rounded off at the corners, and closes the curtain with a distinct, slightly off-centre seam running the full height of the building. It looks like a dress done up with a zip, the bottom of which hangs down into the recessed entrance area and is finished off with a metal "bead" designed as a rainwater gutter. This is indeed a "hem", and to maximise its effect, the facade hangs so low that tall visitors intuitively dip their heads when passing underneath. Or are they are simply aware of how much weight is hanging over their heads?

Loadbearing glass: the sum of all contradictions?

One great motivating factor in architecture is making something appear lighter than it really is. In the end, the dissolution of the mass is one of the driving forces in the development of architecture, and what could be more helpful in this respect than "transparent" glass? Timber and metal constructions required to support the glass can only be reduced to a certain minimum, and the obvious step to the completely "visual" dissolution is to use glass for the loadbearing members as well. Since the 1980s, considerable developments have been witnessed in this constantly booming market but there has never been a real breakthrough. "Structural glazing" has replaced frames and gaskets, vertical glass fins perpendicular to the surface of the glass facade accommodate the wind forces, removing all restrictions to opening up the space. Glass columns and loadbearing glass walls dissolve the horizontal constraints completely in order to remove all limits to space via glass stairs, glass floors and glass roofs in the vertical direction as well.

But glass cannot free itself from its contradictions even when used exclusively. And even if these contradictions do not proliferate, the totally glass building is nevertheless the image of the sum of all the contradictions inherent in glass. The glass house remains, if we close with the terms of the dreams of crystalline architecture, a "natural fantasy".

Further reading
- Neundlinger, Klaus: *Einübung ins Aufbegehren. Ein Beitrag zur Materialgeschichte des Glases*, Vienna, 2005.
- Pfammatter, Ulrich: *In die Zukunft gebaut*, Munich, 2005.
- Quetglas, Josep: *Der gläserne Schrecken. Mies van der Rohes Pavillon in Barcelona*, Basel, 2001.
- Wiggington, Michael: *Glass in Architecture*, London, 1996.

Plastic on the threshold of architecture

Katharina Stehrenberger

Both the architect Gottfried Semper[1] and the philosopher Roland Barthes[2] describe plastic as something that is constantly in motion, something without form. This is a surprising description for a building material, and a statement in which we detect both fascination and mistrust. And this ambivalence appears to accompany the development and use of this building material from its beginnings to the present day.

The readiness for experimentation with plastics that began around 1950 is explained not only by the state of research at that time, but also by the socio-political background. Following the stagnation during the years of World War 2, it was now time to look to the future again. This positive underlying mood generated a social euphoria that was accompanied by a strong belief in technical progress. Standing on the threshold of the exploration of space and weightlessness, the properties of this new type of material, plastic, seemed to be ready to make a contribution to the world of the future.

The search was helped by an open and positive attitude towards this building material, and represented a new, 100% plastic world with a material homogeneity that permeated the entire building inside and outside. A bold vision was delivered by R. Buckminster Fuller in 1960, which he called a "hypothetical geodesic dome for New York City". "Spaceship Earth", as Fuller called our planet, expressed all the promises of this new material: the project appeared like a giant glass cheese dome over Manhattan, was futuristic, transparent, and apparently endless and seamless. It was not only the transparency that fascinated the pioneers; it was also its unrestricted mouldability and the associated possibility of unlimited space-formation. During an early development phase, the chemicals company Monsanto Ltd. produced the prefabricated Monsanto "House of the Future" in which the dreams of organic forms became reality. Both the house-like clover leaf and the UFO-like "Futuro" après-ski

Fig. 33: Plastic carries artificial, transparent and futuristic associations
R. Buckminster Fuller: hypothetical geodesic dome over New York City (USA), 1960

Fig. 34: The world's first mass-produced plastic house
Matti Suuronen: "Futuro" après-ski hut (FIN), 1968

hut by Matti Suuronen employed this mouldable material with skill.

Despite the many experiments over a period of some two decades, many developments made from fibre-reinforced plastics never made it past the stage of unfinished prototypes. The possibility of using plastics for both load-bearing and enclosing functions quickly proved to be a purely theoretical option. The euphoria dissipated, and developments came to a temporary halt during the oil crisis of 1973. The sudden lack of raw materials, the embrittlement and yellowing when exposed to sunlight, the easy flammability, as well as their uncertain disposal put a stop to the exploration of plastics. An awareness of the limits of technology was now coupled with idealistic reservations.

It is only in recent years that the damaged image of plastic has been somewhat revised. This was helped both by the revival of the architectural language of the 1960s and 1970s, and by ongoing technical developments, which helped the material to shake off its murky past. But even though considerable improvements have been made on the visual side, the ecological aspects are still unsatisfactory: a building material that is based on crude oil – a finite resource – and is difficult to recycle remains a material at odds with the demands of sustainable building.

Fig. 31: Fire at Expo '67 in Montreal: the acrylic panels melted in just 15 minutes!
R. Buckminster Fuller (1895–1983) in collaboration with unknown architects: US Pavilion, Montreal (CAN), 1967

Fig. 32: The plastic clover leaf showed how we might live in the future.
Monsanto Ltd.: "House of the Future", prototype in Disneyland, 1957

In addition, the material has not really established any really new spatial or constructional design concepts in its entire history, a fact that would have been critical for the widespread use of this material in architecture. But if we drop the idea of using plastics for the structure *and* the enclosure, a diverse world of envelopes and cladding opens up.

Phenomenological assessment

Depending on the production method and the material composition, plastic can have a matt, rough or a shiny, smooth surface. This has visual and also haptic consequences. Both fibre-reinforced plastics and unreinforced plastics are characterised by a variable degree of translucency, fragility associated with the relative thinness of the material, and sheer limitless mouldability. Almost all factors can be influenced at will and are depend entirely on the desired final product. The spectrum of light permeability stretches from absolutely opaque to transparent, and can create the most diverse moods according to its colouring. For instance, the amber-coloured roof of hollow-box elements in Geislingen, designed by the structural engineer Heinz Isler, generates an almost sacred atmosphere. The translucent effect of plastics primarily depends on the light permeability of the material's molecules and not on the fibres, because correct production melts the fibres completely with the polymers. Whereas non-fibrous acrylic sheet achieves almost 100% transparency, fibre-reinforced plastics are cloudy at best.

All these properties lead to a certain affinity with glass – more direct than with the material's structural relatives, fibre-bonded materials made from wood or cement. Despite different manufacturing processes, different surface temperatures and different degrees of hardness, both plastics and glass are amazingly similar in their expression: both materials can call on a whole repertoire of forms and exploit their easily controllable light permeability. It is precisely because of these characteristics that they are optimum projection materials. "Everything is light and flies, everything is transparent and illuminated," is how Vittorio Magnano Lampugnani

Fig. 36: The rough surface remains visible in the injection-moulding method
Faserplast Rickenbach-Wil company: pipe segment

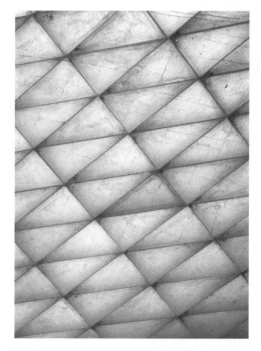

Fig. 37: Sacred effect of translucent hollow-box elements
Heinz Isler: roof, Geislingen (D), 1967

sums up one possible trend in today's architecture. He continues thus: "If we are not considering glass-roofed cities or aerodynamic houses, building complexes keep pace by way of colourful, shimmering, sometimes also talking and singing screen-type facades and multimedia walls."[3] What he is talking about implicitly here are the material properties of both building materials.

Origin and potential

The first experiments with plastics-type materials some 150 years ago were founded on purely vegetable or animal raw materials, such as tar, resin and linseed oil. The covering materials asphalt and linoleum, still used today, were the first "synthetic" products of those days. It was about 100 years after those first natural predecessors appeared that the first truly synthetic products were produced. Durable Bakelite, for example, inaugurated the era of heat-resistant plastics and hence opened up new tasks for the building industry. But the invention of polymers based on crude oil resulted in a veritable explosion in the development of plastics. Today, a built environment without plastics would be unthinkable, and the diversity of applications with reinforced and unreinforced products is almost infinite. For example, as a formless building material, unreinforced plastics can be used as binders or sealants. If aesthetic requirements are relevant, countless products are available for the internal linings or external cladding to buildings. But the greatest quantities of unreinforced plastics are certainly to be found in the concealed durable pipes and cables of building services.

Fig. 35: Shiny smooth skin
Angelo & Dante Casoni: motorway service station, Pratteln (CH), 1978

By contrast, in engineered structures, fibre-reinforced plastics are preferred. Engineers quickly discovered this corrosion-resistant material as a loadbearing envelope for industrial buildings or tower-like structures such as silos or chimneys, in which the beneficial properties of high strength and low weight are relevant. Fibre-reinforced composites can therefore be used as structural materials and exhibit a particular potential in this field. However, an insurmountable conflict arises: the combination of translucency and load-carrying capacity can be exploited, e.g. in the building envelope, for uninsulated components only because otherwise the light permeability is cancelled out, or at best severely restricted, when we add the thermal insulation. When using the material solely as a loadbearing structure, its transparency is also equally difficult to preserve because our modern regulations regarding protection from fire and failure generally demand the use of more resistant, opaque materials. Designing with fibre-reinforced plastics also means developing and using components prefabricated in a factory. The associated difficulties of individual adjustment on the building site increases the work involved in the design and planning process, and demands maximum precision from all participants.

If the comment by the Swiss engineer Heinz Hossdorf that "one litre of polyester is as expensive as a bottle of the best red wine"[4] is taken seriously, then using all relevant properties – load-carrying capacity, translucency, light weight – justifies the use of this expensive building material. It is therefore unsurprising that the developments with fibre-reinforced plastics have faltered, for all these reasons. As a result, the tendency is a shift from over-specified monomaterials to complementary systems in which the unreinforced plastic is used merely as a covering skin. But in the end it is the spatial structuring aspect that is interesting for architecture, and it clearly

plays a secondary role to the visual, phenomenological aspect, as will be seen in the following examples.

Constructional strategies

We distinguish between constructions with a stable or unstable form. Whereas the former retain their configuration permanently, the latter return to their previous form upon losing an external force action. Both single- and double-leaf constructions are to be found in both systems. The developments have been numerous and diverse since the early days, and extend from membranes stretched over frameworks to flexible cushion constructions and rigid sandwich panels. Whereas plastics constructions were once primarily structural, their use is increasingly in the non-structural areas of the building envelope. Nevertheless, there are currently still isolated structural uses that

Fig. 39: Manual skills despite innovative material
Heinz Isler: petrol station canopy, Thun (CH), 1962

often arise out of research projects. But these days it is primarily the phenomenological interest in the image of the semitransparent plastic that determines the construction. Although the new plastic envelopes with their scenic claims still continue to exploit the shaping properties of the material, they employ plastic more as a specific layer than as a universal building material.

Constructions with a stable form: examples

Heinz Isler's petrol station canopy in Thun combines architectural and engineering skills in one structure; the loadbearing structure itself determines and encloses the space. Totally in keeping with the typical tradition of engineered architecture, the translucent canopy exhibits a tendency to dissolve the mass, and pursues the age-old obsession of making the object appear lighter than it really is. This canopy of glass fibre-reinforced plastic (GFRP) built in 1962 has a maximum span of 9 m and consists of a double layer of prefabricated elements that were glued together to form a planar hollow-box slab measuring 14 x 22 m. A permanent connection was achieved by

Fig. 38: Folded-plate structure of glass fibre-reinforced plastic, one of the first structures designed by Renzo Piano
Renzo Piano: salt warehouse, Pomezia near Rome (I), 1966

adding a covering lamination on both sides. This lightweight canopy supported on eight steel columns still stands today; its once immaterial appearance has been severely spoiled, however, by a coat of paint that was added later.

The engineer Heinz Hossdorf designed a large roof with a seemingly sensual shell construction for Expo 1964 in Lausanne. The formal idea behind this exhibition pavilion stems from the image of a field of tulips in an open landscape. The glass-fibre membrane hanging low over the ground turns the two-dimensional roof into a tactile three-dimensional sculpture, the appearance of which makes it assume the language of tent construction with its unstable form. The use of the umbrella principle was developed in structural tests on models, and finally realised in a succession of prestressed hyperbolic paraboloid shells of GFRP measuring 18 x 18 m. The translucent and, at night, illuminated loadbearing construction of steel

Fig. 42: Lightness thanks to translucency
Heinz Isler: petrol station canopy, Thun (CH), 1962

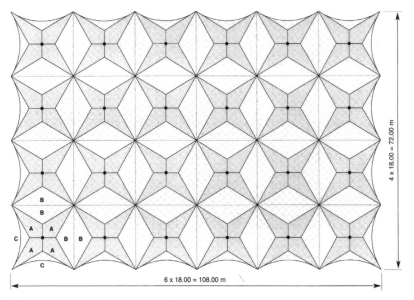

Fig. 40: Glass-fibre hoppers form a translucent spatial sculpture
Heinz Hossdorf: roof for Expo '64, Lausanne (CH), 1964

6 x 18.00 = 108.00 m

4 x 18.00 = 72.00 m

Fig. 41: Plan of the 24 roof segments made from fibre-reinforced plastic
Heinz Hossdorf: roof for Expo '64, Lausanne (CH), 1964

ribs and plastic shells was demolished on the last day of Expo 1964.

The motorway service station in Pratteln built in 1978 to a design by the architectural practice of Angelo & Dante Casoni has achieved cult status owing to its iconographic conciseness. Like virtually no other structure in Switzerland, the "beam" with its anthropomorphous and simultaneously abstract nature reflects the futuristic, technological *Zeitgeist* of the 1970s. A thermally insulating GFRP sandwich construction enabled the erection of an envelope made from elements with extremely thin walls. The rigid panels with their organic openings also satisfy the requirements for a self-supporting component, and were attached directly to the main structural steelwork without the need for any stiffening secondary framework. Recently refurbished, the original polychromatic design has been transformed by a homogeneous coat of paint.

The original idea behind the concept of Graz Art Gallery was called "Pin and Skin" and drew attention to the two main themes of the location of the structure and its distinctive envelope right from the competition stage. The biomorphic bubble structure of the approx. 40 x 60 m "friendly alien" designed by the architects Peter Cook and Colin Fournier seems to be like a living organism

Fig. 43: Prefabricated facade element made from fibre-reinforced plastic
Angelo & Dante Casoni: motorway service station, Pratteln (CH), 1978

Fig. 44: Iconographic architecture for fast consumption
Angelo & Dante Casoni: motorway service station, Pratteln (CH), 1978

obstinately snuggling against the cast-iron frame of the neighbouring historical building. The wall construction of this seemingly lightweight structure completed in 2003 is in the form of a translucent freely formed shell – a self-supporting sandwich construction, which would not have been possible without the close cooperation of the engineers at Ove Arup. Behind the bluish acrylic sheet enclosure there is a steel structure consisting of a shell construction resolved into individual members, which together with the cellular glass insulation, forms the core of the approx. 900 mm thick facade. Sixteen striking overhead openings, the "nozzles", allow daylight into interior; there are no other windows. The expressive architectural language of this Austrian centre of culture is a provocative interjection in the Baroque setting of this part of the city. In addition, the exotic nature of this structure is further

expressed through the multimedia façade, which can be used for all manner of displays.

Constructions with an unstable form: examples

"In the beginning there was the pneumatic tyre." This was the thesis that the German structural engineer Frei Otto took for his work on diverse membrane projects with an unstable form. Together with other pioneers of tension structures, he developed curving stressed-skin constructions using lightweight textiles, in some cases reinforced with plastics.

The membrane roofs for the Olympic Games facilities in Munich, built between 1967 and 1972 to designs by the architectural practice of Behnisch & Partner and the two structural engineers Frei Otto and Heinz Isler, were

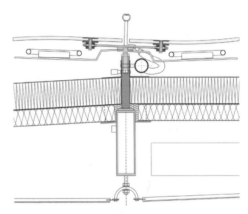

Fig. 45: The facade envelope is an impressive 90–100 cm thick
Peter Cook & Colin Fournier: art gallery, Graz (A), 2003

Fig. 46: Organic architectural form in a historical context
Peter Cook & Colin Fournier: art gallery, Graz (A), 2003

among the first tension structures of that period and exhibited some of the longest spans. The roofscape stretching across the Olympic Park, reminiscent of an abandoned sail, is a logical component in the park design and engages in a dialogue with the undulating landscape. The tent-like roofs are related to the ideals of Heinz Hossdorf's umbrella construction, while being totally different in terms of their constructional realisation. Owing to their complex structure and form, the membrane roofs could only be designed after tests on models. Methods were tried out in Heinz Isler's laboratory in Switzerland and by Frei Otto at the Institute for Lightweight Structures in Stuttgart. The tests finally resulted in a loadbearing structure of stable steel pylons, struts and a system of cable ties. This is the flexible framework for the overlying mesh of spring steel with its movable nodes. Finally, diamond-shaped panels of rigid acrylic sheet form the translucent roof covering providing protection against the weather.

Pneumatic structures, called air-inflated or air-supported domes, are the main group of membrane constructions with an unstable form. Double- or multi-skin membrane roofs prestressed by the internal air pressure can span over wide areas without the need for intermediate support. The US pavilion at Expo 1970 in Osaka had an air-filled membrane roof of PTFE-coated glass-fibre fabric that covered an area measuring almost 10,000 m². The shallow curvature of this roof is typical of such structures. The form of the air-filled cushions was ensured by a mesh of cables on the outside and a circumferential compression ring, which also provided stability. This pavilion, reminiscent of a giant airbed, not only set new standards in terms of size, it also played with the fascination of the seemingly

Fig. 48: Plastic membranes shape the roofscape; model of overall complex
Behnisch + Partner, with Frei Otto and Heinz Isler: Olympic Park, Munich (D), 1967–72

Fig. 49: Membrane structure for an arena without intermediate columns
Walter Bird, Sam Brody, Serge Cherayeff, Lewis Davis, David Geiger: air-inflated dome, Expo '70 in Osaka (J), 1970

ephemeral. This type of construction was soon taken up for warehouses, roofs to tennis courts and sports centres. However, the costs of maintaining the air pressure permanently were so high that such structures disappeared again after a few years.

The appearance of the Allianz Arena in Munich (completed in 2002), designed by the architectural practice of Herzog & de Meuron, is characterised by an envelope of air-filled cushions. In this case, however, it is not the interior that is filled with air and inflated, but rather the space between the two-layer membrane skin. The diamond-shaped cushions (each side 8 m long) consist of extremely stable 0.2 mm thick ETFE sheeting, which is very hardwearing, not readily flammable and, with a light permeability of 90%, virtually transparent. A framework

Fig. 47: Tent construction with covering of acrylic sheets
Behnisch + Partner, with Frei Otto and Heinz Isler: Olympic Stadium, Munich (D), 1967–72

of galvanised steel sections, which are in turn fixed to a reinforced concrete structure, serves as the support for the cushions. Artificial lighting is incorporated between the concrete loadbearing structure and the facade con-

struction, and it is this that sets the scene by turning the stadium into a giant coloured object in the landscape.

The watersports centre for the 2008 Olympic Games in Beijing designed by PTW Architects is inspired by the image of soap bubbles: the building envelope of stretched ETFE membranes is – on a metaphorical level – not unlike the expression of water with all its reflections, plays of light and air bubbles. The air-filled cushions reflect their immediate surroundings and at night serve as a screen for lighting effects and projection. The 3.7 m thick facade of "The Water Cube" National Aquatics Centre consists of a metal, apparently randomly arranged loadbearing construction plus the ETFE air cushions in their aluminium frames. But behind the seemingly chaotic structure there is a rigorous geometry like that inherent to natural systems such as crystalline, cellular or molecular structures. The total weight of this lightweight construction is only a fraction of that of an equivalent structure of steel and glass, and is therefore efficient and economic.

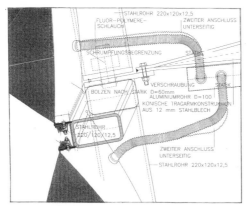

Fig. 50: Air supply and lighting for white ETFE cushions
Herzog & de Meuron Architekten: Allianz Arena, Munich (D), 2002

Fig. 51: Taut membrane cushions form the translucent envelope to the stadium
Herzog & de Meuron Architekten: Allianz Arena, Munich (D), 2002

Fig. 52: Air-filled cushions made from a plastic membrane on the roof of the stadium
Herzog & de Meuron Architekten: Allianz Arena, Munich (D), 2002

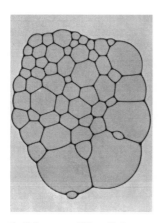

Fig. 53: Foam as a model for architecture; soap bubble formation

Summary

Synthetic building materials have established a place for themselves in contemporary architecture thanks to their diverse application options. Depending on their use, they can have a major impact on the appearance of architecture. But it is still uncertain as to whether this lightweight material will also give rise to a new style of architecture which – like the philosopher Peter Sloterdijk noted in his book *Schaum* (foam) in 2004 – can free itself from the traditional structural elements. Even though the projects of the pioneering days suggested such a course, the dynamic of the latest architectural examples is not generated by a new understanding of the constructional and spatial fundamental premises, but rather primarily by a graphic quality reduced to the external envelope. Plastics therefore meet the obviously virulent needs of contemporary architects to create a setting. A multimedia overstraining of our built environment could, however, lead to a surfeit, similar to the criticism of the growth of the concrete jungle in the cities during the 1970s. Nevertheless, this material with its soft, flexible nature embodies the idea of a dynamic yet ephemeral architecture like no other building material.

From the technical viewpoint, plastics exhibit a considerable potential for further development. The integration of solar cells, microsensors or conductive metals could turn the dream of the intelligent building envelope into reality within a few years. However, there are many disadvantages that speak against the use of plastics. The various environmental influences, their thermal and acoustic isolation, behaviour in fire, ageing process and, finally, the recycling issue are all questions that have not yet been answered satisfactorily.

Notes

[1] Gottfried Semper: Textile Kunst. Stoffe. Kautschuk, in: *Der Stil*, vol. I, 1860, pp. 112–19 (Engl. transl.: Gottfried Semper: *Style: Style in the Technical and Tectonic Arts; Or, Practical Aesthetics*, Harry Francis Mallgrave (ed.), Los Angeles, 2004).

[2] Roland Barthes: Plastik, in ibid.: *Mythen des Alltags*, Frankfurt a.M., 1964, pp. 79–81 (Engl. transl.: Roland Barthes: *Mythologies*, New York 1972, p. 97 et seqq.).

[3] Vittorio Magnano Lampugnani: 2. Telematik im Urbanen: von A wie Arbeiten bis W wie Wohnen, in: *Verhaltene Geschwindigkeit, Die Zukunft der telematischen Stadt*, Berlin, 2002, pp. 21 & 23.

[4] Elke Genzel, Pamela Voigt: Introduction, in: *Kunststoffbauten Teil 1, Die Pioniere*, Weimar, 2005, p. 8.

Fig. 54: Air-filled cushions made from a plastic membrane enable any form of facade design
PTW Architects: watersports centre for the 2008 Olympic Games, Beijing (CN), 2008

Building underground

Alois Diethelm

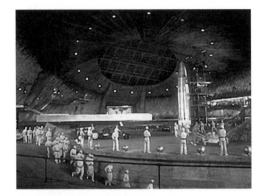

Fig. 1: A secret underground alternative world
Film set in "James Bond 007 – You Only Live Twice", 1967

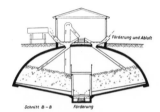

Fig. 2: From outside there is no hint of the existence of a subterranean space – the vault as a structurally ideal form
Swedish-style potato storehouse

Subterranean structures are all around us yet we hardly notice them– a situation that, depending on the circumstances, we find fascinating, matter-of-course or even objectionable. Because it is invisible, complete or partial lack of knowledge about an underground structure leads to suppositions about the actual conditions. We speculate about the city beneath the city as a living organism with the most diverse infrastructures, or in the form of traces of bygone times (e.g. Rome, as the result of destruction and reconstruction), and hope that "secret" structures such as fortifications and bunkers lie behind unassuming doors and hatches. At the same time, modern underground building work in Europe – and in Switzerland specifically – is an expression of a spatial expansion that attempts to preserve our familiar urban landscape. So in existing structures, whose architectural value is to be found not least in the interaction between the building and its external spaces, new space requirements are fulfilled with "invisible" i.e. subterranean, interventions. The same fate awaits those structures that are regarded by the general public as a "necessary evil", concessions to a modern way of life, e.g. basement garages.

What I shall try to do here is to assign the characteristics of underground structures to various categories: on the one hand, in terms of their relationship with the topography, and, on the other, according to the applied principles of creating enclosed spaces. I shall deal with the specific conditions, options and restrictions that accompany building underground. I shall repeatedly pose the following questions: "How do we experience the subterranean world?" "Which concepts are intrinsic to this?" "Where are additional measures required?"

The substructure in the superstructure

Today, in our latitudes every building activity, even those "purely" above ground, starts with an excavation. What we mean by doing this is to found the building on a frost-resistant material capable of carrying the weight of the construction. The easiest way of achieving this – and one which is linked with the advantage of creating additional space – is to provide a basement or a cellar. We dig out the ground to form a large pit and, in a first step, enable the construction of subterranean space according to the principles of building above ground. Effecting the design is the following distinction, whether the building fills the excavation completely, which means that of the sides of the excavation must be appropriately secured (e.g. timbering), or whether the building – even after completion – is positioned as an autonomous edifice detached from

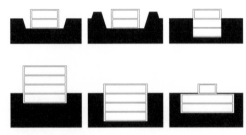

Fig. 4: Underground building in superstructure style
Top (from left to right): the excavation that remains open – with the spoil used to form an enclosing wall – excavation backfilled
Bottom: possible relationships between substructure and superstructure

the sides of the excavation, and so the subsoil exerts no pressure on the walls. The latter approach enables an identical form of construction to be used for both substructure and superstructure, and simultaneously simplifies natural ventilation and daylighting issues. The substructure component in the superstructure still poses the question of the relationship between the parts above and below ground. And this concerns not only the vertical component, which manifests itself in the number of storeys above and/or below ground, but also the horizontal expansion. In other words, we have a structure that, depending on the "depth of penetration", exhibits more or fewer basement storeys, but also a basement extending over a larger area than the storeys above. What we see at ground level is therefore frequently only a fraction of the entire structure – as if it were a submarine at anchor with only the conning-tower protruding above

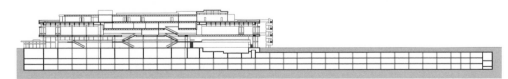

Fig. 3: The internal layouts of substructure and superstructure have developed independently of each other but still use a common column grid.
Roland Rohn: Hoffmann-La Roche staff accommodation, Basel (CH), 1971

Fig. 5: Trees indicating the extent of the
extension below ground
Tadao Ando: Vitra Seminar House, Weil (D), 1993

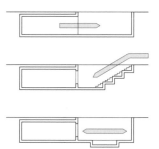

Fig. 6: Horizontal extensions
Relationships (from top to bottom): inside–outside –
outside–inside – centred

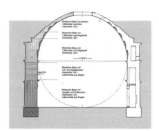

Fig. 7: Fictitious terrain build-up
by Pierre Zoelly
Pantheon, Rome (I), AD 118–128

the water. We can therefore assume that the majority of flat roofs are not be found on buildings but rather over apparently firm soil in the form of roads, plazas and gardens and in this way remain "invisible".

The relationship with the "overworld"

Subterranean space quickly reminds us of damp grottoes with gloomy lighting conditions. But are such images still relevant today when we consider modern methods of construction and contemporary architectural briefs? Only a few forms of use that are met with underground really have to take place underground. The possible reasons for going below ground level were mentioned in the introduction; mostly, they reflect the external perception desired (streetscape/landscape). In such cases the interior gains nothing extra for being underground. On the contrary, the reduced options for admitting daylight are regarded as a disadvantage. As a result, the type of lighting and the degree of contact with the outside world, or rather the world above ground, the "overworld", becomes a decisive criterion for contemporary subterranean structures.

Here, we see the contrast between overhead lighting through openings in the ceiling/floor above and lateral lighting through perforated walls. Interior spaces of any size may be positioned in front of these perforations – openings or walls completely "missing". The spectrum ranges from lightwells with minimum dimensions to larger external spaces that frequently are also accessible. The relationship between these external spaces and the "overworld" fluctuates between a mere visual link and a physically usable space continuum. Points of reference such as buildings, trees and people situated within the field of vision help us to grasp the subterranean external space for what it is, whereas the physically usable connection between "overworld" and "underworld" generates an interweaving of spaces – either with the aim of bringing the surroundings down below ground, or taking the subterranean use upwards into the streetscape or landscape. In contrast to lightwells, which – as their name suggests – merely serve to admit daylight, patio-type external spaces also bring the weather below ground and counteract the feeling of confinement often associated with underground buildings. We therefore question another aspect of our experience of underground spaces: the isolation – when an interior space is perceived as being unaffected by the weather, the seasons or other events. A good example is a military bunker, whose independence is further emphasised by having its own power supply. Recording studios and rehearsal facilities that have to be cut off from the outside world acoustically, or wine cellars in which a constant climate is vital, provide further examples. The consequences of excluding the outside world are mechanical ventilation and artificial light; the latter – like the provision

of rooflights – can also be regarded as intrinsic to the nature of subterranean spaces. But this applies to enclosed spaces above ground too and, generally, to all introverted spaces, something that Pierre Zoelly demonstrates impressively with his modified sectional drawing of the Pantheon, where he continues the terrain up to the oculus. So do we need traces of incoming water on the walls in order to experience the space below ground as subterranean?

Topographical concepts

Detaching ourselves from aesthetic or, indeed, even ideological aspects, building underground – like any other form of building – has its origins in mankind's need for shelter and protection. Protection from the vagaries of the weather (sunshine, rain, wind etc.) or other people or animals. Starting with the actual relevance of these dangers and taking into account the given topographical and

Fig. 8: A ramp links the underground entrance with the surrounding street level.
Renzo Piano, Richard Rogers: Centre Pompidou, Paris (F), 1977

geological conditions, the possibilities range from caves (natural, reworked or man-made) to depressions to soil-covered elevations.

Caves – the solid prehistoric huts

Natural caves or crags were shelters for humans that did not require any special skills to render them habitable. The spatial experience of the solid construction was therefore a solution that was associated with the need for shelter and protection long before humans had learned to use tools to work stone. Closures made from animal skins and woven twigs and branches, frequently reusable furnishings among nomadic peoples, were additions whose technologies (e.g. woodworking) gradually evolved to become significant components of simple construction methods. If caves had to be hollowed out first, the builders chose geological situations that promised easy working, although these usually involved materials with a lower strength. Even today then in constructing galleries and in some cases caverns we still use methods in which timber or steel assemblies are inserted or slid forward in line with progress underground to support the remaining subsoil. In the simplest case this involves strengthening the surface to prevent collapse.

Fig. 9: Exploiting the available topography
Ancient amphitheatre in Stratos (GR), c. 500 BC.

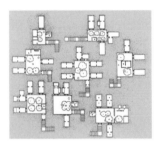

Fig. 10: Courtyards and stairs (1st floor)
Typical village, Xi-an region, China

However, in the case of loose or soft materials this can even become a temporary or permanent primary supporting structure which is replaced by or encased in a loadbearing concrete lining. Depending on the thickness of the material that separates the subterranean spaces from ground level, it is only a small step to open-cut or cut-and-cover working, in which a loadbearing structure is covered with soil only after being completed.

Basically, the cave represents that form of underground building for which the topography is only important in terms of access and, possibly, daylighting. It is frequently a by-product, e.g. in the extraction of natural resources, or is chosen because of climatic or acoustic conditions that are found only at a certain depth.

Depressions – a daylighting concept
Depressions can have connections to other spaces or form their own space. These latter spaces are those topographical depressions suitable for use as, for example, sleeping-places in the open air shielded from the wind – the most primitive form of human shelter. Amphitheatres, like the one in Stratos, exploit the natural, pitlike topography in order to create terracing for spectators with a minimum of reworking, with the floor of the "pit" becoming the stage, the arena. Man-made depressions represent another concept for introducing light and air into adjoining subterranean interior spaces, in some cases also providing access to these. The settlements in the Xi-an region of China with their sunken courtyards are an ideal example of the multiple use of depressions: they form an entrance courtyard for the adjoining chambers, provide these with daylight and also serve as communal areas or living quarters. These generously sized, normally square depressions are, like galleries, the starting point for horizontal space development which, through further excavation, enables the creation of further rooms at any time. It is therefore conceivable that rooms are initially excavated on just two sides, with the other two sides being used only when the need for more space or a growing family makes this necessary.

Viewed from above, Bernard Zehrfuss' extension to the UNESCO complex in Paris is nothing other than one of these aforementioned Chinese villages. Looked at more closely, however, we can see that the principles he has employed follow different functional, structural and urban planning concepts. Whereas in China the depressions mark the start of the building process, in the Zehrfuss concept they are merely undeveloped "leftovers". The UNESCO complex was built using conventional superstructure methods in a cut-and-cover procedure. If underground building is necessary for climatic reasons in some cases, in others it is the surrounding built environment that forces an "invisible" extension.

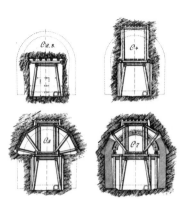

Fig. 11: Securing underground galleries with timber, enlarged upon provision of the lining
Tunnel cross-sections through Albula railway line in the Grisons (CH), 1903

The main building, which Zehrfuss designed in 1958 with Breuer and Nervi, takes on a particular position within the urban environment: to the north it embraces the Place de Fontenay in highly contextual fashion, whereas to the east and west – adhering to the principles of Modernism – it leaves large open areas, the buildings on which form a sporadic, small-scale, random composition. The underground extension managed to preserve the volumetric relationships; however, the character of the external spaces underwent a major transformation. It is therefore wrong to say that subterranean interventions always allow the urban constellation to remain intact.

Elevations – man-made topography
In the examples up to now underground space was created by removing material: directly in the case of the cave,

Fig. 12: Top: UNESCO main building, originally with an open plaza; bottom: later underground extension with courtyards
Marcel Breuer, Bernard Zehrfuss, Pier Luigi Nervi: UNESCO, Paris (F), 1958

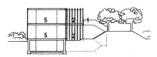

Fig. 13: Spoil used to form an embankment, as noise barrier and to provide access to upper floor
Fritz Haller: Bellach School, Solothurn (CH), 1959

Fig. 14: Timber frame covered with peat
Long house, Iceland

Fig. 15: The building becomes the topography.
Bearth & Deplazes: Carmenna chair-lift, Arosa (CH), 2000

indirectly in the case of structures built in open excavations. Elevations, on the other hand, require the addition of material – in the ideal case spoil (excavated material) that is not removed from the site but instead retained for shaping the land.

Fritz Haller's Bellach School at Solothurn (1959–60) shows us the potential inherent in excavated material, not in the sense of underground building directly but rather in the form of a concept that can be applied to this. Alongside the school an embankment has been built which protects against noise and provides access to the upper floor of this building (which has no internal staircases).

A given topographical situation often invites the creation of subterranean spaces above ground level: an additional hill is added to an undulating landscape, or an existing elevation is raised. Military hospitals or reservoirs function in this way. In doing so, the reservoir, for instance, benefits from the elevated position (pressure), is less exposed to climate-related temperature fluctuations (owing to the enclosing earth embankment), and is less of a "disruption" in the surrounding rural or urban landscape. In both cases – military hospitals and reservoirs – a gently rolling meadow blurs the underlying geometry.

Besides the strategy of incoherence between inside and outside as a traditional form of camouflage, an alternating effect is desired in other cases: interior and exterior appearance have an impact on each other. This is very evident at the valley station of the Carmenna chair-lift in Arosa (Bearth & Deplazes). The gently undulating topography has been transformed into a folded roof form. On the entrance side the folds appear to mirror the outline of the mountain peaks in the distance. However, the longer the distance between the folds on the roof, the less distinctive is the separation between the man-made and the natural topography. The soil covering changes the folds into vaults, and on three sides the roof surfaces blend with the rising and falling terrain. On the mountain side the chair-lift itself and the opening through which it enters the interior of the "hill" are the only evidence of this artificial topography.

Fig. 17: The choice of materials and form allow the building to match the landscape.
Skogar open air museum, Iceland

While in Arosa the fusion with the landscape was a key element in the designer's intentions, it is almost a by-product in the grass-covered peat buildings of Iceland. Owing to the lack of suitable clay for the production of roof tiles, roofs have been covered with peat since Iceland's settlement in the 9th century. Grass grows on the peat roofs and the ensuing dense network of roots forms an interwoven, water-repellent layer, which is adequate waterproofing in areas with low rainfall (approx. 500 mm p.a.). However, the durability of the waterproofing function is directly dependent on the pitch of the roof. If it is too steep, the rainwater drains too quickly, which means the peat dries out and develops cracks

during periods of little rainfall. On the other hand, if the pitch is too shallow, the water seeps through. The peat also regulates the moisture level and assumes various storage functions. A simple timber roof structure (cf. steel frame to valley station in Arosa) serves as a supporting framework for the peat, which is prevented from sliding down the roof slope by the solid external walls. These "green" roofs among the gently undulating landscape look like knolls, whereas the moss-covered brown peat walls recall a geological fault. So the integration is not due to the fact that grass has been laid like a carpet over the structure, but rather through the adaptation of given conditions – the texture of the landscape as well as its rhythm. Examples can be seen in the villages in the valleys of Engadine or Ticino, where the houses are built exclusively of stone. It is a local stone and forms, as monolithic rockface or loose boulders, the backdrop for the houses and retaining walls made from the very same stone; the transitions are fluid. The situation is very similar with Baiao House by Eduardo Souto de Moura, where the rubble stone facades on either side seem to become retaining walls for the neighbouring hillside, and the transition between roof and terrain is unnoticeable.

If what we have here is the naturalness of man-made constructions, then it is the reverse in constructions like the Abu Simbel Temple, where at the entrance stand four

Fig. 16: Silhouette of folded roof against outline of mountains in background
Bearth & Deplazes: Carmenna chair-lift, Arosa (CH), 2000

figures 20 m high which were carved out of the rock, i.e. the artificiality of the natural.

Concepts for creating spaces

In the foregoing the actual construction process for subterranean structures was mentioned only as an aside.

Fig. 18: Interlacing of building and topography with (retaining) walls
Eduardo Souto de Moura: Baiao House, Baiao (P), 1991–93

In the following I shall look at the principles for creating space – from the properties of the single room right up to the three-dimensional development of internal layouts – that arise owing to the special conditions and possibilities that building below ground level open up for us.

Geological concepts

The geological relationships influence the formation of space on various levels. For instance, the dissimilar properties of adjacent rock strata can steer the space development in such a way that the chosen stratum is the one that can be worked more easily (e.g. soft sandstone instead of limestone). Consequently, the actual position of a space or a sequence of spaces can be defined by the economic aspects of the geology. In this case a change in the stratum may in the end form the boundary to our underground expansion; depending on the structure of the adjoining rock, however, the load-carrying capacity and the associated unsupported spans can also limit the dimensions of our underground rooms. In the simplest case we remove only that amount of the "soft" rock necessary to leave walls or pillars supporting the overlying, more

Fig. 19: The natural rockface was reworked here to create what appears to be a man-made block.
Abu Simbel Temple, Egypt

or less horizontal rock strata exclusively in compression without any additional structural means. If the vertical distance between the hard strata is insufficient, we are forced to work the overlying rock into structurally beneficial shapes such as arch-shaped, trapezium-shaped or elliptical vaults or domes in order to create larger spans. Faced with the reverse situation (strata too far apart), the spatial development is subject only to the conditions of one type of rock. Of course, here again – within homogeneous geological conditions – larger spans are achieved by raising the roof.

So the architectural vocabulary can reflect the structural options, on the one hand, but can also, on the other, attest to the construction process. That might be drilled holes for jemmies, or rounded corners due to the circular movements of the human arm when removing material with a pickaxe.

The spread of "geological concepts" during the pre-industrial age was linked directly with rock properties such as ease of working and high strength. From that viewpoint, loess (a marlaceous sand) is ideal; indeed, it gave rise to a tradition of underground building in the Stone Age that is still found today, primarily in China

Fig. 21: Creating open space in solid rock
Left: soft rock – short spans with arches
Centre: hard rock – short spans without arches
Right: hard rock – large span with arch

(Henan valley). Other examples of this can be found in the Matmata region of Tunisia and in Gaudix (Granada province), Spain.

On the other hand, the creation of interior spaces within harder rock formations has only been possible with reasonable effort since the introduction of dynamite (1867) and mechanical mining methods. Admittedly, the Egyptians were constructing extensive rock tombs in the Valley of the Kings as long ago as about 1500 BC, and in the Middle Ages a number of churches were hewn completely out of rock in Ethiopia. This latter example extends from hollowing out the interior to exposing the church on all sides, where the removal of material leaves monolithic walls standing which in turn support the overlying rock forming the roof. Protected by the enclosing rock formations, these churches are difficult to find, but nevertheless exhibit the sort of facades we would expect to see on free-standing churches.

Today, the working of coherent masses of rock is mainly carried out to extract the rock itself, to provide access to deposits of natural resources (e.g. coal, salt etc.), or to remove obstacles (e.g. tunnel-building or

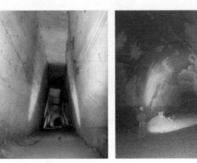

Fig. 20: Vaults in tuff stone, Naples
Trapezoidal (left) and elliptical (right) cross-sections as structurally ideal forms

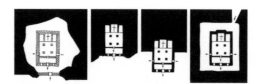

Fig. 22: Classification of Ethiopian rock-hewn churches
From left to right: built-up cave church, rock-hewn cave church, rock-hewn monolithic church

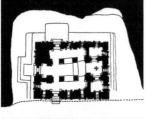

Fig. 23: A Lalibela Church, Ethiopia, c. 1400
The rock has been worked on all sides to create monolithic walls and columns.

conventional mining). Contemporary examples in which the specific properties of the rock are used directly are much rarer. One of these properties is the high storage capacity of rock; in combination with the underground location and hence the independence from the influences of daily and seasonal climatic variations this property offers temperature conditions that can be created and maintained with a minimum of technology.

This fact is exploited, for example, in the Great Midwest Underground (Kansas City, Missouri) – a subterranean cold store, warehouse and production facilities, with a floor area totalling nearly 300 000 m². This example is mainly interesting because, in addition to the storage characteristics of the rock, its good load-carrying capacity was also exploited to the full. As with the aforementioned rock churches, the hollowing-out process produces a monolithic structure (a regular grid of pillars) that need no further strengthening.

Constructional concepts

One decisive factor – and herein lies a considerable difference to building above ground – is the earth pressure that acts on a substructure permanently and from several sides. In this context we can distinguish between two types of construction: autonomous systems, which can simply withstand the pressure, and complementary systems, which function only in the presence of external forces. This latter effect can be seen at the tombs in Monte Albán in south-eastern Mexico, where the slabs of rock forming the roof are not sufficiently stable without the load and the resistance of the overlying soil.

We can divide autonomous systems further into those where the loadbearing elements have an active cross-section or active form. If the size of a component is such that it – obeying the laws of gravity – is itself stable and the horizontal forces present can be carried within its cross-section, we speak of an active cross-section. On the other hand, we can build a more slender structure when the shape of the loaded component corresponds to the flow of the internal forces (element with active form). From this point of view, vaults (cf. tunnels) are ideal structures, the principle of which can be turned through 90° to form an "arched" retaining wall. Like the wall to the tank compound at the aluminium works in Chippis, the plasticity of a series of curved shells allows us to deduce the forces that are at work. However, a shallow curvature guarantees only their buckling resistance, not their stability. That would require additional ribs, an increase in the

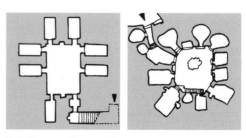

Fig. 25: The courtyard is a central element and can have almost any number of chambers on all sides.
Left: Luoyang, Henan valley (China); right: Matmata (Tunisia)

"rise" or a whole ring of shells. Structures with an active form are generally more labour-intensive, but require less material and render visible the forces within the structure, while structures with an active cross-section consume more materials and "deny" the flow of the forces, but are usually easier – and hence cheaper – to construct.

Structures with an active cross-section also help to stabilise excavations, an aspect that is always relevant below a certain depth. If the area of the excavation is only small, it can be secured with a (welded) ring of walings.

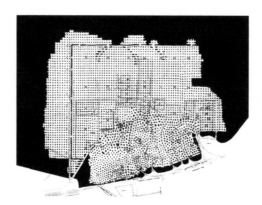

Fig. 24: Monolithic pillars measuring 7.50 x 7.50 m on 19.5 m grid
Great Midwest Underground, started and continually expanded since 1940, Kansas City (Missouri, USA)

Fig. 26: Solid rock hollowed out to create a cold store and warehouse
Great Midwest Underground, started in and continually expanded since 1940, Kansas City (Missouri, USA)

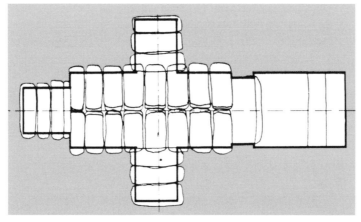

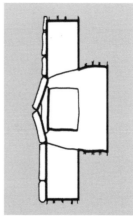

Fig. 27: Large-format stone slabs leaning against each other and wedged into the soil
Tombs (plan and section) in Monte Albán, Mexico

are aesthetic factors relevant, which have an influence on the three-dimensional manifestation of every project that develops from inside to outside. For there is no external form that has to be "attractive". Despite this great design freedom, the majority of contemporary subterranean

If the corner-to-corner distance is too great, the walings themselves must be braced. This can be done with ground anchors provided there are no adjacent buildings or underground services in the way. The walings can be omitted by increasing the number of anchors. But the reverse is also true: the anchors can be omitted if the building under construction is called upon to help stabilise the excavation. Christian Kerez's competition entry for the extension to the Freudenberg Cantonal School in Zurich-Enge demonstrates a very obvious concept – and one which applies generally to building underground. Initially, the plan layout seems to be rather random, but upon closer inspection we realise that this is the maximum usable area between existing structures and trees. The outline includes cranks and curved segments which appear to be elaborate and expensive. But the proposed wall of contiguous bored piles means that the geometry of the building is irrelevant because the connections between the piles always remain the same regardless of any change of direction. In other words, whether the wall is straight or curved is irrelevant to its construction.

Furthermore, walls of contiguous bored piles can carry vertical loads (in contrast to sheet piling), which means they can secure the sides of the excavation and also act as external walls in the finished structure. Kerez exploits this property and uses the main floor slab, carried by the piles, to brace the piles and thus eliminate the need for any ground anchors.

Fig. 28: Retaining wall with "arch" form to resist earth pressure
Tank compound, aluminium works, Chippis (CH)

Fig. 29: Retaining wall with "arch" form
Schematic plans (from top to bottom):
- simple "arches"
- additional ribs provide greater load-carrying capacity
- a greater "rise" also improves the load-carrying capacity

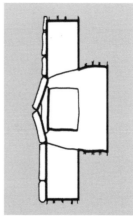

Fig. 30: A seemingly random form, but it reflects the trees and adjoining buildings above ground
Christian Kerez: Freudenberg Cantonal School project, Zurich (CH), 2002

Informal concepts

Actually, building underground allows us to create "uncontrolled", additive, rambling interior layouts because there is no visible external face. By this we mean the provision of rooms and spaces without the effects of the customary external "forces". There is no urban planning context, which as a parameter influencing the form predefines a certain building shape to fit a certain plot, nor

structures are simply "boxes", and only forced to deviate from this by infrastructure (services), plot boundaries and geological conditions because economic parameters generally call for simple shapes. Projections and re-entrant corners only enlarge the building envelope and involve elaborate details. Merely in cross-section, where storey-high set-backs render a terraced excavation possible, the sides of which need not be secured against slippage (e.g. timbering, ground anchors), are such forms economic.

The term "informal concept" is an expression covering all those structures whose properties are due neither to geological nor technical/constructional parameters, but rather reflect the fact that we cannot see them. Compact boxes, rambling interiors (internal forces) and partly "distorted" containers (external forces) fall into this category.

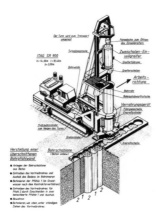

Fig. 31: Wall of contiguous bored piles
Every second pile is installed first and the intermediate spaces filled with concrete afterwards; the soil provides the formwork.

Frequently, the lack of rules is the sole rule – at least the absence of such rules that can be derived from building below ground.

The rambling interior layout unites a wide range of the most adverse conditions. Sometimes it is the result of optimum space and/or operational requirements; sometimes it is an unavoidable consequence of a regular need for additional space which has to be met by underground means owing to restrictions above ground, or in other cases when a scarcity of space becomes evident even at the planning stage but the provision of another basement storey is seen as disproportionate to the requirements. The additional underground rooms are added where they are required or wherever seems most suitable, for whatever reason. So the rambling interior layout would seem to represent an "anything goes" pragmatism but also a precisely controlled arrangement. Informal, i.e. not governed by rules, also means that responses to external forces, like the underground services or changing geological conditions mentioned above, depend on each individual situation.

Conclusion

Jørn Utzon's Silkeborg Museum project (1963) is a good example of how to unite a number of the themes dealt with above. These result in a more or less expansive interior layout with a series or interlacing of "room containers". The onion-shaped shells brace each other; as structures with an active form, their dimensions and the degree of curvature – on plan and in section – reflect the flow of the forces at work. The changes in the cross-sections can be seen clearly at the openings. Together with the overhead lighting and the physical experience of immersion (the route through the museum), both of which – as already explained – are not necessarily linked exclusively with building underground, the Silkeborg Museum, had it been built, would have embodied the "underworld" in conceptional and spatial terms unmistakably and without any romantic transfiguration.

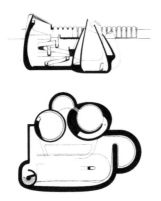

Fig. 32: "Vaulted" walls – as a loadbearing structure with an active form – to resist earth pressure
Jørn Utzon: museum project, Silkeborg (DK), 1963

Further reading
- Pierre Zoelly: *Terratektur*, Basel, 1989.
- Henri Stierlin/Pierre Zoelly: "Unterirdisches Bauen", in: *Werk*, 10, 1975.
- Gerhard Auer (ed.): "Sous Terrain", in: *Daidalos*, 48, 1993.
- Georg Gerster: *Kirchen im Fels*, Zurich, 1972.
- Vincenzo Albertini, Antonio Baldi, Clemente Esposito: *Naples, the Rediscovered City*, Naples, 2000.
- Bernard Rudofsky: *Architecture without architects*, New York, 1964.
- Werner Blaser: *Courtyard House in China*, Basel, Boston, Berlin, 1979, pp. 111–20.

Site preparation
Surveying work

Fig. 33: Staking out a new building

Basic geographical data

In Switzerland digital data from the surveys done by state authorities is available for virtually the whole country. (Grid of X/Y coordinates, origin at Bern Observatory: 600 000 000 m/200 000 000 m.) Switzerland's state surveying authority bases its information on triangulation – a three-dimensional representation comprising a large number of adjacent triangular areas. The most important level of information gained from the official surveys is the real-estate details. These describe the network of parcels (plots of land). These plots are limited (surrounded) by boundary points. Boundary lines join the individual boundary points. Every element (permanent control point, boundary stone, Polygon point, anchor point, corner of building, ground cover, individual object etc.) has been recorded numerically. This means that they are fixed using X/Y coordinates. For permanent control points the height above sea level Z is also known. The official surveys form the basis for the federal land registers.

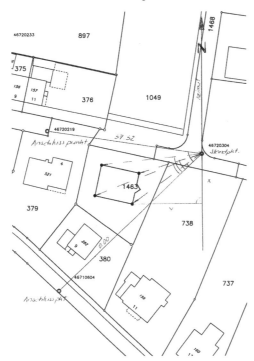

Fig. 34: Cadastral map (block plan showing parcels)
Setting out a building with four local reference points

Setting-out

Once the design has been submitted to the authorities for approval, the new building must be marked out with special poles. The basic form of the building (including projections and re-entrant corners), the shape of the roof (indication of eaves at junction with facade) and, if required, the outline of any later landscaping must be readily visible.

The structure is set out starting from the boundary points (boundary lines) using the boundary clearance dimensions. A surveyor is usually called in for urban projects these days. He or she will set out the coordinates of the planned structure as calculated in the design office and drive pegs into the ground to indicate the intentions of the planners. This setting-out work takes place based on the permanent control points available from the official surveys.

The data prepared in the design office is loaded into the tacheometer (measuring instrument). The orientation on site depends on the local reference points or the church spires visible. The coordinates are called up on the tacheometer and converted into angles and distances. The tacheometer is set up at a suitable point on the site. At least two local reference points are required to complete the setting-out. The surveyor's assistant with the reflector (reflective staff, to measure distances) approaches the desired point until he or she is just a few centimetres from the target. Instead of the reflector, a peg is then driven into the ground.

GPS (Global Positioning System) methods may be used for setting-out if the horizon is relatively free of obstacles (trees, buildings). In order to calculate the exact lengths of the poles, the surveyor is appointed to determine the ground levels during the setting-out procedure. This normally represents only a little extra work. A height-above-sea-level reference in the vicinity of the new structure is helpful so that the contractor can establish the necessary levels at a later date.

Following the setting-out, the level of the base of the excavation and the angle of the sides of the excavation are determined. The edge of the excavation can be marked with loose gravel or spray paint. The contractor can then commence with the excavation work.

Fig. 35: Permanent control point

Fig. 36: Benchmark

Fig. 37: Boundary stone prior to installation

Fig. 38: Boundary stone installed

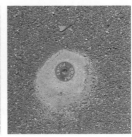
Fig. 39: Boundary point (pin) in pavement

Site preparation
Earthworks

Excavations

The movement of masses of soil is an activity that is difficult to predict, the details of which are normally planned by civil engineers and geologists. Using the results of a soil survey (boreholes), the anticipated quantity of material to be excavated and the strength of the subsoil can be determined. Afterwards, a decision can be made regarding the best type of foundation for the structure.

The earthworks contractor initially removes the uppermost layer of topsoil and vegetation (approx. 30 cm) with a tractor shovel and retains some of this material on site. Afterwards, the actual excavation work begins in stages. If there is room on the site or in the immediate vicinity, excavated material (spoil) is retained for backfilling at a later date because the transport of spoil is expensive and should be avoided wherever possible.

Working with the excavation plant (excavator, tractor shovel etc.) is a skilled job; the operators have to work to an accuracy of a few centimetres

Once the required depth has been achieved, the base of the excavation is covered with a blinding layer of lean concrete (grade PC 150, approx. 5 cm). The lean concrete provides a clean base on which to mark out underground services or the foundations. However, on rocky ground the layer of blinding may not be necessary.

The excavation should generally be about 60 cm larger than the outline of the building all round; 60 cm provides an adequate working space for the contractor. The angle of the sloping sides to the excavation (and if necessary stabilising measures) depends on the properties of the soil. The angle must also be chosen to rule out slippage or collapse and hence guarantee the safety of persons working in the excavation. Depending on the weather conditions and the hydrostatic pressure (slope run-off water or groundwater), any water must be drained away according to the regulations.

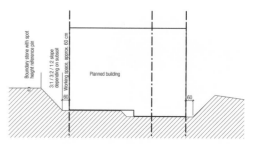

Fig. 41: Schematic section through excavation

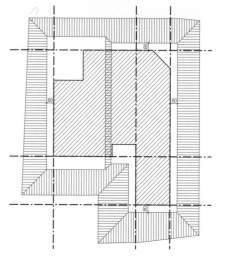

Fig. 42: Schematic plan of excavation (showing sloping sides)

Profile boards

Once the layer of blinding has been completed, the profile boards are set up. The main grid lines or outside faces of the structural shell are established with wires and bricks. The setting-out is the responsibility of the architect and is subsequently checked by the surveyor. By that, he or she refers once again to the existing permanent control points. The surveyor marks the building lines on the profile boards (tolerance ±5 mm). With the help of plumb bobs the plan layout is projected onto the blinding layer of lean concrete. The location of the building is thus fixed. Work can now begin on the drains or the ground slab.

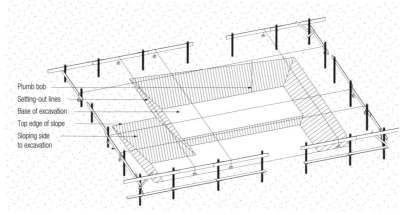

Plumb bob
Setting-out lines
Base of excavation
Top edge of slope
Sloping side to excavation

Fig. 40: Excavation with sloping sides

Fig. 43: Sloping sides stabilised with plastic film

Foundations

The brief

"The contact between the building and the ground determines both the transfer of loads into the subsoil and the interface with the topography... In the simplest case the foundation to a building is a direct consequence of the decisions that were invested in the constructional relationships above ground. But as soon as the terrain in the subsoil region presents difficulties due to its topography or geology, we must react to these circumstances."

Extract from: Heinz Ronner, *Baukonstruktion im Kontext des architektonischen Entwerfens*, Haus–Sockel, Basel, 1991

Influences

Mechanical, biological and chemical effects:

Loads	dead and imposed
Settlement	compression of the subsoil during and after the construction process
Earth pressure	forces acting (primarily horizontally) on the underground walls
Moisture	in the atmosphere (precipitation)
	on the ground (splashing)
	in the ground (moisture, frost, groundwater)
	in the building (vapour diffusion)

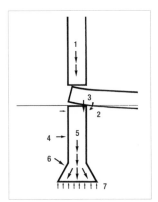

Fig. 44: Load transfer
1 Dead and imposed loads
2 Bending moment at floor support
3 Bearing pressure at support
4 Earth pressure, hydrostatic pressure
5 Foundation load
6 Spread of load
7 Ground pressure (underside of foundation)

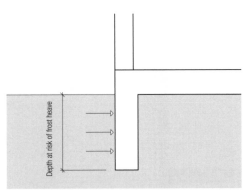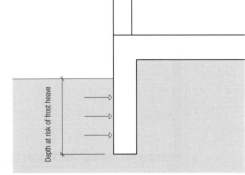

Fig. 45: Stem wall to provide frost protection
No direct structural function; prevents water seeping below the ground slab within the depth subject to frost heave; up to 800 m above sea level frost line = 80 cm below surface; at higher altitudes 1/1000 (i.e. 1.2 m at 1200 m above sea level)

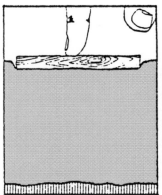

Fig. 46: Shallow foundation
Used when the load-carrying capacity of the subsoil is consistent; depth of foundation = "depth at risk of frost heave" (alternative: provide stem wall)

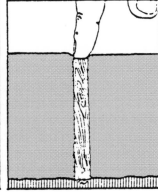

Fig. 47: Deep foundation
Used when the load-carrying capacity of the subsoil is inconsistent or inadequate near the surface; depth of foundation = depth of loadbearing stratum

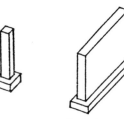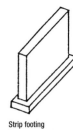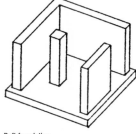

Pad foundation
discrete

Strip footing
linear

Raft foundation
planar

Fig. 48: The foundations project beyond the rising structural member
a) to spread the load
b) to provide a firm, level base for formwork (components in contact with the soil are practically always in concrete these days)

Foundation schemes
Loadbearing layer inside

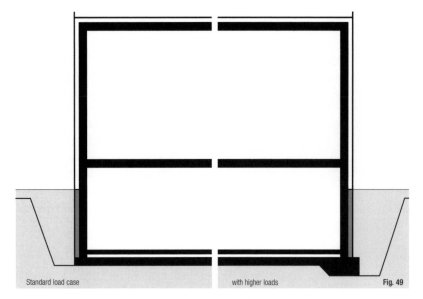

Insulation on cold side, inner skin loadbearing
(normal case)
As a rule, all "underground components" for foundations
are constructed these days in reinforced concrete.

Raft
Building below ground level

Building supported on raft foundation
Thickening below walls with higher loads
Change of material from building to perimeter insulation
Problem at base of wall: thermal insulation interrupted
(heated basement)

Standard load case   with higher loads   **Fig. 49**

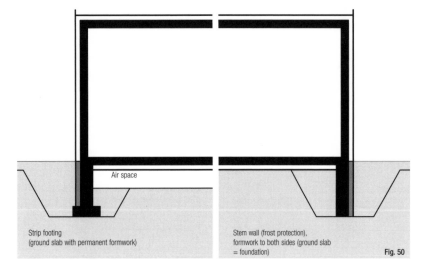

Strip footing, stem wall (frost protection)
Building at ground level (= no basement)

Building supported on strip foundations in the case of:
    a) loadbearing strata at lower level
    b) air space (enables floor construction without
       damp-proof membrane)
Underside of strip footing down to frost line
Stem wall necessary when building supported on
ground slab
Change of material from building to perimeter insulation
Problem at base of wall: thermal insulation interrupted

Air space

Strip footing
(ground slab with permanent formwork)

Stem wall (frost protection),
formwork to both sides (ground slab
= foundation)   **Fig. 50**

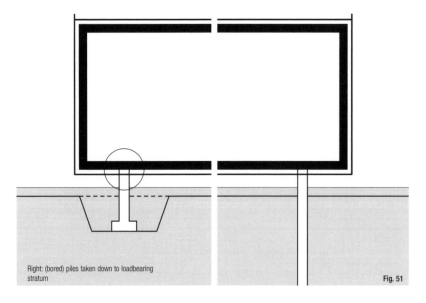

Individual foundations
Building above ground level

Lightweight, pragmatic architecture: e.g. protection against
floods (cf. Farnsworth House, Mies van der Rohe)
Underside of foundation down to frost line or loadbearing
strata (piles)
Problem at column head: insulation penetrated
Lateral stability provided by fixity and/or wind bracing,
depending on height of column

Right: (bored) piles taken down to loadbearing
stratum   **Fig. 51**

Foundation schemes
Loadbearing layer outside

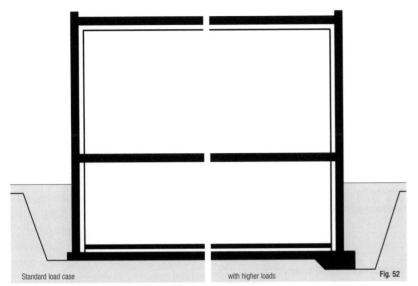

Standard load case   with higher loads   **Fig. 52**

Insulation on warm side, inner skin non-loadbearing
(special case in concrete or timber)

Raft
Building below ground level

Building supported on raft foundation
Thickening below walls with higher loads
In concrete change of material not necessary at
ground level
Problem at floors: thermal insulation interrupted

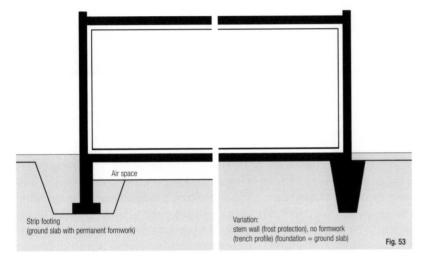

Air space

Strip footing
(ground slab with permanent formwork)

Variation:
stem wall (frost protection), no formwork
(trench profile) (foundation = ground slab)   **Fig. 53**

Strip footing
Building at ground level (= no basement)

Building supported on strip foundations in the case of:
    a) loadbearing strata at lower level
    b) air space (enables floor construction without
       damp-proof membrane)
Underside of strip footing down to frost line
Stem wall (frost protection) necessary when building sup-
ported on ground slab
Advantage: thermal insulation not interrupted/penetrated

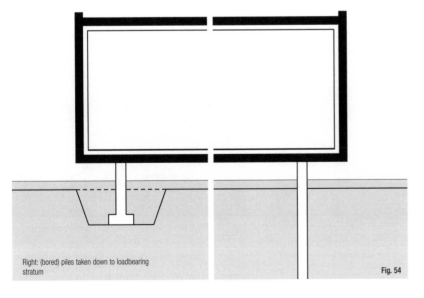

Right: (bored) piles taken down to loadbearing
stratum   **Fig. 54**

Individual foundations
Building above ground level

Building supported on columns, pilotis, piers, etc.
Lightweight, pragmatic architecture: e.g. protection against
floods
(cf. Farnsworth House, Mies van der Rohe)
Underside of foundation down to frost line
Advantage: thermal insulation not interrupted/penetrated
Lateral stability provided by fixity and/or wind bracing,
depending on height of column

The basis for plinths

Alois Diethelm

Fig. 55: The plinth as a platform to prepare the site
Greek temple, c. 500 BC

Fig. 57: Substructure and superstructure as structurally independent constructions with the same use (residential)
Philip Johnson: Wiley House, New Canaan (USA), 1953

The "plinth" regulates the structure–terrain relationship. These days, when talking about a plinth we generally mean an independent building component with different properties to the facade, which either appears as cladding or a solid wall. But conversely we also speak about a "plinth detail" when referrig to an interface with the ground "without a plinth".

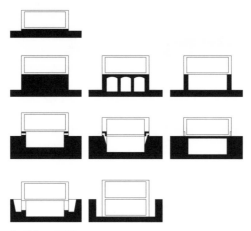

Fig. 56: Types of plinth
From top to bottom: platform, "earth pile", basement, box

The plinth above ground
The historical development of the plinth extends from the pragmatic preparation of the building site to personal protection against external dangers (animals, weather, war etc.), to the architectural, morphology-based apparition of Post-Modernism. Hardly any other building component blends technical requirements and architectural intentions in such diverse ways, the origins of which are no longer distinct. Even in the Greek temple, whose platform is a result of the "cultivation" of the terrain, part of its power is derived from its accessibility and hence its three-dimensional conspicuousness. As it developed further, the "earth embankment" held in place by stones grew to the height of a complete storey (e.g. temple in Nîmes, 16 BC) and it was only a matter of time before this plinth was hollowed out to create usable space.

By the middle of the 19th century the plinth storey only remained a subject for palaces and villas, while all other buildings had normal ground floors indistinguishable from the upper floors (cf. housing in the Middle Ages). Regardless of its use (originally ancillary rooms, later also main rooms), the fortified and solid character continued up to the beginning of the 20th century, sometimes in stone (solid or just a facing) or with less expensive rendering.

The plinth below ground
Other reasons for a visible plinth are underground rooms requiring natural ventilation options and the desire to minimise excavation, both of which led to the ground floor being raised. The basement walls grow out of the ground and appear as independent components because they generally have to satisfy different conditions from the facades above (resistance to moisture, earth pressure etc.). Irrespective of the plinth question, the elevated ground floor is also a theme at the entrance, where the difference in levels that has to be overcome is accommodated either outside the building, within the depth of the facade, or first inside the building, in the lobby or hall. Basement walls hardly distinguishable externally are those that enclose rooms and extend above ground level regardless of the ground floor slab, and introduce light into the basement by way of hopper-shaped openings.

The lightwell functions similarly. Used as an intermittent means, the lightwell is not substantially different from the enclosing walls. To simplify construction, it is available as an add-on, prefabricated element in concrete or plastic, but the disadvantage is that the lightwell creates a hole in the paving, grass, etc., which has to be covered with a grating. Stretched to a linear element running along sections of the facade, the lightwell, provided it is sufficiently wide (1–2 m), is an excellent way of admitting daylight into basements. Basements are thus turned into habitable rooms, with the only difference being the lack of a view.

Fig. 58: Powerful structural link between substructure and superstructure with different uses (residential and prestigious versus basement)
Hardouin-Mansart, de Cotte: Grand Trianon, Versailles (F), 1687

Fig. 59: A raised ground floor leaves room for a basement; natural ventilation and daylight for basement rooms, entrance formed by interruption in plinth
Diener & Diener: Warteckhof, Basel (CH), 1993–99

The "transferred" plinth

If the base of the lightwell drops to the level of the basement floor slab, this creates an accessible external space, an arrangement with a long tradition in the United Kingdom, for instance. Reached separately via an external stair, such basements are suitable as company flats or for use by small businesses. The requirements the "basement wall" has to meet are now no different from those of the facade above. With such an arrangement on all sides we obtain a "tank" in which the building stands untouched by the geological conditions and where all storeys can be constructed according to the same principles (e.g. timber engineering).

Fig. 64: A building growing monolithically out of the hillside
Valerio Olgiati: school, Paspels (CH), 1998

Fig. 60: Lightwell with fully habitable basement rooms
Steger & Egender: Art School, Zurich (CH), 1933

Fig. 61: The "lightwell" here has been extended to form an accessible garden.
Steger & Egender: Art School, Zurich (CH), 1933

The suppressed plinth

In contemporary architecture the plinth theme is mainly relevant only on a constructional/technical level. If the topographical conditions are not conducive to the creation of, for example, a plinth storey, the structural arrangement is suppressed, sometimes at great expense. Increasingly, buildings are being seen more as (art-related) objects than as structures; but they are still built in the same way. We are mostly using the same methods as we did 50 years ago, at best with only minor modifications; the

difference is that on the path to maximum formalisation they frequently ignore the "rules of architecture".

Regarding the building as an object emphasises three principles of the terrain–structure relationship: growing out of the terrain, placed on the terrain, and detached from the terrain. From the viewpoint of building technology, growing out of the terrain presents the greatest problems because the continuous, consistent "outer skin" is subjected to different requirements: weather resistance and protection against mechanical damage above ground level, moisture and earth pressure below. Homogeneous materials such as in situ concrete and render (waterproof render and/or moisture-resistant substrate) present few problems. Jointed constructions left exposed present many more difficulties: masonry, precast concrete elements and timber, sheet metal or other lightweight claddings. The weak spots are leaking joints but also the inadequate moisture resistance of the materials themselves (bleeding, rot etc.).

On the other hand we can detach the building from the ground by employing a whole range of methods, from strip footings above ground to storey-high pilotis, and hence eliminate the "ground-related" effects. Between these two extremes we can place the building on the terrain, an arrangement which through the ground floor slab – and possibly even through a basement – clearly has the effect of anchoring the structure to the ground. However, the fact that the facade cladding stops short of the ground conveys the impression of an object placed on the ground.

Fig. 62: The lightwell as an indication of a basement
Marques & Zurkirchen: Kraan-Lang House, Emmenbrücke (CH), 1994

Fig. 63: A container without an anchorage, "temporarily" parked on the grass
Marques & Zurkirchen: Kraan-Lang House, Emmenbrücke (CH), 1994

Fig. 65: The difference in height on existing terrain is accommodated within the solid plinth for the timber structure above.
Gion Caminada: factory, Vrin (CH), 1999

Fig. 68: The concrete plinth is the visible part of the excavation in which this timber building stands. Horizontal boards positioned at the steps in the concrete cover the concrete/timber junctions.
Peter Zumthor: Gugalun House, Versam (CH), 1994

Fig. 66: Rendered thermal insulation with stone plinth
Dolf Schnebli: apartment block, Baden (CH), 1990

Our image of the plinth

The tendency towards a formalised object is not least a reaction to Post-Modernism, the protagonists of which, with comparable technical means, attempted to create not formalisation but a nonexistent structural versatility in order to achieve the image of the traditional "building" (plinth, standard and attic storey, distinguished only by their surface textures).

Even if only in the form of cladding (just a few centimetres thick), this type of plinth is more than just a way of distinguishing the facade because such an arrangement protects the facade against soiling as well as mechanical damage.

The unavoidable plinth

Ignoring architectural preferences, it may well be that the topography determines the need for a plinth, depending on the type of construction. Whereas on flat ground it is still easy to suppress or reduce the plinth, on sloping ground we are immediately faced by the question of whether the difference in levels can be accommodated by forming a true plinth storey or whether the plinth should follow the line of the terrain. The former suggests storeys with different utilisation, while the latter raises structural issues: is the plinth the foundation for the facade above, and hence loadbearing, or is it a "protective screen" to ward off the problems of earth pressure and moisture?

Fig. 67: Painted concrete and ceramic tiles as protection against weather and soiling, and also providing a figurative plinth function
Otto Rudolf Salvisberg: apartment block, Zurich (CH), 1936

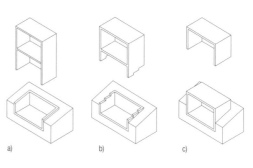

a)   b)   c)

Fig. 69: Plinth forms for sloping sites
a) Building in open excavation ("protective screen")
b) Building, or rather superstructure, supported on sides of excavation
c) "Basement storey" supporting upper floor

External wall below ground
Influences on the building envelope

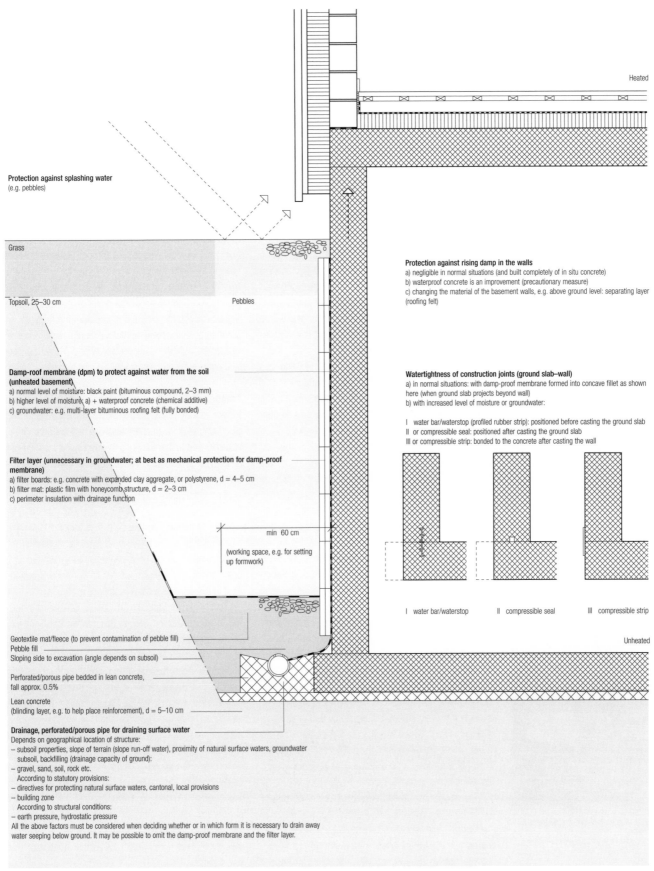

Protection against splashing water
(e.g. pebbles)

Grass

Topsoil, 25–30 cm

Pebbles

Damp-roof membrane (dpm) to protect against water from the soil (unheated basement)
a) normal level of moisture: black paint (bituminous compound, 2–3 mm)
b) higher level of moisture: a) + waterproof concrete (chemical additive)
c) groundwater: e.g. multi-layer bituminous roofing felt (fully bonded)

Filter layer (unnecessary in groundwater; at best as mechanical protection for damp-proof membrane)
a) filter boards: e.g. concrete with expanded clay aggregate, or polystyrene, d = 4–5 cm
b) filter mat: plastic film with honeycomb structure, d = 2–3 cm
c) perimeter insulation with drainage function

min 60 cm

(working space, e.g. for setting up formwork)

Geotextile mat/fleece (to prevent contamination of pebble fill)
Pebble fill
Sloping side to excavation (angle depends on subsoil)

Perforated/porous pipe bedded in lean concrete,
fall approx. 0.5%

Lean concrete
(blinding layer, e.g. to help place reinforcement), d = 5–10 cm

Drainage, perforated/porous pipe for draining surface water
Depends on geographical location of structure:
– subsoil properties, slope of terrain (slope run-off water), proximity of natural surface waters, groundwater
  subsoil, backfilling (drainage capacity of ground):
– gravel, sand, soil, rock etc.
  According to statutory provisions:
– directives for protecting natural surface waters, cantonal, local provisions
– building zone
  According to structural conditions:
– earth pressure, hydrostatic pressure
All the above factors must be considered when deciding whether or in which form it is necessary to drain away
water seeping below ground. It may be possible to omit the damp-proof membrane and the filter layer.

Heated

Protection against rising damp in the walls
a) negligible in normal situations (and built completely of in situ concrete)
b) waterproof concrete is an improvement (precautionary measure)
c) changing the material of the basement walls, e.g. above ground level: separating layer
(roofing felt)

Watertightness of construction joints (ground slab–wall)
a) in normal situations: with damp-proof membrane formed into concave fillet as shown
here (when ground slab projects beyond wall)
b) with increased level of moisture or groundwater:

I water bar/waterstop (profiled rubber strip): positioned before casting the ground slab
II or compressible seal: positioned after casting the ground slab
III or compressible strip: bonded to the concrete after casting the wall

I water bar/waterstop   II compressible seal   III compressible strip

Unheated

Fig. 70: External wall, scale 1:20

The wall

Fig. 1: Erecting the original hut
Excerpt from: Antonio Averlino Filarete: "Treatise on Architecture", 1460–64, Florence, Bibl. Naz., Cod. Magl. II, I, 140 fol. 5v

Cordula Seger

The wall is charged with cultural-historical significance. Popular sayings like "to stand with one's back to the wall" or "to bang one's head against a brick wall" testify to the wall being the visible boundary to a specific space, and the collective agreement to respect this artificial demarcation as binding and meaningful.

Terms are closely attached to language and can be defined only in the context of their boundaries. This means that a word's meaning is defined in context with and by being differentiated from other words and their material correlation. The wall to a room therefore is different from a piece of masonry; flat and thin, the wall possesses neither substance nor relief and thus creates no sense of depth. Contrary to this, masonry reacts on both of its sides and establishes both internal and external boundaries, here and there. As an independent architectural element it has the inherent capability to enclose and define – and thus create – space. A wall, however, is inevitably joined to a floor and a ceiling, or an underlying supporting construction, and in essence relies on the spatial transitions for its existence. In terms of these characteristics a wall belongs to the category of filigree construction (in traditional frame construction apparent as the infilling), whereas masonry is considered to be an element of solid construction. In the German language, the difference between filigree construction and solid construction, tectonics and stereotomy, is accentuated by a linguistic differentiation: "This tectonic/stereotomic distinction was reinforced in German by that language's differentiation between two classes of wall; between *die Wand*, indicating a screen-like partition such as we find in wattle and daub infill construction, and *die Mauer*, signifying massive fortification."[1]

According to Gottfried Semper's theory – developed in *Style in the Technical and Tectonic Arts; or, Practical Aesthetics* – the linguistic distinction between wall and masonry is of vital importance. Referring to etymology, Semper derives the German word *Wand* from *Gewand*

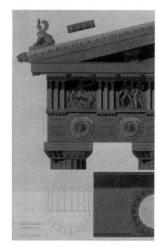

Fig. 2: Brightly painted beam in the Parthenon in Athens
After Gottfried Semper: plate V from *Anwendung der Farben in der Architektur und Plastik*, Dresden, 1836

(garment/vestment) and *winden* (to wind/coil). Semper's classification of the arts is divided into four segments: textiles, ceramics, tectonics (according to Semper mainly apparent in timber construction) and stereotomy, and he lists the wall in the textile category. Within Semper's classification, word origin and ethnographical and developmental determinants are interdependent: "Here, once again, we find the remarkable case of ancient phonetics helping the arts by elucidating the symbols of grammar in their primitive appearance and by verifying the interpretation these symbols were given. In all Germanic languages the word *Wand* (of the same origin and basic meaning as the term *Gewand*) refers directly to the ancient origin and type of a *visibly* enclosed space."[2] This overlapping of language and art has significant consequences; as a basic line of reasoning it runs through Semper's whole theory. In 1860 Semper wrote of the imminence of a fruitful interaction of research into linguistic and artistic form. In Semper's opinion the term enables a more pointed discussion on what is real. In his reflections on architecture the writer Paul Valéry approaches this notion in poetical fashion, "Truly the word can build, as it is able to create, but it can also spoil."[3]

Featuring the wall

Where exactly is the border between the masonry and the wall? As described above, there is a material difference between the masonry's thickness and the expanse of the wall's surface, between constructional autonomy and a corresponding dependency on other constructional elements. However, a transition of form is possible: the masonry can be transformed into the wall. This can be achieved through cladding or with a jointing technique that lends the wall a textile or at least flat appearance.[4] This, however, should not be understood as architectural amusement; the significance lies in the fact that a cladding of any kind generates meaning.

A thin coat of paint, for example, is all it takes to turn the masonry into the wall. In this context the discovery of the colourful Greek architecture in the second half of the 18th century had a significant impact on the architecture theory debate. It is more than the opposing camps of white elegance and restraint versus colourful exuberance. It stands for the transformation of a hitherto plastic concept into a textile one, the conversion from masonry to wall. In the first volume of their *Antiquities of Athens,* published in 1763, James Stuart and Nicholas Revett included drawings of the Palmette and the Lotus frieze they had discovered at the Ilissos Temple – both are brightly painted. In 1806 Quatremère de Quincy supported the new perception of Greek architecture in a widely acclaimed lecture. Consequently, Semper perceived[5] and recognised him as the initiator of this discourse.

Fig. 3: The non-loadbearing columns are part of the wall design.
Karl Friedrich Schinkel: Friedrich Werdersche Church, Berlin (D), 1830

Fig. 4: View of building with iron frame
Viollet-le-Duc: coloured plate from *Entretiens sur l'architecture*, 1812

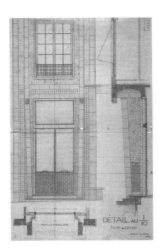

Fig. 5: View and section of entrance door
Auguste Perret: apartment block, 25 rue Franklin, Paris (F), 1903–04

Semper attributes the symbolic aspects of the creation of space to the wall. Visible from both inside and outside, the ornamental envelope to a building carries and unveils the spatial and architectural expression of the construction as a whole. The wall, freed from its loadbearing function, defines the building and conveys meaning. The following quotation illuminates both the differentiation between and overlapping of masonry built for constructional purposes and a wall carrying a more symbolic meaning: "…even where solid walls are necessary, they are nothing more than the internal and invisible framework to the true and legitimate representation of the spatial idea, of the more or less artificially worked and woven assembly of textile walls".[6] In Friedrich Schinkel's Friedrich Werdersche Church in Berlin the symbolic aspect attributed to the wall becomes particularly obvious. The Gothic ribs visible in the nave do not have any loadbearing function, they do not meet at the centre of the vaulting, and where usually the boss should be, a gap hints at the absence of support. Here, the Gothic ribs are part of the wall lining, or rather its setting.

The central importance of the wall in the 19th century also unfolded against the background of a distinction John Ruskin established in 1849, the distinction between "building", the purely assembly aspect of construction, and "architecture", the decorative aspect.[7] This differentiation has its consequences. Architecture's symbolic and communicative claims are stressed as decorative added value in comparison to a solely technical implementation. Expressed more pointedly: cladding is the equivalent of architecture.

Of frames and the framed

In the middle of the 19th century Eugène Viollet-le-Duc developed a structural rationalism. It defined the constructional framework as a necessity. Viollet-le-Duc differentiated between primary and secondary elements: among the former, he lists the mechanics and structure of a building, whereas the latter, like walls and infilling, may be painted and decorated.[8] Such a differentiation incorporates architectural elements into a hierarchical structure – ornamentation and decoration are permissible only when devoid of any constructional function. Viollet-le-Duc's theory was demonstrated in a project for a house with an iron frame, whose loadbearing structure is openly visible, while the gaps are filled with enamelled clay bricks.[9] The topic of infilling appeared in a new light as around the turn of the last century the use of reinforced concrete in combination with a frame increased. This is the case with Auguste Perret and his pioneering use of reinforced concrete in an apartment block at 25 rue Franklin in Paris. Here, Perret formulated and demonstrated the idea of structure and infilling in the sense of frame and framed.

It is quite telling that – according to Perret – the beginning of architecture is marked by the use of timber frames,[10] which in the early 20th century – thanks to the new building material reinforced concrete – was experiencing a contemporary reinterpretation. The frame defines and accentuates the framed and attributes true meaning to it. However, the frame to the rue Franklin building was not a naked concrete construction, it was also made explicit by cladding. In that respect the simple, smooth ceramic tiles were clearly distinguishable from the decorative floral motives of the infilling. The wall is given the significance of a picture enclosed in a constructional frame. It acts as a metaphor for the soft, interchangeable and perpetually changing medium in general. The infilling and its surrounding tectonic structure of construction elements are engaged in a dialogue. Only this dialogue and the discursive intensity of the discussion about the style reveals a building's character and its atmospheric intention. The dialogue defines the building's character – the richness of interrelated, interfering moods, which are able to go beyond a purely practical evaluation – and emphasises it with architecture. So the ceramic cladding enabled Perret to differentiate between the primary and secondary construction elements and at the same time accentuate the logical construction of the building as a whole. In this respect he satisfied both Semper's request

Fig. 6: Playing with variously decorated ceramic panels, view of upper storeys
Auguste Perret: apartment block, 25 rue Franklin, Paris (F), 1903–04

Fig. 7: The central glass rosette above the entrance
Auguste Perret: garage, Société Ponthieu-Automobiles de Paris, Paris (F), 1906–07

The glass wall

Auguste Perret defined frame construction as a development of timber construction and tried to apply the same formula to utility buildings – as in the garage for the Société Ponthieu-Automobiles de Paris, where he, so to speak, aggrandised the principle of infilling and framing with the large central glass rosette. Contrary to this, Walter Gropius consciously tried to break away from the division into framing and infilling with his factory building for the Fagus company in Alfeld an der Leine (1911–14). Gropius placed a box-type facade of glass and steel in front of the line of the columns and – as an architectural quintessence – around the building's corners, thus expressing the desire for transparency.

The glass wall, however, allowing an unobstructed view both of the inside from outside and vice versa, and letting the observer's eye penetrate the surface, once more leads to the question of whether a surface can carry meaning. A transparent glass wall's ability, or inability, to generate architectural meaning first became a relevant topic for discussion with the construction of the Crystal Palace in London in 1851. "Joseph Paxton, gardener and engineer, erected the envelope of iron and glass, whereas the decoration – in the primary colours red, yellow and blue – was contributed by the artist and architect Owen Jones. The decorative forms, and even just the coat of paint covering the iron frame, were intended – at least seemingly – to uphold the traditional functions of architecture as a symbolic expression of society as a whole."[11] Interestingly, the glass infilling itself was not assigned any symbolic function – this had to be added by the architect.

The building as a container for displaying goods spectacularly – as emerged with the Crystal Palace – has

continued in the form of the department store. In the years following the First World War, the use of glass curtain walls in the construction of commercial premises was developed in America. The technological prerequisite here was the development of toughened glass with better load-carrying capacities. As expressed in the term curtain wall, the glass elements hang like textiles from the edges of the concrete floors, which cantilever beyond the line of the columns. Seen from the outside, the glass facade surrounding the building is perceived as an independent skin and thus deviates from the traditional understanding of a wall existing only within a compound floor–ceiling structure.

Viewed from the inside, the transparent glass wall virtually rescinds its ability to delimit a room not only in

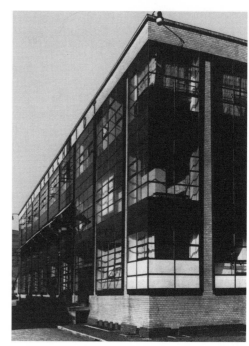

Fig. 9: The first curtain wall in Europe wraps around the corners to enclose the whole building.
Walter Gropius: Fagus factory, Alfeld a. d. Leine (D), 1911–25; view from south-east, condition after 1914

reality, but also symbolically. Wall and window blend into each other in the sense of a structured opening. What the contemporaries of historicism had perceived as a deficit in the Crystal Palace – that the glass envelope itself did not possess any expressive power – is seen as a quality by classical Modernism. It maintains that only "neutral" buildings allow their occupants a sufficient degree of freedom. However, classical Modernism does not refrain from charging the material with ideological meaning: glass stands for light and air, and thus for a positive openness towards the outside.

Economic interests were just as important in encouraging the use and development of the material. In the department store category, introduced at the end of the 19th century, the main issue is the visibility of the goods

Fig. 8: External view of Alhambra Courtyard – structure versus architecture
Joseph Paxton: Crystal Palace, London (UK), 1851

Fig. 10: **The setting for the plate**
Theo van Doesburg, "Maison particulière" (in conjunction with C. van Eesteren), "counter construction" *(Analyse de l'architecture)*, 1923, pencil and ink, 55 x 38 cm

on display. The interior was systematically aligned towards the outside and acted as an information medium for passers-by and potential customers.

The curtain wall is exemplary for the alienation of what a wall traditionally should and must achieve. However, there were also other interesting approaches, like the effort prior to the First World War to use glass as a meaningful construction material and to intertwine the functions of wall and opening. Bruno Taut's "glass architecture", inspired by the writings and aphorisms of Paul Scheerbart, made use of glass bricks, prisms, floor and wall tiles in order to create a differentiated interior atmosphere.

The self-sufficient wall

In the 1920s the "De Stijl" architects amalgamated the principles of filigree and solid construction with the help of thin panels made of reinforced concrete, and elevated the wall plate to a constructional, space-generating and creative principle. Consequently, the hierarchy of primary and secondary building elements was abandoned visually.

When the wall plates are to be accentuated, colour plays a vital role: architects and artists from the "De Stijl" group painted entire walls, and the edges of the painted plates abutted in such a way that the volume of the building became secondary to the concept of a floating structural assemblage. Accordingly, Arthur Rüegg van Doesburg's "Maison particulière" comments: "Looking back, the use of colour, which suggests an open method of space creation, can be understood as progressive criticism of an architecture still defined by the traditional rules of structures and the enclosed room."[12] So while the tinted wall was designed to accentuate the abstract quality of the building and ostensibly denies its importance, it still becomes significant in a historical context through the

attitude it conveys: traditional principles are undermined in order to communicate a new understanding of space.

Intimacy and representation

The wall in the narrower sense of the word is conceived from the interior space. The one, specific space finds its delimitation here: "The wall is the one constructional element that defines the enclosed space as such, absolutely and without auxilliary explanation. The wall gives the enclosed room its presence and makes it visible to the eye."[13] The saying "within one's own four walls" illustrates the strong focus on the enclosed interior space.

As the influence of the middle classes started to grow in the 19th century, interiors gained increasing relevance as a venue for collective self-presentation. Walter Benjamin attributed the "enclosing" power – for which he created the figurative term "sheath" – to the lifestyle in the 19th century. The "dwelling" of a person, Benjamin writes, carries that person's "fingerprints" and can "in the most extreme case become a shell".[14] In the Art Nouveau period with its ideal of an interior designed coherently in all aspects, Benjamin saw a break with the idea of a room as an enclosing structure. "Art Nouveau is rocking the very foundations of the nature of housing".[15] Continuing this train of thought we note that Art Nouveau with its floral and organically curving motifs emphasises the flatness of the wall and directs our attention to visual effects and not to the atmosphere of the space. Accordingly, the interior was flattened to a film around 1900, and the mistress of the house, performing her duties of representation, merges, so to speak, into this surface of social projections. This interpretation is affirmed by a photograph of Maria Sèthes, who, wearing a dress designed by her husband Henry van de Valde, blends in with the room's interior, which was designed as a *Gesamtkunstwerk*. A merger between the wall decoration and the lady's housecoat takes place. Considered in a history of architecture context, this is taking Semper's clothing principle to the extreme. If the interior is perceived as a defined living space, however, the design principles of Art Nouveau are doubly restrictive towards women because the interior has been assigned as their central living space. Adolf Loos was strongly opposed to stylistic art – and he counted the designs of Henry van de Velde, Secession and the Wiener Werkstätten among these. Loos harshly criticised Art Nouveau's dramatic elaborateness and promoted the idea that interior spaces have to reflect their occupant's personality and not express some arty architect's narcissistic self-complacency.

From clothing to cladding and back

The wall's expressive powers today mostly appear to be reduced. The third volume of the *Handbuch der Architektur*,[16] published in 1903 in Stuttgart, dedicated individual chapters to various wall coverings – stone, paper,

Fig. 11: **Roadside elevation showing the entrance at the side**
Gerrit Rietveld: Rietveld-Schröder House, Prins Hendriklaan 50, Utrecht (NL), 1924

Fig. 12: The woman has been photographed in such a way that she seems to merge into the room.
Photo of Vienese fashion designer Mathilde Fröge, c. 1905, with self-designed "Reform" dress. Ms Fröge is standing in front of a cabinet by Kolomann Moser and is wearing jewellery by Josef Hoffmann.

Fig. 13: The clothes and wearer are part of a *Gesamtkunstwerk* setting.
Maria Sèthe, wearing a dress designed by her husband, the architect Henry van de Velde, photographed in their house in Uccle near Brussels, c. 1898.

of reality, of the material, is necessary where form is to emerge as a meaningful symbol, as an independent creation of man."[17] Semper's fondness for carnival was countered by Modernism with its moral request for sincerity, which led to a decline in the fullness of expression. It was left to Post-Modernism to rediscover the communicative potential of the wall and combine the principles of clothing and cladding.

Notes

1 Kenneth Frampton: *Studies in Tectonic Culture: The Poetics of Construction in 19th and 20th Century Architecture*, London, 1995, p. 5.
2 Gottfried Semper: *Der Stil in den technischen und tektonischen Künsten.* vol. 1, Frankfurt/M. 1860, p. 229. – English translation: Gottfried Semper: *Style in the Technical and Tectonic Arts; or, Practical Aesthetics*, vol. 1, (Semper's emphasis).
3 Paul Valéry: *Eupalinos*, Frankfurt/M., Leipzig, 1991, p. 78.
4 See the essay "The pathos of masonry" by Ákos Moravánszky, pp. 23–31. The mixing of solid and filigree construction was initiated by Semper, who assumed that every well-built masonry wall represented a type of weaving due to its jointing principle.
5 Gottfried Semper: ibid., p. 218.
6 ibid., p. 229.
7 The distinction between design and architecture also had repercussions for education around 1800. For example, in France the "Ecole Polytechnique", whose focus was applied technology, was founded in 1795. The growing specialisation provoked a separation between the disciplines, which has had a lasting effect on the understanding of design and architecture, and is only slowly moving towards the necessary union.
8 Robin Middleton: "Farbe und Bekleidung im neunzehnten Jahrhundert"; in: *Daidalos* "In Farbe", No. 51, Berlin, 15 March 1994, pp. 88–89.
9 See Eugène Emmanuel Viollet-le-Duc: *Entretiens sur l'architecture*. Atlas, Paris, 1864, PL. XXXVI.
10 Auguste Perret: *Contribution à une théorie de l'architecture*, 1952, quoted by Frampton 1995, pp. 125–26.
11 Susanne Deicher: "Polychromie in der englischen Architektur um die Mitte des 19. Jahrhunderts", in: *Daidalos*, ibid., p. 91.
12 Arthur Rüegg: "Farbkonzepte und Farbskalen in der Moderne", in: *Daidalos*, ibid., p. 69.
13 Gottfried Semper: *Der Stil in den technischen und tektonischen Künsten*, vol I. Frankfurt/M. 1860, p. 227.
14 Walter Benjamin: *Das Passagen-Werk*. Gesammelte Schriften Bd. V1. Frankfurt/M. 1982, p. 292. – English translation: Walter Benjamin: *The Arcades Project*, Cambridge, Mass.,1999.
15 ibid., p. 292.
16 Hugo Koch: "Ausbildung der Wandflächen", in: idem: *Die Hochbaukonstruktionen. Des Handbuches der Architektur dritter Teil.* Vol. 3, no. 3: Ausbildung der Fussboden-, Wand- und Deckenflächen, Stuttgart, 1903, pp. 101–22.
17 Gottfried Semper: ibid., p. 231, footnote 2.

leather or woven fabrics – and to techniques like painting, wallpapering, incrustation, stucco, mosaics or wood panelling, and to "artistic painting". Contemporary works, however, concentrate mainly on what is intended to be hidden behind the wall.

This shift in the importance and perception of the wall is also reflected on a linguistic level: while the 1903 manual speaks – in line with Semper – of wall clothing, today only the term cladding is in use. The cladding refers to something that is meant to remain hidden or come to the surface in an altered state; thermal insulation, vapour check, air cavity etc. occupy the space between wall and cladding.

Gottfried Semper loved role-playing, which serves as a binding convention and simplifies human interaction. To take part in a public debate he used coded gestures and images. "I believe that *dressing-up* and *masquerade* are as old as human civilisation itself, and the pleasure in both is identical with the pleasure in all the activities that make humans become sculptors, painters, architects, poets, musicians, dramatists – in short: artists. Any kind of artistic creation on the one hand, and artistic enjoyment on the other, require a certain carnival spirit – if I may express it in modern terms. The smouldering of carnival candles is the true atmosphere of art. The destruction

Fig. 14: Entrance beneath fascia of marble and grey granite. The motifs are reminiscent of the early Renaissance and emphasise the central transition to the building.
Robert Venturi, John Rauch: Gordon Wu Hall, new common rooms for Butler College, Princeton University, New Jersey (USA), 1980

The design of the facade

Marcel Baumgartner

Fig. 15: "Bingo" (Cutting): removing the external wall with a power saw, revealing the interior
Gordon Matta-Clark (1943–78): American architect and conceptual artist

The word facade

The word "facade" is ambiguous. It is derived from the Italian word *facciata,* which in turn comes from the Latin word *facies;* it literally means form, appearance, visage, aspect, and hence the external appearance, the physiognomy of the building. Viewed from outside, the facade is frequently designated the building envelope or outer skin. These terms lead us to suspect that the facade tends to be a thin superficial covering, draped like a dress over the underlying skeleton. They make a theme out of the suggestion of the surface, its materiality, structure and configuration. As a result, we combine these surface-related aspects and speak of the surface structure.

On a different level of meaning, the facade is frequently simply referred to as the external wall, masonry or otherwise. And this brings us to two further features of the facade:

On the one hand, in the term external wall the "external" is meant in the sense of a periphery or a termination and hence highlights a spatial property of the facade. The facade defines the separation between internal and external, or rather the spatial limitation of the interior space from the inside and the exterior space from the outside.

On the other hand, the term external wall refers to the constructional nature of the facade. The term wall implies solid construction, but a filigree construction is equally possible. The structure of the facade, revealed by cutting a section through it, depends on the specific form of construction and will be called the inner structure here.

The constructional system of the facade, the inner structure, depending on the form of construction, solid or filigree, forms the constructional basis of the surface structure.

Observation 1: There is an indivisible, mechanical and constructional interdependence between the inner structure and the surface structure of the facade.

Constructional systems

The facade, when understood as a building technology element, fulfils the elementary functions of loadbearing, insulating and protecting. These functions generally occur in this order, considered from inside to outside. The loadbearing function is necessary because, generally, at least a part of the loads from the suspended floors and roof of a building are supported at the edges, i.e. along the periphery, and must be transferred vertically. Insulation is required for the thermal regulation of the interior spaces with respect to the exterior spaces, in some cases to insulate against heat or cold, and depends on the geographical and seasonal climatic situations as well as the requirements for individual thermal comfort. The protective layer protects the building and the facade

construction itself, especially the insulation, from external actions arising from the immediate environment. Seen in the light of these requirements, the facade is certainly the most complex component of a building, and attracts comparatively high production and maintenance costs. The planning and development of a facade calls for an intelligent coordination of the loadbearing, insulating and protective functions to create an efficient total system.

In principle, we distinguish between *synthetic* and *complementary* systems.

Synthetic systems

Synthetic systems fulfil the primary structural and building physics functions of the facade by means of a single, multifunctional layer. A typical synthetic system is monolithic fair-face insulating concrete. This carries loads and insulates by means of one single layer, the surface of which at the same time forms its own protective layer (in some cases assisted by an invisible, additional, hydrophobic coating). In other words, the protective layer simultaneously performs loadbearing and insulating functions. The insulating effect of this system is not achieved via a separate insulating material, but is defined via the thermal conductivity of the building material used. The skill in developing synthetic systems therefore lies in optimising the three interlinked functions. For example, according to modern standards, homogeneous facing brickwork made from weather-resistant hard-fired bricks has an inadequate insulating value.

Observation 2: As the number of functions allocated to the outermost layer – i.e. the protective layer – increases, so the appearance of the facade becomes less easy to change.

What synthetic forms of construction have in common are their immediacy of the expression and associated authenticity. By combining the loadbearing, insulating and protective functions in one single layer, the inner constructional system is directly impressed on the external appearance of the facade. The surface structure of the facade is directly coupled with its inner structure. In facing brickwork, for example, the intrinsic rules of the masonry bond are visible in the courses of bricks in the surface structure. But in monolithic fair-face insulating concrete, the surface structure exhibits a constant quality in all dimensions, which can be influenced only by the formwork, from outside, but not by the inner structure itself.

Complementary systems

In a complementary system, the structural and building physics functions of the facade are allocated to different layers, each with specific monofunctional properties.

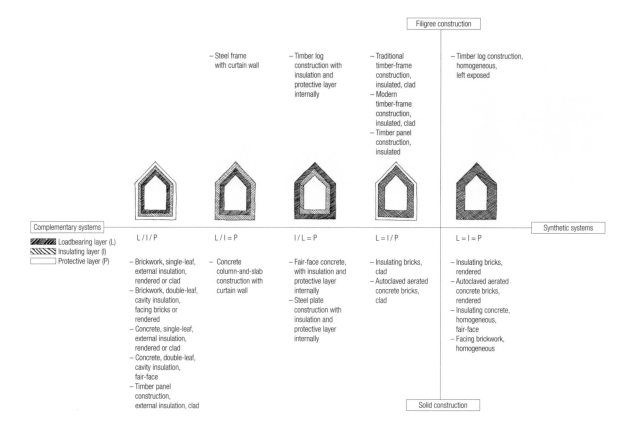

Filigree construction

– Steel frame
with curtain wall

– Timber log
construction with
insulation and
protective layer
internally

– Traditional
timber-frame
construction,
insulated, clad
– Modern
timber-frame
construction,
insulated, clad
– Timber panel
construction,
insulated

– Timber log construction,
homogeneous,
left exposed

Complementary systems

▨ Loadbearing layer (L)
▧ Insulating layer (I)
▢ Protective layer (P)

Synthetic systems

L / I / P

L / I = P

I / L = P

L = I / P

L = I = P

– Brickwork, single-leaf,
external insulation,
rendered or clad
– Brickwork, double-leaf,
cavity insulation,
facing bricks or
rendered
– Concrete, single-leaf,
external insulation,
rendered or clad
– Concrete, double-leaf,
cavity insulation,
fair-face
– Timber panel
construction,
external insulation, clad

– Concrete
column-and-slab
construction with
curtain wall

– Fair-face concrete,
with insulation and
protective layer
internally
– Steel plate
construction with
insulation and
protective layer
internally

– Insulating bricks,
clad
– Autoclaved aerated
concrete bricks,
clad

– Insulating bricks,
rendered
– Autoclaved aerated
concrete bricks,
rendered
– Insulating concrete,
homogeneous,
fair-face
– Facing brickwork,
homogeneous

Solid construction

This is achieved by combining two or three complementary layers.

In three-layer complementary systems, the three monofunctional components are generally in the order of loadbearing, insulation and protection, viewed from inside to outside. One typical example of this is the widely used solid construction with an inner loadbearing leaf of brickwork or concrete enclosed in an insulating material that is then protected by render (thermal insulation composite system), some form of cladding or another leaf of masonry or concrete. Timber panel construction is similar, with an enclosing layer of insulation protected by an outer layer of cladding.

In two-layer complementary systems, one of the two layers performs two primary functions, while the other layer is monofunctional. Such systems can be regarded as variations within the range between three-layer complementary systems and single-layer synthetic systems.

One group of two-layer systems is based on the principle of an external layer of insulation that simultaneously provides protection. This group includes filigree steel frames and solid concrete column-and-slab structures enclosed by some form of non-loadbearing suspended cladding, which forms a self-contained, compact building component, insulating and protecting in one and the same plane.

Another group of two-layer systems reverses the traditional sequence of layers – loadbearing inside, insulation and protection outside – and ensures that the external loadbearing structure also provides protection. Typical examples of this are fair-face concrete construction with internal insulation (solid construction) and timber log construction with internal insulation (filigree construction). While the loadbearing structure is simultaneously the protective outer layer resisting the effects of the weather, such systems will certainly also require a protective inner layer to prevent the layer of insulation being damaged by the users of the building (e.g. driving nails into the wall). This could take the form of an inner lining of plasterboard or wood panelling.

A third group of two-layer systems is based on the principle of an inner layer performing loadbearing and insulating functions, which has to be protected by another layer on the outside. This principle is used in timber construction for externally insulated filigree structures, e.g. timber-frame construction. Thanks to the low thermal conductivity of the timber members, these can be placed in the same plane as the insulation without causing any building physics problems. Such forms of construction are now available in the form of prefabricated sandwich elements, which to some extent form a partially synthetic system comprising loadbearing and insulating functions. In solid construction this principle crops up in masonry structures built from insulating bricks or autoclaved aerated concrete bricks (= loadbearing and insulating functions), which must be protected on the outside with some form of external cladding system with ventilation cavity.

If this same masonry structure is protected by a layer of render instead of external cladding, the construction is generally called a "synthetic system". As the render is bonded to the substrate both mechanically and chemically, the use of this term is certainly correct for the final state of the facade cross-section.

Observation 3: As the number of functions allocated to the outermost layer decreases, so the architectural design freedoms increase.

The use of a complementary facade structure, in particular a three-layer one, modifies the constructional dependency between the surface structure and the inner one. In the extreme, the outermost layer of the facade, which is always at least, a protective layer appears as an apparently independent leaf. It promises to be the immediate, sole layer providing the surface structure and, through a reference to the inner structure, suggests a high degree of exchangeability or autonomy. A closer look, however, reveals certain constructional dependencies that limit the supposed variability decisively. We distinguish between two cases here: the *independent* and the *non-independent* protective layer.

Above a certain height, an independent protective layer must be fixed back to the loadbearing structure using suitable fasteners to guarantee its stability. This means the individual, functionally independent layers are joined in a constructional sense. For example, in double-leaf masonry the external masonry leaf is fixed back to the internal masonry leaf with wall ties to prevent buckling or overturning of the outer leaf. The fasteners (wall ties) penetrate the insulation (the sensitive building physics layer) and pass from the cold to the warm side of the construction. It is therefore important to use only wall ties whose thermal conductivity is interrupted in some way (thermal break).

A non-independent protective layer requires an additional, dedicated supporting framework, which in turn is fixed back to the loadbearing structure. All the loads acting on the protective layer, primarily the vertical dead loads, must therefore be carried by the supporting framework and transferred through the insulating layer to the loadbearing structure. In timber construction this is typically achieved by using a grid of battens to form a suitable framework for what is usually a lightweight cladding; the insulating material is installed between the battens. When using heavyweight cladding materials, e.g. prefabricated concrete panels, the elements are supported from the loadbearing structure by means of heavy-duty anchors and brackets. Such fixings, normally metal, again disrupt

the insulating layer and have to be well protected against moisture, especially condensation, in order to reduce the risk of corrosion.

Summing up, we can see that the true separation of layers in complementary systems always involves a (large or small) number of disruptions, or rather penetrations. The average insulating value of the facade must always take these thermal bridges into account.

Below, we investigate the laws that affect the outermost protective layer of the facade, i.e. the surface structure, from constructional and architectural viewpoints. For this purpose, the term "facade design" can be expanded to cover the development of the surface structure as such. But it should not be forgotten that there is a dependency on the constructional system of the facade in cross-section, the inner structure, which affects the variability of the surface structure.

Materials

Observation 4: The essence of every facade design is its materials.

As a review of the known types of facade types shows, the majority of systems in common use are of the complementary variety. The increase in the demands placed on the insulating layer have helped to promote this fact in recent decades. Among these complementary systems, the majority have a monofunctional, outer protective layer. This protective layer could actually be constructed from a wide range of different materials, provided they guarantee the protection and imperviousness of the system. This contrasts with the loadbearing and insulating layers, where the choice of material is of course severely restricted owing to the specific structural or building physics requirements.

The upshot of this is that the protective layers of today's facade systems exhibit a high degree of design freedom in terms of materials, construction and the relationship with the underlying loadbearing or insulating layer. For example, looked at from the purely technical perspective, a masonry wall with external insulation does not necessarily have to have a protective layer of brickwork; an insulated timber building not necessarily a timber cladding. This has less to do with the loss of "constructional honesty" and more to do with the constructional variability inherent to complementary systems.

Observation 5: The choice of facade material depends on availability, building technology properties, material and abstract values, and economic and ecological sustainability.

Key criteria for the choice of material for the facade surface are the building technology properties of the material plus

Fig. 16: Homogeneous layer in the form of a seamless polyurethane membrane applied with spraygun or roller
NL Architects: WOS8 heat exchanger station, Utrecht-Leidsche Rijn (NL), 1998

Fig. 17: Jointed layer of semi-transparent glass panels
Peter Zumthor: Art Gallery, Bregenz (A), 1997

the knowledge and skills of those working with the chosen materials. Every facade is directly exposed to the actions of its immediate environment. Sun, wind, rain, snow, varying temperatures, mechanical and chemical effects all have to be taken into account when considering materials with respect to maintenance and durability. The statutory provisions with respect to fire protection and acoustics are further, restrictive criteria. In response to this, contractors and industry have developed techniques and constructions to suit the materials. These have become accepted in the profession through planning and production and established as forms of construction or systems.

Owing to its direct presence on the surface, the facade material characterises the identity of a building culture, e.g. the typical timber architecture of certain regions of Switzerland, the Bernese Oberland and Valais, or the distinctive brickwork culture of Denmark. The level of the abstract meaning of the facade material in certain cases exceeds the actual constructional background to the choice of material and finds the justification for its continued usage in the appearance alone. Notions of tradition and *Zeitgeist* are therefore expressed on a formal level via the facade surface.

In addition to the actual protection, the outermost layer of the facade can in some cases be allocated further functions, which increase the technical value of the facade. A familiar example of this is the multimedia facade, which by way of large-scale printing or projection fulfils additional communication tasks. Another example can be found in energy-efficient construction where the protective skin is in the form of hot-water collectors or photovoltaic modules, which contribute actively to solar energy gains.

Division

Observation 6: Every facade, whether of a jointed or homogeneous appearance, is eventually confronted with the problem of division.

In architectural terms, the facade can vary from very thin, skin- or cloak-like, to sturdy, encasement- or masonry leaf-like; from flat, planar right up to sculpted, moulded. In constructional terms, this layer either comprises pieces joined together or it is homogeneous. The term homogeneous in this context relates to the surface structure in the finished state and should not be confused with the term synthetic, the system concept in connection with the inner structure of the facade system.

Most facade materials are made up of individual modules or elements, large or small, joined together. This results in a mechanical bond, which must be appropriately maintained and stabilised.

A homogeneous layer is technically possible with a few materials only. The prerequisite for this is that the

Materials	Jointed layers	Homogenised layers
Stone	– Masonry units – Panels and slabs – Slates	
Concrete	– Prefabricated shaped elements – Panels and slabs	– In situ concrete
Mineral composite materials	– Panels and slabs – Slates	– Render
Brickwork	– Masonry units	
Ceramics	– Panels – Mosaics	
Glass	– Masonry units (glass bricks) – Panes	
Timber	– Joists, planks – Shingles – Panels and boards	
Metal	– Panels, plates and sections – Industrial/tinsmith sheet metal – Fabrics and foils	
Plastics	– Moulded elements – Panels and plates – Fabrics and sheets	– Render – Coatings
Insulating materials	– Transparent thermal insulation elements – Cellular glass boards	
Paints		– Coatings

material can form a permanent chemical bond inherent to the material through processing on the building site. This is the case, for example, with concrete, render, paints or certain plastics, which can be cast, trowelled, applied or welded through a number of operations. The boundaries of these operations are therefore "smeared" into each other, with the transitions sometimes becoming invisible, depending on the methods used.

As a rule, the building technology properties of the material used for homogeneous construction also require the layer of material to be positioned in certain, separate sub-areas that remain visible. The construction of every facade, both the homogenous and the jointed varieties, is therefore essentially characterised by the question of division. In the former, the question of division depends on the processing options on the building site, and in the latter on the production conditions for the module or element in the factory.

Shaping

Observation 7: The shape of the parts of the facade is primarily determined by the material properties, the production process and the logistics.

Shaping is often the result of complex, technical interdependencies. The dimensions of a stone cladding panel, for example, depend primarily on the splitting and sawing tools at the quarry, the dimensions and geometry of a brick on the pressing and firing methods in the brickworks. The

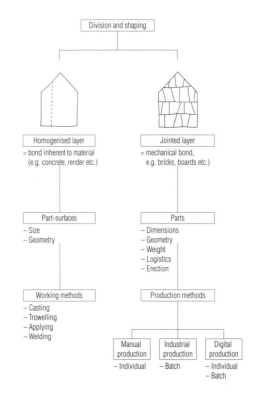

lengths and cross-sectional sizes of solid timber members are limited by the natural growth of the wood, which in turn is controlled by the forestry industry. By contrast, the dimensions of wood-based products are determined by the machines available to the woodworking industry. Usually, the architect can influence these factors and processes to a limited extent only, mostly for economic reasons, and in any case this requires extensive knowledge of the relationships between material properties, production and the final form.

Manual, hand-crafted production offers maximum freedom in the design of a facade, from one-off fabrications to small batches. One example of this is sheet metal work, much of which is still based on a few semi-finished products and is largely carried out directly on the building site.

Industrial production is founded on semi-finished, finished or more complex system products, based in turn on a set of precise geometrical and constructional rules, which are reflected directly in the appearance of a facade. The availability of the components is defined by the manufacturers' catalogues and regulated by the market.

Digital production opens up new perspectives in this context. Thanks to systematic digitising and clarification of the interfaces between the planning and the machine manufacturing processes, it unites the apparent contradictions between individual design and mass production. In the ideal case, forms with complex geometry can be transferred directly from the digital drawing board to component production, which allows the architect to exert

Fig. 18: Batch-prefabricated concrete elements in different, sculpted designs
Miguel Fisac: MUPAG rehabilitation centre, Madrid (E), 1970

Fig. 19: Layering with striking horizontal joints
Herzog & de Meuron Architekten: Ricola
warehouse, Laufen (CH), 1987

**Fig. 20: Continuous development of overlapping
sheet metal with pattern of fine joints**
Gigon/Guyer Architekten: Liner Museum, Appenzell
(CH), 1998

more influence directly on the production process and, in the end, the shaping.

Besides the production, the logistics and time factors play a significant role in the design of facade components. In other words, transport to the building site and the erection conditions on the building site affect the geometry, dimensions and weight of the elements and hence the expression of the facade as a whole. The life-cycle behaviour of a material is critical for the issue of exchangeability, which is again affected by the logistics.

Jointing

Observation 8: The joint articulates the constructional relationship between the parts of the facade.

The bond of a surface structure is derived from the suitable geometrical and constructional jointing of several larger or smaller parts of a facade. A joint inevitably ensues between the parts, and is part of both a technical and an architectural problem.

The joint regulates the constructional relationship between the individual parts of a facade. It is both a separating and a connecting element. Considered as a connection, it controls permeability, considered as a gap, it provides the necessary tolerance between the parts. This latter aspect includes dimensional accuracy during the building process (dimensional tolerance), while offering play for the material to expand due to external influences (movement tolerance).

We distinguish between joints with and without the insertion of an additional jointing material.

Joints without a jointing material are based on the purely mechanical interdependence between individual facade components, e.g. butt, overlap, interlock. The difficulty with such jointing techniques is to guarantee the necessary imperviousness to wind and water. For this reason, an additional impervious layer in the form of a waterproof sheet or airtight membrane is often fitted behind jointed protective layers, e.g. sheet metal with double welted joints.

In joints with jointing material, an additional material is positioned between the parts of the facade and provides the desired connection, separation, sealing or tolerance functions. A typical example of this is the brick facade with its horizontal and vertical mortar joints bonding the individual bricks together, sealing the joints and offering a certain tolerance in the horizontal and vertical dimensions of the wall. Another example is metal facades in which suitable neoprene sealing gaskets are fitted into grooves in the edges of the metal elements. These "compression profiles" are squashed by the contact pressure of the next element (screwed into place) and therefore guarantee the desired imperviousness. A further solution is the widely used permanently resilient putty or silicone joint

which, however, tends to call for expensive maintenance because it does fail in the end.

The jointing of the parts of the facade and hence also the joint itself are subjected to different structural requirements, according to the external wall system. A loadbearing or independent facade is assembled according to the loadbearing principle, whereas a non-loadbearing or non-independent facade can, in principle, be designed without any such constraints. Accordingly, in loadbearing systems the joints are obligatory components of a structural system, are subjected to structural actions, and their design is more constrained than the joints of non-loadbearing systems.

As mentioned above, joints occur in homogeneous facade constructions as well. This is because there is a limit to the panel sizes, which are restricted by the material stresses (elasticity). Like large facade components, the individual panels must be "joined" together to close off the layer over the whole building. The ensuing joints are visible as construction joints, which allow the observer to draw conclusions about the stages of the work. Expansion joints, which anticipate subsequent movement of the individual panels, relieve the panels and prevent stress cracks in homogeneous materials.

The controlled crack (contraction joint) can be regarded as a special form of joint. The crack is not caused by the addition of individual parts, but by the deliberate fracturing of the material at a particular point. The controlled crack, or a multitude of hairline cracks, can be used in homogeneous constructions specifically as a counter-policy to the expansion joint, provided the imperviousness of the facade remains guaranteed. This strategy is used, for example, in fair-face concrete or rendered facades which,

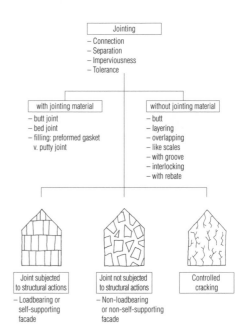

however, calls for a suitable, precise material composition in order to prevent damage.

Openings

Observation 9: The opening arises as a variation or disruption of the facade system.

The potential degree of opening of a building is determined fundamentally and permanently by the choice of loadbearing structure. Solid loadbearing structures generally restrict the range of openings to hole-like types of limited size. Filigree loadbearing structures, on the other hand, can exist, in the extreme case, of virtually nothing but openings. The effective degree of opening is eventually decided by the facade, via the permeability of the outer layer enclosing the loadbearing structure. The outer layer regulates the relationship between open and closed, between transparent and opaque zones. In doing so, the individual opening appears as a variation of a facade part or a joint or perhaps as a disruption of the facade system.

Observation 10: The opening as a variation of the facade system is subsidiary to the constructional and geometrical rules of the facade.

On the level of the facade parts, an opening occurs in the form of an omission, an empty space or a modulation in that the transparency of individual elements is varied by

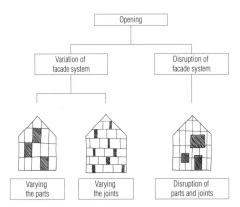

the material or the formal characteristics. A typical example of this is the suspended facade in which we can see the difference between the transparent and opaque glass elements, between perforated and plain sheet metal.

On the level of the joints, the dimensions of the joint space can be varied until the joint is quasi-permeable and itself becomes an opening. This type of opening is found in stables in timber log construction, where the joints between individual logs are left wide open to permit ventilation, which means that a functional compromise has to be made regarding the watertightness.

Observation 11: The opening as a disruption of the facade system prevailing over the constructional and geometrical rules of the facade.

The opening as a disruption of the facade system behaves like an autonomous element in the facade. The junction between the opening and the facade system is often controlled with a type of seam, which neutralises the set of constructional rules for the facade, the materiality, division and jointing at the position of the opening. This measure is seen, for example, in the form of a frame around the traditional window opening consisting of window sill, reveals and lintel. In other cases the opening is simply cut through the facade, similar to a perforation; the boundary of the opening remaining indistinct, at least on the outside.

Composition

The appropriate architectural composition of the means of construction, materials, components, joints and openings leads to the specific appearance of the facade in relation to the building as a whole.

On the level of the materials, the colours and textures, visual and tactile properties, should be coordinated with each other; on the level of the components, joints and openings, the numbers, dimensions, geometries and proportions must be considered. Irrespective of the technical requirements, certain general compositional principles are evident here.

Fig. 21: Window openings as a variation of the facade system (left) or as a disruption of the facade system (right)
Peter Zumthor: Private house, Gugalun, Versam (CH), 1994

Fig. 22: Wave-like development of a glass facade divided vertically; alternating opaque and transparent horizontal bands of different widths
Diener & Diener Architekten: Malmö University (S), 2005

Fig. 23: Free-form composition using different materials (sheet metal and glass), formats, divisions, joints and openings
MVRDV: Silodam housing development, Amsterdam (NL), 2002

Observation 12: The relative, area-related number and size of components, joints and openings regulate the sculpting of the facade.

Very fine sculpting can be achieved by using a large number of small parts. Movements in the two- or three-dimensional sense can be traced accurately and softly. The individual parts seem to merge into the mass. The number of joints increases in proportion to the divisibility. A dense network of joints weaves the surface together visually and often lends it the character of a textile. Appealing examples of this include facades of facing brickwork, whose horizontal and vertical mortar joints, depending on the bond, can remind the observer of a fabric.

By scaling the parts and joints, the texture can be further refined, right up to giving the impression of an almost homogeneous material. For example, evenly laid, small, thin wooden shingles with almost invisible, fine joints and overlaps give the impression of a continuous skin. And in the case of render, a conglomerate of different mineral components, there is a huge range of design choices from visible joints to completely homogeneous surfaces. The appropriate gradation is controlled by the grain size and the method of applying or working the materials.

In contrast to small-format surface structures, a surface comprising just a few large parts seems to have a more pronounced texture. The individual parts and the intervening joints are easier to identify visually. The consequence is that the geometrical, formal composition of the parts plays a greater role and the network of joints dominates, whereas the effect of the building as a whole tends to be additive, fragmentary. Contrast in large-format compositions can be influenced by the width and colouring of the joints in relation to the facade components.

Observation 13: The absolute number and size of the parts, joints and openings regulate the scale effect of a building, whereas their positions influence the legibility of the internal layout.

As a rule, the surface structure provides an indication of the internal organisation of a building, e.g. through division or distribution of the elements revealing the location of individual storeys or rooms. Through the targeted manipulation of the dividing elements, e.g. through unrestricted configuration, coupling or multiplying, it is possible to cover up, blur or cancel out the relationship between the facade structure and the internal layout.

Observation 14: The form of the parts, joints and openings regulates the relationship between the geometry of the surface structure and the geometry of the building.

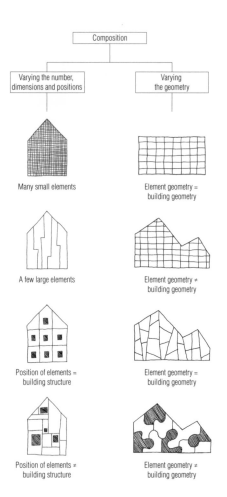

Repetitive parts produce a regular surface structure, a classical grid of panels. A grid is geometrically rigid and cannot respond to irregular building contours. This means either the grid dominates the layout of the building envelope, or the grid is curtailed by the building geometry. In the latter case, the elements at the edges of the panels must be modified and adapted to the building geometry.

Custom parts can be made for specific projects to suit irregular building geometries. In this case, the geometric principle of the shaped parts is achieved by treating the particular building geometry as one element. Irregular geometries along the edges of panels therefore become not the exception, but the rule.

Another strategy is to apply ornamental motifs to the facade structure as required. Such patterns follow their own geometrical logic, which is not derived from the building geometry, or at least not directly. The patterns are distributed at random over the building, a practice that visually alienates the contours and overall form of the building. This is camouflage, disguising our intentions. Employed in the positive sense, it helps to give a facade a multifaceted expression.

Process

The final question is: where does the design of the facade begin? Is the facade design the consequence of the expression, or is the expression the consequence of the facade design?

Observation 15: Like all architectural design processes, the design of the facade is an iterative operation with feedback in which the interdependencies of individual decisions are not always clear, do not always follow a linear course.

In principle, the start of the investigation, the first draft design, can be based on technical or architectural criteria, with no restrictions on the details or the whole. The critical point is the motivation for getting to grips critically with the consequences of the chosen strategy and recognising and understanding the diverse dependencies. The aim here should be to filter out the hierarchy between obligatory and variable, between "hard" and "soft" regulating factors or parameters. The facade design is therefore coupled to the concept of the architectural project.

The quality and complexity of the process as a whole lies in the professional, nonetheless stimulating, handling of both constructional and architectural principles.

Observation 16: The above observations are not commandments, but aids to orientation in order to study the design of the facade more precisely, more systematically. They should support the design process and reveal the relationship between conception, construction and perception in a visual way. This is therefore an attempt to introduce a system, although sometimes breaking the rules intelligently can lead to new findings.

Fig. 24: Heavyweight, prefabricated concrete elements with striking open joints enclosing a sculpted building form
von Ballmoos Krucker Architekten: primary school, Obermeilen (CH), 2007

Further reading
- Andrea Deplazes, Jürg Fischer: *Lignatec Fassadenbekleidungen*, Lignum Zürich, 11/2008.

For and against the long horizontal window
The Perret – Le Corbusier controversy

Bruno Reichlin

"Mr Auguste Perret reports on the architectural section of the *Salon d'Automne*." That was the headline used by the *Paris Journal*[1] for an interview with Auguste Perret on the section dedicated to "Architecture and Town Planning" at the *Salon d'Automne* (1 Nov to 16 Dec 1923). According to journalist Guillaume Baderre, this section in particular evoked great curiosity among the visitors: "Some people greeted our young architects' bold designs with great enthusiasm, others were genuinely shocked, but nobody was indifferent… First and foremost, the numerous models[2] by Messieurs Le Corbusier and Jeanneret sparked off controversial debate. These architects employ a new and outstanding technique that throws all traditional rules overboard."[3]

This interview gave Perret the opportunity to launch a direct and quite malicious attack on Loos, Le Corbusier and Jeanneret. The arguments brought forward by "our

avant-garde architects", as Perret mockingly called them, were redirected towards themselves. According to Perret they were cultivating a new formal academism that closely resembled the one they pretended to oppose and was likewise totally insensitive to the functional aspects of residential living. Perret contended that "for the benefit of volume and wall surface, these young architects repeat the very mistakes that in the recent past were made in favour of symmetry, the colonnade, or the arcade… They are bewitched by volume, it is the only issue on their minds, and suffering from a regrettable compulsion they insist on devising combinations of lines without paying attention to the rest." Perret continued with his accusation thus: "These *faiseurs de volume* [creators of volume] reduce chimneys to pathetic fragments that no longer allow the fumes to disperse. They do not even refrain from eliminating the cornices and consequently subject the facades to exposure and rapid decay… This complete denial of all practical principles is simply amazing." And this, Perret furiously concluded, "is especially obvious with Le Corbusier of all people, an architect representing the principle of practicability *par excellence* – or at least pretending to represent it."

The criticism of Perret that sparked off the most far-reaching consequences was directed, as will soon be revealed, at the form of the openings in the wall surfaces. And it was this criticism that prompted a passionate response from Le Corbusier. In the course of the ensuing controversy between Perret and Le Corbusier, two diametrically opposed positions were defined.

In addition to the purely technical and aesthetic arguments, two contrasting conceptions of residential living came to be established – or even of two cultures, if the term culture is defined in its broadest, almost anthropological sense. But let us look at the contradictions in question – meticulously and chronologically. During the interview, Perret kept referring to the contradiction between form and function within Le Corbusier's architectural framework of ideas: "The function necessitates the form, but the form must not supersede its function… However, we see in Le Corbusier's work a tendency to use clusters of windows to achieve volume, which leaves large wall areas in between completely blank; or, on an artistic whim, he constructs awkward window shapes, windows with an excessive horizontal elongation. From the outside this may make an original impression, but I fear that from the inside the impression is much less original because the result is that at least half of the rooms are without any natural light, and I believe this is taking originality too far."

This criticism cut Le Corbusier to the quick. Deeply insulted, he retaliated twice in the same *Paris Journal*: "A visit to Le Corbusier-Saugnier", undertaken once more by Baderre ("the other side must also be heard"),

Fig. 1: Franz Louis Catel: Schinkel in Naples, 1824

published on 14 December 1923, gave him the first opportunity for a riposte:[4]

Le Corbusier admitted that he was dismayed by Perret's lack of loyalty – a colleague after all – and accused him of publishing not only insulting but factually incorrect arguments against him. After cursorily touching on the criticism regarding chimneys and missing cornices, he directly addressed the question of the openings: "And here is the final insult from Mr Perret: my windows don't let in enough light. This accusation really infuriates me as its falseness is more than evident. What does he mean? I strive to create well-lit interiors…, this is my prime objective, and this is exactly why the external appearance of my facades might seem a little bizarre in the eyes of creatures of habit. Mr Perret upholds that I intentionally create bizarreness. Exactly –'intentionally'. But this is not for the sake of the bizarre itself, but in order to allow a maximum of light and air into my houses. This so-called whim is nothing else than my wish to comply with the occupants' most elementary needs."

In the *Paris Journal* of 28 December 1923, there was another contribution from Guillaume Baderre, entitled "Second visit to Le Corbusier".[5] This time the journalist voiced his own opinion. He takes Le Corbusier's side and sums up all the arguments in favour of long horizontal windows, and anticipates all the papers and lectures that later made it popular. In short, the traditional vertical window is the result of outdated construction standards (stone and brick). These windows were limited in width and required massive walls. The enlargement of the window surfaces in prominent buildings thus necessitated a disproportionate increase in height – both for the openings and the rooms they serve. The use of reinforced concrete, however, allows for greater spans, wider clear openings, a significant reduction in the supporting elements – and thus the long horizontal window. "This [window] is much more practical," Baderre wrote, "because it admits more light into a room even if its area is the same. In fact, its shape focuses all the incoming light at the occupant's eye level. With windows of the old type, about half of the light is lost. Of course a room's floor should be well-lit, but the greatest amount

Fig. 3: Marcel Duchamp: "Fresh window", assemblage, 1920

of light should occur in the middle of the room, in its most vivacious part, i.e. between the heads and feet of its occupants."

What made Baderre's article particularly significant, however, was the simultaneous publication of the first sketches – floor plans and general views – of the small villa in Corseaux on the banks of Lake Geneva, which Le Corbusier and Jeanneret designed for the architect's parents.[6] The plan for this little house was a real challenge for Perret. "Only one side of the house has a real window, but this window occupies the whole width of the facade." Despite its being the only one, Baderre continued, the window sufficiently illuminates the whole living space because "not only its dimensions admit enough light, but at both ends it meets the adjoining side walls at a right-angle. These white walls direct the view straight towards the scenery outside, unobstructed by window reveals. They are truly flooded with light."[7] Perret had hardly uttered his verdict – and through him as a mouthpiece the "institution" ("a true authority in the field of architecture", Baderre had written in deferential regard, with Le Corbusier echoing ironically in a biting letter to Perret that "an Olympic god is about to speak"[8]) – when Le Corbusier reciprocated with a work that virtually lent the disputed object the character of a manifesto. Even in this booklet, published 30 years after the construction of the house on Lake Geneva, Le Corbusier did not hesitate to describe the long horizontal window as "the main protagonist of the house",

Fig. 2: Le Corbusier: La Roche-Jeanneret House, Paris (F), 1923

Fig. 4: Le Corbusier and Pierre Jeanneret: small house in Corseaux on Lake Geneva, Vevey (CH), 1923

or even "the sole protagonist of the facade".[9] Whereas, up until then, the discussion on the pros and cons of the long horizontal window seemed to revolve mainly around "technical" aspects – direction of the light, constructional options, savings in space – something quite different was now cooking in the pot: Le Corbusier's aim was to work the long horizontal window of the *petite maison* into his continuing controversy with Perret. And, not surprisingly, the discussion was rekindled six months later when Perret built his "Palais de Bois" art gallery. In the *Almanach*, Le Corbusier describes the *petite maison* and then once more returns to the dispute under the title "Brief contribution to the study of the modern window".[10]

On two successive pages Le Corbusier juxtaposes a photograph showing a panoramic view of the lake as it can be enjoyed from the window and a sketch showing Perret seated in an armchair in front of the *fenêtre en longeur* which illuminates the bar of the "Palais de Bois". The sketch depicts the circumstances of an encounter between Perret, Jeanneret, and Le Corbusier. Perhaps out of spite the draughtsman shows the walking-stick of the venerable master pointing straight at the long horizontal window. Pleased about having "caught" Perret sitting peacefully in front of the building's sole long horizontal window, Le Corbusier congratulated him – "very

pretty, your long horizontal windows" – and expressed satisfaction at the discovery that the old master, too, is employing this type of window. Perret, for his part, did not react to this humorous allusion, but returned to the attack: "Actually, the long horizontal window is not a window at all. (Categorically): A window, that is man himself!" And when Jeanneret stated that the human eye can only capture a horizontal view, he dryly retorted: "I detest panoramas".[11]

When Perret claimed that a window was "like a human being" he did so because he recognised an anthropomorphic analogy. In his book on Perret, Marcel Zahar elaborated on this: "The vertical window gives man a frame in line with his silhouette…, the vertical is the line of the upright human being, it is the line of life itself".[12] Behind Perret's convictions lies a cultural framework of ideas, documented through centuries of pictorial and literary tradition and still valid today. How not to be reminded of the first verses of the second and fifth poems from Rainer Maria Rilke's cycle "The windows":[13]

N'es-tu pas notre géometrie, fenêtre,
très simple forme
qui sans effort circonscris
notre vie énorme?

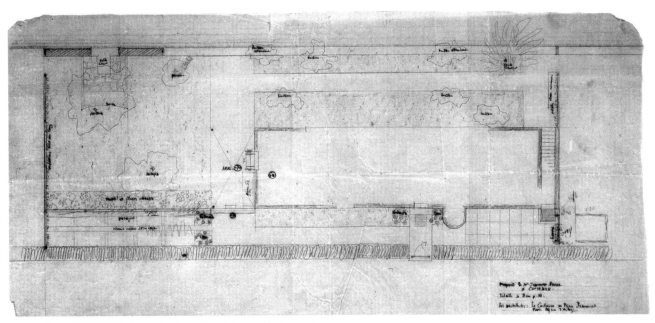

Fig. 5: Le Corbusier and Pierre Jeanneret: location plan for small house in Corseaux, Lake Geneva (CH), 1923

Comme tu ajoutes à tout,
fenêtre, le sens de nos rites:
Quelqu'un qui ne serait que debout,
dans ton cadre attend ou médite.

Perret was opposed to long horizontal windows because for him they indicated a momentous change, a change that questioned the values deeply rooted in culture, especially in the "experience" of the interior. And this is probably why he believed that Le Corbusier was "destroying the beautiful French tradition".[14]

The traditional window opens up the inside towards the outside; at the same time, however, the window defines the space and acts as a threshold, "excluding" in a physical as well as a figurative sense. Whereas the long horizontal window "condemns us to look at an eternal panorama", Perret observed, the vertical window is a stimulant "as it shows us *un espace complet* [a complete space]: street, garden, sky". But what matters most is that these openings can also be closed.[15]

According to Le Corbusier the long horizontal window – in contrast to the traditional window – was acting as a mediator between inside and outside because the opening itself cancels both the threshold and its own boundaries. And this is the true meaning of the photograph of the long horizontal window at the *petite maison* published in the *Almanach*, a photograph in which everything that constitutes the physical elements of the building diffuses into an indistinct, dark background, a framework

that allows the euphoric picture of "one of the world's most beautiful panoramas"[16] to emerge. "The scenery is right there – it is just like being in the garden."[17]

Whereas the traditional window limits the view to a section of the continuum of the landscape, thus "manipulating" it by giving it the aura of a *veduta,* the long horizontal window is answering the request for "objectivity" – one of the main goals of "Modernism" and "purism": to depict the scenery as it is. "The window with its length of 11 metres

Fig. 6: Le Corbusier: lighting sketches, 1923

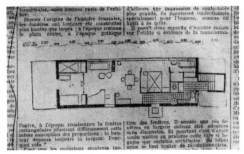

Fig. 7: Article about the small house in Corseaux by Le Corbusier and Pierre Jeanneret
Excerpt from *Paris Journal,* 28 December 1923

Fig. 8: Le Corbusier: sketches for the small house on Lake Geneva, 1923

allows the vastness of the outside world into the room, the unadulterated entity of the lake scenery, in stormy weather or brilliant serenity".[18]

But is it true that a long horizontal window does *not* manipulate the view? Perret contended that the vertical window (in other languages not just by chance called a "French window") renders a complete "three-dimensional impression" because it allows a view of street, garden, and sky. Marie Dormoy, Perret's faithful supporter, elaborated on this: "A window in the form of an upright rectangle makes a room much more cheerful than a horizontal one because this form permits a view that includes the foreground, the most colourful and vivacious segment of a view."[19] This comment reminds us of the particular preference for the window picture that dominated the world of painting from the days of Romanticism through to our times, and the important role it played in the development of the modern picturesque interior. The vertical window allows the eye of the observer to wander downwards to the first and nearest spatial levels – street and garden – and horizontally to the middle and deeper levels – houses opposite, trees, hilly background – and upwards into the unlimited expanse of the sky. The vertical window shows a pictorial cut-out of maximum perspective depth as well as great variety and gradation in terms of dimension, colouring, and brightness. But it is also an ideal conveyor of manifold atmospheric impressions: the perception of the immediate and familiar surroundings creates a feeling of quiet and calm, and looking out from the elevated position of the window provides the necessary detachment and the discretion of seclusion.

"The view from the window is one of the privileges of house-dwellers, mainly the middle classes, as they live in apartments in the towns and cities... The window is... a place of silent monologue and dialogue, of reflection on one's own status between the finite and the infinite."[20] It is obvious that Perret prefers the vertical window for the very same reasons that painters are fascinated by the window as a motif.

The window motif is also an important experimental field in modern painting. This happened at the very latest when artists more or less consciously turned away from the painting as a peep-show, thus questioning the principle – which goes back to the Renaissance – that claims any painting in the original sense is a "window picture". "In order to force all elements of a painting into the picture's frame"[21], painters gradually withdrew from the absolutisation of linear perspective, renounced the space of aerial perspective, and stopped rendering the tactile – and later the apparent materiality of the subject. Painting also abandoned the absolute colour of the object and the relative apparent colour as well as graphic detail

Fig. 9: Le Corbusier: August Perret seated in an armchair in front of the long horizontal window *(fenêtre en longeur)* of his art gallery, the "Palais de Bois", 1924

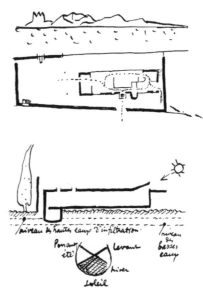

Fig. 10: Le Corbusier: location plan (top) and sketches (bottom) for the small house on Lake Geneva, 1923

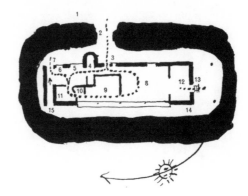

Fig. 11: Le Corbusier: sketch of functions (north at the top), 1923

and the exact rendering of anatomical and perspective proportions.

As far as the window motif and its role in these drastic sublimation processes is concerned, J.A. Schmoll, known as Eisenwerth, drew the conclusion that "the window motif in the paintings of the 19th and 20th centuries has paved the way for an understanding of a purely two-dimensional, abstract depiction devoid of illusory concepts of depth (as Matisse's painting "Porte-Fenêtre" already suggested as early as 1914). The representation of perspective in Western art began with the assumption that the depth of a room is generated by a view through a window, and ended with the notion of recognising the form of the window itself as the principle behind a two-dimensional, pictorial architecture."[22]

Against the backdrop of this summary of the role of the window motif as an important pioneer of modern painting, we will once more return to the long horizontal window...

Perret was opposed to the long horizontal window because it did not facilitate a full view of the outside space – garden, street, sky – "particularly the segment of the sky, most of the time lost through the horizontal window", as Margherita G. Sarfatti remembers.[23] And, indeed, the long horizontal window does limit the perception and correct depth evaluation of the scenery that is visible. This impression is emphasised by the extreme distance between the vertical boundaries to our view, even more so if – as in the first sketches for the *petite maison* – all the elements that delineate the room, i.e. the side walls and the ceiling bordering on the openings, are altogether hidden from sight. In other words: the long horizontal window breaks through both sides of the pyramid of vision horizontally and thus itself disappears from the visual range of the observer. Consequently, the window picture loses the characteristic of a *veduta* framed by a window, and the window frame its function as a *repoussoir*.

Fig. 12: Le Corbusier and Pierre Jeanneret: View through the long horizontal window of the small house on Lake Geneva, contemporary photograph

Fig. 14: Le Corbusier: View through the long horizontal window of the small house on Lake Geneva, 1923

Fig. 13: Le Corbusier and Pierre Jeanneret: View through the long horizontal window of the small house in Corseaux on Lake Geneva, present-day photograph

Fig. 15: Le Corbusier: Interior of the small house on Lake Geneva, 1923

But if the long horizontal window is the opposite of the perspective peep-show with its characteristic steeply sloping sides and the traditional window frame, it must be considered as one of those constructional measures that played a vital role in architecture's gradual disentanglement from the traditional perspective environment. In looking at the conception and effect of the interior, the long horizontal window thus plays a similar role to the pictorial experiments that, based on the window motif, led to "a transformation from the panel painting to the prevalence of painting on canvas."[24]

"The scenery is there", in its direct immediacy, as if it were "glued" to the window because either a detached and calming effect is denied, or the "transition from the nearby, familiar objects to the more distant ones is hidden from view, which significantly reduces the perception of three-dimensional depth."

"The paradox of the window – the modern, completely transparent one which simultaneously opens up towards the outside and admits but also confines"[25] – resulted in some embarrassment for interior designers and architects at the end of the 19th and beginning of the 20th century. It encouraged Dolf Sternberger to dedicate a whole chapter of his book *Panorama of the 19th century* to "The Disruptive Window". And Cornelius Gurlitt begins his chapter on windows, as published in his comments on art, the artistic crafts, and interior design,[26] with some cursory comments on the window's recent development: the gradual enlargement of both the opening itself and the individual panes of glass: "Goethe's cry from his deathbed for 'More light!' rang through our living quarters." But he also makes a complaint: "The large window bonded the room too closely with the outside world. Man's deftness in creating large, fully transparent walls grew to such an extent that the border between the room and the outside world was altogether blurred to the human eye, which greatly impaired the artistic consistency of the room." For Gurlitt both the use of brightly coloured curtains towards the end of the 18th century and the

Fig. 16: Caspar David Friedrich: View from the Artist's Studio,
Window on the Left, 1806

Fig. 17: Henri Matisse: Open Window, Collioure, 1905

Fig. 18: Robert Delaunay: Window on the City, 1910

Fig. 19: Max Beckmann: Interior with Mirror,
1926

more recent fashion of blinds and bull's-eye panes are means employed in order to restore a room's original feeling of "inner seclusion", which was disturbed both by an excessively obtrusive relationship with the outside world and by the incoming flood of too much consistent daylight that deprived the room of twilight's charms. "Far removed is all that goes on outside" – this should apply to the interior as Gurlitt wishes to restore it: "We feel alone in it, be it with our own thoughts or with our friends."

The same kind of criticism comes from Baillie Scott[27] in his sarcastic comment on the fashion of large windows spreading to English suburban mansions: "From the outside we instantly note the enormous breaches in the walls, calculated for their external effect just like shop windows. There is the table with the vase, there are the lace curtains, and so on, it all reminds us of a 'shop display'. And inside there is this harsh, merciless light that destroys all feeling of calm and shelter."

"The interior", writes Walter Benjamin in his "Arcades Project",[28] "is not only a private person's universe, but also his protective shell." The shadowy, phantasmagorical half-light of the interior softens the all-too-physical reality of things, while the objects' mainly symbolic existence "erases" their utility value, their concrete and commercial substantiality. In this environment furniture, furnishings, and personal knick-knacks turn the room into a safe haven for ideological and sensual identification because the

gentle deception hovering at the centre of this microcosm has been created by the room's occupant himself in accordance with his very own spiritual disposition.

But along comes Le Corbusier's long horizontal window to tear open the "protective shell of the private person" and let the outside world invade the interior. In the tiny living room of the lakeside villa, nature in all her glory is within reach, through the whole cycle of weathers and seasons. "A window with a length of 11 metres establishes a relationship, lets in the light... and fills the house with the vastness of a unique landscape, comprising the lake and all its transformations plus the Alps with their marvellous shades of colour and light."[29]

"Then the days are no longer gloomy: from dawn to dusk nature goes through her metamorphoses."[30] No longer shut out by walls and curtains, the light pours in through this opening and de-mystifies the room and the objects; the sentimental objects regain their original, solid, prosaic quality of practical tools.[31]

The interior has taken flight – this time into the open. *True nature* is a place of genuine memories, a euphoric object of desire with uplifting and consoling abilities. The house on Lake Geneva is a tiny hideaway protected within nature's bosom.

But the *petite maison* does not constitute the typical "hut" with thick walls creating a protective square around the interior. The long horizontal window, opening up wide

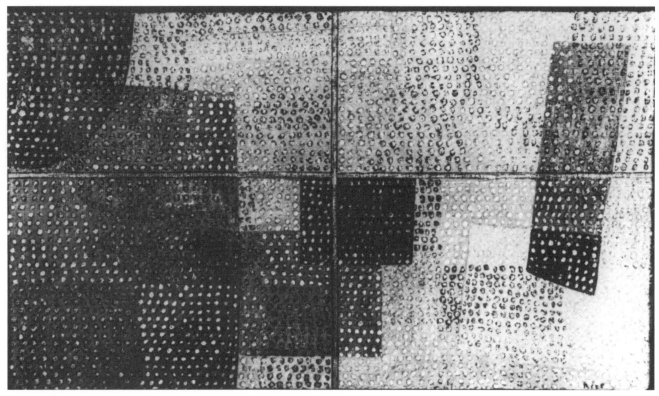

Fig. 20: Paul Klee: "Through a Window", c. 1932

towards the scenery, enforces an unusual visual and psychological "omnipresence" on the occupant.

On the borderline between two antithetical interiors, the place of physical presence and the place of spiritual longing, the human being – in the latter case forced into the role of a passive observer exactly when the all-embracing intimacy of objects and the room has disappeared – experiences the psychological and symbolic conflict within the modern "interior", which architecture can, at best, only strive to elucidate and illustrate.[32]

Excerpt from: *Daidalos* 13, "Zwischen innen und aussen", June 1984.

Notes

[1] *Paris Journal* of 1 Dec 1923. The document is in the Le Corbusier Foundation collection (hereafter: LCF doc.), Paris.
[2] However, the catalogue of the Salon d'Automne 1923 speaks of two *hôtels privées* models (p. 344).
[3] All prior quotations of Auguste Perret appeared in the *Paris Journal*.
[4] *Paris Journal* of 14 Dec 1923 (LCF doc.)
[5] *Paris Journal* of 28 Dec 1923 (LCF doc.)
[6] Parts of the diary of Le Corbusier's father, Georges-Edouard Jeanneret, are in the library of the La-Chaux-de-Fonds Villa. The entry for 5 Sept 1923 includes a first reference to the building plans. The proposal "d'une maison puriste, forme wagon" is first mentioned on 27 Dec 1923.
[7] *Paris Journal* of 28 Dec 1923.
[8] Letter from Le Corbusier to Auguste Perret, 13 Dec 1923 (LCF doc.).
[9] Le Corbusier: *Une petite Maison – 1923*, Zurich, 1954, pp. 30–33, 36.
[10] Le Corbusier: *Almanach d'architecture moderne*, Paris, 1926, pp. 95–97.
[11] This opinion of Perret is taken from: Marcel Zahar: *Auguste Perret*, Paris, 1959, p. 15.
[12] ibid.
[13] Rainer Maria Rilke: "Les Fenêtres", Paris, 1927.
[14] Notes by Le Corbusier on an undated sheet concerning a view Perret had expressed to the publisher of *L'Architecture Vivante*, Feb 1926 (LCF doc.).
[15] After Marcel Zahar, ibid.
[16] Le Corbusier: *Une petite Maison*, ibid.
[17] Le Corbusier: *Almanach*, ibid.
[18] Le Corbusier: *Sur un état présent de l'architecture et de l'urbanisme*, Paris, 1930, p. 30.
[19] Marie Dormoy: "Le Corbusier", in: *L'Amour de l'Art*, Paris, March 1930, No. 5, p. 213ff.
[20] J. A. Schmoll (known as Eisenwerth): "Fensterbilder – Motivketten in der europäischen Malerei", in: *Beiträge zur Motivkunde des 19. Jahrhunderts*, Munich, 1970, p. 152.
[21] Georg Schmidt: *Kleine Geschichte der Modernen Malerei*, Basel, 1955
[22] Eisenwerth: ibid., p. 150.
[23] Margherita G. Sarfatti: "Perret", in: *L'Architecture d'aujourd'hui*, 1932, p. 11.
[24] Eisenwerth: ibid. p. 151.
[25] Dolf Sternberger: *Panorama of the 19th Century*, New York, 1977.
[26] Cornelius Gurlitt: *Im Bürgerhause*, Dresden, 1888.
[27] M. H. Baillie Scott: *Houses and Gardens*, Berlin, 1912, p. 35.
[28] Walter Benjamin: *The Arcades Project*, Cambridge, Mass., 1999.
[29] Le Corbusier: *Précisions*, ibid., p. 130.
[30] Le Corbusier: *Almanach*, ibid., p. 94.
[31] Le Corbusier: *L'art décoratif d'aujourd'hui*, Paris 1925, chap. "Besoins-types", p. 69ff.
[32] J. A. Schmoll: ibid., chap. "Schlussbemerkungen und literarische Aspekte".

Fig. 21: Henri Matisse: "Glass Doors", 1914

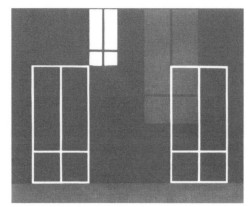

Fig. 22: Josef Albers: "Windows", 1929

The window – opening package

The brief

An aperture in a wall, floor or roof is known as an opening. Openings join spaces for functional and/or visual reasons and thus establish a relationship between them. In the following we shall restrict our observations to openings in vertical external walls. The surfaces within the depth of a wall created by forming an opening are known as *reveal* (vertical), *sill* and *head/lintel* (horizontal).

The window is a building component for closing off an opening. It consists of outer and sash frames plus the glazing and is fitted into the structural opening. Together, window and opening therefore form an indispensable *constructional package*. The window is both an element of the package and the divider between interior and exterior.

The light permeability of the glazing promotes visual links between inside and outside, and also admits daylight into the interior. Consequently, the position and size of the opening is a key element in the design of the interior. Furthermore, if the incoming light – divided into direct sunlight and diffuse daylight – is also directed and regulated, this has a particular influence on the design concept.

In terms of the performance of the building, the window must provide a viable separation between the interior and exterior climates, and to do this it must exhibit certain thermal insulation characteristics. The main load on a window construction is that due to water and moisture in all their states, both from inside (moisture in the air, vapour diffusion and condensation) and from outside (rainwater, snow, meltwater). Essentially, the window design should prevent water from entering, but if it does enter it should be able to drain away in a controlled fashion (waterproofing). The airtightness of the window–opening

package also needs to be given attention. After all, the window assembly must guarantee comfortable conditions inside the building, and that involves thermal and sound insulation issues.

When preparing the working drawings the *tolerances* must be taken into account. As windows can be produced with considerably tighter tolerances than, for example, masonry, it must be possible to accommodate the tolerances when fitting the window into its structural opening. But the window manufacturer can use the as-built dimensions and hence construct a window to the exact size required.

At the window head it is necessary to leave space for a *sunshading system*, which will have an effect on the window head and lintel design.

The principle of the opening rebate

The opening rebate is a peripheral step or shoulder in the structural opening and thus forms the contact face between outer frame and structural opening. The window is fitted up against this step, fixed with screws and sealed. To avoid stresses caused by temperature-related movements, the frame must be built in with minimum tolerance. All fixings must be protected against corrosion.

The principle of the frame rebate
(see full-size details)

The biggest problem with the window is keeping out water and wind. The rebate in the structural opening and the rebates in the frame members are therefore the most important elements in this battle. Special attention must be paid to the tightness of the joints between outer frame and opening, and outer frame and sash frames.

The weatherstripping between outer frame and sash frames remains in the same position around the entire periphery and is sealed at the corners. There are two different sealing positions in a window element:

Outer frame–opening

– water and wind
– accommodation of climate-related movements in the masonry

Outer frame–sash frames

The *rebate* is intrinsic to the design of windows with opening lights, i.e. *opening windows*:

– joint permeability for controlled air change rate between sash frames and outer frame
– protection against driving rain, water and wind

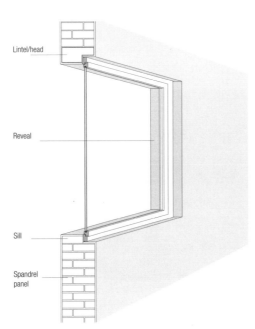

Lintel/head

Reveal

Sill

Spandrel panel

Fig. 23: Perspective view of opening rebates

Position of window, opening rebate forms

The position of the window within the depth of the opening and the opening rebate form have considerable influence on the architectural expression of a building. Windows fitted externally, flush with the facade, lend the envelope a compact and enclosing appearance, which emphasises the form of the building. Contrasting with this, windows fitted further back within the depth of the opening create relief due to the play of light and shade, which breaks up the volume of the building. Depending on the opening rebate form, the part of the frame visible externally can be suppressed or featured. Viewed from the inside, a window fitted on the outside can create an alcove, thus extending the usable floor space, whereas windows fitted on the inside generate a distinct enclosure to the interior and possibly even the impression of a thin outer skin. Apart from the extreme positions of windows fitted flush with the inside or outside faces, the position of the window does not depend on the opening rebate form. We distinguish between two principal opening rebate forms.

Fig. 24: Window opening inwards (top), opening outwards (bottom)

View from inside   View from outside

Window opening inwards

Such windows are usually fitted from inside. The entire width of the outer frame is visible internally, whereas from outside it might be that only the sash frames can be seen. The window can be fitted flush with the inside face of the wall. As the window is always fitted back from the face of the facade by a distance equal to at least the depth of the step or shoulder, it is relatively well protected against the weather. The connections do not present any problems because they are essentially covered and protected by this step or shoulder.

View from inside   View from outside

Window opening outwards

The entire width of the outer frame is visible externally. The window can be fitted flush with the outside face of the wall; however, that does mean that the glazing and the frames are fully exposed to the weather. The connections must satisfy enhanced aesthetics and quality requirements because they are readily visible and very exposed, especially when the window is fitted flush with the outside face.

The window as a component – frame sections

Materials for outer and sash frames

Untreated wood

The following measures must be taken to ensure the durability of wooden windows:

Choose suitable, resistant species of wood such as pine, spruce, fir and larch. Ensure that water can drain away from all sections and surfaces.

Ensure protection by providing an appropriate surface treatment: priming is a preventive measure protecting against discolouring mould growth. Impregnation prevents rotting caused by moisture.

Painted wood

Wood can be painted many different colours. Opaque paints have a lower water permeability than mere impregnation and they protect against rot. Problems: resistance to ultraviolet radiation, vapour pressure from inside (in the case of thick coats of paint on the outside of the window).

Wood/metal

This is the combination of a loadbearing construction of wood on the inside and an aluminium facing on the outside. The latter protects the wood, but the architectural expression of the window varies from inside to outside.

Plastics

PVC is the most common material for the production of plastic windows. The material of the frame sections is initially white; it can be dyed or coated, but not painted.

The frame sections are hollow (single- or multi-chamber systems), with various forms readily available. Despite the inclusion of metal stiffeners to strengthen the chambers, plastic windows are known for their relatively low structural strength.

Aluminium and steel

Metal windows have a high thermal conductivity and so the frame sections must include a thermal break.

Aluminium windows: Stability is relatively good and so aluminium is suitable for large elements. As a rule, the surface is treated because otherwise the irregular oxidation of the material leads to blemishes.

We distinguish between mechanical surface treatments, e.g. grinding, brushing and polishing, and the electrochemical anodising process, which produces a consistent oxide layer. Stove-enamelling involves bonding a coat of paint to the metal surface by firing.

Steel windows: Mainly used for industrial buildings. Much more stable than aluminium windows. Large window assemblies, especially together with the glazing, are very heavy (installation problems).

The biggest disadvantage is the risk of corrosion, which can be reduced by painting or galvanising. Like aluminium windows, steel windows can be given a stove-enamelled finish.

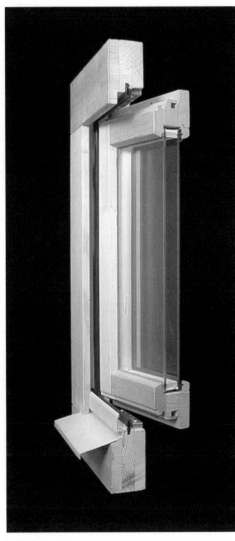

Fig. 25: Window sample
Frame: untreated wood; insulating glazing

The window as a component – glass

Types of glass

Various types of glass are available, distinguished by the method of manufacture:

– *Float glass* is today the most common form of glass and has a flat surface.
– *Window glass* was the forerunner of float glass and is characterised by a slightly undulating surface (cf. window panes in old buildings).
– *Rolled or patterned glass* has a textured surface and is therefore translucent, not transparent.
– *Wired glass* includes a wire mesh inlay, which enhances the fire resistance and binds together the fragments of a broken pane.

In addition to these basic types, diverse coatings and surface treatments are possible. The choice of glass and its coating or treatment influences the architectural expression and the quality of light entering the interior (direct, diffuse, coloured) plus building performance and security aspects. We distinguish glazing primarily according to mechanical and thermal treatments:

– standard glass,
– toughened glass,
– toughened safety glass,
– laminated glass,
– laminated safety glass,
– fire-resistant glass,
– heat-treated glass,
– insulating glazing,
– heat-absorbing glass,
– solar-control glass

Current thermal insulation and comfort requirements have made insulating glazing the number one choice for almost all windows.

Insulating glazing consists of at least two panes of glass bonded to an aluminium or plastic spacer. The adhesive also seals the cavity between the panes.

The thermal insulation properties of insulating glazing essentially depend on the cavity and the quality of its filling (various gases), also any coatings that have been applied.

Important parameters

U-value: This designates the thermal transmittance value of glasses and building components. The lower the value, the better the insulation. Customary values are 1.0–1.1 W/m^2K, but values as low as 0.2 W/m^2K are possible (SILVERSTAR glass, glass with special interlayer).

g-value: This defines the total energy transmittance through the glazing. This value is important for controlling heat transmission gains and heat protection. The g-value specifies how much energy from the incident solar radiation passes through the glazing into the interior. It is made up of two components: the direct radiation transmission and the secondary heat emissions. This latter phenomenon results from the fact that the incident solar radiation heats up the glass, which in turn releases this heat both inwards and outwards (panes of glass with plastic interlayer: the interlayer controls the energy transmittance).

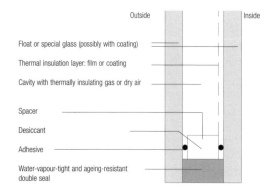

Outside | Inside

Float or special glass (possibly with coating)

Thermal insulation layer: film or coating

Cavity with thermally insulating gas or dry air

Spacer

Desiccant

Adhesive

Water-vapour-tight and ageing-resistant double seal

Fig. 26: Schematic diagram of insulating glazing construction

Further reading
- Christian Schittich, Gerald Staib, Dieter Balkow, Matthias Schuler, Werner Sobek: *Glass Construction Manual*, Basel, 1998.
- Bruno Keller, Stephan Rutz, professor for building physics, Zurich ETH: *pinpoint. Fakten der Bauphysik. Zu nachhaltigem Bauen*, Zurich, 2007.
- Glas Trösch AG: *Glas und Praxis*, Bützberg, 2000.

Window – horizontal section, 1:1

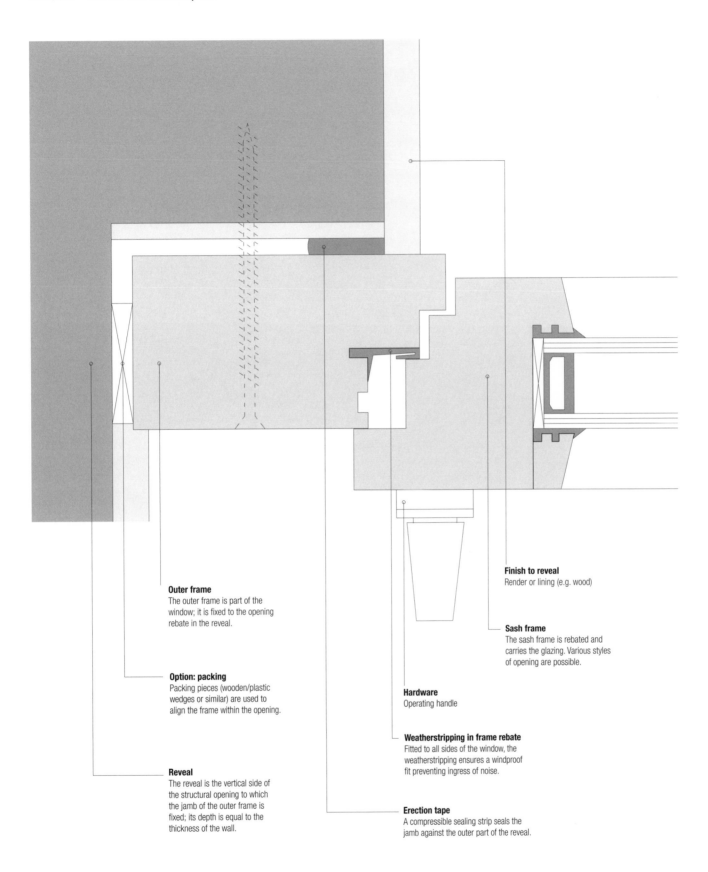

Outer frame
The outer frame is part of the window; it is fixed to the opening rebate in the reveal.

Option: packing
Packing pieces (wooden/plastic wedges or similar) are used to align the frame within the opening.

Reveal
The reveal is the vertical side of the structural opening to which the jamb of the outer frame is fixed; its depth is equal to the thickness of the wall.

Finish to reveal
Render or lining (e.g. wood)

Sash frame
The sash frame is rebated and carries the glazing. Various styles of opening are possible.

Hardware
Operating handle

Weatherstripping in frame rebate
Fitted to all sides of the window, the weatherstripping ensures a windproof fit preventing ingress of noise.

Erection tape
A compressible sealing strip seals the jamb against the outer part of the reveal.

Fig. 27

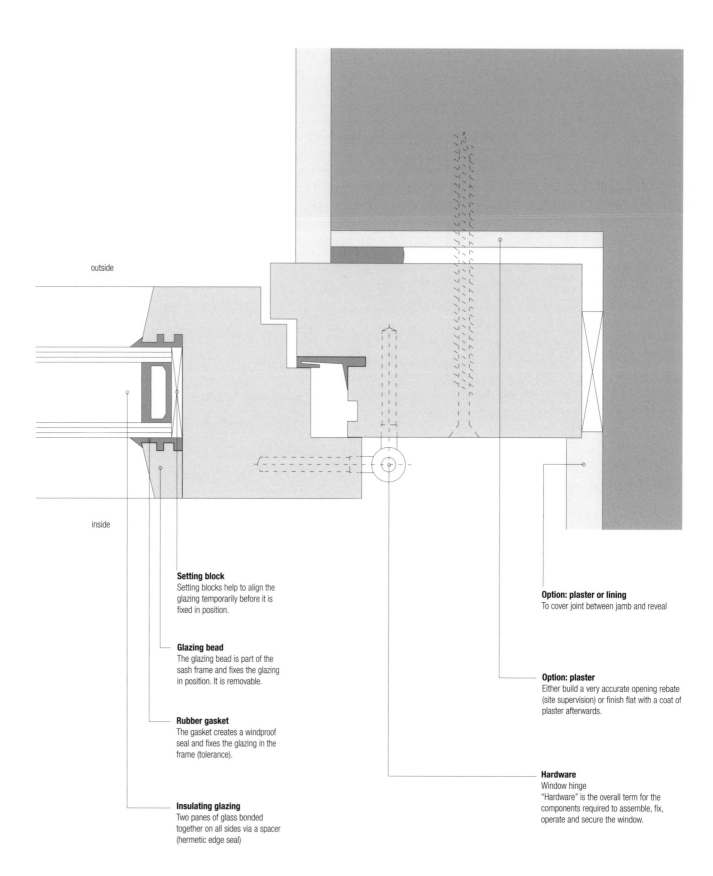

outside

inside

Setting block
Setting blocks help to align the
glazing temporarily before it is
fixed in position.

Glazing bead
The glazing bead is part of the
sash frame and fixes the glazing
in position. It is removable.

Rubber gasket
The gasket creates a windproof
seal and fixes the glazing in the
frame (tolerance).

Insulating glazing
Two panes of glass bonded
together on all sides via a spacer
(hermetic edge seal)

Option: plaster or lining
To cover joint between jamb and reveal

Option: plaster
Either build a very accurate opening rebate
(site supervision) or finish flat with a coat of
plaster afterwards.

Hardware
Window hinge
"Hardware" is the overall term for the
components required to assemble, fix,
operate and secure the window.

Fig. 28

Window – vertical section, 1:1

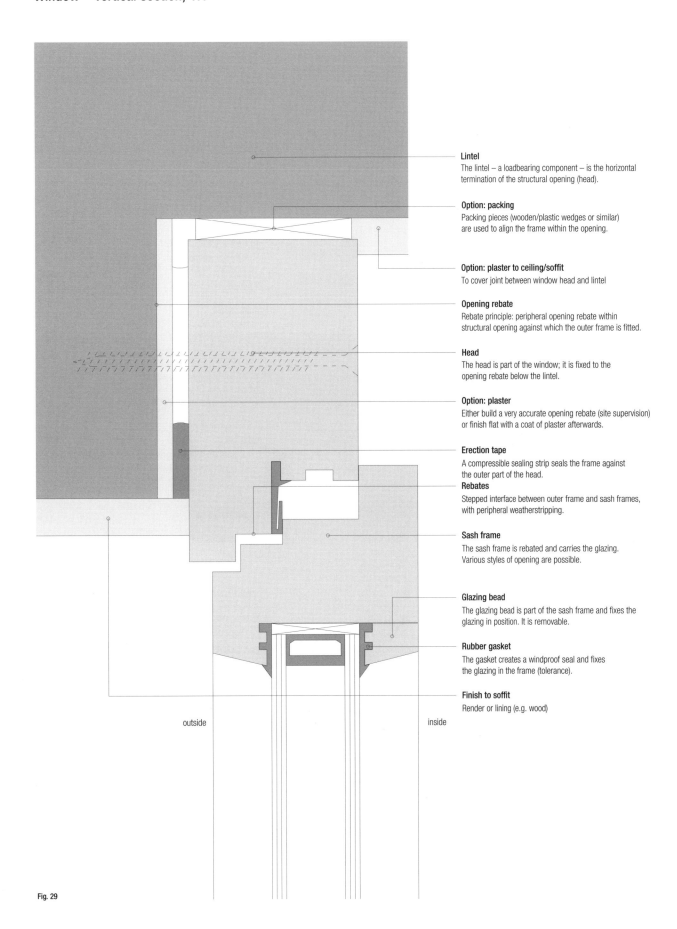

Lintel

The lintel – a loadbearing component – is the horizontal termination of the structural opening (head).

Option: packing

Packing pieces (wooden/plastic wedges or similar) are used to align the frame within the opening.

Option: plaster to ceiling/soffit

To cover joint between window head and lintel

Opening rebate

Rebate principle: peripheral opening rebate within structural opening against which the outer frame is fitted.

Head

The head is part of the window; it is fixed to the opening rebate below the lintel.

Option: plaster

Either build a very accurate opening rebate (site supervision) or finish flat with a coat of plaster afterwards.

Erection tape

A compressible sealing strip seals the frame against the outer part of the head.

Rebates

Stepped interface between outer frame and sash frames, with peripheral weatherstripping.

Sash frame

The sash frame is rebated and carries the glazing. Various styles of opening are possible.

Glazing bead

The glazing bead is part of the sash frame and fixes the glazing in position. It is removable.

Rubber gasket

The gasket creates a windproof seal and fixes the glazing in the frame (tolerance).

Finish to soffit

Render or lining (e.g. wood)

outside   inside

Fig. 29

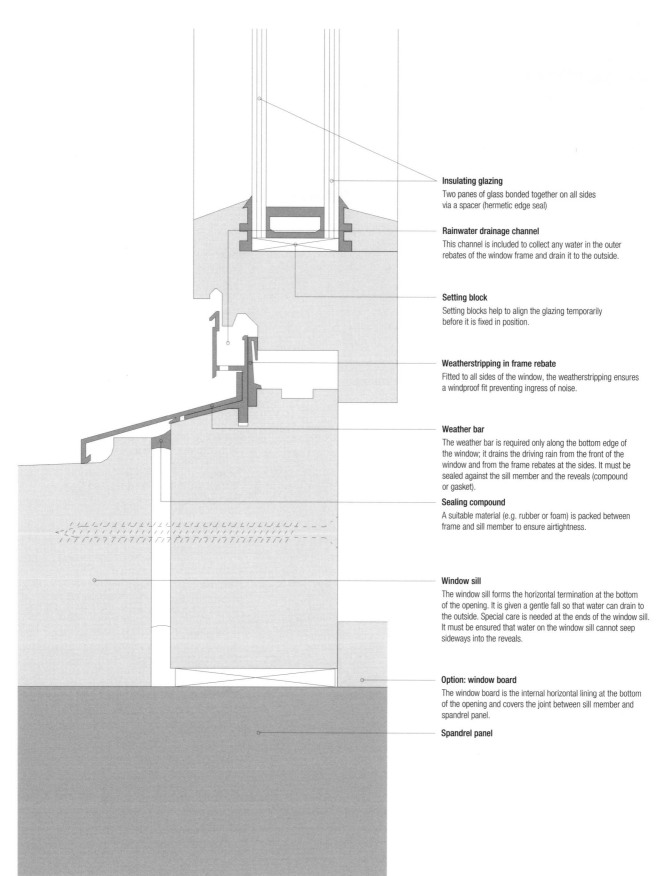

Insulating glazing

Two panes of glass bonded together on all sides
via a spacer (hermetic edge seal)

Rainwater drainage channel

This channel is included to collect any water in the outer
rebates of the window frame and drain it to the outside.

Setting block

Setting blocks help to align the glazing temporarily
before it is fixed in position.

Weatherstripping in frame rebate

Fitted to all sides of the window, the weatherstripping ensures
a windproof fit preventing ingress of noise.

Weather bar

The weather bar is required only along the bottom edge of
the window; it drains the driving rain from the front of the
window and from the frame rebates at the sides. It must be
sealed against the sill member and the reveals (compound
or gasket).

Sealing compound

A suitable material (e.g. rubber or foam) is packed between
frame and sill member to ensure airtightness.

Window sill

The window sill forms the horizontal termination at the bottom
of the opening. It is given a gentle fall so that water can drain to
the outside. Special care is needed at the ends of the window sill.
It must be ensured that water on the window sill cannot seep
sideways into the reveals.

Option: window board

The window board is the internal horizontal lining at the bottom
of the opening and covers the joint between sill member and
spandrel panel.

Spandrel panel

Fig. 30

The opening as a hole

Fig. 31: Embedded in the steep coastal cliffs
Adalberto Libera: Casa Malaparte, Capri (I), 1941

Adalberto Libera: Casa Malaparte

Besides the numerous small openings in the facade, Casa Malaparte has four large, carefully positioned openings. From inside, whether sitting or standing, these permit an unrestricted view of the steep, rocky coastline of the island of Capri. The inside of each opening has an elaborately carved chestnut frame, giving the effect of a "painting". The glass, as the physical separation between inside and outside, has no frame and is fitted flush with the outside face of the wall, which enables the thickness of the external wall to be experienced from inside. From the outside, however, this flush arrangement emphasises the homogeneity of the envelope.

Fig. 32: View of the steep coastal cliffs framed as a "painting"
Adalberto Libera: Casa Malaparte, Capri (I), 1941

Rudolf Olgiati: Van Heusden House

The tower-like appearance of this building is reinforced by the limited number of "punched" openings in the walls. The deep "hoppers" suggest mass and promise a solid, monolithic form of construction. On the contrary, the walls are thin skins. Only a section through the building reveals this to be a contemporary design using a minimum of materials. The inward projection of the window "hoppers" either frames the view of the outside world or focuses the incoming daylight.

Fig. 34: Cantilevering glass oriels enable good views of the street below.
Alejandro de La Sota: Calle Prior apartment block, Salamanca (E), 1963

Alejandro de La Sota: Calle Prior apartment block

The Calle Prior is a narrow street that does not permit any balconies with a useful size. Nevertheless, tenants are still given the chance to "keep an eye on the street".

Glass "showcases" protrude from the facade to enable a view of the entire street. They are glazed on all four sides and therefore stand out quite clearly from traditional oriels or windows. When looking out of the window the feeling of stepping out into the street is reinforced by this design and becomes an architectural feature.

Fig. 33: The deep, splayed window openings suggest a solid envelope.
Rudolf Olgiati: Van Heusden House, Laax (CH), 1964

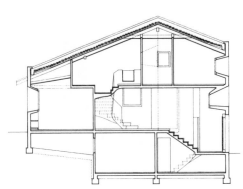

Fig. 35: The splayed window openings extend into the rooms.
Rudolf Olgiati: Van Heusden House, Laax (CH), 1964

The opening as a horizontal strip

Fig. 36: Different horizontal strip windows lend the facade a distinct hierarchy.
M. Ponsett, E. Salas: "La Fabrica" furniture manufacturer, Barcelona (E), 1961

M. Ponsett, E. Salas:
"La Fabrica" furniture manufacturer

The internal organisation of this building is clearly legible on its facade. At ground level it is almost entirely one large display window. And this generous transparency is repeated for the working areas on the three stepped-back floors above.

In between, the high-level, continuous strip windows to the display areas extend across the full width of the facade. These have the effect of dividing the facade horizontally, storey by storey, and thus underline the hierarchy in a simple way.

Herzog & de Meuron: House in Tavole

Like an abandoned child, the building stands amid olive groves. The delicate concrete frame forms a fragile envelope denoting the floors. The infill panels are of rubble stone.

Whereas the individual windows submit to the rules of stratification, the mullioned continuous horizontal strip window separates the solid coursing of the envelope from the oversailing eaves. The window extends around three sides to admit light into an interior that is heavily influenced by the omnipresent landscape.

Fig. 40: The dominant horizontal strip window on the upper floor reveals the loadbearing structure.
Otto Rudolf Salvisberg: First Church of Christ, Scientist, Basel (CH), 1937

Otto Rudolf Salvisberg:
First Church of Christ, Scientist

The church is located in a courtyard plot set back from the road. The entrance is through an open foyer which is defined by the cantilevering assembly hall on the upper floor.

A finely divided horizontal strip window dominates the facade. The ensuing transparency reinforces the curving shape of the hall. A consistent level of daylight is able to reach deep into the building.

Separated from the facade, the loadbearing structure of individual columns becomes distinct, having absolutely no effect on the facade itself.

Fig. 37: The landscape seen through the horizontal strip window has a clear influence on the interior.
Herzog & de Meuron: House in Tavole (I), 1988

Fig. 38: The horizontal strip window separates the roof from the solid walls.
Herzog & de Meuron: House in Tavole (I), 1988

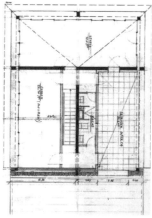

Fig. 39: Plan of upper floor
Herzog & de Meuron: House in Tavole (I), 1988

The opening as a joint

Fig. 41: The vertical "joints" distinguish the cells.
Harry Weese: Metropolitan Detention Centre,
Chicago (USA), 1975

Harry Weese: Metropolitan Detention Centre

This prison in the centre of Chicago is a triangular high-rise block built completely in reinforced concrete. At first sight the facades look like giant punched cards for computers owing to the pattern of the windows, which appear as storey-high joints between the masonry panels of irregular width extending vertically between the regularly spaced floors of the building.

Upon closer inspection we discover that the width of the windows has been calculated exactly to rule out the need for any bars. The reveals splay outwards, thereby maximising the angle of view from each cell. Horizontal openings for the plant rooms halfway up the building and the exercise yard on the top floor represent the exceptions. These horizontal dividers add scale to the monumental appearance of this "prison tower".

Fig. 44: Wall panels joined by diagonal corner window "hinge"
Louis Kahn: Richards Medical Research Centre, Philadelphia (USA), 1965

Louis Kahn: Richards Medical Research Centre

The complex comprises several buildings in an interlinked linear arrangement. Towers abutting the main buildings house access and service shafts.

One tower, which provides sanitary facilities, lifts and stairs for several storeys, forms a dominant terminus. The square tower comprises four wall panels which are joined in such a way as to create continuous slits at the corners. However, with the two-storey-high diagonal corner windows it seems as though the panels are joined via a hinge.

Fig. 42: Tall windows create a link between old and new building.
Diener + Diener: Pasquart Centre, Biel (CH), 1999

Fig. 43: Positioning the window in the corner leads to different lighting effects.
Diener + Diener: Pasquart Centre (museum), Biel (CH), 1999

Diener + Diener: Pasquart Centre

The extension by Diener + Diener sets itself apart from the existing building by appearing as its "poor relation". But the use of tall windows, a characteristic feature of the existing building, nevertheless creates a powerful link between the two.

Whereas the openings in the facade appear as traditional holes, from inside they become slits stretching from floor to ceiling, allowing ample light into the rooms. Positioned at the corners, the windows create two interior zones near the facade, characterised by their different lighting conditions. They therefore encourage a particular layout of the exhibits.

The opening as a transparent wall

Figs 45 & 46: Inner courtyard as "sundial"
Luis Barragan: Casa Antonio Galvez, Mexico City
(MEX), 1955

Luis Barragan: Casa Antonio Galvez

Situated within a plot enclosed by high walls the Casa Antonio Galvez offers the most diverse relationships with its surroundings and, through the positioning of the openings, plays with different degrees of intimacy and changing moods.

For instance, a small patio extends an ancillary room to the living room and in a certain way functions as a light source. Depending on the position of the sun, light enters the room either directly or after being reflected from the wall opposite. The view out the window becomes a view of a "sundial". The aim here is not to dissolve the boundary between interior and exterior, but simply to distinguish the two sides distinctly through the use of colour and material.

Fig. 49: Using the same materials to dissolve the boundary between inside and outside.
Eduardo Souto de Moura: Algarve House, Quinta do Lago (P), 1989

Eduardo Souto de Moura: Algarve House

The living room of this single-storey holiday chalet opens up to the garden across its full width. The material and surface treatment of floor, wall and ceiling continue unchanged from inside to outside, thus blurring the boundary between interior and exterior, indeed dissolving it altogether.

The glazed facade that spans the entire width and height of the room is a climatic necessity. The sliding doors reduce the divisive effect of the glazing when open.

Bo + Wohlert: Louisiana Museum

Louisiana Museum is a series of pavilion-type exhibition units situated within tree-covered parkland. Linking the pavilions are glazed corridors, which enable visitors to study the sculptures dotted around the park, which thus becomes an extension of the internal exhibition space.

The pavilion shown here overhangs the top of a slope which leads down to a lake. The proximity of the natural surroundings, enhanced by the lack of spandrel panel and lintel, and the floor raised clear of the ground convey the impression of a treehouse. But the mullions prevent the scene being perceived merely as a painting.

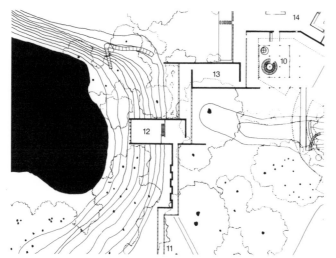

Fig. 47: Exhibition room (12) pointing like a "cannon" towards the lake
Bo + Wohlert: Louisiana Museum, Humlebaek (DK), 1958

Fig. 48: Nature almost within reach thanks to the omission of spandrel panel and lintel
Bo + Wohlert: Louisiana Museum, Humlebaek (DK), 1958

About the door

Cordula Seger

The door is our link between inside and outside, and creates a relationship between different spheres. Together with the threshold it denotes a significant crossing-place. In many cultures this transition from one space to another, which questions the physical presence of the person passing through the door, is accompanied by symbols. In doing so, the physical and the implied figurative transition from one social position to another are superimposed. Those who may pass through a certain door identify themselves as members of a community.[1]

As a crossing-point the door also represents the beginning of our journey through the building and, as we enter, prepares us for what follows. In doing so, the visual and the haptic experiences play an important role: Does the door handle fit snugly in the hand? Do we have to use our body weight to push open the door, or does it swing open easily? Does the door close with a satisfying clunk, or does it grate against the frame?

The height, width and design of the door indicate the degree of prestige and openness to the public. An entrance door with a generous opening and interesting design is an inviting gesture. However, the design of the entrance is often ignored, especially in residential developments. This deficit is reinforced by minimal ceiling heights – the correspondingly "squashed" doors look oppressive and uninviting. Within a multi-occupancy apartment block the entrance door to each apartment separates the semi-public corridor or landing from the private living quarters. Often provided with a wide-angle door viewer, which guarantees a view out but not in, the door demonstrates that not every visitor is welcome. We expect the entrance door to provide protection, whether against unwanted noise, intrusive looks, heat losses or even intruders. It is therefore built accordingly – solid, satisfying increasingly higher demands. It is really the internal door that separates the private areas and creates a hierarchy of spaces: the more intimate the function of the room, the more impenetrable is the door. After all, a jib-door is hardly noticeable; let into the wall to be as invisible as possible, it conceals secrets.

For its part, the type of door indicates the anticipated flow of visitors and the manner in which these are to be guided. The automatic sliding door obeys the wishes of a constant flow of people. In a department store, for instance, such a door enables an unhindered flow of shoppers in and out. On the other hand, the revolving door to a hotel spins invitingly into the street. Its circular movement represents a constant coming and going but allows every guest to arrive and depart individually. The swing door is also a traditional part of the hotel. It links the public sphere with that behind the scenes, e.g. the restaurant and the kitchen. Opened with a trained kick, the door moves in the desired direction to permit the unhindered passage of the busy waiter or waitress.

Fig. 50: Bold colours distinguish the entrance and so the door is singled out as a key design element
Bruno Taut: Hufeisen estate, Berlin-Britz (D), 1925–27

Fig. 51: Link between private and sacred: a miniature shrine above the wooden lintel distinguishes this entrance
Old farmhouse in Villa di Zoldo, Dolomites (I)

Fig. 52: The revolving door as a trademark of a grand hotel, Olive Street entrance,
The Biltmore Hotel, Los Angeles (USA), 1923

Fig. 53: View of one of the large entrance portals on the northern facade
Hans Kollhoff and Christian Rapp: residential development, KNSM-Eiland, Amsterdam (NL), 1991–94

In his *The Poetics of Space* the philosopher Gaston Bachelard asks: "And then, where to? To whom are the doors opened? Are they opened on to the world of people or the world of loneliness?"[2] In architectural terms this question can be answered at least partly: in the private part of the building the door opens inwards and guides the incoming person into the protective space. There are many figures of speech containing references to doors either opening or closing, showing the importance of this opening in the wall, and indicating that we should not cross the threshold too lightly when the door opens inwards. But in buildings in which large numbers of people congregate the doors must open outwards, in the direction of escape. However, the question of "where to?" concerns more than just the direction of opening. It points to the quality of the space into which the door opens. The positioning of the door – whether it emphasises the symmetry and leads us into the centre of the room, or is close to a wall and leaves space for furniture – has a crucial influence on the utilisation and atmosphere of interior spaces.

Notes

[1] See Arnold van Gennep: *Übergangsriten* (1909), Frankfurt a.M., 1999, p. 184.
[2] Gaston Bachelard: *Poetik des Raumes*, Frankfurt a.M., 1994, p. 222.
– English translation: Gaston Bachelard: *The Poetics of Space*, Boston, 1969.

Doors – types of opening

Fig. 54: Types of opening
scale 1:100

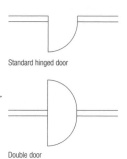

Standard hinged door

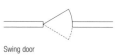

Double door

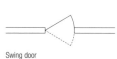

Sliding door (in front of wall)

Sliding door (within wall)

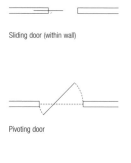

Pivoting door

Swing door

Folding door (fitted between jams)

Folding door (fitted in front of opening)

Revolving door

The opening form

The most common type of door is the hinged, single-leaf door. Together with the swing door and the double door it has hinges on one side. As the weight of the door leaf acts directly on the hinge like a lever, the use of such doors is limited to standard door widths, although in the form of a double-leaf door twice the standard width can be accommodated.

The hardware for sliding and folding doors is less dependent on the weight and so can be used for larger openings as well. In contrast to the hinged door a sliding door needs less space around the door because the door leaf does not swing out into the room. However, space adjacent to the side of the door is necessary to accommodate the door leaf as it slides. Sliding doors are often used internally to subdivide a large room, e.g. for dividing a living room, or separating a dining area from the kitchen.

When used as an internal door to a bedroom it must be remembered that a sliding door cannot achieve the same sound insulation value as a hinged door. If good acoustic insulation is necessary, e.g. doctors surgeries, a double door is advisable.

Automatic sliding doors have become established for buildings open to the public where there are large flows of people. Such a door guarantees an optimum throughflow. Another type of door is the revolving door. Its efficiency depends on its diameter. The advantage of revolving doors over automatic sliding doors is that they obviate the need for a lobby.

Standard hinged doors

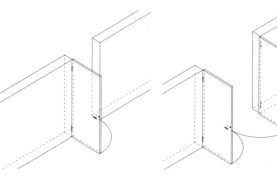
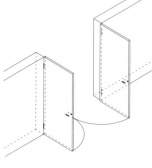
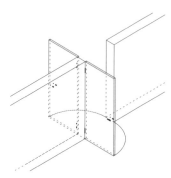

Fig. 55: Single-leaf hinged door, hinges on left   **Fig. 56: Double-leaf hinged door**   **Fig. 57: Double door**

Sliding doors

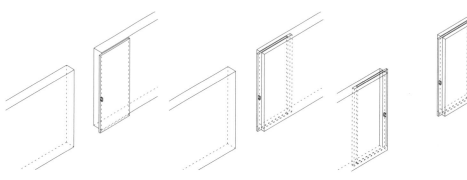

Fig. 58: Single-leaf sliding door (in front of wall)   **Fig. 59: Single-leaf sliding door (within wall)**   **Fig. 60: Double-leaf sliding door (within wall)**

Doors – types of door stop

Fig. 61: Types of door stop
scale 1:50

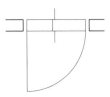

Lining and architrave
raised threshold

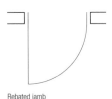

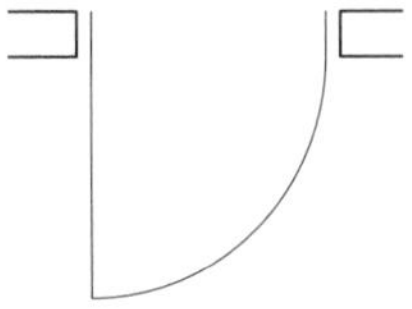

Rebated jamb
no threshold

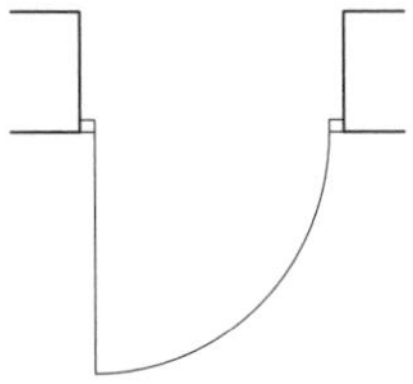

Frame in opening, finished flush
no threshold

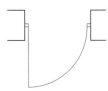

Frame in opening, centred in reveal
no threshold

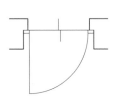

Frame clear of opening, either side of wall
step in floor

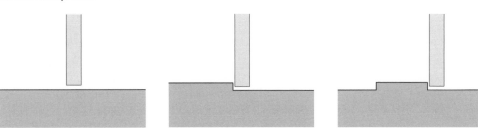

Frame clear of opening, against shoulder in
reveal, step in floor

The door stop form

The door stop is the meeting point between the door leaf and the component in which the door opening is located. Its form depends on the technical, circulation and architectural requirements that the door has to fulfil.

The door frame is manufactured from a dimensionally accurate material, e.g. wood, steel, so that, once fitted into the structural opening in the wall, it can accommodate the dimensional discrepancies in the wall. The frame also serves as a member to which the door hardware, e.g. hinges, tracks, is attached.

If a door has to be waterproof and windproof, and meet a certain standard of thermal and acoustic insulation, a peripheral frame is indispensable. Special care is required at the threshold. On the one hand it must be waterproof, but on the other, crossing it should be as convenient as possible, whether on foot or in a wheelchair.

The form of the door stop changes the visual perception of a door. A frame finished flush with the wall and painted the same colour as the wall disguises the opening. If the frame is fitted within the reveal, it forms an inviting recess. A door that includes lining and architrave emphasises the opening as a "framed" aperture, an impression which can be further underpinned by including a raised wooden threshold.

Whereas the raised wooden threshold was very popular in the past, the preference these days is for internal doors without any threshold to interrupt the floor finishes. A change in the floor finish is covered accordingly with a thin strip of metal or plastic. If sound insulation is important, a vertical seal is included in the bottom of the door leaf.

Jamb stop detail

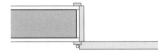

Fig. 62: Lining and architrave (internal door, also external door in timber frame construction)
rebated door leaf

Fig. 63: Rebated jamb (internal door)
no rebate in door leaf

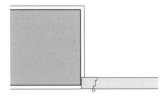

Fig. 64: Frame in opening, finished flush (internal and external doors)
rebated door leaf flush with frame

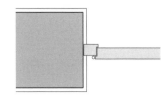

Fig. 65: Frame in opening, centred in reveal (internal and external doors)
rebated door leaf

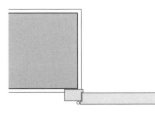

Fig. 66: Frame clear of opening, fitted to either side of wall (internal and external doors)
rebated door leaf

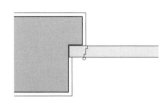

Fig. 67: Frame clear of opening, against shoulder in reveal (external door)
rebated door leaf flush with frame

Threshold stop detail

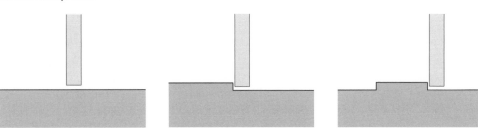

Fig. 68: No threshold

Fig. 69: Step in floor

Fig. 70: Raised threshold

Doors – hardware

Hinged single leaf steel-framed glass door
e.g. Forster Profilsysteme, Arbon (CH)

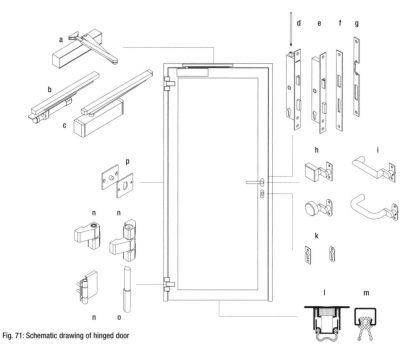

Fig. 71: Schematic drawing of hinged door

Door closers
a   Door closer with articulated arm
b   Concealed door closer
c   Door closer with fixed track

Door locks
d   Mortise lock (leaf) with latch and dead bolt plus additional bolt to door head
e   Mortise lock (leaf) with latch and dead bolt
f   Striker plate (frame)
g   Striker plate (frame) for electrical door opener

Door handles
h   Square or round door knob
i   Angular or rounded door handle
k   Escutcheon

Seals
l   Vertical seal in underside of door leaf
m Threshold with seal

Door hinges
n   Screwed on (weight of door critical)
o   Welded on

Hinge bolts
p   A hinge bolt, positioned centrally between the hinges, prevents the door being forced open on the hinge side.

Sliding wooden door
e.g. HAWA-Junior hardware

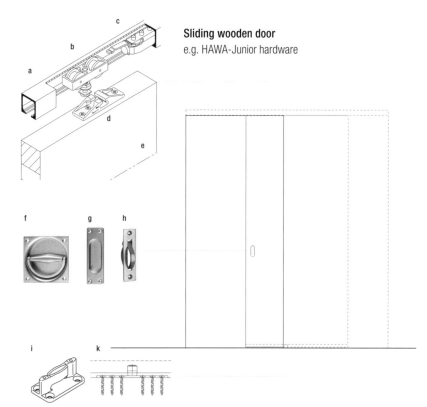

Fig. 72: Schematic drawing of sliding door

Hardware for single-leaf sliding doors
a   Track fixed to lintel or ceiling or soffit
b   Trolley with nylon rollers
c   Buffer with retaining spring
d   Hanger for left- or right-hand opening
e   Door leaf

Door handles
f   Recessed with ring
g   Recessed
h   On front edge

Floor guides
The floor guide profile is fitted adjacent to the opening at the start of the slot in the wall and runs in a track let into the base of the door leaf.
i   T-form floor guide (no play)
k   Guide pin

Wall – opening
Influences on the building envelope

1. Rain
Wall
Erosion of outer leaf, risk of saturation of outer leaf, frost risk
a) Masonry (monolithic, two leaves or with external insulation): render/paint.
b) Fair-face masonry: clay/hard-fired bricks are water-repellent and frost-resistant, special mortar required (seal joints), possibly a ventilation cavity.
c) Lightweight construction (steel, timber): cladding, shingles, planks, boards; if the loadbearing construction is positioned externally, it must be protected (paint, cladding, canopy).
d) Exposed concrete facades: concrete is essentially waterproof, but the problem of carbonation must be considered: carbon dioxide and moisture in the air react with the alkaline components in the cement, which leads to corrosion of the reinforcement and subsequent spalling of the concrete surface.

Window
Rain striking the window is drained via a weather bar on to the window sill. Rebates in the window frame must always be formed to prevent water collecting. The joints with the spandrel panels at the sides are particularly vulnerable.

2. Sunshine
Wall
Measures to combat ultraviolet radiation and temperature rise. Untreated timber facade elements exposed to direct sunlight are particularly vulnerable to deformation, cracking and sometimes "scorching" as well. Nevertheless, timber is regarded these days as a building material presenting few problems. Paints, glazes and impregnation are additional measures that can be taken to prevent water entering porous building materials. Dark finishes are a problem because they heat up too much and so are unsuitable for facades with external insulation.

Window/opening
Measures to combat glare and heat gains, and to provide privacy
– Flexible sunshading systems, external:
a) Louvres (aluminium, position of louvres variable) integrated into window head or housed in surface-mounted box on facade
b) Roller shutters (wood, aluminium, fabric) integrated into window head or housed in surface-mounted box on facade
c) Hinged, folding or sliding shutters of wood or sheet metal (folding against reveals, hinged or sliding in front of facade)
– Fixed measures, external (*brise-soleil*, canopies, fixed louvres)

3. Noise
Wall
Owing to their lack of mass, lightweight buildings (timber or steel systems) are more vulnerable to noise. Discuss with a specialist if necessary, but not a problem in normal cases.

Window
Thickness of individual panes, total thickness of glazing and airtightness of joints depend heavily on the level of noise to be expected. Opening the windows for ventilation is hardly possible when noise levels are high, so mechanical ventilation will be required.

4. Wind
Wall
Generally, all facade constructions made from small-format, jointed elements, and primarily timber wall constructions, will require the inclusion of an airtight membrane in order to overcome the problem of any gaps that occur in the joints due to swelling/shrinkage.

Window
The rebates in the window frame must be windproof; window frames and glass can be subject to severe wind loads.

5. Soiling of the facade, water entering horizontal joints
Wall, window
Rain in conjunction with upward air currents can force water into horizontal joints. Therefore, horizontal components such as lintels, window sills and cornices must be provided with rainwater drips.

6. Temperature
(The thermal transmittance, and hence the minimum thickness of various constructions, is specified in standards.)
Wall
Thermal insulation materials guarantee protection against high temperatures in summer and low temperatures in winter. Depending on the system, the layer of insulation is separate, the material provides both loadbearing and insulating functions (single-leaf masonry), or the insulation requirement is integrated into the building component (timber platform frame construction).

Window
a) Insulating glazing
b) Double window
possibly with insulated frames

7. Vapour diffusion from inside outside
Avoiding saturation of the construction by condensation water
Wall
Possible measures:
a) Ventilation cavities (drying out and dissipation of moisture in an air gap outside the layer of insulation with the help of natural convection)
b) Vapour barrier/check on the warm side (inside) of the insulation for components vulnerable to moisture
c) Vapour-proof internal loadbearing layer, e.g. in situ concrete
d) Moisture-resistant insulation, e.g. cellular glass
e) Whole construction open to vapour diffusion, e.g. single-leaf masonry

8. Mechanical damage
Wall, window
Soft surfaces (paint, some types of wood) are vulnerable to mechanical damage. Rendered external insulation is particularly susceptible (principally at base of wall, i.e., from ground level up to a height of about 2.00 m).

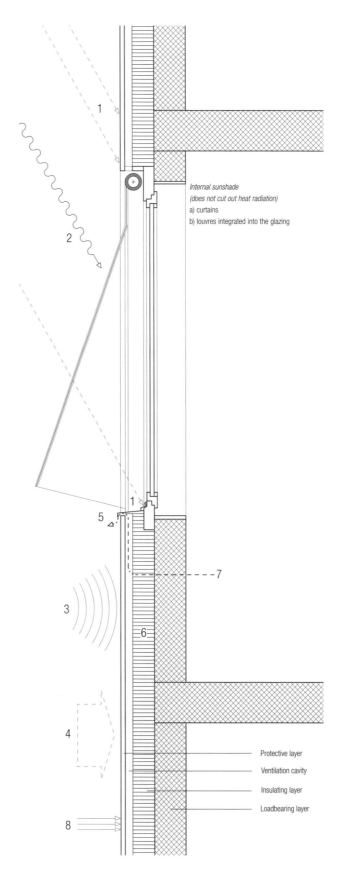

Internal sunshade
(does not cut out heat radiation)
a) curtains
b) louvres integrated into the glazing

Protective layer

Ventilation cavity

Insulating layer

Loadbearing layer

Fig. 73: Schematic section, scale 1:20

Cutting out sunlight and glare

Patric Allemann

Protection against sunlight and glare is provided by additional elements around the opening. The task of these elements is to regulate the amount of daylight and solar radiation entering the interior, perhaps even exclude it completely. A secondary function is to provide privacy at night.

There are many ways of incorporating sunlight and glare protection measures into the architecture of a building. However, certain building performance aspects must be considered if efficient, functioning protection is to be achieved.

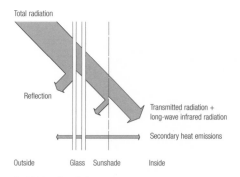

Fig. 75: Internal sunshade

Sunshading: the brief

Depending on the geographical location of a building, its exposure and the construction of its facades, solar energy can enter through the openings and lead to overheating of the interior in spring, summer and autumn. We prevent this by installing a suitable sunshading system. Basically, sunshades reduce the amount of heat radiation admitted by reflecting it. The total energy transmittance (g-value) is the means we use to assess the effectiveness of the protection, or to compare it with other systems. The g-value is the total of radiation transmitted plus secondary heat emissions to the inside and is determined through measurements or calculations. An efficient sunshade is distinguished by a high degree of reflection, which reduces the g-value accordingly. To prevent overheating of the interior, this reflection must take place before the radiation strikes the glass. If the solar radiation passes

facade design. One advantage of the fixed sunshade is that the visual relationship with the outside world remains essentially undisturbed. Depending on the form of the sunshade, an interesting intermediate layer can also be created between inside and outside which can even provide useful floor space (e.g. loggia). However, a fixed sunshade can respond to the changing solar trajectory (daily and seasonal) to only a limited extent.

A movable sunshade can be constantly adjusted to suit the position of the sun and to regulate the incoming sunlight according to individual needs. Owing to the diversity of types many design options are conceivable. During the planning it is important to consider the minimum and maximum dimensions of the respective systems. However, these dimensions vary only slightly among manufacturers of the same systems. Whereas the minimum dimension

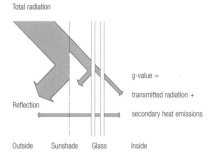

Fig. 74: External sunshade

through the glass first, some of this radiation is absorbed by the internal sunshade and converted into long-wave infrared radiation. This radiation can no longer be reflected back through the glass and promotes a temperature increase inside the building. Optimum sunshading can therefore only ever be fitted externally.

Types of sunshading

Sunshades can be designed as movable or fixed components. Examples of fixed sunshades are canopies, horizontal and vertical screens (*brise-soleil*), loggias and fixed louvres. Such elements form a vital part of the

Fig. 76: Fixed sunshade as a tangible intermediate layer with *brise-soleil* (top) and loggia
Le Corbusier: Unité d'habitation, Marseille (F), 1947

depends on the size of the opening, the maximum dimension mainly depends on the properties of the materials employed and the degree of exposure to the wind.

Various types of movable sunshading

Roller shutters: These consist of non-adjustable slats guided in channels at the sides of the opening. When not in use the slats are rolled up around a spindle mounted near the window/door head or folded into a bunch (folding roller shutter). The degree of light transmittance is determined by the slat profile (interlinked or separate), the reflection by the material and its colour. Today, the slats are usually of aluminium, which combines a high degree of reflection with minimum maintenance. By contrast, the wooden shutters often preferred in the past require more maintenance. As an option, roller shutters can be pivoted outwards and upwards to allow indirectly reflected daylight to enter the room. The maximum/minimum dimensions for roller shutters without this feature are approx. 50/450 cm for the width and 50/400 cm for the height. During planning, the maximum permissible area of approx. 10 m² must be considered. The maximum dimensions must be considerably reduced on facades exposed to high winds (e.g. high-rise blocks).

Louvres: In contrast to the slats of the roller shutter, the angle of each louvre can be varied about its longitudinal axis, which enables flexible control and redirection of the incoming light. The louvres, which are made exclusively of aluminium, are guided in channels or by thin steel wires. When not in use the louvres are stored as a compact bunch at the window/door head. The minimum dimensions are similar to those for roller shutters, but the maximum dimensions depend on the louvre profile. Special care must be taken with louvres exposed to high wind loads.

Roller blinds: These are made of fabric and when not in use are rolled up at the window/door head. Light transmittance and degree of reflection are determined by the type of fabric. Light-coloured fabrics can scatter the incoming light considerably and cause glare. Unlike the roller shutter, there is no option for pivoting a vertical roller blind outwards and upwards. The maximum/minimum dimensions are approx. 40/300 cm for the width and 40/400 cm for the height. The maximum permissible area is approx. 8 m², the ideal width-to-height ratio 1:3.

Semi-awnings: This is an elaborate variation on the vertical roller blind which, thanks to an additional roller plus stays, can be pivoted outwards and upwards to permit a partial view of the surroundings. Apart from

Fig. 77: The components of the sunshading system are housed behind an aluminium fascia and are therefore concealed when not in use.
Gigon/Guyer: Broëlberg development, Kilchberg (CH), 1996

Fig. 83: Semi-awnings to the windows, straight-arm awnings and vertical blinds to the balconies
Max Ernst Haefeli: Rotach development, Zurich (CH), 1928

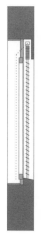

Fig. 78: Louvre blind
integrated into the wall
access from outside

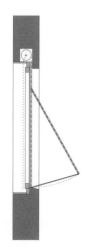

Fig. 79: Roller shutter with angled
positioning option
integrated into the wall access from inside

Fig. 80: Semi-awning
surface-mounted
access from outside

Fig. 81: Straight-arm awning
mounted below the lintel
access from outside

Fig. 82: Articulated-arm awning
surface-mounted on soffit
of balcony slab

Fig. 84: Large articulated-arm awning forming a movable canopy
Oliver Schwarz: factory building, Ebikon (CH), 1996

a minimum height of 120 cm, the maximum/minimum dimensions and maximum area are the same as for vertical roller blinds.

Straight-arm awnings: Two straight stays, their outer ends connected to a tube, unroll a fabric blind by means of gravity and position this at a certain angle to the facade. This type of shading was often popular for balconies in the past. The fact that the window is not completely covered guarantees a link with the outside world. The maximum/ minimum dimensions and the maximum area correspond to those of vertical roller blinds; the length of the straight stays is 80–150 cm.

Articulated-arm awnings: Two or more articulated arms enable a fabric blind, which is rolled up when not in use, to be extended to any desired position between minimum and maximum. An additional hinge enables the angle to be adjusted as well. This is the most popular type of sunshading for balconies and patios and is also employed for shading large (display) windows. Widths of between 2 and 7 m are possible, the maximum arm length is 4 m.

Hinged, folding and sliding shutters: These, the archetypal movable sunshades, are usually made from wood or aluminium. When not in use, the leaves are folded together adjacent to the reveal or stored in front of a plain part of the facade. The dimensions depend on the particular window.

Insulating glazing with integral louvres: In this arrangement a louvre blind is integrated – gastight – between the two panes of an insulating glazing unit. As explained above, this system does not provide optimum protection against heat radiation because the temperature rises in the cavity between the panes and some of the excess heat is emitted inwards in the form of long-wave infrared radiation. However, the system is suitable for high-rise buildings because fitting the blind between the panes of

Fig. 85: Folding shutters providing sunshading for balconies
Baumschlager & Eberle: Hötting Estate, Innsbruck (A), 1999

glass protects it against wind forces and soiling. A defect in the blind results in the entire glazing unit having to be replaced.

Surface-mounted or flush?

With the exception of the last two examples all the other types of sunshading can be installed as surface-mounted elements visible on the facade or integrated into the window/door head detail. The latter variation results in the sunshading element being essentially concealed when not in use. One hybrid solution is the installation below the window/door head behind a fascia panel flush with the facade. Articulated- and straight-arm awnings are frequently fitted beneath the balcony of the floor above.

If the sunshading element is integrated into the window/door head detail, easy access for maintenance and replacement must be guaranteed. Furthermore, the continuity of the layer of thermal insulation must be taken into account.

Antiglare measures: the brief

Glare is caused by direct sunlight and its reflection by internal surfaces, but also by daylight reflected by external objects (e.g. light-coloured buildings, snow-covered surfaces, etc.). In contrast to the sunshading issue, in which the heat radiation comes from a precisely defined direction, the incidence of the light and the resulting glare depends on diverse factors related to the particular conditions.

Fig. 86: Surface-mounted roller shutter boxes as a design element on the facade
Ernst Gisel: housing and studios, Zurich (CH), 1953

Glare is also an individual, subjective reaction influenced by the activities of the person concerned. For example, persons working at computer screens are more sensitive to glare than those writing manually at a desk.

Changing demands placed on the internal functions calls for a fine regulation or redirection of the incoming daylight, even complete blackout measures (e.g. classrooms).

As with sunshading, antiglare measures also involve limiting the view of – and relationship with – the outside world. This affects both the architecture (unwanted introvertedness) but also the human psyche (feeling of being excluded).

For these reasons antiglare measures should be (re) movable wherever possible. Although some of the sunshading forms described above can also prevent glare (e.g. louvres), antiglare measures are advantageous when fitted internally – for glare still occurs during the heating period when solar energy gains are undoubtedly desirable.

Types of antiglare measures

There are two main ways of preventing glare, which, however, can be subdivided into a number of variations.

Curtains: This traditional form of preventing glare and creating privacy is made from a fabric, which can be chosen to determine the light permeability. The level of incoming light can be controlled by using two or more layers of curtains with different light permeability (e.g. net curtains during the day, opaque curtains at night). However, as curtains can be moved only horizontally and not vertically, which would be necessary to track the sun properly, they must be drawn completely in order to prevent glare. Modern variations made from efficient high-tech textiles are available which achieve good reflection but with little loss of transparency. Vertical louvres, which can be rotated about their longitudinal axis, are the only form of "curtains" that permit the incoming light to be adjusted to suit the position of the sun.

Blinds: Vertical blinds with a corresponding opaque coating are often used to darken classrooms or other teaching facilities. Louvre blinds enable precise regulation of the incoming light, right up to complete exclusion. A relationship with the outside world is maintained by adjusting the angle of the louvres. The colour and material of the louvres have an influence on the quality of the light as perceived subjectively in the room, e.g. wooden louvres close less tightly but establish a warm light. Aluminium light-redirecting louvres guide incoming light through appropriately positioned louvre profiles into the depths of the interior and achieve consistent illumination plus a gain in passive solar energy through storage of the heat in solid parts of the building – and without any glare component.

Fig. 87: Curtains for preventing glare and for partial exclusion of the surroundings
Ludwig Mies van der Rohe: New National Gallery, Berlin (D), 1968

Fig. 88: Internal louvre blinds achieve diffuse interior lighting effects, the surroundings become blurred outlines
Alvar Aalto: Villa Mairea, Noormarkku (FIN), 1939

The doubling of the sky

Sascha Roesler

Only when we stare at the ceiling at night do we really first appreciate it. The dream of the insomniac is that the ceiling above will finally disappear. A whole genre of 20th-century literature was dedicated to the ceiling being the counterweight to the ruminations, doubts, worries, and anticipations of the insomniac, and turned the ceiling into the canopy over the modern soul. "It is a special type of sleeplessness that produces the indictment of birth." (E.M. Cioran) The fact that in reality today we have to think in two dimensions, without structure, when considering the answer to this, is the outcome of a rationalisation process that has given birth to the flat slab of reinforced concrete being the normal case. The primary job of a floor today is to carry loads over typical spans. For economic and not architectural reasons we therefore almost always resort to flat slabs. The majority of all building tasks, residential and office buildings, are characterised by their flat slabs. Prestressing techniques mark the culmination of a technological evolution during which thinking in terms of joists and beams shifted step by step towards thinking in terms of slabs and plates. Even downstand beams, the leftovers of the old timber joists, are regarded as a disruption in modern concrete construction, not only from the economic viewpoint, and are avoided wherever possible.

In the architectural sense the flat slab of the "Dom-Ino" house type developed by Le Corbusier in 1914 was programmatic. Its combination of frame and flat slab suggested a hitherto unknown degree of freedom in the design of the plan layout. The *plan libre* propagated through this system was, however, still restricted to a certain extent because the floor slab used by Le Corbusier at that time was a Hourdis-type hollow clay block assembly and the staircase was still linked to the internal beam arrangement. Concentrating the design work on the plan layout, which was finally achieved with the arrival of the flat slab, favoured the progressive neutralisation of the modern floor slab and determined the wall as the space-defining component. The view of the soffit and the plan on the floor had become merely backdrops to the space structured by the walls. Homogeneity, flatness and an indifference to direction determine not only the architectural expression of the flat slab, but are today normally the abstract prerequisites for this in order to elicit the economic efficiency of the space. And of course the floor area is also the yardstick with which the economics of an architectural project is calculated.

Today, the question is how the diversity of possible floor forms can be reintroduced into everyday building tasks. The timber joist floor, a popular method of support since ancient times – and up until the Second World War still the dominant method in the Western world – was supplanted step by step by steel beams and reinforced concrete slabs. A quick review of the historical development prior to the flat slab shows the diversity of design inherent in this process of development. The works of Claude Turner in the USA and Robert Maillart in Switzerland provided sufficient momentum to propel design in the direction of the flat slab with its indifference towards direction. The difference between the traditional floor supported on beams or joists, as François Hennebique used for his concrete structures, and the flat slab with flared column heads is that the flow of forces into the columns can be recognised.

No less decisive was the change in society that accompanied these engineering developments. The upsurge of the services and consumer society plus housebuilding for the masses led to the development of new types of construction – office towers, shopping centres, high-rise apartment blocks – and to a hitherto inconceivable manipulation of the interior environment. Building services of all kinds – sanitary and electrical lines, ventilation, lighting – are today, whether clad or left exposed, the matter-of-course elements of the modern floor. So the floor has turned into a complex "flooring system", the horizontal component upholding the interior environment. Polytechnical versatility – regardless of the material of the loadbearing structure – has now become the technological characteristic of the floor (and hence the ceiling). Layer upon layer, above and below, the structural floor designed to carry loads has been given new functions over the past 100 years in order to meet all the newly emerging social needs. To the layman the "ceiling" is the soffit of a horizontal layer of the building – the surface that spans over our heads. But considered as a complex, multi-layer component, the ceiling is also the underside of the floor to the next storey. Impact sound problems from above or a fire demonstrate not only the separating but also the bonding character of this component. Accordingly, we must distinguish between – and consider the mutual dependency of – the phenomenology of the soffit as a boundary and the technical treatment of the floor as a component that includes the floor construction of the storey above. This mutual dependency becomes especially clear in expansive interiors where the floors span considerable distances. The "underside" must be and is visible but direct access is not possible. The sheer expanse of the floor component calls for ingenious structural solutions. Starting from this double meaning – the floor as soffit and as component – I shall discuss three conceptual approaches in the following, approaches that characterise the architectural handling of floors – and soffits – to this very day. Irrespective of the particular materials used, these approaches seem to me to show the correlation between the visibility and technicisation of the floor, an aspect that increased with Modernism.

Fig. 1: Flared-head columns in reinforced concrete (diameter varies with storey, or rather load)
Robert Maillart: grain warehouse, Altdorf (CH), 1912

Fig. 2: The roof as a "baldachin"
Frank Lloyd Wright: office building for Johnson Wax company, Racine (USA), 1940–50

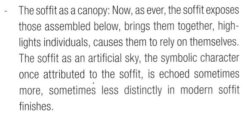

Fig. 3: Structure of a steel cellular floor deck dating from the 1950s
from bottom to top: fire-resistant suspended ceiling, cellular floor deck, transverse duct for services, floor covering

- The soffit as a canopy: Now, as ever, the soffit exposes those assembled below, brings them together, highlights individuals, causes them to rely on themselves. The soffit as an artificial sky, the symbolic character once attributed to the soffit, is echoed sometimes more, sometimes less distinctly in modern soffit finishes.
- The stacking nature of the storeys: As the construction of high-rise structures started to evolve, the stacking of the storeys became not only a technical challenge to many advocates of Modernism but also a social Utopia. Architectural expression and social consciousness can be found in the repetition of the floors.
- The longing for a different spatial order: The opposite nature of walls and floors seems to be obvious in everyday building. But in fact since the dawn of Modernism we have seen, again and again, attempts to dissolve this oppositon, to create continuity between wall and floor, wall and soffit, above and below, inside and outside.

Baldachins

"Baldachin" is another word for canopy and is derived ultimately from *Baldacco*, an early Italian name for Baghdad. Originally, it was the name of a precious silk which was imported into Europe from Baghdad. Owing to the exclusivity of this silk material, it was used as an ostentatious textile ceiling over the heads of the powerful and important. The simple supporting framework, four poles were enough, reinforced the notion of a surface floating free in space. The baldachin made possible a wall-less space within a space, and it was precisely this that showed those underneath to be unapproachable. The idea of an individual sky for those persons who have to be protected, those whose outstanding individuality has to be emphasised, is unmistakable here. Portable versions of the baldachin (testers) are still used today in religious processions. What has remained, however, is not such temporary sky imitations but instead permanent, domelike canopies of timber or stone to cover the bodies of the living – the thrones of kings, the testers of bishops, the beds

Fig. 4: Convertible umbrellas in the courtyard of the Mosque of the Prophet
Frei Otto, Bodo Rasch, Jürgen Bradatsch: Mosque of the Prophet, Medina (Saudi Arabia), 1971

of princes – and the substitutes for the dead – statues on tombstones.

Looked at in this way, the baldachin is a reduced form of covering, a gesture of presentation and not a mere utility surface. This distinguishes the baldachin of the Middle Ages from our present perception of the soffit. The baldachin creates a symbolic space below itself, but not an accessible surface above. To access the "floor" above – to walk on it – would be regarded as a symbol of its profanity! To this day, the floor–soffit coalition still remains in this dilemma, trapped between symbolic meaning and profane use.

Cladding

The suspended ceilings used today in so many different building projects remind many of the baldachin, rendering visible a will to present the modern individual in his

Fig. 5: Wavy soffit
Alvar Aalto: public library, Viipuri (RUS, formerly FIN), 1927–35

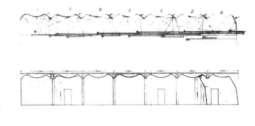

Fig. 6: The sections show the wave-like shape of the suspended ceiling. Acoustic considerations governed the shape of this wave.
Alvar Aalto: public library, Viipuri, (RUS, formerly FIN), 1927–35

or her daily business and lend him or her comfort and security. Even the simplest suspended ceilings in open-plan offices are evidence of the attempt to harmonise complex interior environment requirements with a certain degree of architectural representation. In many places it is the suspended ceiling and not the soffit of the load-bearing floor component that is seen internally. And this boundary layer meanwhile has to fulfil countless functions. As the spatial expression of technical necessities (fire

Fig. 7: Perspective view: all services are routed within the depth of the lattice floor construction.
Eero Saarinen & Associates: General Motors Corporation Research Centre, Warren, near Detroit, Michigan (USA), 1951–57

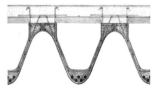

Fig. 8: Detail of floor construction: V-shaped precast ferrocement elements; wall thickness: 3 cm; total depth of floor (incl. floor finish): 50 cm
Pier Luigi Nervi: Galbani office building, Milan (I), 1955/56

protection, sound insulation, lighting units, loudspeakers, sprinkler systems etc.), the finished ceiling in architectural terms is all too often merely a compromise. The double effect of a suspended ceiling – it is a form of cladding and at the same time creates an intermediate space – results in an architectural effect whether we like it or not.

The cladding character of this layer favours an inherent logic unconnected with the loadbearing structure, which was nevertheless attributed to it again and again in the history of building. Whether the textile-like timber soffits of Alvar Aalto or the pictures projected onto the ceilings of a hotel in Lucerne by Jean Nouvel, the soffit as architecture becomes an image, and the soffit cladding the *leitmotif* for the whole building.

The textured soffits like those devised and used by Robert Maillart, Pier Luigi Nervi, Frei Otto, Heinz Isler and Santiago Calatrava also take on a similar, clad character. The difference between loadbearing structure and cladding has become obsolete in the works of these engineers. Gottfried Semper was surely the first to press for such a view of architecture. He recognised the link

Fig. 9: Galbani office building Milan (I), 1955/56
Reinforced concrete floor by Pier Luigi Nervi
Design: E. Soncini, A. Pestalozzo

between the German words *decken* (to cover), *entdecken* (to discover) and *Decke* (the German word for floor component *and* ceiling), which showed the gestural nature that had once accompanied the origin of these things and so permeated architecture as well. The ceiling, a covering, enclosing, protecting structure, is simultaneously tangible and intangible. Its textile nature as given by the language undermines the image of a heavyweight floor structure above us. Semper shrinks the three-dimensional separating layer to an incorporeal surface – skin, textile, clothing, coating: "In all Germanic languages the word *Wand* [wall] (of the same origin and basic meaning as the term *Gewand* [garment/vestment]) refers directly to the ancient origin and epitome of a visible space termination. Likewise, cover, cladding, barrier, seam, and many

other technical expressions are not symbols of language applied late to building, but rather certain indications of the textile origins of these components."

In buildings with extensive services the various media – electricity, heating, water, ventilation – require their own zone, which can occupy a considerable depth, in some cases even the full height of a storey. In the Salk Institute in La Jolla (Louis Kahn, 1965) the services zone became an accessible room in order to ensure simple maintenance and upgrading.

In an architectural sense the Centre Pompidou in Paris (Rogers and Piano, 1976) marks the culmination of the progressive technicisation of the building. This structure witnessed the first-ever application of the preliminary ideas of Archigram and others stretching back 15 years. The building services were no longer the shameful thing that must be hidden but instead had become the governing spatial principle of the building. Le Corbusier's vision of the modern building as a machine had been turned into a hands-on experience here by displaying the technical infrastructure – the building as a stage for the building services.

Stacking

If the thread towards the profane means an advancing utilitarianistion – becoming secular, worldly – of things, then the modern floor–soffit conglomerate is the place where this process has become particularly effective. Defying all handed-down symbolism, it is the most profane of all building components. No other component has been transformed to such an extent in the course of the technical and functional developments of Modernism. The brief and the technologies have changed radically within a very short time and opened up new design opportunities for

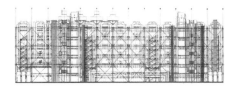

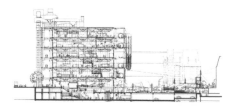

Fig. 10: Lattice beams at 13 m centres each span 48 m without any intermediate columns and therefore ensure maximum flexibility for the interior. The building houses a museum of modern art, a centre for industrial design and a public library.
Renzo Piano & Richard Rogers: Centre national d'art et de culture Georges Pompidou, Paris (F), 1976

Fig. 11: The cantilevering floor slabs, used as balconies, reinforce the layered nature of the two towers.
Bertrand Goldberg: Marina City, Chicago (USA), 1959–64

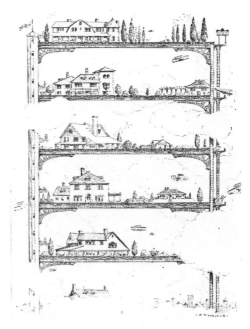

Fig. 13: Rem Koolhaas: "The skyscraper as utopian device for the production of unlimited numbers of virgin sites on a single metropolitan location."
Reproduction of a caricature taken from *Life Magazine*, published in 1909

architects and engineers. It was also the arrival of the skyscraper at the start of the 20th century that characterised the structure and significance of the floor and its soffit decisively. They became a "separating layer" in a vertical stack and an "infrastructure zone" for horizontal services.

"Everything is devoid of gods" is how Cioran succinctly expressed the terminus of this increasing profanisation – and in doing so forgot that it is precisely this absence that prepares the ground for religious input. The glorifying of the profane, which had been elevated to a precept by the beginning of the 20th century, would have been inconceivable without the increasing technicisation of living conditions. Right from the start this glorification was charged with Messianic characteristics, the salvation of the individual. Within this, "feasibility thinking" tallied with the far more vague notion of "homelessness". Both were embodied symbolically in the new high-rise buildings. No other type of building inspired such flights of fancy as the skyscraper rising skywards. Like no other type of building before, the high-rise block embodied the realisable opportunities of a society fascinated and surprised by modernisation. In all this, the floor component has become the platform for these opportunities and the dominating structural element in the facade. It was only the multiple stacking of the floors that had rendered both of these architectural phenomena visible. Peter Sloterdijk called the "serialism" of such stacking as the "transition between elementarism and social Utopianism". Stacking leads to both architectural and social added-value.

The floor component becomes the structuring principle of the facade; the building rising vertically is given a horizontal component. The Marina City towers in Chicago designed by Bertrand Goldberg are excellent examples of this. Here, the cantilevering floor slabs reinforce the layering of the building. This pair of towers represents a rare example of high-rise architecture using balconies.

Multiple stacking establishes a direct relationship between the repetition of identical storeys and the appearance of the entire building. Rem Koolhaas devised a formula for this: the greater the number of storeys, the more lasting is the impression of the overall form. In his famous study of the skyscraper architecture of New York (*Delirious New York*) he includes a caricature of a skyscraper that appeared in *Life Magazine* in 1909. The building, drawn as an iron frame, consists merely of a stack of country houses and their associated gardens. The underlying thought of a storey-by-storey stacking of different worlds turns architecture into the infrastructure for individual, storey-related fantasies. The building, generally conceived as a functional unit for a principal usage, dissolves into disparate storeys for this or that function. The floor becomes an artificially created, empty island that can be occupied and made habitable from time to time. The inheritance of this architectural development – the storey as an array of opportunities and a standardised element in a greater whole – has brought benefits for low-rise buildings, too. A faithful implementation of this concept could be seen at the World Exposition EXPO 2000 in Hanover in the form of the Netherlands pavilion

Fig. 12: The floor providing texture on the facade
Hideo Kosaka: Post Office Savings Bank, Kyoto (J), 1954

Fig. 14: Stacked landscapes ("Isn't the issue here new nature?")
MVRDV: Netherlands pavilion at the World Exposition EXPO 2000 in Hanover (D)

designed by MVRDV. The floors in this pavilion functioned as platforms for man-made, independent landscapes visible to visitors even from afar.

Möbius strips

In 1865 the German astronomer August Ferdinand Möbius described an infinite, curved surface in three-dimensional space that has just one edge and hence no distinguishable top and bottom. If we run a finger along the Möbius strip, we reach the other side of our starting point. This is due to the twist in the surface within its development. Depending on the position on the surface, what was formerly inside is now outside, the outside turned to the inside. Orientation in a conventional sense is not possible with such a figure because every segment of the surface is given an opposite meaning during the development. Conventional terms for describing spaces, like above and below, left and right, front and back, do not apply.

Just how much architecture is duty-bound to observe such terms in its thinking is demonstrated in practice, where the basic building blocks are walls and floors. The Möbius strip is therefore an example of a three-dimensional anti-world whose description and realisation depends on discovering new terms. Levels and no longer storeys, inclines and no longer walls and floors, fluid transitions and no longer enclosed spaces will probably dominate this anti-world. Landscapes and urban lifestyles are the models for an architectural realisation. Attempts to render such different spaces conceivable have accompanied the modernisation of architecture from the very beginning. The dream of the levitating surfaces of Russian Constructivism

was also the dream of a floor that had discarded its supporting structure. Even the laws of gravity were relieved of their validity at this moment of social upheaval.

Diagonals

An awareness of vertically stacked interior spaces was Adolf Loos' starting point and goal, and he hoped that his breakthrough would come with the new frames of reinforced concrete. Loos developed his method of design, which was intended to overcome the traditional thinking in independent storeys and which only became known as the "spatial plan" later, in the 1920s, in the premises of Goldman & Salatsch in Vienna (1911). Levels made visible and storeys no longer separated from each other characterised this building. The floors became effective interior design elements, more space-generating than space-enclosing objects. The various functional zones were differentiated by way of distinct storey heights – 2.07 m for the seamstresses seated at their machines, 3.00 m for the cutters standing at their tables, 5.22 m for the steam-filled pressing room – and this had to be compensated for constantly through mezzanine floors, galleries and landings, the edges of which were therefore exposed internally. This constant up and down gave the connecting stairs the character of a route, a path. The principle of stacking the storeys, so fundamental to modern architecture, had been conceived for the first

Fig. 15: Different levels made visible
Adolf Loos: Goldmann & Salatsch premises, Vienna (A), 1909–11

time – alternatively – as an intertwining of vertically stacked levels.

Whereas Loos's floors were designed as platforms that lent his architecture its specific interior atmosphere, some 40 years later the French architect Claude Parent elevated the terrain to the space-forming fundamental principle. The ground, regardless of whether it was natural or man-made, established an abstract space continuum and contrasted a world of functional, separate spaces with another one involving fluid transitions and networking. Parent, like no other architect before him, placed the slope – the reflex to a terrain seen as sculpted – at the focus of his architectural creativity. He proposed the incline

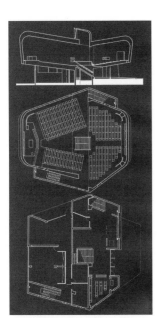

Fig. 16: The first implementation of the *fonction oblique:* **the nave is dominated by two sloping roof slabs.**
Claude Parent & Paul Virilio: Saint-Bernadette du Banlay à Nevers (F), 1965

Fig. 17: "Life on the slippery slope!"
Claude Parent: Sketches for *fonction oblique* (structure of living area)

Fig. 20: The Möbius strip as a code for hitherto unknown geometry
Foreign Office Architects: Virtual House, project 1997

plane (*fonction oblique*) as a possibility for a different experience of space contrasting with the three-dimensional Cartesian system represented in architecture by walls and floors. Imbalance and destabilisation, the consequences of living on sloping planes, were Parent's guarantee for space perceived once again as authentic and corporeal. The architecture should thus contribute to testing a new, hitherto unknown experience of space.

It was only after the introduction of CAD for architects on a wide scale that the designs proposed decades before by Loos, Parent, and others began to find wider acceptance in everyday architectural practice. Furthermore, since the beginning of the 1990s we have seen the publication of architectural designs that elevate the landscape to a new model of urban architecture. Thinking in layers creates continuous surfaces extending beyond storeys and buildings, and in doing so distinctions such as floor and wall, inside and outside, lose their significance. It is no mere coincidence that architectural practices such as UNStudio and Foreign Office Architects are experimenting with the Möbius strip as a code for hitherto impossible geometry. Floors and walls are losing their horizontal and vertical definitions, are becoming curves, ramps, diagonals and folds, and since then persist in a zone of indistinguishability.

Fig. 18: Plan of Möbius House
UNStudio/Van Berkel & Bos: Möbius House, Amsterdam (NL), 1993–98

Further reading
- E.M. Cioran: *The Trouble With Being Born*, New York, 1976.
- Gottfried Semper: *Der Stil in den technischen und tektonischen Künsten*, vol. 1, Frankfurt a.M., 1860. – English translation: G. Semper: *Style in the Technical and Tectonic Arts; or, Practical Aesthetics*, vol. 1, Munich, 1860.
- Peter Sloterdijk: *Spheres III – Foams*, Frankfurt a.M., 2004.

Fig. 19: Wall and floor, inside and outside lose their significance as distinguishing features.
UNStudio/Van Berkel & Bos: Möbius House, Amsterdam (NL), 1993–98

The roof

Francesco Collotti

Flat or pitched roof? We are not interested in pedantically reconstructing the position of this or that person, and we certainly do not intend to play the game of those who, taking the form of the roof as their starting point, distinguish between good and bad, progress and tradition, vernacular architecture and International Style. If we had been alive in the early 1930s, we would have been forced to take sides in favour of one tendency or a tendency of a tendency. We would have chosen Modernism or perhaps even those deliberate exaggerations that prevent moderate positions in revolutionary moments. Or we would have chosen another, more traditional Modernism that was pursuing the ancient myth of architecture and trying to evocate already forgotten briefs for this discipline.

Today, we no longer have to do make such categorical decisions and can permit ourselves the liberal pursuit of a non-dogmatic eclecticism which allows us to assemble dissimilar and sometimes contrasting worlds of forms in one and the same composition. We can therefore reconstruct – with a leisurely calmness and cheerfulness – the arguments of one or other position with respect to new trends. On the one hand, we acknowledge the ability of Modernism to re-establish the discipline, but at the same time we are conscious of the dogmatic inflexibility that precluded the "Neues Bauen" movement from inspiring permanent, local monuments and turning them into stone. On the other hand, now that we have had time to reflect on the ideological polemics we can recognise the motives of that rearguard action that was in the position to conduct a dialogue with tradition, the local monuments and the slow passage of time, which for their part are linked with habits and an everyday life consisting of repetitive gestures, of normality, banality, coincidence.

The wise and moderate stances appear today to be more durable than the categorical avant-garde, also more convincing than the exasperated reactionary. In the flat-versus-pitched-roof debate everybody claims to have good reasons for underpinning the validity of his or her own proposal, and everybody wants an appropriate roof which protects and is simple. But what is an appropriate roof? Is it a roof that covers well? Or is it a roof that finishes off the building? Or is it a roof that conveys the impression of covering well and finishing off the building by remaining in the background as far as possible? Or is it a roof that beyond being a good covering and finishing off the building also presents a protective and powerful form?

Few speak about the roof as one of the archetypal and generating motifs of building work, the roof as an intrinsic form and image. The roof is related to the myth of construction and with the original instinct to protect ourselves. Perhaps the origin of the roof has something to do with the ancient idea of space, namely, the tent (in its most primitive or most cultivated forms, e.g. Asplund or Lewerentz). The nomads as tent-users and the settled

tribes who built earthen or stone terraces and pyramids represent two different and separate worlds. But both can be seen in the same picture. The roof goes hand in hand with the myth of construction, this oldest of all human gestures, to cover and protect ourselves. According to the extraordinary portrayal by Piero della Francesca, the cloak of the Madonna is simultaneously protection, house, tent and roof. And even if there is apparently no roof, i.e., also if it is not clearly present, it exists (consider the well-contrived house without a roof from the exercises of Paul Schmitthenner).

So the roof is a longing on the part of the building, a desire for a covering, the promise of protection, as well as completion. The roof finishes off the building. In some countries raising the roof is celebrated. This holds even for those flat roofs that some would like to banish from the family of roofs altogether for ideological reasons, for the simple reason that we do not see them. On the contrary, we sense flat roofs, even when they are not directly visible, or we try to make them noticeable. Sometimes all the good architect needs is a delicate cornice, subtle profiling, a narrow joint in the render, a small strip of sheet zinc or copper to convey the impression of the roof. At the Tuscolano Estate (Rome, 1950–54) Adalberto Libera used the remnant of the roof, a sensitive, interrupted, gently animated line, to mark the end of the facade – and the start of the roof. It is a lightweight wing ready for take-off, a discreet but important symbol. For Le Corbusier in an apartment for Charles de Beistégui in Paris (1930–31), the roof is reconquered space, the place for a modern hanging gardens, a place removed from the tight-fisted sellers of roofing tiles and slates. It is a wonderful place, natural and artificial, a space in the city but at the same time above it, outside the hustle and bustle of the metropolis. The height of the walls that enclose the terrace is such that only some Parisian landmarks are visible – the most important ones. A place in which the city seems surreal, the object of abstract contemplation, cleansed of and alienated from context. The roof, the open hall of the house (the flat roof as living space – Sigfried Giedion).

In any case the roof is related to the mythical archetypal forms which – even after successive metamorphoses, transfigurations and alterations – are still recognisable in the elements of architecture. For centuries the gable was a reminder of the roof in the facade (e.g. Heinrich Tessenow).

The roof is loaded with significance: it can be indiscreet. In some cases it will do anything to become visible. The roofs of ancient Greek temples on Sicily were announced through colourful architectural features rich in motifs, metopes and triglyphs, which for their part told of even older wooden temples that used decorative elements to preserve the memory of construction techniques (the little lion half-head gargoyles on the long sides spouting the water from the hipped roof surfaces). The roof includes figures and symbols, it terrifies those who threaten the sanctuary (Norwegian stave churches with dragons' heads; the roof as the protective shell of an animal).

It is not just by chance that the roof suggests similarities between building and shipbuilding (in the arsenal at Venice the roof also serves as a crane for building ships). In theatre design the roof becomes a very complex part of the stage machinery, a place for producing special effects and illusions (Friedrich Weinbrenner, Karl von Fischer).

The roof and the locality: the roof always generates symbols, distinguishes one place from another, and not just for reasons of climate. The roof and its materials invoke a certain town, a certain atmosphere. The copper roofs of Paris call forth the idea of city architecture. All impressions that characterise a certain town or region are expressed through their roofs. The roof covering Giovanni Michelucci's Borsa Merci in Pistoia can never be seen in its entirety. It is a drawn shadow. As in other towns in Tuscany it is a fine line, an obviously lightweight structure with a great overhang, dark, rich in shade. We feel that the roof fulfils its function, but we see only the underside of the gutting eaves.

Mario Ridolfi regards the roof as a masterpiece of craftsmanship with an ancient origin, a traditional form that again and again is made more complex and adapted to suit the demands of the plan. A thick body of terracotta tiles, a powerful motif whose principal components are the ridge and all the elements of a cultivated, hand-crafted tradition. (There is something Baroque in all this, as if Borromini had been reborn in small architectural constructions.)

Jože Plečnik created an urbane figure out of the roof by converting a nonuniform terrace of houses into large-scale urban architecture (Trnovo, 1944). The roof can unite the spirit and soul of a people: a great hall in which a whole community can recognise itself again and to which it is called at important moments (Tessenow, community assembly hall, 1941/42, and local government forum, 1941). The roof is an unmistakable place in the centre of the town, the *coperto* tradition in Lombardy: a collective urban place covered by a roof supported on columns where we sometimes find a fountain, or benches for discussing, voting, recognising ourselves as a community, or, in a pragmatic way, for exchanging goods, buying, trading. In this case the roof, as an architectural element, can become a style. The changes to and rationalisation of the *coperto* reappear in many neoclassical works. Fluctuating between a vernacular architecture that is ennobled by various architectural features, and an enlightened, cultivated and, in a way, deprovincialised architecture, such neoclassical works embody a certain ambivalence. The roof as a boundary condition, as an interrupted figure between town and country... (the Coperto dei Figini in the cathedral square in Milan, destroyed c. 1850).

Roof, character, identity: In converting many palaces and large country houses Karl Friedrich Schinkel modified the form of the roof. This gesture demonstrates an attempt to transform the rural character of the aristocracy into a learned and less provincial one.

The roof can be a structure totally independent of the building it covers, but also an inseparable element fundamental to the functioning of the construction. A room in which to dry grain and cereals, a room for the tackles, winches and pulleys for hoisting, for vehicles and bales of straw. In some examples in the Alps the roof descends from the highest point of the house to support the timber beams that run past the solid, white-rendered walls. Consequently, the roof is transformed. It is perforated; it is a thin textile material consisting of horizontal bars and a transparent timber lattice, filtering the light.

The vulnerable roof: a body that reacts to the weather, is sensitive to the prevailing wind and rain (Lois Welzenbacher's house in Grödnertal). In other situations the roof opens up to gather the sunlight from the valley, to provide a view of the mountains (Gio Ponti's Hotel Valmartello or Jože Plečnik's mountain house).

Provisional conclusions (with less certainty, many doubts and various unanswered questions): in Modernism a number of rich and fruitful positions dealing unreservedly with the subject of the roof exist and prosper alongside the official position and classification. We have noted that further in-depth research, like the current treatment of the roof, may never be ultimate, categorical or rigid. For the roof, as in the past with the facade or ornamentation, it is the attempt to find a solution that is important, not the stubborn pursuit of a principle. Take the work of Ignazio Gardella. During his life he was a protagonist of the fight that led the architectural culture of our century to renew its vocabulary, but together with others – Rogers, Samonà, Quaroni – he tried to prevent the vocabulary of Modernism from becoming a new style. Modernism is an intellectual attitude, a way of behaving with respect to reality. So Gardella's flat roofs of the 1930s, when the aim was to take up a demonstrative position, are almost a manifesto; but then we have in the postwar years his roof to a church in Lombardy, the roofs to workers' houses in Alessandria, gently placed on the buildings, the variation on a traditional form of roofing to the house of a vineyard owner between the vines on the slopes...

It is for all these reasons that the roof and its form cannot be reduced to a single slogan. I believe we have to read all the forms extant in Modernism, not only those of the avant-garde. The various souls of Modernism. It is to recognise the fact that we can no longer wallow in the belief that architectural experience begins and ends with Modernism. Today, Modernism can relate to monuments in a new light, reflect in a new way on the total architectural experience over the course of time. And it will continue to learn from these.

Excerpt from:
Francesco Collotti: *Architekturtheoretische Notizen*,
vol. 1 of the *Bibliotheca series*,
pub. by Martin Tschanz, Lucerne, 2001

Pitched roof
Functions of layers

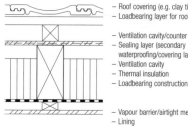

– Roof covering (e.g. clay tiles)
– Loadbearing layer for roof covering

– Ventilation cavity/counter battens
– Sealing layer (secondary
  waterproofing/covering layer)
– Ventilation cavity
– Thermal insulation
– Loadbearing construction

– Vapour barrier/airtight membrane
– Lining

Fig. 1: Pitched roof with secondary waterproofing/covering layer of overlapping sheets
(cold deck)

– Roof covering (e.g. clay tiles)
– Loadbearing layer for roof covering

– Ventilation cavity/counter battens
– Sealing layer (secondary
  waterproofing/covering layer)
– Loadbearing layer for sealing layer
  (decking)
– Thermal insulation
– Vapour barrier/airtight membrane
– Loadbearing layer for vapour barrier
  (in this case decking acts as lining)

– Loadbearing construction

Fig. 2: Pitched roof with seamless secondary waterproofing/covering layer
(warm deck)

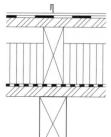

– Roof covering/sealing layer (sheet metal)
– Separating layer (e.g. roofing felt)
– Loadbearing layer for roof covering
– Ventilation cavity/loadbearing ribs

– Thermal insulation
– Loadbearing construction

– Vapour barrier/airtight membrane
– Loadbearing layer for vapour barrier (in
  this case decking acts as lining)

– Loadbearing construction

Fig. 3: Pitched roof without secondary waterproofing/covering layer
(cold deck)

Designation of layer	Function	Materials, thicknesses
Roof covering	– Protection against the weather (rain, hail, snow) – Protection against fire – Reflection (solar radiation) – Arrangement of the roof surface (on plan)	– Clay or concrete roof tiles, slates, fibre-cement, sheet metal (approx. 2–40 mm)
Supporting layer for roof covering	– Battens or decking for fixing the roof covering	– Roof battens, 24 x 48 mm (primarily for all small-format roof coverings), spacing approx. 15–30 cm, depending on roof covering – Timber decking, 27 mm (primarily for thin, sheet-like roof coverings)
Ventilation cavity (in counter batten layer)	– Ventilation of roof covering – Ventilation of timber battens (keeping them dry) – Dissipation of air heated up by solar radiation in summer (primarily a problem with dark roof coverings)	– Counter battens, 24 x 48, 48 x 48 or 60 x 60 mm, spacing approx. 60 cm
Sealing layer (secondary waterproofing/covering layer)	– Protection against soiling (dust, soot, drifting snow, wind) – Protection for layers underneath (thermal insulation) – Draining of water that has penetrated an overlapping roof covering (ponding) – Temporary protection to structural shell during construction until roof is completed	– Bituminous felt, 3 mm, on 27 mm timber decking – Special plastic sheeting, vapour-permeable, 0.2 mm, on 27 mm timber decking – Fibre-cement sheets, approx. 4 mm, laid with overlaps – Timber boards, 6–24 mm (waterproof hardboard)
Ventilation cavity (cold deck only)	– Dissipation of any external moisture that may have penetrated the secondary waterproofing/covering layer – Dissipation of warm, moist internal air in winter (prevention of condensation) – Dissipation of air heated up by solar radiation in summer	– min. 40 mm or as calculated
Thermal insulation	– Protection against or delay of cooling in winter and temperature rise in summer – Insulation can be laid above, below or between loadbearing members (problem: sealing of joints with rafters)	– Mineral wool, foam plastic (PUR + PS), min. 150 mm or as calculated
Loadbearing construction	– Carries dead and imposed loads (snow, wind etc.)	– Timber, steel, reinforced concrete, cross-section according to structural analysis
Airtight membrane, vapour barrier	– Protection against uncontrolled ventilation losses in the voids above and the associated condensation – Protection against warm, moist interior air diffusing into the roof construction – Protection against formation of condensation in cooler zones	– PE and PVC sheeting, kraft papers, approx. 0.2 mm – PE and PVC sheeting, aluminium foil, approx. 0.2 mm
Lining	– Termination of internal space, inner surface to roof void – Protection against surface condensation (moisture buffer) – Stores internal heat (avoids "stuffy" climate)	– Timber – Gypsum (plasterboard) – Wood-based materials – Plastered – Wood-cement boards – Wood panelling

Flat roof
Functions of layers

– Protective and drainage layer (rounded gravel)

– Waterproofing layer

– Thermal insulation

– Vapour barrier, separating layer, slip plane
– Layer for levelling and falls for minimum roof pitch

– Loadbearing layer

Fig. 4: Flat roof without ventilation (warm deck)
not accessible

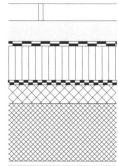

– Accessible wearing course (e.g. quarry tiles on chippings)
– Protective and drainage layer (rounded gravel)
– Waterproofing layer

– Thermal and impact sound insulation
– Vapour barrier, separating layer, slip plane
– Layer for levelling and falls for minimum roof pitch

– Loadbearing layer

Fig. 5: Flat roof without ventilation (warm deck)
accessible

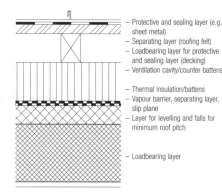

– Protective and sealing layer (e.g. sheet metal)
– Separating layer (roofing felt)
– Loadbearing layer for protective and sealing layer (decking)
– Ventilation cavity/counter battens

– Thermal insulation/battens
– Vapour barrier, separating layer, slip plane
– Layer for levelling and falls for minimum roof pitch

– Loadbearing layer

Fig. 6: Flat roof with ventilation (cold deck)
not accessible

Designation of layer	Function	Materials, thicknesses
Wearing course	– For foot or vehicular traffic – Vegetation layer, extensive or intensive planting systems	– Roof suitable for foot traffic: quarry tiles, asphalt or concrete on drainage layer, approx. 6–20 cm
Protection and drainage layer	– Protection of sealing layer (or thermal insulation in upside-down roof) against mechanical damage and ultraviolet radiation, provides ballast for underlying layers (wind suction) Single- or multi-ply layer to seal the structure against rain, snow and meltwater	– Roof unsuitable for foot traffic: rounded gravel (no sand owing to possible plant growth), approx. 6 cm – Extensive planting: 6 mm filter layer, approx. 8–15 cm plant-bearing substrate, approx. 6 cm vegetation – Intensive planting: 3 mm protection layer, approx. 12–15 cm water retention layer, 3 mm filter layer, approx. 7–20 cm soil or humus, 6–50 cm vegetation
Separating layer	– Sheeting laid on sealing layer as initial protection before installing protection layer and wearing course – Protection against mechanical damage to waterproofing (caused by chippings)	– Fleece
Sealing layer (moisture barrier, waterproofing) **Ventilation cavity** (cold deck only)	– Wherever possible, wearing course and protection layer should be able to move independently of each other (separating layer)	Conventional waterproofing systems for warm decks: – Bitumen sheeting, 3 layers; consisting of 3 layers of bituminous felt (backing layer: dry felt, jute fabric, glass fibre or aluminium foil), 2 intermediate layers of bitumen and 1 bitumen top coat (total thickness 7 mm), SNV 556 – Polyester-based bitumen sheeting, 2 layers (backing layer: jute fabric or glass fleece), total thickness min. 5 mm, SIA 218 – Synthetic sheeting, polyester-based, 1 layer, compatibility with adjacent materials must be guaranteed otherwise a separating layer must be included, SIA 280: Sarnafil, Gonon etc.
Thermal insulation	Layer of insulating material with defined thermal conductivity	– Mineral-fibre materials (limited compressive strength), glass wool, rockwool – Porous materials (high compressive strength), cellular glass (foam glass), vermiculite, perlite (Fesco Board, Heraperm) – Organic materials (high compressive strength), polystyrene foam (expanded or extruded), polyurethane foam, polyethylene foam, PVC foam
Impact sound insulation	Only required on roofs subject to foot or vehicular traffic	– Organic materials (high compressive strength), cork, insulating board, expanded polystyrene foam, approx. 2–4 cm – Mineral-fibre materials (high bulk weight and high compressive strength required), glass wool, rockwool, approx. 2–4 cm
Vapour barrier	– Layer with defined vapour permeability, prevents saturation of thermal insulation, not necessary on upside-down roof – Intermediate layer providing permanent separation between two incompatible materials	– Bitumen sheeting, hot bituminous compound 85/25, F3, with talcum powder, F3 and hot bituminous compound, V 60, with talcum powder, aluminium 10 B, polyester-based bitumen sheeting, aluminium foil both sides, Sarnavap 1000, Golfi D 2.1, polyethylene, butyl rubber
Separating layer, slip plane	– Intermediate layer enabling independent movement of individual layers of flat roof make-up – Layer that compensates for roughness or unevenness in the underlying construction	– Diverse oil or kraft papers, PE-coated
Levelling layer (falls layer)	– Layer added to achieve the required falls (min. 1.5%) in the underlying construction – The falls layer can be omitted when the loadbearing construction is already laid to falls.	

Flat roof
Warm deck – conventional systems

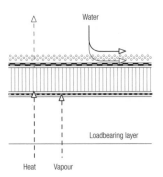

Fig. 7: Schematic drawing of building performance parameters

The conventional warm deck is a single-skin roof which contains one each of the necessary functional layers (loadbearing, waterproofing, thermal insulation, possibly sound insulation for accessible roofs). Various functions can also be combined in one material layer, although the waterproofing is always placed above the thermal insulation. When selecting materials, ensure that the components are compatible with each other and the building performance values are correct (use tried-and-tested combinations of products). Warm decks have a seamless roof covering. To prevent damaging condensation it is vital to install a vapour barrier on the inside (warm side) of the thermal insulation above the loadbearing layer. The vapour permeability resistance of this vapour barrier must be coordinated with the other layers of the roof construction. A layer of gravel, paving flags, road surfacing material or planting is suitable for protecting the waterproofing against the weather and mechanical damage. It is usually advisable to install a separating layer, e.g. fleece, between the waterproofing and this layer of protection. The necessary falls (min. 1.5%) can be produced in the loadbearing layer, in a layer specifically incorporated for this purpose or in the thermal insulation.

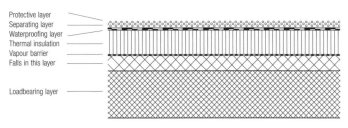

Fig. 8: Section through warm deck (synthetic roof covering)

Warm deck (synthetic materials)
The waterproofing here is a single layer of synthetic roofing felt with torched or bonded overlapping joints. The resistance to ultraviolet radiation is generally limited and so a protective layer must be added.

Various rigid products can be used for the layer of insulation. However, care must be taken to ensure that they are compatible with the waterproofing. Polystyrene, for instance, must be separated from the synthetic roofing felt (migration of softener). On accessible roofs it is important to ensure that the compressive strength of the thermal insulation is adequate.

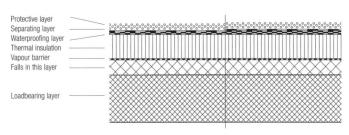

Fig. 9: Section through warm deck (bituminous roof covering)

Warm deck (bituminous materials)
The waterproofing here consists mostly of two layers of polyester-based bitumen felt. The first layer is laid loose on the thermal insulation and all further layers are then fully bonded together. When using pure bitumen sheeting at least three layers are necessary.

Various rigid products can be used for the layer of insulation. On accessible roofs it is important to ensure that the compressive strength of the thermal insulation is adequate.

Flat roof
Warm deck – special systems

The conventional warm deck systems have given birth to special flat roof constructions – for reasons of aesthetics and/or specific products. These are single-skin roofs and so follow the same layering principle as a conventional flat roof: the waterproofing is seamless and is placed above the thermal insulation. A vapour barrier installed on the inside of the thermal insulation prevents damaging condensation. Here again, the necessary falls (min. 1.5%) can be produced in the loadbearing layer, in a layer specifically incorporated for this purpose or in the thermal insulation.

Compact roof

The compact roof evolved specifically from the use of cellular glass and only works with this material. All the layers apart from the protective layer or wearing course are fully bonded together and to the loadbearing layer; together they provide the waterproofing, vapour-imperviousness and thermal insulation functions.

The insulation consists of vapour-tight cellular glass laid in a hot bituminous compound on the loadbearing layer, and this also functions as the vapour barrier. The joints are simple butt joints filled with a hot bituminous compound. Two layers of bitumen roofing felt, again fully bonded, serve as a waterproofing layer. As on a conventional warm deck, a layer of gravel, paving flags, road surfacing material or planting serves as a protective layer or wearing course. The compact roof is an expensive system. However, with a loadbearing construction of in situ reinforced concrete (as rigid as possible) it guarantees a high standard of reliability with regard to preventing ingress of water.

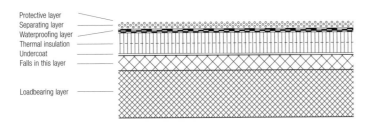

Protective layer
Separating layer
Waterproofing layer
Thermal insulation
Undercoat
Falls in this layer

Loadbearing layer

Fig. 10: Section through compact roof

Uncoated roof

Uncoated roofs are flat roof systems without a protective layer or wearing course. The omission of this protection means that the "exposed" roof covering must withstand various influences.

The make-up of the waterproofing can employ either bituminous or synthetic roofing felts (number of layers as for a conventional warm deck). In each case the manufacturer of the materials must confirm that the roof covering is suitable in terms of its resistance to ultraviolet radiation. It must also be incombustible (fire rating No. 6). The omission of the protection (ballast) also means that the roof covering is exposed to the wind. It must be ensured that all layers are fixed together (bonded or mechanically) such that the forces can be transferred. Mechanical fixings must be covered. Edges and junctions must be specially secured (wind suction). Uncoated roofs are sensitive to loads and are thus unsuitable for foot traffic. They must be approved – also by the local fire brigade. It is essential to check the waterproofing function of such roofs at regular intervals.

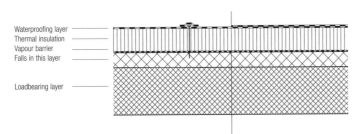

Waterproofing layer
Thermal insulation
Vapour barrier
Falls in this layer

Loadbearing layer

Fig. 11: Section through uncoated roof

Flat roof
Upside-down roof

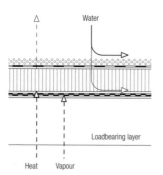

Fig. 12: Schematic drawing of building performance parameters

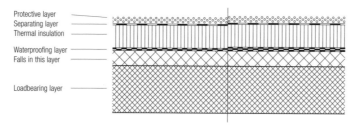

Fig. 13: Section through upside-down roof

Upside-down roof

The upside-down roof is a non-ventilated flat roof system with the obligatory functional layers. However, the sequence of the layers is different from a conventional warm deck.

The layer of thermal insulation is placed above the waterproofing and must therefore itself be waterproof (extruded polystyrene). This is a single layer of material and must therefore incorporate rebated joints. As the insulation is laid "in the wet" it must be 20% thicker than is necessary to satisfy the actual thermal insulation requirements.

A separating layer of fleece above the insulation prevents the gravel infiltrating the joints in the thermal insulation. The use of a special separating fleece which allows most of the water to drain away enables the 20% extra thickness to be reduced to just 3%.

The seamless waterproofing can consist of bituminous or synthetic roofing felt (number of layers as for a conventional warm deck) and is laid beneath the insulation, directly on the loadbearing layer. This also acts as a vapour barrier, and its position below the thermal insulation means that it is adequately protected against any damage.

A protective layer is absolutely essential on an upside-down roof. It prevents damage to the thermal insulation and also serves as ballast to prevent the insulation lifting off the layers below. As on a conventional warm deck a minimum fall of 1.5% must be incorporated, which can be achieved in the loadbearing layer or in a layer specifically incorporated for this purpose.

Flat roof
Cold deck

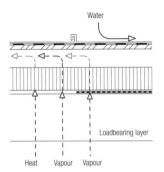

Fig. 14: Schematic drawing of building
performance parameters

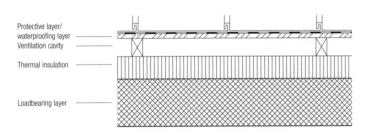

Fig. 15: Section through cold roof

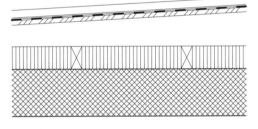

Fig. 16: Section through cold roof

Cold deck

The cold deck is a double-skin roof construction consisting of a lower, enclosing and thermally insulating skin with a separate airtight membrane, and an upper, weatherproof skin designed to carry wind, snow and imposed loads. Between these two there is a ventilation cavity – the size of which is determined by building performance parameters – with appropriate inlets and outlets. The cross-sectional area of this ventilation cavity must be min. 1/150 of the roof area, the minimum depth must be 100 mm. The total area of inlets/outlets must be at least half the size of the minimum cross-sectional area of the ventilation cavity itself. This ventilation arrangement ensures a balance in the vapour pressure between interior and exterior climates, especially in winter, and that in summer the temperature rise caused by solar radiation ("stuffy" climate) is dissipated by convection. One specific example of a ventilated roof is the Davos-style roof; the ventilation cavity in this roof is designed as a crawl space which enables the waterproofing to be inspected from inside.

The layer of insulation is placed over the loadbearing layer and must consist of a vapour-permeable material (mineral or glass wool). Incorporating the ventilation above the thermal insulation obviates the need for a vapour barrier on the inside of the insulation. However, such a vapour barrier is included with a loadbearing layer that is very open to diffusion (timber or steel) and this acts as a diffusion-retardant airtight membrane. The layer of insulation need not be vapour-permeable because it is positioned above the ventilation cavity. However, it requires its own loadbearing layer (double-skin construction). Gravel or sheet metal are suitable materials for the protective layer above the insulation; the minimum roof pitch for a sheet metal roof covering with double welt joints must be 3%. The fall in the cold deck is usually achieved within the ventilation cavity (loadbearing layer or waterproofing layer). Such an inclined boundary surface promotes the thermal currents in the ventilation cavity.

Pitched roof

The multiple pitched roof

The crystalline form of the Böhler house harmonises in an obvious way with the mountainous landscape. The volume clings to the slope like a boulder, the irregular roof form underscoring its amorphous character. The animated silhouette of the slate-covered roof surface seems to emulate the outline of the mountains. Similar to the design of the facades, which are determined by a seemingly traditional fenestration but whose arrangement is actually a departure from tradition, the roof form oscillates as well between expressive gestures and hand-crafted traditions. The transition to the masonry is not abstract but instead employs the classical overhanging eaves, which protect the facades against rain and melting snow.

Fig. 19: Hans Leuzinger: Glarus Art Gallery (CH), 1952

Fig. 17: Heinrich Tessenow: Private house (Böhler), St Moritz (CH), 1918, destroyed 1989

The integrative pitched roof

The extension to the school in St Peter integrates seamlessly into the local setting. The new buildings supplement the local built environment, which is characterised by a precise, functional positioning of the buildings and a choice of materials heavily influenced by the type of construction. Nevertheless, the pitched roofs of the new solid timber buildings achieve a certain autonomy thanks to subtle differences. Their roof surfaces are somewhat shallower than those of the neighbouring buildings and are finished with sheet metal. Wood-based boards replace the purlins of these couple roofs at the overhanging canopy, resulting in a delicate verge detail. The likewise slim eaves detail is characterised by a gutter that continues beyond the junction with the verge and acts as a spout, discharging the rainwater in a visible, thin, splashing stream directly into a gravel soakaway.

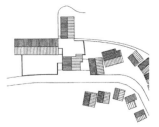

Fig. 18: Site plan
Conradin Clavuot: School in St Peter (CH), 1997

The pitched roof as a geometric element

Boasting different sizes, the exhibition wings of the Glarus Art Gallery dominate this L-shaped complex on the southeastern edge of a park. The one- and two-storey pavilions appear as simple, rectangular buildings. Three exhibition rooms, one lit from the side and two from overhead, are the focal points. The rectangular brick volumes are each crowned by fully glazed pitched roofs whose architectural design emphasises the will to reduce the form. Although the overhang of the roof on all sides is minimal, it still generates a shadow on the walls below and hence reinforces the independence of the roof form. The glazed roofs illuminate two of the exhibition rooms, separated only by a dust screen.

Fig. 20: Conradin Clavuot: School in St Peter (CH), 1997

Flat roof

Fig. 21: Adalberto Libera: Casa Malaparte, Capri (I), 1941

The accessible flat roof

Perched on a clifftop, Adalberto Libera's Casa Malaparte has an imposing form, its red paint finish creating an artificial addition to the topography. A tapering external staircase in a form not dissimilar to the building itself links the natural with the man-made environment. From this flat roof platform there is an all-round view over the sea and the rocky coastline of the island of Capri. The exposed nature of this site is further reinforced by the complete absence of safety barriers. The finish to the roof surface is in the same colour as the facades so that the building presents a monolithic appearance. An elegantly curving screen of white-painted concrete ensures privacy for the solarium and is the sole enclosed part of the rooftop terrace.

Fig. 22: Adalberto Libera: Casa Malaparte, Capri (I), 1941

The roof garden

The Villa Savoye is raised above the ground on columns and stands in a gently sloping forest clearing near Paris. The set-back ground floor facade helps the upper floor and the sculpted rooftop structures to appear more dominant. In contrast to the main floor, which is open to its surroundings on all sides thanks to the long ribbon windows, the roof garden of the Villa Savoye is enclosed by sculpted walls and offers only partial views of its surroundings. This results in an interior space open to the sky with a charming, introverted character. Unlike the platform of the Casa Malaparte, the protected rooftop terrace here serves as an extension to the living quarters in the summer. In his *Five Points of a New Architecture*

Fig. 24: Le Corbusier: Villa Savoye, Poissy (F), 1929

Fig. 23: Le Corbusier: Villa Savoye, Poissy (F), 1929

Le Corbusier regards the roof garden as a substitute for the ground area occupied by the building itself.

Fig. 25: Herzog & de Meuron: "Auf dem Wolf" locomotive depot, Basel (CH), 1995

The apparently corporeal flat roof

The four parallel bays of the "Auf dem Wolf" locomotive depot in Basel are separated by in situ concrete walls. Corporeal roof structures span over these concrete walls. The glass-clad lattice beams also form a monitor roof profile, which provides good illumination throughout the interior despite the excessive interior depth in some places. In architectural terms the rhythm of the translucent monitors can be interpreted as the regular positioning of sleepers, the rails being represented by the longitudinal walls, albeit with the positions reversed.

The roof as an independent large-scale edifice

Visible from Potsdamer Strasse is the ground-level section of the New National Gallery in Berlin, which is practically reduced to two architectural elements. A flat roof assembled from steel beams supported on eight columns soars over and beyond the reception area and ground-floor exhibition areas. But the other element, the set-back glass facade on all sides, is hardly noticeable. The roof spans 42 m and sails far beyond the glass walls. It comprises a two-way-spanning beam grid of 1.8 m deep H-sections which together weigh 1250 tonnes.

Fig. 26: Ludwig Mies van der Rohe: New National Gallery, Berlin (D), 1967

The roof as a folded plate

Fig. 27: Gigon & Guyer: Extension to art gallery in Winterthur (CH), 1995

Fig. 28: View during construction
Gigon & Guyer: Extension to art gallery in Winterthur (CH), 1995

The sawtooth roof as a light-directing layer

The art museums in Appenzell and Winterthur, both by Gigon & Guyer, are excellent examples of two fundamentally different methods for dealing with the framework conditions of sawtooth roofs.

The extension to the art gallery in Winterthur can be divided into three horizontal layers. The unheated, ventilated ground floor is for parking only. The exhibition rooms are located above this on the true main floor. And above the exhibition level a sawtooth roof ensures the necessary illumination. This layering of the functions is reflected in the facade design, which is likewise divided into three parts, with the exhibition level – framed, as it were, by the parking level and the sawtooth roof – being given most emphasis. The rhythm of the sawtooth roof matches the grid of the steel frame, but depending on the size of the exhibition areas, three, four or five "teeth" of the roof are allocated to each area. Internally, in contrast to the facade, the subdivision into exhibition area and lighting layer is suppressed by the use of a seamless lining. The effective height of the sawtooth roof is thus added to the exhibition area and can therefore be appreciated directly. As the glazed surfaces of the sawtooth roof face almost exactly north, no direct sunlight enters the building.

Fig. 29: Gigon & Guyer: Liner Museum, Appenzell (CH), 1998

The sawtooth roof as a sculptural element

The Liner Museum in Appenzell has a sawtooth roof for a completely different reason. The zigzag profile of the roof provided the chance to create an expressive, large-scale silhouette which, when viewed from close up, lends the museum an abstract quality. Only when we look down on the art museum and the town from the surrounding hillsides does the sawtooth roof blend in with the roofs of the neighbouring industrial buildings. In this case each "tooth" of the roof is allocated to a separate exhibition area, which means that from inside we see not a sawtooth roof but instead what appears to be an asymmetric pitched roof. The rhythm of the interior spaces (and hence the sawtooth

roof) narrows towards the north. So as the pitch of the roof slope remains the same, the height of each section decreases. This, together with the design of the ends of the building and the homogeneous cladding, promotes the alienation of the external expression of the sawtooth roof theme. Sandblasted chromium-steel sheets, overlapping like tiles, clad the whole of this monolithic structure, leaving no distinction between wall and roof surfaces. They thus lend the finished building a corporeal expression.

The roof as an irregular folded plate

The Carmenna chair-lift takes day-trippers from the valley station, which is located above Inner-Arosa near the late-Gothic mountain chapel, via an intermediate station to the side of the Weisshorn.

To preserve the landscape, the relatively large volume of the valley station is partly buried in the rising slope of the mountainside. A thin layer of soil lies like a carpet on the tent-like, multiple-folded roof and thus produces a seamless connection with the landscape. The conspicuous angularity of the roof form, supported by a lightweight steel frame, nevertheless reveals that this is an artificial continuation of the natural terrain. But in winter the scale of the roof form, appropriate to the topography, and the layer of snow over everything results in an almost complete fusion between the natural and the man-made elements.

The picture is completely different when looking from the valley side. The multiple folds of the entrance facade remain completely visible; it looks like a cross-section through a sculpted landscape. Blurred outlines of the interior workings can be made out behind the semi-transparent "Scobalit" facade. The left half serves for the night-time storage of the four-person chairs. The right half is for dispatching the winter sports fans on their way up the mountain. This latter half, the actual valley station for the lift system, is in the form of a bright, neon orange-painted tunnel.

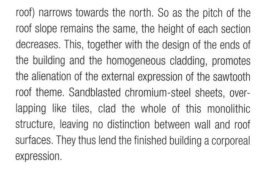

Fig. 31: Bearth & Deplazes: Valley station of Carmenna chair-lift, Arosa (CH), 2000

Fig. 30: View from mountain side
Bearth & Deplazes: Valley station of Carmenna chair-lift, Arosa (CH), 2000

Barrel-vault roof and shell roof

The barrel-vault roof

The – on plan – symmetrical, three-part Kimbell Art Museum is given its rhythm by the barrel-vault roofs perpendicular to the axis of symmetry. The character of the building, both internally and externally, is essentially determined by the roof form. The barrel vaults with their cycloidal cross-section each span 30.5 m in the longitudinal and 6.7 m in the transverse direction, and are supported on just four square columns at the corners. All the segments have identical, large dimensions and, when placed together, form very large areas without any intervening columns. However, these areas can be subdivided by means of portable, non-loadbearing partitions. The unusual illumination is also due to the roof form. At the crown of the vault there is a longitudinal slit which admits daylight. As direct daylight is unsuitable for displaying works of art, a reflector mounted below the slit redirects the incoming light such that the soffit of the vault is illuminated. At the gables there is a glazed gap, varying in width, between the non-loadbearing, semicircular travertine infill panel and the stiffened edge of the barrel vault, and this renders visible the geometry of the cross-section.

Figs 35 and 36: Eero Saarinen: TWA Terminal, New York (USA), 1958

Fig. 32: Louis I. Kahn: Kimbell Art Museum, Forth Worth (USA), 1972

Fig. 33: Louis I. Kahn: Kimbell Art Museum, Forth Worth (USA), 1972

The expressive shell roof

In contrast to the assembly of different shells at Sydney Opera House, the expressive roof form of the TWA terminal is a single symmetrical, large-scale arrangement. Although sculptural thinking was central to Eero Saarinen's design for the terminal and working drawings were not produced until the final form had been decided upon, the building benefits from the structural possibilities of the three-dimensional shell, transferring the weight of the roof to just four colossal columns. The dynamic shape, which explores the frontiers of formwork for in situ concrete, plays with the aesthetics of the propeller aircraft prevalent at the time of the building's construction.

The additive shell roof

Fig. 34: Jørn Utzon: Sydney Opera House (AUS), 1973

Sydney Opera house is located at a prominent position on a peninsula in Sydney Harbour. Jørn Utzon developed his design wholly based on this specific situation. Three groups of intersecting shells – containing concert hall, opera and restaurant – rise out of a massive, apparently monolithic plinth. The contrast between the heavyweight, earth-bound foundation and the lightweight, elegant shells helps to emphasise the functional separation between the ancillary spaces located underground and the public foyers and auditoriums above. At the same time, the plinth forms an artificial topography for the terracing, as in ancient Greek theatres.

Fig. 37: Jørn Utzon: Sydney Opera House (AUS), 1973

Criteria and relationships

Fig. 38: Cold deck
pitched roof
cold roof space
(screed)

Fig. 39: Cold deck
pitched roof
two ventilation cavities

Fig. 40: Cold deck
flat roof
accessible roof space

Fig. 41: Cold deck
flat roof
air cavity in roof
construction

Fig. 42: Warm deck
pitched roof
one ventilation cavity

Fig. 43: Warm deck
flat roof
no air cavity

Two layering principles

Apart from the fundamental protective function of the roof, i.e., providing shelter for human beings, keeping the water out is the main task of the roof. External influences (sunshine, rain, wind) but also those from inside (water vapour pressure) and the resulting problem of water vapour diffusion give rise to further strains in the roof construction. In order to do justice to these diverse demands, a multi-layer structure is necessary, which has led to two layering principles. One of these systems is chosen depending on the given overriding conditions, the roof form, the loadbearing structure, the conditions at junctions with other parts of the structure and at the edges of the roof.

Cold deck

In the cold deck the waterproofing layer is so far removed from the layer of thermal insulation that a dry air cavity is formed between the two. This captures the water vapour diffusing out of the insulation and carries it away.

A pitched cold deck has two air cavities: one between the roof covering and the secondary waterproofing/covering layer, and one between this latter layer and the insulation, although it is this second cavity that actually qualifies the roof to be called a "cold deck" (see "Pitched roof" on p. 218).

Warm deck

In the warm deck the waterproofing layer or a diffusion-retardant layer, e.g. in a pitched roof a secondary waterproofing/covering layer, is laid immediately above the thermal insulation. The water vapour diffusing out of the insulation could therefore condense on the non-ventilated cold side of the insulation and saturate this. A vapour barrier installed on the inside prevents the warm, vapour-saturated air entering the insulation and thus prevents any damaging condensation.

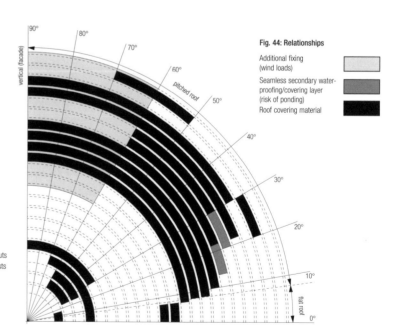

Thatch
Flat overlapping elements

Profiled overlapping elements
Flat sheets
Profiled sheets

Sheet metal
Flexible sheeting

Straw, reed
Loose stone slabs
Wooden shakes/shingles
Fibre-cement slates
Clay/concrete tiles
Clay/concrete tiles
Glass
Fibre-cement
Metal
Metal (standing seam)
Bitumen
Synthetic materials

Couple roof
Purlin roof   with queen struts
                   with queen posts
                   trussed
In situ reinforced
concrete roof

Fig. 44: Relationships

Additional fixing
(wind loads)

Seamless secondary water-
proofing/covering layer
(risk of ponding)

Roof covering material

Relationships between roof pitch and roof covering material

The pitch of the roof depends on the roof covering material, the roof form, the fixings and the type of jointing. A flat roof must exhibit a seamless, waterproof roof covering.

On the other hand, a roof covering of overlapping elements with its high proportion of joints is better suited to a pitched roof. The more watertight the roof covering element and its joints with neighbouring elements, the shallower is the allowable pitch.

Flat roof – pitched roof
Repercussions for the building envelope

1. Rain
Flat roof
a) Waterproofing: The waterproofing and water run-off layer must exhibit, depending on the system, a minimum fall of between 1.5% (upside-down roof) and 3%. The waterproofing layer is generally the topmost layer or the second layer below any wearing course or protective layer. The exception is the upside-down roof, where the waterproofing layer is beneath the thermal insulation. In this case it must be assured that the insulating material is moisture-resistant (various systems available).
b) Drainage: Rainwater is drained to a downpipe or gulley outlet at the lowest point on the roof surface and then inside or outside the building to a soakaway or drainage system. The provision of an upstand (parapet) around the edge of the roof is intended to prevent water running over the edge of the roof and down the facade during periods of heavy rainfall. Such a parapet must be at least 12 cm high (measured from top of wearing course or protective layer to topmost component of parapet – e.g. top of sheet metal capping) and must be absolutely watertight (SIA 271).

Pitched roof
a) In contrast to the flat roof, the water run-off layer on a pitched roof must be rainproof but need not be waterproof (e.g. thatched roof). The drainage of the water must take place via the uppermost layer, which can consist of sheet metal, clay/concrete roof tiles, stone, glass etc. The pitch varies depending on the material. However, the pitch must always be steep enough to ensure that rainwater drains without ponding. The secondary waterproofing/covering layer functions as a temporary roof should the roof covering become damaged and also helps during severe weather.
b) Drainage: A gutter is essential along the edge of the roof (eaves); it can remain visible (external downpipe) or it can be incorporated in the edge of the roof (internal downpipe).

General
a) Oversailing eaves and verges protect the wall–roof junction against rain. The joints between roof covering and wall are exposed to extreme conditions (hydrostatic pressure). Underneath the eaves/verge the resulting eddy that develops, however, generates a countercurrent and lowers the risk of water penetration.
b) The dimensions of roof gutters and the number of downpipes are calculated according to the area of roof and the quantity of precipitation expected.

2. Sunshine
Flat roof
Some waterproofing materials are vulnerable to ultraviolet radiation (e.g. bitumen sheeting) and must be covered and protected by a layer of gravel or similar material.

General
In a lightweight roof a "stuffy" climate (a build-up of heat below the roof) is prevented by the circulation of air in the cavity, and in a heavyweight roof it is the mass of the loadbearing layer, which absorbs the heat, that prevents this problem.

3. Wind
Flat roof
Wind suction is primarily a problem on uncoated roofs because the roof covering is not weighted down by gravel or other similar materials. The roof covering must be fixed to the loadbearing layer at individual points. Parapets around the edge of the roof (not suitable for cold deck systems) reduce the wind suction on large areas. The outer protective layer also has the task of providing ballast (e.g. gravel, concrete flags) for the layers below.

Pitched roof
On roofs with overlapping elements wind suction can be a problem, depending on the pitch and the weight of the materials. Wooden shakes/shingles or thatch must always be securely fixed. Owing to their weight, tiles can usually be simply laid in place without fixing, but at pitches of 60° and more they must always include an additional mechanical fastener.

General
Lightweight roofs must always include an airtight membrane.

4. Temperature
General
Standards stipulate the thermal resistance and hence the minimum thickness of the various constructions. The climatic conditions of Central Europe mean that a layer of insulation to the enclosing envelope of rooms designed for occupation is always necessary. The type of insulation and its position within the roof construction depend on the system chosen.

5. Vapour diffusion from inside to outside
General
It must be guaranteed that moisture is not introduced into the layer of insulation through saturation of the construction due to vapour diffusion from inside to outside. Many insulating materials are poor insulators when wet! Saturation can be prevented by using concrete for the loadbearing layer (vapour-tight), including a vapour barrier/check on the warm side of the insulation, or employing moisture-resistant insulating materials.

6. Snow
Flat roof
A parapet around the periphery of the roof (min. 12 cm) prevents fallen snow from penetrating the roof edge detail and creates a reservoir for meltwater.

Pitched roof
Snowguards must be fitted to prevent snow sliding off the roof.

General
The loadbearing construction must be designed to carry a certain snow load depending on the pitch of the roof and the location/altitude of the site.

7. Mechanical damage
Flat roof
It is primarily the uncoated roof that is vulnerable to mechanical damage – also due to hail. On a bituminous warm deck it should be ensured that the protective layer of rounded gravel does not contain any sand because this provides nutrients for plants. The small roots of plants gradually penetrate the waterproofing and render it useless. On an accessible upside-down roof the thermal insulation is especially sensitive to point loads.

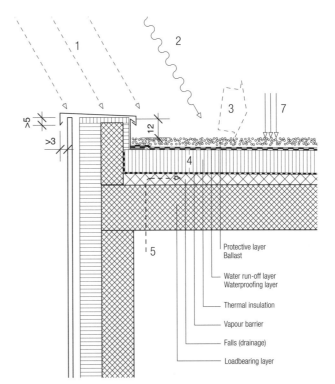

Protective layer
Ballast

Water run-off layer
Waterproofing layer

Thermal insulation

Vapour barrier

Falls (drainage)

Loadbearing layer

Fig. 45: Flat roof, warm deck, scale 1:20

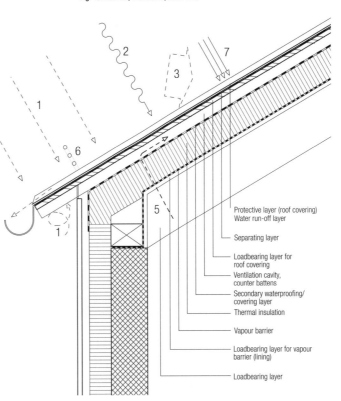

Protective layer (roof covering)
Water run-off layer

Separating layer

Loadbearing layer for roof covering

Ventilation cavity, counter battens

Secondary waterproofing/covering layer

Thermal insulation

Vapour barrier

Loadbearing layer for vapour barrier (lining)

Loadbearing layer

Fig. 46: Pitched roof, ventilated sheet metal, scale 1:20

For current Swiss and German standards on roof construction see www.sia.ch and www.bauregeln.de.

249

Flights of fancy

Daniel Gut

The staircase as a multiplier of the horizontal plane

Space for human movement is practically limited to two dimensions because gravity pins us to the ground. Our bodies cannot explore the space overhead. Accordingly, our perception of the world takes on a horizontal orientation. Architecture has been drawing its conclusions from this for thousands of years and arranges the functions horizontally. The staircase is therefore one of the important inventions in the history of architecture because it offers us the chance to link conveniently the vertical multiplication of areas for human movement by dividing the difference in height into small units that human beings can negotiate.

Every staircase renders two fundamentally different, opposing movements possible. And not only in physical terms: ascending and descending are terms loaded with mythological and psychological meanings as well. In Christian mythology, for example, the connection between places of good and places of evil are given extra significance by using the word pairs above–below and light–dark. This has consequences for the psychological dimension of the terms ascending and descending. These opposites firmly anchored in the human mind have been transferred directly into the secular world. The stairway to Heaven has become a ladder of knowledge, a ladder of

Fig. 1: Giovanni Battista Piranesi: Carceri, plate VIII, 2nd ed., 1761

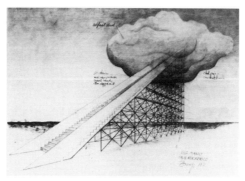

Fig. 2: Haus-Rucker-Co: Big Piano, 1972

virtues; the higher position in the hierarchy is better; we ascend to the top league or descend into madness.

Piranesi makes use of extravagant, enigmatic staircases in his architectural vision *Carceri* in order to lend his gloomy spaces an element of psychophysical disunion. The stairs lead into the depths of the dungeons and symbolise a world out of balance.

Ascending and descending movements, in relation to moving in the horizontal plane, represent a change of rhythm which has subconscious psychological repercussions. In the slowing of the rhythm as we ascend our spirit tends to want to hurry ahead of our bodies, to tackle our destination, or rather our immediate future. The German language even has an everyday specific, stair-related

word for this: *Treppengedanke* – a forethought; likewise a word for the opposite direction: *Treppenwitz* – an afterthought – a thought that occurs to us only after starting to descend the stairs while our minds are still upstairs dwelling in our immediate past.

Human beings have become accustomed to the artificial character of a succession of horizontal planes. Every child, having mastered the art of walking, then has to deal

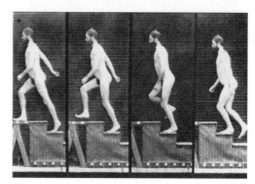

Fig. 3: Eadweard Muybridge: Human and Animal Locomotion, 1887

with climbing stairs. Over the years this motion becomes a programmed movement mechanism. But because this ritualised sequence of movements, in contrast to moving on a horizontal plane, is inextricably linked with the geometry of the step, the staircase enjoys increased attention. What this means for the architect is a chance to use materials to satisfy this enhanced focus. Apart from the fact that the architect can determine the rhythm of future movements by choosing a particular step geometry, he or she knows that the floor covering will be trodden upon with just a touch more care and awareness, that the handrail will be consciously perceived and that a rotational movement into the prescribed direction will take place on any landings necessary.

In the following I shall use word pairs to represent the contradictory characters or design concepts for stairs to demonstrate the potential opportunities and consequences of architectural decisions. The choice of these word pairs is intentionally arbitrary. The vista of possible options is too broad to want to cover everything.

The generating component of a project or building

Vertical access can be coupled with the three-dimensional concept of a building to the extent that it forms a permanent component or even the pretext for the concept. It is therefore an early topic in the design process and can be anchored in the design task. The design and choice of materials for vertical access are derived directly from the structure of the building or form a permanent component in this. Removal or repositioning during the ongoing design process becomes ever more difficult and practically impossible in an existing building without changing or destroying the entire concept. The enhanced

Fig. 4: Le Corbusier: Apartment block,
24 rue Nungesser et Coli, Paris (F), 1934

Fig. 5: Frank Lloyd Wright: Guggenheim Museum, New York (USA), 1959

Fig. 6: Adalberto Libera, Curzio Malaparte: Casa Malaparte, Capri (I), 1941

potential for spatial quality is paid for by a loss of flexibility and is therefore suitable only for building projects that can accept a rigid spatial fabric.

One example of a stair, or rather ramp, structure that forms the crucial pretext for the concept can be found in the Guggenheim Museum. The three-dimensional concept of this museum is based on a spiral ramp whose arrangement is directly reflected in the external appearance of the building. All the exhibition rooms are attached to this spiral ramp. Visitors are taken by lift to the top of the building from where they descend via the ramp at a leisurely pace, imperceptibly, determined by the works of art.

The Casa Malaparte on the island of Capri approaches the theme of the design-generating staircase from a totally different angle. The expressive power of the elongated, "crouching" volume situated on the rocky peninsula is reinforced by the fold in the silhouette caused by the monumental staircase. Because the stair, and with it the volume, ends at the lowest point between the mainland and the peninsula, it seems as though the building literally grows out of the rock. This distinctive point is the termination of the picturesque stair we have to descend in order to reach the house from the mainland.

In structural terms staircases in buildings have a more or less complementary character, depending on whether they have been devised as an accent, as part of a composition of various elements, or as a continuation of the

building structure. In comparison to the aforementioned stairs they appear later in the design process. Their positioning and architectural expression are allowed much more flexibility. This applies to the design process and also to later changes to the existing building although, of course, the strategic positioning of a staircase remains crucial. The permanence within the building provides potential for a deliberate, relatively independent architectural statement which, in turn, can permit a fusion with the surroundings in numerous ways.

One example of this approach can be seen in the entrances to St Jakob Park – trunk-like staircase "hoppers" which, like mobile steps for aircraft passengers, are appended to the facade. The logic of the resulting flexible positioning could be adapted to suit the functional requirements. In terms of the materials employed, however, the translucent cladding to the staircase entrances ensures integration into the theme of the facade with its transparent plastic "rooflight" elements, which the nighttime illumination changes into a shimmering skin.

On the other hand, the spiral staircase in Le Corbusier's maisonette apartment is inserted like an artefact into the plan layout. Hidden in the base is the staircase leading down to the floor below. The permanence is expressed in the materials. While the strings blend in with the plastered surfaces of the apartment, the flight itself appears to be part of a composition of inserted elements.

Fig. 7: Herzog & de Meuron: St Jakob Park, Basel (CH), 2001

251

Fig. 8: Harbour steps in St Augustine (USA)

Fig. 9: Alvaro Siza: House of Dr A. Duarte, Ovar (E), 1985

Staircase as event or staircase as obstacle

There are stairs that invite the observer to use them. But there are others that we pass without noticing, and if forced to use them we get the feeling of being unwanted guests. One critical factor here appears to be the change in the degree of openness upon starting to use the stair or stair shaft. If this openness remains unaffected or is enhanced when using the stair, the stair tends to gain a more public character. The stair becomes an event. Numerous measures can be employed to manipulate this impression. The effective mass of the stair and its relationship with the surrounding space play a role. Three-dimensional settings can be devised in order to turn the ascent into a sensation or a social occasion. A dignified design and expensive materials can (but need not) emphasise the event of ascending the stairs.

Spatial and organisational decisions have turned the main staircase at the public library in Viipuri into an event. Visitors are initially channelled up a narrow stair before arriving at a broad landing in the very centre of the library. Although the handrail steers the visitor directly to the upper level, he or she senses the spatial extent of the symmetrical staircase on the central axis of the interior. The skill with which the handrail has been incorporated turns this stair into a combination of entrance and means of internal circulation, creates a prestigious staircase occupying the middle of the building.

In Balthasar Neumann's proposal for the Hofburg Palace in Vienna the ascent of the stair is celebrated as a primary spatial attraction. This monumental staircase is accommodated in the largest room in the Hofburg Palace and is located in a prominent position on the central axis of the complex, lit from the two courtyards at the sides. Starting at entrance level, two flights lead up into the great staircase hall where several flights and landings branch off almost like a labyrinth. This almost intimidating staircase seems to symbolise the feudal claims to power.

Just as interesting is the question regarding the opposite situation: How do we prevent a passer-by from

ascending a stair? How do we express, with architectural means, that a stair is not to be used? Reducing the degree of openness to a more private character, or providing spatial or geometrical restrictions, turns the stair into an obstacle. The more abrupt this change, the more obvious this statement becomes. In addition, the architectural expression of the stair can help it to be overlooked or create an off-putting effect. Steep steps or the omission of safety features (balustrade) can enhance this impression. A similar effect can be created by embedding the stair construction "incidentally" into its surroundings and using the same materials, especially if this homogenisation presents a contrast to the more public space.

The photograph of the harbour steps in St Augustine (Fig. 8) shows quite clearly that this is not a descent for public use, that it is reserved for fishermen and sailors who need to reach their boats. The clarity of this architectural statement is the result of the abrupt change in scale between the expansiveness of the quayside and the confinement of the steps, promoted by the choice

Fig. 11: Alvar Aalto: Public library, Viipuri (FIN, today RUS), 1935

of material for the steps – the same sandstone as the quay wall.

In the house of Dr Avelino Duarte, Alvaro Siza employs nuance-filled means for the stairs leading to the private area of the house to indicate that the stair transcends a barrier to the more private living quarters. While the bottom steps, belonging to the half-public room, appear to be cut out of the material of the high plinth, the floor covering to the stair itself, a warm wood, together with a narrowing of the width draws a clear line between public and private.

Three-dimensional spatial fabric or stair core

Stair cores wind upwards over any number of storeys while their plan area remains equal or similar. They are usually quasi-autonomous shafts within buildings which

Fig. 10: Balthasar Neumann: Proposal for the Hofburg Palace in Vienna (A), 1747

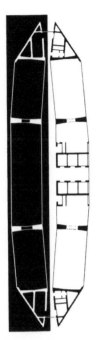

Fig. 12: Gio Ponti: Pirelli Headquarters, Milan (I), 1961

join, or separate, the individual floors. Although the extent of the spatial separation can be manipulated by the type of connection between the stair shaft and the individual floors, or the vertical spatial "transparency" of the core, the stair shaft remains the symbol of movement between the essentially independent floors via the "neutral" stair shaft. The solution is economic because it permits an optimum relationship between access space and usable floor space and, through repetition of identical building elements, enables a rational construction process. Above a certain height of building this makes stair cores indispensable.

Stair shafts, or rather their outer walls, which are often solid to comply with the thermal, acoustic and fire requirements, can be used to brace the building, as the plan of the Pirelli Headquarters shows. The system of walls separating stair shafts and ancillary rooms brace the building in the longitudinal direction. As main access is via the lifts in the middle of the building, the stair shafts occupy only a minimum area and are located in poché-type spaces at the ends of the curved blocks.

By way of contrast to the above emergency stairs we should consider the stair shaft of the Palazzo Barberini. This stair shaft is an impressive combination of the goals of a spectacle and a rational, vertical connection. The size of the stairwell creates an effective three-dimensional space extending over six storeys.

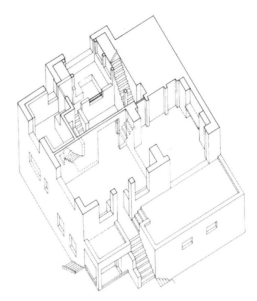

Fig. 14: Adolf Loos: Müller House, Vienna (A), 1928

The three-dimensional interior layout attempts to minimise the contrast between vertical and horizontal movement by merging horizontal and vertical circulation areas within a three-dimensional continuum. The spatial barriers between the storeys can be broken down further by introducing split levels, inclined planes and ramps. This permits almost unlimited manipulation of the hierarchy among the storeys. A *promenade architecturale*

Fig. 13: Francesco Borromini: Palazzo Barberini, Rome (I), 1633

Fig. 15: OMA: Jussieu University library project, Paris (F), 1993

Fig. 16: Paris Metro, stairs

is created: the topmost storey becomes the end of a promenade, a lift becomes a time machine.

The spatial plans of Adolf Loos were one attempt to overcome the conventional breakdown into storeys, to achieve a three-dimensional interior layout. It became possible to give different spaces different ceiling heights according to their usage. The offsets between the individual levels resulted in plenty of freedom in the design of living quarters. Numerous short stairs formed a route through the interior, leading gradually to more private areas.

Some of the designs from OMA are related to these spatial concepts although they stem from a completely different *Zeitgeist*. Contemporary technology enables us to deform the floor slabs at will, to overcome the classical subdivision of horizontal and vertical, and to allow the ground floor to flow upwards as a continuous band without a real staircase.

Thoroughfare and stopping-place

Stairs that are reduced to their practical function form vertical bridges between different levels and are designed purely as thoroughfares. We stop perhaps only briefly to exchange words with another staircase-user, or for a rest. Otherwise, such staircases are purely circulation areas and lead from one place to another. Depending on the ratio of the anticipated foot traffic and the dimensions of the stair, stopping for a moment can hinder the flow of people, even endanger their safety. In fact, specific measures can cultivate or influence the nature of the flow of people on a stair. Countless stairs in underground stations throughout the world demonstrate how a flowing movement of the mass can be promoted with an additional dynamic parallel with or in the direction of the flow.

What turns a staircase into a stopping-place or a place for communication? In terms of their actual width and steepness, the stairs leading to the entrances of the Bouça publicly assisted housing development are no different to the thoroughfare stairs described above. However, people are happy to sit here, to while away the hours with

Fig. 19: Greek theatre in Epidaurus (GR), 4th century BC

chitchat. Critical aspects are the proportions of the flights and the relationship between the foot traffic expected and the width of the stair. Whether a stair acts as a catalyst for communication of course depends on the utilisation at both ends of the stair and how it relates to its immediate environment. The lighting, the microclimate and, possibly, the view can represent animating factors. Who doesn't prefer a wide open view to a confined perspective?

However, the stair also offers the advantage of being able to see beyond the person in front, a fact which has been exploited for thousands of years in the arrangement of audiences. These places normally serve one-way communication; those on the grandstand are the consumers. The steeper the terracing, the better our view and the greater the feeling of being exposed to what is being offered; it is harder to hide behind the person in front. However, if we place two grandstands opposite each other, multiple communication is possible. The discussion forums of history made use of this arrangement, a fact that is copied by contemporary televised discussions. One variation on this type of collective communication is the singing by blocks of fans in sports stadiums; this is only possible thanks to the stepped, grandstand form.

Fig. 17: Edward Hopper: Sunlight on Brownstones, 1956

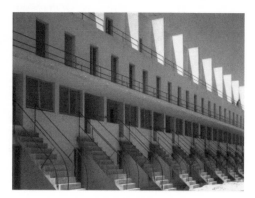

Fig. 18: Alvaro Siza: Bouça publicly assisted housing project, Porto (P), 1977

Further reading
- Karl J. Habermann: *Staircases – Design and Construction*, Basel, Boston, Berlin, 2003.
- John Templer: *The staircase Vols 1+2*, Cambridge, Mass., 1992.
- Cleo Baldon: *Steps & stairways*, New York, 1989.
- Walter M. Förderer: "Treppenräume", in: *Daidalos*, No. 9, 1983.
- Wolfgang Meisenheimer: "Treppen als Bühnen der Raum-Anschauung", in: *Daidalos*, No. 9, 1983.
- Ulrich Giersch: "Auf Stufen", in: *Daidalos*, No. 9, 1983.

Excerpt from the *Bauentwurfslehre* (Building Design Textbook) by Ernst Neufert

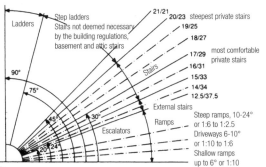

(1) Pitches for ramps, external stairs, private stairs, plant access stairs and ladders

Storey height	Two flights		One and three flights, building entrance	
	Shallow (good) pitch		Shallow (good) pitch	
	No. of steps	Rise	No. of steps	Rise
a	b	c	f	g
2250	–	–	13	173.0
2500	14	178.5	15	166.6
2625	–	–	15	175.0
2750	16	171.8	–	–
3000	18	166.6	17	176.4

(2) Storey height and stair pitch

Type of building	Type of stair		Usable stair width	Rise $a^{2)}$	Going $a^{3)}$
Residential buildings with no more than two apartments[1]	Stairs deemed necessary by the building regulations	Stairs leading to rooms suitable for permanent occupation	≥ 80	17 ± 3	28^{+9}_{-5}
		Basement and attic stairs that do not lead to rooms suitable for permanent occupation	≥ 80	≤ 21	≥ 21
	(Additional) stairs not deemed necessary by the building regulations, see DIN 18064, Nov 79, section 2.5		≥ 50	≤ 21	≥ 21
(Additional) stairs not deemed necessary by the building regulations within one apartment			≥ 50	No stipulations	
Other buildings	Stairs deemed necessary by the building regulations		≥ 100	17^{+2}_{-3}	28^{+9}_{-2}
	(Additional) stairs not deemed necessary by the building regulations, see DIN 18064, Nov 79, section 2.5		≥ 50	≤ 21	≥ 21

[1] Also includes maisonette apartments in buildings with more than two apartments.
[2] but not < 14 cm. [3] but not > 37 cm = definition of rise/going ratio a/a

(3) Stairs in buildings, DIN 18065

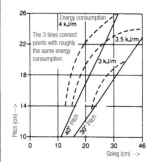

(4) Energy consumption for an adult climbing a flight of stairs

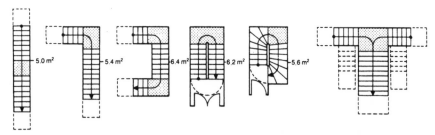

Figs 5-16: 16 risers 17/29, 17.2/28.1, storey height 2.75 m, width 1.0 m

(5) – (11) All forms of stairs without landings cover practically the same plan area, but the distance from leaving the last step of a lower flight to reaching the first step of the next flight upwards can be considerably shortened by using winders -> 6–10 or spiral stairs. Therefore these are preferred for multistorey buildings.

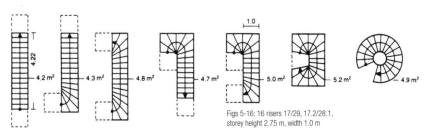

(12) – (16) Stairs with landings cover the plan area of a single flight + landing area - 1 tread area.
Stairs with landings are necessary for storey heights ≥ 2.75 m. Landing width ≥ stair width.

(17) Stair with three flights: expensive, impractical, wastes space

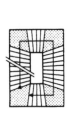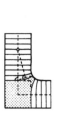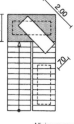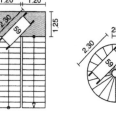

(18) Diagonal first step and distorted steps save space

(19) Curving the steps in narrow stair shafts saves on landing width

(20) Minimum space requirement for transporting furniture

(21) Space requirement for stretcher

(22) Spiral stairs: space requirement for stretcher

STAIRS

DIN 18064, 18065, 4174

The range of possibilities for stairs and means of access is broad: from the design options for the most diverse types of residential stairs to spacious external stairs to those on which ascending and descending calls for big strides. Using a stair requires, on average, seven times more energy than walking normally along a horizontal plane. When ascending a stair the physiologically favourable "climbing work" is given by a pitch of 30° and a rise/going ratio of

$$\frac{\text{step height (rise) } H}{\text{step depth (going) } T} = \frac{17}{29}.$$

The rise/going ratio is determined by the step length of an adult (approx. 61-64 cm). To determine the favourable rise/going ratio with the minimum energy requirement use the following equation:

$2h + t = 63$ (1 step).

Besides the aforementioned relationships, the overriding functional and architectural purposes of the stair are very important for the dimensioning and design of stairs. It is not just the gain in height that is important but rather the way in which that gain in height is achieved. A low rise of 16 cm (with 30 cm going) is preferred for external stairs designed for use by large numbers of persons simultaneously. On the other hand, steps in offices or escape stairs should render possible a rapid change in height. Every stair deemed necessary must be placed in a continuous stair shaft which, including its entrances and exits to the outside, should be positioned and designed in such a way that it can be used safely as a means of escape. Exit width ≥ stair width. The distance from any point within a room designed for occupation or a basement storey to a stair deemed necessary or an exit may not exceed 35 m. If more than one stair is necessary, they should be distributed so that the means of escape is as short as possible. In stair shafts the openings to basements, roof spaces not designed for occupation, workshops, retail areas, storage areas and similar areas must be fitted with self-closing doors, fire resistance classification T 30.

Fig. 20: Source:
Ernst Neufert: *Bauentwurfslehre*, Braunschweig/Wiesbaden, 2002. – English translation: Ernst and Peter Neufert: *Architect's Data*, Oxford, 2004.

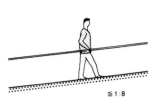

① Step length of an adult on a horizontal surface

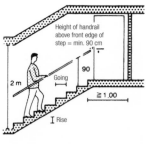

② An inclined, rising surface shortens the step length; comfortable gradient: 1:10 to 1:8

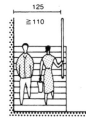

③ Favourable standard rise/going ratio 17/29; step length = 2 going + 1 rise = approx. 62.5 cm

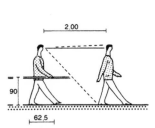

④ Step ladder with balustrade

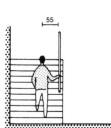

⑤ Standard stairs 17/29, max. 18 steps

Handrails and balustrades can be omitted on stairs with ≤ 5 steps.

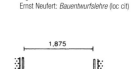

Handrails can be omitted on stairs with a pitch < 1:4.

⑥ Stairs without handrail(s)

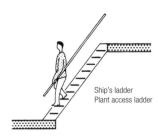

⑦ Stairs can save space when positioned properly one above the other.

⑧ If rafters and beams run in the same direction as the stair flight, it is possible to save space and expensive trimmers.

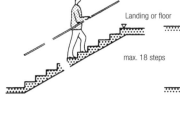

⑨ Basement entrances and trapdoors should be avoided; however, the above combination is advantageous and presents no risks.

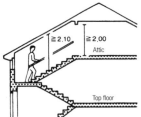

⑩ On spiral stairs the distance from the line of going to the outside of the string should be 35–40 cm.

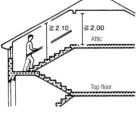

⑪ On straight flights the distance from the line of going to the balustrade should be 55 cm.

⑫ Stairs on which two persons can pass without difficulty

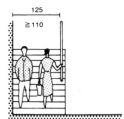

⑬ ≥ Minimum width for three persons

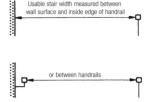

⑭ Minimum dimensions for stairs

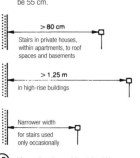

⑮ Measuring the usable stair width

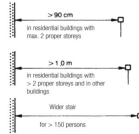

⑯ The rise/going ratio of a stair may not change within a flight.

STAIRS

DIN 18064, 18065, 4174

Stipulations covering the design of stairs vary among the building codes. DIN 18065 covers the main requirements to be satisfied by stairs.

Residential buildings with no more than two apartments: usable width min. 0.80 m, rise/going ratio 17/28; stairs not deemed necessary by the building regulations: 0.50 m, 21/21; other stairs deemed necessary by the building regulations: 1.00 m, 17/28. Stairs in high-rise apartment blocks: 1.25 m wide. Stair width in public buildings must also take into account the desired escape time p. 466 "Theatre". Length of stair flight: ≥ 3 steps, ≥ 18 steps 5. Landing length = n times step length + 1 tread depth (e.g. for 17/29 rise/going ratio = 1 x 63 + 29 = 92 cm or 2 x 63 + 29 = 1.55 m). Doors opening into a stair shaft may not impair the statutory width.

A shallow, comfortable pitch for external stairs in gardens etc. is achieved by including landings every 3 steps. This ensures that a stair in a theatre or an external location is ascended and descended slowly, i.e., it could be even shallower. But a stair to an ancillary entrance or escape stairs should enable a rapid change in height.

Fig. 21: Source:
Ernst Neufert: *Bauentwurfslehre* (loc cit)

The geometry of stair transitions

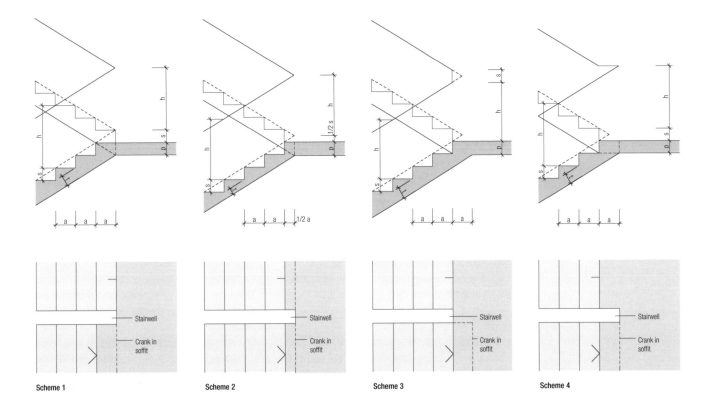

Scheme 1   Scheme 2   Scheme 3   Scheme 4

Fig. 22: Schemes (above)
a   Going (step depth)
s   Rise (step height)
h   Height of balustrade
p   Thickness of landing slab
t   Thickness of stair slab

Relationship between stair member thickness, handrail geometry and landing geometry

The designer has to deal with numerous geometrical relationships when designing a staircase. These change depending on the type of staircase construction and the handrails. The schemes shown above therefore do not represent universally valid solutions but rather use the example of a monolithic staircase to demonstrate the typical relationships between step geometry, handrail geometry and thickness of landing and flight members.

Scheme 1

Shifting the last step of the lower flight back by one going (a) towards the stairwell places the stairwell, the crank in the soffit and the change of direction of the handrail all in one line. However, the exact position of the crank also depends on the ratio of the flight slab thickness to the landing slab thickness (p/t), but this can be adjusted within structurally reasonable limits to match the geometry. The change of direction of the handrail is paid for by raising the height of the intersection of the two handrails by one rise (h + s). Any horizontal handrails required at this point would therefore also need to be positioned at a height of h + s.

Scheme 2

If the top step of the lower flight and bottom step of the upper flight are each shifted towards the stairwell by half of one going (a/2), the stairwell, the crank in the soffit and the change of direction of the handrail all lie in one line. Again, the exact position of the crank depends on the ratio of flight slab thickness to landing slab thickness (p/t). However, the change of direction of the handrail is only raised by half of one rise (h + s/2).

Scheme 3

Aligning the top step of the lower flight and bottom step of the upper flight with the end of the stairwell shifts the crank in the soffit (of a monolithic stair) of the lower flight into the landing by approximately one going (a). The intersection of the handrails moves into the landing by half of one going (a/2). This problem can be overcome by using a curved handrail or interrupting the handrail, depending on the width of the stairwell.

Scheme 4

If the top step of the lower flight and bottom step of the upper flight each shifted towards the stairwell by one going (a), the crank in the soffit of the lower flight coincides with the end of the stairwell. The handrail then needs to change direction twice in order to achieve the same height again.

Balustrades and spandrel panels
Extract from Swiss standard SIA 358, 1996 edition

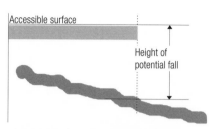

Fig. 23: Definition of height from which a person could fall

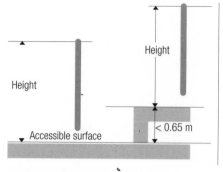

Fig. 25: Height of safety elements

Objective of protection

Balustrades, spandrel panels and handrails must constitute constructional measures to prevent persons falling
from a higher level to a lower level. Protection against a
risk of falling is given when suitable measures reduce the
risk to an acceptably low level.

Strength

The design and construction of balustrades, spandrel
panels and similar safety elements should be such that
they can withstand the loads and stresses anticipated.
This requirement shall also apply to the associated fixings
and infill panels.

Materials

Materials that may corrode or may be adversely affected
by the weather must be suitably protected and maintained. Risk of injury caused by damage to infill panels of
glass, plastic and similar materials must be prevented by
choosing a suitable material.

Arrangement of safety elements

Balustrades and spandrel panels

Every surface that may be used by persons, i.e. every surface accessible to persons, in normal circumstances and
that could constitute a risk of falling must be protected
by a safety element. A risk must generally be assumed
when a person could fall from a height of more than
1.0 m. Said height is the vertical difference between the
edge of the accessible surface and the adjoining surface
at a lower level. If there is an increased risk of falling,
safety elements may be necessary even at lower heights.
Safety elements for heights up to 1.5 m can be provided
in the form of measures that simply restrict access to the
edge of the accessible surface, e.g. planting.

Handrails

Stairs with more than five steps shall generally be provided with handrails. Escape stairs and stairs with more
than two steps that are normally used by disabled, elderly
or infirm persons shall generally be provided with handrails on both sides.

Requirements to be satisfied by safety elements
Height

The height is measured from the accessible surface, in
the case of stairs perpendicular from the front edge of the
step to the top edge of the safety element.

In the case of spandrel panels, the top edge of the
fixed part of the bottom member of the window frame
obtains.

Components, e.g. copings, radiators, in front of the
safety element with an accessible surface less than 0.65 m
above the primary accessible surface shall be regarded
as accessible. In such a case the height of the safety element is measured above the higher surface. The normal
height of a safety element is at least 1.0 m. In the case
of permanent spandrel panels at least 0.2 m thick the
minimum height shall be 0.9 m.

Spandrel panels and balustrades along a flight of
stairs shall exhibit a minimum height of 0.9 m. For reasons of serviceability (avoidance of feelings of insecurity
and dizziness), the height of safety elements should be
increased in the case of extreme heights from which persons could fall.

Geometric arrangement

Balustrades, spandrel panels and similar safety elements
must prevent persons from falling through them. The
minimum requirement is a longitudinal member at the
highest point plus an intermediate longitudinal member
at half height or vertical members at a maximum spacing
of 0.3 m. In buildings to which unsupervised children of
pre-school age have access the following special requirements shall apply:

Openings in safety elements up to a height of 0.75 m
may not permit the passage of a sphere with a diameter
of 0.12 m. This requirement shall also apply to openings
between safety elements and between safety elements
and adjoining building components (exception: openings between edge of step and balustrade). On stairs
the distance between front edge of step and balustrade may not exceed 0.05 m. Climbing on the safety
elements shall be prevented or made difficult by suitable
measures.

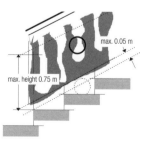

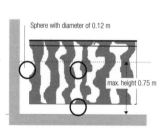

Fig. 24: Geometry of safety elements

Lifts

Fig. 26: This lift installation fits in the stairwell.
Arne Jacobsen: Søllerød Town Hall (DK), 1942

Lifts enable persons and loads to be transported vertically between the storeys of a building. Lifts are always considered part of the infrastructure. Their positioning depends directly on the vertical and horizontal circulation areas for persons in the building, and is not necessarily associated with other building services.

Unlike staircases, which spread out vertically and horizontally and can change position from storey to storey, lifts are housed in vertical shafts for reasons of support and fire protection. Lifts constitute circulation interfaces for persons and goods on every single floor and are therefore located close to the stairs, which also makes them easier to find.

The requirements placed on lifts are essentially governed by the use and function of the building. We distinguish between passenger lifts and goods lifts. However, the requirements of the market and technological developments result in indistinct boundaries between different types of lift.

ISO 4190 specifies that a lift must have a floor area measuring at least 1.40 x 1.10 m and a door opening at least 0.80 m wide in order to accommodate a wheelchair. All lift manufacturers can supply a standard model with these car dimensions and a load-carrying capacity of at least 630 kg for max. eight persons. Such a lift has enough space for most types of wheelchair, plus one other person. The space in front of lift doors should be large enough to accommodate persons waiting for the lift; a minimum landing size of 1.40 x 1.40 m is recommended.

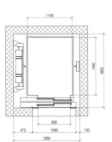
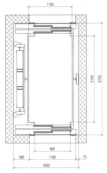

Passenger lift (wheelchair-compatible) Lift car and shaft dimensions

Passenger lift (wheelchair-compatible)
Minimum dimensions for barrier-free lifts

- Residential and office buildings
- Load-carrying capacity: 630 kg
- Car dimensions: 1.40 x 1.10 m (depth x width)
- Door width: 0.8 m
- Car for 8 persons, wheelchair/pram and accompanying person
- Door on one or two sides
- 2-part sliding door

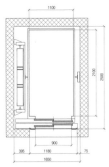

Passenger/goods lift (fire-fighting lift) Lift car and shaft dimensions

Passenger/goods lift
Minimum dimensions for fire-fighting lifts

- Residential and office buildings
- Load-carrying capacity: 1000 kg
- Car dimensions: 2.10 x 1.10 m (depth x width)
- Door width: 0.8 m
- Car for 13 persons, wheelchairs, stretchers,
- 1 pallet on manually operated pallet truck
- Door on one or two sides
- 2-part sliding door

Fig. 27: Lift car and shaft dimensions
Schindler Aufzüge AG

Bed/goods lift Lift car and shaft dimensions

Goods/special lift
Bed lifts, large goods lifts

- Hospitals and industry, warehouses
- Load-carrying capacity: 1600 kg
- Car dimensions: 2.40 x 1.40 m (depth x width)
- Door width: 1.3 m
- Car for 21 persons, beds, pallets
- Door on one or two sides
- 4-part, centre-opening sliding door

Fig. 28: The inside of a lift shaft

Lift shafts

Shafts for lift installations can be built in reinforced concrete, masonry or steel, and often contribute to the overall stability of a structure. Apart from the structural requirements, it is the sound insulation and fire protection specifications that determine the design and construction of lift shafts inside buildings. To improve sound insulation, lift shafts are isolated from the rest of the structure.

Headroom
There is extra space at the top of the shaft above the topmost floor served by the lift. This headroom allows for overrun and is the location of the ventilation opening and possibly the drive motors depending on the type of system.

Maximum structural opening: panels over entire shaft width and storey height with door frame, doors and call button panel inset

Moderate structural opening: door frame and doors remain visible, call button panel integrated into door frame

Minimum structural opening: door frame concealed, only doors visible, call button panel separated and brought forward from frame

Fig. 29: Landing doors
Different designs for landing doors with minimum or maximum structural opening

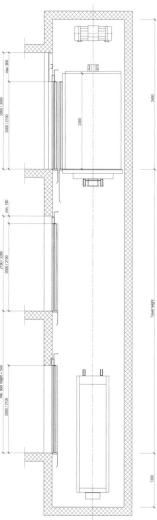

Lift pit
A lift pit to allow for overrun is located below the bottommost floor served by the lift. The pit should be approx. 1.0–1.5 m deep.

Fig. 30: Lift car and shaft dimensions in section
Schindler Aufzüge AG

Heat losses through lift shafts

Lift shafts often represent weak points in the thermal insulation concept of a building: a permanent opening at the top of a shaft leads to uncontrolled heat losses. Gaps between the landing doors allow hot air to flow unhindered from the heated parts of the building into the shaft, which then acts like a chimney, forcing the hot air up and out of the permanent openings at the top. This problem can be solved by fitting automatic ventilation flaps, which saves a considerable amount of heating energy (see "Energy-saving measures" on p. 262).

In addition to the lift manufacturer's specific recommendations, the following fundamental requirements are important when designing lift shafts:

- The lift shaft must be ventilated to ensure an adequate air quality in the shaft. An opening leading directly to the outside at the top of the shaft should therefore be provided.
- To prevent smoke building up in a lift shaft in the event of a fire, the Swiss VKF and SIA fire regulations require a smoke vent to the outside (unobstructed area of opening at least 5% of cross-sectional area of shaft, but max. 0.16 m^2).
- No services other than those required for the lift itself may be routed through a lift shaft.
- The temperature in the shaft must be between +5 and +40°C.
- The given shaft dimensions are basic or finished dimensions that must be adhered to (max. tolerance ±20 mm). In addition, any vertical misalignment measured over the entire height of the shaft may not exceed ±20 mm.
- Below the counterweights, the lift pit must be founded on suitable, undisturbed subsoil. If this is not possible, the necessary measures must be specified together with the manufacturer at the design stage.
- The shaft must be provided with electric lighting that ensures a level of illuminance of min. 50 lx over the whole shaft.
- It will normally be necessary to include fixings in the roof to a shaft for attaching a block and tackle.
- Access to the drive systems and the control cabinet must be possible at all times, using a standard key if necessary. Access through private rooms is not permitted.
- Electrohydraulic lifts require an oil-tight lift pit.

Lift drive systems

We make a fundamental distinction between electromechanical (traction) and electrohydraulic lifts.

The former type, with its wire ropes, counterweights and drive integrated into the lift shaft, is very popular these days. Various gear ratios are available to reduce the driving power, or for lifting heavier loads. The speed can be varied accordingly. Their simple drive system makes these lifts suitable for fast speeds and tall buildings.

Electrohydraulic lifts have fallen out of favour because of their limited speed and travel height. Such lifts are suitable for low-rise buildings and very heavy loads. Their advantage is that the drive can be positioned almost anywhere around the shaft.

Drive and control for electromechanical (traction) lifts

The drive for an electromechanical lift can be accommodated in the headroom at the top of the lift shaft. An extra lift motor room is therefore unnecessary. Access for servicing the compact control unit is integrated directly into the standard door frame. Such a design simplifies lift maintenance, ensures easy handling and saves space.

Drive and control for electrohydraulic lifts

The drive and control for an electrohydraulic lift are located in a separate room or control cabinet that can be positioned on any convenient floor within a radius of 10 m from the lift.

Fig. 31: Lift door types

The doors are equipped with an electronically actuated drive so that they operate quickly and reliably. Telescoping sliding doors are available in various forms, with the two- or four-part designs being the most common.

2-part side-opening sliding door
Side-opening door systems are preferred in residential buildings because they require the least space.

4-part centre-opening sliding door
Centre-opening doors are used in office buildings because they open faster and can therefore achieve greater carrying capacity.

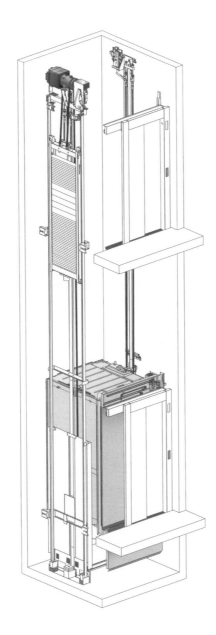

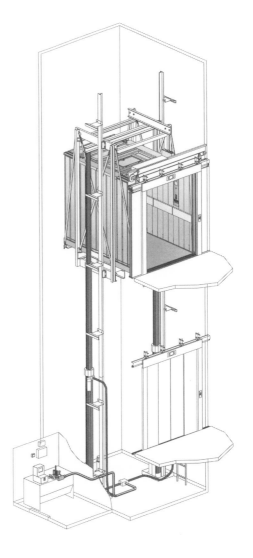

Fig. 32: Electromechanical (traction) lift

The drive is integrated into the shaft. Maintenance is carried out via the lift car. Arranging the drive in this way makes a lift motor room on the roof unnecessary.
Travel height: up to approx. 60 m
Speed: approx. 1.0–2.0 m/s

Fig. 33: Electrohydraulic lift

The hydraulic drive can be located in a separate lift motor room that can be positioned on any convenient floor within a radius of 10 m from the shaft.
Travel height: up to approx. 18 m
Speed: approx. 0.6 m/s

Energy efficiency

Energy efficiency is a subject that is becoming increasingly important for lift installations as well. Ever stricter safety standards plus demands for greater convenience and barrier-free access call for more and more electronics in modern lifts. The total energy consumption of a lift is made up of the energy required during travel and that required during standby.

Standby and travel requirements

Two figures indicate the standby and travel requirements, and both can be measured on an installed lift and thus verified. Depending on how the lift is used, it is worthwhile optimising the system for standby or travel consumption.

Five usage categories lead to the proper weighting. The figures for standby and travel plus the usage category give us the energy efficiency value, which is the main piece of information on the energy label.

Energy-saving measures

It is not the individual lift components, but rather how innovative subassemblies interact that guarantees the energy efficiency of the overall system. Energy recovery methods can be employed to reduce energy consumption when the lift is moving.

Energy recovery

Energy is produced during braking and is recovered by converting it into electricity instead of letting it be wasted as heat. Two operating states enable energy to be gained in this way.

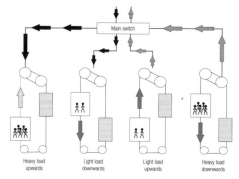

Fig. 34: Sketch of energy recovery principle
Energy recovery takes place in the two scenarios on the right.

Energy is recovered when:
– the loaded car travelling upwards is lighter than the counterweight, or
– the loaded car travelling downwards is heavier than the counterweight.

As energy recovery is impossible when the car is stationary, these methods are especially popular for lifts that are constantly in use.

In the case of well-used lifts and great travel heights, the energy recovered can be fed directly into the building's electricity network. A building always has an underlying energy requirement and so the electricity gains are not usually fed into the public grid. Energy recovery from lifts can therefore reduce a building's overall electricity consumption.

The level of energy recovered depends on the power of the drive system and the number of journeys or the travelling times.

Automatic ventilation flap

Automatic ventilation flaps can reduce the problem of heat losses through lift shafts and save a noticeable amount of heating energy. Thermostats regulate the automatic flaps, opening them only after the temperature has reached 35°C or in the event of a fire or failure of the electricity supply. Switches for opening the flaps manually are located adjacent to the building's main entrance and in the lift motor room (if there is one).

Fig. 35: Automatic ventilation flap at top of lift shaft

Destination control

Destination control means that the lift system knows the exact destination of each passenger in advance and therefore provides the best lift car for that journey. This method of control for groups of lifts has been growing in popularity ever since Schindler, the Swiss lift manufacturer, introduced the first practical destination control system more than 30 years ago.

Being able to sort passengers beforehand and minimise the number of lift car stops enables lift installations with destination control to achieve a much higher level of efficiency than conventional lifts.

Swiss standards and directives containing further information
SN EN 81-1/SN EN 81-2 Safety rules for the construction and installation of lifts –
Part 1: Electric lifts / Part 2: Hydraulic lifts
SIA 180/370 General conditions for lifts, escalators and moving walkways

SIA 181 Sound insulation in buildings
SIA 500 Barrier-free buildings
VKF Fire protection guidelines for lift installations
VKF Fire protection commentary for fire-fighting lifts

The staircase as an assembly of simply supported beams

Burkard Meyer Architekten: Services centre in Winterthur (CH), 1999

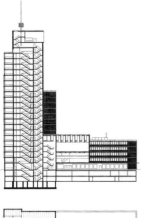

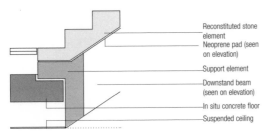

Figs 36 and 37: Section and plans

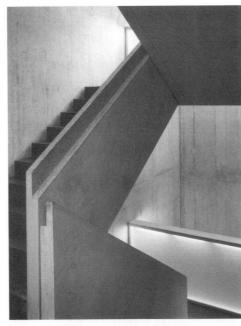

Fig. 38: Staircase
Burkard Meyer Architekten: Service centre, Winterthur (CH), 1999

The mainly single flights of stairs in the access tower to this high-rise block connect storey heights of up to 4.5 m. This results in large spans for the individual stair flights, which are made from precast, solid, dark reconstituted stone.

As the load-carrying capacity of this reconstituted stone material is less than that of conventional concrete, four precast concrete elements are responsible for the loadbearing functions of the stair flights. These act as primary beams spanning between the supports. While one of these beams is in the form of a conventional downstand beam, the other is in the form of a deep beam and simultaneously acts as the balustrade. At the ends these beams are supplemented by two support elements (L-shaped in section). The reconstituted stone stair elements are laid on these loadbearing elements, with neoprene pads ensuring that no impact sound is transferred to the primary loadbearing members. The verticality, the physical presence and the accuracy of the precast elements determine the expression of the stair shaft.

Fig. 41: Section through stair shaft

Reconstituted stone element
Neoprene pad (seen on elevation)
Support element
Downstand beam (seen on elevation)
In situ concrete floor
Suspended ceiling

Fig. 39: Detail of support

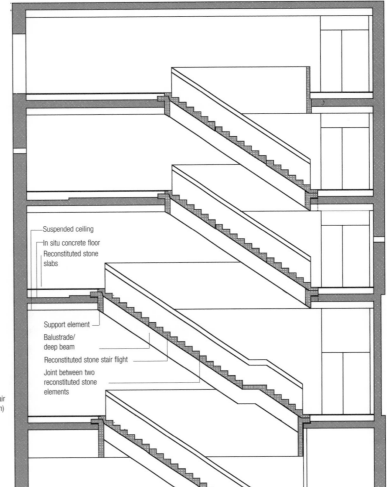

Suspended ceiling
In situ concrete floor
Reconstituted stone slabs

Support element
Balustrade/ deep beam
Reconstituted stone stair flight
Joint between two reconstituted stone elements

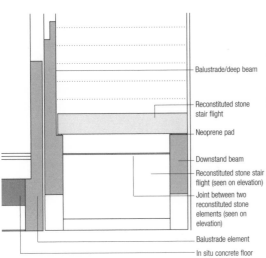

Balustrade/deep beam

Reconstituted stone stair flight

Neoprene pad

Downstand beam
Reconstituted stone stair flight (seen on elevation)
Joint between two reconstituted stone elements (seen on elevation)
Balustrade element
In situ concrete floor

Fig. 40: Cross-section through stair

The staircase as a monolithic, organic form
Herzog & de Meuron: Küppersmühle Museum in Duisburg (D), 1999

Fig. 42: The seemingly organic stairwell

Fig. 43: No joints are visible.

As an expressively designed vertical edifice, the external stair tower with a pentagonal plan shape forms a deliberate contrast to the modest statements of the exhibition rooms of this converted industrial building.

The cantilevering fair-face concrete stair construction winds its way up between the angled external walls around a seemingly organic stairwell. This space has been given its homogeneous character by ensuring that no joints are visible between the various concrete pours.

The external concrete walls were constructed first before casting the concrete balustrade and the stair flight in one operation. This meant that an L-shaped cross-section had to be cast. However, that made compaction very difficult because it is impossible to pass a poker vibrator around a 90 degree angle. The surfaces affected, i.e. the steps and the floor, were subsequently covered with a similarly homogeneous terrazzo finish. The vertical boards used as the formwork for the balustrade and the boards for the soffit formwork enabled the construction joints, which are essential over such a length of stair flight meandering over four storeys, to remain concealed. The top of the balustrade was the only surface that had to be finished (in this case ground) subsequently.

All the fair-face concrete parts have a red-brown colouring and hence reflect the colour of the brickwork of the existing building. The terrazzo finish likewise makes use of the same colour, which results in a monochromic space and enhances the monolithic effect of the construction.

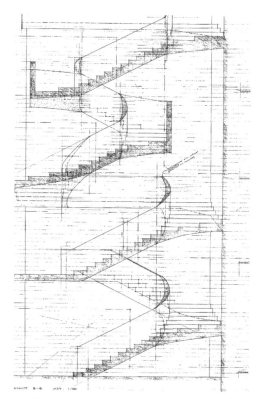

Fig. 44: Section

Fig. 45: Plans of ground floor, 1st floor and 2nd floor

The staircase as a space frame
Otto Rudolf Salvisberg: District heating power station, ETH Zurich (CH), 1935

Fig. 46: General view of stairs

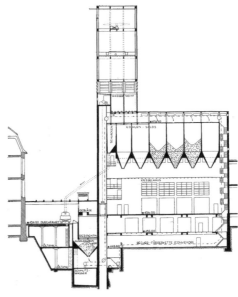

Fig. 50: Section through boiler house

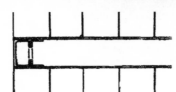

Fig. 47: Detail of stairwell

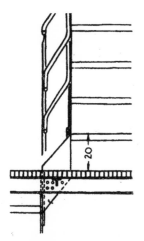

Fig. 48: Detail of stair/landing junction

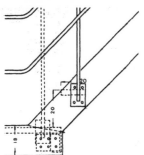

Fig. 49: Detail of connection between outer string and landing

Two "transparent" steel staircases with open-grid landings and treads were built in the boiler house. These stairs lend some texture to the elongated interior space surrounded by solid concrete walls and the silo hoppers but without occupying any space.

Situated in the corner, the three-dimensional structure climbs in dog-leg style up to the dizzy heights of the silo-charging level. Below the silo hopper openings steel beams and open-grid flooring panels make up the "transparent" mezzanine floor which stretches right across the interior, allowing workers access to the silo outlets.

Steel strings 18 cm deep are used as the primary loadbearing members for the stair flights and landings; these are bolted directly to the concrete walls. The stair string at the landing is bent into a loop around the stairwell without having to change the pitch in the transverse direction. This defines the geometry of the transitions at the landings and leads to an unconventional, welded crank in the outer strings that ist nonetheless a harmonious complement to the detail of the inner strings when seen as a whole. The treads made from open-grid flooring are bolted directly between the strings without the need for any secondary loadbearing members and therefore seem to dissolve into the background. Steel flats and fixing plates join the tubular uprights of the balustrades to the strings. Where the tubular handrails and intermediate rails meet the concrete wall they are simply bolted directly to the wall.

Apart from the "lightweight", simple form of construction, the direct connections between the stair components and the walls also play a major role in creating the effect of a space frame.

The staircase as a solid timber construction
Conradin Clavuot: School in St Peter (CH), 1998

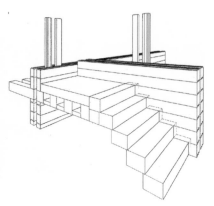

Fig. 55: Perspective view

Fig. 51: The ends of the steps

Fig. 52: General view of stair

The interior of the school in St Peter is determined by the material presence of the pine beams in log construction. The design of the staircase blends seamlessly into this constructional concept. The steps are made from untreated beams which appear to grow out of the module of the solid timber wall, running between wall and balustrade. While the steps were shown let into the wall in the early drawings (see Fig. 55), this was not carried out on site because the solid timber wall is one of the shear walls of the building whose structural action would have been interrupted by the inclusion of such members. The support on the wall side was therefore accomplished with a mortise and tenon joint additionally secured on the far side of the wall with metal bolts (see Fig. 54). The steps are suspended on bolts (concealed by dummy tenons) from the balustrade, which is also made from solid timber members and spans the distance between the floors. The individual members of the balustrade are joined by a number of threaded bars so that the balustrade acts as a deep beam and can span the full distance between floors.

Solid timber undergoes contraction and hence settlement in the first years of the life of a structure. In this school the settlement per storey was up to 10 cm. This resulted in the balustrade, which runs between the floors, undergoing a minimal (calculated) rotational movement. That in turn subjected the steps to a certain amount of torsion because their two supports were each subjected to different movement caused by the settlement. This factor and the contraction of the individual components of the staircase has led to small but noticeable gaps between the individual timber components. However, this in no way impairs the overall character of the construction. The elegant rawness of the solid components easily accommodate this phenomenon; indeed, it tends to emphasise their expressive character.

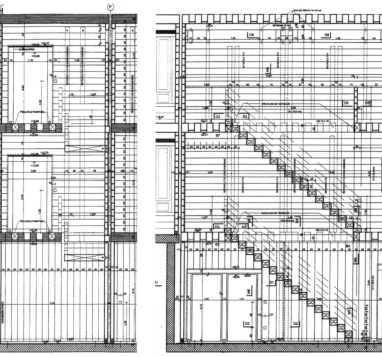

Fig. 53: Section

Fig. 54: Longitudinal section

STRUCTURES

Courtyard house versus veranda house

Andreas Kohne,
Andrea Deplazes

The courtyard house and the veranda house are architectural archetypes. As converse and complementary prototypes, they form the basis for numerous variations and combinations. As food for thought, they help us to understand the built environment, and illustrate and comprehend planned or unplanned growth processes. Current issues concerning the subject of urban density can therefore be presented in a plausible way – and their relationships explained – on different scales (S, M, L), ranging from the individual unit to the urban structure.

1. Basic types and schemes

The courtyard house

The courtyard house has been used as a form of shelter for thousands of years. Such houses can be found around the Mediterranean, in North and West Africa, and right across Asia from the Middle East to China. In the classic, prototypical courtyard house there is an area open to the sky in the centre of the building. The house is organised around this area, which, depending on the cultural region, is known as a courtyard, yard, atrium, patio, peristyle or *riad*. The outer boundary is defined by an enclosing wall, which, however, does not enjoy the status of being a facade facing the surroundings beyond. The clear demarcation makes the central area mostly a very private "inner world", often totally different and screened off completely from the surrounding "outside world". Accordingly, the courtyard house is an introverted housing form.

Fig. 1: Simple and extended courtyard house schemes

The house itself is accessed either directly from outside via one or more entrances, thus preserving the character of the courtyard as an extremely private place, or via the courtyard, which then becomes a semi-public space, a sort of forecourt. The rooms can be accessed directly from here or via an ambulatory running around the sides of the courtyard, a sort of intervening layer reminiscent of a cloister or arcade. The outcome is a sequence of public, semi-public and private spaces.

The size of the courtyard depends on functional criteria; in addition to fundamental purposes it is often also representative. Light, shade and ventilation have a great influence on the dimensions depending on climate, location and culture. Those dimensions in turn determine the height and depth of the building in relation to and depending on the storey height. The depth of the building results from the maximum natural illumination possible.

Fig. 2: Josep Lluis Sert: Casa Sert, Cambridge, Massachusetts (USA), 1958

Fig. 3: Private house, "al sohemi", Cairo (Egypt)

According to a universal rule of thumb (the so-called schoolhouse standard), with daylight from one side and a 3 m clear ceiling height, sufficient daylight can reach the farthest corners of a room 7–8 m deep. Inevitably, the courtyard assumes a certain size so that sufficient daylight reaches the rooms arranged around it. Where ventilation is the prime concern, small "perforations" are often sufficient, which means each open area cannot be referred to as a courtyard as such, but rather as a shaft, even a chimney. The interior layout of the courtyard house is very much dependent on climatic circumstances such as the trajectory of the sun over the day, or the building physics characteristics of the materials, especially the heat storage capabilities of heavy materials. For example, in subtropical regions the bedrooms are mostly positioned along the outer, solid, plain enclosing walls; the walls absorb the heat from the sun during the day and release it into the interior at night. The courtyard itself is partly in the sun or lies in the shade of the walls of the building.

The plan layout of a courtyard house corresponds to the principle of "protection": heavyweight walls closed to the outside world surround an inner space that is not visible from the outside. The boundaries gradually disappear from outside to inside and open up towards the centre, the courtyard. This shelter principle is found in monasteries, mosques and caravanserais, or the workplaces of craftspeople. They are structures that are segregated from the outside for functional, historical or cultural reasons, and are protected from or screened off from public spaces.

Fig. 4: Plan layout of courtyard house, shelter principle

The veranda house

The opposite of the courtyard house in terms of its typology is the veranda house, which can be regarded as an extroverted house. Its outward orientation results in distinct facades,[1] which portray, and therefore represent, the building and its interior to the outside world. The veranda house can also be described as a "point-block" with a garden or a building surrounded by a peripheral, open walkway and garden, e.g. the bungalow common in many regions. Etymologically, the English word "veranda" (or "verandah") stems from the Bengali *(bārāndā)* or Hindi *(varandā)* languages. However, as this term was used very frequently in Portuguese (in 1498 at the latest) and Spanish texts from very early times, it presumably found its way via these languages to India (Portuguese: *varanda*, originally Tamil: *veruntharai: verun* [empty] + *tharai* [floor, space]). In the veranda house the outermost boundary of the plot is mostly open or denoted by enclosures such as fences and hedges, or is merely the cadastral boundary. The difference between this and the courtyard house is that the rooms occupy not the periphery of the plot, but rather form its focus or centre. The grounds therefore become a private garden, or semi-public external space if they form part of the access to the building.

Fig. 5: Simple and extended veranda house schemes

In contrast to the courtyard house, access is not completely and directly from outside, but via the grounds, i.e. garden or veranda, which means that these areas inevitably lose their privacy and are exposed to the public and the neighbourhood. Access within the interior is usually via individual, vertical shafts, i.e. stairs, in a core with little daylight. Only a limited number of units per storey can be accessed via one stair.

The general, simplified plan layout of the veranda house reveals how the external boundary is broken up; layers form around the innermost, partially closed core (cella). Those layers become more and more open as we approach the outside and merge with the surrounding landscape. This principle is known as a "temple" layout.

Fig. 6: Plan layout of veranda house, temple principle

In the veranda house, openings in the facades serve as entrances and admit daylight. The maximum building depth depends directly on the question of illumination and explains the greatest possible and customary dimensions for this type of building. According to the rule

Fig. 7: Private house with private grounds

Fig. 8: Watanabe House, Sekigawa (J)

Fig. 9: Several homesteads, Batina Oasis (Oman)

of thumb mentioned above, with light from one side only, a room up to 7–8 m deep can be provided with adequate daylight. So with light from two sides, a building depth of 14–16 m is possible, a dimension that is often encountered in veranda houses. The distance between two adjacent buildings is likewise regulated by lighting aspects: the necessary minimum distance to the nearest neighbouring building must be such that an adequate amount of daylight is guaranteed (on the ground floor, too) and is not spoiled by shadows. Shadows cast by adjacent buildings are particularly problematic with taller structures. It is this circumstance that encourages low-density developments with defined spacing rules and fewer buildings, totally in contrast to developments with courtyard houses. Shading to protect against direct sunlight is relevant only on the side facing the sun and can be achieved by providing shades for the veranda layer or by designing a veranda of suitable depth.

The very different ways of handling light (heat) and shade (sunblinds) as well as private and public areas allows us to draw a first general conclusion regarding the distribution of these two house types. Courtyard houses tend to be found in regions in which an absolutely private place to which people can withdraw plays a very important role, as in Islamic cultures or in areas where the climate is such that protection against the sun and heat is essential. Veranda houses, with their overhanging roofs, are chiefly encountered in the tropics, with maximum shade and darkness because the interior has hardly any windows, or in temperate or subpolar zones with facades open to the outside world in order to capture daylight and solar radiation.

2. Variations on the schemes

The two basic types and schemes represent idealised forms. These archetypes can, however, be varied, minimised or undergo radical changes while still maintaining their intrinsic qualities. This results in a number of courtyard and veranda house subtypes that are frequently used. They form the basis for combinations and growth processes through the addition of similar or hybrid subtypes.

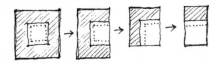

Fig. 10: Courtyard house variations (subtypes)

A U- or L-shaped courtyard house can be derived from the original courtyard house – with its central open area and surrounding access or ambulatory layer – by removing one or two sides of the house and replacing them

with plain walls. Further reduction eventually leads to the simple courtyard house – a house with adjacent yard enclosed by walls on three sides. All courtyard house variations – even in their most minimal form – always correspond to the introverted house type.

In its most fundamental configuration, the courtyard house consists of just an open enclosed space with no room layers. In other words, an inner or "empty" space enclosed by walls – the "very first architectural space" as the result of territorial appropriation and demarcation from the open landscape. In terms of development, it is the enclosing of a yard or garden with the help of a wall (Persian: *pairi-daeza*, a garden enclosed by a wall; later: paradise) to screen off the surroundings. The wall demarcates the plot from the outside world and defines land ownership. Depending on family additions and the needs of the occupants, compartments are built within the enclosed yard one by one to match requirements. The various compartments occupy the yard and divide it into smaller interior spaces with varying degrees of interrelationship. Far more elaborate is the yard enclosed by walls in which the individual compartments are appended to the outside. Ultimate fulfilment of this design principle is achieved when there is a complete ring of individual rooms grouped around a large courtyard, e.g. the Moroccan courtyard house, which represents the perfect variation.

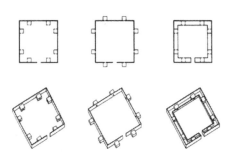

Fig. 11: Sketches by Donald Judd
Houses within a wall or outside or between two walls

The artist and architect Donald Judd looked into these courtyard development principles when suggesting ideas for a house to his sister: "I suggested [that she] simply build a wall around a city-block ... Then as money was available structures could be built against the wall on a scheme or at random according to the functions necessary. The center would remain fairly large and empty, since the area was established by the city-block ... Or a second inner wall could be built and the necessary structures built between the two walls, further enclosing the gardens. Or, additional structures could be built toward the center against the second wall."[2]

Fig. 12: Rapp & Rapp: Leland Building, Detroit, Michigan (USA), 1927

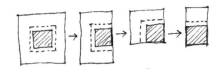

Fig. 13: Veranda house variations (subtypes)

Similar operations are possible with the veranda house. The building positioned in the centre of the plot can be moved so that one side is on the boundary of the plot, or to one corner, or interpreted as a single house with a front garden. In contrast to the minimal courtyard house with its yard enclosed by three walls, the house with a front garden is an extroverted design because the open external space is defined by minimal means only and not by walls. Taken to the extreme, the minimalist veranda house mutates to a point-block without a veranda, which faces the public spaces on all sides directly and abruptly. In contrast to the enclosed open areas of courtyard houses, these are solitary edifices within public spaces.

3. Growth processes (S, M, L)

The multiplication of the courtyard or veranda house type is triggered by additive growth processes, which can be in the form of horizontal or vertical expansion. Three, four or more veranda or courtyard houses at scale S become neighbourhoods at scale M. And grouping several neighbourhoods results in urban districts, towns or cities at scale L. In the end the question is: How can urban infill

strategies be discerned and devised with targeted horizontal or vertical growth processes?

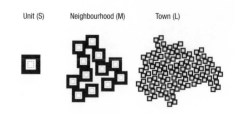

Unit (S)   Neighbourhood (M)   Town (L)

Fig. 15: Courtyard house growth processes

Growth processes for courtyard houses

As courtyard houses, with their closed, external, walled boundaries, can be joined together to form a row in any direction, such houses can be built very close together while still complying with access requirements. This encourages high-density developments with houses and fire walls abutting each other directly. Gaps in the development create the necessary spaces for access and precisely framed alleys, roads or open spaces. This type of horizontal growth allows the spread of urban developments that, at first sight, seem to have a very high density. In Islamic cultures, however, buildings are normally only two to four storeys high, which means that private houses can be occupied by a single family or clan. But the Chinese round and courtyard houses, the Tulou, are much larger. These buildings, mostly three to five storeys high and with diameters exceeding 100 m, house several

Fig. 14: Old quarter (medina) of Fes (Morocco)

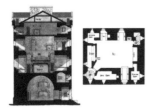

Fig. 16: Comlongon Castle, Dumfries (Scotland), 15th century

Fig. 17: Le Corbusier: Immeubles Villas project, 1922

Fig. 18: G. Candilis, V. Bodiansky, S. Woods: apartment block, Casablanca (Morocco), 1952

clans, and with their metre-thick external walls also served as fortifications in the past.

Allowing courtyard houses to expand vertically is impossible if they are to retain their intrinsic characteristics. Introducing different levels, e.g. simply stacking apartments around an open courtyard, robs that inner area of its privacy, allows others insights into the private sphere; the courtyard becomes a semi-public space. Therefore, vertical growth processes for courtyard houses must be arranged differently. For example, stacking several two-storey courtyard houses results in covered inner areas, i.e. high rooms or halls, instead of the courtyard originally open to the sky. The central, private hall is surrounded by (ancillary) rooms with a minimum depth and provided with daylight via alcoves and galleries – a principle we have already encountered in the Scottish tower houses of the 15th century (Comlongon Castle, Dumfries). Le Corbusier, too, used the principle of stacked apartments with an extra-high private external space. His Pavillon de L'Esprit Nouveau was built in 1925 as a prototype for the Immeubles Villas project. The apartments on top of each other are actually separate villas arranged around inner gardens below a high roof. This block of villas embodies the idea of a new type of urban living, with private gardens that can be placed at any level above the street. The position of the courtyard is the theme of another vertical growth approach in which the private courtyard space is shifted to the outside of the building, a variation we have met before in the shape of the minimal courtyard house

with its yard enclosed by three walls. This space is closed off with a high wall in order to preserve its introverted character. The offset arrangement and two-storey apartments ensures that these courtyards allow enough daylight to reach the apartments. This principle was used for an apartment block in Casablanca designed by Bodiansky, Candilis, Woods (1954) and in a similar way for the housing development on Paul-Clairmont-Strasse in Zurich by Gmür & Steib Architekten (2006).

Growth processes for veranda houses
Owing to their peripheral grounds, horizontal growth processes for veranda houses tend to consume considerable amounts of land. The result is roads lined by fields with individual buildings. Local building regulations usually dictate two rows with a regular distribution and a low-density development. A denser layout can be achieved by building the individual houses adjacent to each other to create terraces with two open sides. Access is from the road, and the gardens lie between the rows of houses. An alternative

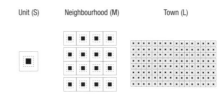

Fig. 19: Veranda house growth processes

Fig. 20: Residential estate of detached houses (USA)

Fig. 21: High-rise buildings in Hong Kong (China)

Fig. 22: Cluster, housing cluster
from: Stefano Bianca: *Urban Form in the Arab World: Past and Present*

is to create back-to-back terraces with access and light via the (front) garden only and, consequently, houses open on one side only. Such terraces, which, theoretically, can be extended *ad infinitum* in the longitudinal direction, can take on any plan form or be arranged in squares or rectangles, so-called perimeter block developments.

In contrast to the courtyard house, vertical development is possible with the veranda house, right up to high-rise buildings with a minimal footprint. Private external spaces are reduced to terraces and the spaces between the buildings become public areas with some level of urban identity.

Access principles
Corresponding access principles can be derived from the various development structures created by these growth processes. Although we might suspect that there are many different options, these can be reduced to a few basic rules, which are made up of roads and alleys irrespective of the type of house, courtyard or veranda:
a) Parallel roads: Individual units combined to form (back-to-back) terraces must be provided with access. Parallel roads allowing direct access to the houses are created between the buildings.
b) Cul-de-sacs: As soon as the plots between the roads are enlarged to accommodate a second or third row of houses, cul-de-sacs become necessary. These branch off from the linear roads to provide access to the houses behind the main rows. A hierarchy of primary and secondary roads evolves.

c) Grids: A grid-type layout results in parallel roads in two directions. The roads can be identical or divided into primary and secondary arteries. In Manhattan, for example, the roads in the north-south direction are called avenues, those in the east-west direction streets. The grid structure defines the maximum dimensions of the building plots by creating so-called blocks.
d) Cluster/tree structures: This type of access follows a distinct hierarchical principle. Clusters of houses, like those of Islamic cities, form a tree structure. The roads and approaches branch off and become more contorted as they become ever finer – according to the principle of fractal geometry – until they finally terminate in a dead end or courtyard. As the public orientation decreases, so the private one increases.
e) Combinations of a–d: All these principles may be combined with each other, a fact that can be checked again and again by viewing urban structures through an aircraft window.

4. Combination strategies

Looking beyond the laws that govern development, we can ask the question as to how maximum urban density can be achieved. The individual forms of variation are often insufficient for this; instead, combinations that link courtyard and veranda types are necessary. We encounter such hybrid forms everywhere.

A skilful combination strategy calls for simple means to increase density and minimise the space required

Fig. 23: Ildefonso Cerdá: perimeter blocks, city expansion, Barcelona (E), 1850

for access. For example, as mentioned above, rows of houses can be in the form of back-to-back developments with external spaces in front, or they can be in double rows with external spaces in between. By increasing the area for development or introducing a further, central row of houses accessed via cul-de-sacs, it is relatively easy to achieve a higher density. In this case, external space and privacy is achieved with houses with a walled courtyard in the second row, while the first row along the road is composed of such houses again or houses with a front garden. A combination strategy, in this case choosing the right type of house (courtyard or veranda) enables all the units to be accessed but also have a private external space.

5. Metamorphosis phenomena

Assigning individual structures to the courtyard or veranda house type using the aforementioned attributes is usually relatively obvious on the level of the respective scale or treatment (S, M, L). But combinations and variations, or, specifically, when changing the scale in connection with growth processes, it can certainly happen that one type "transforms" into the other.

As an example, let us look at a veranda house open on two sides on the individual unit scale (S). An additive process turns the individual house into a row, which in a further step is combined with others to form a perimeter block development. On the neighbourhood scale (M), the perimeter block development – characterised by its internal courtyard – belongs to the courtyard house type. The first metamorphosis has taken place. Strictly speaking, this is a type with a semi-public courtyard surrounded by (through-)apartments with two open sides. It therefore differs from the original type, which has rooms clearly facing the courtyard. The transformation to the next scale involves a further metamorphosis. Several perimeter block developments with intervening roads form an urban district on the level of the town or city (L). The courtyard house type has now reverted to a veranda house type with individual blocks facing the public thoroughfares.

6. The urban typology

On the scale of the town or city (L), we are once again faced with the question of the maximum density possible and the laws governing development, plus the underlying motivation: Just how dense can an urban area be when it is developed according to the principles of the courtyard house or the veranda house?

In planned municipalities, the density is defined indirectly in advance via the access routes, the division into building plots, determining the depths of buildings and the number of storeys, with climatic, topographical and cultural aspects being considered as well. In Dubrovnik, for instance, the compact urban structure – the back-to-back arrangement of the veranda houses – evokes an access principle with primary roads (*stradun*), lateral alleys and open squares. Tokyo, on the other hand, is based on the principle of separate veranda houses, but nevertheless achieves an extremely high density. The houses are of different heights and each one is open on all sides. This essentially low-density development form is intended to

Fig. 24: Unauthorised development in Cairo (Egypt), 2009

reduce the risk of earthquake damage. Often, only the very narrowest of intervening spaces separate the individual houses and so this leads to an incredible density and proximity, which presumes a particular culture of co-existence.

Whereas some European towns and cities are currently experiencing shrinkage processes, Cairo is one of those huge cities that is literally bursting. Unauthorised settlements result in neighbourhoods with an astonishing density. New buildings are erected on huge areas – settlements in the desert and on agricultural land – without prior planning and unauthorised, totally in contrast to planned urban development. These (veranda) houses are often six or more storeys high and use the classic hybrid form of construction found everywhere in Cairo: a framework of columns and slabs in reinforced concrete with plain red brick walls. Infill developments in both the horizontal and vertical direction result in a very high density. Public spaces, however, are confined to minimal access routes between the buildings; public squares or open areas are completely absent.

Kowloon Walled City ("city of darkness"), formerly a district of Hong Kong, holds the record for the greatest building density in the world. A former Chinese military base, a settlement planned by the authorities, was expanded upwards and outwards by its occupants over the years. The situation became so ridiculous and dangerous that the entire development was demolished for safety reasons in 1993.

Towns and cities with veranda houses are very much dependent on their direct surroundings. Owing to the form of the veranda house, the open areas between the buildings become the defining element. The precise configuration of squares, streets and external spaces becomes an obligatory component of high-quality and compact urban planning. Towns and cities with courtyard houses, which are primarily still encountered in Islamic cultures, deal with the issue of density and external spaces by using just a few basic types: the courtyard style for housing, schools (*madrasah*), tradesmen's premises and mosques. These types generate a direct coexistence between urban vitality and quiet public spaces, e.g. in the form of mosques. Transitions between the lively and quiet areas are often very abrupt and unexpected.

Fig. 25: Old quarter of Dubvronik (Croatia)

Fig. 26: Tokyo (J)

Fig. 27: Kowloon Walled City, city district of Hong Kong (China) prior to 1993

[1] Latin: *facies* = visage; Italian: *la facciata* = face
[2] Donald Judd: *Architektur*, Münster, 1989, pp. 40–41.

An attempt to classify horizontal and vertical space development

Christoph Wieser,
Andrea Deplazes

Architecture creates spaces. How these are roofed over is to some extent written as a code in the plan; the spread of the spaces in the horizontal direction is very closely tied to the question of how they are roofed over. This dependence leads to a description of the horizontal and vertical space development in three steps. Starting with the needs of an individual or a community, single compartments are created, mostly of modest size. The second step expands their plan area. The maximum expansion is defined by the respective type of roofing, the limits of which, even today, cannot be pushed beyond a certain point because the work and cost of the roofing increases exponentially. This is how the third step arises: the addition of spaces and hence the perforation of the individual compartments to produce connections between spaces. The enlargement of the room conglomerate is carried out in the horizontal and vertical directions according to the needs. But what principles do we apply for the expansion of the compartment to form complex room conglomerates? How do these growth processes affect the construction?

First part: nucleus and theoretical model

This investigation will focus on the interdependencies between the spatial and constructional structure of a building. In order to analyse these interactions, we shall take a single compartment as our theoretical model and then investigate the possible expansion strategies. This simplified approach is intended to focus attention on the underlying principles. This is not a history of developments or cultures, but rather an approach derived from the aforementioned conditions. The examples chosen serve to illustrate the theories and place them in a context. The development asserted here does not pretend to be universally applicable; in reality, far more complex sequences and hybrid forms of all kinds can prevail in everyday situations, influenced by various factors.

For the sake of simplicity, let us imagine our compartment to be square on plan and measuring about 4 x 4 m and with a height of 2 to 3 m.

The effective dimensions of ancient shelters, tents, wooden or stone huts are about this size and can be regarded as being clearly related to the radius of action of our arms, and to human strength. It therefore takes on something of a "genetic" quality. However, human beings have always known how to exploit the options available to them depending on the materials available.

Let us take a closer look at this compartment. In contrast to a pure body such as a cube, which comes closest to our chosen model, the compartment does not have six equal bounding surfaces, but boundaries of various "orders" which according to Bodo Rasch, and in line with the sequence of building operations, exhibit the following hierarchy: the first-order element is the partition or wall, the second-order element is the roof and the third-order the floor.[1]

Breaking down the enclosure into various orders indicates the different functions these parts must fulfil – from both the symbolic and the constructional perspectives. Let us concentrate on the wall and the roof because these two elements are critical for presenting horizontal and vertical space development. Various techniques are used depending on whether we employ filigree or solid construction, but in the end both types of construction achieve the same effect.

Roofing over

The roofing over of spaces has always been an extremely demanding task because the effect of gravity makes itself felt without remorse: every mistake leads to collapse. Whereas in solid construction the roof and the suspended floors are often carried out in a filigree form of construction in order to save weight, this typical change of materials is absent from filigree construction for obvious reasons. Filigree construction makes use of heavyweight infill panels here and there, e.g. frame building, but the roof construction is kept as light as possible and is not subjected to unnecessary loads. The choice of one or other type of roof was governed in early times by the materials available, and even to this day material properties are an important factor in terms of construction, as well as architecture. Heavyweight domes exhibit different properties from those of folded-plate structures or floors in timber or steel, or the other possibilities provided by flat slabs of reinforced concrete since the beginning of the 20th century.

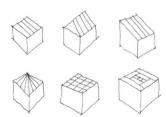

The roofing over of a single compartment is carried out in filigree construction with linear members – originally branches from trees. These are usually directional systems, which include all the different types of flat, monopitch and duopitch roofs. The common feature is that there are walls that serve as supports and walls that do not carry roof loads.

This differentiation renders it possible to include generous openings in the end walls, indeed, even omit them completely, provided transverse stability is guaranteed in some other way.

However, filigree construction also includes non-directional roofing types, which are used for conical huts or tents; these include pyramid roofs – very elaborate constructions with concentrically arranged trimmers, or coffered slabs, although these should actually be designated bi-directional.

Various types of non-directional roof constructions are used in solid construction: corbelled domes of loosely coursed stone slabs – like those that still exist today, the "Bories" in Gordes – pyramid-type roofs, domes, as well as flat slabs in reinforced concrete, which can be designed as directional or non-directional, according to the arrangement of the reinforcement. Barrel vaults are also directional systems.

Fig. 28: Corbelled dome made from courses of stone slabs
Bories, Gordes (F)

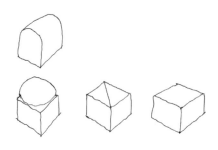

Openings

The wall, whether of lightweight or heavyweight construction, must fulfil partly contradictory conditions: it has a loadbearing function, but openings for windows and doors must also be provided – for connecting individual compartments to form room conglomerates, a well as for lighting and ventilating the interior. In filigree construction, a framework is first erected, which is surrounded by space, and it is not until the second step that the room enclosures are added, the non-loadbearing walls. Openings are accordingly of the structural kind, and the procedure consists of a partial "filling-out" of the framework. The situation is different in solid construction, where the openings are formed in the loadbearing walls. As they weaken the loadbearing behaviour of the wall, the degree of perforation is limited.

There are various reasons behind the desire to enlarge the openings, or to increase their number. Besides improving the interior lighting conditions, some uses such as garages or shops need large openings. On the ground floor in particular, the desire for maximum openings to

create openness is in conflict with the structural requirements because the greatest forces are concentrated here. Over the millennia, various methods have been devised to handle such demands, in both filigree and solid construction, and these will be dealt with in the third part.

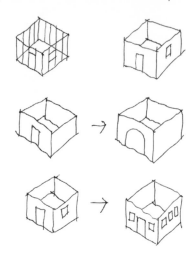

Second part: horizontal growth processes

The desire to enlarge the plan area leads to horizontal growth processes. Starting with the single compartment, space development takes place essentially in two forms: by increasing the volume of a single compartment or by adding additional compartments, which are then linked together.

1. Single-space strategies

The original reason behind enlarging a compartment to form a hall or a shed was certainly to create a place of assembly for festivities and other purposes The various types of longhouses and open halls, like those of the Vikings, in which whole clans lived are well known. If the volume is enlarged, however, the dimensions of the structural parts also have to increase: the structural depth of the roof and the thickness of the external walls. But this is possible only up to a certain level – until the load-carrying capacities of the materials are reached, thus forcing a change to the construction system There is a conflict of interests from a structural viewpoint: to span over large distances we need more material, which leads to an increase in weight and hence to complications in the loadbearing system, which in turn affects the maximum span possible.

This problem can be illustrated using the design and construction process of the dome to Florence Cathedral as an example. The dimensions of the nave and the crossing were stipulated long before Filippo Brunelleschi finally managed to find a solution for the vaulting overhead. He proposed a double-skin dome, which enabled him to achieve two things: the very thick, existing stone tambour

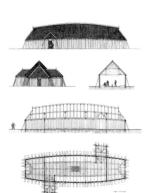

Fig. 29: "Fyrkat"
Reconstruction of a large Viking hall

Fig. 30: Section through double-skin dome
Filippo Brunelleschi: Santa Maria del Fiore,
Florence (I), 1418–36

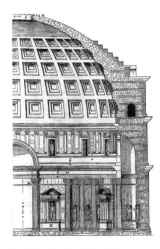

Fig. 31: Section after Palladio, 1570
Pantheon, Rome (I), 118–128 AD

**Fig. 32: Filigree loadbearing structure based
on a modular arrangement and standardised
member length**
Konrad Wachsmann: model of a three-dimensional
(space) frame

could be continued without steps inside and outside and at the same time the weight reduced to such an extent that the substructure was capable of carrying the loads – for there was a span of 42 m to be built.[2]

Depending on their properties, loadbearing structures can be designed with an "active cross-section" or an "active form". In constructions with an active cross-section, the forces flow within an unspecified cross-section that is partially oversized and hence includes structurally inactive zones. To save weight, the lightest material possible is therefore often used. For example, the Pantheon in Rome, whose circular dome consists of ever lighter concrete mixes as it approaches the crown. This is accompanied by a decrease in the shell thickness, which makes the dome of the Pantheon a partly optimised loadbearing structure with an active form. In such structural systems the flow of forces becomes a form-finding parameter and the structure is reduced until only the structurally relevant parts remain. Typical examples of this are frames of all kinds, from simple trusses to the experiments of Konrad Wachsmann, whose ingenious node design enabled him to devise ever bolder space frames in steel.

Even high-tech loadbearing structures for spanning over a space without intervening supports reach the limit of the technical feasibility of their age at some point. And they are often totally inadvisable for reasons of proportions. The basilica was an early form of shed structure whose multi-bay arrangement distributes the loads in an ingenious way: the thrust that ensues from spanning over the nave is resisted by the aisles. This solution produces not only a single large interior space, but the distribution of the loads enables a construction with more slender members, which in Gothic church-building led to a spectacular resolution of the structure. The spectacular interiors flooded with light are paid for with a row of flying buttresses which, "transferred" to the outside, guarantee the necessary equilibrium of forces.

2. Multiple-space strategies

The Basilica brings us to another type of horizontal space development, to the multiple-space strategies, which comprise two main groups. Depending on the type of expansion, we distinguish between the non-directional and the directional addition of spaces.

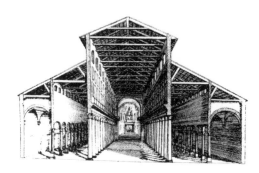

Fig. 33: Section through five-nave basilica
Earlier building on site of St Peter's, Rome (I), 4th century AD

Non-directional addition

By adding further rooms to expand the nucleus, we create a room conglomerate. If this takes place in a non-hierarchical way, i.e. if all the rooms tend to be treated equally, we speak of non-directional addition. Everyday needs trigger this type of horizontal development: the range of spaces available has to be expanded. At the same time, there is the option of differentiating the individual spaces because the additional compartments need not have the same form or the same dimensions.

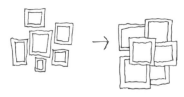

Such spontaneously ensuing room conglomerates have a characteristic tendency to be flexible with regard to further extensions. The ancient principle of the geometrically unconstrained networking of individual spaces can be seen in traditional loam buildings and igloos. Every single igloo consists of a sequence of higher and lower, larger and smaller rooms; the grouping of several igloos to form a cluster of rooms has also been observed.[3] A conglomerate of chambers with the most diverse proportions and dimensions can be compacted to such an extent that there is no wasted space. Hadrian's villa in Tivoli (118–134 AD) illustrates how this principle is artistically and enthusiastically celebrated, particularly in the small thermae.

The example of non-directional, additive interior space development is based on the assumption that individual compartments, independent in terms of layout and structural factors, are joined together to form a conglomerate.

However, this results in filigree construction in a doubling of the columns, and in solid construction a doubling of the walls, which does not of course take place in reality because it would be an uneconomic use

Fig. 34: Building an igloo

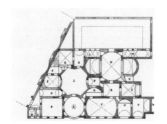

Fig. 35: Plan of small thermae
Hadrian's villa, Tivoli (I), 118–134 AD

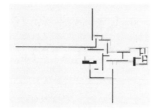

Fig. 36: Ludwig Mies van der Rohe: brick
country house project, 1923–24

of resources. Consequently, the extensions, in structural terms consist solely of wall segments of all shapes and sizes. Only in conjunction with the existing walls do they achieve the necessary stability. In principle, the flowing spatial concepts of De Stijl or Mies van der Rohe's design for a brick country house (1924) could be interpreted as a radical further development of this method. The enclosing structure of the adjoining wall segments has been resolved, the walls and returns stand separately and define the intervening rooms only vaguely.

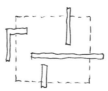

The roof over the interior spaces is also realised differently. Although in traditional building every compartment is often roofed over individually for practical and economic reasons, the roof in other situations acts as a coherent loadbearing structure, as a plate that permits cantilevers to a certain extent.

Non-directional suspended floors are very easy to build in reinforced concrete, although the designation "non-directional" does not describe the relationships accurately. Flat slabs are mostly directional loadbearing structures – it's just that we can no longer see this after the concrete has been cast around the reinforcing bars.

Besides the modern variation of a non-directional covering, or even better the bi-directional or multi-directional roof, there are also traditional forms of construction employing such ideas. These include constructing vaulting over the compartments in the form of a dome, e.g. in madrasahs, or building a timber floor. Owing to their relatively limited span of about 5 m, timber joist floors without glued laminated members are suitable for room conglomerates with essentially self-contained compartments. To improve the transverse stiffness, it is advisable to turn the joists through 90° from room to room. On the other hand, steel floors enable extensive resolution of the structure because steel beams can be easily designed to span long distances, over more than one compartment. However, these usually employ a hierarchical structure and are hence directional.

Compartments with dome roofs can also be assembled in modular form to create complex internal layouts. If the intermediate walls are resolved into columns, this produces one room or several large rooms. One characteristic feature of such interior spaces is the fact that the importance of the individual compartment is still apparent, or at least implied, because the dome has a strongly centralising effect. Aldo von Eyck used this property in an ingenious way for a children's home in Amsterdam. Taking an African souk as his model, he designed a honeycomb-like configuration whose compartments are spanned by domes. To distinguish special spaces he used larger dimensions, as well as individual or ring-shaped rooflights. In addition, he exploited the flexibility of the open room structure to expand the plan layout to meet the respective requirements.

Directional addition

The second group of multiple-room strategies for extending buildings horizontally is based on linear or radial growth. In the linear method, individual walls or partitions are set up side by side to form a compartment-like structure. There is a hierarchy in this structure: loadbearing longitudinal walls and non-loadbearing stabilising or infill walls. This creates obvious, elongated, rectangular rooms which, apart from the first and last compartments, can receive their daylight only through the end walls or the roof. If the loadbearing walls are roofed over with barrel vaults or separate duopitch roofs, the effect of this already very directional structure is further enhanced.

The orientation of the interior spaces runs parallel with the walls. In this direction the individual spaces may also be extended *ad infinitum,* while in the transverse direction a complete "unit" must be added every time. The distances between individual walls could vary, depending on the type of roof, but this would not change the primary direction of the plan layout.

Fig. 37: Honeycomb-like, dome-vaulted structure
Aldo von Eyck: children's home, Amsterdam (NL), 1955–60

In architectural and structural terms, the connections between these elongated chambers perpendicular to the walls are interesting.

Permeable in all directions, almost "naturally", are the grid-like structures of filigree construction – apart from timber log construction, which functions like solid construction in terms of creating interior spaces. The desire, or rather the need, to connect the individual compartments led at an early date, e.g. the Trajanic markets of the Romans, to an opening being cut in the front part of each wall, or rather the addition of a transverse access corridor. A related principle can be seen in the old quarter of Bern, where covered roadside walkways create a public zone linking the narrow, deep buildings.

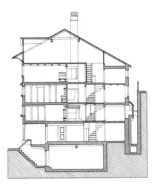

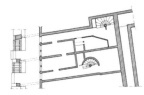

Fig. 38: Narrow houses in the old quarter of Bern (CH)

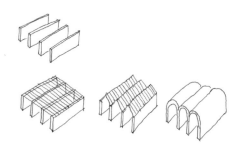

Increasing the degree of transparency in the transverse direction can be achieved by resolving the walls into arches and eventually into columns.

An early example of a barrel-vaulted building with elongated compartments turned into one large interior space is the bathing house of the palace of Qusayr Amra (711 AD), which today stands in the middle of the Jordanian desert. The entrance hall is roofed over by three

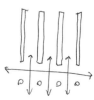

parallel barrel vaults supported on walls resolved almost completely into arches. Nevertheless, the longitudinal orientation of the barrel vaults determines the layout. This superimposition of the longitudinal and transverse direction is also fascinating in the prayer halls of colonnade mosques, such as the Great Mosque in Cordoba (785–961), which was extended in various phases to create an overwhelming interior space with 600 columns. As in the majority of colonnade mosques, there are flat timber ceilings between the walls. The roof construction consists of timber trusses and the duopitch roofs trace the wall structure below.

Fig. 39: Box-frame structure with barrel-vault roof
Bathing house of the Palace of Qusayr Amra (JO), 711 AD

A modern variation of the maximum resolution of a wall structure, roofed over with reinforced concrete barrel vaults each of which is supported on four columns, was designed by Louis I. Kahn in 1972 for Fort Worth in Texas. Here, at the Kimbell Art Museum, Kahn plays consciously with the dominance of the longitudinal vault form by placing the main direction of movement of visitors at 90° to it. Arriving at the main entrance in the centre of the longitudinal facade, visitors are first channelled transversely to the structure and only then in the longitudinal direction of the exhibition rooms. These are arranged

Fig. 40: Barrel-vaulted compartmentalised structure
Louis I. Kahn: Kimbell Art Museum, Fort Worth, Texas (USA), 1972

Fig. 41: View of the large hall transverse to the drastically resolved wall structure consisting only of columns and arches
Great Mosque, Cordoba (E), 785–961

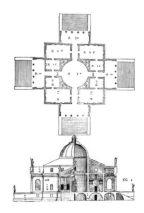

Fig. 42: Plan and elevation
Andrea Palladio: Villa Capra "La Rotonda", Vicenza
(I), 1567–91

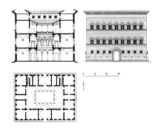

Fig. 43: Plan, section and elevation
Giuliano da Sangallo: Palazzo Strozzi, Florenz (I)
1489–1539

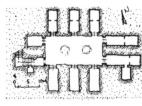

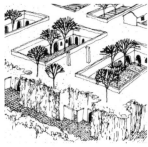

Fig. 44: Sunken-court dwellings in China

with their principal dimensions transverse to the walls so that, once again, visitors have to move mainly across the structure.

The group of directional room conglomerates includes all those buildings with radial expansion, i.e. proceed outwards from a central space.

Buildings arranged around a central space often exhibit a hierarchical, often essentially symmetrical form. Such buildings include palaces and many churches with their prayer niches and side-chapels, as Paul Frankl illustrated in simple schematic drawings in his 1914 book *Die Entwicklungsphasen der neueren Baukunst* (The development phases of modern architecture).[4] But secular buildings, too, such as Palladio's Villa Rotonda (1571) near Vicenza, are frequently organised in this way.

At the Strozzi Palace in Florence, probably built to a design by Giuliano da Sangallo in 1489–1539, it becomes clear that the central space can also be a courtyard. Chinese and Tunisian sunken-court dwellings are interesting in this respect: individual chambers grouped around a central courtyard excavated in the ground. Further rooms can be created as required until the entire periphery of the courtyard is exhausted, at which point another access, light and ventilation court must be excavated. There is a direct relationship between the width of the rooms and the loadbearing capacity of the loamy or loess-like soil.

If the addition of spaces radially is regarded as hierarchical, this is primarily related to the spatial organisation with a central principal space and peripheral annex spaces. But in structural terms, too, the principal room is often treated differently from the others, which without doubt is because of the different dimensions

to be roofed over. In church-building, for instance, the stone dome combined with timber roof structures for the smaller interior spaces is a familiar sight. This change of system is, however, alien to filigree construction; the different requirements with respect to the spans can be responded to in the roof construction and the spacing of the columns, and their dimensions.

Third part: vertical growth processes
As has already been mentioned in the enlargement of the compartment to form a hall, the increase generally

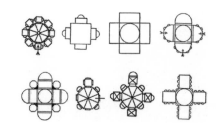

Fig. 45: Radial room conglomerate
from: Paul Frankl, *(Die Entwicklungsphasen der neueren Baukunst)*, 1914

takes place not just in the horizontal direction, but also vertically. This is principally connected with questions of use, proportions and comfort. Considered purely from the constructional viewpoint, this relationship is not obligatory – low, large rooms can be spanned over in the same way as high, large rooms. In order to use the material efficiently, increasing the height of the partitions or walls is associated with a change in their cross-section – batters or steps in solid construction or changing column cross-sections in filigree construction bear witness to this.

Furthermore, above a certain height some form of scaffolding is necessary, which can be called an independent, temporary structure. Although a scaffold is dismantled when the building is complete, it can leave behind tell-tale marks, as on the town hall in Siena (1288–1309), where on the rear of the building and on the tower (1338–48) the pockets for the ends of the scaffold poles are still visible as an irregular pattern of holes in the surface of the clay brick walls The building of high-rise buildings led to the development of forms of construction that do not require any scaffolding – not least for reasons of cost. Giuliani Hönger turned this requirement into an architectural theme at the "Bahnhof Nord" University of Applied Sciences building in St Gallen: the facade elements are designed as prefabricated fair-face concrete frames consisting of two leaves in such a way that the elements can be plugged into each other storey by storey and the overlapping makes subsequent filling of the joints superfluous. Afterwards, the coupled windows are fitted from inside – and they fit exactly thanks to the dimensionally stable prefabricated frames.

The third part of this classification primarily concerns the stacking of individual spaces and space conglomerates to form multi-storey buildings. Questions regarding the respective type of roof can be ignored because they have been dealt with already. On the other hand, the design of the intermediate floors is very relevant. Vertical room development can also be divided into two main groups, which in turn embrace various options. Critical for the allocation to one or other group is in each case the concept for carrying the vertical loads.

Fig. 46: The pockets for the ends of the scaffolding poles are easily visible on the rear of the building
Town Hall, Siena (I), 1288–1309, with the Torre della Mangia, 1338–48

Fig. 47: Facade elements made from prefabricated fair-face concrete frames
Giuliani Hönger: "Bahnhof Nord" University of Applied Sciences Building, St Gallen (CH), 2003–10

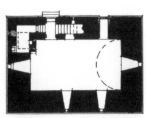

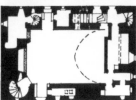

Fig. 48: Scottish tower house
Elphinstone Tower, c. 1440, ground floor and 1st floor

1. Stacking spaces

The simplest option for extending the space vertically has proved to be the stacking of spaces with an identical loadbearing structure.

Expressed simply, in this method the plan shape of the ground floor is multiplied, with the loadbearing walls or columns aligned vertically in all storeys. If a multi-storey building is achieved through simple stacking, each storey is a separate constructional unit. However, the increase in the loads as we approach the ground floor must be considered in the design of the walls or columns.

One example of a two-storey structure with vaulting is the Ksar Ferich fortified storehouse and market in Tunisia, which consists of a succession of barrel-vaulted *ghorfas* (Arabic: space), each of which belongs to one family. The floors to the upper storey are not flat because the rounding of the underlying vaulting is not fully made up into a level floor.

Although the addition of vaulted spaces to form multi-storey, sometimes complex, structures is undoubtedly fascinating, e.g. Elphinstone Tower, a Scottish tower house dating from the 15th century, this form of construction is uneconomic these days – the intermediate floors consume too much space and material. For example, in the Royal Keep in Vincennes, built in 1361, the vaulting occupies half the depth of a storey! For this reason, the intermediate floors were replaced by flat timber joist floors whenever possible, which enriched solid construction with the principles of filigree construction and led to the ongoing development of a pragmatic, hybrid form of construction.

Additive versus divisive strategies

This had repercussions not only for the construction; in conceptual terms, too, such solutions belong to a second subgroup of buildings with identical loadbearing

structures. Whereas in the first group the vertical and horizontal elements are equivalent, at least when considering our simplified model, in the second group a hierarchy appears: walls and columns are primary elements, suspended floors secondary elements.

This reappraisal can be seen in filigree construction just as much as in solid construction. Conventional frame construction is a storey-by-storey concept; the American balloon frame, on the other hand, usually includes timber studs continuing over two storeys, to which the intermediate floors are attached. The situation is simi-

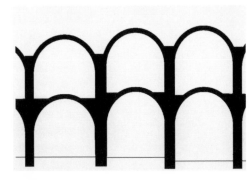

Fig. 49: Section
Ksar Ferich, fortified storehouse (Tunisia)

lar in metal structures, where we find both forms of construction. For example, the Crystal Palace in London designed by Joseph Paxton for the Great Exhibition of 1851, a magnificent, pioneering structure in cast and wrought iron and glass, was built storey by storey. The building systems of Fritz Haller are based on the same principle and exhibit amazing similarities to Paxton's pioneering structure in formal terms – even the design of the lattice beams for the intermediate floors. The Crystal Palace had timber floors, but trapezoidal profile steel sheeting has long since replaced the timber joists for the intermediate floors of steel buildings. To improve the acoustics and gain valuable mass for energy purposes, the steel sheeting is given a topping of concrete. Developments are moving further and further away from timber joists with infill elements and are approaching the look of the flat slab of reinforced concrete. However, the main problem of all filigree structures has not been solved: the simplest possible provision of trafficable surfaces by secondary elements.

In solid construction it is apparent that, in contrast to the first subgroup, buildings in the second subgroup are divisive and not additive: the intermediate floors are inserted between the loadbearing walls running the full height of the building, a fact often revealed through a change of material, e.g. mediaeval towers. The construction work of course still proceeds storey by storey, with the timber joists helping to stabilise the masonry during

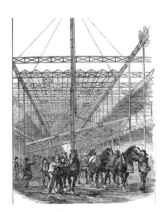

Fig. 50: Joseph Paxton: Crystal Palace, London (UK), 1851
Building for the Great Exhibition

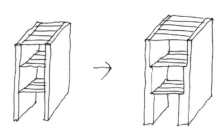

Fig. 52: Adolf Loos: house with one wall, 1921

construction. The characteristic feature of the hybrid form of construction really comes to the fore in a design by Adolf Loos: in 1921 he "invented" a "house with one wall", for which he applied for a patent. It requires only one loadbearing wall because it is designed as a terrace house; the second loadbearing wall is provided by the adjoining house! Timber joist floors span between the walls and the timber facades are attached to the sides of the timber floors.

Loos used this complementary, extremely economic principle in a modified form for his famous detached houses. Rooms of different sizes are fitted into a compact room conglomerate. In terms of construction, the spatial plan is not additive, a conclusion we might draw from the way we experience the interior, but divisive. Loos obviously started with a simple, regular volume, preferably similar to a cube, and divided it into individual parts; their spatial effect and interaction was his prime objective.[5] An

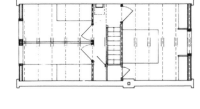

analysis of the constructional framework provides substance to this notion: all external masonry walls plus one or more central columns are loadbearing, which reduces the spans substantially. Interior spaces are formed step by step.

First of all, the loadbearing structure in solid construction is supplemented with downstand beams (usually timber) where necessary. The timber intermediate floors are laid on them. The room terminations on plan are created by non-loadbearing timber or plasterboard walls. It is amazing to see the complex room conglomerates that can be achieved with such a simple constructional system. Müller House in Prague,[6] built in 1932 to a design

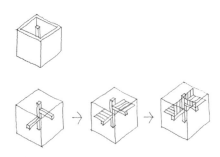

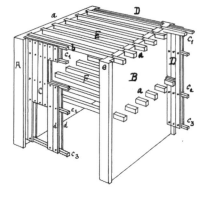

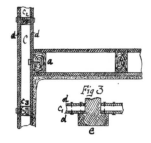

Fig. 53: Plan and construction details
Adolf Loos: house with one wall, 1921

Fig. 51: Fritz Haller: "midi" lattice beam system

Fig. 54: View from living room into dining room at higher level
Adolf Loos: Müller House, Prague (CZ), 1930

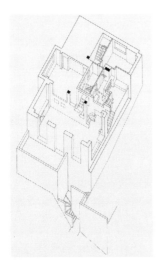

Fig. 55: Axonometric view showing main rooms and reinforced concrete columns (shaded black)
Adolf Loos: Müller House, Prague (CZ), 1930

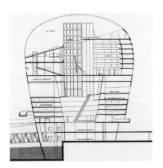

Fig. 56: Section through competition project
OMA, Rem Koolhaas: ferry terminal, Zeebrugge (B), 1989

Fig. 57: Competition model
OMA, Rem Koolhaas: Jussieu Library, Paris (F), 1993

by Loos, is a particularly impressive example, although he modified his system to suit the spans: four reinforced concrete columns with downstand beams, in conjunction with the external masonry walls, form the primary structure into which the room enclosures of timber or plasterboard were inserted.[7]

Vertical versus horizontal orientation

Let us remind ourselves of the constructional features of the second subgroup: the introduction of a hierarchy between the horizontal and vertical elements produces familiar hybrid forms of construction in which intermediate

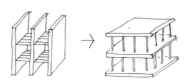

floors in filigree construction are inserted between solid walls. The variability of the system in the vertical direction is thus considerable, as the buildings of Loos show, but in the horizontal direction the design freedoms are restricted by the loadbearing walls.

The invention of the column-and-slab system in reinforced concrete in the early 20th century led to a complete reappraisal – and so we come to the third subgroup of the stacking of spaces with an identical loadbearing structure.

Vertical orientation and permeability is superseded by the stacking of almost autonomous storeys whose plan layouts can be divided up as required but are clearly limited in the vertical direction by the spacing between the intermediate floors. Le Corbusier described this reappraisal with his "Dom-Ino" system of 1914 and expanded it into an architectural programme in his famous book *Five Points of Architecture* in 1927. Spatial penetrations in the vertical are also possible with this system, of course. They are, however, more awkward, which is why in low-cost

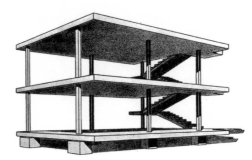

Fig. 58: Sketch of principle of column-and-slab system
Le Corbusier, "Dom-Ino" construction system, 1914

building the horizontal layering prevails, as a look at any contemporary office building will show.

Interesting attempts to overcome the horizontalness of the column-and-slab system can be seen in a number of projects by Rem Koolhaas and OMA.

One example is his design for a ferry terminal in Zeebrugge (1989), in which he strives to introduce a dynamic into the room conglomerates by using a complex layering of the floors inserted between the column grid. Or the competition entry for Jussieu Library in Paris (1993), where horizontal layering is transformed into a continuous ribbon of inclined levels.

2. Changing loadbearing structure

The second group of vertical growth processes comprises all the options that result in a changing loadbearing structure from storey to storey. Here, too, there are three subgroups. The first is also the oldest because in terms of construction it is the easiest to handle. It comprises concepts based on a step-by-step "thinning" of the loadbearing structure as we proceed up the building.

The principle is plain to see: wherever the greatest loads occur, that is where the format of the loadbearing structure is smallest. The spacings of the loadbearing elements can be increased from storey to storey because the loads to be carried decrease. The smallest rooms are therefore on the ground floor, the largest on the top floor. Certainly the earliest example of this type is the "Saalgeschosshaus" of the Middle Ages, a building with two or more storeys and a low, frequently vaulted ground floor of lower value plus a large prestigious hall on the first floor and, either above or adjacent, the living accommodation. Access to the hall was usually via an external stair. The Bayeux Tapestry (c. 1077) includes a very attractive illustration of the differences between the storeys. The use of the term *piano nobile* for the first floor is a remnant of that usage, and remains with us today.

However, we do not have to rely on history to provide examples of close-grid ground floors with larger and higher rooms above – Staufer & Hasler have transferred this principle to a contemporary timber building for a school in Wil. They based their idea on the town hall in Augsburg, which contains three halls, one above the other, and the largest of these, the "Golden Hall", is on the second floor. In Wil, a similar type of vertical layering is visible, primarily in the four-storey entrance zone. The auditorium is located above the entrance hall and above

Fig. 59: Bayeux Tapestry, c. 1077

Fig. 60: Augsburg Town Hall, section

it, on the second floor, the library and the music room, which are not only large areas, but high as well. So the third floor consists of just a void over the aforementioned halls plus a gallery around the library.

Uninterrupted ground floor

Although positioning large rooms on the upper floors might be very obvious from the constructional viewpoint, a building's use often calls for these relationships to be reversed. The contradiction between the heaviest loads on the ground floor and the simultaneous desire for permeability, especially in the urban context for increasing the degree of openness, has already been pointed out. We shall now investigate which strategies can be used to realise this desire. And so we come to the second subgroup, which enables a reversal of the space hierarchy by using a transfer structure over the ground floor.

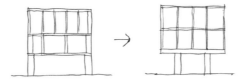

There are various types of "table structures". In structural terms, however, they all face the same problem: the loads of the upper storeys must be grouped together at the latest in the suspended floor above the ground floor, and transferred to the foundations via a few walls or columns. It is not only the bracing to the building that is important, but also solutions for lifts, stairs and vertical building services. It was for this reason that Le Corbusier designed the "tabletop" over the open ground floor of his Unité d'habitation in Marseille (1952) as a trafficable plant floor *(terrain artificiel)*.

The design for Leutschenbach school in Zurich by Christian Kerez appears particularly bold. Although the landscape does not actually "flow" through the ground floor, as Le Corbusier called for, the school building stands on only six 3-leg steel columns. The generous cantilevers are not achieved via a box-like design of the suspended floor, but rather by multi-storey trussed girders in steel, which in structural terms work as plates (see Chapter Buildings).

Jürg Conzett has explained the principle of plate designs for solid construction in an interesting text and

Fig. 61: Staufer & Hasler: school, Wil (CH), 2004

illustrated this using the example of the Volta School in Basel by Miller & Maranta.[8] In this building the largest room, the basement gymnasium, projects one storey above the ground. Above that, there are four storeys containing the classrooms. Spanning over the gymnasium without any intervening columns is made possible by using prestressed concrete wall plates, whose structural depth extends over all four storeys.

Plate designs

The relatively new method of plate design leads us to the last group of options for handling different structures in different storeys. The plates of suspended floors and masonry walls work together structurally and at the same time are "hard" elements that define the interior spaces in an unmistakable way – or suggest it, similarly to the aforementioned brick country house project of Mies van der Rohe. The load transfer from storey to storey is not generally uniform over the full length of the individual plates. Instead, there are zones with heavier and lighter loads. Taken to the extreme, we could say that all vertical loads are transferred at individual points in the form of storey-height "virtual columns".

However, as these are no longer aligned vertically like in a traditional column-and-plate structure, individual loading zones ensue which vary from storey to storey. Characteristic of the interaction of the loadbearing elements in the vertical direction is not only the storey-by-storey displacement of the loadbearing system, but also its synthetic nature: all elements are interrelated and coordinated in such a way that only after building the final masonry wall do we achieve the necessary equilibrium of forces.

In terms of the interior layout, various concepts are conceivable, from compartmentalised to plate-like resolved plan layouts. One example of the first principle is Giuliani Hönger's Sihlhof building for the University of Applied Sciences in Zurich, with its two offset internal courts. In the cardboard model, which deliberately omits the floor slabs, the only partial coincidence of the loadbearing masonry walls becomes obvious. Christian

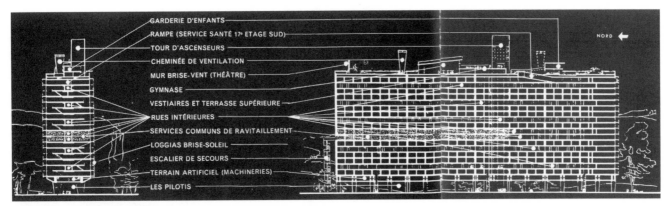

Fig. 62: Le Corbusier: Unité d'habitation, Marseille (F), 1952

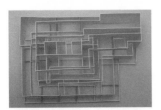

Fig. 63: Cardboard model
Giuliani Hönger: Sihlhof, University of Applied
Sciences, Zurich (CH), 2003

Fig. 64: Christian Kerez: private house,
Zurich (CH), 2003

Kerez's private house in Zurich is resolved into vertical plates at right angles to each other, which only coincide around the staircase. As the facade is fully glazed, the play of the storey-by-storey change in position of the masonry walls is also visible in the finished building.

Conclusion

There is a good reason for the numerous references to the effect of a certain loadbearing structure, especially in the third part: gravity has more far-reaching effects, spatially and structurally, for vertical space development than for horizontal space development. Its effects must always be properly gauged. However, there is also the desire to overcome, at least apparently, the influence of gravity by means of ever more ingenious constructional solutions because gravity contradicts the urbane forces. Design is not – as this study shows once again – a subject that can be considered on its own, but is an integral constituent of architectural thinking. The spaces of architecture are built from real materials. To do this, architecture needs inventive spatial and constructional concepts, which belong together like conjoined twins.

Notes

[1] Rasch, B.: Baukunst: Gestaltendes Begrenzen. Ein Plädoyer für die Moderne, in: *Daidalos* No. 18, Dec 1985, p. 102.

[2] See Saalman, H., Brunelleschi, F.: *The Cupola of Santa Maria del Fiore*, London, 1980.

[3] See Nabokov, P., Easton, R.: *Native American Architecture*, New York, 1989, pp. 196–97.

[4] Frankl, P.: *Die Entwicklungsphasen der neueren Baukunst*, Leipzig/Berlin, 1914, pp. 23–98.

[5] This stems, for example, from Loos's statement that the design is subordinate to the space idea. See: Loos, A.: Das Princip der Bekleidung, 1898, reprinted in: Lampugnani, V. M., Hanisch, R., Schumann, U. M., Sonne, W. (eds): *Architekturtheorie 20. Jahrhundert. Positionen, Programme, Manifeste*, Ostfildern-Ruit, 2004, pp. 25–29.

[6] For details of Müller House and its design, see: Kühn, C.: *Das Schöne, das Wahre und das Richtige* (Bauwelt Fundamente 86), Braunschweig/Wiesbaden, 1989; and: van Duzer, L., Kleinmann, K.: *Villa Müller. A Work of Adolf Loos*, New York, 1994.

[7] Albrecht, U.: *Der Adelssitz im Mittelalter. Studien zum Verhältnis von Architektur und Lebensform in Nord- und Westeuropa*, Munich/Berlin, 1995, pp. 22.

[8] Conzett, J.: Tragende Scheiben im Hochbau, in: *werk, bauen + wohnen*, 9-1997, pp. 35–39.

Structural shell, fitting-out and premium structural shell

Christoph Wieser,
Andrea Deplazes

In all definitions, the structural shell is described only as the indispensable prerequisite for the completion of the building by means of the fitting-out. But there are buildings that quite deliberately turn this apparently transitional stage into a permanent state, not out of necessity it must be said, but rather for architectural reasons: the structural shell in the form of the *premium* structural shell has established a place for itself in contemporary architecture. The reasons for this and what the terms structural shell and fitting-out are all about, plus their relationship with each other, are the topics of the following pages.

First part:
Structural shell and fitting-out

Structural shell

First of all, the structural shell is the part of the construction that in the normal case is at best only partly visible upon completion of the building: the vital structural framework. Depending on the definition, further operations can be added, certainly the construction of the roof. The Swiss Building Costs Plan (BKP), which over many years has become established as a planning tool for tenders for construction operations, goes significantly further and under structural shell lists everything that is connected with the structure and the external appearance of the building, right up to the external painting works and the roller shutters. The building services (electrics, HVAC, pipework, lifts etc.) are inserted between the structural shell and fitting-out phases as what we might call "buffer trades". The breakdown reflects the sequence of operations on site. There is no distinct border between the content of each because fitting-out work normally follows on from the structural shell without a break; sometimes both progress alongside each other.

Despite such overlaps, construction is an essentially linear process that ceases only temporarily upon completion of the building. Considering the lifetime of a building as a whole results in the following (schematic) life cycle: design – start of construction – structural shell – fitting-out – completion – conversion/refurbishment – demolition. Life cycle analyses provide information about the various planning horizons to which the individual phases and components can be sensibly related in terms of their building technology, social and economic aspects. In his book *How Buildings Learn*, Stewart Brand distinguishes between six such "shearing layers of change" whose persistence decreases with each stage. His "six S's" are: "site", "structure", "skin", "services", "space plan" and "stuff".[1]

Another thing that makes this list interesting is the fact that it is not purely architectural, i.e. at the start and finish in particular – when it comes to the urban situation and the use of the building, the things that are put in

it – it includes parameters that are outside the architect's sphere of influence. Therefore, the question as to which role the structural shell or the fitting-out is to play is closely tied to the question of the degree of control given to the architect regarding the appearance of a building. In our fast-moving times, in which the interior designer seems increasingly to be taking the place of the architect, the premium structural shell is a tempting option for limiting the loss of control that threatens.

But back to everyday building in which the structural shell – seen totally pragmatically – is vital if we are to complete the building with the help of the fitting-out. The structural shell is therefore not the target, but an interim condition, the end of a stage that, traditionally, is celebrated with the topping-out ceremony. As a "rite of passage", this ceremony marks the termination of one phase and the beginning of another. The import inherent in this expression in terms of time and space also plays a key role in construction. And although the timing of this ritual is defined, it is not an abrupt transition from one state to another, but rather a process that proceeds differently depending on the type of construction. In this sense, the structural shell is both an auspicious and a vague state: not everything is yet defined, but the view is clearly forwards; we can see what is coming, the conceptual design is becoming a physical reality. But not until the fitting-out is in place are we sure about our success.

Fitting-out

The layer principle is suitable for describing the entire system and for characterising the fitting-out too. The works normally included in the fitting-out are those that clad the structural shell, turn it into a functioning entity and hence convert it into a "fully fledged" building. The fitting-out can be called a cultural layer, an ambience provider that is necessary to give the interior spaces their definitive impression. Fitting-out is therefore vital for the perception and evaluation of an interior and determines whether we enjoy being in certain rooms or find them "cold", "warm", "hard" or "soft".

Putting these words between inverted commas shows us that such feelings need not necessarily have anything to do with the physical circumstances, but have emotional causes – we need only to think of the diverse views on concrete or the psychological effect of colours, for instance. Gernot Böhme has tackled such issues in great detail under the heading of atmosphere and has also pointed out the similarities and dissimilarities between architecture and scenery design for the theatre.[2] According to Böhme, stage sets are always "spaces of atmosphere", communicating with the audience in a direct and emotional way. Architectural spaces can and should be that too. However, in architectural spaces there is not just one view of events. Instead, they are first and foremost

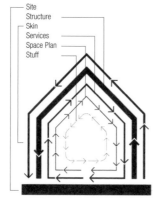

Site
Structure
Skin
Services
Space Plan
Stuff

Fig. 65: "Six S's"
from: Stewart Brand: *How Buildings Learn*

Fig. 66: Anamorphic distorted baroque frescos
Balthasar Neumann: Neresheim abbey church
(D), 1750–92, frescoes by Martin Knoller

vessels in which we are able to move around at will. Nowhere is this clearer than in baroque churches, which stipulate the route we should follow: their *trompe-l'œils* (French: deceive the eye) seem amazingly realistic only when they are viewed from the right position; looked at from other places they appear flat or distorted.

But in a certain way the architect is also a scenographer, which is revealed in the term "promenade architecturale" coined by Le Corbusier, a route through a building devised for its spatial effect, and in the works of interior designers, who give a room this or that ambience depending on their clients' requirements. We could also mention those currently popular television programmes in which an average home is turned into what is often a seemingly theatrical showpiece by a well-rehearsed team in a very short time. The unease that such actions provoke is certainly linked to the fact that we can perceive no connection between the packaging and the underlying structure. The fitting-out is degraded to witty decoration, whereas the goal in architecture is always to create a serious cohesiveness between fitting-out and structural shell, or to imply it.

Dependencies

Maximum directness, in other words a close tie, between these two worlds is the aim of the premium structural shell – a heroic undertaking in the light of the realities of today's building physics. Looser relationships are based on Karl Bötticher's concept of "core form" and "art form", or Gottfried Semper's "structural scheme" and "artistic scheme".[3] Equating the core form and the structural scheme with the structural shell, the art form and the artistic scheme with the fitting-out would be akin to abbreviating these theories. Nevertheless, the comparison shows that both Bötticher and Semper assumed, as a matter of course, a hierarchical relationship between the loadbearing framework and its cladding: in their eyes only the art form, or artistic scheme, elevate a construction to a work of architecture. The fitting-out, as the outermost and hence representative layer, refines the structural shell provided solely according to its constructional necessities.

Bötticher and Semper were thus attempting nothing other than to attach an architectural logic to the centuries-old relationship between structural shell and fitting-out, which had been established primarily for economic reasons. The philosopher Georg Friedrich Hegel goes even further. In a piece written somewhat earlier in the 19th century, he writes of not only a metaphorical, but a very real connection between the two spheres. Furthermore, in the following quotation he refers to the scope that the interplay between structural shell and fitting-out initiates. He saw in Greek sculptures the realisation of an architectural principle: "The mantle especially is like a house in which a person is free to move. It is carried indeed, but

fastened at only one point, e.g. the shoulder, but otherwise it develops its own particular form according to its own special weight; it hangs, falls, and runs into folds spontaneously, and the particular modifications of this free formation depend solely on the pose of the wearer."[4] Through the arrangement of the folds of this cloak it is therefore possible to surmise the physiognomy of the wearer, which it traces discreetly, but at the same time develops its own life due to the properties of the material and cut of the cloth, for example.

Fig. 67: The folds of the mantle
Daniel Schwartz: from the one-off exhibition "Metamorphosen. Griechische Photographien", Kunsthaus Zurich, 1986

Questions of allocation

Before we investigate the relationship between structural shell and fitting-out further, in the light of the above quotation we must ask ourselves the following question: The furnishings of interiors are without doubt part of the fitting-out; but what about the "mantle", i.e. the facades, the building envelope? Are they not part of the structural shell, as the Swiss Building Costs Plan suggests? The layered construction of the facades dictated by today's building physics requirements points in another direction, however: multi-layer designs encourage fitting-out strategies. Even contemporary stone facades, which thanks to elaborate and skilful detailing give the impression of being solid, cannot hide the fact that in most cases they are merely cladding, tied back to the concrete loadbearing layer behind. This is the case, for example, with Max Dudler's IBM Building in Zurich-Altstetten (2006), whose walls on the ground floor of the tower wing are 1 m thick, and still 75 cm thick on the upper floors; but the stone slabs themselves measure only a few centimetres.

Undoubtedly, the allocation of such facades to the fitting-out has something to do with the fact that the slabs are suspended a considerable distance in front of the loadbearing wall and therefore do not enter into a direct tectonic bond with the inner concrete leaf.

Voids, it seems, are one of the most important ingredients in fitting-out strategies, whether in the form of narrow joints, the construction tolerances necessary to

Fig. 68: The solid impression of a facade
suspended in front of a ventilation cavity
Max Dudler: IBM Schweiz, Zurich-Altstetten (CH),
2006

Figs 69, 70: Fitting-out retained
Gottfried Semper: auditorium at the ETH Zurich
(Swiss Federal Institute of Technology), ceiling
paintings by Jean Baptiste Philippe Bin,
Zurich (CH), 1861

**Figs 75, 76: Xenix Cinema, Helvetiaplatz,
Zurich (CH)**
Refurbishment and extension: Frei + Saarinen
Architekten, 2006–07

absorb dimensional deviations at changes of material, or
in the form of larger margins such as suspended ceilings
for ventilation ducts, pipes and cables, or, as in this case,
in the form of a facade with a ventilation cavity. System
facades are generally also designed to be as light as possible so that penetrations through the layer of insulation
can be minimised. However, the current energy efficiency
debate results in ever thicker insulation and hence ex-
acerbates the problem of decoupling the loadbearing and
protective layers, which means that in fitting-out strategies the "interior design" now seems to be increasingly
joined by "exterior design" with an "unattached facade",
as it were. The situation is totally different with single-leaf
fair-face concrete, which reverses the layer principle. On
the outside it displays the naked structural shell. On the
inside, several fitting-out layers clad the profile. The addition of further layers in the course of the life of a building
is seen again and again when renovating old buildings,
where many a surprise awaits us beneath the surface.
Like an onion, we can peel away the layers, and in the
conservation of buildings the difficult question is: which
of the layers found should be placed on top? On a two-
dimensional level we see this principle again in the coats
of paint that have been applied to the backing materials
over the course of decades or centuries.

Permanence and change

The fitting-out is regarded as less permanent than the
structural shell: surface finishes are renewed every five to
ten years, whereas the loadbearing structure is designed
for a life of about 100 years. But there are contrary examples, such as the Hall of Mirrors in the Palace of Versailles,
or the ceiling in the Semper auditorium at the ETH Zurich
(Swiss Federal Institute of Technology), which is one of
the few original elements still remaining.[5]

In order to describe the phenomenon that some fitting-
out designs are retained while others survive for a few
years only, Stewart Brand introduces two expressions in
his book *How Buildings Learn:* "low road" and "high road".
Put simply, it is about the difference between a studio
and a temple.

Robust constructions that are constantly adapted and
used totally differently are described by Brand as "low
road".[6] These are buildings that allow their users or occupants plenty of scope, which positively invite a change
of use, change of owner, e.g. garages, sheds.

One such example is the timber shed on the site of the
Kanzlei School in Zurich, which was built about 100 years
ago as a temporary measure to relieve the congestion in
the classrooms and since the 1980s has been serving as
a cinema and bar. Recently, Frei + Saarinen Architekten
designed an extension to the building that manages to retain the original character but at the same time do justice
to the new requirements. To do this they chose a collage

Fig. 71: "Jules Barsotti's Garage", 770 North Point, San Francisco, interior
view, 1925 …

Fig. 72: … exterior view, 1955 …

Fig. 73: … exterior view, 1990 …

Fig. 74: … and interior view, 1993. The workshop has been adapted to a
retailer of outdoor goods; structural shell remains, fitting-out adapted.
from: Stewart Brand: *How Buildings Learn*

Fig. 77: Salisbury Cathedral, Salisbury (GB), interior view around 1754 …

Fig. 78: … around 1865 …

Fig. 79: … around 1929 …

Fig. 80: … and 1965.
The furnishings and the fitting-out are adapted to the circumstances, whereas the structure remains unaltered.

technique that either supplements or replaces the fabric of the building in a totally pragmatic way and depending on needs. Despite rigorous stipulations, the intervention seems amazingly relaxed and matter of course.

Contrasting with this, Brand also has his "high road" buildings,[7] which remain virtually unchanged over long periods of time because their uses adapt to the building and not vice versa – in a quite lively manner and without conservation. "High road" buildings are cared for and refined; changes are carried out cautiously and with consideration for the original fabric, in a sense "serving" the original. This form of longevity is particularly conspicuous in churches, which often seem as though they have not been altered for centuries.

Second part:
The relationship between structural shell and fitting-out

The uncertainty – definitely not unproductive – as to what belongs to the structural shell and what to the fitting-out comes from the fact that the relationship between structural shell and fitting-out for solid construction is totally different to that for filigree construction. Solid construction can be declared a structural shell strategy because the erection of the loadbearing structure at the same time defines the interior. Although the interior spaces "are all there" already, another fitting-out phase is still required in order to provide the desired surface finishes and to install the building services. As buildings from the past, other cultures or other geographical locations show us, there are conditions in which we could certainly leave it at the structural shell.

Filigree forms of construction, on the other hand, are far more dependent on the fitting-out measures. As a complementary form of construction, it is quite clear that the interior spaces are created only after filling in the loadbearing structure. The layer principle is therefore a genuine constituent of the system and is used even during the erection of the structural shell. Accordingly, filigree construction encourages cladding strategies. The reality is more complex, however, than this somewhat simplified description suggests. For example, in practice we see a convergence between the two forms of construction, and that leads to the originally "pure" forms being "contaminated" to a greater or lesser extent. The result is not only growing complexity in the relationship between solid and filigree construction. Much more significant is the fact that this development often leads to a close interaction between structural shell and fitting-out: complementary, interferential and synthetic systems can be used to designate the three levels that range from heterogeneous connection right up to homogeneous integration of the parts.

The "classic" approach is complementary: the structural shell provides a framework that is clad during the fitting-out phase. Structural shell and fitting-out exhibit different tolerances corresponding to the construction operations; the sequence of the work leads from raw and coarse to worked and fine. If the order is reversed or if components installed at an early stage are intended to remain visible on completion, then appropriate protection is necessary. Fair-face concrete always poses this problem, especially at delicate edges.

So that brings us to the interferential systems, which are characterised by elements that belong to both structural shell and fitting-out. Fair-face concrete or facing masonry are good examples of this, but also the wall panels of timber panel construction, which, if left in their raw state, belong to the structural shell in terms of their loadbearing function but to the fitting-out in terms of their visual effect. The blurring of the boundaries between the two is particularly obvious in system building, where elements are prefabricated and then installed on site. Those elements combine structural shell and fitting-out components to form complex subassemblies, in some cases complete with the surface finishes. In contrast to our third group, the synthetic systems, the connections between the components of this group are, however, reversible. This means that a series of mostly monofunctional components and building materials is assembled in an additive process to form one element.

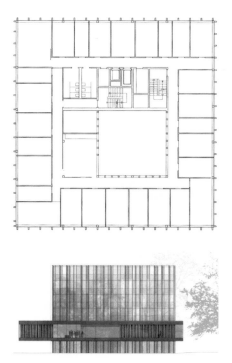

Figs 81, 82: E2A: Heinrich Böll Foundation, Berlin (D), 2008

Synthetic systems, on the other hand, are character-ised by inseparable connections between the individual parts. Such an amalgamation promises many advan-tages, e.g. in the realm of lightweight building materi-als, because the skilful combination of different materials brings together the most diverse functions in one ele-ment in an efficient way. From the ecological viewpoint this is not unproblematic because such elements can-not be easily recycled, if at all. The specification for the new premises for the Heinrich Böll Foundation in Berlin (2008), which is closely associated with the Bündnis 90/ Die Grünen political party, required the architects of E2A to refrain from using wood/metal window frames and also adhesive joints as far as possible. That means, for example, that the carpets in the offices are merely laid, not stuck down. Welded joints are also problematic from the ecological standpoint. However, synthetic systems are limited to relatively small items: even now, a ready-to-use house cannot be made in one piece!

Convergent and divergent solutions

The question of the spatial relationship between structural shell and fitting-out is interesting from the architectural viewpoint. In this context it is worth highlighting two dif-ferent strategies: convergent and divergent. A convergent relationship exists when the fitting-out is added to the structural shell; in other words, when it covers or encloses the structural shell like a second skin in the form of a lin-ing or cladding. The second strategy entails placing the fitting-out in a divergent relationship with the structural shell. Such buildings deliberately exploit the spatial separ-ation between structural shell and fitting-out by empha-sising instead of concealing the ensuing interstices.

Convergent solutions are certainly the normal case because they are created through simple addition: sec-ondary items are added to primary items, the service layer is added to the supporting layer. One typical example of an economic approach (because it saves space) is the Spir-garten retirement home in Zurich-Albisrieden, designed by Miller & Maranta. On the ground floor the reinforced concrete structure is clad in elmwood, which lends the public zones an elegant atmosphere. All pipes, cables, radiators and ventilation ducts are hidden in the voids behind the smooth wooden surfaces. However, the geom-etry of the loadbearing structure itself is not concealed, simply reproduced at a certain distance.

Accessible intermediate spaces, frequently found in the hidden attics of churches and museums, are exciting solutions.[8] If we can look "behind the scenes", the dif-ferent specifications, e.g. in terms of quality of finish, for structural shell and fitting-out become especially evident. Introducing a joint, be it small or large, between structural shell and fitting-out provides a scope we can exploit and which Hegel described by means of ancient sculptures.

Figs 83–85: Kisho Kurokawa: Nagakin Capsule Tower, Tokyo (J), 1972

Figs 86–89: Miller & Maranta, Spirgarten retirement home, Zurich-Albisrieden (CH), 2004–06

Fig. 90: Herman Hertzberger: Ministry of Social Affairs & Employment, The Hague (NL), 1990

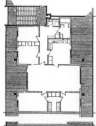

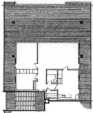

Figs 91–94: Erik Friberger: "Däckshus", Gothenburg (S), 1960

Exploiting this scope to configure the structural shell and the fitting-out in different ways is the principal feature of divergent strategies. Most of the buildings employing this strategy date from the 1960s and 1970s, when the "plug-in" concept was in its heyday. Nagakin Capsule Tower (1972) by Kisho Kurokawa, where the rooms in the form of prefabricated capsules are hooked onto the primary reinforced concrete structure, is a prime example. Herman Hertzberger, a founder of structuralism in the 1960s, always presented structural shell and fitting-out as two different worlds. This was also the case for the Ministry of Social Affairs & Employment in The Hague, Netherlands (1976–90), in which the unitised and prefabricated load-bearing structure of reinforced concrete was assembled cluster-like to form a large complex. The structure remains visible between the various infill elements.

The separation between structural shell and fitting-out is especially obvious in Erik Friberger's experimental "Däckshus" in Gothenburg (1960).[9] As the name suggests, the building consists of a stack of decks, a three-storey reinforced concrete structure with three stair shafts. The columns were positioned in such a way that the individual apartments, using prefabricated timber elements, could be arranged as required on each floor, leaving a balcony zone on both sides. Service shafts are incorporated alongside the stairs. Friberger's idea was to provide neutral "plots" that could be built upon over the years depending on the needs of the occupants – but all the owners used the entire area at their disposal (144 or 210 m^2) right from the start. As the apartments are shallower than the storey height (4 m), a void remains between the top of an apartment and the soffit of the floor slab above. This fact plus the disparate materials of the apartments and the load-bearing structure emphasise the different characters of the structural shell and the fitting-out. The spatial separation between structural shell and fitting-out, the allocation of different spheres, spells out the different rules they have to obey. Whereas this approach creates maximum diversity, a *premium* structural shell tries with suitable means to make the fitting-out superfluous by integrating those means into the structural shell.

Third part:
The fascination of the premium structural shell

What is so fascinating about buildings that seem to be elementary, that apparently consist of nothing but the structural shell? Stanislaus von Moos has called such buildings "inverted ruins", testifying to an optimism for the future.[10] Indeed, even today there is a peculiar romanticism attached to ruins. "White elephants" was the name given to buildings erected in post-colonial Africa with international help but never used. Such "new" ruins can be found all over the world, and they exude a queer

fascination that the photographer Christian Helmle has captured in a recent book of photographs.[11] It was the paintings of the ruins of Eldena Abbey by Caspar David Friedrich that played a key role in the emergence of the romanticism surrounding ruins around 1800. He painted them with different, often dramatic, lighting effects, aiming to evoke various moods in the observer.

Fig. 95: The decaying Dutch pavilion (Expo 2000)
from: Christian Helmle: *White Elephants*

Fig. 96: Caspar David Friedrich, *Abbey in the Oakwood*, 1808–10

Fig. 97: Caspar David Friedrich, *Ruins of Eldena*, 1825

Fig. 98: Christian Kerez, two-unit dwelling, Zurich (CH), 2007

Fig. 99: Valerio Olgiati, Bardill studio, Scharans (CH), 2007

Figs 100, 101: Fuhrimann Hächler, house and studio, Zurich (CH), 2004

Fig. 102: Valerio Olgiati, K + N private house, Wollerau (CH), 2005

Elementary, genuine, permanent

Refined structural shells elicit strong emotions. The directness of the material, the genuineness of what the observer sees, is a total contrast to the modern practice of using all possible material imitations – from laminated floors to wood panelling made from embossed sheet metal and self-adhesive stone-effect wallpapers. In an age characterised by surrogates, genuine solid stone and heavyweight wood-block floors, whose thickness is not only visible but also tangible with every step, seem oddly anachronistic. But it is precisely because the pressure to renew, to modify, is constantly on the increase in the building sector that we are happy to attribute a special aura to natural materials in particular – fully aware of the fact that even the most expensive materials are no longer a guarantee of durability; if the funding is available, even those materials are replaced by others long before their time is up. Patination as the "kindly traces of time",[12] as Georg Mörsch has described it, has a chance to mature in a few instances only.

The premium structural shell attempts to give its users a good feeling of being able to escape from a fast-moving world. Durability, authenticity and solidity are an attempt to counteract the ever thinner, quickly worn surface finishes. And unlike brutalist architecture, which certainly also confirms the powerful effect of the materials, the premium structural shell does not attempt to challenge the senses, but rather to calm them, not to unsettle, but to express security.

Going beyond the intellectual condensing of an architectural idea, the aim is to convey elementary experiences. Examples are the two-unit dwelling in Zurich-Witikon by Christian Kerez (2007) and the studio for Linard Bardill in Scharans by Valerio Olgiati (2007). The elaborate reduction of the building to its structural shell has nothing to do with minimalism in these cases, but much more with the search for timeless interior spaces and the desire for purity. Contrasting with these examples, the honeycombed fair-face concrete of Fuhrimann Hächler's apartment block in Uetliberg (2004) testifies to a brutalistic understanding of leaving the structure exposed and supplementing the structural shell with unpretentious materials.

There are buildings that look unfinished and hence invite occupation, e.g. the Zurich studio (1932) of the sculptor Hermann Haller, with its simple, white-painted, rough-sawn board formwork walls. These simple measures make the joints between the boards even more obvious, but the white paint turns the imperfection into a system and the joints are not regarded as a lack of precision. Premium structural shells, on the other hand, are only apparently unfinished. As the structural shell has been refined and supplemented by accurately detailed and material elements, e.g. the walnut woodwork

Fig. 103: Hermann Haller studio, Zurich (CH), 1932

in Valerio Olgiati's house in Wollerau (2004), it emanates an authority that is not intended to be changed. Kunsthaus Bregenz (1997) by Peter Zumthor is an example where a method first had to be found for covering up the holes drilled in the fair-face concrete walls (needed for each exhibition) before the curators dared violate the perfection of the walls.

High design demand

The term premium structural shell also indicates the considerable input required on the design side so that the fitting-out can be reduced to a few elements. What looks simple on the outside is often complicated on the inside. Integrating all the pipes and cables into the structural shell calls for meticulous planning so that everything ends up in the right place and no power sockets are forgotten. The mechanisation of buildings in the early 20th century nurtured the development of fitting-out strategies because spaces were necessary for the optimum distribution of pipes, cables, ducts etc.; shafts, suspended ceilings and raised access floors are witness to this. In buildings with high services requirements, e.g. laboratories, a considerable part of the storey height is reserved for services. Where vertical distribution is not concentrated in a few places, but spread over many shafts to shorten the horizontal distances, then the effect on the space requirements and the plan layouts is considerable. We therefore speak of section- or plan-based solutions, depending on how the services are organised.

If we believe Hansjürg Leibundgut, professor of building services at ETH Zurich, the space requirements for building services will be substantially curtailed in the future owing to the miniaturisation of the components.[13] Once miniaturisation is combined with decentralised distribution instead of the central rooftop or basement plant rooms customary today, then the space requirements will drop even further.

However, if the majority of the components are integrated into the structural shell, e.g. ventilation ducts (and not just the electric cables, which have long since been routed through the structure), that has consequences for space requirements and the envisaged service lives of the components. Services that are inaccessible must either be designed for zero maintenance or the life expectancy of the structural shell must be reduced. This tendency is actually well advanced in some countries. In the UK, for example, loadbearing structures are designed for a 50-year life, which is only half of what is regarded as standard in German-speaking countries.[14]

Powerful structures

It is no coincidence that premium structural shells are, in the first instance, associated with solid forms of construction, where owing to the systems used it is much easier to incorporate a maximum number of fitting-out elements. In addition, solid construction has another advantage that has already been mentioned: they essentially fix the interior layout and so the architect's influence on the look and feel of the building, especially the interior, is significantly greater. Even when buildings are converted and altered, their spatial character is retained to a greater degree than is the case with neutral, column-and-slab structures.

However, this does not necessarily limit the flexibility, as Toyo Ito's new library for Tama Art University in Tokyo (2007) shows. Ito has designed an open-plan layout that is determined by a sequence of arches at different spacings in the longitudinal and transverse directions instead of a regular grid of columns. The expressive structural shell design results in a powerful system that is both open and defining. It is open and hence flexible in the sense that the spatial associations and boundaries have been chosen very freely and can be altered again and again – it is enough to close off one tympanum and open up another in order to create a new interior space configuration. However, crucial to the spatial effect of the building is the structure that has been chosen, which gives the building an unmistakable character regardless of the internal layout.

Looked at in constructional terms, the fair-face concrete turns out to be a fitting-out material. This is because the loadbearing structure of the arches is formed by steel plates and beams that are encased in concrete for aesthetic and fire protection reasons only. So we have come full circle, and the relationship between structural shell and fitting-out, and what belongs to one or the other, benefits from yet another facet.

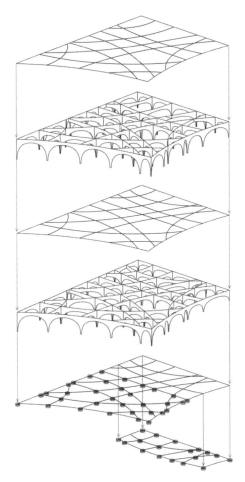

1. Stewart Brand: *How Buildings Learn. What Happens After They're Built*, New York, 3rd ed. 1995 (1st ed. 1994), p. 13.
2. See, for example: Gernot Böhme: "Atmosphere as the Subject Matter of Architecture", in: Philip Ursprung (ed.): *Herzog & de Meuron: Natural History*, Zurich, 2005, pp. 410–17.
3. See: Karl Bötticher: *Die Tektonik der Hellenen*, Potsdam, 1844; Gottfried Semper: *Style in the Technical and Tectonic Arts: or, Practical Aesthetics*, Brighton, UK, 2004.
4. Georg Friedrich Hegel (trans. T. Knox): *Lectures on Fine Art*, vol. 3, "The Ideal of Sculpture; Draping [or Clothing]"; cited by: Bettina Köhler: "Shell", in: Dietmar Eberle, Pia Simmendinger (eds): *From City to House. A Design Theory*, Zurich, 2007, p. 145.
5. See: Andrea Deplazes, Sascha Rösler: "Lebenszyklen und ihre Bauweisen", lecture, "Rohbau versus Ausbau" conference, 7/8 June 2007, ETH Zurich, unpublished manuscript, p. 5.
6. Brand: op. cit., pp. 24–33.
7. Brand: op. cit., pp. 34–51.
8. Christoph Wieser: "Verborgen vorhanden. Vergessene Räume im Dach" (Concealed Existence. Forgotten spaces in the roof), in: *werk bauen + wohnen*, 4/2006, pp. 18–27.
9. For details see: Claes Caldenby, Gunilla Linde-Bjur, Sven-Olof Ohlsson: *Guide till Göteborgs arkitektur*, Stockholm, 2006, p. 234.
10. Stanislaus von Moos: "Rhetorik der Baustelle. Die Entdeckung der Stadt als Prozess", in: *NZZ*, 22/23 Sept 2007, B 2.
11. Christian Helmle: *White Elephants*, Berlin, 2007.
12. Georg Mörsch: "Patina – die freundlichen Spuren der Zeit" (Patina or the kindly traces of time), in: *werk bauen + wohnen*, 5/2006, pp. 4–11.
13. See: Hansjürg Leibundgut, lecture, "Rohbau versus Ausbau" conference, 7/8 June 2007, ETH Zurich.
14. Brand: op. cit., p. 12.

Figs 104–106: Toyo Ito, Hachioji Library, Tama Art University, Tokyo (J), 2007

Structural issues
The relationship between interior structure, loadbearing structure, and infrastructure

Alois Diethelm, Andrea Deplazes

Interior structures, loadbearing structures, and infrastructures are factors relevant to the design which, depending on the utilisation structure, influence each other to differing degrees, or activate various relationships. Whereas interior structure and loadbearing structure form a pair of concepts that can be applied just as well to the primitive hut as to a modern-day building, infrastructure – by which we mean fundamental facilities for the circulation of persons and media, but primarily in conjunction with building services – is meaningless for vernacular buildings because in the majority of pre-industrialisation buildings it existed only temporarily (e.g. in the form of an open fire) or not at all. Although, it is well known that the Romans already possessed highly developed supply structures such as underfloor heating and water pipes, these accomplishments remained virtually meaningless to everyday building work until the Industrial Revolution. From that time onwards they started to influence design more and more, owing to the mass production that became possible and also because of the drive to improve the poor hygienic conditions of 19th-century towns and cities.

From then on, client and architect were therefore confronted with defining the degree or scope of services and the associated usage. If the level of comfort demanded is low, an old building such as those built before the 20th century will still satisfy the needs of many different users. A conversion, if deemed necessary, is relatively simple because the service lines are seldom concealed in the walls or floors, and there are not many of them anyway. Bernoulli realised as early as 1942 that "in today's new buildings it is precisely their systems, devised and installed for very specific situations, that must herald their downfall, must shorten their lives, because a complicated construction cannot be adapted to changing conditions as easily as a simple one."[1] Since then services have multiplied to become an ever denser nerve system infiltrating virtually every building component. Modern buildings would be unthinkable without the tasks they perform. In some cases simplification may be possible, but essentially it must be accepted that contemporary buildings are complicated, according to Bernoulli's definition. The question of adaptability no longer affects just the loadbearing structure, but also the infrastructure to an equal extent. And the fact that adaptability is desirable is proved again and again in practice – throughout the design phase. That was the reason behind the question posed by Marcel Meili recently in an interview. He asked how usage should materialise, "if there is no layout any more because the building afterwards is to appear on the investment market?"[2]

In the light of this, the structural issue should be investigated during three phases:
1. Prior to commencing work on site,

2. After completion (short-, medium- or long-term),
3. During construction.

Differentiated flexibility
We are not interested here in the *absolute flexibility* that fulfils every conceivable adaptation or conversion, but rather design strategies that withstand the conditions of economics-based practice and might supply answers to

Fig. 107: Loadbearing structure with potential for expansion
Apartment block in the centre of Tirana (Albania), 2002

possible medium- or longer-term needs. This opinion is to some extent contrary to the mentality widespread in the present economic climate (in the building industry), a mentality that believes in keeping capital costs down in the knowledge that the follow-up costs after completion will have to be paid by somebody else. Of course, it is always a question of weighing up whether, when, and to what extent intervention is necessary; for the more time that elapses before the first intervention, the less significant is the easy adaptability of the building. This is precisely the situation when the building's original function no longer applies, e.g. disused factories converted into housing, offices, schools etc., where frequently everything apart from the loadbearing structure is torn down because all other components have become obsolete. Infrastructures become outdated after 30, 40, or 50 years; a facade no longer complies with the thermal insulation regulations, a previously harmless building material has proved in the meantime to constitute a health risk. Consequently, the only constant is the loadbearing structure.

And its suitability for new uses depends on the degree of coupling with the interior structure.

If the interior layout must be flexible, it is usually necessary to create rooms, or room segments, of different sizes within the same utilisation. The connectable rooms (separated by sliding doors) in housing or the grid dimensions in offices are traditional. We are talking here about *flexibility of use*, which is relevant only after the building is completed.

On the other hand we have the *flexibility of planning*, which is based on the fact that certain components, e.g. vertical circulation, are declared as immovable from the very start, whereas other parts, which once construction starts are equally permanent, can still be influenced at the outset – up to a certain point of no return; e.g. in house-building the sizes of wet rooms and, very occasionally, their positions. If the internal partitions are loadbearing, the interior structure that can still be influenced at best is subjected to a floor span defined as economic and openings in the facade. Burkard Meyer Architekten exploited most of the flexibility of planning options in their apartment blocks on Martinsbergstrasse in Baden (1998/99). The plan layout is based on a loadbearing facade and a

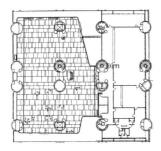

Fig. 108: Columns with space for toilets, stairs etc.
Kenzo Tange: communications centre, Kofu (J), 1964–67

Fig. 109: Only the location of the staircase was established prior to starting work on site.
Burkard Meyer Architekten: apartment blocks, Martinsbergstrasse, Baden (CH), 1998/99

Fig. 110: Flexibility in planning: the position of the windows was determined by the buyers of the apartments.
Burkard Meyer Architekten: apartment blocks, Martinsbergstrasse, Baden (CH) 1998/99

central access core, while the remaining internal configuration, which included bathrooms and kitchens, could be determined by the buyers of the individual apartments. It was unusual that even the positions and sizes of the storey-high windows could be influenced by the buyers.

Fig. 111: Loadbearing structure and infrastructure combined in shafts
Kenzo Tange: communications centre, Kofu (J), 1964–67

However, once work had started on site, the flexibility in the unsold apartments was reduced drastically because the plan layouts had been more or less fully configured by the positioning of openings and locating of building services, i.e. the sanitary installations. The immovability of services is due to the senseless casting-in of the pipes, which is still customary, especially in housebuilding. This reduces the options for adjustments during construction and makes replacement difficult when the system has served its useful life, not to mention any changes of use.

Hollow columns – slender floors

Assuming that we wish to convert a multi-occupancy block into a guest-house or hotel, this raises a number of questions. The existing horizontal circulation within the apartments, possibly only a vague notion, has to be changed to a corridor and form a separate fire compartment. The denser occupancy may well call for additional escape stairs, and the increased number of decentralised wet rooms questions the feasibility of a central service core. Structuralists like Kenzo Tange have tried to find answers to such questions by coupling the vertical infrastructure (services, stairs, lifts) with the inevitable loadbearing structure. The slender columns of traditional column-and-floor systems are transformed into shafts. The predecessors of multifunctional building components can be seen in the industrial buildings of the late 19th century, where vertical lines were routed between pairs of columns.

A similar effect can be seen in the grouping of flues along the fire walls of the multistorey apartment blocks of the 19th and early 20th centuries. The decentralised arrangement of the flues minimises the horizontal service components or, at the very least, renders them superfluous. Relieved of horizontal services, the constructional properties of the floors have to satisfy only loadbearing and sound insulation requirements. Prior to the introduction of reinforced concrete slabs and the possibility of casting services inside these, the exclusively vertical routing was the most obvious (in housebuilding).

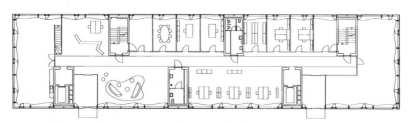

Fig. 112: Column-free plan layout with loadbearing facade and cores (lifts, wet rooms or stairs)
Bearth & Deplazes: ÖKK offices, Landquart (CH), 2001/02

Fig. 113: Grouping versus decentralisation
Schemes with stove and bathroom combined in the centre of the house (left: short service lines), and a decentralised layout (right: many service lines)

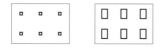

Fig. 114: Hollow columns – slender floor slabs
Schemes showing loadbearing structure (top) and interior fitting-out (bottom); the wet rooms are linked to the loadbearing structure containing the services.

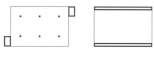

Fig. 115: Slender columns – hollow floors
Schemes showing loadbearing structure (top) and interior fitting-out (bottom); the wet rooms are positioned independently of the loadbearing structure. Multistorey circulation is via perimeter shafts which can also function as vertical loadbearing elements, (see also figs 130–133).

Although the structuralists were trying to achieve the opposite, even Tange determined the uses to a certain extent because the apparently neutral shafts accommodated first a lift, then stairs and finally also wet rooms and ventilation ducts. In other words: the structure is no longer 100% flexible, even though this might seem to be the case at first glance. The plan layout is, on the one hand, dependent on the existence of the appropriate infrastructure components at the desired locations; on the other, the physical cores form a framework to the plan layout that no longer extends from facade to facade but rather stakes out individual internal bays between the cores. But if every core contains stairs, lifts, wet rooms and service shafts, this obviously leads to a system with an "overdesigned" infrastructure and a building whose flexibility is substantially reduced because of the larger cores.

For example, in Tange's building (see fig. 111) – like the ÖKK offices in Landquart (CH) by Bearth & Deplazes – there is no hierarchy among the cores. They form compartments in which the infrastructure uses, e.g. toilets, face inwards. The opposite approach employs a continuous vertical shaft that is only just large enough to accommodate the necessary pipes, cables, and ducts. The shaft forms the starting point – or the backbone – for the development of the plan layout, which might be different on every floor. It is interesting to note that when asking the question "Centralised vertical services plus intensive horizontal distribution, or decentralised vertical services with less horizontal distribution?" vertical access by means of stairs and lifts is not affected because the location and number of these vertical circulation routes are defined by the maximum permissible distance to a means of escape, i.e. by fire regulations.

Slender columns – hollow floors

The outcome of a more or less dense network of continuous vertical components – be they parts of the infrastructure or loadbearing structure – is that uses that call for different interior structures from storey to storey are feasible only when such interior structures are based on a small format. In the opposite direction, pipe runs, ventilation ducts, and columns restrict the usability of the interior spaces.

Therefore, essentially unrestricted planning of individual storeys presupposes a centralised vertical infrastructure from where the local horizontal distribution takes place in cavity floors, suspended ceilings, or within the depth of the floor construction. The point at which at least two service lines cross, e.g. a cable duct and a ventilation duct, determines the overall depth of such hollow spaces. Besides aspects such as easier accessibility for installation and maintenance, it is precisely the intention of avoiding the crossing of services that has led to the simultaneous use of cavity floor plus suspended ceiling.

Combined with a reinforced concrete floor slab, such constructions can reach a total depth of 70–80 cm; however, only 25–30 cm of this is required for loadbearing purposes. This is a waste of potential because the individual layers of the separate functional parts of the floor do not benefit from each other. It would be possible to double the structural depth while retaining the same overall depth by using a "hollow" loadbearing system in steel, concrete or timber, e.g. the MINI, MIDI and MAXI systems of Fritz Haller. This would in turn result in larger spans and, consequently, more flexible utilisation configurations. Whereas in the past the crossing of service lines alone determined the depth of the hollow space, the falls of waste-water pipes is just as important, if not more so. This is particularly relevant when there are different numbers of wet rooms at different locations on the individual floors. The larger hollow spaces of such structures have a positive effect on the horizontal distribution of services.

In Louis Kahn's Salk Institute the floors to the laboratories themselves became accessible for maintenance and upgrading of the numerous installations. The Vierendeel girders, wall plates without openings, and reinforced concrete floors form a rigid hollow box that spans the rooms below without the need for intermediate columns. Service floors are also not unknown in high-rise buildings (e.g. PSFS Building, 1932, Howe & Lescaze) in order to reduce the transport distances for treated media (air and water). Louis Parnes's design for a department store has several storey-high, long-span floors housing

Fig. 116: Services in the plane of the loadbearing structure
Fritz Haller: SBB Löwenberg Training Centre, Murten (CH), 1980–82

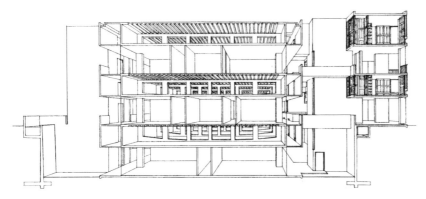

Fig. 117: Storey-high floors to accommodate services
Louis I. Kahn: Salk Insitute, La Jolla (California, USA), 1959–65

not only services but also storerooms for the respective sales areas above.

Comfort and technology

Human shelter is essentially designed to provide protection from the weather and other persons or animals. In many regions of the world protection against cold weather is a key issue. The open fire is the most primitive form for meeting this requirement, its very nature uniting the generation and output of heat at the same place. The stove and the oven make use of this principle, either singly as the only source of heat in the centre of the house, or distributed among several rooms. The unlimited autonomy that the functional unit of heat generation plus output suggests is spoiled by the associated, vertical flues (the situation is different with sources of heat that do not produce exhaust gases, e.g. electric fires). The flue conveys the smoke and exhaust gases and in multistorey buildings brings warmth to adjoining rooms as well. Another line of development began with the Roman *hypocaust* hot-air heating system in which the fire providing the heat is located outside the room to be heated because an

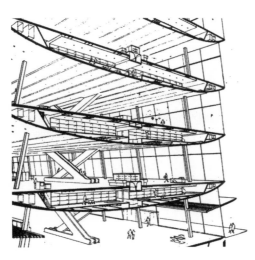

Fig. 118: Storey-high floors as storerooms for the respective sales areas above
Louis Parnes: department store project, c. 1947

open fireplace was regarded as dangerous. The hot air is fed via a sort of cavity floor to flues built into or in front of the inner faces of the walls. This ensured that floor and walls were heated equally. It anticipates central heating and underfloor heating in one system and the principle of supplying heat to the places where the heat is lost most readily. In addition, as a form of pure radiant heating, the heat provided by the *hypocaust* system is more efficient than modern radiators or convectors and also does not suffer from dust-disturbing convection currents. (For a contemporary reinterpretation of the *hypocaust* system see the description of the Gallery for Contemporary Art in Marktoberdorf by Bearth + Deplazes, 2000.)

Rayner Banham saw the technical possibilities of heating rooms or individual components directly as the basic principle for implementing the new interior layout concepts of Modernism.[3] The critical aspect of reduced comfort due to large windows could now be compensated for by the heating. Banham cites the north-facing windows of the draughting rooms at Mackintosh's School of Art in Glasgow (1896-99) as an example. For Frank

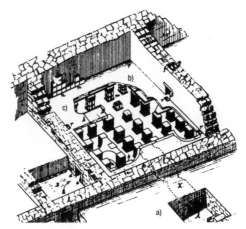

Fig. 119: Roman *hypocaust* heating system
a) fireplace outside the building, b) cavity floor, c) flues (*tubuli*)

Lloyd Wright the hot-water heating system with a central heat source and decentralised distribution presented the chance to realise more complex volumes: "This enabled the form of the various parts of the building to be developed more fully, they would gain light and air from several sides."[4] Building services – whether in terms of heating in winter or cooling in summer – could now be called upon to compensate for the poor insulating properties of the building materials, i.e. the glass. This situation continued until the oil crisis of the 1970s and growing environmental awareness in the 1980s led to investigations into how the use of technical systems could be reduced through materials technology. Although insulating glass coated with heat-absorbing film and noble gas in the cavity had been known since the 1950s, it has undergone a phenomenal development since then and glass is now no longer seen as a synonym for high energy losses.

The growing use of central heating in the first half of the 20th century meant that the necessary infrastructure, for heat distribution or heat output, was being added to or integrated into building components more and more. Whereas up until that time the established services in housing had been restricted to the sanitary facilities in individual ancillary rooms, building services now started to appear all over the house. The way in which architects handled this new challenge varied from the pragmatic approach of routing the services in full view, to the opposite approach in which all pipes and radiators were concealed behind some form of screen or cladding. Yet another approach was employed by those architects who saw the technical heating components as a configuration option – whether in the form of special featuring (colour, arrangement etc.) or through combining with other functions (balustrade).

For Bruno Taut the unpretentiously positioned, but coloured, radiators and pipes represented contrasting elements in a polychromaticism that encompassed the whole interior. The heating in the Kenwin Villa in Veney (1929) by Hermann Henselmann was in the form of several parallel

Fig. 122: Heating pipes grouped to form a surface
Alexander Ferenczy, Hermann Henselmann: Kenwin Villa, Vevey (CH), 1929

Fig. 123: Underfloor heating plus hot-air ducts supplied from the cellar (in front of French windows)
Ludwig Wittgenstein: house in Kundmanngasse, Vienna (A), 1928

Fig. 120: Undesirable building services: the reality with radiators!
Hans and Wassili Luckhardt: house on Rupenhorn, Berlin (D), 1928

Fig. 121: Undesirable building services: photo with radiators discreetly erased!
Hans and Wassili Luckhardt: house on Rupenhorn, Berlin (D), 1928

pipes imitating the course of the long horizontal window above and thus became a horizontal, profiled surface. But in a house in the Kundmanngasse in Vienna (1928) by Ludwig Wittgenstein hidden underfloor heating was specified for the non-private rooms on the ground floor and air ducts fed from the cellar in front of the French windows. According to Christoph Bürkle two photographs of the interior of the house on Ruppenhorn in Berlin (1928) by the Luckhardt brothers testify to the fact that architects sometimes regard radiators as a nuisance; in the photograph used for publication the radiators have been discreetly erased.

Over the years, to relieve the interior of technical components convectors, mounted in the floor to guarantee unrestricted transparency, started to replace radiators

more and more. This unrestricted transparency also applies to ceiling and floor heating systems in which the invisible pipes no longer have to be clad but are instead encased in concrete and cement screed respectively. It is interesting that underfloor heating seems to suggest an evenly distributed heating surface indifferent to types of use, but in practice the spacing of the pipes plus their positioning in individual zones is just as dependent on the actual interior layout as a heating system employing discrete radiators. For instance, the number of heating pipes in the floor is increased, i.e. their spacing is reduced, local to storey-high windows, and deep rooms are divided into zones with their own temperature controls depending on the different amounts of incident solar radiation.

The facade as an infrastructure medium

Up until the beginning of the 1960s building services held really little significance for the design of the facade and, at best, could be made out behind a more or less transparent glass curtain wall because until then the services were all on the inside. However, from that point on they started to assume a more active role in the configuration of the facade. In the buildings of the Brutalism movement solid, usually concrete, shafts surround groups of pipes, cables, and ducts, and combined with stairs and other

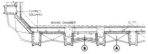

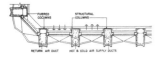

Figs 124, 125, 126:
Top: every third "column" is non-loadbearing
Centre: section through spandrel panel
Bottom: section through window
Paul Rudolph, with Anderson, Beckwith & Haible:
Blue Cross Building, Boston (Mass., USA), 1958

"use-related" bulges add relief to the building envelope. In a reverse approach, exponents of high-tech architecture – and prior to this the Metabolists – created their aesthetic out of the fact that services remained on view or essential functional units were granted autonomy. However, components on the outside must inevitably penetrate the climate boundary, and in the light of the higher standards of thermal insulation now required, external services hardly find favour any more.

Between these two extremes – building services as a styling element on the one hand and invisible necessity on the other (whose common denominator is the unmistakable separation from the loadbearing structure) – there exist concepts in which there is an amalgamation between loadbearing structure, building services and interior fitting-out elements in a multifunctional arrangement. A good example is the Blue Cross Building in Boston (1958) by Paul Rudolph in association with Anderson, Beckwith & Haible. This 13-storey office block in the centre of Boston is based on a loadbearing facade whose facing leaf of vertical columns at a spacing of 1.53 m appears to reflect the loadbearing structure. However, the "columns" that are "missing" at ground floor level, are non-loadbearing. Every third column is therefore hollow and the entire cross-section is used as an exhaust-air duct. Even the neighbouring loadbearing columns are not quite what they seem because half of the depth of each column is reserved for a fresh-air duct. And as the spandrel panels function as mixing chambers the ventilation system therefore spreads like a net over the entire facade – a principal that is not dissimilar to that of the exposed services of high-tech architecture. However, the difference is that the lines of the services coincide with the loadbearing structure and the interior structure. The air duct in the form of a column can therefore accommodate

Fig. 129: Amalgamation of loadbearing structure and vertical service ducts
Paul Rudolph, with Anderson, Beckwith & Haible: Blue Cross Building, Boston (Mass., USA), 1958

junctions with internal partitions, likewise window frames. The visible facade relief is made up of precast concrete elements just a few centimetres thick which appear as cladding owing to the type of jointing. Whereas this type of cladding represents an improvement to the surface of the (Swiss) lattice facade of the 1950s, applied directly to the substrate, on Rudolph's building it forms a hollow backdrop. However, we must ask whether concrete is the

Fig. 127: Sculpted services shaft, in materials to match the facade
Greater London Council, Hubert Bennett: Queen Elizabeth Hall, London (UK), 1966

Fig. 128: Exposed infrastructure as the characterising motif
Renzo Piano & Richard Rogers: Centre Pompidou, Paris (F), 1971–78

Fig. 133: Floor slab without intervening columns, with ventilation ducts and lighting units between the ribs
SOM: American Republic Insurance Company, Des Moines (Iowa, USA), 1965

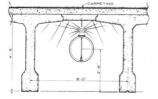

Figs 130, 131, 132:
Top: facade without openings as loadbearing plate containing services
Centre: ground and basement floors as an autonomous block
Bottom: section through floor, scale approx. 1:60
SOM: American Republic Insurance Company, Des Moines (Iowa, USA), 1965

right material because the cranks in the spandrel panels are reminiscent of the stiffening folds of sheet metal panels.

On the Blue Cross Building loadbearing structure, building services and windows form a network that is identical on all sides of the building. However, the functions are separated on the building for the American Republic Insurance Company in Des Moines by Skidmore Owings & Merrill (1965): services housed in loadbearing concrete plates without openings on the longitudinal sides, storey-high glazing on the ends of the building. The topic of hollow loadbearing construction, which is characteristic of the facade, is repeated in the floor, where 1.36 m deep concrete T-beams span 30 m across the whole building without any intermediate supports. These beams form a box-like relief with the air ducts accommodated between the stalks of the Ts. Mounted on top of the circular air ducts are fluorescent lights that use the underside of the ribbed floor as a reflector. In addition to their function as an infrastructure medium, the wall plates (without openings) are designed as deep beams spanning between four columns at the base. In section the building looks like a bridge spanning a two-storey object slipped underneath – the fully glazed cafeteria and refectory block free from all loadbearing members. This addresses the change in structure that affects every larger building owing to the different interior needs of ground floor and upper floors.

Structural change

Even monofunctional buildings often provide for a different usage at ground floor level, above all in city-centre locations. The reasons are obvious: the direct relationship with public spaces favours profit-making uses such as shops, restaurants, etc., and the location level with the surrounding ground means that the ground floor is even accessible to vehicles (cf. fire station, Zurich). In Germany the cast iron columns on the ground floor that

support the downstand beams of joist floors in buildings from the late 19th century are especially classical. This is a type of structural change that is hardly noticeable. But the situation is totally different in a building with a transfer structure which tracks the change in the loadbearing members with expressive force. The high-rise block "Zur Palme" in Zurich by Haefeli Moser Steiger (1961–64) is a good example. The windmill-plan shape of this tower is carried on a concrete platform 12 m above the ground supported on wedge-shaped columns – space enough for an independent two-storey structure underneath.

Lina Bo Bardi took a different course at the Museum of Modern Art (1957–68) in São Paulo, where the storeys are not elevated above ground level, but instead suspended. At least the enclosing concrete frame, with its span of 50 m, conveys this picture. In fact there is another pair of beams within the glass building, so that only the bottommost floor is really suspended. In any case, the whole area beneath the building remains open, in the form of a covered plaza.

Buildings like the school in Volta by Miller & Maranta prove that a structural change is possible without displaying the structural conditions. The in situ reinforced concrete loadbearing structure devised in conjunction with the consulting engineers Conzett Bronzini Gartmann makes use of wall plates on the upper floors that are rigidly connected to the floor slabs. This arrangement functions as a monolithic construction spanning the full 28 m across the sports hall, and cantilevers a further 12 m on the entrance elevation. The wall plates, which incidentally are not continuous from facade to facade but instead consist of two separate parts, line up on all the floors of the school. Jürg Conzett explained in an article that it is sufficient "when the wall plates [above one another] make contact at any one point".[5] Consequently, this principle permits different interior structures from storey to storey, which in the case of the school in Volta is only

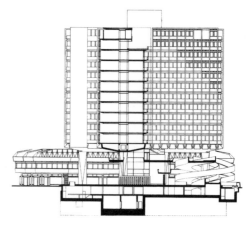

Fig. 134: High- and low-rise buildings, each with its own loadbearing structure
Haefeli Moser Steiger: "Zur Palme" Tower, Zurich (CH), 1961–64

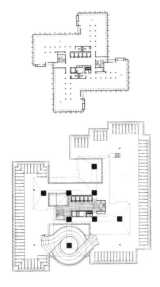

Figs 135, 136, 137:
At parking level (bottom) massive columns trace the windmill-plan shape of the upper floors (centre); general view of building (top).
Haefeli Moser Steiger: "Zur Palme" Tower, Zurich (CH), 1961–64

consummated when supplemented with non-loadbearing walls. It might be exciting to investigate at which phase (prior to beginning work on site, during construction, or after completion) which degree of flexibility can be achieved with this system.

Alternatives

At the start it was said that the complexity of contemporary buildings has to be accepted. But this is only partly true of course. More and more intelligent low-tech concepts are appearing, particularly in the realm of building services, concepts that are based on centuries-old knowledge and are "only" coming to the fore again or being reinterpreted. The stack effect (thermal currents), which is being exploited these days in order to achieve a natural change of air, e.g. in office buildings, was already common for cooling buildings in India in the 15th century, accomplished by means of internal courtyards and an open ground floor. People exploited the physical effects provided by the building elements and spaces that were unavoidable. So building services in traditional buildings is not an appendage rich in technology, but rather an integral part of the interior structure and loadbearing structure. And last but not least, the "air shaft" provides the obvious additional function of allowing light to reach the adjoining rooms!

Fig. 139: Frame with suspended floors
Lina Bo Bardi: Museum of Modern Art, São Paulo (BR), 1957–68

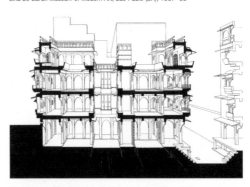

Fig. 140: Exploiting the stack effect: fresh air flows through the open ground floor and rises in the internal courtyard.
House, Jaisalmer (India), 15th century

Notes

1 Hans Bernoulli: "Vom Altwerden der Häuser"; in: *Die organische Erneuerung unserer Städte*, Basel, 1942; cit. in Fredi Kölliker (ed.): *Zahn der Zeit – Baukonstruktion im Kontext des architektonischen Entwerfens*, Basel, 1994.
2 Marcel Meili: "Dinglichkeit und Idee", Marcel Meili in conversation with Hubertus Adam, J. Christoph Bürkle and Judit Solt; in: *archithese* 2003/1, p. 7.
3 Rayner Banham: "Die Architektur der wohltemperierten Umwelt", in: *ARCH+*, Feb 1988, p. 36.
4 Frank L. Wright, 1910; cit. in: Rayner Banham, op. cit., p. 43.
5 Jürg Conzett: "Raum halten"; in: *Werk, Bauen und Wohnen*, 1997/9, pp. 34–39.

Fig. 138: Only the positioning of the windows provides evidence of the structural change.
Miller & Maranta: Volta School, Basel (CH), 1999

Vertical loadbearing structures in solid construction
Cross-section concepts

The principle of solid construction exploits the physical phenomenon of gravity:

– mass – self-weight
– interlocking of wall elements: the "zip" principle (bricks, stones, hybrid forms)
– jointing mortar between wall elements: the "glue" principle, increasing the frictional resistance (adhesion) between the wall elements
– stability and load-carrying capacity: the "wide base, narrow top" principle; objective: optimised use of materials

Fig. 145: Base of wall approx. 6 to 7 m wide, top of wall 4 to 6 m; masonry "external walls" with rubble infill
Great Wall of China, c. 700–100 BC

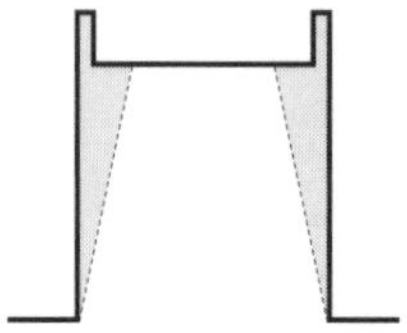

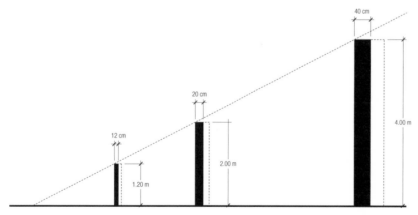

Fig. 141: Straight wall
Excessive cross-section

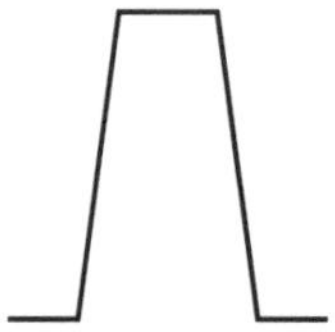

Fig. 142: Tapered wall
Optimised cross-section

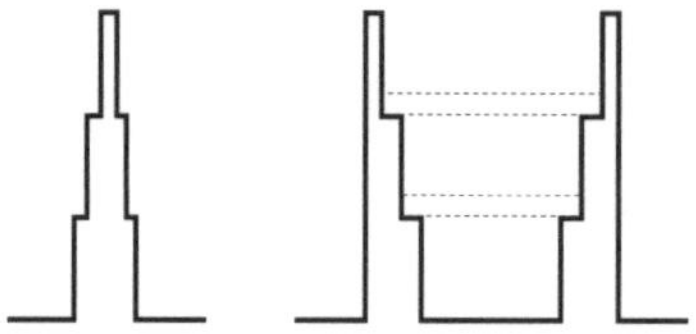

Fig. 143 Stepped wall
e.g. providing support for beams/joists

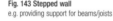

Fig. 144: Sizing after Rondelet (*Theoretical and Practical Treatise on the Art of Building*)
Principally: the taller a free-standing wall, the wider its cross-section. Rule of the thumb for free-standing brick walls subject to wind loads only (average stability):
b = 1/10 h; built of rubble stones, factor approx. 1.75; ashlar stones, factor approx. 0.75

The form of the wall cross-section depends on various factors. The first critical factor is whether the wall is free-standing or whether it is braced or stiffened by other walls; this factor influences the width of the base. In any case, however, the cross-section will reduce with the height in order to optimise the use of materials because both the self-weight of the construction and the imposed loads resulting from the use of the construction gradually diminish further up the wall.

The variation in the cross-section can be either linear or stepped. It depends on the form of construction – with or without mortar, homogeneous or heterogeneous construction – and the building process (height of scaffold lifts), but is generally governed by utilisation considerations. For example, in a multistorey building it is sensible to step the cross-section at the level of the floors (and use the steps to support the floor beams/joists).

As the cost of labour in past decades has increased at a faster rate than the cost of materials, a building whose wall thickness decreases with the height is a rarity these days, with the exception of special structures such as retaining walls and dams. In the solid form of construction the larger wall loads of the lower storeys normally determine the size of the wall cross-section of all the upper storeys; this is especially true when we are stacking identical plan layouts one on top of the other.

Fig. 146: Multi-leaf wall with filling of loose, low-quality material (section)
Trulli – traditional solid stone buildings of southern Italy, Sovero (I)

Vertical loadbearing structures in solid construction
Plan concepts

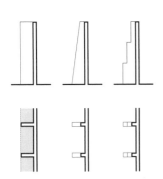

Fig. 147: Walls reinforced with ribs for increasing the inherent stability
sections (top) and plans (bottom)

Fig. 148: Cob construction with timber reinforcement (internal frame) with protective covering of cob (transverse ribs)
Traditional construction of the Dogon people (Mali)

Fig. 152: Concrete half-cylinders 25 m high (d =25 cm); the tie bars at the top guarantee the stability of the form.
Maarten Struijs: windbreak in Rotterdam Harbour (NL), 1985

Fig. 153: Wall forms for stability: L-shape, curve, cranked and winding forms

Looked at in terms of economy of material usage, various plan concepts are conceivable for stabilising the walls. For example, the stability and buckling resistance of the walls can be increased by including transverse ribs, which are either formed by adding the same or a different material, or by dividing, i.e. by omitting superfluous material, above all with very wide wall cross-sections (see plan of the Pantheon).

Changes of direction such as corners, cranks and curves also have a stabilising effect. Here, the height and length of the developed wall governs the number of changes of direction. The reduction in material can go so far as to make it essential, above a certain height, to include auxiliary structural members (see fig. of the windbreak above).

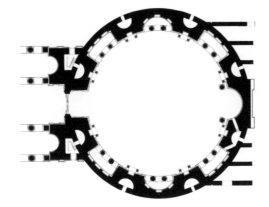

Fig. 149: Omission of material to form alcoves in circumferential wall, which creates a ribbed effect
Pantheon, Rome (I), 118–125 AD (right), loadbearing structure (left)

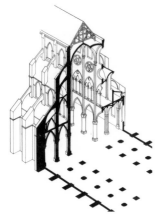

Fig. 150: Flying buttresses to transfer thrust, e.g. from vaulting
Axonometric cut-away view of a Gothic cathedral

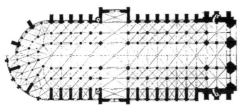

Fig. 151: The external loadbearing structure (flying buttresses) resulted in recesses which were later converted into chapels (along bottom edge of plan).
Notre Dame Cathedral, Paris (F), begun in 1163

Vaulted loadbearing structures in solid construction
Compression structures: arches and barrel vaults

Fig. 154: Succession of stacked arches: sectional concept in order to omit superfluous material. The arch construction is sensible from an engineering and an economic viewpoint.
Pont du Gard, Roman aqueduct at Nîmes (F), 1st century AD

Fig. 157: Brickwork vaulting as permanent formwork to concrete above, with tie bars to accommodate thrust. The vaulted construction here has an architectural, space-forming value.
Le Corbusier: Jaoul houses, Paris (F), 1955

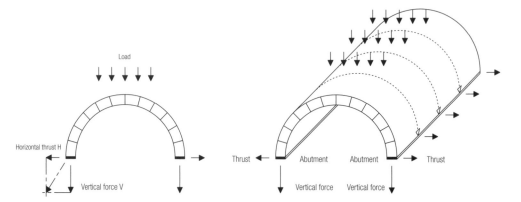

Fig. 155: Arch (as door or window lintel, for large spans)

Fig. 158: Barrel vault

A compression structure allows the "disadvantage" of the weight of the construction to become an inherent advantage of the loadbearing structure.

Fig. 156: The reinforced concrete tie accommodates the thrust and relieves the wall below.
Louis I. Kahn: Indian Institute of Management, Ahmedabad (India), 1962–74

The erection of arched and vaulted constructions follows identical criteria, also because a barrel vault is nothing other than an arch-shape curved surface, or rather a succession of parallel arches. The question of lateral stability is more significant with an arch because it is usually part of a wall subject to the aforementioned conditions (see "Vertical loadbearing structures").

In the example of Louis I. Kahn's Indian Institute of Management in Ahmedabad the double arches relieve the wall below and concentrate the forces at the supports. But the wall does not need to be strengthened as a result of this because the reinforced concrete tie beneath the arches takes the thrust so that all the loads are transferred vertically. The hopper-like reduction in thickness of the wall below the arches merely indicates those parts of the wall that carry practically no vertical loads.

The lateral thrust increases as the rise of the arch decreases. The shallow barrel-vault roofs of Le Corbusier's Jaoul houses were therefore reinforced with steel tie bars. At the aqueduct in Nîmes, on the other hand, such tie bars were unnecessary because a succession of identical arches – irrespective of the rise – results in the coincidence of opposing identical horizontal forces and hence purely vertical loads. However, the end bays need special treatment.

Vaulted loadbearing structures in solid construction
Compression structures: domes

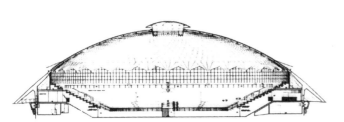

Fig. 159: The tension ring is below ground underneath the column foundations (abutments).
Pier Luigi Nervi: Palazetto dello Sport, Rome (I), 1957

Fig. 162: The dome is resolved into a ring of Y-shaped raking columns
Pier Luigi Nervi: Palazetto dello Sport, Rome (I), 1957

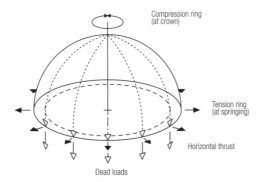

Fig. 160: Dome (body of revolution)

As with barrel vaults and arches, in domes we are always faced with the question: How is the thrust to be accommodated, reduced and taken down to the foundations?

At the Pantheon in Rome the designers employed various features to handle this problem. The weight of the dome decreases as we approach the crown, which is achieved not only by reducing the cross-section but also by using lighter materials further up the dome. The dimensions of the dome are such that the flow of forces starting from the crown remains within the cross-section of the dome. The extra wall height externally adds weight and hence allows the tensile forces to be accommodated in the wall. Likewise, a steel strap acting as a tension ring would also have been conceivable.

Pier Luigi Nervi's Palazetto dello Sport makes use of a complex dome: the concrete shell is reinforced with folds and is resolved into Y-shaped raking columns, which accommodate the thrust by extending the dome and beneath the apex of the Y have a vertical column to transfer the forces vertically into the ground. In the ground there is a circumferential reinforced concrete tension ring. This allowed Nervi to create an interior space completely free from any intervening vertical loadbearing elements.

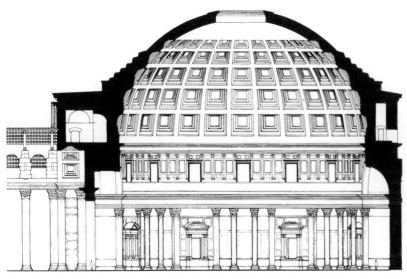

Fig. 161: Dome with voids to reduce weight and consumption of materials (omission of superfluous material). This creates a grid of stiffening loadbearing ribs. In addition, lighter materials were employed further up the dome.
Pantheon, Rome (I),118–125 AD

Fig. 163: An early example of construction with Roman concrete (*opus caementitium*). Pantheon, Rome (I), 118–125 AD

Of heavy mass and apparent heaviness

Martin Tschanz

Resistance

Mass is a fundamental property of material which expresses itself in the mutual attraction of bodies and in their inertias. The former results in the heavyweight, age-old problem of architecture, the latter allows mass to generate resistance. Both of these aspects are illustrated in the pier of the Wipkinger viaduct in Zurich. Its heaviness enables it to stand securely on the edge of the river bed, also resisting the highest floodwaters. However, the builders of this pier were not satisfied with this effective mass but instead emphasised this aspect with decorative additions: a not quite regular and relatively coarse yet careful cutting of the stones; a visual enlargement of the volume, which appears to extend far beyond the bridge supports (particularly when seen from a distance) and finally gently sloping sides, a stepped plinth and particularly coarse, almost rustic, masonry at the sides above the waterline. Furthermore, a carefully constructed, stocky arch indicates the loads to be overcome and, together with small openings at the sides, demonstrates that what the observer sees is perhaps not as massive as it appears at first sight. This vaulting was later fortified to form a bunker, which itself has recently been filled with concrete. A tumour-like protrusion of solid concrete should, with its inert mass, resist the impact of any projectiles. The rounded forms are only understandable as martial shows of strength because grenades would be deflected directly onto the structure they are trying to protect! They demonstrate the sculpted, moulded mass. The heaviness and inertia of the mass in the modest bridge pier are, on the one hand, necessary to carry out the tasks, and on the other, the themes of the design. In this way, its appearance conveys stability and obstinate resistance.

In architecture advocating a large mass, in terms of the primary functions, tends to be the exception. We usually think of retaining walls, dams, bunkers, avalanche protection and similar structures. In other words, structures that are generally the province of the engineer, who can guarantee the desired results. But architects, for

Fig. 164: Bridge over River Limmat, Zurich-Wipkingen. East pier

their part, can also convey and express the idea of the security and safety achieved.

Massiveness

For most, this interest goes beyond the physical and, above all, formal properties of mass or the associated connotations. Massive material can be sculpted, and moulded. Its relative homogeneity and stability enable us to hollow it out or model it, so to speak. A massive wall, for example, invites us to make it thinner by creating local recesses, or to provide texture in the form of profiling. These possibilities are shown in an exemplary way by Mario Botta in his church in Mogno. His elliptical cylinder encloses a space that unites the non-directional basic geometric forms of square and circle with the directional forms of rectangle and ellipse. The architectural means to this end is the plastic formation of the mass of the walls. Recesses allow the square to become legible, additionally emphasised by the diagonal relationship established by the cylindrical column on the axis of the entrance; a continual reforming and thinning-out allows the rectangle on plan to transform gradually to an ellipse at the start of the glass roof, the ellipse itself terminating at the curving roof.

Of course, the idea of forming a space through plastic modelling of the mass of the walls is not new. Frequently, the external volume of a building does not obey the same laws as the design of the interior spaces – there is on the one hand the requirements of urban planning, on the other the utilisation conditions inside the building. This leads to an unavoidable conflict, particularly when functional or "scenic" aspects, rather than, for example, tectonics, determine the architectural approach, which correspondingly wishes to express these conditions. The mass of the walls is often a suitable place for dealing with this conflict. Baroque architecture, in particular, provides virtuoso examples of this. However, unlike in the case of the church in Mogno, the aspect of massive material forming the "grey area" between the spatial boundaries is usually of secondary importance. This is more often the place, besides the loadbearing structure, to embed the functions and all possible technical necessities. "Mass" in this sense is indeed precisely confined but its structure and composition less defined and vague. Whether the mass consists of voids or material, it is equivalent to the appearance of the material as a body, whose internal structure is hardly relevant, at least for everyday considerations.

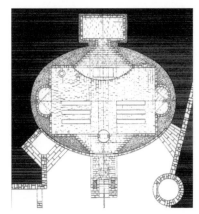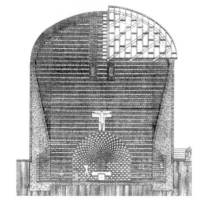

Fig. 165: Plan (above), section (right)
Mario Botta: church in Mogno (CH), 1986–95

Fig. 166: Cassina de Camadra, Blenio Valley

Fig. 167: Rudolf Fontana, Christian Kerez: Oberrealta Chapel (CH), 1994–95

We understand massiveness to express the (relative) homogeneity of the material of a body. It lends it interesting properties. Without immediately having to think of a "ruin", it lets objects age with dignity, and gives them a claim to durability and longevity. In addition, it permits simple, direct design. Impressive in this sense are, for example, the Alpine buildings built entirely of stone (as can be found in southern Switzerland), where walls and roof are layered with the same gesture and are made from the same materials found more or less in the same place. Christian Kerez may well have had such buildings in mind when he designed the chapel at Oberrealta. His design concentrates fully on the essentials: a protective envelope in a trusted form, a door with threshold and a window form a structure which is both a man-made symbol of a house absolute and hence also a symbol of shelter and protection. This embodiment of familiarity and extreme abstraction, the simple, well-proportioned form and the solid materiality give this building a sacred dignity which does justice to the function and the location. This concentration would be inconceivable without a material "from one mould", which enables such a construction without details.

Monoliths and "monoliths"

"One of the most prominent features of the bunker is that it is one of the few modern monolithic forms of architecture.

"While the majority of structures are bonded to the ground through their foundations, the bunker has none at all; its centre of gravity replaces them. This explains its ability to achieve a certain mobility..."

Thus Paul Virilio begins his chapter entitled "The Monolith" in *Bunker Archeology*[1], providing in the same breath a convincing definition for architectural monoliths which remains very close to the term itself: a building like a stone that behaves like one as well. However, there are hardly any forms of architecture that do justice to the term used in this way. It is understandable that the term is also used for structures that only appear to be monoliths, even when they exhibit conventional loadbearing behaviour. Here is the definition of Rodolfo Machado and Rodolphe el-Khoury given in their catalogue *Monolithic Architecture*:[2] "We understand monolithic to signify monolith-like..." That is on the one hand in the sense of an exaggeration – although they call this form metaphorical – for not actually monolithic, and really extraordinarily homogeneous and solid objects; and on the other, also in an "allegorical" sense as well "for buildings that do not have the physical material properties of the monolith, but that seem, 'pretend' or 'act' as though they do. In this allegorical mode the term monolithic has more to do with representational strategies than material qualities."

Monoliths in this sense are compact architectural objects which appear to be hermetic and reveal nothing of their content. They are stand-alone, often remote structures, but may well form points of orientation in themselves. They are objects without scale which have an imposing, characteristic, individual form and, accordingly, are frequently personified, so to speak, and given a name. Their materials are often confined to a thin envelope which has nevertheless to demonstrate the appearance of a certain homogeneity. The design of the volume should suggest mass, which is mostly achieved by heightening a plastic deformation, preferably under the apparent influence of gravity or some other force.

The relationship between inside and outside is always problematic with such objects. The similarity with a massive body implies that the configuration of the interior, as a diffuse "mass", is uninteresting. It plays no role in the building's outward appearance, which in this sense is the only relevant aspect. This fact may well have contributed to the success of such hermetic architecture. In order to avoid reducing the design totally to the volume and the surface, the external form in the aforementioned sense has to be balanced by a similarly imposing interior. This might allow such forms to start resembling the bunkers described by Virilio once again, perhaps best shown by the designs for the National Library of France by OMA and the Tokyo Opera by Jean Nouvel. Nevertheless, the term

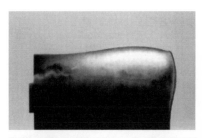

Fig. 168: Jean Nouvel: National Theatre project, Tokyo (J), 1986; view of model (left) and longitudinal section (right)

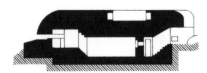

Fig. 169: Bunker in French Atlantic Wall "buried" in the sand (left), longitudinal section (right)

One kilo…

Not everything is what it appears to be. Even mass itself has many surprises in store. Schaffhausen-based artist Katharina Bürgin, for instance, shows us a work which, even without a title, we recognise immediately as a house, owing to its simple, distinctive shape: the chalky, slightly blemished white surfaces, the somewhat worn edges, which are not quite straight, slightly bulging, and the sides, which lift the work clear of the underlying surface, causing it to float almost. The work manifests itself to us as solid, cast; we are reminded of plaster models. The "large" in the title "Large House" could relate to a scale, for at 48 cm long the object is not exactly large. If we dare to touch it, we are initially surprised by the silky softness and warmth of the surface, but then shocked: where is the weight? The work is massive yet frighteningly light in weight, moulded from papier mâché. So, what is a kilo now?[3]

"monolithic" does not seem to be at home in this figurative sense; the association with the enclosing sensual qualities of solid materials, which are not confined to viewing from remote distances and can hardly be limited, is too strong. It would seem to be more advisable to speak of hermetically or plastically formed solitary objects.

Notes
[1] Paul Virilio: *Bunker-Archäologie*, Munich, 1992 (1975), p. 37. – English translation: Paul Virilio: *Bunker Archeology*, New York, 1994.
[2] Rodolfo Machado, Rodolphe el-Khoury: *Monolithic Architecture*, Munich, 1995 (catalogue of The Heinz Architectural Center, Pittsburg, 1995/96), pp. 15–16.
[3] This is how the text by Gertrud Ohling ends in the catalogue to the Manor-Kunstpreis 1994: *Katharina Bürgin, Objekte 1992 bis 1994*, Museum zu Allerheiligen, Schaffhausen 1995.

Fig. 170: Katharina Bürgin: "Large House"
(1993)
Paper, 28 x 48 x 26 cm

Ksar Ferich
A fortified storehouse in southern Tunisia

Fig. 171: Ksar Ferich
Development of the first courtyard

Fig. 173: Ksar Ferich
The completely unbroken perimeter of the complex

Fig. 172: Ksar Ferich
The ksar is located between an inhabited region and the Sahara desert

Fig. 174: Inner courtyard
View towards the entrance

Fig. 175: Inner courtyard
Complex at the centre of the ksar

Ksour and ghorfas

The ksour (plural of ksar) of southern Tunisia are fortified living and storage complexes which were preferably built high up on the mountain plateaus or on steep mountain slopes. The centre of the complex is frequently a kalaa (a fortification). Grouped in the rocks below are the houses or caves and these are always accompanied by honeycomb-like, barrel-vaulted ghorfas (Arabic: ghorfa = space), often built in several storeys, one above the other. These serve mainly as storage rooms.

Isolated true ghorfa complexes built in the landscape are also called ksour. These (usually) rectangular complexes are surrounded by a continuous high wall interrupted by only one door, and convey a good defensive impression. They functioned primarily as collective warehouses for a clan while the nomadic tribesfolk were moving from pasture to pasture with their herds. Official guards, but also the sick and the old who could not travel with the herds, lived in and guarded the ksar. There were often hundreds of storerooms, some of which were up

to six storeys high, grouped like the honeycombs of a beehive around one or more internal courtyards.

Every family owned an appropriate number of these vaulted constructions – up to 10 metres deep, about three metres wide and about two metres high, secured with small doors of palm wood – to store their personal provisions. Rickety external stairs without balustrades, steps or timber joists cantilevering from the walls led to the upper entrances. Relief-type decoration in the internal plaster, e.g. in the shape of a hand or foot, ornamentation or lettering, is found in some places. A ksar was a place of trade and assembly in times of peace, a refuge in times of war. Thanks to the provisions stored within and a draw-well in the internal courtyard, a ksar could also survive longer sieges if necessary.

The large ghorfa complexes began to lose their significance as the nomads started to build permanent settlements. They decayed or had to be demolished to make way for new buildings (e.g. in Medenine, where more than 30 such ksour were razed to the ground). Many fortified storehouses have in the meantime decayed to such an extent that great care is needed when exploring them. Some are still used as storage rooms or stalls, others have been converted into simple accommodations for tourists. Occasionally, the visitor comes across well-maintained or restored complexes which, even today, are still occupied, or have been reoccupied, by local people.

Excerpt from: Dorothy Stannard, *Tunesien*, Berlin, 1992

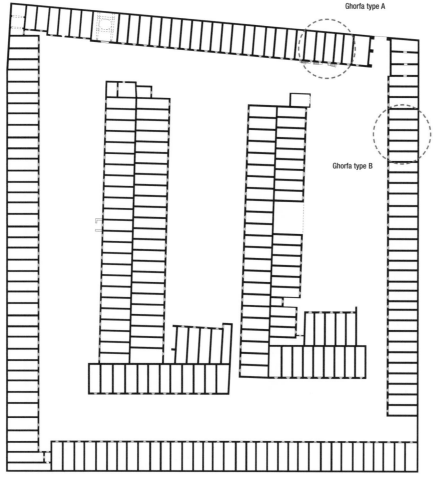

Ghorfa type A

Ghorfa type B

Fig. 176: Ksar Ferich
Plan of ground floor, 1:1000

Fig. 177: Ghorfa type A
Section, 1:200

Fig. 179: Ghorfa type A
Longitudinal section, 1:200

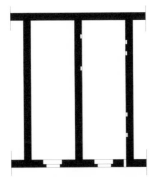

Fig. 178: Ghorfa type A
Plan, 1:200

Fig. 180: Ghorfa type A
Front facade

Fig. 181: Ghorfa type A
Side facade

Fig. 182: Ghorfa
Detail of partially rendered facade

Fig. 183: Ghorfa type B
Front facade

Fig. 186: Ghorfa type B
Elevation, 1:200

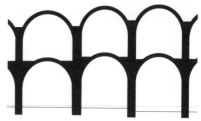

Fig. 187: Ghorfa type B
Section, 1:200

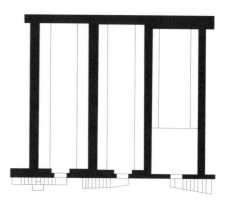

Fig. 188: Ghorfa type B
Plan, 1:200

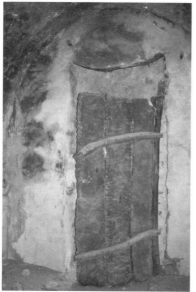

Fig. 184: Ghorfa
Interior view, ground floor

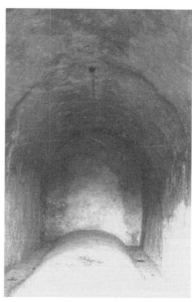

Fig. 185: Ghorfa
Interior view, upper floor, with vaulted floor

How to make a ghorfa:

Throughout the south of Tunisia grain was stored in small stone cells known as ghorfas. They were each about 2 m high and 6–10 m in length. More units were added as required both at either side and above, sometimes reaching up to 8 units in height. Eventually, the whole formed a courtyard, the blank outside walls deterring raiders. A skill you might just require – how to make a ghorfa:

1. Build two walls of rock and mud about 2 m apart and 1.5 m high.
2. Place vertically between the walls two straw grain baskets packed with earth. These must fit exactly between the walls to support them. Place a third straw grain basket of earth horizontally on top of the first two.
3. Over this place a previously manufactured plaited reed/straw mat to make an arch.
4. An arched roof of rocks held by a fine clay and gypsum mortar can then be gradually constructed, using the matting and grain baskets as support.
5. Construct a rear wall if necessary. Remove the supporting baskets and plaster the internal walls with lime and mud. Decorate if required with figures and handprints or fish to ward off the evil eye.
6. Construct a front wall with a wooden access door of palm.

Excerpt from: Anne & Keith McLachlan: *Tunisia Handbook*, Bath, 1997

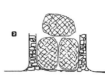
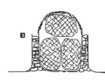

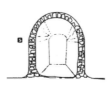

Fig. 189

Books on Tunesia:
- Jellal Abdelkafi: *Tunesien: Geographie – Geschichte – Kultur – Politik*, Stuttgart, 1994.
- Myron Goldfinger: *Villages in the Sun*, New York, 1969.
- Derek Hill: *Islamic Architecture in North Africa*, London, 1976.
- Peter Andreas Kroehnert, Josef Schramm: *Tunesien, Land zwischen Sand und Meer*, Freilassing, 1969.
- Hans-Georg Roth, Anne Brakemeier: *Tunesien*, Breidenstein, 1995.
- Konrad Schliephake: *Tunesien: Geographie – Geschichte – Kultur – Religion – Staat ...*, Stuttgart, 1984.

Sculpted architecture
The Scottish tower house

Nik Biedermann, Andrea Deplazes

Fig. 190: Neidpath Castle, Peebles (Scotland), 14th century

Fig. 191: Montebello Castle, Bellinzona (CH), 14th century

The fortified house

Typical of Scottish architecture is the tower house of the Middle Ages, a combination of castle and residence in a compact, vertically organised space. Early examples of this typically Scottish form were plain, the reflection of a poor land characterised by internal unrest and regional wars between rival clans. Constant rebuilding was unavoidable. As peace gradually gained the upper hand over the countryside, the external appearance of these tower houses became more decorative, picturesque, "romantic" – reflecting the needs of their owners at that time to express their prosperity. By contrast, the need for fortifications was gradually relegated to the background, transforming the keep into a fortified manor house. The topicality of these tower houses over a period of three centuries (13th to 16th century) led to hybrid forms characterised by regional influences. However, the original form always remains clearly recognisable in these numerous variations.

The core of this work is a study of the architecture of tower houses, not their chronological development and the other facets that occurred simultaneously. The selection that follows does not claim to be exhaustive but does allow an insight into their variety, the wealth of space in these tower houses and their specific idiosyncrasies.

Tower house versus castle

The Scottish tower house is surprising in that it is conceived as a free-standing solitary edifice. The entire defensive system corresponds to the "principle of the chestnut": wooden, unprotected ancillary buildings grouped to form a courtyard like the prickly but soft shell; in the middle stands the tower house as the tough core, serving as the fortified residence and place of work of the Lord of the Manor, and the final, sole place of refuge. Depending on the topographical situation, the building was protected against enemies by simple palisade fences, walls or ditches. In certain situations suitable rocky hillsides – as at Smailholm Tower – or rocky escarpments – as at Neidpath Castle – replaced some of the elaborate

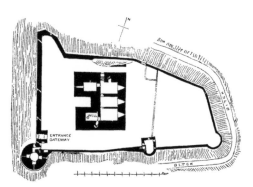

Fig. 192: Plan of whole complex
Borthwick Castle, Midlothian (Scotland), 15th century

defensive structures. The defensive strategy provided for retreating from the poorly fortified ancillary buildings to the tower, which could serve as living accommodation for a long period.

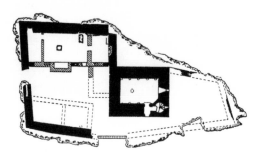

Fig. 193: Plan of whole complex
Smailholm Tower, Roxburgh (Scotland), 16th century

In contrast to the Scottish tower house, the castle complexes built during the same period on the European mainland employed the "onion principle", i.e. the keep, as the heart of the complex, was protected by several concentric defensive rings. Every ring was defended to the utmost because both residential and ancillary buildings extended over several rings. The keep, on the other hand, functioned purely as a (normally) unoccupied, defensive tower, from where the final defence of the complex could be organised. Compared to the Scottish tower house, designed for occupation at all times, the continental keep was, on plan, a much more compact affair. It is therefore also clear that the Scottish tower house was organised vertically and, as a result, had to evolve upwards. The defensive principle is founded on the difficulty of capturing storeys, i.e. the ease of being able to defend narrow spiral staircases.

Architectural observations
Mass and void

The Scottish tower houses, at least the early examples, stand today like eroded outcrops of rock on the hillsides. They appear to be straightforward, solid and elementary. Merely the few irregularly placed openings, which seem to follow no rules, give any hint of internal life behind the mass of stone. In fact, these immovable boulders are hollow inside and their enclosing walls are partly hollow, or even downright thin. The hidden chambers offer the occupants comfort and security against the harsh environment. To the outside world these structures appear to be highly fortified, while inside there is a surprising homeliness thanks to the numerous different spaces. The specific character of the Scottish tower houses is based on this apparent paradox – the combination of, in terms of space, most compact and most efficient form of residence and fortification.

Fig. 194: Eduardo Chillida: "Lurra" G-306, 1994

Eduardo Chillida

Like the sensation of heat can only be appreciated by first experiencing cold, architectural space can only be perceived through its physical boundaries. The mass of the building becomes, oddly enough, more compact once something lightweight is placed alongside, or is perforated by the inclusion of voids and compartment-like rooms.

This principle also characterises the work of the Spanish artist Eduardo Chillida, who calls himself an "architect of empty space". In his fine-grained clay sculptures in particular, the "Lurras", heaviness and massiveness are increased through implied or real spatial inclusions, through incisions which suggest a hollow interior. A rich dialogue between mass and space, heaviness and lightness ensues. As already intimated, the Scottish tower houses can also be interpreted in this way. They are excellent examples of how the fusing of opposites helps to reinforce the idiosyncrasies of the individual components.

Inside and outside

The external form of the Scottish tower house generally corresponds to the form of the main internal room, the hall. This coincidence of content and expression is not compulsory, as Baroque churches demonstrate, for instance. In a building external form and internal space often obey different masters. This is understandable in an urban context, with the chance to respond to external conditions prescribed by the location and locality. However, it is interesting to note that in the tower house there is a secretive "in between", a "massive" layer in which we find the most diverse spatial inclusions – "*poché* spaces": vertical access routes, small, sometimes interlinked chambers, but also mere protrusions of the main room to form window alcoves.

In the early types of tower house with external walls up to four metres thick and few rooms within this thickness, it would be better to speak of "masonry armour" than a conventional external wall. Their unusual, indeed incredible, size is the direct consequence of their task – to protect the living accommodation. The gradual transfer of compartments into this masonry appears to contradict this purpose at first sight. But this forms our "in between", a layer of individual rooms adjacent to the central hall, without weakening the masonry critically. Owing to the lack of openings the extent of this hollowing or thinning out cannot be seen from outside. The extra space gained in this way enables all secondary living functions to be transferred into the walls themselves. The central, main room is relieved and the size of this room can grow accordingly without having to increase the overall volume of the tower house. This achieves a clear separation between main room and ancillary rooms or – in the language

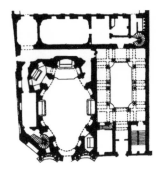

Fig. 195: Plan
Francesco Borromini: San Carlo alle Quattro Fontane, Rome (I), 1634–67

of Louis I. Kahn – "servant" and "served" rooms. This division becomes clear when the resulting interior layout is considered without the enclosing walls (like a "negative"). All the interior spaces, starting from the central, main room, appear to spread out or branch off like vectorised tentacles working to an inherent code.

Spatial inclusions

These ancillary rooms are actually the result of the main room "boring" into the surrounding walls and can be distinguished according to their specific functions. Looking at the alcoves of the main room raises the question of whether these should be regarded as part of the main room or as autonomous spaces. It is clear that all alcoves (for secluded seating, window seats or access to loopholes), with the exception of fireplaces, face outwards, i.e., face the light. Alcoves on the same level as the main room would seem to support the view that they are extensions of the main room. In contrast to these, alcoves reached via steps, and in some cases with fixed furnishings, could be classified as autonomous

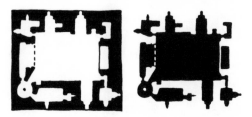

Fig. 196: "Positive" and "negative"
Comlongon Castle, Dumfries (Scotland), 15th century

Fig. 197: Separate alcove with seating
Comlongon Castle, Dumfries (Scotland), 15th century

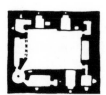

Fig. 198: Comlongon Castle

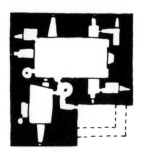

Fig. 199: Cessford Castle

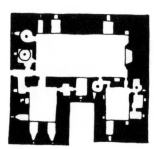

Fig. 200: Borthwick Castle

Fig. 201: Dundas Castle

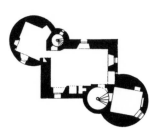

Fig. 201: Claypott Castle

compartments. More obviously separate are the rooms concealed completely within the walls, which are reached through small openings leading off the main room or, indeed, only via alcoves. These rooms adhere to the principle of compartmentation because the direct connection with the main room is clearly interrupted by the intervening walls.

Openings

Admitting light into the central hall enclosed on all sides imposes different conditions on the design and form of the light-admitting alcoves. Basically, we distinguish between two types of opening:

Openings with splayed reveals

Through reflection the narrow, deep openings with their splayed reveals distribute an even, diffuse light throughout the interior. They are not confined to a certain horizon and can therefore respond better to functional conditions. Ingenious location of these windows in the corners or end walls of the hall can promote strong sidelighting of the longitudinal wall, which thus becomes a bright "light wall" – as at Borthwick Castle. The orientation of the main room is thus underpinned not only by its geometry but also by the play of light and dark wall surfaces. With just a few, precisely located openings the lower part of the enclosed main room is illuminated surprisingly effectively, while the upper part forms a dark ceiling.

Alcoves

The daylighting effects are totally different in the deep seating alcoves. These alcoves tend to adhere primarily to the right-angled geometry of the plan disposition but prevent optimum scattering of the incoming daylight. They create high-contrast, exciting "inner" hall facades with light and shade, but above all with visual relationships with the surroundings so that the hall – contrary to the gloomy external expression – appears extraordinarily expansive, bright and homely. That is the real surprise that we never expected before studying the plans!

Vertical penetration and organisation

It is remarkable that the storey-by-storey plan concept is organised without corridors, apart from a few exceptions. The numerous spiral stairs can be regarded as a vertical corridor system (as Hermann Muthesius describes in his book *Das Englische Haus*), which, as a rule, are positioned in the corners of the external wall or at the junctions with later extensions. The characteristic aspect of this "corridor system" is that no staircase links all storeys. Generally, spiral stairs connect rooms over several storeys only in the case of unavoidable, functional requirements. The result is a complex three-dimensional labyrinth.

Confusion and error is the key to the vital defence of the tower house once an enemy has gained access. Narrow spiral stairs can be readily defended by switching the position of and direction of rotation of the flights, the "eye of the needle" effect of narrow entrances and exits. Different connections between the floors at different places aggravate this loss of orientation. No additional measures are needed to create this confusion; it is integral to the access concept of the tower house. And the concealed escape routes should not be underestimated, allowing the unexpected and sudden retreat of the defenders in many ways.

Organisation

Access to the early tower houses was not at ground level like the later examples but rather via an external wooden stair or bridge at the side, which led directly onto the first floor. The typical vertical arrangement with one main room per floor meant that the ground floor contained the storage rooms and prison (= dungeon, later donjon), the first floor the main, prestigious hall for daily activities, the second floor the private rooms of the Lord, the third floor the rooms for the family and their servants, and above that the battlements.

Plan layout

The unique plan arrangements (rectangular, L-, C-, H- or Z-types) are essentially based on the progress in means of defence together with the growing needs for additional living areas on the individual floors. Starting with a basic form (a simple rectangle), tower houses were always extended according to the same pattern: the existing enclosing walls were extended so that a new, smaller "main room" with similar features was enclosed. It was usually the most important ancillary rooms that were transferred from the confines of the walls into this new space. However, the majority of tower houses did not obtain their plan layouts through changes to existing buildings; most were demolished and rebuilt over existing fragments according to the latest findings of contemporary ideas on defence and the current living and prestige needs of the owners.

Metamorphoses

As the defensive nature of the tower house diminished and the demands for a prestigious appearance grew, so the hitherto concealed alcoves and chambers within the outer walls started to become protrusions on the facade (as though they had become, so to speak, solid bodies trying to burst through the outermost skin and thus forcing this outwards). The originally massive, tranquil appearance of the fortified house became a sculpted body with projections. On the facade and in cross-section it can be seen that these projections preferably begin above the topmost floor with, in each case, coincident main rooms. A number

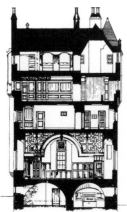

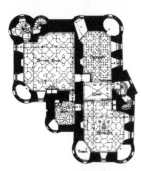

Fig. 203: From top to bottom: facade, section, 4th floor plan, 1st floor plan
Craigievar Castle, Aberdeen (Scotland), 17th century

of corner turrets and rooftop structures distinguish the silhouette of the building, which has become a three-dimensional crown. From now on the picturesque, romantic architecture of the later tower houses primarily followed the most diverse, fashion-oriented currents of each age and omitted any superfluous defensive measures.

Likewise, the internal organisation, as at Craigievar Castle, changed to a cluster-type conglomerate of spaces. The main rooms were now no longer directly one above the other but instead faced in different directions on the upper floors and were further subdivided and oriented according to specific needs. Larger ancillary rooms can be recognised on the facades as additional divisions of the L-shaped body of the tower. This vertical succession of spaces can be reached from the main rooms or may connect these directly. The multi-layer access and interconnection principle of the interior layout, still organised storey by storey, continues via various stairs and their horizontal and vertical branching throughout the building. The originally distinct hierarchy of main and ancillary rooms had become compressed into a complex "room conglomerate".

Morphological deductions

Thick walls enclose an elongated, rectangular space. The thickness of the walls and their geometry are not really identifiable, neither internally nor externally. However, the interior space is defined with geometric precision by the four corners.

It is only the openings in the walls that create a spatial reference with the outside world. At the same time, the enclosing walls are divided into individual L-shaped fragments. Their thickness becomes apparent through the depth of the reveals to the openings. As soon as the openings are positioned in the enclosing surfaces, the original geometry of the space becomes clearly recognisable.

However, if the openings are positioned at the internal corners and more or less match the height of the storey, so that some enclosing surfaces are extended by the reveals, the interior space begins to "drain away" and lose its distinct geometry. The fragments of wall will tend to become linear bodies; they lose their capacity to "enclose" the space.

If, in addition, the fragments of wall contain chambers, this has, on the one hand, little influence on the spatial properties of the main room; but on the other hand, from an economic viewpoint, this is a clear gain in floor area, which depends on the maximum possible reduction in the wall mass and hence the loadbearing structure. However, the true content of the apparently solid walls can be seen only by looking directly into these chambers. If the geometry and extent of these chambers varies (to suit functional requirements, for example), their influence on the interior and exterior spaces remains small. Only when the thinning of the walls containing rooms becomes quite

Fig. 204: Schematic plan layouts
Enclosed space – Openings – Openings in the corners

Fig. 205: Schematic plan layouts
Individual chambers – Various room inclusions – Maximum use of wall thickness

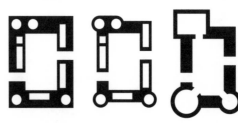

Fig. 206: Schematic plan layouts
"True" basic plan – Extended basic plan – Sculpted surfaces

extensive and these spaces start to "protrude" outwards do the various chambers become readily visible. In doing so, they create a sculpted surface through which the original angular basic shape is still recognisable.

If, however, the chambers enlarge at the corners and protrude beyond the confines of the wall to a much greater extent, we reach the point where the original basic shape is no longer recognisable. We arrive at a new composition which is determined by the large chambers within the walls and is hardly akin to the original basic shape. On the other hand, the geometry of the interior, the central hall, oddly enough remains unchanged, which underpins the validity of the hypothesis related here regarding the spatial growth of Scottish tower houses.

Serial expansion concept

It is unusual that, contrary to developments in England and on the European mainland, the vertical organisation of the tower houses continued to hold sway in Scotland for the "castles" of later times. Extra wings (called "jams") were added to promote horizontal expansion, but no longer in the form of additional rooms but by interlocked "tower houses". (We get this impression on the outside but in fact the interior layout of the wings employed simple principles of subdivision.) Glamis Castle is a good example of how the "L-type" nucleus was added in the 17th century to rise above the jams on both sides.

Fig. 207: Total complex, plan of 1st floor
Glamis Castle, Tayside (Scotland),
13th–17th century

Fig. 208: Total complex, plan of ground floor
Craigmillar Castle, Edinburgh (Scotland),
14th–16th century

Jams in the style of French palaces

Craigmillar Castle is a good example of another phenomenon which is not unusual in the history of tower houses with their surrounding complexes. The original tower house was of course incorporated into the sequence of spaces of the new complex. But in contrast to Glamis Castle the tower house was "ensnared". Only a horizontal section reveals the thick external walls which have been woven into the overall complex.

Adolf Loos and Scottish tower houses?

The plain expression and simple, cubic, vertical emphasis of the middle-class urban villas of Adolf Loos dating from the late 1920s awaken strong associations with Scottish tower houses. These urban villas are impressive on the one hand because of their elaborate space enclosures appropriately lined to suit their uses, and on the other because of the rich variety of spatially complex connections corresponding with classical notions of space hierarchies.

Tower houses are similar. Originally plain and unornamented on the outside, their interiors developed from functional to mazelike internal configurations with a rich hierarchy. In terms of interiors it is the most recent tower houses, e.g. Craigievar Castle, that are interesting in connection with Loos. Their spatial complexity and carefully detailed internal surfaces, especially the stucco to the vaulting over the main rooms and the wooden linings to the rooms protruding into the external walls, are comparable with the linings of diverse materials in the aforementioned urban villas.

Spatial plan
Adolf Loos used this term to conceive a horizontal and vertical interlacing of spaces. It is tempting to search for this strategy in the tower houses. However, in reality in tower houses the notion of the spatial plan is confined to the main room and its various alcoves plus the associated galleries, just the same.

Loos made a theme of the interdependency of variously sized and hence variously tall rooms. His argument was spatial economy, the need to compress them into a dense conglomerate with compact external dimensions. Precisely positioned openings link these spaces and define, through their size, the spatial and hierarchical coherence.

Despite the disparate organisation, we can detect a relationship between the tower house and a Loos villa. Both are devoid of corridors in the main spaces or storeys and both have several staircases which do not connect all storeys. In the tower house this is clearly explained by the need to confuse attackers, while in the Loos house it is the need to set the scene for the sequence of internal spaces. As in the tower house with its central, main room, the expansion of the main storey is legible in the Loos designs.

Fig. 210: Section, plan of 1st floor
Adolf Loos: Moller House, Vienna (A), 1928

Fig. 209: Part of model of main floor, undergraduate study, ETH Zurich, 2002
Adolf Loos: Moller House, Vienna (A), 1928

Fig. 211: From top to bottom: facade, inner hall, peripheral study alcoves
Louis I. Kahn: Phillips Exeter Library, Exeter (New Hampshire, USA), 1968–72

Louis I. Kahn and Scottish tower houses?

The Castellated and Domestic Architecture of Scotland, a work in five volumes by David MacGibbon and Thomas Ross, is regarded as the standard work of reference on Scottish castles. We can assume that Kahn knew at least the first volume of this work very well indeed because he often refers to Comlongon Castle, which is well documented in this publication.

Kahn's obvious fascination with the simple, lucid, almost ancient classification of a space enclosed by a defensive wall which itself contains chambers (as is the case with the early Scottish tower houses) can be seen in his work. It was probably not the mass itself as such but rather the conception of spatial inclusions in the walls, which surround a main space and allow the creation of differentiated spatial references, that awakened Kahn's interest. The simple but readily comprehensible hierarchy of a main space and several clearly ordered peripheral ancillary spaces characterise Kahn's work.

Phillips Exeter library

Two rings of spaces surround a multistorey hall in the axially symmetrically organised square plan form of the Phillips Exeter Library (1968–72). The inner ring spans four access and service cores marking the corners. The outer ring seems to surround this without any regard for the regularity of the small-format facade arrangement. Only at the corners of the building do the rings meet.

The spatial compression, from the hall linking the floors to the bookshelves on each storey to the peripheral two-storey reading and study zones, responds accurately to the specific requirements of the brief. It is only the plasticity of the study alcoves – furniture-like enclosures inserted between the window reveals – that reinforce the periphery of the building.

The classification of main and, apparently, randomly created ancillary rooms in the defensive walls of tower houses is interpreted by Khan in the form of a strict hierarchy of concentrically arranged and differently compacted layers of spaces.

Outside, the building appears as a "body", with thick brick walls whose piers taper towards the top. The resulting openings with their different heights divide the building up according to the classic rules of architecture into pedestal, column, and entablature. The chamfered corners of the building reveal the (sometimes) open internal spaces behind.

Although this measure does prevent the perception of continuity over the entire building, it enables the depth of the outer ring to be seen at the corners. The apparently compact mass of the building is softened by the fact that the outer walls do not meet at the corners. And this allows the richness of the interior to be made legible on the surface.

Comparisons with current housebuilding: Japan
Small house forms in Japan

In the heavily populated districts of Japanese conurbations, which owing to the ever-present risk of earthquakes have spread out like carpets around their city centres, unique small-format houses are erected in the interstices. The enormous economic pressure and the resulting consequences for (exploitation of) the building

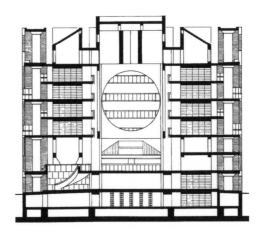

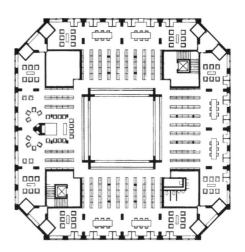

Fig. 212: Section, plan of 3rd floor
Louis I. Kahn: Phillips Exeter Library, Exeter (New Hampshire, USA), 1968–72

regulations lead to plan sizes that cover virtually the full extent of the small plots of land. This calls for economic forms of construction, but far more critical is the need for a type of construction that can respond to these very confined spatial relationships. What these "mini-houses" appear to have in common is that their spatial response is basically introverted because externally there is hardly any space for the development of facades (Italian: faccia = face). The reasons for this can be found in the compact

Fig. 213: Hermetically sealed object with shafts apparently driven into the mass
Jun Tamaki: Hakama House, Kyoto (J), 1998

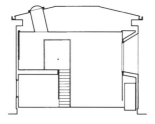

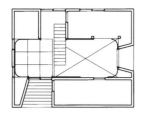

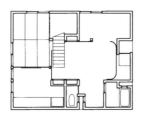

Fig. 214: Section, plans of ground and upper floors
Jun Tamaki: Hakama House, Kyoto (J), 1998

development structure with minimum clearances between buildings, or simply the placing of buildings in the gaps between existing buildings, which itself leaves little space for facades.

Hakama House

Jun Tamaki's Hakama House (1998) in Uji-shi, Kyoto, stands on a small road between an older house and the entrance to a plot of land further back from the road. Outwardly, the building responds autistically to its immediate surroundings. It is a monolithic object topped by a flat roof which is separated from the walls by a wide joint. The seemingly monolithic design of the building is reinforced by the few hopper-shaped openings driven deep into the apparent mass. Some of them are just on the limit of threatening to produce a visual weakening of the building. Even though the house does have a number of flush-fitted openings, their size and position turns them into minor players compared with the distinctive hoppers, and they do not relieve the monolithic effect. The principle of a central, two-storey hall and a surrounding ring of ancillary rooms is therefore sensible here because the reference to the outside world in this location is not really significant. Much more important is the "captured" main room, its lighting and its references to the neighbouring rooms.

One-room house?

The central hall renders possible access without corridors, but also acts as a circulation area and a habitable room. From here, the upper floor is reached via the single staircase. This conflict is handled by providing curtains to close off the main room or leave it open to the alcoves behind. This enables the occupants to choose between the almost sacred "one room" with the curtains closed and the more far-reaching aspect that continues to the periphery and makes the interior appear larger than it really is.

Twin tower houses

In her diploma thesis of 1999 Catherine Gay grappled with the notion of discrete, compact building using the high-rise structures at Kreuzplatz in Zurich as an example. There are two massive high-rise buildings among the trees of Arterpark, which stretches to the edge of the road at Kreuzplatz. The two structures are positioned in such a way that they divide up the park at this point and form an entrance from Kreuzplatz to the actual park itself. Their heavyweight appearance is due to the choice of solid sandstone facing masonry with its regular perforations; the set-back in the facade at the top reinforces the impression of height. The interior remains concealed behind this rigid lattice facade and is not revealed until we enter one of the towers.

Loadbearing structure versus spatial structure

The loadbearing structure of each tower is in the form of a giant shaft within the outline of the tower itself ("tube-in-tube" principle), which results in a ring of interior spaces with different depths surrounding hall-type spaces. Solid concrete floors separate the rings horizontally storey by storey, while the hall in the central shaft of the tower can be divided at various heights with floors of lighter

Fig. 215: Extent of main room with curtains drawn back
Jun Tamaki: Hakama House, Kyoto (J), 1998

Fig. 216: Main room bounded by drawn curtains
Jun Tamaki: Hakama House, Kyoto (J), 1998

Fig. 217: Catherine Gay: Towers at Kreuzplatz,
Zurich
(diploma thesis, ETH Zurich), 1999

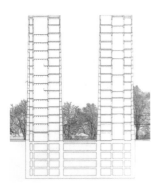

Fig. 218: Section through towers
Catherine Gay: Towers at Kreuzplatz, Zurich
(diploma thesis, ETH Zurich), 1999

Fig. 219: Inner hall lit from three sides
Catherine Gay: Towers at Kreuzplatz, Zurich
(diploma thesis, ETH Zurich), 1999

construction. The disposition of the plan layout more or less coincides with the loadbearing structure and can be modified by subdividing the ring spaces and changing the height of the central hall.

Use options

The standard floors have a "traditional" layout comprising two apartments, with the rooms, loggias, kitchens, and bathrooms, plus the continuous lift and stair shafts, grouped around the central halls. Owing to their size, the halls are primarily habitable rooms, a fact that is illustrated by the solid enclosing masonry piers and the floor of the hall placed at a slightly lower level. In contrast to the textile curtains of the Hakama House by Jun Tamaki, the space-defining boundaries are solid here and conspicuous by their immovableness. The hierarchy is created not only by location and size but also by the properties of the boundary elements.

The principle of the vertical stacking of twin-wall rings around enclosed halls and non-loadbearing partitions enables a multitude of uses. For example, besides apartments, these high-rise blocks could accommodate offices, restaurants or nurseries without having to make any major changes to the loadbearing structure. The individual utilisation units can extend not only horizontally across the floors but also vertically through the halls, which helps to reinforce the spatial associations beyond a single storey.

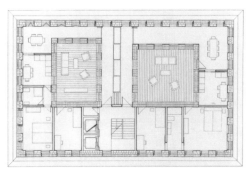

Fig. 220: Plan of standard floor
Catherine Gay: Towers at Kreuzplatz, Zurich
(diploma thesis, ETH Zurich), 1999

Provision of services during planning work

Project phase	Services	Fee in % to SIA 102	Drawings sent to...	Which drawings?	Scale(s)	Accuracy of costs		Method of calculating costs	Dates, key parameters
Strategic planning	Formulation of needs, solution strategies	Reimbursement of costs							
Preliminary study	Definition of project, feasibility study, selection procedure	Reimbursement of costs	Client	Location drawings, block plans	1:10,000 1:5,000 1:2,000				
Draft project	Survey of potential options and rough estimate of costs	3%	Client, authorities, some consultants	Site plans, cadastral surveys, plans, sections, elevations	1:1,000 1:500 1:200	Rough estimate	±25%	Building volume (m³), components	Preliminary clarification, preliminary decisions
	Draft project and estimate of costs	6%–9%				Estimate	±20%	Building volume (m³), components	
Building project	Building project	13%	Client, authorities, consultants, specialists	Site plans, cadastral surveys, plans, sections, elevations	1:1,000 1:500 1:100				
	Detailed studies	4%		Detailed sections, detailed plans, detailed elevations	1:20 1:5 1:1				
	Estimate of costs	4%–21%				Estimate	±10%	Components, company prices	
Approval procedure	Approval procedures	2.5%	Client, authorities	Site plans, cadastral surveys, plans, sections, elevations	1:1,000 1:500 1:100				Application for building
Tenders	Tender drawings (provisional working drawings)	10%	Client, consultants, contractor(s)	Plans, sections, elevations, earthworks, drainage	1:50				Approval for building
	Issuing and comparing tenders, award of contract(s)	8%–18%				Tender for work required			
Detailed design	Working drawings	15%	Client, contractor(s)	Publication and detailed drawings, plans, sections, elevations, earthworks, drainage, details of kitchens and sanitary facilities	1:50 1:20 1:5 1:1				
	Contracts with manufacturers	1%–16%				Preparation of contract principles			Release for construction
Construction	Design supervision	6%							Start on site
	Site supervision and cost control	23%–29%				Cost control by means of estimate(s)			
Completion	Commissioning	1%							
	As-built documentation	1%	Client, authorities	As-built drawings, drawings for publication	1:500, 1:200, 1:100 as required				
	Management of guarantee work	1.5%							
	Final invoice	1%–4.5%				Final invoice			
Management	Operation, maintenance	Reimbursement of costs							

Notes

The services listed here are taken from *Swiss standard SIA 102*, 2003 edition
(Regulations Governing Architects' Services and Fees). In Germany the *HOAI*
(Scale of Fees for Architects and Engineers, www.hoai.de) applies similarly.

The sequence of building operations

Preliminary work	BKP 1	–Soil surveys	
		–Clearance, preparation of terrain	
		–Setting up common site facilities	
		–Earthworks	
Structural shell 1	BKP 2	–Duties of site manager	
		scaffolding	
		drainage to buildings	
		concrete, reinforced concrete work	
		masonry work	
		–Erection of concrete/steel/timber structures	
Structural shell 2	BKP 2	–Windows, external doors	
		–Flashings	
		–Roofing work	
		–Special seals and insulation	
		–Rendering	
		–Treatment of external surfaces	
		–Sunshades, external finishing work	
Media/infrastructure	BKP 2	–Electrical installations	
		–Heating, ventilation, air conditioning	
		–Sanitary facilities	
		–Transport installations (lifts)	
Fitting-out 1	BKP 2	–Plastering	
		–Metalwork	
		–Joinery	
Fitting-out 2	BKP 2	–Floor finishes	
		–Wall finishes	
		–Ceilings	
		–Treatment of internal surfaces	
		–Drying out	
		–Cleaning	
External works	BKP 4	–Landscaping	
		–Structural and fitting-out works	
		drainage to external facilities	
		retaining walls	
		roads and hardstandings	
		–Gardens	
		planting	
		fences	
		equipment, appliances	

Notes
The above extract shows the stages of work more or less corresponding to the sequence on the building site. Of course, the individual steps do not run strictly chronologically but are often carried out simultaneously. Several operations often have to be performed at different times in order to complete certain stages of the work.

This list corresponds to the breakdown into various operations according to the Building Costs Plan (BKP) of the Swiss Central Office for Building Rationalisation (CRB).

The following standards apply similarly:
in Germany DIN 276 "Building costs"
in Austria ÖNORM B 1801-1 "Building costs – cost breakdown".

Compartmentation

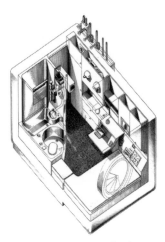

Fig. 221: Axonometric cut-away view of one capsule
Kisho Kurokawa: Nakagin Capsule Tower, Tokyo (J), 1972

Kisho Kurokawa: Nakagin Capsule Tower

The Capsule Tower by Kisho Kurokawa is an assembly of 144 identical units stacked around two stair towers. The prefabricated units correspond to the dimensions of standard freight containers and contain a bathroom, kitchenette and bed.

The arrangement of the building is an expression of the design and construction principles, which are essentially congruent. The external form is not rudimentary but rather a product – as a variation on the stacking principle; the different orientation of the units is also noticeable.

Fig. 224: External view; the taller staircase tower is clearly visible.
Kisho Kurokawa: Nakagin Capsule Tower, Tokyo (J), 1972

Fig. 222: Plan of 1st floor, on the right the terrace above the studio
Rob Mallet-Stevens: Martel Villa, Paris (F), 1926–27

Fig. 223: External view with studio in foreground and exposed staircase core
Rob Mallet-Stevens: Martel Villa, Paris (F), 1926–27

Rob Mallet-Stevens: Martel Villa

The additive and the divisive forms of interior design can be seen in this building. The plan is based on a rectangle with a central circular stair tower linking all floors. The rooms are attached to this central spine like individual compartments, the number of which diminishes as we go higher up the building, and this leads to the creation of rooftop terraces.

The unifying render finish, which deliberately suppresses the construction joints, and the positioning of the openings are the manifestation of a sculptural approach to the design of the envelope. Accordingly, not only is the overall form a product of the internal spatial composition; it has an effect on this as well.

Box frame construction

Fig. 225: Shear walls form the party walls between the maisonettes (left: main floor; right: upper floor)
Atelier 5: Flamatt 1 residential development, Bern (CH), 1957–58

Fig. 227: The south facade reflects the shear wall structure.
Atelier 5: Flamatt 1 residential development, Bern (CH), 1957–58

Atelier 5: Flamatt 1 residential development

The apartment block shown here, designed by the Atelier 5 team, illustrates a typical use of parallel shear walls (or cross walls). They separate the individual apartments and on the standard floor determine the dimensions of the living room. The south facade reflects this loadbearing structure, which limits the openings on all sides (structural opening). The inclusion of loggias further emphasises the principle of the box frame construction.

The shear walls and the floors form the primary structure and are built of in situ concrete, while the partitions within the apartments consist of storey-high, precast concrete elements.

El-Azhar Mosque in Cairo

The prayer halls of the Islamic world are the earliest examples of large open-plan interior spaces. They are based on an orthogonal column grid square – and hence unidirectional – in the case of the El-Azhar Mosque.

Nevertheless, the linear arches do lend the interior a certain directional quality which, however, is in turn weakened again by the transverse beams (for lateral stability), which seem to introduce an intermediate level. In terms of the loadbearing structure this is a classical box frame with parallel longitudinal walls and floor bays spanning the space below. However, the shear walls have been dissolved to the barest essential as columns and arches thus giving the impression of a wide open space.

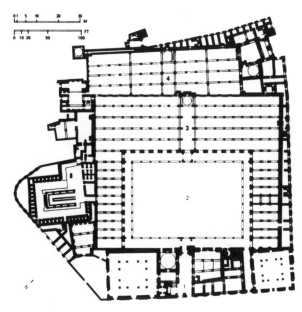

Fig. 226: On plan the walls resolved into arches are the dominant feature...
El-Azhar Mosque, Cairo (Egypt), c. 970

Fig. 228: ...while the prayer hall appears to be less directional owing to the transverse beams.
El-Azhar Mosque, Cairo (Egypt), c. 970

Frame construction

Fig. 229: The steel structure is a visible form criterion ("lattice structure").
Craig Ellwood: Smith House, Los Angeles (USA), 1957–58

Fig. 231: Steel frame with beams at the same level, floor bays as subsystem
Fritz Haller: canton school, Baden (CH), 1962–64

Craig Ellwood: Smith House

This private house is based on a steel frame without any hierarchy in the structural assembly. Although the columns and beams are of different sizes, they appear to be of equal value. Only the diagonal bracing is quite obviously smaller.

A comparatively lightweight construction without expensive earthworks and foundations has been achieved as the steel frame evens out the topographical situation. Horizontal and vertical infill panels are fitted between the modular loadbearing structural members to form the individual rooms.

Fritz Haller: canton school, Baden

A square column grid forms the starting point for this steel frame designed by Fritz Haller, which develops identically in both directions on plan. As the photograph shows, the columns are not erected storey by storey but are instead continuous over several storeys. The horizontal beams are seated on cleats on the columns before being bolted into place.

The floor bays are formed by a subsystem spanning between and at the same level as the beams. The lattice floor members save weight and also enable easier horizontal routing of services (heating, waste etc.).

Artaria & Schmidt: Schaeffer House

During construction, a clear distinction between primary and secondary loadbearing structures could be seen in the steel frame in this example. There are the longitudinal direction yokelike frames, consisting of two circular columns joined by an I-beam; steel angles as erection aids join the frames in the sense of a secondary loadbearing structure.

However, the form of construction cannot be deduced from the finished building with its enclosing rendered masonry. The structural steelwork is a means to an end and may well have been used purely to facilitate rapid construction.

Fig. 230: The primary loadbearing structure is a horizontal and vertical succession of separate yokes.
Artaria & Schmidt: Schaeffer House, Riehen (CH), 1927–28

Fig. 232: All traces of the structure are concealed behind masonry panels and render.
Artaria & Schmidt: Schaeffer House, Riehen (CH), 1927–28

Column-and-slab systems

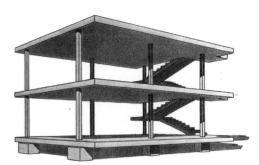

Fig. 233: Loadbearing structure in concrete, with cantilevering floor slabs and bracing provided by the staircase
Le Corbusier: Dom-Ino project, 1914

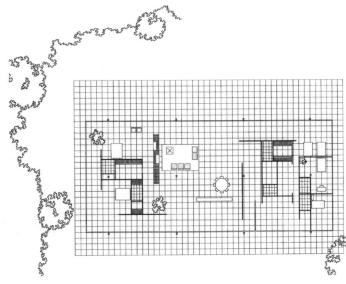

Fig. 234: Transparent, "flying" living room at the front stabilised by compartment-type bedrooms at the rear
Lina Bo Bardi: Casa de Vidro, São Paulo (BR), 1951

Fig. 235: Fluid space continuum, the fusion of interior and exterior
Ludwig Mies van der Rohe: Caine House project, 1950

Le Corbusier: Dom-Ino project

Le Corbusier took a Hennebique-type frame, in which the in situ concrete columns are placed at the very edges of the concrete floors, and moved the columns back from the edges. Firstly, this resulted in a shortening of the span (and as a result a reduction in the depth of the slab) and, secondly, it enabled openings to be positioned independently of the loadbearing structure. The ribbon windows advocated by Le Corbusier later, or indeed the curtain wall (*façade libre*), is closely linked with this form of construction.

In line with Le Corbusier's proposal for reconstruction after the war in Flanders, relieving the facade of its loadbearing function enables low-quality materials with poor loadbearing characteristics (e.g. debris from destroyed buildings) to be used.

Lina Bo Bardi: Casa de Vidro

This, the architect's own house, is situated on the side of a hill. It unites the column-and-slab system and the compartmentation approach. Supported on circular columns, the expressively cantilevering living room is formed by two slabs, with the glazing of the facade spanning these like a skin and conveying an image of maximum lightness.

The necessary stability is provided by the bedrooms at the back, which employ the compartmentation principle. They are arranged in two rows with the garden between. The open ground floor forms a forecourt to the garage and provides access to the living room.

Ludwig Mies van der Rohe: Caine House project

The definition of space in this design for a bungalow makes use of non-loadbearing wall plates arranged at random within the column grid. The way in which the walls relate to each other enables the creation of clearly defined compartments but also fluid, interconnected spaces. Depending on the occupant's position, he or she can seem to be in two or even three rooms at the same time!

In the project shown here there is a certain compaction on the right-hand side, with some of the rooms for domestic staff and children directly adjacent to the facade. However, the facade remains uncluttered over the remaining floor area.

The fully glazed column-and-slab system was proposed here in order to achieve the illusion of maximum possible fusion between interior and exterior.

Single-storey shed forms

Fig. 236: MAXI steel building system, (above) before adding the cladding, (right) with associated facade system
Fritz Haller: USM plant, Bühl (D), 1983–87

Fig. 237: Modular building system

Fritz Haller: USM plant, Bühl

The MAXI modular structural steelwork system devised by Fritz Haller, as used for the USM plant, includes facade and roof elements as well as the loadbearing structure.

The maximum column grid is 14.40 m for a two-way span arrangement or 9.60 x 19.20 m for a one-way span. Not unlike Jean Prouvé's "Palais des Expositions", the floor also consists of lattice beams but in this case is not an independent system. The floor is made up of main beams, which span from column to column, and intermediate beams at the same level at right-angles to these (beam grid).

The non-loadbearing facade is connected to a secondary framework on a 2.40 m grid and conceals the primary loadbearing structure. Fritz Haller has also designed MIDI and MINI modular systems with correspondingly reduced spans.

Salt warehouse

The single-storey shed shown here illustrates the use of glued laminated timber (glulam) members and the aspect of partial prefabrication.

Basically, the bonding of timber boards to form beams evens out the natural irregularities (inhomogeneity) of the wood but also enables to achieve lengths far beyond those that trees can achieve naturally. The shape of the members used for this salt warehouse match the flow of the forces and form a three-pin arch.

Pairs of parallel members, together with wind and stability bracing, are assembled to form a half-shell, which is then erected against another half-shell (providing mutual support). The bracing and purlins between the arches are added on site and, in the final building, disguise the form of erection.

Jean Prouvé: Palais des Expositions

With a column grid of 36 m the "Palais des Expositions" extends over a floor area of 23 800 m². The primary structure was conceived as a platform with rigid connections between the columns and the 1.5 m-deep steel beams.

The columns themselves are each made up of five steel tubes which fan out from a common base and thus provide the necessary bracing effect. Resembling a table-top, the space frame, constructed of intersecting lattice beams, sits like a secondary structure on the beams. The space frame was assembled in sections on the ground before being lifted into position and fixed.

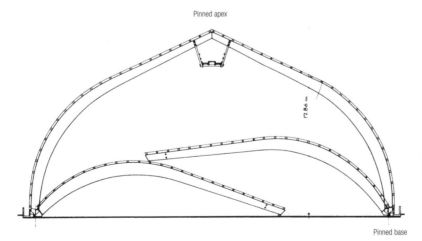

Pinned apex

Pinned base

Fig. 238: Beams as primary and stressed skin as secondary loadbearing structure
Salt warehouse

Fig. 239: Erection of prefabricated half-shells
Salt warehouse

Prefabrication
System building

Alois Diethelm

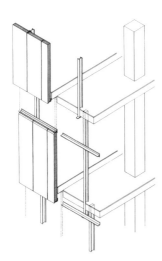

Fig. 240: Axonometric view: FCW warehouse
Durisol panels attached to secondary structure

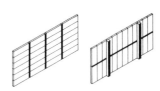

Fig. 241: Durisol system
Horizontal panels between loadbearing columns, or
vertical panels as curtain wall

Every form of construction is founded on a set of rules stemming from, initially, the properties and conditions of the materials employed and the requirements they have to meet. The specific properties of a building component are after all the product of a process of cognition drawn from both the empirical and analytical experiences gained. As a result, these experiences generate rules for their use or processing ("the rules of architecture"). Consequently, every form of construction involves building with a system.

Directives – standards
The impetus behind systemised building (a term which still has to be defined) is due to many reasons. However, it is always accompanied by the desire to achieve optimised working procedures, whether in the planning, production or processing. One example of this is the dimensional coordination of masonry units (see the essay "Types of construction"), which the architect can use as his or her dimensional basis, the brickwork manufacturer for producing larger batches, and the bricklayer for building practical bonds.

A minimal but relatively widely supported consensus on the dimensions of building components forms the basis for the modern building industry. So we can speak of systemised building because the quality and dimensions of individual components (primarily semi-finished goods, e.g. wood-based boards, metal sections, etc.) are defined by the relevant standards (SIA, DIN etc.).

Types of prefabrication
The difference between systemised building and system building is connected with the various degrees of prefabrication. This gradation leads to motives for the choice of a particular form of construction. Generally, prefabrication is associated with cost- and time-savings plus improved workmanship. However, only when looked at in terms of additional criteria is it possible to choose an optimum system for a specific project.

These days, small- to medium-sized construction projects can employ two fundamentally different prefabrication principles: a) dimension-related systems with kitlike modular coordination, and b) individual prefabrication with specified jointing principles (e.g. timber platform frame construction). Both systems have, in the meantime, become highly developed – thanks to large-scale production. But otherwise they could not be more different! Modular construction is designed to permit the exchange of individual elements (easy adaptation to suit changing or new conditions) and this generates the architecture. The modular coordination relieves the architect of the need to make sometimes arbitrary decisions derived from aesthetics, e.g. the size and position of a window, but at the same time could be regarded as limiting the degree of

design freedom. At best, the surface finishes of the elements can be selected independently.

It is essential to make a distinction between self-supporting systems and those that need a loadbearing frame, and to include the form of the elements (2D/3D). Apart from just a few exceptions, we shall consider only those systems that fulfil all the requirements (thermal and sound insulation, weather protection) in one and the same ready-to-use building component, be it a sandwich panel with a multi-ply construction or a monolithic – "synthetic" – construction.

Non-loadbearing elements – facades
Most of the systems that require an independent loadbearing structure are 2D elements for facades. They are popular because they permit the use of diverse loadbearing systems and interior layouts. However, a secondary framework for fixing the elements will be necessary, to suit the size of the elements and the position of the columns. The Durisol system, which enabled two different forms of construction with the same panels, was a good example in many ways; horizontal elements positioned either between or in front of the loadbearing columns at a spacing of 1.5 m; alternatively, vertical elements suspended from a secondary framework like a curtain wall. The success of the Durisol system (Durisol element: impregnated, cement-coated wood fibres formed the core for the factory-applied waterproof render outside and hard plaster inside) may well be due to the fact that it represented a rudimentary, easily understood system and, apart from the panels, was not restricted to particular

Fig. 242: Facade using Durisol system
Rudolf Kuhn and Heinz Ronner: FCW warehouse, Zurich (CH), 1954–55

products or manufacturers. It was thus comparable with a masonry unit, a brick. In contrast to the sheet metal panels widely used for single-storey sheds today, where the architectural input is mainly confined to the external cladding, Durisol facades bore a direct relationship with their tectonic properties. The design potential inherent in the Durisol system (compare Max Bill or Rudolf Kuhn with Heinz Ronner and others) can be attributed to its being a "soft" system (few parameters), a direct consequence of the small, directional format of the panels. The method of using customary products in an uncustomary way manifests itself here.

Self-supporting elements – room units

The 3D systems, where complete room units are suspended from or supported on a loadbearing frame, exhibit exactly the opposite behaviour. Adaptation to changing conditions or renewal from time to time (due to wear or fashion-driven obsolescence) require the replacement of the complete unit. Whereas in the 1960s the idea of exchanging units was primarily the outcome of a desire for social utopias (cf. Metabolism), today it is mainly production techniques. However, the aspect of large-scale production is usually confined to repetitions within the same structure; the universal application of such units is practically equal to zero. The situation is different with units that are not part of a primary structure but instead function autonomously. The best-known examples of these are prefabricated garages and standard (freight) containers used as temporary site accommodation.

In addition, the room unit exhibits the greatest degree of prefabrication. Like a caravan it is fully finished internally and is more or less ready to occupy after it has been transported to the building site. In the 20th century caravans, but also railway carriages, aircraft and ships, provided endless inspiration for various attempts trying to create compact, multifunctional units as the most compressed form of minimal shelter. Borne along on the euphoria of the plastics age, the late 1960s saw the appearance of diverse kitchens and bathrooms that could be inserted into the interior like furniture. Plastics enabled seamless transitions from, for example, a shower tray to the rising wall, and saved weight. However, the

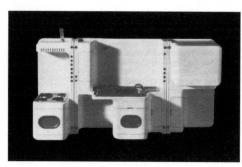

Fig. 243: Room unit interpreted as plastic furniture; the photo on the left shows the kitchen in the closed condition.
Masonari Umeda: mobile kitchen, 1968

limited radius of action of mobile bathrooms (pipes and cables!) and the fact that plastics can only be renewed by replacing them may explain why these room units never became very popular. Fully fitted sanitary compartments installed storey by storey – coupled with the progress on

site – have been in use for some time (primarily in hotels). These concrete units can be fitted with ceramic tiles and appliances in the conventional way to suit the client's specification. This is clearly an attempt to optimise quality of workmanship and costs. The aspect of prefabrication concerns neither the replaceability nor the aesthetic relevance.

Fig. 244: Container (e.g. as meeting room) supported on steel frame
Dollmann + Partner: office building, Fellbach (D), 1999

Loadbearing elements – floor, wall and roof

When we speak of individual prefabrication, meaning that form of construction where a building is broken down into transportable segments and subsequently reassembled in such a way as to disguise the reassembly, we initially think of timber platform frame construction. However, we also see this method being used for more heavyweight forms of construction, above all in Germany, where brick walls are supplied as storey-high elements. As the prefabrication does not alter the constructional conditions significantly, this form of construction does not create its own specific architecture. The situation was different with the heavyweight panel construction that was widespread in the Warsaw Pact countries. Those elements were supplied completely finished (paint, plaster or tiles) and lifted into position. The exposed joints – whose degree of sealing left much to be desired – reflect the internal layout (the elements span from floor to floor and from wall to wall). Openings are generally holes within a panel, with the omission of whole panels and their replacement with glass, e.g. for an entrance or staircase, being the exception.

Rudolf Schindler turned these "empty spaces", or rather introduced clearance between the panels, into a standard on his own home in Los Angeles (1922). Large expanses of glass at the corners alternate with slit-like windows fitted between uninsulated concrete elements. An answer to the current building performance requirements is

Fig. 245: Storey-high clay elements with loadbearing and insulating functions; (left) erection of loadbearing structure at ground floor level, (above) finished building
Tectône: hotel training school, Nivilliers (F), 1999

supplied by elements like the clay products of the French manufacturer Guiraud Frères in Toulouse. The storey-high elements, which are equally suitable for use as walls and floors, are available with and without core insulation. They may be used without render/plaster, e.g. at the hotel training school in Nivilliers, and in this way are a direct reflection of the tectonic qualities.

Loadbearing elements – room segments
Positioned halfway between our two-dimensional elements and room units are those elements that are indeed three-dimensional but need to be joined to create a complete interior space. These are a) repetitions of identical room segments, or b) the combination of identical but also different elements. The L-shaped elements represent a

Fig. 246: The concrete panels were cast on the ground (top) and afterwards lifted into position (bottom).
Rudolf Schindler: Schindler House, Los Angeles (USA), 1921–22

hybrid form where one leg forms the wall and the other the roof; as separate units these belong to category b), but assembled in pairs they are similar to category a).

The advantages are the simplified handling, helped by the smaller dimensions, and – as a direct result of this – the saving in weight. The space-forming principles extend from single L-shaped elements fixed in the ground (e.g. bus stops), to mutual support, to support on one side provided by, for example, in situ concrete walls or beams. The use of such L-shaped elements is interesting where the horizontal leg forms the roof – in single-storey structures or the topmost storey of a multistorey building. The structural and thermal insulation demands placed on both legs are then almost identical, so the surfaces can also be identical. And if they are identical, it is possible to achieve a seamless transition from roof to wall and hence overcome a number of weak points in the construction (change of material).

Fig. 247: Shell-type building envelope made from polyurethane
Addition of self-supporting room segments

Loadbearing elements – room units
The fundamental prerequisite for every room unit is that it must be self-supporting. When we speak of "loadbearing" room units we mean the ability to stack them. The absence of a primary, independent loadbearing structure means that the aspect of interchangeability no longer applies but the possibility of temporary usage takes on more prominence. As the units are joined like building blocks, they can also be dismantled without damage and re-erected elsewhere. Examples of this form of construction are building site accommodation and temporary school classrooms.

On the other hand, building with room units has also been used where neither replaceability nor temporary usage were relevant. In such cases cost-savings and a better quality of workmanship were the decisive factors. Whereas other methods permit the assembly of individual walls, floors, and roofs to form interior spaces of virtually any size, in this method the room unit is coupled with the transport options. At HABITAT 67 the size and weight of the units (19.75 x 5.35 x 3.65 m; 85 t) meant that prefabrication had to be carried out in situ.

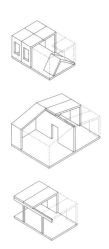

Fig. 248: Room segments: L-shaped elements
Formation of interior spaces by fitting segments together or to a supporting structure

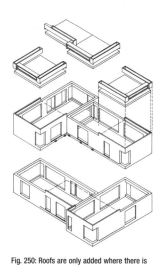

Fig. 250: Roofs are only added where there is no unit above.
Moshe Safdie: HABITAT 67, Montreal (CAN), 1966–67

Fig. 249: Plastic walls and roof
James Stirling: Olivetti training centre, Haslemere (UK), 1969

Stacking units so that they face different directions creates open terraces but also covered external spaces. And stacking has an effect not only on the external appearance; internally, maisonettes are often the result.

Outlook for the near future

Reduced to constructional aspects, prefabrication can be broken down into the categories "complementary systems" and "synthetic systems". The former are systems that consist of a multitude of complementary, partially autonomous layers, the latter those whose components are quasi-permanently connected and that may well result in a material that satisfies the "loadbearing–insulating–protecting"

Fig. 251: Stacking of concrete room units ("heavyweight prefabrication")
Moshe Safdie: HABITAT 67, Montreal (CAN), 1966–67

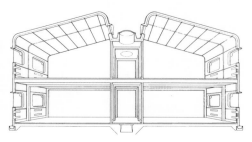

Fig. 252: Intermediate floor with loadbearing structure of linear members; roof and wall elements are loadbearing
James Stirling: Olivetti training centre, Haslemere (UK), 1969

requirements simultaneously. If a "complementary system" can be regarded as a mechanical assembly, then a "synthetic system" is something like a "contaminated agglomeration", which of course immediately raises the question of its recyclability. They are usually classed as special waste.

The objective of current materials technology research is therefore to guarantee reuse or at least recyclability. The first attempts in this direction involve trying to replace the plastics by suitably refined organic materials. In this case prefabrication is aiming to solve an ecological problem, a tendency whose significance for system building is set to grow.

Fig. 253: The units are erected as "structural shells" without any roof.
Moshe Safdie: HABITAT 67, Montreal (CAN), 1966–67

Sustainability
Fundamentals of architecture

Andrea Deplazes

Fig. 1: Hans Kollhoff: High-rise office block, Potsdamer Platz, Berlin (D), 1999

Fig. 2: Jean Nouvel: Arts and Congress Centre, Lucerne (CH), 1999

Fig. 3: Solid construction, stereotomy

Fig. 4: Filigree construction, tectonics

Two high-profile antipodes of architecture – whose positions on the subject of "sustainability and the self-image of architecture" could not be more different – met during the 3rd Architecture Symposium in Pontresina, albeit not in a direct debate. Hans Kollhoff from Berlin, whose office skyscraper in hard-fired brickwork on Berlin's Potsdamer Platz has already attracted considerable attention, and Jean Nouvel from Paris, who presented an illustrated discourse of epic proportions on the Lucerne Arts and Congress Centre, besides other projects. These two rivals represent a – there's no other way to describe it – diverging cread in terms of the relevance of architecture and its consistence today and in the future. Kollhoff will not desist from returning the fundamentals of architecture to solid construction (stereotomy) and filigree construction (tectonics) while calling for good workmanship, craftsmanship, and sustainable architecture. In his words: "The real question is which structures will still be around 75 years from now. Just look at the works of Jean Nouvel; in five years time they'll be ready for pulling down!" Jean Nouvel, on the other hand, describes such criteria as 19th-century thinking and retaliates with the observation that the building process has changed radically, that modern technologies of architecture demand a completely new concept and attitude, due to industrial production and assembly, for example: "Whoever builds with bricks and inserts little windows must be very limited upstairs!" So much for the initial statements marking out the lines of battle.

Of course we know that Hans Kollhoff tends to favour solid construction. After all, it is precisely the filigree constructions of Jean Nouvel and others that he so despises. The terms solid construction and filigree construction, and their architecture theory equivalents stereotomy and tectonics respectively, are the names of two categories of architecture which are fundamental in morphological and phenomenological terms. If we do not wish to approach critical comparisons in architecture from a historical–contemporary or stylistic angle, but rather, for example, consider the structural characteristics of different cultures, then we quickly discover some surprising coincidences.

The pisé/cob form of construction in China and modern European reinforced concrete construction, in terms of the production process ("mould" plus "casting") and the finished appearance of the wall ("pattern of the mould"), are identical. The only differences lie in the materials and the technology of the moulds. The concrete plays the role here of a further developed, processed, and therefore permanent "cob". Both contain solids such as gravel and sand in different grain sizes, plus dustlike fine constituents, silts or cement, which form a mineral "glue", when water is added. Whether simple wooden panels or the very latest large steel formwork systems have been used is reflected merely on the surface of the finished wall.

Similarly, we can compare the frame of a yurt from the Caucasus with a traditional timber-frame building in Switzerland and the three-dimensional lattice made from industrially manufactured steel sections forming the loadbearing structure of an American skyscraper. We discover that there are almost identical tectonic principles that enable us to assemble linear members to form a two- or three-dimensional framework. The only differences are in the spans and the stability of the linear members (because we are comparing debarked sticks, sawn squared timber and rolled steel I-sections), the detailed design of the connections between the members (which are either axial or eccentric, tension- or compression-resistant or both), and the means of fastening required. Many other examples could be added to these, whose differences would then have to be fleshed out and explained; but that is not the intention of this essay.

We can draw two initial conclusions from this: the two categories stereotomy and tectonics are certainly suitable for describing the fundamental structural and building process characteristics of architecture and – comparing location, time, and culture – demonstrating the foundations of the origin and evolution of architectural form. They are not, as Jean Nouvel obviously believes, dust-laden, outdated dogma from the history of architecture. Further, these comparisons show that where different cultures have had access to the same resources of usable materials, they have developed surprisingly similar forms of building more or less independently of each other.

In reality the development of building techniques and the interplay between science, research, and technology exert a great influence on the building process and, consequently, on the visible architectural result. However, this concerns only the optimisation and refinement of the production and processing methods, i.e. the workmanship or the industrial production process, and hence the product, the building materials, of course. These have always been subject to ongoing improvements in order to make them either more *durable* or *stronger*, which is not necessarily the same thing. In striving to attain climate and weather resistance, timber was swapped for stone, an organic for a mineral substance, which triggered a completely different type of building process. (Consider the "theory of metabolism" of Gottfried Semper, which is less concerned with building techniques themselves and more concerned with the consequences for architectural style at the time of the change from tectonics to stereotomy, a sort of transfer of timber construction to solid construction. I call this conflict "technological immanence versus cultural permanence".)

Fig. 5: Reversal process from solid to filigree construction from about 1800 onwards, provoked by industrial production

Fig. 6: Chicago
The steel frame to a "solid" high-rise block

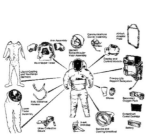

Fig. 7: Moon suit
Structure and components

So the trend was to favour solid construction whenever possible, which resulted in the increase in value of public architecture, in monumentalism, but also in the sense of a pragmatic approach to traditional timber construction, where the open panels between the timber members were filled with brickwork and the facades sometimes covered with a mineral lime render like the skin. And building materials became stronger in order to improve the *relationship between loadbearing capacity and material consumption*. The upshot of this was that the building elements became ever more refined and more slender, which first happened with the introduction of steel sections into architecture around 1800. It is not difficult to imagine what a fundamental upheaval this meant to the architect's self-conception; the sudden replacement of solid, real(!) structures with stone and brick walls by filigree lattices of steel sections with more or less permanent infill panels of masonry and stone cladding. That was what happened in Chicago with the invention and erection of the first high-rise buildings. And that marked the reversal from solid construction to filigree construction, provoked by industry.

Moreover, the technicians and engineers of structural steelwork faced a new problem, one which is still with us today: corrosion. The measures required to protect steel sections and panels against rust are immense and a considerable cost factor in the upkeep of a steel structure. And Jean Nouvel's Arts and Congress Centre in Lucerne has not been spared this problem; constant maintenance and renewal of the corrosion protection system is the only way to keep rust at bay.

This leads to a dilemma because, although building materials technology is always trying to achieve durable *and* strong materials, as yet no suitable synthetic, answer-to-everything building material has been found. We are saddled with similar problems in the corrosion that attacks reinforcement in reinforced concrete. But even indestructible stone, the incunabulum of stereotomy and the reason for the immortality of historical structures, is showing the signs of erosion caused by acid rain and aggressive urban atmospheres, particularly softer varieties such as sandstone, tuff, or limestone. So even stone is not our answer-to-everything building material, even if it is more durable than steel.

So in this sense Nouvel's plea in favour of modern technology as a generator of contemporary architecture and an answer to the acute demands of sustainability – of course, not as the only criterion – does not go far enough. This is because it is not a third category but rather an ingredient contained in both stereotomy and tectonics.

However, if we consider Nouvel's stance in the light of the fact that technology has tended to develop ever stronger and hence thinner building elements, which led in steps to our glazed filigree construction (from solid walls to slender brick or concrete shells, from multi-layer double windows to thin insulating glass membranes), then we might dare to suggest an adventurous hypothesis:

If the present glass technology and the associated curtain wall facade systems advance as rapidly as they have done in the past decade, ten years from now we shall surely reach the point at which we can no longer sublimate the substance. What this means is that we would then have facade films in the nano-molecule range, e.g. two film-like skins with aerogel between spanning ultralightweight carbon fibre structures.

If that seems unbelievable, take a quick look at the technology of space travel, which triggered the aforementioned rapid progress in glass technology. The space suits worn by the astronauts on the moon were multi-layer designs. Each layer had to guarantee a different protective function. The *moon suit* was therefore a *complementary system of monofunctional components* with the undesirable side-effect that it was heavy and restricted the astronauts' movements considerably. By contrast, the *Mars suit* will be a *synthetic system* comprising just a few, perhaps just one *complex* layer of high-tech textiles which will perform *multiple functions*. Now if that doesn't have an effect on our facades…

But how does that serve architecture?
Somehow, listening to Nouvel's lecture in Pontresina, I was reminded of the film "Déjà Vu", with its illuminated glass towers covered in writing and pictures, celebrating the play of multi-layer transparency and the reflective parallaxes in the aurora of the artificial light of the illuminated city – all brilliant projects in a virtuoso presentation. Take note! Nevertheless, what remains apart from the *"two-dimensional image"* of architecture? Where do we go from here – if not mere imitation – with this extreme reduction to "projection"? What is there left to invent that has not already been tried? Is the final "kick" really just the leap into the virtual world of fantastic, animated illusion? At any rate this road towards technological and architectural sublimation will only leave room for recurring variations! A horror vision for today's architects asking the question of what will really be relevant for their discipline in the next three to five years!

So if filigree construction seems to be heading towards a temporary dead-end, solid construction – following a sort of genetic programme of compensation – may be heading for unforeseen new honours simply because it promises a broad fallow field site for architectural discovery.

As an example let us assume that we overcome the already *outdated building performance standards of the 1970s*: from multi-leaf facade construction to monolithic-synthetic. Not because I wish to praise this technology (but a corresponding minimum expertise is important for architects), but because unforeseen possibilities for the *plastic modulation* of building mass and spatial inclusions, of massiveness and solid walls, of layering and opening are waiting for us; all extraordinarily rich and elementary architectural themes.

Again and again I am amazed by the spatially clear conception of the Scottish donjons (or keeps), with their rooms built within the three-metre-thick walls: a maximum defensive stance with minimum use of materials, true "clearings". This is not about massiveness and monumentality in a historical sense or style but rather about a source of architectural design strategies which, with the present conditions and signs, are worth sounding out. In comparison with this Le Corbusier's beacon for overcoming cell-like, plain interior spaces by using reinforced concrete columns and flat slabs, his famous sketches from *Five Points of Architecture*, are rather consumptive, although I must admit that his and also Mies van der Rohe's fascination with an open progression of spaces and glazed membranes (the term "facade" is questionable here) was undoubtedly new and justified. But that is already 70 years ago, which is why Nouvel's statement must inevitably be regarded as anachronistic.

Why should Kollhof's solid construction be antiquated and Nouvel's filigree construction contemporary?

Let's look at the essential features of both categories and their structural differences in order to discuss their suitability for and relationship with the issue of sustainability. Obviously, *the term "architectural structure"* has something to do with visions of durability, inertia, rigidity, changeability, and flexibility.

In solid construction, as the name suggests, solid, uniform walls are erected first and perforated (to create openings) immediately afterwards, or at least during the building process. This is the direct creation of interior space, whose arrangement has been establihed on the plans and sections, as well as the separation from the outside world. Solid construction appears to be erratic and permanent, or looked at another way, inflexible and rigid. This concept is obviously also carried over to the usability of a solid structure, and even to the assessment of its *usefulness*.

In filigree construction a lattice of slender linear members is erected first. This framework projects into the surrounding, natural space, but without us being able to distinguish between interior and exterior. As soon as it is erected it is covered with a skin or the open spaces between the linear members are filled in to create surfaces. This is the only way of distinguishing between interior and exterior, above and below. Which bay is closed off or not is not prejudiced by the lattice structure, which gives rise to the impression of increased flexibility, during utilisation as well.

Now, we know that every generation is accompanied by changes in values which characterise that generation and distinguish it from others. And by this I certainly do not mean fashions, which are extremely short-lived. In the indistinct mix of concurrent values that characterise our modern pluralism, the problem would seem to be the lack of a sufficiently adaptable concept for distinguishing and assessing vital criteria. There are also biological re-evaluations and changes, e.g. a couple moves into an apartment together, they have children, and those children grow up in that apartment, departing when they reach adulthood. It hardly needs to be explained that such changes exert a direct influence on the concept of and the desire for adaptable architecture which matches situations throughout life.

What this means for solid construction is that despite a defined internal layout, sufficient *flexibility of utilisation* must be incorporated. This is nothing other than designing interior spaces not for specific purposes but instead leaving them "open" to allow for various utilisation options. In this way not every change of function will lead to a conversion, plus the associated energy requirements and disposal problems. On the other hand, this concept risks introducing monotonous, stereotyped, uninteresting architecture, which in turn proves to be a permanent problem in urban, everyday situations. (Astoundingly, it was precisely the classicism of the 19th century that provided a credible solution to this dilemma.)

The situation is completely different with filigree construction in which the *flexibility of the interior spaces* appears to be, so to speak, inherent within the system. The problem of "adaptable" utilisation does not arise here (the specific internal layout requirements can be met completely individually), but instead the question of the provision of permanent and flexible components for dividing the interior space, for creating rooms, and their environmentally compatible disposal and/or re-use. It seems that we have to introduce a new scale of values at this point: the classification into short-, medium-, and long-term lives of building materials and building elements which are dependent not only on such factors as climate and weather, load-carrying capacity and stability, but to a large extent on the *utilisation demands*. This is also a welcome occasion, albeit perhaps late, to dispense with the rather didactic distinction between solid construction and filigree construction, or at least to blur the distinction to allow for the newly introduced criteria to apply to both categories. (Of course, solutions between these two poles have been attempted

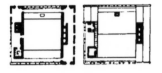

Fig. 8: Comlongon Castle,
Dumfries (Scotland), 15th century

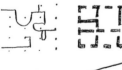

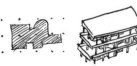

Fig. 9: Le Corbusier:
sketches from *Five Points of Architecture*

continually throughout the history of building. What is a Gothic cathedral if not a solid construction of most sublime filigree design? What are the temples of the ancients if not the most solid tectonics? But I don't want to discuss the considerably more complex architecture theory term "tectonics" here.)

So we are talking about the *half-life* of a building and the realisation that the basic fabric of a structure has a governing influence on the extent of the finishes and fittings. In solid construction the structural shell corresponds to the finished construction to a large extent (basically only the services, closures to openings and surface finishes are missing). But in filigree construction the permanent, structural proportion is, by contrast, so small that considerable work is required to subdivide the interior space and add the finishes and fittings. In the light of this it is worthwhile classifying building elements according to three priorities: the basic fabric of a structure, the structural shell, comprises the loadbearing structure and, possibly, the building envelope. This has a long lifetime (target: 100 years) and therefore cannot be changed, i.e. is permanent. This is called the *primary structure*. The interior subdivision, the interior finishes and fittings and the building services constitute the *secondary structure*. These have an average life-span of about 20 years, which is why they must be conceived as adaptable and variable. The *tertiary structure* is made up of equipment, technical apparatus and furnishings with short lifetimes (on average five to ten years). These items are easily changed and flexible. These three time-related conceptual stages are characterised by clear demarcations between the different structures and components. It must be possible to install, disassemble, or reassemble secondary and tertiary systems subsequently without disrupting the intact whole. The "seams" also guarantee recycling sorted according to material. I am not advocating, for example, a self-contained building system (I certainly do not wish to repeat the history of industrialised prefabrication through standardisation), but instead wish to demonstrate further strategies for architectural design, a long-term concept for the development of flexible design and form-finding criteria.

This brings me to the last point in my comparison of solid and filigree construction. It would seem that, led astray by the building insulation requirements of the 1970s, we have paid too little attention to the mass of the building. Today we know that the absorption of heat by solid components, particularly in well-insulated buildings with plenty of windows, has to be given special attention to avoid overheating of the interior in summer. There are two methods in low-energy design: the *storage concept* and

the *insulation concept*. Both approaches exploit the system-related properties of solid construction and filigree construction. The storage concept works, as you might expect, with the solid components that are needed anyway: floors, walls, etc. These form heat storage units in which, for example, passive solar energy entering through large south-facing windows can be stored (e.g. school in Vella).

Contrasting with this, in filigree construction, e.g. in a modern timber house (platform frame or panel construction, e.g. Bearth-Candinas private house, Sumvitg), the mass of the building is missing, such that windows facing south tend to lead to overheating. In this case it is much better to fill the spaces between the timber members with a thick layer of insulation and to distribute the windows over all facades in order to achieve an advantageous balance between heat gains and heat losses.

Finally, I shall draw a couple of conclusions which I hope will provide food for thought:

Sustainability is a basic ingredient of architecture. In the ideal case it does permanent good on various levels of human culture – in society, in urban planning, in economic and ecological matters, in the creation of living space (a juncture that is part of human life just as the snail's shell is part of the snail), in aspects of energy and materials audits, etc., i.e. *in the complex totality*. In this respect success or failure is not governed by having the highest level of technology: transparent thermal insulation, solar collectors, and mechanical ventilation do not automatically guarantee a conscious, sensible use of energy, particularly when we know that in the operating phase of a state-of-the-art building, i.e. after the energy-intensive production phase, the consumption of valuable electrical energy plays a far greater role in an environmental audit than the heat losses. These technical accomplishments, similar to the ingenious but expensive sorting concepts of recycling, stand at the end of a chain of decisions and processes whose success essentially depends on whether a *clear, architectural concept was present at the beginning*. In the light of this the issue of sustainability must be used as a chance to develop new design strategies within the discipline of "architecture", with which the debate surrounding the architectural relevance of purely formal observations, as are often to be found in schools and in practice, is transformed. The discussion is then:

"Which known and proven architectural principles can be renewed in conjunction with contemporary technology? What is the potential for new creations of architectural themes that can be derived from this? In all this, what is really relevant for the architects of today?"

Lecture on the occasion of the discourse *Novatlantis* for the 2000-Watt Society, ETH Zurich, November 2000

Fig. 10: Storage concept
Bearth & Deplazes: school complex, Vella (CH), 1997

Fig. 11: Insulation concept
Bearth & Deplazes: private house
(Bearth-Candinas), Sumvitg (CH), 1998

The problem of heat flow and vapour diffusion

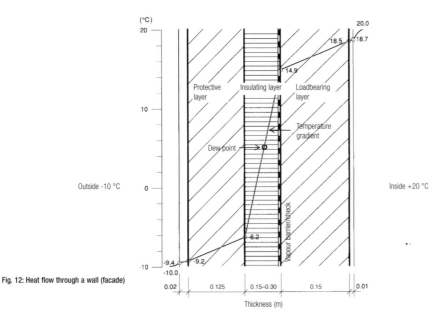

Fig. 12: Heat flow through a wall (facade)

The phenomenon of vapour diffusion
Cold air contains little water vapour
(outside – dry air),
hot air contains considerable water vapour
(inside – high humidity).

When hot air meets cold air or is quickly cooled, moisture in the air condensates as water (dew point). This can happen as a result of the temperature gradient within a layer of insulation ($\Delta t = 21.1$ °C) within the construction.
Moisture in the construction leads to damage to the building fabric:
- rotting (wood),
- mould growth,
- breakdown of the microstructure (materials),
- disruption to the loadbearing structure,
- damp thermal insulation is useless.

Condensation within the construction (interstitial condensation) must therefore be prevented, or all moisture must be allowed to dry out or escape.

Basic principles
A "vapour barrier/check" must be integrated in order to prevent condensation. Two rules must be observed in conjunction with this:
- The vapour barrier/check must be attached to the warm side (inside) prior to fixing the thermal insulation.
- The imperviousness (to vapour) of the materials must decrease from inside to outside. "Sealed loadbearing layer on the inside, vapour-permeable protective layer on the outside."

The following symbol is used on drawings to indicate the position of the vapour barrier/check:

Measures
Specific technical measures to prevent interstitial condensation, in the thermal insulation especially, are as follows:

Measure 1
Internal loadbearing layer made from a vapour-tight material, e.g. in situ concrete, glued panels (sandwich panels in timber construction), internal lining of sheet steel;

or

Measure 2
Vapour barrier membrane attached on the warm side directly in front of the thermal insulation;

or

Measure 3
Thermal insulation made from a vapour-tight insulating material, e.g. cellular glass;

or

Measure 4
Ventilated cavity between insulating layer and protective layer;
condition: good air circulation (thermal currents) in the cavity, width of cavity: 3–4 cm

Insulation concepts
Diagram of layers

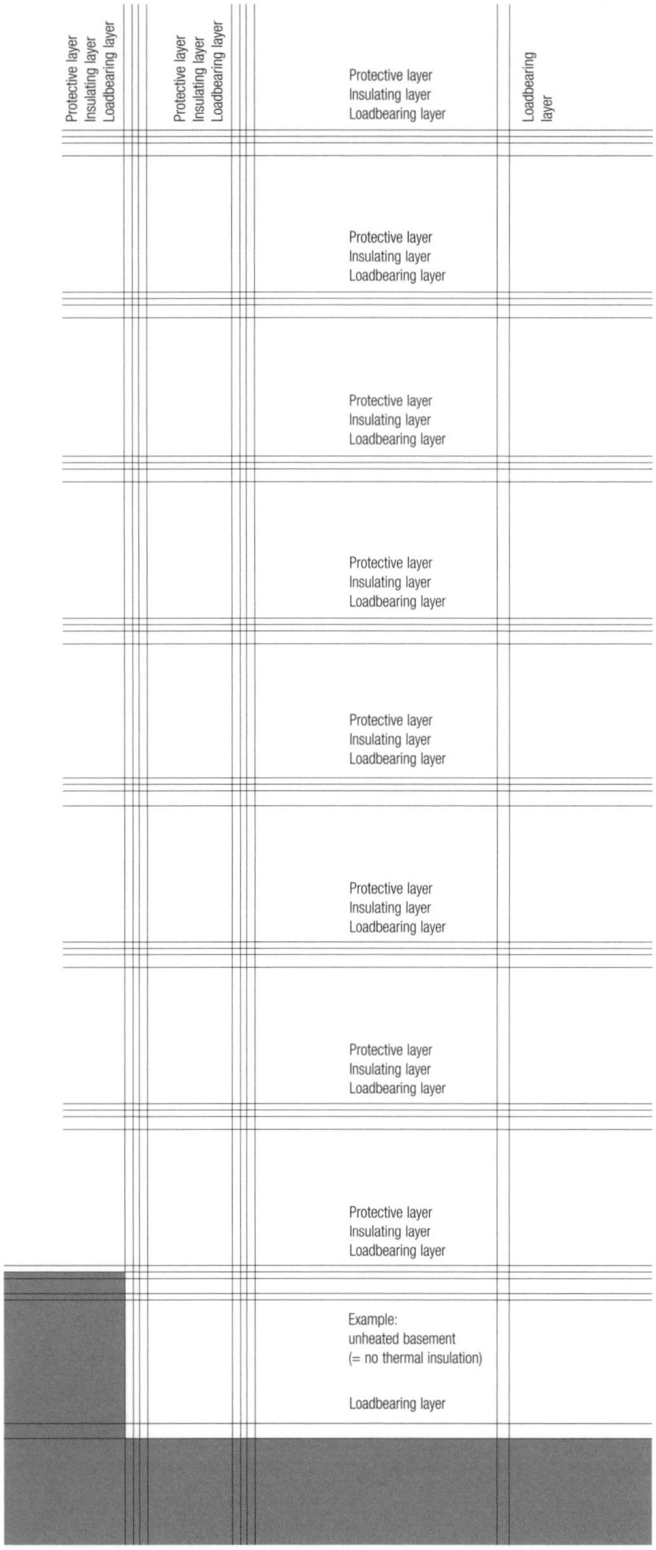

Protective layer
Insulating layer
Loadbearing layer

Protective layer
Insulating layer
Loadbearing layer

Protective layer
Insulating layer
Loadbearing layer

Loadbearing layer

Protective layer
Insulating layer
Loadbearing layer

Protective layer
Insulating layer
Loadbearing layer

Protective layer
Insulating layer
Loadbearing layer

Protective layer
Insulating layer
Loadbearing layer

Protective layer
Insulating layer
Loadbearing layer

Protective layer
Insulating layer
Loadbearing layer

Protective layer
Insulating layer
Loadbearing layer

Example:
unheated basement
(= no thermal insulation)

Loadbearing layer

Fig. 13: Diagram of layers (template)
External walls, floors and roofs are first drawn schematically with three layers. The dimensions of the individual layers are not defined here, they are determined by building performance, structural and architectural criteria.

In finalising a draft design the question of a suitable insulation concept arises in conjunction with the intended architectural appearance of the building. Insulation is not automatically "thermal insulation" but can also include sound insulation, for example. Thermal insulation between the interior and the exterior climates is used above all in the facades, in the roof and in the foundations, or rather the "floor over the basement". Sound insulation is employed primarily between the storeys (in the floors) or in the walls between sound compartments, e.g. between apartments, offices, etc. At the start the architect is faced with the choice of a thermal insulation system. In synthetic systems or compact systems individual elements provide several functions, e.g. insulating and load-carrying. Examples of this are single-leaf masonry walls and timber panel elements. By contrast, there are complementary systems split into a hierarchy of layers with the functions of loadbearing, insulating, and protecting. Starting with the position of the structural elements in relation to the insulation, complementary systems therefore require a further refinement of the insulation concept according to "loadbearing layer inside" or "loadbearing layer outside".

When choosing a complementary system the diagram of layers serves as a reference for the constructional analysis of a building. It is suitable for checking the continuity and coherence of the insulation concept and for localising problems. Loadbearing layer, insulating layer (thermal and sound insulation) and protective layer are shown schematically on plan and in section, with the rule being that the individual layers should not be interrupted. Openings (doors, windows), changes of direction (projections, rooftop terraces, etc.) and nodes (junctions) in the layers demand special attention. The insulation concept is elaborated when these key points are designed in detail, or – if particularly serious disadvantages are discovered – the concept is discarded.

Insulation concepts
Complementary systems – loadbearing layer inside

In this concept the loadbearing layer is exclusively on the "warm side", completely enclosed by the layer of insulation. The outermost layer serves, in the first place, to protect the insulation against mechanical damage and climatic effects and has no loadbearing function. Various materials may be used, from a thin layer of render to suspended stone slabs to facing brickwork or fair-face concrete. Accordingly, the thickness of the protective layer can vary considerably. Penetrations through the thermal insulation are confined to the fasteners for the insulating material and the external cladding or the ties attaching a self-supporting external leaf to the loadbearing layer. The ensuing thermal bridges are minimal.

Owing to the uninterrupted development of the insulation layer and the minimal thermal bridges, the "loadbearing layer inside" concept does not present any problems in terms of the building performance and is one of the most common facade arrangements. It is also frequently used in the refurbishment of uninsulated or poorly insulated buildings.

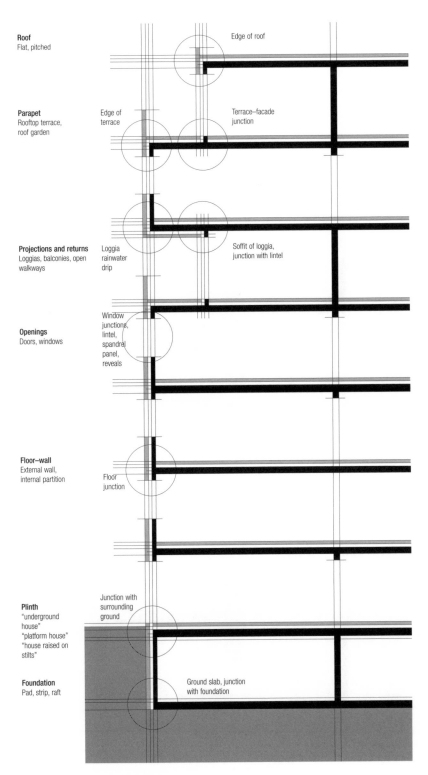

Roof
Flat, pitched — Edge of roof

Parapet
Rooftop terrace, roof garden — Edge of terrace — Terrace–facade junction

Projections and returns
Loggias, balconies, open walkways — Loggia rainwater drip — Soffit of loggia, junction with lintel

Openings
Doors, windows — Window junctions, lintel, spandrel panel, reveals

Floor–wall
External wall, internal partition — Floor junction

Plinth
"underground house" "platform house" "house raised on stilts" — Junction with surrounding ground

Foundation
Pad, strip, raft — Ground slab, junction with foundation

Fig. 14: Diagram of layers, loadbearing layer inside
The insulating layer continues uninterrupted as a "second leaf". The circles designate the transitions where the different layers are joined together; these key details must be resolved in detailed drawings.

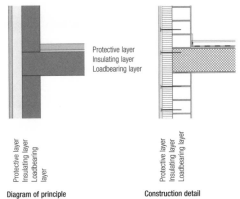

Protective layer / Insulating layer / Loadbearing layer

Diagram of principle — Construction detail

Fig. 15: Case study: rendered external insulation, wall–floor junction
The protective layer consists of render applied to the insulation. This form of construction results in a thin wall but the protective layer provides little defence against mechanical damage, which can lead to problems around the plinth in particular (damage to the insulation caused by feet, vehicles etc.).

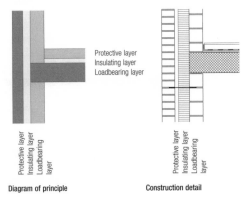

Protective layer / Insulating layer / Loadbearing layer

Diagram of principle — Construction detail

Fig. 16: Case study: double-leaf masonry, wall–floor junction
The protective layer is realised as a self-supporting masonry leaf, e.g. using clay or calcium silicate bricks, and partial tying back to the loadbearing layer is necessary owing to the instability of the non-loadbearing external leaf in the case of multistorey buildings. The use of double-leaf masonry results in the thickest wall construction.

341

Insulation concepts

Complementary systems – loadbearing layer outside

The "loadbearing layer outside" concept is used primarily on buildings with a fair-face concrete or facing masonry external facade, or those with a single interior space.

The insulation in this case is on the inside. The transfer of loads from floors to the external loadbearing structure in multistorey buildings means that the insulation layer is interrupted at every floor. To reduce the ensuing thermal bridges the soffits of the intermediate floors have to be insulated for a distance of at least one metre around the perimeter. Combined thermal and impact sound insulation can be incorporated on the top of the floor. Fair-face concrete structures can also make use of corrosion-resistant chromium steel anchors which enable a structural connection between wall and edge of slab but also leave a cavity which can be filled with a compression-resistant insulating material. The continuity of the insulating layer is guaranteed here, but the (closely spaced) anchors do represent discrete thermal bridges.

Owing to their "false vapour-tightness sequence" (most permeable layer on the inside, densest layer on the outside), constructions with internal insulation must include a vapour barrier on the inside of the thermal insulation in order to prevent condensation.

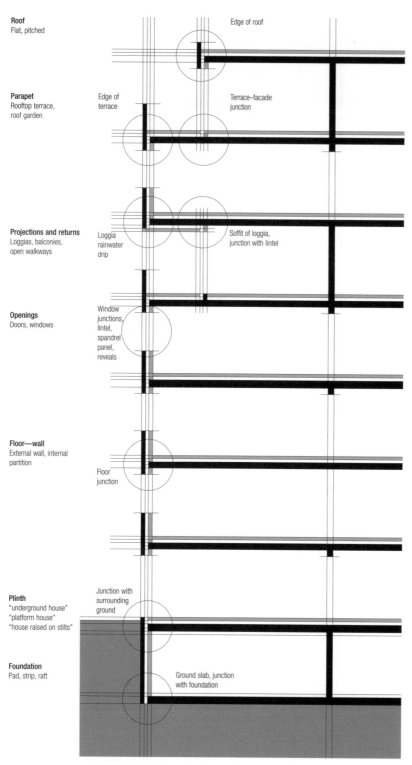

Roof
Flat, pitched

Edge of roof

Parapet
Rooftop terrace,
roof garden

Edge of
terrace

Terrace–facade
junction

Projections and returns
Loggias, balconies,
open walkways

Loggia
rainwater
drip

Soffit of loggia,
junction with lintel

Openings
Doors, windows

Window
junctions,
lintel,
spandrel
panel,
reveals

Floor—wall
External wall, internal
partition

Floor
junction

Plinth
"underground house"
"platform house"
"house raised on stilts"

Junction with
surrounding
ground

Foundation
Pad, strip, raft

Ground slab, junction
with foundation

Fig. 17: Diagram of layers, loadbearing layer outside
The system chosen for the floor connections (with chromium steel anchors) makes possible an uninterrupted insulating layer. The circles designate the transitions where the different layers are joined; these key details must be resolved in detailed drawings.

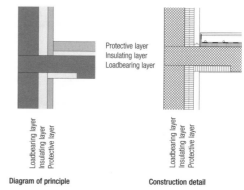

Protective layer
Insulating layer
Loadbearing layer

Loadbearing layer
Insulating layer
Protective layer

Loadbearing layer
Insulating layer
Protective layer

Diagram of principle   **Construction detail**

Fig. 18: Case study: floor support not separated, discontinuous insulating layer
To compensate for the interruption in the insulation layer a strip of insulation at least 100 cm wide must be attached to the soffit around the perimeter (either laid in the formwork or fixed to the underside of the floor). Disadvantage: the soffit must be plastered or lined ("facing quality"). Combined impact sound/thermal insulation must be incorporated on top of the floor. The vertical loadbearing layer can be in concrete or masonry.

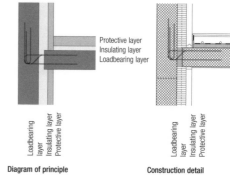

Protective layer
Insulating layer
Loadbearing layer

Loadbearing
layer
Insulating layer
Protective layer

Loadbearing
layer
Insulating layer
Protective layer

Diagram of principle   **Construction detail**

Fig. 19: Case study: floor support separated, continuous insulating layer
This type of construction is only possible in reinforced concrete because the chromium steel anchors must be integrated into the wall and floor reinforcement. Compression-resistant insulation must be incorporated between the face of a wall and the edge of the floor. Such insulation is often included with the respective anchor system (e.g. Schöck-Isokorb).

Seven rules for the design of a low-energy house

What are the key factors when planning a low-energy house? The following seven rules are intended to provide an overview and a guide.

1. Work according to a concept

The form, location, and interior layout of a building have a major influence on the energy consumption. Strive for clear, simple solutions. If you are not inventive by nature, assemble your house (intelligently) from inexpensive, readily available parts.

2. Plan a high degree of insulation…

The thermal insulation of a low-energy house is at least 20 cm thick. Depending on the type of construction, the complete external component can be between 25 and 60 cm thick in total.

… and avoid thermal bridges

The problem of thermal bridges occurs wherever the insulated building envelope is penetrated by components which allow the passage of heat from inside the building. Many buildings lose more heat via avoidable thermal bridges than over the entire uninterrupted wall. Transitions and junctions require special care:

- between window and wall, roof and other windows,
- between door and wall,
- between wall and roof,
- between roller shutter and wall,
- via shafts and flues at wall and roof,
- via thresholds, window sills, lintels at floor and wall,
- via fasteners, e.g. for balconies.

3. Exploit solar heat gains

Include large windows on the side facing the sun, provided their energy audit is positive. Adequate storage capacity is necessary in order to absorb the radiation. This means that a heavyweight form of construction is preferable for internal partitions and floors. Position permanently habitable rooms, e.g. living room, children's rooms, on the sunny side whenever possible.

4. Build airtight…

No house without convection safeguards! The occupants breathe, not the walls, nor the roof. Ensure airtightness and check the workmanship, particularly at troublesome details.

… and install mechanical ventilation

This will increase the quality of life in the house and reduce energy consumption because the heat losses can be recovered (heat exchanger). The ventilation plant must be carefully sized, and disturbing noise can be reduced with sound attenuation.

5. Cover the residual heating requirements with renewable energy media

Solar energy, wood, and ambient heat are ideal for low-energy houses because small installations (heat pumps, collectors) are adequate for low energy requirements, or only a small amount of fuel (wood) is necessary.

6. Store and distribute the heat with a low temperature level…

The lower the temperatures of the heating media, the smaller the losses; this applies to both the generation and the distribution of heat.

… install the heat storage media in the heated part of the house…

Every storage medium loses heat; this heat must be used in a low-energy house.

… and insist on short lines

In some low-energy houses the supply and return pipes (due to their large surface area) heat up more than the radiators being supplied. This can lead to problems in the regulation of the heating system and to unnecessary energy losses.

7. Use energy-saving household appliances

The use of energy-saving household appliances reduces emissions and environmental loads at the power station locations.

Excerpt from:
Othmar Humm: *NiedrigEnergie- und PassivHäuser*, Staufen near Freiburg, 1998

Low-tech – high tectonics

Andrea Deplazes

Camouflaged energy concept

One example for energy-saving construction within the costs framework of conventional building methods: What was originally intended as a conventional school design at the tender stage changed during the planning phase to a concept complying with the Swiss "Minergie" Standard. In doing so it was possible to avoid delegating the energy problem to the building services and instead to achieve a synthesis with the tectonics of the structure.

A visitor to the school in Vella would be unable to discover anything that could be deemed unusual in a school. The buildings employ a solid form of construction, with fair-face concrete walls internally and solid timber wall panelling for the classrooms and the sports and assembly halls. The buildings are enclosed in a layer of thermal insulation 12 cm thick, which in turn is protected by a layer of render about 3 cm thick – exactly as used in the traditional timber houses not far from the school, which are clad with a thin render "membrane". The internal layout corresponds exactly with typical school requirements.

But upon closer inspection our attentive visitor would make a few discoveries: no radiators in the rooms, no centralised heating plant in the basement, no solar collectors anywhere in the building or on the roof! Instead, a mechanical ventilation system ensures a supply of fresh air with a low air change rate (0.5) and is intended to prevent uncontrolled ventilation losses (e.g. windows left open unintentionally). A heat exchanger has been installed downstream from this system to introduce waste heat from the exhaust air into the incoming fresh air. That is it, the only technical component in the school; this belongs to the – in architectural terms – less interesting part of the concept. More conspicuous are the ribbed concrete floors, the solid floor finishes of Vals quartzite stone slabs (also in the classrooms) and the large-format windows with their hopper-shaped reveals whose timber frames are screened externally by the thermal insulation. This is where the inconspicuous energy concept begins – with the use of passive solar energy.

A technical problem?

Soon after beginning the planning it was discovered that the location of the new school would be really ideal for exploiting solar energy. Although nothing of this kind had been allowed for in the budget, the local authorities approached us, the architects, with the wish to integrate solar collectors into the roof surfaces. ("However, it mustn't cost more.")

We were not impressed by the idea of the "badge of enlightened energy consciousness", which all too often is placed conspicuously in the foreground. After all, the addition of technical equipment to the building would have disturbed not only the architectural surroundings of this mountain village with its splendid, archaic houses. To greater extent it disturbed our understanding of our role as architects – trying to combine diverse, often conflicting parameters in the design process – in that we would have to come to terms with an aesthetically successful integration of collectors into roof and other surfaces.

A tectonics solution

We therefore developed the concept of storing the solar energy in solid components. The appealing notion here is that we can use the same wall thicknesses and floor depths as in a conventional design – provided that the components are of solid construction so that they can absorb the incoming solar radiation (through the windows) as quickly as possible and thus prevent overheating in the interior. However, as the walls in the classrooms would be needed for all sorts of blackboards, magnetic notice boards, cupboards and showcases, and hence would not be available as a storage medium, we opted for ribs on the absorption surfaces and the optimisation of the floor mass distribution in line with the recognition that the dynamic penetration of heat radiation into solid components is about 10 cm (primary storage). During periods of good weather lasting a few days in the winter the storage media can be continually charged (secondary storage).

Multiple use strategy

This is coupled with additional, satisfying multiple uses. Provided with ribs, the floors easily span the 7.5 metres across the classrooms with little material consumption. At the same time, the profiled soffits create an extremely effective acoustic diffusion so that other acoustic measures

Figs 20 and 21: School building and multipurpose hall (left), south facade with large area of glazing (right)
Bearth & Deplazes: school complex, Vella (CH), 1997

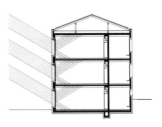

Fig. 22: Section through classroom wing

(absorption) are unnecessary. Inexpensive energy-saving lights are easily installed between the ribs without creating any glare. And finally, the ribbed floors create a rich architectural motif which can certainly be regarded as a transformation of the Baroque ceilings in the aforementioned houses of this district. Just one last component was missing in order to redirect the maximum amount of solar radiation up to the soffit – light-redirecting louvres on the inside of the window panes.

But as specially designed light-redirecting systems would have been too expensive, we made use of conventional aluminium louvres which we threaded onto the operating cords and rotated 180°. These louvres are let down in winter just enough so that the pupils nearest the windows are not disturbed by the shallow, intense incoming sunlight, which is heightened by snow on the ground. However, the foremost one-third of the floor surface directly adjacent to the windows can still absorb heat and correspondingly "charge up" like a sheet of blotting paper across the depth of the room. The louvres can be rotated into position to reflect the sunlight over the heads of the pupils and up to the underside of the ribbed floor slab. This allows not only the heat absorption of the floor slab to be exploited to best effect, but also improves the natural lighting across the depth of the room, which in turn reduces the amount of electrical energy required for lighting. And the fact that in this position the louvres are still "open" and thus permit a view of the surrounding countryside should not be underestimated.

Versatile concept

As a concept for the use of solar energy through storage in solid components such as floors and walls, which have to be constructed anyway, this method is not confined to schools. The multiple use strategy of components is the condition that must be fulfilled in order to remain competitive – in terms of price – with conventional methods of building. It could be the right time to switch from the modernistic understanding of complementary architectural systems comprising monofunctional individual parts to synthetic, complex, polyfunctional components. That is what we call holistic thinking. Only in this way can we achieve added value in economic, energy, and cultural terms "in one fell swoop", which is nothing other than "sustainability". The entire energy concept with solid storage media would have been architecturally meaningless for Vella if the necessary massiveness could not have been combined with the theme of plasticity and the "monolithic mass" of the building, in the play of the surfaces, interior depth, and thin-wall facade skin, both in the corporeal expression of the building and in the motifs of the detailing, and with the urbanistic structure of this mountain village and its powerful, cubic, stocky houses.

Fig. 23: Classroom with ribbed concrete soffit

Project:	School complex with multi-purpose hall, Vella (CH)
Client:	Local authority of Vella, Lugnez (CH)
Architects:	Valentin Bearth, Andrea Deplazes, Chur
Energy concept:	Andrea Rüedi, Chur
Building services:	Nold + Padrun, Chur

Key parameters

Recommendations of SIA 380/1 "Energie im Hochbau", 1988 edition; target value : 260 MJ/m²a

SIA brochure D 090 "Energiegerechte Schulbauten":
standard target value: 150 MJ/m²a
optimised target value: 76 MJ/m²a

Value calculated for Vella according to "Handbuch der passiven Sonnenenergienutzung",
SIA/BEW document D 010: 24 MJ /m²a
Measured results for Vella (IBT diploma thesis 98/99): 34 MJ/m²a

The deviation of the measured energy consumption values from the calculated ones for the school complex in Vella lies within the tolerances of the method of calculation.

Storage capacity (reserve for poor weather):
During a period of poor weather lasting 4 days, an outside temperature of -5 °C and decreasing solar gains the storage media discharges from an average 21 °C to 19 °C. At this point the descending temperature gradient intersects with the preheated (with the heat exchanger) air temperature curve of the mechanical ventilation system such that the value can be maintained. (Measured values from 12–15 Jan 1999, measurements taken in winter 1998/99)

Excerpt from:
Bulletin, Magazin der Eidgenössischen Technischen Hochschule Zurich, issue No. 276, "Energie – im Umbruch", January 2000, pp. 32–33

BUILDINGS

Apartment blocks, Martinsbergstrasse, Baden
Burkard Meyer Architekten

Alois Diethelm

Situation, theme

This development occupies the south-east corner of the Merker district, a former industrial site in the centre of Baden. The three separate blocks, two of which were built in the first phase of the project, reflect the style of the detached houses along the Martinsbergstrasse, which date from the early 20th century.

The main entrance on Martinsbergstrasse is via a small forecourt enclosed by concrete walls and hedges. In keeping with the urban situation, the private external areas are covered in gravel and screened off from the public road by walls. The road at the rear gives access to the garages and also to the "Merker" meadow, an open recreational area which, like the two apartment blocks, forms part of the development plan for the whole area.

Whereas the buildings appear to be solitary when viewed from the south side, the lower ground level on the north side exposes the basement and reveals the fact that the buildings are part of the same unit. The sequence of open car parking areas below the blocks and closed garages between forms a sort of chequer effect as they alternate with the buildings and intervening open spaces above. Although there is a variation of material (fair-face concrete and facing brickwork) in the basement parking level and the apartments above, continuity between them is maintained.

Architects: Burkard Meyer Architekten, Baden
Construction period: 1998–1999
Project managers: Roger Casagrande
Alois Diethelm
Structural engineers: Minikus Witta Voss, Zurich

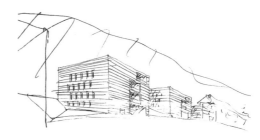

Fig. 2: Stark volumes in an urban context
Sketch

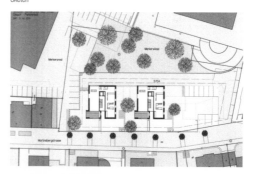

Fig. 3: Situation without third block
Point-blocks on the opposite side

Fig. 1: View from the "Merker" meadow
The difference in levels reveals the basement.

Layout and loadbearing structure

With the exception of block A, where the topmost apartment occupies one-and-a-half storeys, each block contains four apartments, one on each floor, organised around a central access core. This core divides each apartment into two areas: a bedroom wing with a ceiling height of 2.46 m, and a living/dining wing with ceiling heights up to 3.06 m. This latter wing, which spans across the full depth of the building from facade to facade, changes from one side of the core to the other on every floor. This enables the lower ceiling height of the group of rooms above or below to be exploited. This "stacking" principle is visible in the facade by way of the staggered floor slab edges.

The living room opens out onto a veranda. Although this is not heated, it is fitted with double glazing on the facade. This creates a buffer zone which can be opened up virtually over its full area in the summer.

The masonry of the facade and the concrete access core, together with the in situ reinforced concrete floors, form the loadbearing structure. The remaining walls are non-loadbearing plasterboard on timber studding.

Fig. 6: Wooden model
Shows the different ceiling heights and how the apartments are "stacked".

Fig. 4: Plan of 1st floor
The living room extends from one facade to the other.

Fig. 5: Plan of 2nd floor
The small apartment and the penthouse share the 2nd floor.

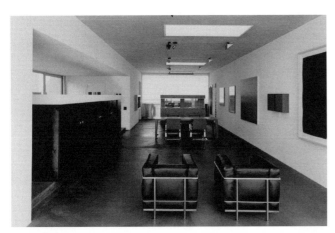

Fig. 7: Penthouse
View towards kitchen; interior lit by rooftop terrace and rooflights.

Fig. 8: Penthouse
Multimedia furniture serves as room divider; the rooftop terrace can be seen in the background.

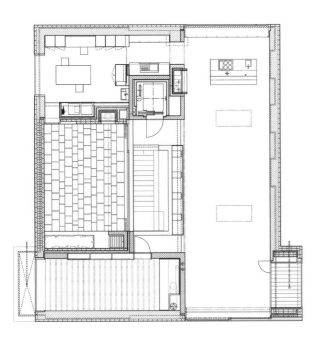

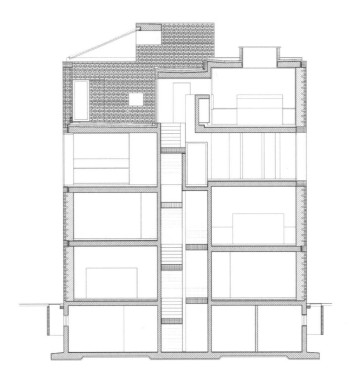

Fig. 9: Plan of 3rd floor
Living room without veranda

Fig. 10: Section
Showing rooftop terrace to penthouse

Openings and loadbearing structure

Some of the openings are intrinsic to the layout and others may be located to suit the owners' requirements. What both have in common is that they span between the edges of the floor slabs.

Openings of the former type are to be found on the north and south elevations, forming extensions to the living rooms. Their interaction reflects the principle of the mirrored plan layouts. With a span of about 4.60 m, however, they are on the limit of feasibility because the adjoining Optitherm masonry, which owing to its porosity has a lower compressive strength than normal brickwork, can only just carry the loads that arise.

On the other hand, the east and west elevations are characterised by the storey-by-storey alternation between "frameless" windows flush with the facade and French windows set in deep reveals. Spanning between the floor slabs, these openings turn the masonry into shear walls which, owing to the fact that the floor slab edge elements distribute the loads, stand virtually separately from the sections of wall above and below. From a design point of view this meant that the position of the windows could in fact remain variable right up to shortly before work started on site.

Fig. 11: External view of block A
The garden wall along Martinsbergstrasse can be seen in the foreground.

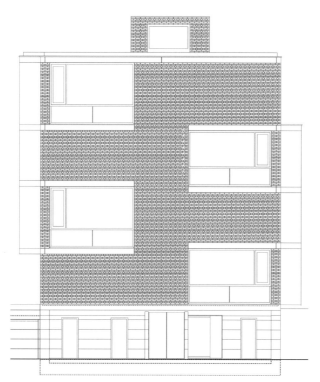

Fig. 12: North elevation

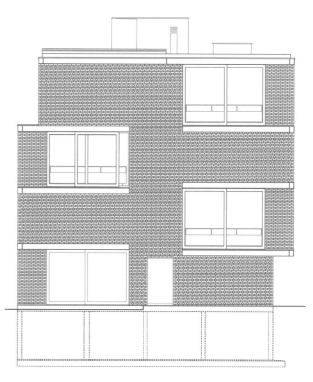

Fig. 13: South elevation

Fig. 14: Ground floor wall at the position of the window flush with the outside face
The masonry bond can be clearly seen.

Design and realisation I

The brickwork of the facades is based on the combination of Optitherm and Kelesto masonry developed by the architects and first used on Brühl School in Gebenstorf.

The walls are made up of 400 mm thick Optitherm units (insulating bricks) in a masonry bond plus 120 mm Kelesto units (facing bricks fired below the sinter point). The two leaves of masonry, which are built simultaneously, are connected at every fourth course by means of a row of headers to form an inseparable bond. The wall requires no further insulation (U-value 0.38 W/m²K). No insulation is inserted into the voids that are created between the bricks.

Besides the advantages for the interior climate that result from such an inert wall construction (phase shift effect), this design also benefits from the fact that – in contrast to conventional facing masonry in a twin-leaf arrangement and cavity insulation – the interlacing of the courses means that expansion joints are unnecessary. The sculpted appearance of the building (no interruptions at the corners and in the middle of the elevations) is primarily due to this component.

The facing masonry and the type of joints were chosen based on performance criteria. According to these, it is important to guarantee the migration of the vapour diffusion but also to protect against driving rain. The mortar joints on the outside face were therefore compacted with an electric vibrator as the wall was built because any water penetrating the joints cannot be drained away as there is no ventilated cavity as such. Joints simply struck with a trowel would have been inconceivable. Likewise, facing

bricks with a high vapour diffusion resistance would have been unsuitable because the backing of Optitherm bricks is open to diffusion; a hard-fired facing brick would have been too dense.

In terms of its elasticity, Optitherm masonry is regarded as moderately soft. For internal plastering work this means that it is not possible to use a pure cement plaster. Instead, a lime-diluted undercoat (hydraulic lime plus cement) or a lightweight undercoat must be used. The Optitherm bricks themselves are normally used in conjunction with a lightweight mortar, which exhibits better thermal insulation properties owing to the expanded clay- sand content but has a lower loadbearing capacity. Their use together with facing masonry, where a lightweight mortar would be unsuitable because of the high water infiltration, meant that for both the Optitherm and the Kelesto units a facing-grade mortar was used throughout in order to create the same structural relationships for both types of masonry.

During construction great care had to be exercised by all involved to ensure that the masonry was kept dry because the highly porous Optitherm bricks (thermal insulation) quickly absorb any water. The upshot of this is that any moisture present migrates outwards during the first heating period and in doing so liberates lime from the bricks, which appears on the surface in the form of efflorescence. However, this is quickly washed away by the rain.

Another building by Burkard Meyer Architekten employs similar masonry but with impregnated Kelesto bricks. The idea behind the impregnation is to prevent the efflorescence.

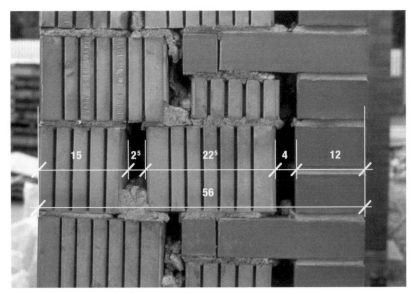

Fig. 15: Close-up of masonry
Combination of Optitherm and Kelesto facing masonry

Design and realisation II

The edges of the floor slabs, which characterise the appearance of the facades, consist of prefabricated concrete elements which, in the standard case, are supported on the outer half of the masonry cross-section. This means that the cross-section at the French windows, which open inwards, is doubled because of the formation of a lintel plus sill.

Although these bands offer almost unlimited freedom for positioning openings during the design phase, the opposite is true during the construction phase. The desire to create complete concrete soffits or lintels throughout the thickness of the masonry had the effect of limiting the repetition of elements because of the unrestricted positioning. Prefabrication was therefore chosen because it produces a better surface finish and not because it achieves rational construction.

The contractor used the concrete elements as permanent formwork which, owing to its relatively high "self-weight", did not require any further fixings. A 10 mm cavity between the strip of extruded polystyrene insulation along the edge of the slab and the concrete elements guarantees that floor slab and elements can move independently. Gypsum boards act as spacers during placing of the concrete and are later removed.

Polyethylene film both above and below the concrete elements separates them from the masonry so that both materials can move independently. Accordingly, the joints are sealed with putty.

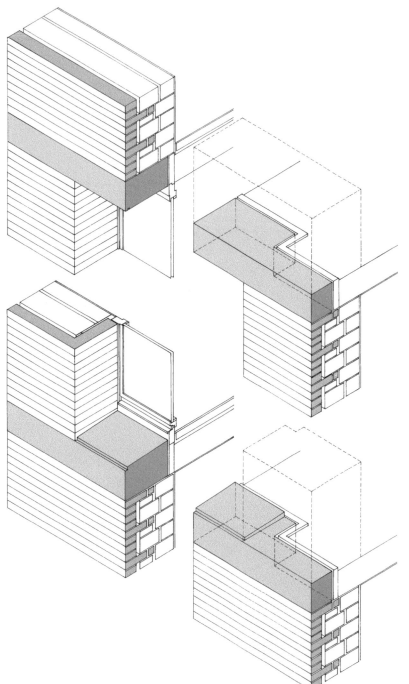

Fig. 16: Axonometric view
"Thickening" of slab edge elements adjacent to window

Fig. 17: Close-up of formwork
The slab edge elements act as a permanent formwork; gypsum boards provide a space for the insulation.

Fig. 18: 1st floor slab
The returns in the slab edge elements indicate the positions of the French windows.

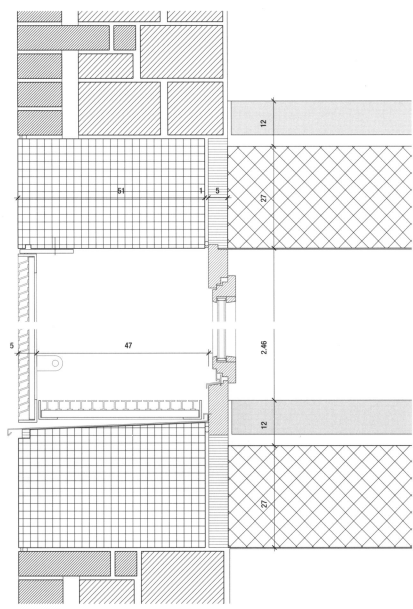

Fig. 19: Section, 1:10

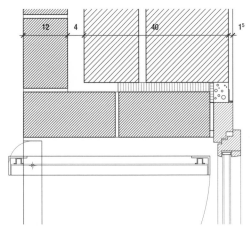

Fig. 20: Plan, 1:10

Design and realisation – the French window

The window opens inwards and is a simple painted wood version because of its less exposed position. The lower section of the external anodised aluminium weatherproof screen, fitted flush with the facade, serves as a balustrade; the upper section guarantees privacy by means of two shutters which pivot inwards. The space between screen and window therefore becomes – like the veranda – a transition zone, useful as a balcony for smokers but also as a rainproof area for airing clothes. The position of the shutters changes the expression of the facade from an absolute plain one without any relief to a more sculpted one exposing the full depth of the masonry.

The construction of the reveals in Kelesto bricks, which have a considerably poorer insulation value than the Optitherm masonry, and attaching the window frames to these bricks meant that it was necessary to include a strip of extruded polystyrene insulation between the Optitherm and Kelesto units.

Slab edges
- Prefabricated concrete element, 500 x 290/340 mm
- Anodised aluminium sill, d = 3 mm, bonded to smooth-finish concrete element; turned up at junction with reveal masonry
- Aluminium open-grid flooring laid in stove-enamelled steel frame; finished level with apartment floor

Fig. 21: Close-up of French window
Weatherproof screen acts as balustrade and shutter.

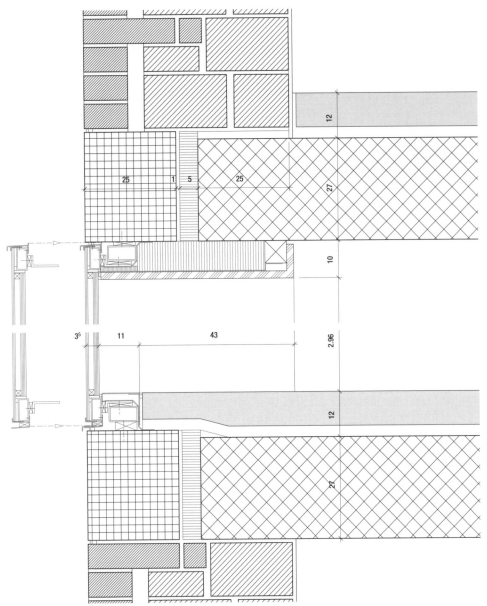

Fig. 22: Section, 1:10

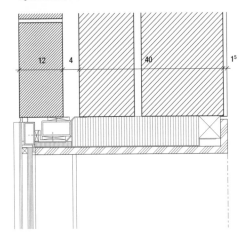

Fig. 23: Plan, 1:10

Design and realisation – the "frameless" window

The window, fitted flush with the facade, enables the full depth of the masonry to be appreciated from the inside and gives the matt but, owing to the brickwork bond, strongly textured facade a highly abstract highlight. This effect is accentuated by the use of stepped insulating glass which gives the impression of a window without a frame.

To create a safety barrier, the inner pane is of laminated safety glass; a separate balustrade, which would have lessened the effect of the direct transition to the outside world, is therefore unnecessary.

The linings to reveals and lintel conceal both the supporting framework for the window and the insulation.

Fig. 24: View of "frameless" window from inside
The reveals enable the thickness of the masonry to be appreciated.

Window element
- Stepped insulating glass bonded to aluminium frame (prefabricated structural sealant glazing)
- Glazing beads top and bottom serve as additional mechanical fixings
- Window element fitted into steel frame installed beforehand

Design and realisation – the sliding window

The two leaves of the window, which owing to its exposed position is a wood/metal composite design, slide in front of the masonry and enable the window to be opened to virtually its full width. The veranda, which in spring, autumn and winter also serves as a climate buffer zone, therefore becomes a proper balcony.

Unlike conventional sliding windows, there is no rectangular frame here; in other words, the window has been reduced to guide tracks top and bottom. This lends the facade relief at these points thanks to the juxtaposition of window and masonry within the depth, a relief that would otherwise only be possible by varying the building envelope.

The reduction of the wall thickness by the width of the guide track, and the desire to have walls in facing masonry on the inside of the veranda as well, led to the use of a twin-leaf masonry arrangement locally.

Floor construction, studio

Floor covering	10 mm
Cement screed	80 mm
Impact sound insulation	30 mm
Polyurethane thermal insulation	50 mm
Concrete slab	240 mm

Edge of slab

Prefabricated concrete element	120 x 290 mm
OMEGA anchors	
Extruded polystyrene slab edge insulation	50 mm

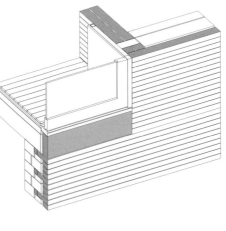

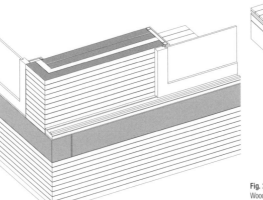

Fig. 25: Axonometric view of sliding window
Wall behind sliding window built as twin-leaf masonry, otherwise combination masonry

Fig. 26: Floor construction, veranda

Wooden grid (Douglas fir)	27 mm
Rubber mat bonded to insulation underneath (for stability)	
Extruded polystyrene thermal insulation	150–300 mm
2 layers of bitumen roofing felt	
Concrete slab laid to falls	220–240 mm

Fig. 27: Ground floor veranda
The sliding doors opening onto the veranda lend depth to the facade.

Fig. 28: Veranda
Unheated intermediate zone acts as extension to living room and also as balcony.

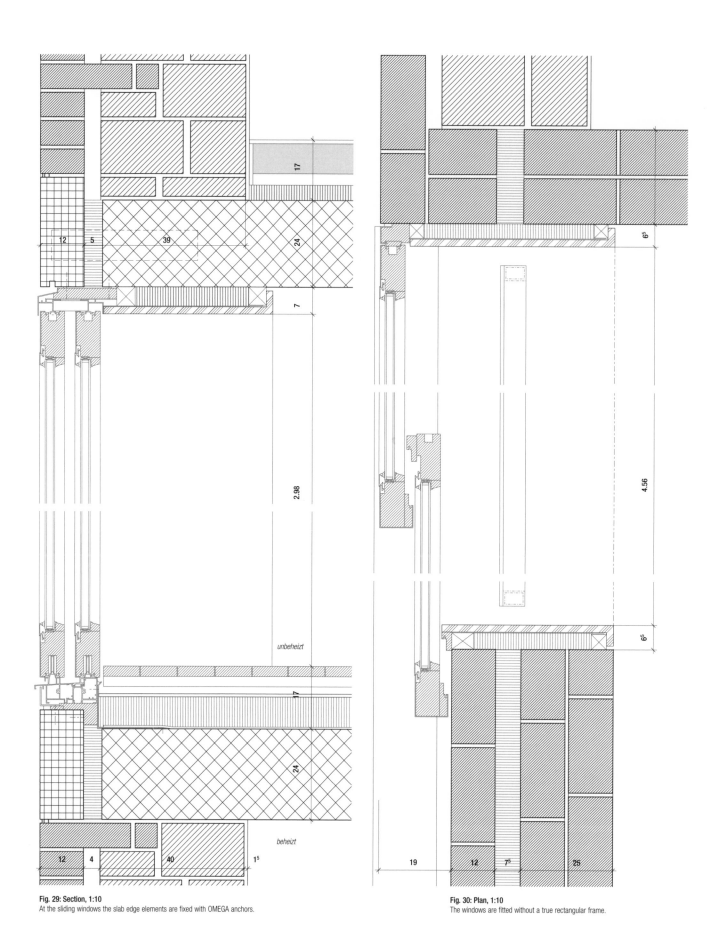

Fig. 29: Section, 1:10
At the sliding windows the slab edge elements are fixed with OMEGA anchors.

Fig. 30: Plan, 1:10
The windows are fitted without a true rectangular frame.

Gallery for Contemporary Art, Marktoberdorf
Bearth + Deplazes

Katharina Stehrenberger

Fig. 1: View from north side

Situation and theme

Positioned between the town hall and private villas that date from the 1920s, the art gallery of the Dr Geiger Foundation stands in the centre of Marktoberdorf in Germany's Allgäu region. Its multifunctional qualities make it equally ideal for special exhibitions, the presentation of the Foundation's own collection or for use as a studio. This detached building nicely integrates into the environment of individual buildings so typical of Marktoberdorf. However, its stark cubic form also distinguishes it from the surrounding houses. The composition with the existing Foundation building maintains the internal logic while achieving optimum utilisation within the plot. What appears to be an empty forecourt – a quadrangle enclosed by walls – within the complex is in fact a space for exhibiting sculptures; it thus forms a pivotal point and hence a central element. The two brickwork cubes forming the structure are of different heights and slightly offset sideways. Each measures 10 x 10 m on plan. The special feature is the compactness of the building envelope made from red-brown, flush-pointed hard-fired facing bricks. With facing brickwork also used on the inside, this art gallery takes on a sort of workshop-like character and expresses the idea of a "living" gallery whose purpose – just for once – is not to act as a neutral room housing works of art.

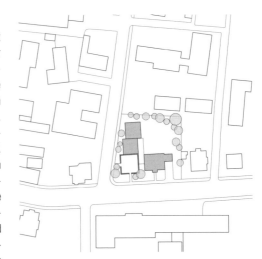

Fig. 3: Site plan, 1:2500

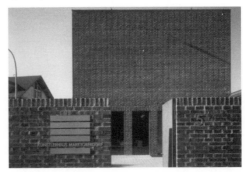

Fig. 4: Main entrance with forecourt

Architects: Bearth + Deplazes, Chur
Construction period: 1998–2000
Project manager: Bettina Werner
Structural engineer: Jürg Buchli, Haldenstein

Fig. 2: View from the town hall

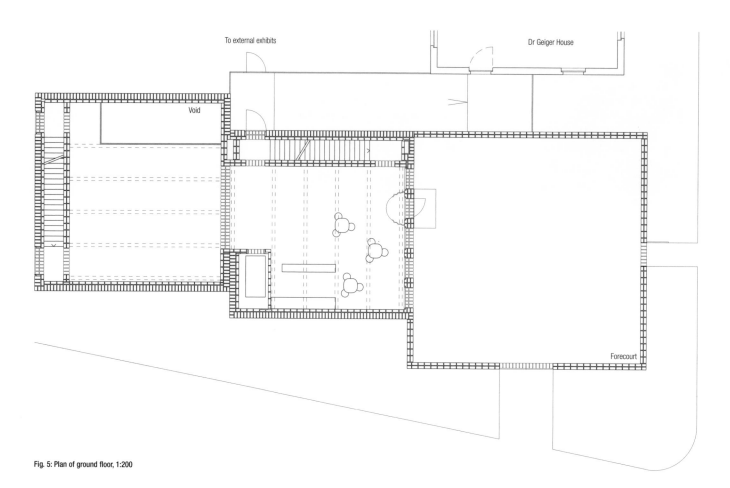

Fig. 5: Plan of ground floor, 1:200

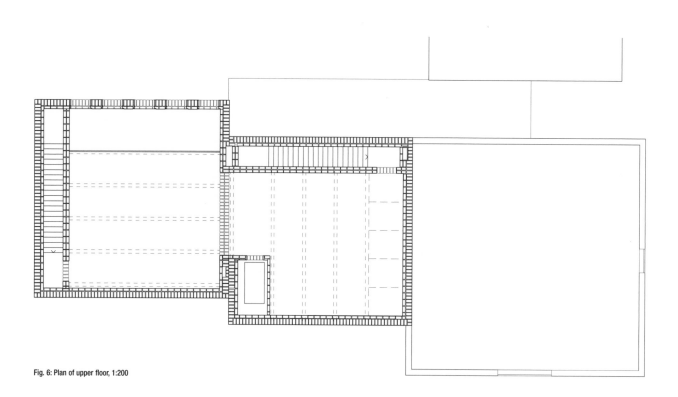

Fig. 6: Plan of upper floor, 1:200

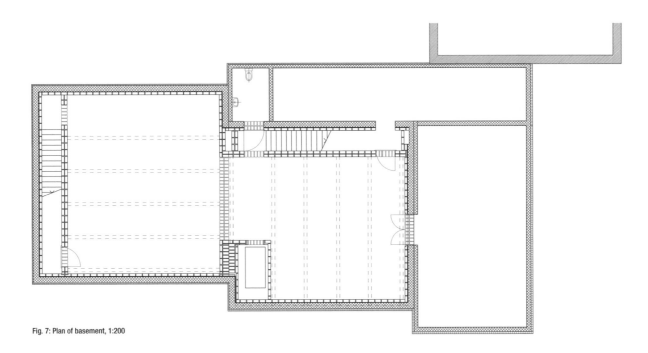

Fig. 7: Plan of basement, 1:200

Loadbearing structure

In terms of classification, the building consists of two identical volumes, one of which is turned 90° and butt-jointed to the other. The seam between the two parts is rendered visible by way of the change in direction of the span of the beams and the double thickness of wall. The layout concealed behind the masonry shell obviously facilitates the unrestricted use of the exhibition areas and deliberately omits any internal core or partitions. Stairs and service shafts blend into the enclosing walls in order to create coherent exhibition areas of maximum size. Basically, the building is reduced to the interplay between a self-supporting envelope and the floors is surrounds, which are borne on steel beams. The monolithic basement and the roof functioning in a similar way to the intermediate floors provide a logical conclusion to the brickwork envelope.

The foundation of the gallery structure extends below ground level in the form of a brick-clad tank; this gives the impression that the masonry envelope has been sunk into the ground. The actual building envelope in solid masonry is built up off the basement. The clay masonry functions as a "brick–mortar composite section" with high compressive and low tensile strength. The actual loadbearing capacity results from the interaction of the two materials in all three directions. Minimal intermediate floors of tightly fitting spruce planks integrate into the vertical layout of the interior space without impairing the masonry shell. From the outside this solid masonry structure thus preserves an impression of having no internal floors.

Fig. 8: Masonry enclosing walls

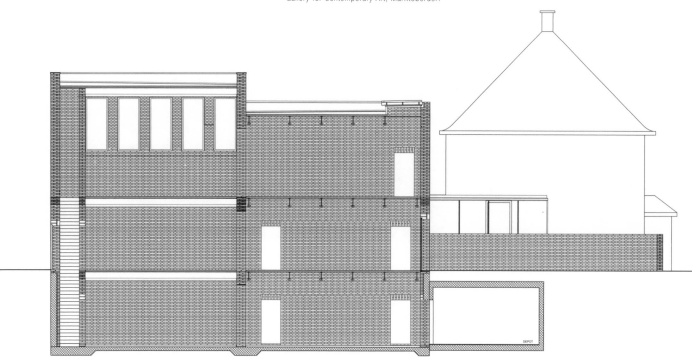

Fig. 9: Longitudinal section, 1:200

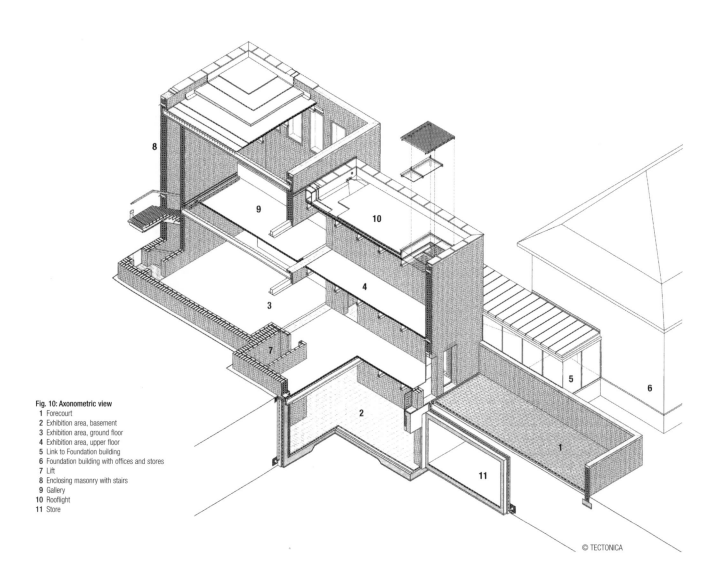

Fig. 10: Axonometric view
1 Forecourt
2 Exhibition area, basement
3 Exhibition area, ground floor
4 Exhibition area, upper floor
5 Link to Foundation building
6 Foundation building with offices and stores
7 Lift
8 Enclosing masonry with stairs
9 Gallery
10 Rooflight
11 Store

© TECTONICA

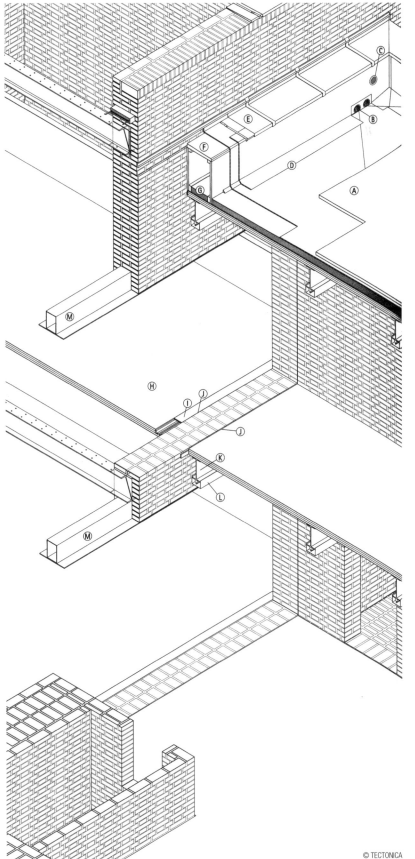

Floors, roof, roof edge and loadbearing structure

The steel beams of the cubes abutting at 90° run parallel to the openings in the masonry. The fusing together of the two volumes makes it necessary to introduce a "dummy roof edge" to complete the parapet. This is a timber construction covered in sheet metal imitating a solid parapet. Inside the building, beams fabricated from a hollow steel section plus steel plate are used to support the floor beams (IPE sections) above the large openings between the two parts of the gallery. From inside, only the bottom flange is visible in the opening. The incoming steel floor beams are incorporated in the first course of the masonry in English cross bond. Pins anchor the beams to the masonry. This means that the floors are incorporated into the masonry without seriously defacing the inner skin of the building envelope.

The wall was built first up to the level of the beam support. Round steel bars were then incorporated in the mortar bed at the position of the floor beams. Afterwards, the wall was continued upwards in the normal way. A space was left around the end of the beam so that it could be subsequently separated from the external masonry by means of 30 mm polystyrene. The beam pocket was finally filled with concrete.

Fig. 11: Bearing for floor beam

Fig. 12: Axonometric view
A 50 mm gravel
B Drainage outlets
C Ventilation outlet
D 2 layers of bitumen roofing felt, 3 mm
E Sheet metal capping on mortar laid to falls
F Supporting construction of water-repellent wood-based board
G Rockwool thermal insulation laid to falls, 150 mm
H 3-ply core plywood, 95 mm
I Cable duct with removable cover (for electric distribution)
J Separating strip, 1.5 mm
K Steel beam, IPE 360
L Fluorescent tube with transparent plastic diffuser
M Beam: 200 x 300 x 8 mm rectangular hollow section +
     495 x 12 mm bottom flange

© TECTONICA

Fig. 13: Special reveal bricks prior to fitting door

Fig. 15: Daylight enters through the large rooflight

Openings

The care taken with the way the floors are integrated is also evident in the arrangement of openings for doors and windows. Used only sparingly, they reinforce the monolithic character of this art workshop. The economical positioning of windows and the sometimes narrow, low-height openings give the effect of broad, mostly uninterrupted wall surfaces for the presentation of the exhibits. To be able to incorporate door and window frames flush with the wall surfaces, special bricks with corresponding rebates were prefabricated. Structural masonry cambered arch door and window lintels, which effectively distribute the wall loads of the masonry above, were built in situ with the smallest possible rise.

Fig. 14: Detail section
1 Sheet copper capping
2 Hard-fired facing bricks, 320 x 145 x 65 mm, lava texture, brown
3 Reinforced concrete ring beam
4 Window lintel, clay
5 Damp-proof course
6 Roof construction:
  – 50 mm gravel
  – waterproofing
  – thermal insulation
  – vapour barrier
  – 95 mm glulam planks
7 Steel beam, IPE 360
8 Textile sunblind
9 Fluorescent tube with transparent plastic diffuser
10 Heating pipes bedded in mortar
11 Glulam planks, fir/spruce, 95 mm, oiled with white pigment
12 Sealing strip
13 Basement wall construction:
  – plastic sheeting
  – peripheral insulation
  – waterproofing
  – 330 mm reinforced concrete
  – hard-fired facing bricks, 320 x 145 x 65 mm
14 Brick slips, 320 x 15 x 65 mm
15 Floor construction:
  – hard-fired facing bricks, 320 x 145 x 65 mm
  – 105 mm mortar bed
  – separating layer

Lighting

The cubes are divided into three levels. This creates three floors with different levels of lighting. Whereas the basement – the floor of the cube – is characterised by hard-fired facing bricks and artificial light, the exhibition rooms above are flooded with daylight entering through tall windows on one side. The decision in favour of artificial lighting in the basement and at ground floor level was quite deliberate. Only on the upper floor does daylight enter through windows and rooflights. The simple structural concept also requires a neat solution for the artificial lighting. And so in the gallery the artificial lighting is fitted beneath the white-painted steel beams. The lighting units are of fluorescent tubes with transparent plastic diffusers which can be controlled individually.

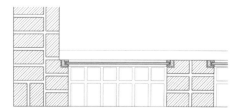

Abb. 16: Horizontal section through window showing special reveal bricks

Fig. 17: Daylight enters through the tall windows on the upper floor.

Fig. 19: Artificial lighting fitted to bottom flanges of beams

© TECTONICA

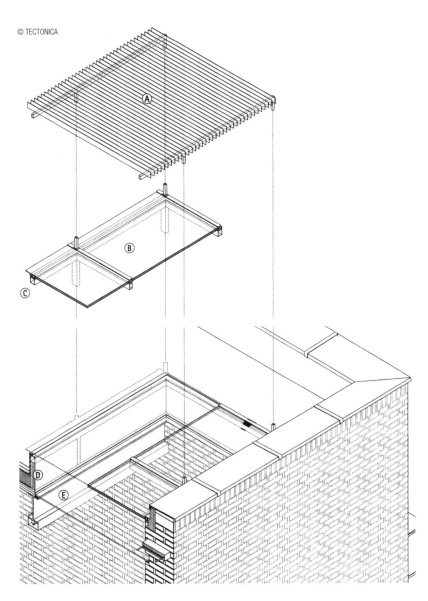

Internal surfaces

In the basement the floor finish to the cube is of hard-fired facing bricks with wide joints. Contrasting with this, the floors above are formed by steel beams and timber planks. The arrangement is very "proper" and thrifty: solid, 80 mm thick, finely glazed spruce laid on white-painted steel beams without any further floor finishes. This results in sound transmissions that propagate vertically throughout the building. However, this has been accepted in order to retain the minimalist concept of the architecture.

Fig. 18: Exploded diagram of rooflight
A Aluminium louvres as thermal insulation, also providing protection against glare and sunlight
B Laminated safety glass: 8 mm glass, 15 mm cavity, 8 mm toughened safety glass
C Steel frame of rectangular hollow sections, 80 x 50 x 2 mm
D Loadbearing sandwich element with integral posts of 7 mm sheet steel and 70 mm rockwool
E Laminated safety glass, 16 mm, coated

Fig. 20: Corner showing toothed intersection

Design and realisation in clay brickwork

The Bavarian hard-fired facing bricks used for the gallery resemble the materials employed in this region in the Middle Ages, although, strictly speaking, Marktoberdorf does not lie within the actual clay brickwork catchment area. Besides this local reference, the material – in historical terms – is well suited to this workshop-type building. The building envelope is built from high-strength hard-fired clay facing bricks in the Bavarian format of 320 x 145 x 65 mm with an animated, irregular lava texture surface, left exposed internally and externally, and used consistently throughout. The use of hard-fired facing bricks, which ensure some relief themselves and not just an attractive appearance, is an intrinsic component in the overall monolithic design. The irregular texture of the clay bricks and the coarse-grained mortar also create a wall surface that calls to mind a woven textile. Their stability and inertia with respect to climatic influences underscores the aesthetic qualities of these bricks. These factors determine the design of the building as a monolithic masonry structure, approx. 540 mm thick, built in English cross bond. Besides the climatic advantages of an inert wall construction, this thick uniform shell offers an advantage, i.e. no expansion joints are necessary. Such continuous vertical joints in a solid brick wall are normally required to prevent uncontrolled cracking (caused by disparate loadings, settlement or thermal movement of individual components). However, owing to the limited dimensions of the facades, such joints are unnecessary here. The lack of interruptions in the wall considerably helps the sculpted effect.

Of great significance in the masonry bond is the way the joints harmonise with the brick themselves, not only in terms of their size (30 mm perpends, 10 mm bed joints), but also in terms of colouring and texture. In order to break up the seemingly archaic-looking expressive force of the red-brown brickwork, both internally and externally, grey, grainy joints were chosen. Another prime advantage of the choice of clay masonry for an art gallery is that the humidity of the internal air – so crucial for preserving the exhibits – always remains constant. The humidity hovers around the level that is acceptable for both gallery visitors and exhibits alike.

This clay masonry building owes its existence to expertise imported from the Czech Republic (knowledge of old masonry bonds and sound knowledge about the building of facing brickwork). About 100,000 bricks of 18 different types were used, including solid and facing bricks plus specials at lintels and reveals.

Toothing at corner

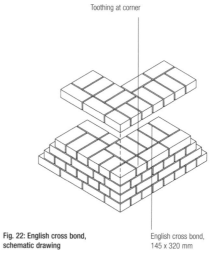

Fig. 22: English cross bond, schematic drawing   English cross bond, 145 x 320 mm

Fig. 21: English cross bond with wide joints

10 mm bed joints

30 mm perpends

Fig. 23: The wall plinth heating is totally invisible!

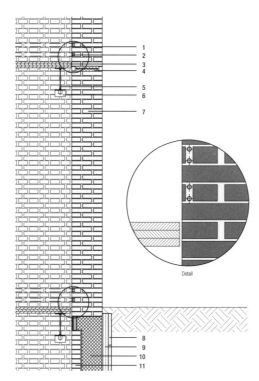

Detail

Fig. 24: Wall construction
1 Copper pipes, D = 18 mm, flow and return fully surrounded by mortar
2 Brick slips, 5 mm thick
3 Glulam planks, 95 mm thick
4 Ring beam (for horizontal stability)
5 Steel beam, IPE 360, built into masonry
6 Fluorescent tube with transparent plastic diffuser
7 Masonry, 495 mm
8 Cementboard
9 Cellular glass thermal insulation, 100 mm
10 Reinforced concrete, 320 mm
11 Facing brickwork, 145 mm

From *hypocaust* to wall plinth heating

The object of this observation is primarily the interaction of building mass (masonry) and the principle of space heating. If air-filled capillaries in porous building materials are good thermal insulators, then air must be a totally unsuitable medium for transporting heat.

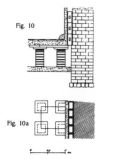

Fig. 10

Fig. 10a

Fig. 25: *Hypocaust*, section and plan

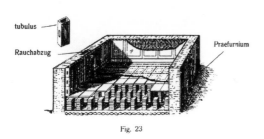

tubulus

Rauchabzug

Praefurnium

Fig. 23

Fig. 26: Isometric view of *hypocaust (hypocaust ≈ heating from below)*

Nevertheless, convector heaters (unrestricted movement of interior air) are still installed, with the disadvantage of intensive heat generation, and the drawback that the interior air is set in motion together with all fine particles such as dust and microbes. The principle of heating by radiation (controlled movement of interior air) was invented by the Romans, with their underfloor heating, called *hypocaust*. The heat generated at a source (*praefurnium*) is fed into a cavity floor where it subsequently rises into the interior rooms through clay flues (*tubuli*) and radiates from the inner surfaces of the walls by taking the path of least resistance: the radiation penetrates the air virtually without loss, while within a masonry body it can only propagate from molecule to molecule by way of vibration, i.e. has to perform work. The consequence is that the majority of the heat can be used for space heating without being lost within the cross-section of the wall. This is backed up by the solar radiation incident on the outside face, which is stored in the uniform masonry body, uninterrupted by thermal insulation.

Wall plinth heating

The *hypocaust* concept was considerably simplified for the gallery in Marktoberdorf without, however, relinquishing any of its effectiveness. Instead of an internal wall layer comprising vertical clay flues through which the hot air rises, two circuits of water-filled copper pipes have been integrated into the masonry walls just above each floor level to act as a heat transport medium. A conventional oil-fired boiler generates the heat for this system.

Consequently, the wall plinth heating uses only the principle of radiated heat in the loadbearing masonry. Heat source, transport medium and building measures are considerably different to those of the *hypocaust* underfloor heating system. The wall heating has proved to be amazingly effective. Owing to the inertia of the solid masonry, the controllable heat radiation is sufficient to guarantee a controlled interior temperature. A lower water temperature and hence less expensive heating is the outcome of the more even heat distribution of this heating by radiation. Such an installation is particularly viable for art galleries and museums. Until now, the interior climate necessary in such buildings containing valuable and highly sensitive works of art had been regulated mainly by way of extremely cost-intensive technology. But instead of complex building services and an air-conditioning plant, this building merely requires a network of copper pipes let into the external walls just above each floor level. The internal surface of the masonry radiates the heat evenly and ensures a comfortable interior climate. This combination of single-leaf wall construction and wall plinth heating has proved to be simple but effective.

Detached family home, Grabs
Peter Märkli

Thomas Wirz

Situation and theme

Grabs, the kind of scattered settlement, that is typical in Switzerland, lies in the flat land of the St Galler Rhine valley. Peter Märkli's house stands in a gentle depression between farms and other detached houses. It faces south and access is from the north side, via a narrow asphalt road.

At the start the design work was marked by an intensive analysis of the location and the interior layout, always keeping in mind the needs of the occupants. In the course of the design process the aim was to focus on a few themes – "one decides in favour of a whole". One sketch finally embodied all the essential factors of the design.

Märkli responded to the given situation with a solitary, compact building. The house does not attempt to fit in with the existing buildings; it distances itself, so to speak, from its environment. It achieves this through abstraction. The intent here is not "minimal art" or a "new simplicity", but rather a directness of expression in which all parts of the whole are visualised together.

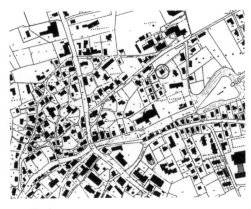

Fig. 1: Site plan

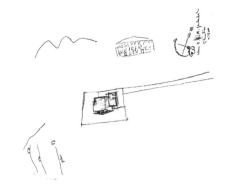

Fig. 2: Sketch showing location and context

Architect: Peter Märkli, Zurich
Construction period: 1993–1994
Project manager: Gody Kühnis, Trübbach
Structural engineer: Kurt Gabathuler, Scuol

Fig. 3: The house stands like sculpture on the open ground.

Relationship with the terrain

The open ground on which the house is built had to remain intact as far as possible. Therefore, the cantilevering part of the veranda seems to float above the ground. All the elements grow out of the envelope itself, which lends the building an autonomous, even introverted expression. It was not intended to be a house with external facilities competing with the neighbouring farmyards. The house is different from its surroundings, or as Ines Lamunière says: "It possesses a certain austerity which confines people either to the inside or the outside." A private garden in the normal sense of the word would be inconceivable here; the private external space – the veranda – is part of the house.

Fig. 4: The veranda is seemingly cut out of the volume.

Fig. 5: The veranda "floats" above the ground.

Fig. 6: The veranda – external and yet enclosed

Interior layout

The plan evolved around a focal point along the lines of the "onion skin principle". A few steps lead up from the covered entrance area to the hall, from where stairs lead to the upper floor and basement. The living room and kitchen are arranged in an L-shape on two sides of the hall. The large sliding windows allow a good view of the veranda and the seemingly distant surroundings beyond. The sliding aluminium shutters, providing privacy and protection from direct sunlight, help to reinforce this effect. Owing to the relationship between the corner and a section of wall, the interior space becomes opened up. This space then, devoid of any intervening columns, with the folding dividing wall between kitchen and living room, and a cement screed floor finish throughout, achieves an astounding expansiveness.

The interior layout on the upper floor also makes use of the L-shape. The south-facing rooms in the "L" are reached from a central hall, brightly lit via rooflights. The rooms, cantilevering out over the veranda, are of different sizes and are separated by plasterboard walls and built-in cupboards. The tiled bathrooms have been placed on the north side of the building.

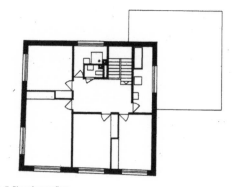

Fig. 7: Plan of upper floor

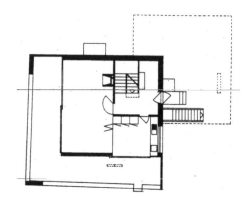

Fig. 8: Plan of ground floor

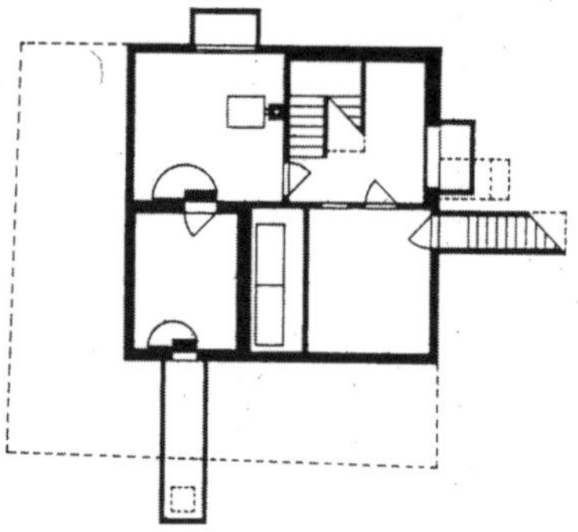

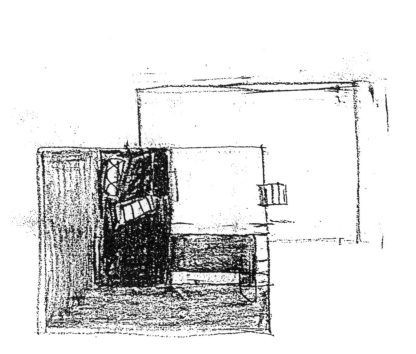

Fig. 9: Plan of basement

Fig. 10: Sketch showing interlacing of rooms

Construction and structural aspects

The use of in situ concrete is underscored by the non-right-angled geometry of the building, "which allows the cast form to be seen as bordering on the ideal, so to speak". The homogeneity of the cube is achieved by a constructional separation. The outer skin of concrete is structurally independent, with the loads being carried through prestressing and cantilevers. The inner skin is of plastered masonry. The concrete wall at ground floor level is the sole free-standing structural element. Besides its loadbearing function, it lends structure to the plan layout and marks the limit of the living room.

Fig. 12: Entrance elevation

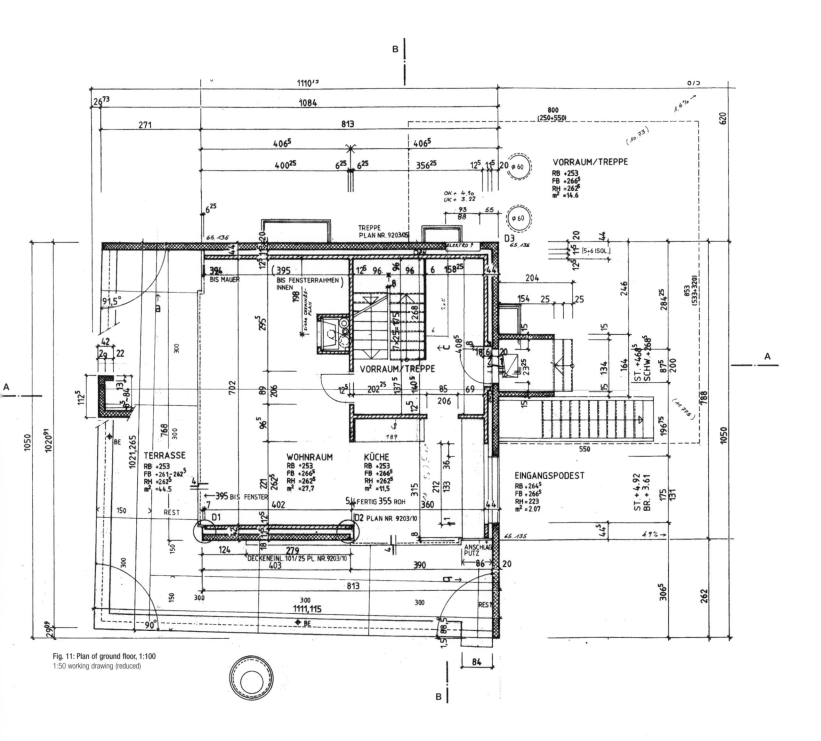

Fig. 11: Plan of ground floor, 1:100
1:50 working drawing (reduced)

The inner skin, masonry and concrete floors could be removed at a later date; the outer concrete envelope is totally separate from these in a structural sense. The point in the floor slab over the ground floor where the inner and outer skins meet (circled in fig. 103) is the point at which the large sliding windows to the veranda are incorporated. The use of such large window elements, without employing any cover strips, required a high degree of precision (tight tolerances) during manufacture and installation.

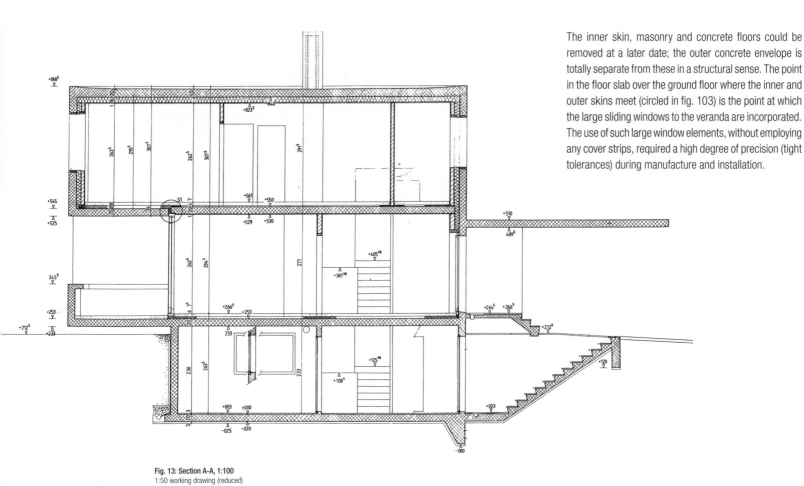

Fig. 13: Section A-A, 1:100
1:50 working drawing (reduced)

Fig. 14: Section B-B, 1:100
1:50 working drawing (reduced)

Roof

Triflex waterproofing	
Concrete	200 mm
Extruded polystyrene	80 mm
Rockwool between metal framing	80 mm
Vapour barrier	
Plasterboard	15 mm

External wall, upper floor

Plaster, smooth finish	10 mm
Brickwork	100 mm
Extruded polystyrene	140 mm
Concrete	200 mm

Slab over ground floor

Epoxy resin floor covering	
Cement screed	40 mm
Extruded polystyrene	(outside 80 mm)
Concrete	200 mm

External wall, ground floor

Plaster, smooth finish	
Brickwork	125 mm
Extruded polystyrene	120 mm
Concrete	200 mm

Slab over basement

Granolithic concrete floor covering	
Cement screed	75 mm
Extruded polystyrene	60 mm
Concrete	200 mm

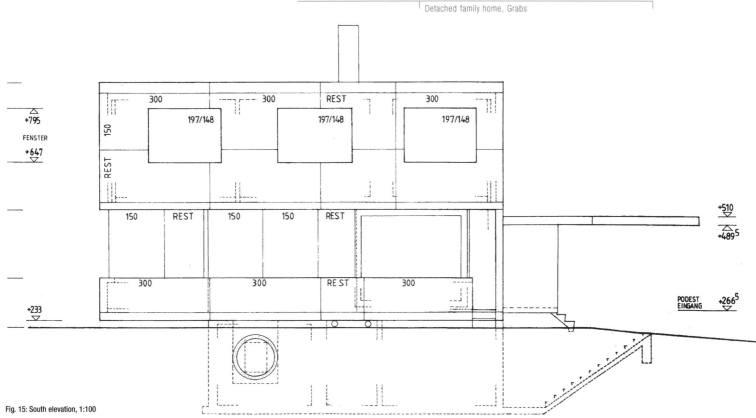

Fig. 15: South elevation, 1:100

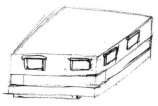

Fig. 16: Sketch showing facade proportions

Fig. 17: East elevation, 1:100

Facades

Here again there is no clear hierarchy among the components. As with the interior layout the most important thing in this case is the proportions. The relationship between the parts and the whole, between the parts themselves, and between openings and wall surfaces are crucial influences on the expression of the building. Internally, Märkli

also controls the elevations and the positions of openings in every single room by means of a consistent system of dimensions. At the lowest hierarchic level we have the pattern of formwork joints, which itself is subservient to the surface.

Small sketches showing two elevations were used to check the relationships.

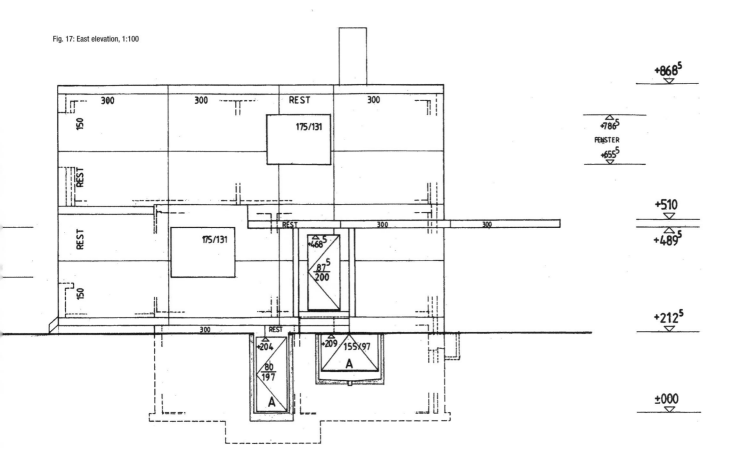

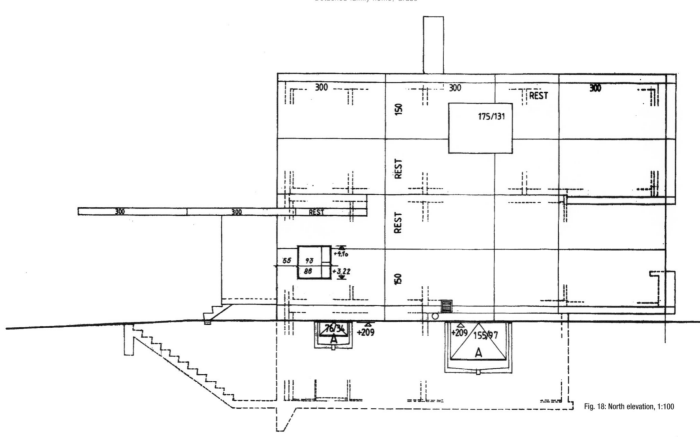

Fig. 18: North elevation, 1:100

Märkli works according to visual rules. The north elevation, for instance, is dominated by the two divergent cantilevers – the canopy over the entrance area and the veranda – and these add a certain tension to the facade. But the openings are positioned in such a way that the visual balance is restored. What this means is that the "centre of gravity" for the viewer comes to rest within the outline of the building (one can check this with the view towards the corner).

A single element like the long cantilevering canopy always has more than one function. Besides the architectural use already mentioned, it also serves as a symbol for the entrance, protects the entrance from the weather and acts as a carport.

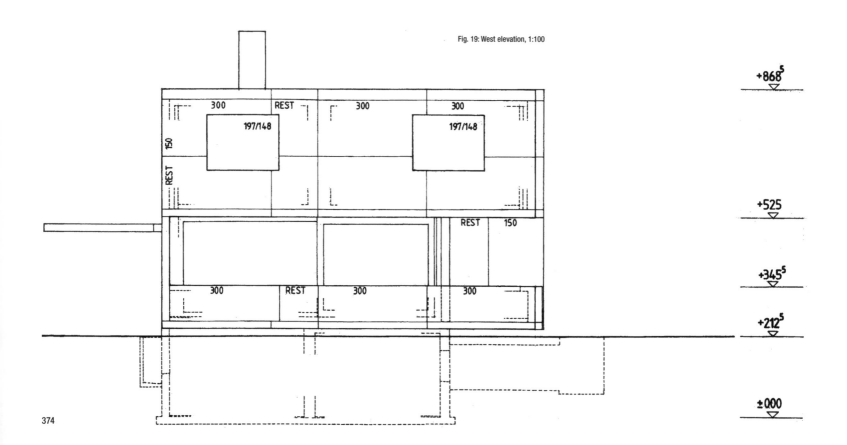

Fig. 19: West elevation, 1:100

Openings

For tectonic reasons, the windows finish flush with the outside face, which helps to emphasise the coherence of the envelope. This results in deep internal reveals, whose "archaic" nature would not normally suit the character of such a house. Märkli solves this problem by including a wooden lining on the inside with a recess for storing the shutters. With the lighting units also being positioned above the window, the technical elements are concentrated around the opening. The walls and ceilings therefore remain intact, a coherent whole.

There are two different types of window, in both cases horizontal pivot windows in aluminium frames. In the rooms above the cantilevering veranda the "wooden box", fitted with folding shutters of imitation leather, projects into the room. On the north side, in the kitchen and in the bathrooms, this box is fitted flush with the inside wall. It houses painted folding wooden shutters to provide privacy and protection against direct sunlight. All the folding shutters are standard products easily integrated into the whole thanks to their accurate design and fabrication.

Fig. 20: Window flush with facade surface
Fitting the window in this way calls for carefully controlled details in terms of sealing against driving rain and wind pressure (rebated joints).

Fig. 21: Aluminium horizontal pivot window

Fig. 22: Window with "imitation leather bellows"

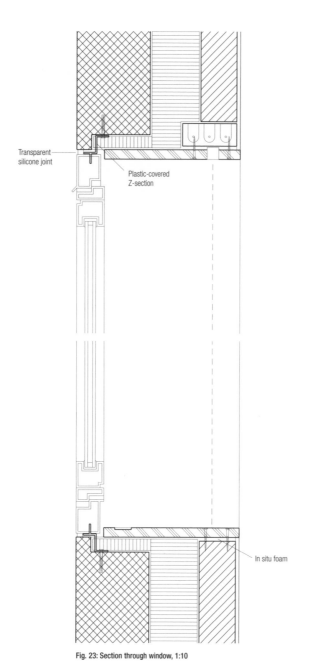

Transparent
silicone joint

Plastic-covered
Z-section

In situ foam

Fig. 23: Section through window, 1:10

Fig. 25: Window type I

Fig. 26: "Imitation leather bellows" from outside

Fig. 27: "Imitation leather bellows" from inside

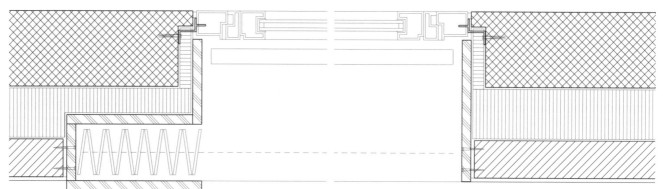

Fig. 24: Horizontal section, 1:10

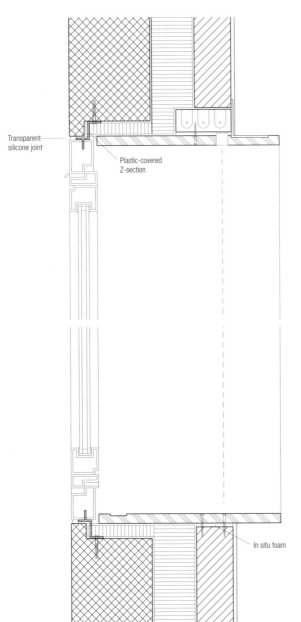

Transparent silicone joint

Plastic-covered Z-section

In situ foam

Fig. 28: Section through window, 1:10

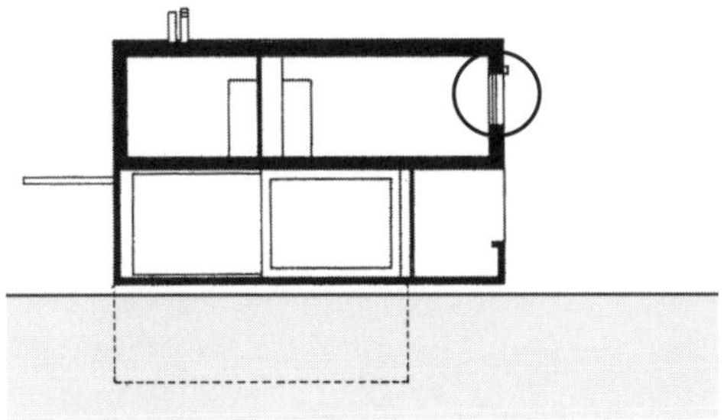

Fig. 30: Window type II

Fig. 31: Horizontal pivot window from outside

Fig. 32: Horizontal pivot window from inside

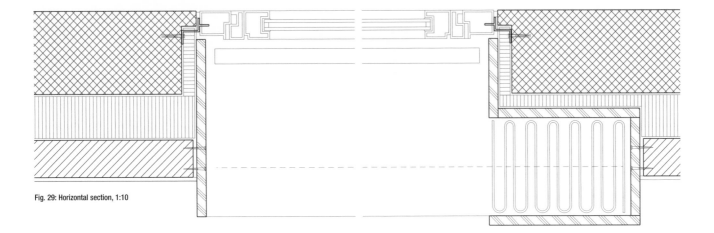

Fig. 29: Horizontal section, 1:10

Paspels School
Valerio Olgiati

Martin Tschanz

Paspels School

The school is located at the top end of Paspels village, which clings to a slope facing south-west. The three individual buildings of the existing school complex are joined in a row along the contour line of the slope, each one positioned to suit the local topography. They integrate seamlessly then into the scattering of buildings that make up the village.

Following the same logic, the new, separate school building is added on at the top end of the village. A distorted square on plan, with sides not quite at right angles to each other, this building and its roof pitch, which tracks the line of the slope, exudes a very compact expression. It seems to be moulded from a viscoplastic material that has changed shape under the effects of gravity.

Starting from a central corridor at ground floor level, the two floors of classrooms above are each reached by single flights of stairs. There are three classrooms and one ancillary room on each floor, arranged in the four corners of the building and thus facing in a different compass direction. This results in a cross-shaped common area lit from all sides, with a north-eastern arm that widens out to form an area used by the pupils at break-times. A diffuse daylight prevails here, contrasting with the changing direct sunlight in the three other arms of the cross.

As the doors to the classrooms are positioned at the far ends of the arms, each room gains its own lobby. The irregular geometry is especially noticeable in these areas because the inside corner of each room indeed forms a right angle and the short side of each room also joins the facade at a right angle.

The layout of the rooms on the two upper floors is not identical. This means that although the rooms may appear

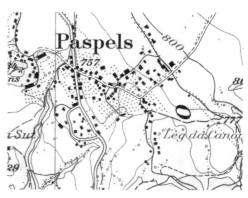

Fig. 2: The scattered layout of the village

the same, the changing lighting effects essentially create different rooms. On the outside this repositioning results in a sort of play on symmetry. Window frames in costly bronze make for a noble contrast with the crude simplicity of the concrete walls.

In terms of its construction, the school follows on the traditions of the houses of the Grisons canton. Solid concrete walls form the loadbearing structure, which contrasts starkly with the homely effect of the wood-lined rooms. The different characters of the rooms are thus highlighted: the warmth and intimacy of the classrooms contrasting with the hard, cool common areas (transition zones); a quiet, even muffled acoustic contrasting with resonance, warm brightness contrasting with differentiated light directed into the depth of each space.

Without any stylistic preferences, this school building, in terms of its character and construction, as well as in the nature of its interior, fits in perfectly with its location.

Extract from: *Archithese* 2.97

Architect: Valerio Olgiati, Zürich
Construction period: 1996–1998
Assistants: Iris Dätwyler
         Gaudenz Zindel
         Michael Meier
         Raphael Zuber
Site manager: Peter Diggelmann, Chur
Structural engineer: Gebhard Decasper, Chur

Abb. 1: Two sculptural elements project beyond the cube of the building: the canopy over the entrance and the water spout

Concept

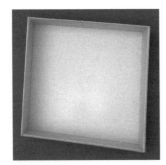

Fig. 3: External envelope

Fig. 4: The meandering internal skin around the classrooms forms a complete loop.

Fig. 5: Inner layer of insulation

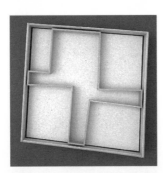

Fig. 6: The structural system chosen permits a rearranged layout on the floor above.

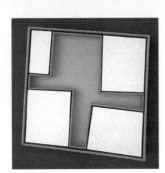

Fig. 7: The classrooms are lined with wood panelling.

Draft project

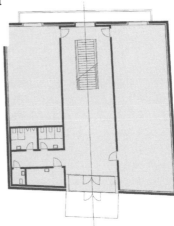

Fig. 8: Draft project, plan of ground floor

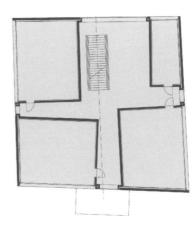

Fig. 9: Draft project, plan of 1st floor

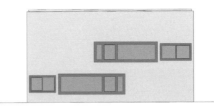

Fig. 10: Draft project, east elevation

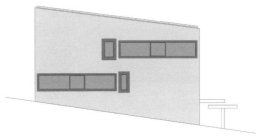

Fig. 11: Draft project, north elevation

Gebhard Decasper

Structural aspects
The engineer's report

The architectural concept called for the inside of the building to be separated from the external facade by 120 mm of thermal insulation without erecting a second loadbearing wall to support the floor slabs. This in turn called for an optimum engineering solution in order to transfer the support reactions from the walls and floors to the external facade.

The answer was to use high-strength double shear studs.

At ground floor level the two walls to the left and right of the stairs are the primary structural elements supporting the first floor. The inner walls of the first and second floors are the structural elements for the floor and roof above respectively. The interaction with the floor and roof slabs (walls as webs, slabs as flanges) is taken into account. All the support reactions are transferred at the wall junctions transverse to the external walls. Double shear studs, one above the other, were incorporated in the facade at these junctions. The number of shear studs required depends on the loadbearing capacity of a single stud.

In order to eliminate the deflection of the unsupported slab edges (spans between 8.0 and 10.0 m) along the facade, additional support points with shear studs were incorporated in the centre of each slab edge span and at the corners of the facade.

Special attention had to be given to transferring the shear forces at the shear studs.

The thermal insulation had to be reduced to 50 mm around the shear studs; however, this was acceptable in

Fig. 14: Cage of reinforcement with shear stud positioned ready for casting in

terms of the thermal requirements. In order to prevent – as far as possible – the formation of cracks in the external walls, particularly around the long horizontal windows, considerable additional longitudinal reinforcement was fitted in the areas at risk. The structural analysis of this new building represented a real challenge for the engineer.

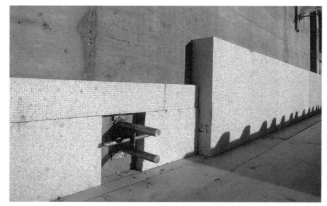

Fig. 12: The thickness of thermal insulation is reduced around the shear studs.

Fig. 13: Row of shear studs in the internal corridor

Fig. 15: 2nd floor, south-facing classroom

Fig. 16: Common area on 1st floor

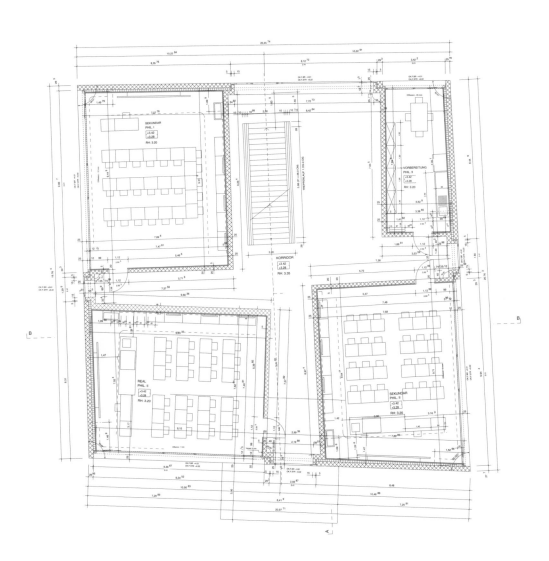

Fig. 17: Plan of 1st floor, 1:200
1:50 working drawing (reduced)

Fig. 18: Common area on 2nd floor

Fig. 19: Corridor, 2nd floor

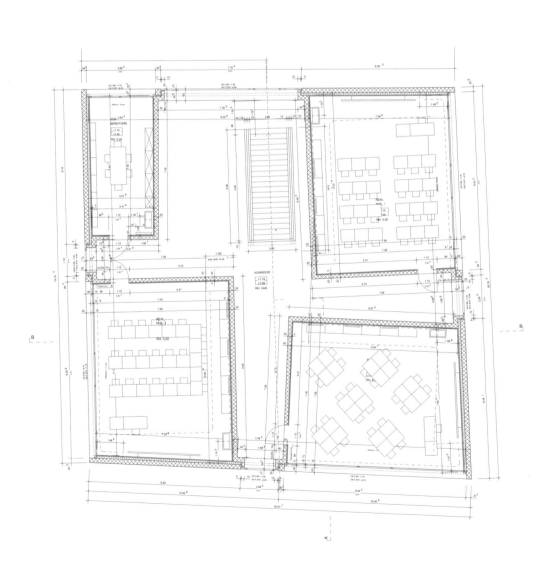

Fig. 20: Plan of 2nd floor, 1:200
1:50 working drawing (reduced)

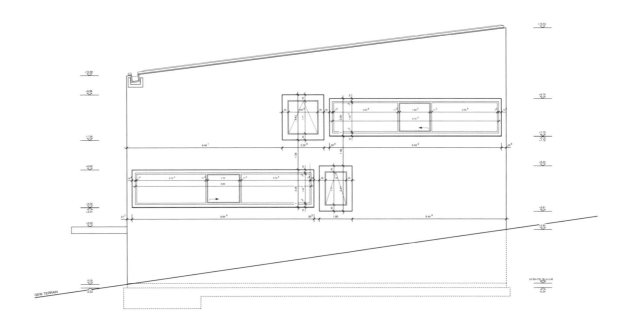

Fig. 21: South elevation, 1:200
1:50 working drawing (reduced)

Fig. 22: Section, 1:200
1:50 working drawing (reduced)

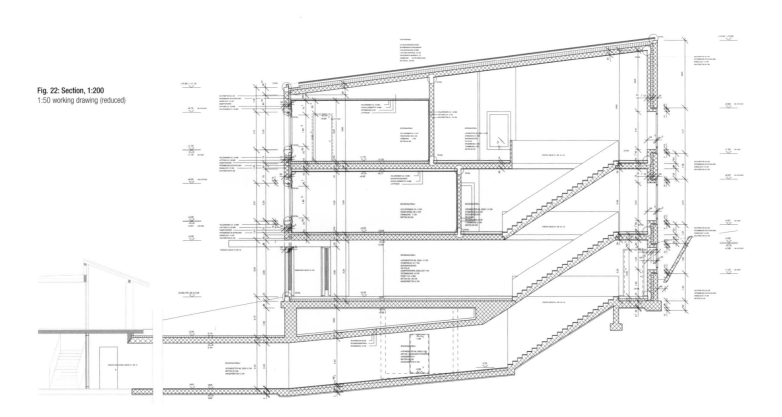

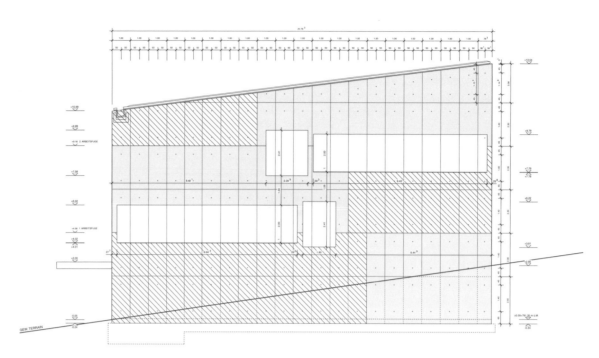

Fig. 23: South elevation, formwork layout, 1:200
1:50 working drawing (reduced)

Fig. 24: South facade

DETAIL 13

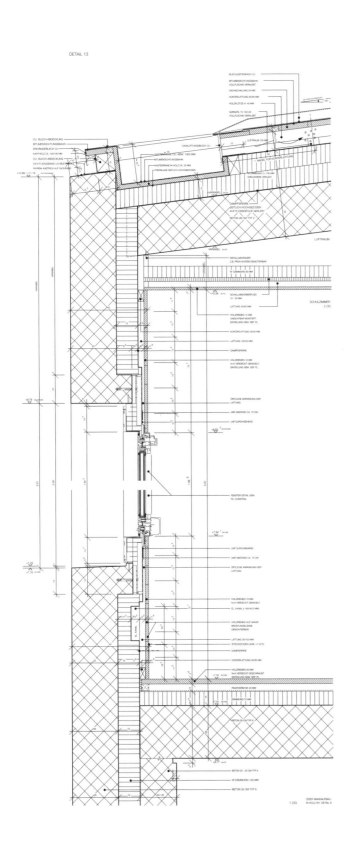

Fig. 25: Section through classroom window, 1:20
1:5 working drawing (reduced)

Fig. 26: Inward-opening classroom windows from inside

Fig. 27: Inward-opening classroom windows from outside

Floor construction

Tongue and groove boards fixed with concealed screws,	26 mm
Pavatherm NK impact sound insulation	40 mm
Thermal insulation	74 mm
Concrete, type 6	280 mm

Wall construction

Concrete, type 5	250 mm
Thermal insulation	120 mm
Vapour barrier	
Counter battens	30/60 mm
Tongue and groove boards fixed with concealed screws	18 mm

Roof construction

Sheet metal	
Bitumen roofing felt, fully bonded	
Boarding	29 mm
Counter battens	60/60 mm
Battens	40 mm
Sarnafil TU 122/08, fully bonded	
Thermal insulation, 2 layers laid cross-wise	2 x 100 mm
Vapour barrier	
Concrete, type 2	260 mm

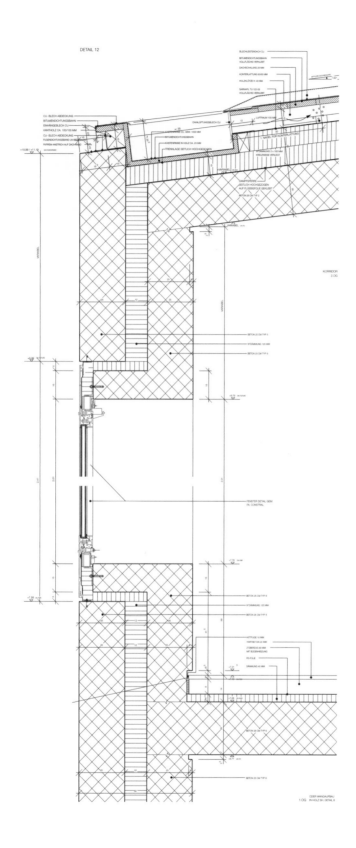

Fig. 28: Section through corridor window, 1:20
1:5 working drawing (reduced)

Fig. 29: Windows in common areas open outwards

Fig. 30: Contrast between inward- and outward-opening windows

Floor construction

Granolithic concrete	20 mm
Screed with underfloor heating	80 mm
Polyethylene sheet	
Thermal insulation	40 mm
Concrete, type 6	280 mm

Wall construction

Concrete, type 5	250 mm
Thermal insulation	120 mm
Concrete, type 5	250 mm

Roof construction

Sheet metal	
Bitumen roofing felt, fully bonded	
Boarding	29 mm
Counter battens	60/60 mm
Battens	40 mm
Sarnafil TU 122/08, fully bonded	
Thermal insulation,	
2 layers laid cross-wise	2 x 100 mm
Vapour barrier	
Concrete, type 2	260 mm

Volta School, Basel
Miller + Maranta

Judit Solt

Situation and theme

The St Johann district of Basel is a tense clash of different scales. Residential blocks, the Novartis industrial area, the northern ring road and the St Johann inland port on the Rhine are all found in close proximity. And between these two extremes lies a perimeter block development stretching mercilessly without interruption, plus the massive volume of a former coal warehouse, which has housed oil tanks for the nearby district heating power station since the 1960s.

The reform of the Basel school system and the large influx of newcomers to this part of the city in recent years resulted in an urgent need for new educational facilities here especially. In 1996 the local authority, Basel-Stadt, organised a design competition for a school building containing 12 classrooms, the related ancillary rooms and a large sports hall.

The project as constructed is not an attempt at inner-city rehabilitation, but rather the opposite; it highlights the fragmentation of the urban structure at this point in the city. But it mediates with great sensitivity between the various types of use and conflicting architectural scales that meet here.

The powerful presence of the warehouse, which dominates this district, was the starting point for the design. The new school building has been built on the site of a former heavy oil tank. It adjoins the remaining warehouse directly and assumes the same building lines; the only difference is that the new building is taller. The 6 m deep excavation that remained after removing the oil tank has been used to accommodate the sports hall. The open area in front of the school, with its gravel underfoot and canopy of leaves overhead in the summer, is used by the

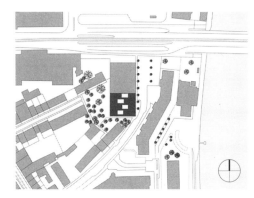

Fig. 2: Site plan

pupils at break-times but also serves as a common area for the local community.

The fair-face concrete facades help to establish the school building as an interface between the residential and industrial elements. Thanks to the layout of the form-work panels, the facades lend the building a monolithic character, even though the east and west elevations contain large openings. This compactness and the use of wood/aluminium windows fitted flush with the outside face are references to the neighbouring industrial structures, for instance the district heating power station. However, this is not a case of thoughtless industrial aesthetic. Like the adjoining warehouse, the facade concrete's pale yellow colouring has a warm, weathered feel, yet at the same time its fine, smooth character shows it to be something totally distinct.

Extract from: *Archithese* 1.01

Architects:	Miller + Maranta, Basel
Construction period:	1997–2000
Assistants:	Peter Baumberger
	Othmar Brügger
	Michael Meier
	Marius Hug
Structural engineers:	Conzett Bronzini Gartmann, Chur

Fig. 1: Entrance elevation fronting the open area

Jürg Conzett

Interior layout

The main access to the school is from the open area used by the children at break-times. Much of the entrance hall which runs the full width of the building, can also be opened up to merge with the open area. On one side a staircase leads down to the first basement level containing a viewing gallery for the sports hall and the cloakrooms, and from there a second staircase leads down to the sports hall at the second basement level. The stairs to the first floor, which accommodate common areas, are on the other side of the entrance hall. Two smaller staircases lead to the other floors above.

The layout of the other floors is essentially determined by the depth of the building and the loadbearing walls. The four room "bands" have a simple form: a classroom on the facade and the adjoining generously sized atrium, opposite this a room for special teaching requirements. However, the result is complex: a maze of corridors spreading out from the atria, but providing interesting views – into the atria, into the surroundings, into the classrooms and often even straight through several room "bands". This guarantees orientation at all times, but is also a spectacular demonstration of the unique character of an urban district split between residential and industrial uses.

Fig. 4: Classroom and atrium, with a view of the inland port on the Rhine in the distance

The entrance to the school building is on the "residential side" of this district, where small structures prevail and where only the district heating power station with its 100 m chimney provides a clue to the abrupt alternation in the structure of the local developments. We see more and more of the other side of the city as we climb higher and higher within the school. We can see as well the industrial buildings and the cranes of the inland port on the Rhine, whose unexpected size suddenly makes us realise how near they are. This setting helps to illustrate the impressive change of scale and opens up new perspectives for this district in the truest sense of the word.

Fig. 3: Access corridor with atria on both sides

Interior layout

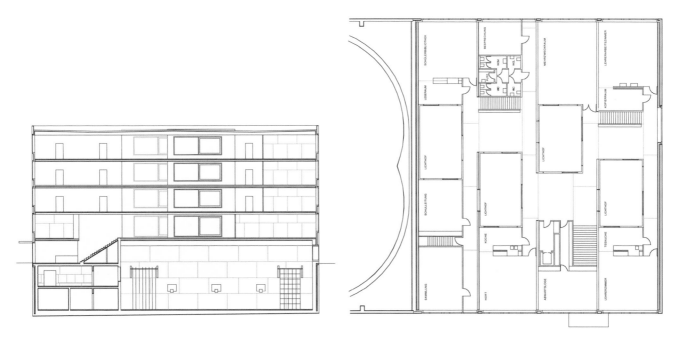

Fig. 5: Section, 1:500

Fig. 6: Plan of 1st floor, 1:500

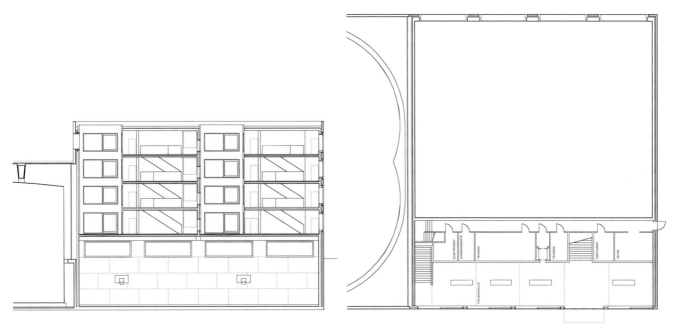

Fig. 7: Longitudinal section, 1:500

Fig. 8: Plan of ground floor, 1:500

The structural system

The mixed usage of the building – the large open sports hall with several storeys of smaller room units above – and the large depth of about 40 m led to an unconventional reinterpretation of monolithic construction. The structural system developed in conjunction with the Chur-based consulting engineers Conzett Bronzini Gartmann AG involves the composite action of concrete flat slabs (i.e. no downstand beams) and walls. The two parallel walls of the sports hall carry a slab which spans 28 m and cantilevers 12 m in the direction of the open area fronting the school. This slab in turn supports the loadbearing walls which divide the building into four room "bands". Bending moments are resisted by prestressing.

The man-made link between separating and supporting – intrinsic to monolithic construction – leads to a particular concentration of significance for every single element. This is especially relevant when, as with this building, the structural concept and internal layout are conceived as a single entity. It is interesting that the construction principle employed here permits walls to be supported only at a certain place, and hence reveals new interior layout options in monolithic construction that are worth exploring.

The construction principle behind this building remains discernible without becoming oppressive. The facades ensure the stability of the building in the longitudinal direction; however, they are non-loadbearing and are connected to the loadbearing structure only at discrete points. One of the places where this can be seen is on the west elevation, where the grid lines are displaced.

Fig. 10: Shear wall showing reinforcement and prestressing tendon

The materials used also point to the structural principles: the loadbearing elements – slabs and walls – are in fair-face concrete, contrasting with the non-loadbearing elements employing lightweight construction techniques.

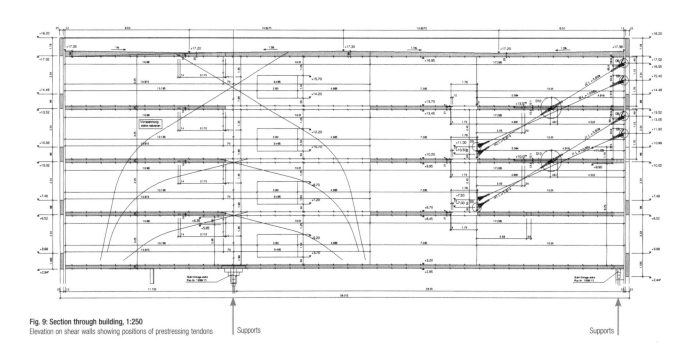

Fig. 9: Section through building, 1:250
Elevation on shear walls showing positions of prestressing tendons   Supports   Supports

Fig. 11: East facade

Fig. 12: Atrium

External and atrium facades

External facades

The design of the facades is not essentially dictated by the internal layout behind. The facade is basically a single-leaf construction attached to the loadbearing wall behind only at individual places. Without expansion joints and structurally autonomous, it embraces the loadbearing walls like an independent skin. Using the same material for the facade and the walls prevents an ambiguous, fragmented realisation.

Neither the internal layout nor the enormous room depths are apparent on the fair-face concrete facade. The metal-framed windows are arranged in horizontal bands.

Internally, the contrast between structure and fitting-out is reduced to the simple complementary elements of shell and lining, which means that the structural efforts are hardly perceptible.

Atrium facades

The atria have a cladding of wood-based panels in a mother-of-pearl colour and wooden windows fitted flush with the outside face. Together, these create the effect of polished, compact inclusions in a concrete monolith.

Fig. 13: East elevation showing layout of formwork panels, 1:500

External and atrium facades

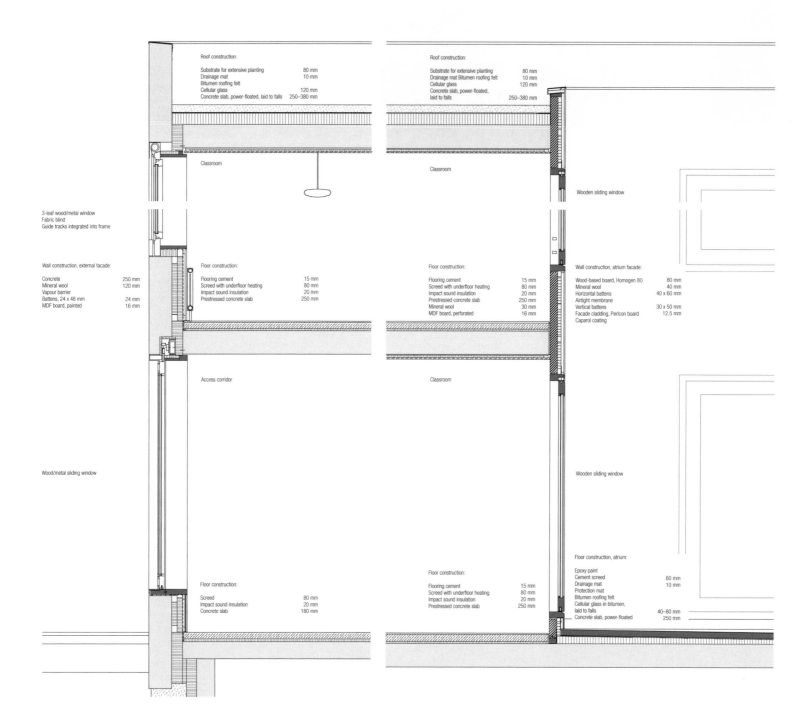

Roof construction:

Substrate for extensive planting	80 mm
Drainage mat	10 mm
Bitumen roofing felt	
Cellular glass	120 mm
Concrete slab, power-floated, laid to falls	250–380 mm

Classroom

3-leaf wood/metal window
Fabric blind
Guide tracks integrated into frame

Wall construction, external facade:

Concrete	250 mm
Mineral wool	120 mm
Vapour barrier	
Battens, 24 x 48 mm	24 mm
MDF board, painted	16 mm

Floor construction:

Flooring cement	15 mm
Screed with underfloor heating	80 mm
Impact sound insulation	20 mm
Prestressed concrete slab	250 mm

Access corridor

Wood/metal sliding window

Floor construction:

Screed	80 mm
Impact sound insulation	20 mm
Concrete slab	180 mm

Fig. 14: Section through external facade

Roof construction:

Substrate for extensive planting	80 mm
Drainage mat Bitumen roofing felt	10 mm
Cellular glass	120 mm
Concrete slab, power-floated, laid to falls	250–380 mm

Classroom

Wooden sliding window

Floor construction:

Flooring cement	15 mm
Screed with underfloor heating	80 mm
Impact sound insulation	20 mm
Prestressed concrete slab	250 mm
Mineral wool	30 mm
MDF board, perforated	16 mm

Wall construction, atrium facade:

Wood-based board, Homogen 80	80 mm
Mineral wool	40 mm
Horizontal battens	40 x 60 mm
Airtight membrane	
Vertical battens	30 x 50 mm
Facade cladding, Perlcon board	12.5 mm
Caparol coating	

Classroom

Wooden sliding window

Floor construction, atrium:

Epoxy paint	
Cement screed	60 mm
Drainage mat	10 mm
Protection mat	
Bitumen roofing felt	
Cellular glass in bitumen, laid to falls	40–80 mm
Concrete slab, power-floated	250 mm

Floor construction:

Flooring cement	15 mm
Screed with underfloor heating	80 mm
Impact sound insulation	20 mm
Prestressed concrete slab	250 mm

Fig. 15: Section through atrium facade

0   1   2.5 m

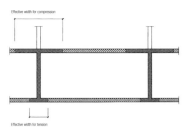

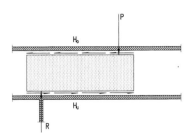

Fig. 16: Shear wall schemes
Loadbearing shear walls acting as transfer structures for individual columns
(elevation and section)

Remarks on the structural system
"Shear diaphragms in buildings"

The idea of using walls and floor slabs as interconnected, loadbearing elements in buildings is not new. This principle, however, is used mainly only locally, when other options prove inadequate, e.g. in transfer structures or cantilevers for heavy storeys. But when employed systematically as a constructional concept for a building, this approach can result in useful solutions, particularly with complicated internal layouts, and thus present a rational alternative to a framed building.

We shall start by looking at a reinforced concrete wall plate constructed monolithically with the floor slabs above and below. Such a wall plate can be considered, for example, as an I-section beam, transferring the loads of a row of columns into the external walls (fig. 168). Far more interesting and more versatile applications are, however, possible if we exploit the fact that in most instances the floor slabs of a building are supported on an internal core and external walls such that they are held in position horizontally. If this condition is satisfied, then it is sufficient to support a wall plate at just one point, any point, in order to turn it into a stable, unyielding loadbearing element (fig. 169). The beam in fig. 168 can therefore be split into two individual wall plates of different sizes without suffering any loss in load-carrying capacity (fig. 170).

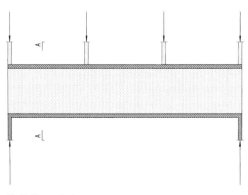

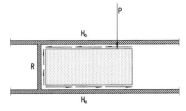

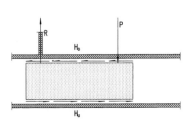

Fig. 17: Shear wall schemes
Shear wall as unyielding structural element with single discrete support. The rotational effect of load P and support reaction R is eliminated by the horizontal couple H_o and H_u generated in the floor slabs.

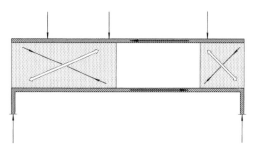

Fig. 18: Shear wall scheme
Beam consisting of two non-identical shear walls

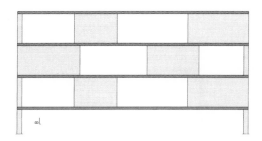

Fig. 19: Planar unyielding wall systems (system A)

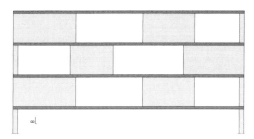

Fig. 20: Planar unyielding wall systems (system B)

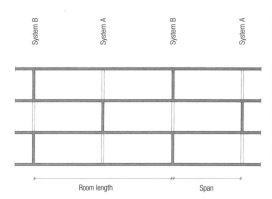

Room length   Span

Fig. 21: Section B-B through a row of several systems as shown in Figs 171/172

However, keeping in line with the aforementioned condition, the unequal horizontal forces that are transferred from the wall plates into the floor slabs must be able to continue down to the foundations via stiff cores or external walls. The floor slabs are loaded in two different ways: on the one hand they act structurally as slabs which transfer the forces from distributed loads to the loadbearing wall plates by way of bending (this is the conventional structural action of floor slabs), and on the other they also act as plates in conjunction with the walls (and in doing so assume a role similar to that of the flanges of a rolled steel beam section). The floor slabs become then interactive loadbearing elements which realise several structural functions simultaneously. Interactively loaded components have long since been common in bridge-building. For example, the road deck of a box girder bridge acts as a slab transferring the wheel loads transverse to the axis of the bridge into the webs of the box, while at the same time acting as the upper flange in the longitudinal direction of the bridge. In buildings the stresses due to the plate effect are generally so low that conventional design based on bending of the slab is sufficient to determine the thickness of the floor slab. The plate forces then need to be considered only when sizing the reinforcing bars.

An unyielding wall plate can also serve as a support or suspension point for another plate. In this way we can build complete systems of unyielding plates (figs 171 and 172). As already mentioned, it is sufficient when the plates make contact at one – any – point. The floor slabs are either supported on or suspended from the wall plates. Wall plates above or below are equally useful as supports; by choosing complementary wall plate systems the span of the floor slab can be reduced, possibly to just half the length of the room (fig. 173).

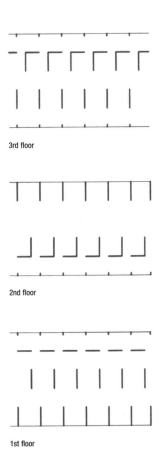

3rd floor

2nd floor

1st floor

Fig. 22: Plans on schemes in axonometric view below

Systems of unyielding wall plates are not confined to just one level. Individual plates can be cranked or rotated with respect to each other without diminishing their structural effect or making them more complicated to build (fig. 175). As long as we maintain the conditions of the horizontally unyielding floor slabs and the wall plates held at one point at least, numerous combination options ensue. Nevertheless, only the components already provided are used to transfer the forces; ribs, downstand beams or linear structural members are unnecessary.

Several examples investigated in detail show that in buildings of three or more storeys unsupported spans of up to 40 m are possible without any inappropriate effort. The thickness of the concrete wall plates in these cases is between 200 and 350 mm. The planning and execution of such a system is simple and economic, but does require close cooperation between architect and engineer from the very beginning, and leaves little room for improvisation.

Excerpt from: *Werk, Bauen+Wohnen* 9/97

Fig. 23: Axonometric sketch showing the principle of a three-dimensional system of unyielding shear walls

Sihlhof School, Zurich
Giuliani Hönger

Lorenzo Giuliani, Christian Hönger,
Patric Allemann

Architect: Giuliani Hönger, Zurich
Construction period: 2001–2003
Project management: Lorenzo Giuliani
                        Christian Hönger
                        Marcel Santer
Site management: Bosshard + Partner, Zurich
Structural engineers: Dr Lüchinger + Meyer, Zurich

Concept, urban integration

The concept is distinguished by the great complexity of the brief: two different polytechnics with very extensive and – when planning started – not fully defined interior layouts had to be realised within a single building in a central location. In order to minimise the design and building time, this large new building had to comply with the applicable building regulations; there was insufficient time to apply for a lengthy architectural design approval procedure. Nevertheless, the aim still was to create a convincing urban and architectural statement within this heterogeneous context.

Starting with the maximum volume allowed by the building regulations, the building was given a distinctive form compared with its variegated surroundings. A five-to seven-storey facade in a large-scale format was built facing Lagerstrasse. This abuts an office building – protected by a preservation order – dating from the 1950s by way of a respectful "joint". At the back the building steps down towards the smaller neighbouring buildings, thus matching their scale. The projections allowed for in the building regulations enabled this terracing effect to be devised in such a way that the building gains a sculpted character but still appears as a coherent unit. Exploiting the outlines more or less to the full results in

Fig. 2: Site plan

the maximum possible volume for the ambitious interior layout.

Like the shape of the building, the facade also interprets its urban context. On the one hand, the beige-coloured reconstituted stone cladding enables the building to blend into its surroundings. While on the other, the minor variations in the width of the piers between the windows, the dominant feature of the facade, leaves a slightly odd impression and thus enables the university building to take on its own character.

Fig. 1: View from Kasernenstrasse
The main entrance is emphasised by the cantilevering lecture theatre above. On the left the "joint" between the new building and its neighbour.

Fig. 3: View of rear of building

Internal layout

Two offset atria help to handle the great depth of this building. The two are connected at one point and so become a coherent structure which – in a similar way to the atria at Zurich University and in the central hall in the main building of the ETH – creates a powerful identity. Depending on the observer's position and viewing angle, this element is perceived either as one "cranked" internal space or as two separate inner courtyards. In line with this dual usage each atrium is associated with one of the polytechnics. Whereas the Business and Management School is arranged around the upper atrium (lit from above), the Teacher Training College surrounds the lower atrium (illuminated by diffuse light from the sides). With their generous vertical dimensions, these are quality urban inner spaces ideally suited to the inner workings of such an educational establishment.

The single, large lecture theatre is positioned over the entrance so that it can be reached from both polytechnics via a small foyer but is also accessible to external users. By projecting a little beyond the line of the facade it helps direct the eye towards the main entrance and defines the entrance area before this expands upwards in the form of the first atrium.

Whereas the lecture theatre, a special-purpose room, is slotted into the plan like a piece of a jigsaw, the seminar and study rooms trace the lines of the various facades. Winding access corridors are the outcome of this plan layout, the atria and the adjoining ancillary rooms. The facade steps back as we proceed up the building, as

Fig. 4: Lower atrium
At top right the entrance to the foyer of the lecture theatre

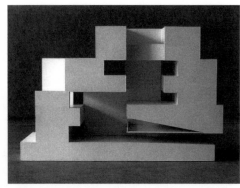

Fig. 5: Sectional model
Upper and lower atria join to form one interior space

do the positions of the corridors. Their layout also has to take account of the two atria. But thanks to the recurring references to the atria, orientation remains straightforward despite the complexity of the internal layout. To minimise the space for the staircases, these are kept simple, which is a boon to the atria. All three staircases also serve as escape routes.

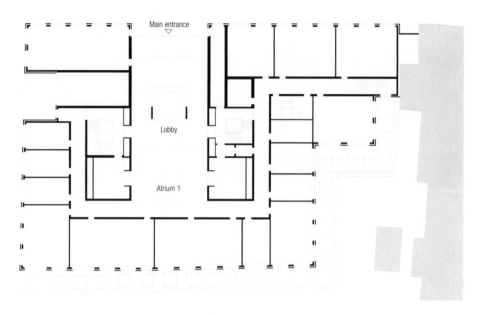

Fig. 6: Plan of ground floor, 1:600

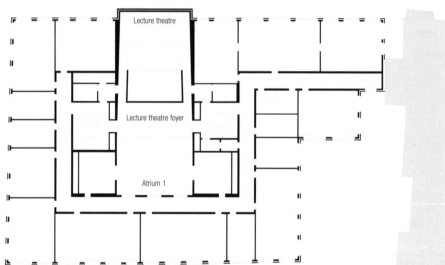

Fig. 7: Plan of 1st floor, 1:600

Fig. 8: Plan of 2nd floor, 1:600

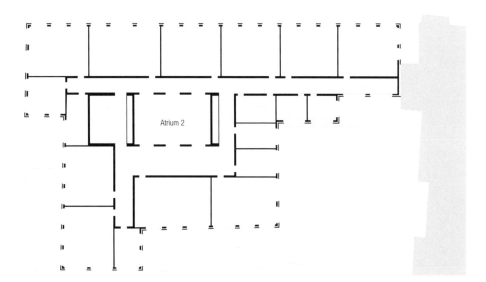

Fig. 9: Plan of 3rd floor, 1:600

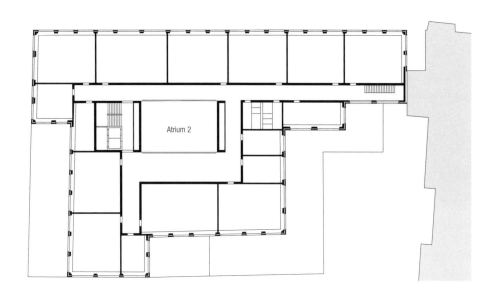

Fig. 10: Plan of 4th floor, 1:600

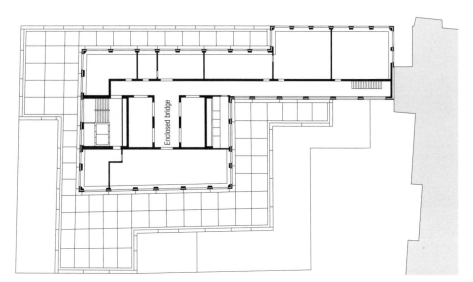

Fig. 11: Plan of 5th floor, 1:600

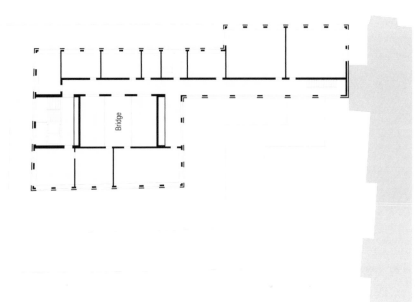

Fig. 12: Plan of 6th floor, 1:600

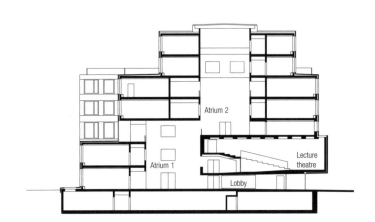

Fig. 13: Section, 1:600

Fig. 14: Longitudinal section, 1:600

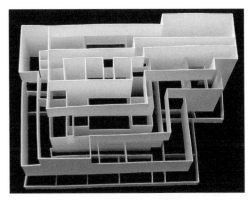
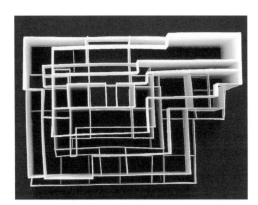

Figs 15 and 16: Model showing principle of vertical loadbearing structure
The loadbearing walls are stacked in different positions with respect to each other and intersect storey by storey.

Fig. 17: Upper atrium, looking down towards entrance level
The walls without intermediate supports act as storey-high deep beams.

Loadbearing structure

The terracing at the back of the building and the offset atria leaves the structure with only a few vertical load-bearing walls that pass through all storeys. Loadbearing walls of reinforced concrete stacked cross-wise make up the primary vertical loadbearing elements. At the same time these act as the facades and the fair-face concrete walls to the meandering access corridors (see figs 15 and 16). The loads are directed into the loadbearing walls and then accumulate at the intersections, from where they continue on their downward journey to the foundations.

In this system the door and window openings in the wall plates represent a problem. In order to maintain the structural integrity it is necessary to include top and bottom chords (door and window lintels, door thresholds, spandrel panels) at all openings and/or adequately sized floor slabs. Therefore, on the terracing at the back of the building the severely perforated loadbearing walls in the facade act compositely with the 300 mm thick reinforced concrete floor slabs. Around the atria the concrete walls have fewer openings and can therefore span further. Some of the slabs, e.g. over the lower atrium or the floor of the lecture theatre, are suspended from these loadbearing walls.

Despite the ambitious structural aspects the strict architectural requirements governing the formwork layout and the surface quality requirements for the fair-face concrete walls internally still had to be fulfilled.

The groups of seminar and study rooms can be flexibly subdivided, despite the monolithic construction, within the limits imposed by the fenestration and the doors in the walls to the corridors.

Fig. 18: Working drawing of 1st floor, 1:50
(reduced here to 1:200)

Materials and design

Both the facade and the terraces are clad with prefabricated polished reconstituted stone panels. The beige-yellow colouring of the Jurassic limestone exposed by the polishing provides a reference to the colours of neighbouring buildings like the post office and the office building on the corner (protected by a preservation order). The facade makes use of vertical piers and horizontal spandrel elements of a similar size suspended like a curtain wall in front of the structural members. The joints are sealed. At first sight we appear to be viewing a large-scale structural facade. But owing to the displacement of the piers from floor to floor, attributable to the internal layout, a closer inspection reveals a new type of appearance which,

Fig. 20: Seminar room

compared with conventional grid-like facades, loses much of its rigidity. The edges of the 120 mm thick reconstituted stone panels are never visible. All corners and edges are formed with three-dimensional elements, which reinforces the corporeal appearance of the building.

The three different sizes of window employ the double window principle. Whereas the inner window completes the building envelope in terms of thermal performance requirements, the outer window provides acoustic insulation and protection for the sunblinds fitted between the inner and outer windows. The windows are set back with respect to the cladding, which establishes a delicate relief and introduces a subtle play of light and shade on the facade.

Light-coloured fair-face concrete walls and stone floor finishes in Venetian trachyte make it very clear that the architects intended the atria and access zone to serve as urban spaces. Taking up this logic, the lecture theatre – a place of assembly – employs the same materials. To contrast with this, the seminar rooms have linoleum or carpeting on the floors, white-painted glass-fibre wallpaper on the walls, wooden doors and wooden window seats to create a more homely atmosphere. The floor slab thickness of 300 mm necessary for structural reasons meant that all floor finishes could be laid directly on the floated concrete without the need for impact sound insulation or screeds. The (long) drying time normally required for screeds was thus unnecessary and this shortened the construction time considerably.

Fig. 19: Terracing at rear of building
Terraces and facades are finished with polished reconstituted stone panels;
corner and edge pieces are three-dimensional elements.

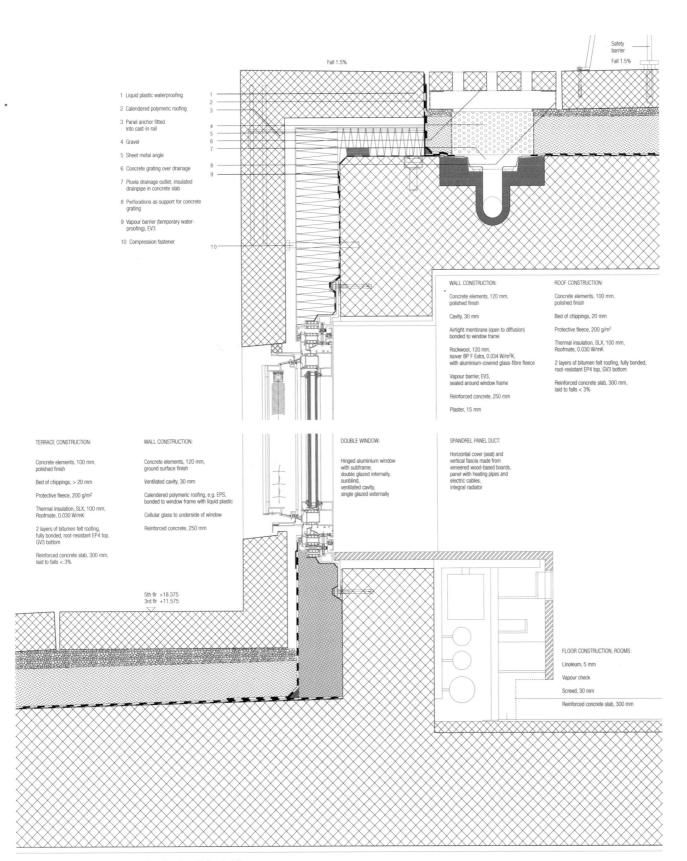

1 Liquid plastic waterproofing

2 Calendered polymeric roofing

3 Panel anchor fitted
   into cast-in rail

4 Gravel

5 Sheet metal angle

6 Concrete grating over drainage

7 Pluvia drainage outlet, insulated
   drainpipe in concrete slab

8 Perforations as support for concrete
   grating

9 Vapour barrier (temporary waterproofing), EV3

10 Compression fastener

Fall 1.5%

Safety
barrier

Fall 1.5%

WALL CONSTRUCTION:

Concrete elements, 120 mm,
polished finish

Cavity, 30 mm

Airtight membrane (open to diffusion)
bonded to window frame

Rockwool, 120 mm,
Isover BP F Extra, 0.034 W/m²K,
with aluminium-covered glass-fibre fleece

Vapour barrier, EV3,
sealed around window frame

Reinforced concrete, 250 mm

Plaster, 15 mm

ROOF CONSTRUCTION:

Concrete elements, 100 mm,
polished finish

Bed of chippings, 20 mm

Protective fleece, 200 g/m²

Thermal insulation, SLX, 100 mm,
Roofmate, 0.030 W/mK

2 layers of bitumen felt roofing, fully bonded,
root-resistant EP4 top, GV3 bottom

Reinforced concrete slab, 300 mm,
laid to falls < 3%

TERRACE CONSTRUCTION:

Concrete elements, 100 mm,
polished finish

Bed of chippings, > 20 mm

Protective fleece, 200 g/m²

Thermal insulation, SLX, 100 mm,
Roofmate, 0.030 W/mK

2 layers of bitumen felt roofing,
fully bonded, root-resistant EP4 top,
GV3 bottom

Reinforced concrete slab, 300 mm,
laid to falls < 3%

WALL CONSTRUCTION:

Concrete elements, 120 mm,
ground surface finish

Ventilated cavity, 30 mm

Calendered polymeric roofing, e.g. EPS,
bonded to window frame with liquid plastic

Cellular glass to underside of window

Reinforced concrete, 250 mm

DOUBLE WINDOW:

Hinged aluminium window
with subframe,
double glazed internally,
sunblind,
ventilated cavity,
single glazed externally

SPANDREL PANEL DUCT:

Horizontal cover (seat) and
vertical fascia made from
veneered wood-based boards,
panel with heating pipes and
electric cables,
integral radiator

5th flr +18.375
3rd flr +11.575

FLOOR CONSTRUCTION, ROOMS:

Linoleum, 5 mm

Vapour check

Screed, 30 mm

Reinforced concrete slab, 300 mm

Fig. 21: Section through edge of terrace (top) and junction with facade, 1:5
(reduced here to 1:10)

Building services

The use of thick, solid floors increases the active storage mass significantly and, thanks to the heat storage capacity, improves the comfort in the interior at all times of the year. All seminar rooms are mechanically ventilated for reasons of comfort (high noise levels on Lagerstrasse), but natural ventilation (by opening the windows) nevertheless remains possible. Air-conditioning is used in the lecture theatre and the IT training rooms. Louvre blinds provide sunshading which is controlled according to the level of daylight. This helps to achieve an optimised energy balance. Heat generation and distribution is by conventional means. As the use of the building calls for the temperature control to respond rapidly, space heating is by means of radiators fitted along the spandrel panels.

Supply- and exhaust-air ducts are routed in the suspended ceilings over the access corridors. Electric cables, heating pipes and the IT network cables run in the ducts along the spandrel panels.

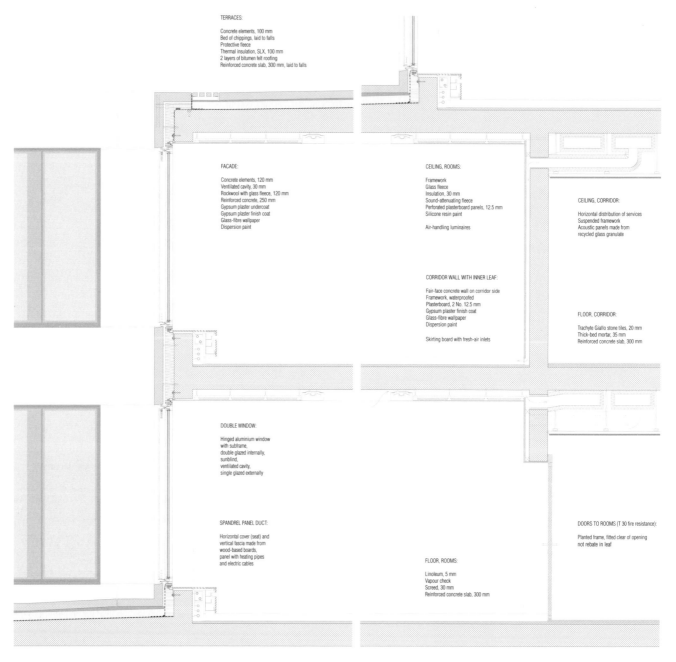

TERRACES:

Concrete elements, 100 mm
Bed of chippings, laid to falls
Protective fleece
Thermal insulation, SLX, 100 mm
2 layers of bitumen felt roofing
Reinforced concrete slab, 300 mm, laid to falls

FACADE:

Concrete elements, 120 mm
Ventilated cavity, 30 mm
Rockwool with glass fleece, 120 mm
Reinforced concrete, 250 mm
Gypsum plaster undercoat
Gypsum plaster finish coat
Glass-fibre wallpaper
Dispersion paint

CEILING, ROOMS:

Framework
Glass fleece
Insulation, 30 mm
Sound-attenuating fleece
Perforated plasterboard panels, 12.5 mm
Silicone resin paint

Air-handling luminaires

CEILING, CORRIDOR:

Horizontal distribution of services
Suspended framework
Acoustic panels made from
recycled glass granulate

CORRIDOR WALL WITH INNER LEAF:

Fair-face concrete wall on corridor side
Framework, waterproofed
Plasterboard, 2 No. 12.5 mm
Gypsum plaster finish coat
Glass-fibre wallpaper
Dispersion paint

Skirting board with fresh-air inlets

FLOOR, CORRIDOR:

Trachyte Giallo stone tiles, 20 mm
Thick-bed mortar, 35 mm
Reinforced concrete slab, 300 mm

DOUBLE WINDOW:

Hinged aluminium window
with subframe,
double glazed internally,
sunblind,
ventilated cavity,
single glazed externally

SPANDREL PANEL DUCT:

Horizontal cover (seat) and
vertical fascia made from
wood-based boards,
panel with heating pipes
and electric cables

FLOOR, ROOMS:

Linoleum, 5 mm
Vapour check
Screed, 30 mm
Reinforced concrete slab, 300 mm

DOORS TO ROOMS (T 30 fire resistance):

Planted frame, fitted clear of opening
not rebate in leaf

Fig. 22: Section through seminar room and corridor
Services are routed in ducts along the spandrel panels and
above the suspended ceiling over the corridor.

Training centre, Gordola
Durisch + Nolli

Andreas Kohne

Urban planning

The training centre of the Swiss Building Industry Association was conceived in the 1960s as a campus. It is located in the marshes of the Magadino Plain on the edge of the small town of Gordola, very close to an industrial estate, the A 13 motorway and the nature conservation area on the banks of Lake Maggiore. A two-stage architectural competition was held for the new premises needed to complement the existing buildings. The new building had to provide training rooms and workshops for metalworkers, joiners and plumbers, all protected against flooding. The convincing aspect of the winning design is that it employs stilts instead of an embankment to raise the building, situated on the edge of the site, above potential floodwaters. The new building, positioned across the line of the valley, redefines the boundary between the landscape and the grounds of the training centre. It does this, however, without interrupting the broad plain, at the same time creating a new balance between existing and new.

The project

This long building containing workshops and classrooms is characterised by a striking sawtooth roof form that recalls the familiar industrial shed. All the rooms required are housed in this 140 m long building, which is raised almost 3 m above the ground. Elevating the complete building guarantees highly effective protection against floods. However, this design idea also results in a spacious, open outdoor area. The large covered area beneath the building is suitable for a variety of uses: a shady place for working

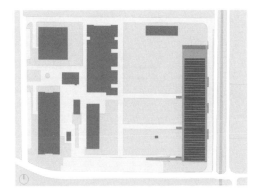

Fig. 2: Location plan
The existing complex with the new building on the western boundary

or relaxing in summer, a large car park, storing materials, etc. Access to platform and building is via three wide stairs plus a long ramp on the west side. These lead directly to the workshop entrances. There is also a large lift for goods and mobility-impaired persons at the northern end of the building. The open platform on all sides connects the individual entrances. During breaks it is used as a terrace from where students can enjoy the view across the grounds to the mountains beyond the plain.

Each entrance opens onto a corridor that crosses the building and terminates in a glass door that admits daylight into the entrance zone. The corridors widen in the centre to form small foyers. The three entrance areas divide the building into three large training workshops, the "laboratori". Based on a grid of 3 m, which is ideal in this case, the workshop areas measure 27 m wide and

Architects: Durisch + Nolli Architetti
      Sagl, Massagno/Lugano
Project managers: Pia Durisch, Aldo Nolli
Competition: 2004
Construction: 2008–2010
Structural engineer: Jürg Buchli, Haldenstein
      (d. 2010)

Fig. 1: View of the new building from the north-west
The precise, shiny metal "workpiece" lying on the "workbench"

407

Fig. 3: Longitudinal section, 1:1200

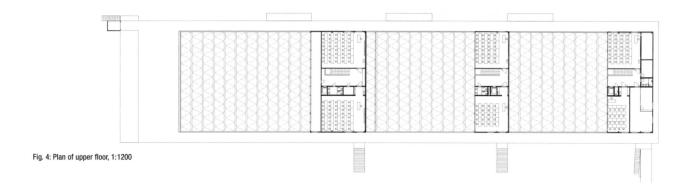

Fig. 4: Plan of upper floor, 1:1200

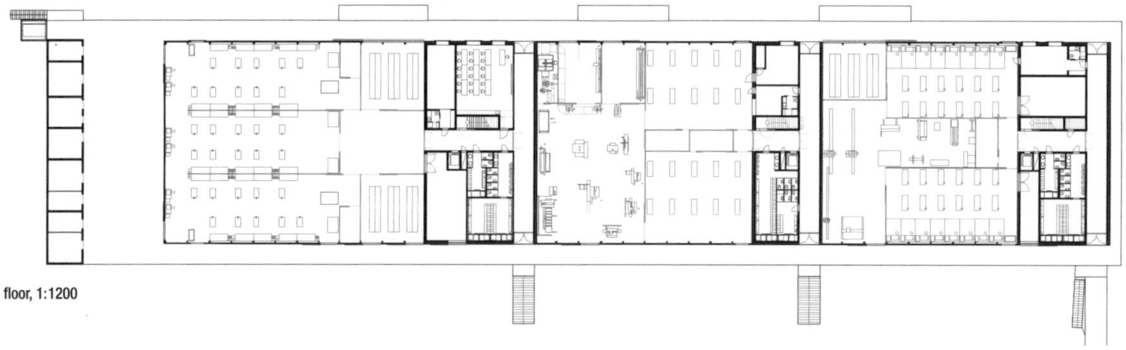

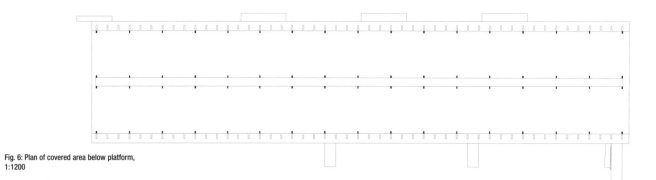

Fig. 5: Plan of ground floor, 1:1200

Fig. 6: Plan of covered area below platform,
1:1200

are between 27 and 33 m long. These large rooms, with about 800 m² floor area, can be subdivided into separate teaching zones by means of transparent partitions. The introverted working areas, free from intervening columns, are illuminated via the translucent northlights of the sawtooth roof and thus present optimum conditions for exacting operations on the machines. Such a design fosters every student's concentration. In addition, openings in the longitudinal facades frame specific, picturesque views of the immediate surroundings. Changing rooms and sanitary facilities plus ancillary and plant rooms are located adjacent to the entrance areas, which are accessible from both sides. Each classroom for theory lessons on the upper floor is reached via a central stair or lift accessed from the foyer below. The classrooms are also lit via the sawtooth roof and square windows in the walls. The long zigzag line of the roof rises in these areas to indicate the presence of the classrooms and emphasise the entrances.

The structure

The structure of the building is memorable, simple and efficiently formulated: rising above the large, open "workbench" in fair-face concrete is the building containing the training workshops in lightweight, shiny steel representing a precisely machined "workpiece".

Fig. 8: The lattice beams for the roof prior to erection

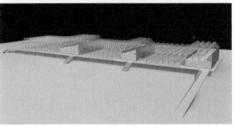

Figs 9, 10: Models of the structure
The roof is a folded trussed framework covering the entire building.

Fig. 7: Erecting the steelwork
Lattice beams span the full width of the building and, together with the facade columns, constitute the exposed loadbearing structure.

Fig. 11: Classroom on upper floor

Roof construction

Profiled sheet metal type SP,	
45 x 900 x 0.8 mm	45 mm
Supporting framework	60 mm
Underlay, Sarnafil TU 111	
Thermal insulation, Flumroc PARA	2 No. 80 mm
Vapour barrier, Sarnavap 1000E	
Flat sheet, Montana SP 59 x 900 x 1.00 A	59 mm
Trussed framework / metal frame	

Wall construction

Profiled sheet metal type SP,	
45 x 900 x 0.8 mm	45 mm
Supporting framework, top-hat sections	2 No. 40 mm
Thermal insulation, Isover Cladisol	120 mm
Metal tray, Montana MK 80 x 500 mm	80 mm
Steel column, HEA 200	190 mm
Total	475 mm

Floor construction

Floor covering, granolithic finish	160 mm
Thermal insulation	40 mm
Reinforced concrete slab (Cobiax system)	400 mm
Total	600 mm

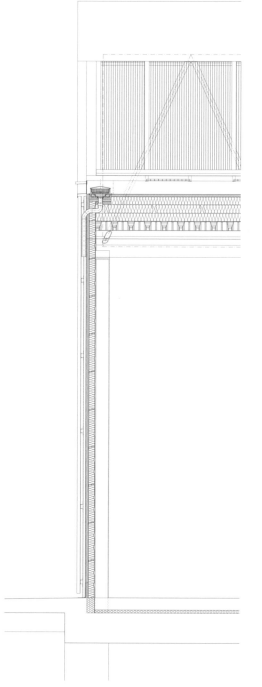

Fig. 12: Section through facade, 1:50

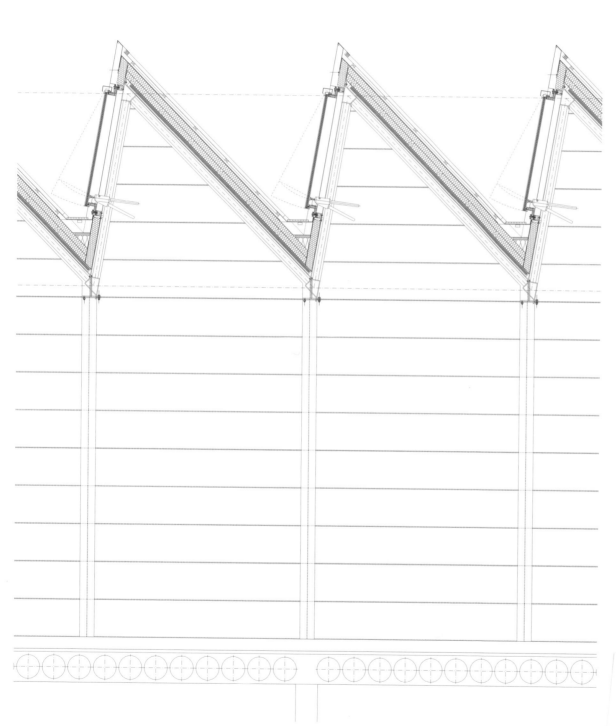

Fig. 13: Section through roof and northlights, 1:50

The 68 reinforced concrete columns of the "table" are arranged on a grid that is ideal for both loadbearing structure and flexibility of use. All columns are founded on pad foundations because of the alluvial gravel of the subsoil. The 40 cm thick reinforced concrete slab, the "tabletop", supported by these columns, has a maximum span of 12 m. Large spherical void formers (Cobiax system) were cast into the reinforced concrete slab between the top and bottom reinforcement to save weight and material.

Erected on this slab is an extremely slender steel structure with HEA columns on a 3 x 27 m grid. A folded steel frame was developed for the roof and used to cover the whole building. This delicate "lacework", as the designers called it, can span the building width of 27 m without the need for any intermediate columns, and repeats over the entire length of the structure. Shear walls in reinforced concrete alongside the access zones stabilise the building and also divide it into fire compartments. The folded shape of the roof enables the inclusion of northlights, which together with the north-south orientation guarantee optimum glare-free illumination in the workshops and classrooms. Simple opening panels in the acrylic sheets of the northlights enable the large rooms to be ventilated naturally. All pipes, cables and ducts are suspended from the members of the roof construction and left exposed. The lightweight partitions, made from Duripanel cement-bonded frame panels with large areas of glazing, divide the rooms into their functional units, but in no way diminish the directness and openness of the interior. The brightly lit workshops are designed for a high level of flexibility and good working conditions.

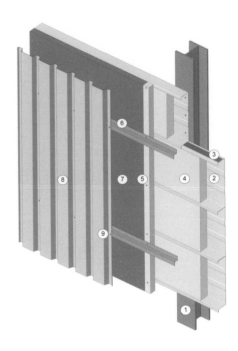

1. Steel column
2. Metal tray
3. Sealing tape
4. Thermal insulation
5. Vertical battens
6. Z-section cladding rail
7. Additional insulation
8. Trapezoidal profile sheet metal cladding attached vertically
9. Cladding fastener

Fig. 15: Facade construction principle
Montana Bausysteme AG

Fig. 14: Erecting the building envelope
The layered facade construction was readily visible during erection.

Building envelope and materials

Its obvious lightness allows this structure to enter into a dialogue with the sheds and greenhouses of the surroundings. Both inside and outside it is reminiscent of a factory building. The materials selected and their precise fabrication, a key factor in the character of the building, correspond to the vocations being trained within. Using reinforced concrete for the loadbearing structure to the elevated platform keeps the design simple and practical. A lightweight, delicate steel structure on top of this was chosen in order to minimise the load on the platform. The structural steelwork, left exposed internally, is finished on the outside with conventional lightweight metal cladding. Both facade and roof use a simple metal tray system, Montawall (Montana), which is commonly used for industrial buildings. These metal liner trays, visible inside the building, are filled with insulation on the outside and clad with profiled metal sheeting. In this building the trays for the roofs above the classrooms are perforated in order to improve the room acoustics. On the outside the entire building is clad with thin trapezoidal profile chromium steel sheets fitted in front of a ventilation cavity. The individual sheets are fixed to the supporting steelwork with overlaps. The reflective chromium steel, which replaced the copper facade originally envisaged, has a shiny look and emphasises the sharp contours of the building.

The training centre in Gordola mainly uses materials and fabrication principles well known from conventional industrial buildings. The result, however, looks nothing like one of those trivial structures we see on anonymous industrial estates. Instead, it is a calm, extremely precisely formulated training facility in which the students can learn and prepare for their later careers in a working environment that is as natural and pleasant as possible.

Fig. 17: Building on stilts
Protection against flooding and a covered outdoor space

Fig. 16: Workshop
Northlights guarantee even, glare-free illumination in the workshops.

New Monte Rosa Hut
Monte Rosa Studio (ETH Zurich), Bearth + Deplazes

Andrea Deplazes
Marcel Baumgartner

Location, concept

The defining element in the architectural concept for the new Monte Rosa Hut is its "splendid isolation". The building is situated amid a mountainous landscape that can sometimes be as breathtakingly brutal as it is breathtakingly beautiful, with a climate that is extreme and far remote from the convenient infrastructure of the civilised world. Nevertheless, this new edifice is a product of an extraordinarily urban culture. The new Monte Rosa Hut must be as autonomous as possible, i.e. function without help from outside. These boundary conditions directly influenced the design and construction of the structure, the building site logistics and operations and the infrastructure, and play a crucial role in the operation of this facility.

The architectural form is based on the idea of a point-block placed in an exposed position on a massive ridge of rock. Modelled on the ideal of a sphere or a cylinder, the structure has a maximum volume but at the same time a minimum surface area, so that as little heat as possible is lost via the building envelope. A specific, polygonal geometry was necessary for the project so that it could be built from flat wall and floor elements. The result is

Fig. 2: Monte Rosa massif
The site amid the untouched mountain landscape

a building footprint based on an irregular octagon and ideally adapted to the irregular shape of the rock underneath. This prominent structure functions as a point of orientation in this wild landscape, a "lighthouse" guiding walkers across the glacier.

The new Monte Rosa Hut is a joint project of ETH Zurich (Swiss Federal Institute of Technology, project manager Prof. M. Eberle) and the Swiss Alpine Club (SAC), Monte Rosa Section.

Architecture, concept:	Monte Rosa Studio, ETH Zurich
	Department of Architecture, ETH Zurich, Prof. Andrea Deplazes, Marcel Baumgartner (project manager), Kai Hellat
Detailed design:	Bearth + Deplazes Architekten AG
	Daniel Ladner, general manager
Draft design:	2003–2006
Detailed design:	2007–2009
Construction:	April–September 2009

Fig. 1: The new Monte Rosa Hut
View of south facade with photovoltaic array and Matterhorn in background

Monte Rosa Studio (design as evolution)

The Monte Rosa Studio at the ETH Zurich (Swiss Federal Institute of Technology) provided the opportunity to try out an evolutionary design procedure over several semesters. A total of 33 students took part in the process. Design ideas were developed and discussed in a kind of open competitive procedure, with the adoption of others' ideas and intelligent combinations permitted. What counted every time was the better concept, regardless of where it came from. Contributors' claims were intentionally blurred, and sensitivity towards the actual design process was fostered. The studio management took on the role of critical yet motivating discussion partner, coaching the participants and steering the development in the "right direction" as necessary. Intensive collaboration with professional specialists helped to push back the boundaries of the academic design studio in the direction of practical construction.

Fig. 3: Students surveying the site …

Fig. 4: … and in the design studio

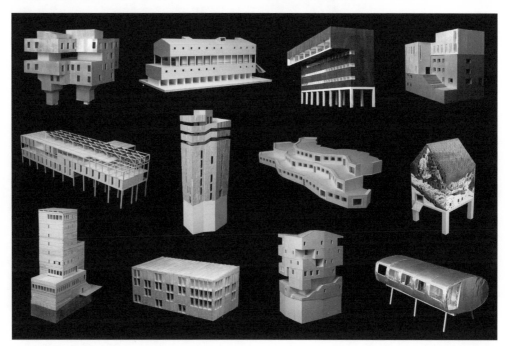

Fig. 5: A selection of designs submitted by students of the Monte Rosa Studio
Issues related to topography, structure and typology were explored in conjunction with aspects such as transport logistics, energy balance and water balance.

Fig. 6: Sketch of basic concept
The route upwards from the dining room via the
peripheral stair with its continuous window strip

Internal layout

The internal layout is star-shaped, i.e. has a radial form
and is identical in all directions. Starting with this centric
form, the building was then divided into 10 segments on
plan. This layout and structural system, which extends
over all five storeys, results in a compact arrangement
for 50 trapezoidal compartments in total.

The building's footprint is determined by the interior
spaces with the largest areas, the dining room and the
kitchen, which for operational reasons must be on the
ground floor with a direct link to the outside terrace, which
is used during good weather. At the same time, this footprint was kept as small as possible so that the foundations
on the rugged rock could be achieved with relatively little
excavation work.

The plant rooms are housed in the basement, which
protrudes out of the rock on the valley side. This is also the
location of the main entrance with cloakrooms, shoe room
and winter room. The bedrooms for guests are situated
on the upper floors.

Typically, the stairs in a building with such a radial
layout would be in the centre so that a maximum number
of habitable rooms could benefit from natural ventilation
and daylight. However, owing to the compact layout of the
rooms and the relatively small plan area, the core of the
new Monte Rosa Hut is simply too small for stairs plus
the necessary landings providing access to the individual
rooms. Therefore, the stairs were moved to the periphery,
directly behind the facade. The outcome is a cascade-like
stair that introduces a surprising three-dimensional effect
into the otherwise small compartmentation of the interior.
All in all, the spiralling stair extends over five storeys and
encompasses an angle of 250° on plan, thus forming,
so to speak, the spatial and conceptual backbone of the
project.

Fig. 7: Model study
Stacking 50 compartments in the form of a modular system

Accompanying the stair is a continuous window strip
that winds around the whole building. Visitors therefore
get a breathtaking view in all directions, can watch the
landscape, the light and the weather from this safe haven.
At night, bright light shines out through this strip of glazing
to provide orientation. Furthermore, it serves as a "solar
heat trap" – more of which later.

Along the facade, single flights of stairs span from
floor to floor, from grid line to grid line, rising in a clock-
wise direction. Between each pair of flights one segment
serves as a landing providing access to the core. On plan
each storey is therefore offset by two segments. Taken
as a whole, this series of flights forms a cascade-type
three-dimensional sequence that rises continuously from
the first basement level, with the main entrance, to the
third floor. At this point the visitor is directly above the main
entrance again, facing the Matterhorn.

Placing the stairs on the periphery like this leaves a
space in the centre of the building that becomes a lobby
providing access to the individual bedrooms. All pipes,
cables and ducts are also routed through this central space
in service shafts positioned in the ends of the radial walls.

Fig. 8: Landing between stair flights and panoramic view through continuous window strip

Fig. 9: Dining room on ground floor

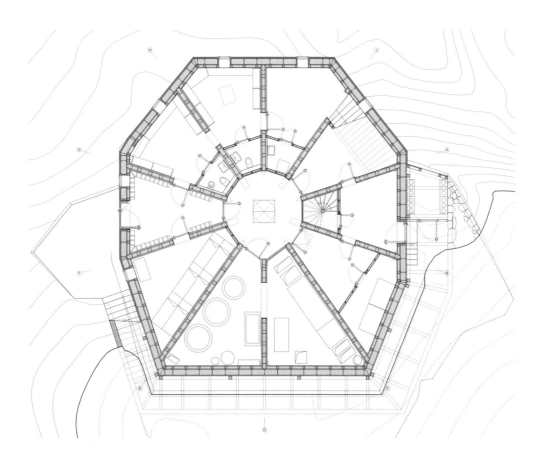

Fig. 10: Plan of 1st basement level, 1:200

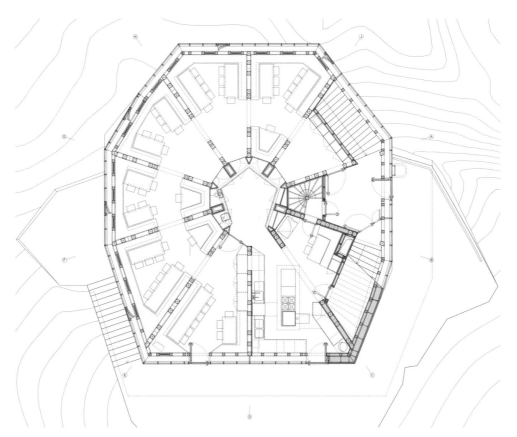

Fig. 11: Plan of ground floor, 1:200

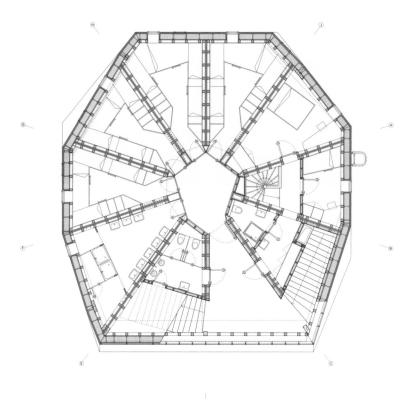

Fig. 12: Plan of 1st floor, 1:200

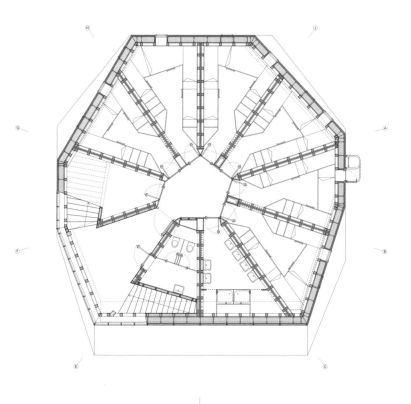

Fig. 13: Plan of 2nd floor, 1:200

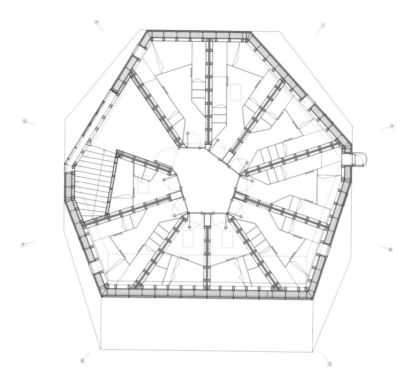

Fig. 14: Plan of 3rd floor, 1:200

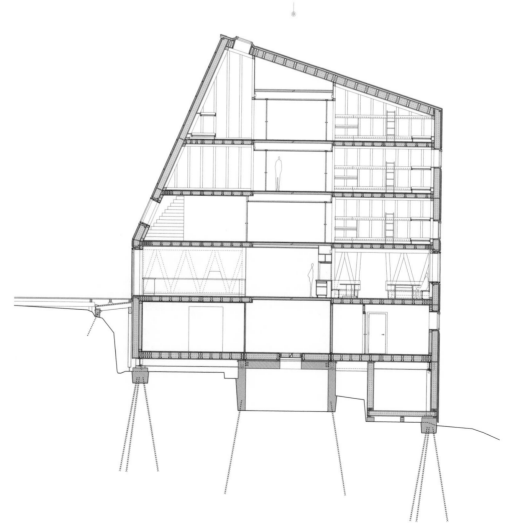

Fig. 15: Section, 1:200

Fig. 16: Assembling the truss

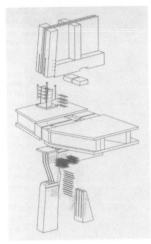

Fig. 17: Axonometric view
Connection between radial walls on ground and 1st floors

Loadbearing structure

The new Monte Rosa Hut is not founded directly on the rock, as we might expect. Instead, it is founded on something resembling "piles". The whole building is a response to the irregular, steeply sloping terrain. A horizontal platform of steel beams raises the building above the rock and protects the permafrost below. This platform consists of 10 radial beams in a star formation that are supported on one pad foundation in the centre and 10 around the periphery. The radial beams support the loadbearing wall plates above. A peripheral beam traces the contour of the structure on plan and transfers the loads of the external walls to the radial beams and from there to the pad foundations. This approach enabled the concrete for the foundations (and the associated helicopter journeys) to be kept to a minimum.

Rising above this is the structure itself, which is made from digitally prepared and machine-fabricated timber wall and floor elements and forms the interior spaces directly. Instead of a typical frame structure with an infilling of thermal insulation and sheathing both sides, a new form of timber frame construction open on one side was developed for both external walls and internal partitions. The sole plates, head plates, studs and other members of these walls are open to the inside. The studs carry the vertical tensile and compressive forces, whereas the sheathing on one side, a three-ply core plywood, ensures stability by resisting the horizontal forces. The precision jointing between elements was achieved with timber-to-timber connections or integral steel parts depending on the loads.

The 10 internal partitions in their star formation form the primary structural system of the building. Steel connectors join all these walls together throughout the height of the building to form shear walls.

The stair cuts through the grid lines and thus turns the structure into a three-dimensional experience. However, the stairs also penetrate the radial walls and therefore interrupt the vertical load path locally, which does weaken the plate effect and entails a structural conflict. The reduced plate effect is compensated for by the opposite wall plate on the projection of the corresponding grid line. A sturdy post in the facade carries the vertical loads. On the ground floor the axial plates are in the form of timber trusses. The cumulative vertical and horizontal forces from the three upper floors are transferred to the basement via sturdy struts connected by large gusset plates.

Timber construction, fire protection

Work at the site of the new Monte Rosa Hut 2883 m above sea level could only be carried out from mid-May to late September. Owing to this short time slot and the elaborate logistics involving transport by rail and helicopter, the five-storey building was conceived as a fully prefabricated timber structure. Timber is a comparatively lightweight building material that can be prefabricated with the very latest production technology and so achieve a form of construction that is efficient in terms of costs and time. The new building was therefore assembled like a large 3D puzzle of 420 timber elements that were flown by helicopter to the site, where they were positioned and installed immediately. The timber construction had to be derived from a complicated structural geometry formed by 10 grid lines, an octagonal shape on plan, irregular angles in the facade, plus the cascade-like staircase. The architects also intended the form of construction

Fig. 18: Foundations
Steel platform on pad footings

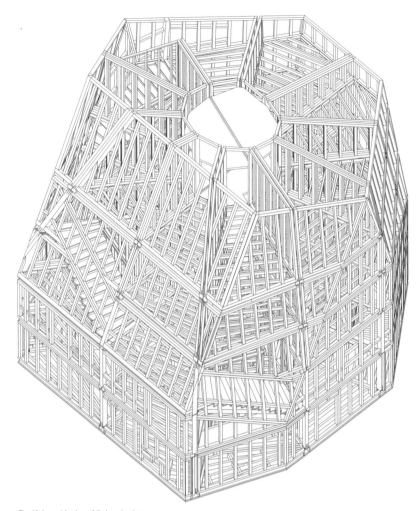

Fig. 19: Isometric view of timber structure
The frame made up of 420 separate elements

Fig. 21: Central lobby before adding finishes

to remain visible. It was for this reason that a reversed form of frame construction was devised for the external and radial walls. Contrasting with classic frame construction, the members here remain visible internally and the sheathing closes off the construction externally. The framing members and the studs thus form recesses that can be used for storage, fixtures or services. Using this approach, the delicate form and the structural nature of timber become tangible. The vibrancy of the surface lends the interior an atmosphere of security and creates a reference to the SAC's first wooden mountain huts.

In the basement, the radial walls, like all other internal and external walls plus the floors, are clad with gypsum fibreboard for fire protection. Likewise, the stairs are lined from top to bottom with gypsum fibreboard so that they can be used as a fire escape. With the lining, the peripheral staircase is turned into a sculpted, tube-like structure that extends unbroken from the main entrance in the basement right up to the third floor.

Fig. 20: Erection of timber structure on site
The helicopter functions as means of transport and crane

Fig. 22: Prefabricated timber elements
Interim storage of elements marked with exact position and weight details

Wall construction, bedrooms

1 Sheet metal facade

- Untreated aluminium sheets joined with double welt standing seams at 400 or 320 mm spacing
- Sheathing, spruce/fir shiplap, 27 mm
- Ventilation cavity, battens, spruce/fir, 30 x 60 mm
- Facade underlay with sealing tape over nails
- Sheathing, spruce/fir shiplap, 27 mm
- Studs, 300 mm
- Mineral insulation, 300 mm
- 3-ply core plywood, spruce/fir, 30 mm
- Structural timber, spruce/fir, 120 x 140 mm

2 Window

- Velux-type window, pine frame, clear lacquer finish
- Triple glazing, 32 mm
- External flashing, titanium-zinc
- Flashing element, untreated aluminium
- Lining, solid spruce/fir, 27 mm

3 Floor construction

- Textile floor covering, Kugelgarn®
- Subfloor, gypsum fibreboard, 2 No. 12.5 mm, with 10 mm mineral insulation, 35 mm
- 3-ply core plywood, spruce/fir, 30 mm
- Structural timber, spruce/fir, 80 x 180 mm
- Mineral insulation, 180 mm
- 3-ply core plywood, spruce/fir, 30 mm

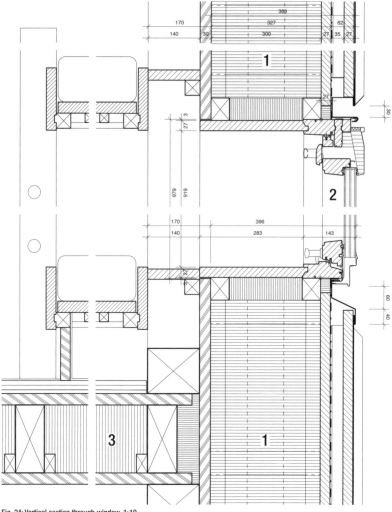

Fig. 24: Vertical section through window, 1:10

Fig. 23: Bedroom with small windows

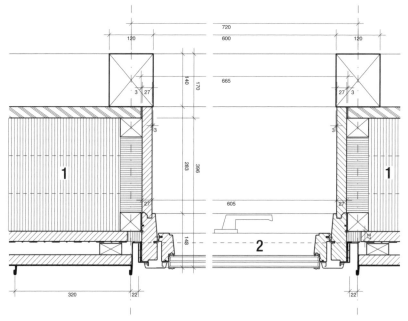

Fig. 25: Horizontal section through window, 1:10

Wall construction, stair

1 Photovoltaic array

– Post-and-rail system, aluminium, black
  anodised finish, 50 mm
– Bespoke photovoltaic panels, laminated
  safety glass, black enamel finish, 14 mm
– Ventilation cavity, 30 mm
– Facade underlay with sealing tape over
  nails
– Sheathing, spruce/fir shiplap, 27 mm
– Studs, 300 mm
– Mineral insulation, 300 mm
– 3-ply core plywood, spruce/fir, 30 mm
– Structural timber, 120 x 140 mm
– Mineral insulation, 140 mm (stair)
– Gypsum fibreboard, acrylic paint, pale
  gold, 15 mm (stair)

2 Continuous window strip, stair

– Post-and-rail system, aluminium,
  untreated, 50 mm
– Triple glazing, 44 mm
– U_g-value 0.7 W/m²K,
  U_w-value 1.2 W/m²K,
– g-value 0.27–0.5 depending on
  orientation
– Gypsum fibreboard lining, acrylic paint,
  silvery, 15 mm
– Structural timber, spruce/fir,
  140 x 140 mm

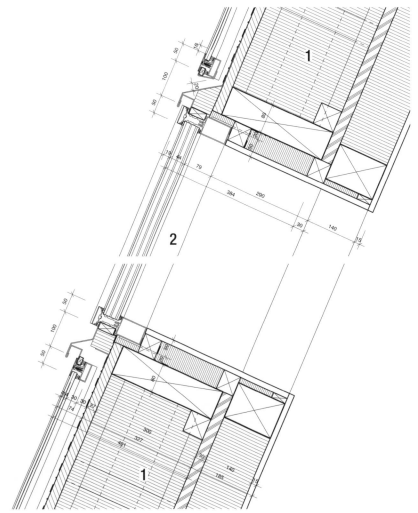

Fig. 27 Vertical section through continuous window strip, 1:10

Fig. 26: Peripheral stair and panoramic view through continuous window strip

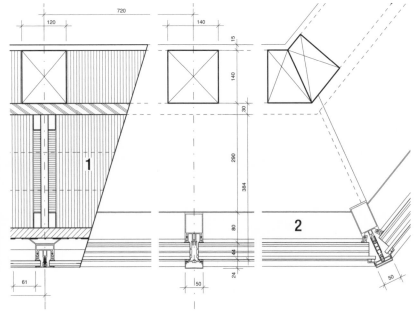

Fig. 28 Horizontal section through continuous window strip, 1:10

Building envelope, facade design principles

The facade concept is based on a combination of energy-saving and energy-gaining strategies. On the one hand, a minimal, highly insulating facade surface was required in order to minimise heat losses. On the other, the strip of glazing that follows the stairs as they wind around the building has been maximised such that the best possible solar gains are achieved from direct and indirect sunlight. The entire building is heated exclusively with these solar gains.

The 30 cm thick external insulation around the timber structural shell was applied on site and afterwards clad with a thin layer of untreated aluminium as protection (leaving a ventilation cavity between insulation and aluminium). This layered facade construction solved the problem of the joints between the elements and how to seal them.

The aluminium cladding to the facade guarantees sound, long-lasting protection against water, wind and weather. The aluminium was attached in individual sheets in the traditional way, with double welt standing seams joining the sheets. The intentionally rough, untreated aluminium allows the faceted structure to glisten in the most diverse colours and reflections.

The south facade is the power plant of the new Monte Rosa Hut. It is clad entirely with photovoltaic panels that provide the electricity the building needs. The entire photovoltaic array seemingly slices through the structure such that it takes on a square form.

The individual bedrooms – almost resembling cave-like wooden chambers – are only provided with small windows. From inside, these small openings, with the glass finishing flush with the aluminium cladding, seem to be punched through the thick outer cloak of the facade. The legibility of the floors and the scale of the structure are blurred by the varying positions of the small windows above the respective floor level, turning the building into a prismatic body.

And cutting through all this is the continuous window strip following the stairs, flush with the aluminium and lending the structure a special symbol. At ground floor level it is like a horizontal visor marking the *piano nobile*, so to speak. As it traces the stair, the band of glass rises, bends twice at every flight and unrolls itself around the corners of the facade. Together with the small individual windows, it awakens associations of a castle or fortified tower.

Fig. 29: Facade assembly
Attaching the individual aluminium sheets to the sheathing

Fig. 30: The new mountain hostel amid the monumental mountain landscape
The facade design awakens associations of a fortified tower.

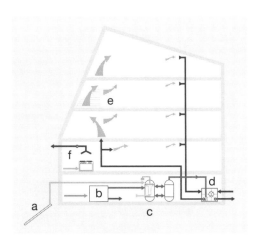

Fig. 31: Heating and ventilation concept
warm water produced by means of solar thermal collectors (a), cogeneration
plant (b), heat store (c), central ventilation plant with heat recovery (d), controlled
ventilation of the rooms (e), ventilation system kitchen (f)

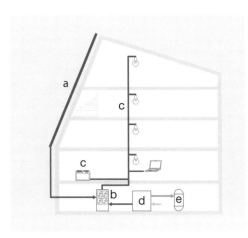

Fig. 32: Electricity supply concept
obtaining power from the photovoltaic system (a), batteries (b), appliances (c),
cogeneration plant for back-up supply of power and heat (d), heat store (e)

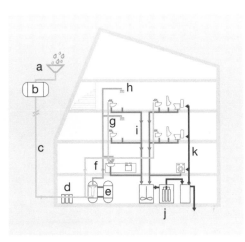

Fig. 33: Water supply concept
capturing melt water (a), rock cavern (b), feed pipe (c), disinfection (d), heat store (e),
fresh water kitchen (f), washstands (g), showers (h), waste water (i), microbiological
treatment plant (j), grey water (k)

Building services, building automation

The remoteness of this facility urges thrifty use of resources. To minimise the need to fly in supplies, the building must be essentially autonomous in terms of energy
and water supplies.

The building's heating requirements are covered by
the passive solar gains through the continuous glazing
along the stairs. The solar collectors, 60 m² of absorption
area facing south-west and mounted on a rock face away
from the building, heat a tank of water for hot water and
space heating requirements. To distribute the heat and for
reasons of comfort, but also to avoid damage to the building due to excess moisture, a mechanical ventilation system (with heat recovery) has been installed throughout.
Depending on the temperature of the water in the tank, a
combined heat and power system (CHP – to cover peak
demand and act as a backup system) can be switched on
via a separate set of pipes.

Some 90% of the electricity requirement is covered by
the photovoltaic panels integrated into the facade. During
periods of bad weather or full occupancy, the CHP backs
up the supplies. Near the building there are no springs
available all year round and so meltwater is collected in
the summer and stored, protected against freezing, in a
200 m³ rock cavern 40 m above the site. The natural gradient ensures adequate water pressure. Inside the building, the water is filtered and disinfected.

Waste water is treated in the facility's own microfilter
sewage plant on a biological basis. It is used for flushing
toilets and in washing machines, and following further
treatment is discharged back into the environment as
clean water.

The main aspect of the building automation is the use
of a predictive control system. Based on weather fore-
casts, the number of visitors can be estimated in advance.
The energy consumption of individual components, e.g.
waste water plant, recharging the batteries with electricity
or maintaining the water temperature, can therefore be
better coordinated, which means that the CHP only has
to be operated when really necessary.

Abridged article taken from
ETH Zurich: *New Monte Rosa Hut SAC – Self-Sufficient Building in High Alps,*
Zurich, 2010.

Vocational Training Centre, Baden
Burkard Meyer Architekten

Thomas Schwendener

Fig. 1: Bruggerstrasse elevation
New training building with roadside access ramp

Architects:	Burkard Meyer Architekten BSA, Baden
Feasibility project:	2002
Construction:	2004–06
Project management:	Daniel Krieg, Andreas Stirnemann
Assistants:	Tobias Burger, Boris Hitz, Christiane Illing, Marianne Sigg, Corinna Wanner
Site management:	Burkard Meyer Architekten, Markus Gersbacher
External works:	Schweingruber Zulauf Landschaftsarchitekten, Zurich
Facade consultant:	Mebatech, Baden
Structural engineers:	Wolf, Kropf & Partner, Zurich
HVAC engineers:	Waldhauser Haustechnik, Basel
Electrical engineers:	Herzog Kull Group, Aarau

Situation

The headquarters of the multinational ABB company founded in 1891 has made a lasting impression on the townscape of Baden. As traditional branches of industry were restructured and outsourced in the 1980s and 1990s, the chance arose to redevelop brownfield sites in many industrial locations in Switzerland. The public sector showed its commitment to making Baden a centre for training and business by locating the three sections of the ABB Vocational Training Centre in the town. The different parts of the complex were inserted competently into the industrial townscape by the Burkard Meyer architectural practice.

The conversion of the former BBC welfare centre enabled what was once clearly identified as the company's own meeting place for meals, training and entertainment to be retained as a significant highlight of the complex. This is being transformed into a training, administration and infrastructure building; built in 1951–54 to a design by the architect Armin Meili, the director of the 1939 Swiss National Exhibition, and an important example of Swiss post-war architecture, it will thus continue to be a significant feature in this urban setting.

Directly adjacent to the welfare centre, slipped into the foot of the Martinsberg, is the sports complex with its gymnasia. Built above two parking levels, the building when viewed from the industrial quarter looks like a tall plinth. Further up on the plateau, where the entrances to Martinsberg School and the sports complex itself are located, the building has only one storey. A staircase located between the complex and Meili's building cuts

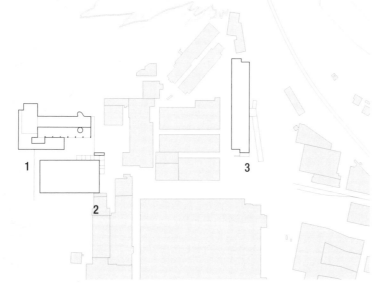

Fig. 2: Site plan of the industrial quarter of ABB, Baden
1 Former BBC welfare centre, 2 New sports complex, 3 New training building on Bruggerstrasse

Fig. 3: Armin Meili: Former BBC welfare centre
Baden (CH), 1951–54

through the plinth and links the upper level with the level of the industrial buildings, where the new building housing the classrooms is located, on Bruggerstrasse.

The new building for the Vocational Training Centre, which owing to its position nearer the town marks the start of this area, still permits a view of the ABB structures beyond and the Martinsberg. The observer sees a slim, elongated structure with fully glazed main elevations and closed end elevations, and on the long sides a joint separating the building from the ground. A plinth-like ramp structure in front of the building visually anchors the volume firmly to its location. During the day, the impressive internal workings of the building can be only roughly discerned from outside. But at night, it becomes a sort of illuminated showcase enabling the internal activities to be rendered legible to the outside world.

Fig. 6: View of sports complex from industrial quarter

Fig. 7: Interior of upper sports hall with overhead lighting

Fig. 4: Night-time view of new Bruggerstrasse training building

Interior layout

The true surprise of this building lies in its interior layout and loadbearing structure, which are derived from a combination of contemporary teaching ideas and energy-efficiency demands plus fire protection and acoustics requirements. The result explores uncharted territory in school building. The classrooms – contrary to normal conventions – are not located along the facade, but instead are concentrated in the middle and stacked over several storeys. Access, on the other hand, is via external corridors along the glazed elevations. This unusual concept means that the classrooms form blocks and therefore direct interior relationships are possible in the longitudinal and transverse directions, which allows the rooms to be used for various pedagogic models. The acoustic and climatic separation between the rooms and the access corridors is by way of clear glass, which at the same time guarantees natural lighting but also views into the classrooms. The communal areas, staircases, lifts and ancillary rooms are designed as open zones spanning from facade to facade, which divide the building into three usage zones in both the plinth and the four identical floors above.

Fig. 5: Concept and study model
Loadbearing structure and interior layout with simulation of incoming daylight

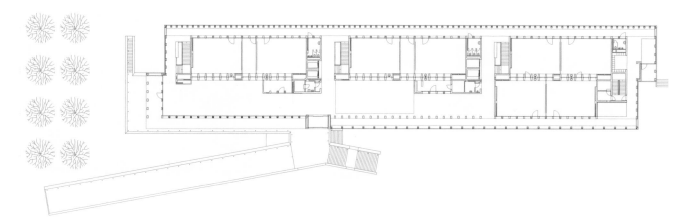

Fig. 8: : Plan of 1st floor, 1:800

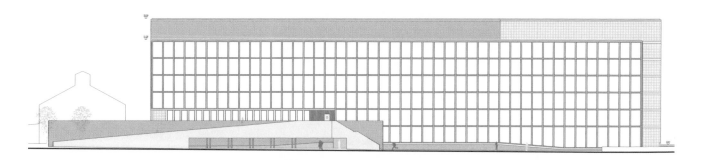

Fig. 9: Plan of the 3rd floor, 1:800

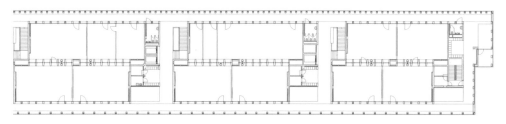

Fig. 10: East elevation, 1:800

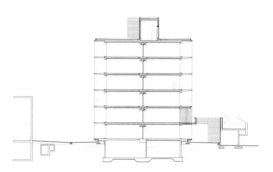

Fig. 11: Section, 1:800

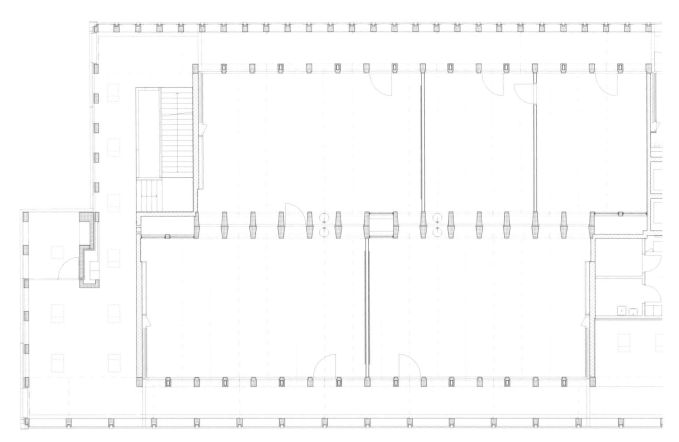

Fig. 12: Part-plan of classroom storey, 1:200

Loadbearing structure

The plan typology, usage and loadbearing structure of
the Bruggerstrasse training building are very closely
linked and are also mutually dependent. With the exception of the basement and the access cores required
for stability, the entire building consists of prefabricated
reinforced concrete elements. The filigree architecture,
in the form of columns and slabs, creates both the loadbearing and the interior structure. The building consists
of five rows of columns, which have a space-forming
effect owing to their repetitive nature and close spacing. The primary columns in the centre and also the
secondary columns between corridors and classrooms
were joined by beams at the works to form prefabricated frames. The 120 mm thick slab elements placed
on these serve as permanent formwork for the concrete
topping and simultaneously form the soffits complying
with the acoustics and lighting specifications. Additional
cantilever slab elements are used in the corridors. The
function of the outermost row of columns on each side
is to brace the facade construction.

Fig. 13: Access corridor
The incoming light from the side reinforces the effect of depth.

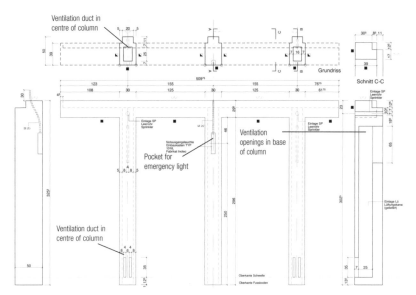

Fig. 14: Drawing of three-column units

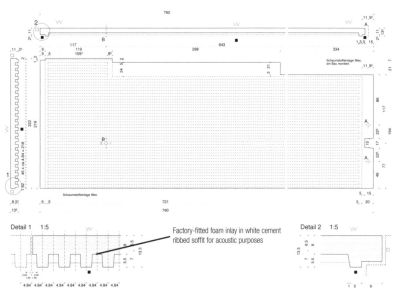

Factory-fitted foam inlay in white cement ribbed soffit for acoustic purposes

Fig. 15: Drawing of suspended floor elements/ribbed soffit

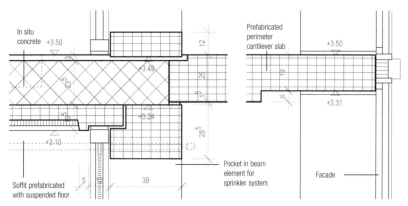

Fig. 16: Jointing of elements, external row of columns, 1:20

Fig. 17: Erection of loadbearing structure
Three-column units held in position with temporary raking props

Fig. 18: Erection of floor elements
Prefabricated perimeter floor element being lowered into position

Fig. 19: Concrete topping to floor elements
Three-column units and prefabricated floor elements prior to pouring the concrete topping that bonds the prefabricated parts into one composite construction.

Fig. 20: Overall view of structural works during construction

Building services

The mechanical ventilation required from the energy view-point for the rooms in the middle of the building goes hand in hand with the development of a new type of building, and which eventually led to an autonomous architectural expression.

The services are placed entirely in the central zone. Vertical distribution routes are positioned between the individual columns. From here, the fresh air is supplied to the rooms, which from there escapes into the corridors via leakage-air ducts in the columns. The corridors are used, so to speak, as part of the extract-air system. The outermost rows of columns serve as an internal *brise-soleil*, their close spacing reacting to the changing exposure to the sun. The ends of the building can be opened up for night-time cooling – the air bricks guarantee the necessary security. The thermo-active system (TABS) installed in the concrete suspended floors provides the system with the required inertia and permits "Minergie"-compliant wintertime heating and summertime cooling of the building mass. Whereas the classrooms exhibit a relatively constant temperature in summer and winter with a low energy input, the temperature of all the access areas fluctuates.

Fig. 21: Outer column – head of column with ventilation duct, acoustic soffit

Fig. 22: Outer column – base of column with ventilation duct

Fig. 23: Night-time cooling via concrete air bricks
Hinged flaps in the communal zones ensure night-time cooling.

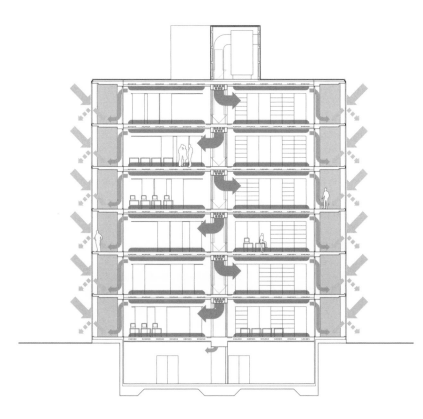

Fig. 24: Ventilation concept
Fresh air is introduced into the rooms in the centre of the building and exhausted, cascade-fashion, via the corridors behind the facades.

Fig. 27: East elevation
Transparency with closely spaced columns

Fig. 29: West elevation
Transparency with widely spaced columns

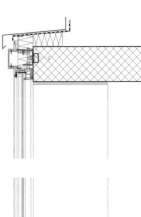

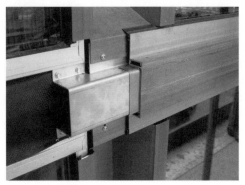

Fig. 28: Detail of facade construction
Connection of extruded bronze window frame sections

Fig. 30: The materials of the classrooms
View towards central row of columns and the classrooms beyond

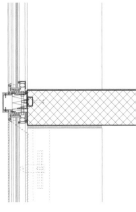

Fig. 25: Section through facade, 1:20

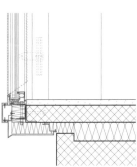

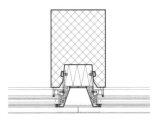

Fig. 26: Horizontal section through facade
column, 1:20

Design and materials

The facade of the building reflects its internal structure with its strict layout. Storey-height fixed glazing framed by extruded bronze sections form a continuous grid on each longitudinal facade. The envelope comprises conventional double glazing units and therefore guarantees an energy- and cost-efficient form of construction. The spacing of the facade columns is different on the east and west sides; they therefore react to the different lighting and solar radiation conditions. External sunshades are unnecessary because the corridors act as buffer zones. The ends of the building are finished with concrete air bricks concealing the interiors behind. The concrete is visible on the outside and therefore links the roof construction with the end of facade and the ramp structure.

Internally, the architectural expression is determined by the use of just a few materials. The loadbearing members are left fully exposed everywhere. The rows of concrete columns with glass infill panels between characterise the interior atmosphere. The columns provide shade, define the rooms and also accommodate the building services. Their finely grooved surfaces remind the observer that concrete is a mouldable material and lend the heavy pre-fabrication a certain elegance. Furthermore, depending on the viewing angle, the columns form a closed wall or allow an unrestricted view into the adjoining area. The superimposed multi-layer idea of facade, columns and usage zones create different images in different lighting conditions; the glass alternates between opaque, transparent, reflective and translucent. The intention behind the ambiguous but primarily transparent design of the walls is to encourage exchanges and communication between the various vocational disciplines.

The soffits in the classrooms are in the form of pre-fabricated elements with white cement ribs. Floor finishes in self-levelling screed and flooring cement emphasize the homogeneous, robust choice of materials. Thanks to the suspended floor dimensions and their corresponding mass, conventional impact sound insulation was unnecessary. Shades of red here and there supplement the minimal materials concept and accentuate selected areas within the structure.

Wall construction, main facade

Bronze section
Waterproof sheeting
Thermal insulation, 120 mm
Double glazing insulating unit with low E glass
Prefabricated column, 400 mm

Roof construction, 5th floor

Concrete flags in bed of chippings/mineral substrate, 50 mm
Separating layer
Bitumen felt waterproofing
Rigid thermal insulation, 200 mm
Vapour barrier
Concrete topping, 265 mm / falls
Prefabricated element, white cement soffit, 135 mm

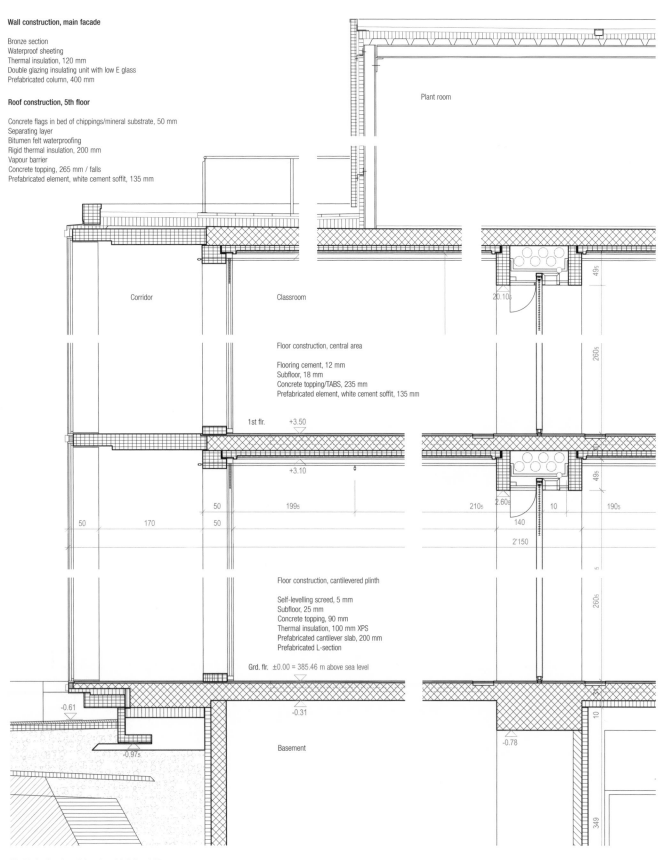

Plant room

Corridor

Classroom

Floor construction, central area

Flooring cement, 12 mm
Subfloor, 18 mm
Concrete topping/TABS, 235 mm
Prefabricated element, white cement soffit, 135 mm

1st flr.   +3.50

+3.10

Floor construction, cantilevered plinth

Self-levelling screed, 5 mm
Subfloor, 25 mm
Concrete topping, 90 mm
Thermal insulation, 100 mm XPS
Prefabricated cantilever slab, 200 mm
Prefabricated L-section

Grd. flr. ±0.00 = 385.46 m above sea level

Basement

Fig. 31: Section through facade and building, 1:60
Extract from original 1:50 working drawing

Teacher Training College, Chur
Bearth + Deplazes

Valentin Bearth, Andrea Deplazes,
Alois Diethelm

Situation and theme

The science wing is an extension to the Grisons Teacher Training College. Its architectural vocabulary – four concrete platforms stacked one upon the other – and its division into teaching and preparation rooms reflect the terse operational space and economic criteria.

The total transparency of the interior and facades is presumably meant to make clear for all to see the purpose of science. The precise clarity of a crystalline lattice or a molecular structure as the building block of life or nature to be studied has been transformed into the rational scientific structure of an angular, polished glass box planted in the cultivated greenery of its surroundings. Rational artificiality in the midst of romantic artificiality. A "reflection" of nature next to the "model" of nature.

The absence of colour – within the building there exist only shades of grey on grey ("laboratory grey") – increases our perception of the artificiality of the science laboratory as a total contrast to the intensive, diverse, dense "illustrative" greenery of the vegetation in the area. Trees, bushes, vines, ferns etc. extend right up to the glass box itself. Unexpectedly, observer and observed exchange places.

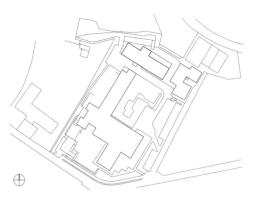

Fig. 2: Site plan
The new building at the foot of the Hoffelsen in Chur

Architects: Bearth + Deplazes, Chur
Construction period: 1997–1999
Project manager: Bettina Werner
Structural engineer: Fredy Unger, Chur

Fig. 1: South facade
Viewed head on, it is possible to see right through the building!

Internal layout and loadbearing structure I

The loadbearing structure of in situ concrete consists of four platforms stacked one upon the other, the conglomerate braced by an access tower on one side. Each row of columns is coupled with downstand beams to form a frame-like, five-bay "yoke" running parallel to the length of the building. A suspended ceiling spans the two yokes, hemmed in by the beams.

In contrast to beams that are positioned perpendicular to the length of the building, this arrangement permits a straightforward horizontal distribution of the services required (electricity, water, waste water, gas and laboratory media). Apart from the tower, the structure does not initially imply any particular use or internal layout. The division into teaching, ancillary and access zones is primarily by way of non-loadbearing walls – glass in the longitudinal direction (for transparency). Across the building the main rooms are demarcated by walls of built-in cupboards between the appropriately sized columns (600 x 600 mm).

The user-defined and – possibly – temporary arrangement of walls, for which the loadbearing structure is ideal, is somewhat restricted however by the position of risers and waste pipes. The shafts for these vertical service runs are located on the two columns to the left and right of the tower and cannot be altered (see "a" in plan of ground floor below). On the other hand, the building services on the platforms are autonomous. Use of the tower as

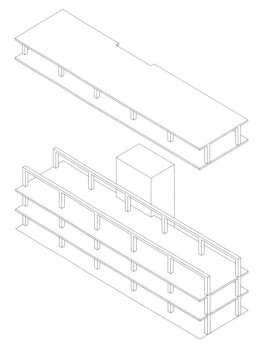

Fig. 4: Axonometric view of structural system
Stacked concrete "platforms"

a possible services shaft, which would mean elaborate perforations in the downstand beams in this area and the need for a suspended ceiling, is therefore superfluous and favors the concept of the platforms.

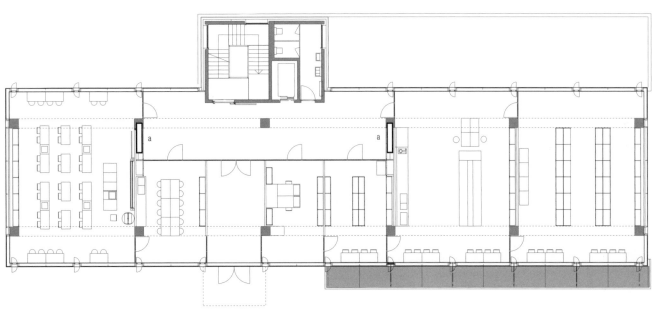

Fig. 3: Plan of ground floor
The rooms are reached without the need for corridors.
a) Vertical service shafts

0   1   5 m

Internal layout and loadbearing structure II

Fig. 5: Seminar room
A suspended ceiling between the downstand beams, but only the bare concrete
soffit adjacent to the facade (see section)

Fig. 6: Seminar room
Views of the outside are still possible even when the awnings are extended.

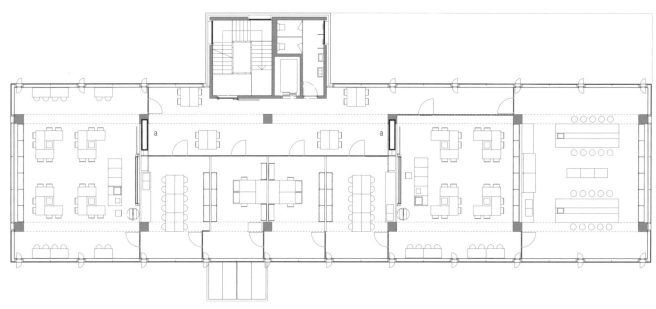

Fig. 7: Plan of 1st floor
Lobby adjacent to staircase and corridor to room at east end of building
a) Vertical service shafts

0 1   5 m

Internal layout and loadbearing structure III

Fig. 8: North facade
Staircase tower bracing the whole structure; frameless glass curtain wall

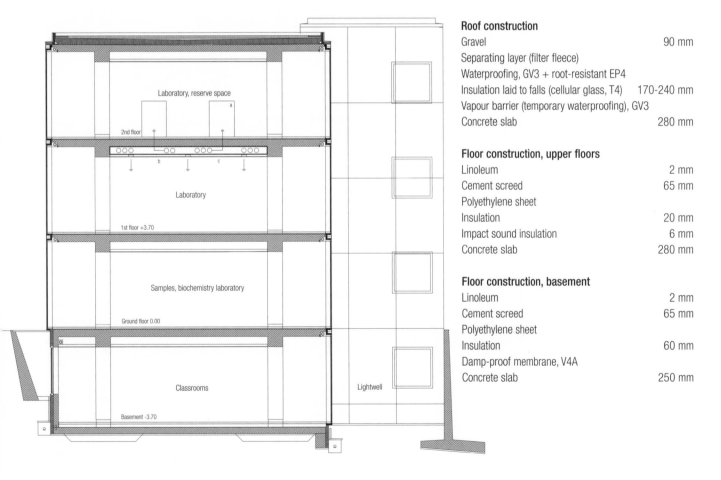

Fig. 9: Section
The stacked concrete "platforms" and staircase tower, which in the basement is coupled with the lightwell.
a) Laboratory benches/media supply points; b) horizontal media zone/distribution; c) lighting unit

Roof construction

Gravel	90 mm
Separating layer (filter fleece)	
Waterproofing, GV3 + root-resistant EP4	
Insulation laid to falls (cellular glass, T4)	170-240 mm
Vapour barrier (temporary waterproofing), GV3	
Concrete slab	280 mm

Floor construction, upper floors

Linoleum	2 mm
Cement screed	65 mm
Polyethylene sheet	
Insulation	20 mm
Impact sound insulation	6 mm
Concrete slab	280 mm

Floor construction, basement

Linoleum	2 mm
Cement screed	65 mm
Polyethylene sheet	
Insulation	60 mm
Damp-proof membrane, V4A	
Concrete slab	250 mm

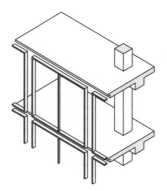

Fig. 10: Concrete members (primary loadbearing structure) with lightweight metal
frames (secondary structure)
Frames fitted to edges of floor slabs

Design and realisation – the curtain wall

The facade is based on a system of nearly square frames, each fixed top and bottom to the edges of the floor slabs. The frames (post-and-rail construction) are positioned relative to each other so that there are spaces in between. The horizontal spaces house the external awnings, the vertical spaces the ventilation flaps.

A vertical T-section in the middle of the anodised aluminium frames halves the width of the glass and hence considerably reduces the price of the glass. Laminated safety glass is used for the inner panes of these double-glazed units and thus renders any form of balustrade (safety barrier) unnecessary. Natural ventilation is provided by the aforementioned inward-opening flaps. The outer louvres guarantee ventilation regardless of the weather (e.g. night-time cooling in summer, protection against driving rain), but also prevent intruders gaining access to the building. The outer centre flap is a response to the teaching staff's wish for a physical link with the outside world.

Using the spaces between the frames in this way (for awnings and ventilation flaps) allows the glass to finish flush with the frames and so create a skin-like development – glass and frames in the same plane. The corners employ stepped glass (the panes meet without any frame) and this reinforces the idea of the developed facade. All the engineering components are built in, which causes the whole facade construction in the end to function together like a clockwork.

Nevertheless, at CHF 970/m^2 (including awnings, ventilation flaps, connections and terminations and internal blinds; index 1999) this is a cost-effective solution for a curtain wall system.

Fig. 11: Close-up of facade
Frameless corner detail (stepped glass)

Facade construction

1 Aluminium facade sections, 60 x 180 mm
2 Double glazing, inner pane of laminated safety glass
3 External patent glazing fitting for mechanical fixing of glass
4 Recess: 60 mm rockwool thermal insulation plus sheet aluminium lining
5 Awning as external sunshading (acrylic fabric)
6 Internal blackout blind fitted into recess in soffit
7 Room-height ventilation flap (recess similar to No. 4 above)
8 "Psychological" opening flap

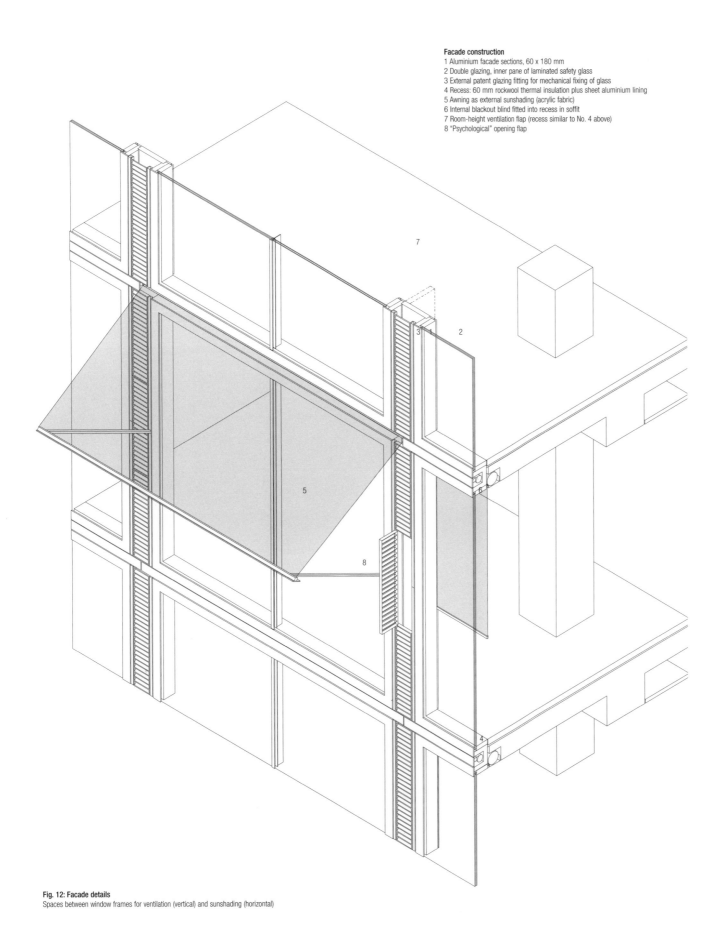

Fig. 12: Facade details
Spaces between window frames for ventilation (vertical) and sunshading (horizontal)

Fig. 13: South facade with entrance
External ventilation flaps open

Facade construction

a Aluminium facade sections, 60 x 180 mm
b Bracket and cast-in rail for attaching facade sections
c Double glazing, inner pane of 8 mm laminated safety glass, outer pane of 8 mm float
   glass (outer pane at frameless corners: 8 mm toughened safety glass)
d External patent glazing fitting for mechanical fixing of glass (b = 60 mm)
e Extra-wide cover strip (b = 120 mm)
f Rockwool, 60 mm, plus sheet aluminium lining
g Front edge of awning
h Straight awning arm
i Internal blackout blind fitted into recess in soffit
j Fluorescent lights recessed into soffit

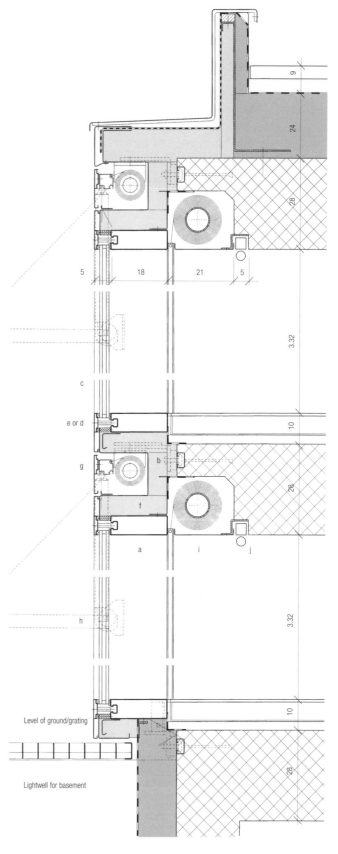

Fig. 15: Vertical section

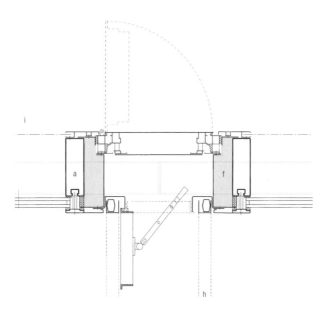

Fig. 14: Horizontal section
Vertical joint with internal and external
ventilation flaps

0   10   50 cm

Design and realisation – the sunshading

Protection against direct sunlight is an integral part of the building services concept which, despite the fully glazed facades, does without mechanical air-conditioning. In contrast to vertical blinds, which, when in use, stretch like a skin over the facade (but cannot be integrated flush), these straight-arm awnings lend the building form and relief. Depending on the position of the awnings the building takes on two different appearances. (This changing appearance is also reinforced by the fact that the awnings are fitted only on the southern side and hence represent a stark contrast to the otherwise glass-only facades.)

Once extended, the cantilevering awnings still allow the facade behind to remain visible – an unconventional, inviting gesture not possible with the majority of sunshading systems. Even more significant is the way they separate inside from outside to a greater or lesser degree. But here again, the visual relationship is still preserved. However, the drawback of this type of awning can be seen at the end of the building where, depending on the position of the sun, the incident sunlight can still reach the glass. Another drawback is their vulnerability to the wind when extended.

The same architectural expression could have been achieved with articulated-arm awnings. However, they present a weakness that repeated buffeting by the wind can alter the adjustment over time.

These electrically operated awnings roll up into the spaces between the window frames. The same cover strip (w = 120 mm) as used on the adjoining post-and-rail construction conceals the standard horizontal edge section of the awning. Channel sections were fitted over the arms so they too fit flush between window frame and ventilation flap. Apart from the window frames in standard anodised aluminium, all the exposed parts of the facade have a black stove-enamelled finish, which minimises the presence of the joints and the louvres of the ventilation flaps.

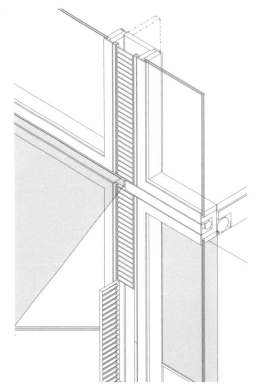

Fig. 17: South facade with awning extended
Maximum extension of straight arm = horizontal

Fig. 16: South facade with awnings retracted
The same appearance on all sides

Fig. 18: South facade with awnings extended
The facade is given relief; the omission of one awning marks the entrance (fixed canopy).

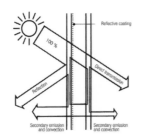

Fig. 19: Shading – the radiation relationships
Source: "Glas und Praxis", Glas Trösch AG, 2000

Energy concept – the greenhouse problem

The specific problem of glazed buildings – which basically applies as well to any window in a fenestrate facade – is that in winter glass provides less protection against heat losses (although this is more than made up for by the solar energy gains during the heating period, primarily with large areas) and in summer admits too much (unwanted) energy. If nothing is done about this, the consequences are all too well known: overheating in summer, overcooling in winter.

Until the 1980s full air-conditioning in glazed buildings was therefore the most common answer to this problem. But our changing environmental awareness and the resulting growing rejection of air-conditioning systems has meant that since that time various solutions have been applied to make the continued use of large expanses of glass possible. These involve, on the one hand, optimised materials (e.g. changing the properties of glass) and, on the other, optimised design concepts (structure, building services, building performance).

The main thrust of development in glass production has been improvements to thermal insulation (U-value) and total energy transmittance (g-value). Technical means of achieving this involve (colourless) films for thermal insulation and shading, plus gas fillings (e.g. argon). The influence of the g-value should not be underestimated because extreme shading measures can exclude the heat-giving solar radiation just when it is wanted, i.e. passive use of solar energy in winter. At the same time, however, good shading measures can protect against excessive temperature increases if sunblinds cannot be extended because of high winds, for example.

Because of the large areas of glass, the teacher training college uses a glass with a very good shading value (south facade: g-value 38%) without reducing the solar energy gains significantly. Of course, the flow of energy from outside to inside is also reduced by good thermal insulation (see diagram), which can lead to the decision to exploit solar energy gains in winter by using south-facing glazing with a poorer U-value. At the teacher training college double glazing with a U-value of 1.0 W/m^2K and a light transmittance of 70% was used on all sides. Logically, the g-value on the north facade – at 55% – is lower than that of the south facade.

Design criteria involve the orientation or positioning of a building and hence a ventilation concept, which inevitably also includes the choice of building materials. At the college the south-facing orientation guarantees optimum utilisation of solar energy. However, because the rooms span the building (i.e. in a south–north direction), this orientation also sets up thermal currents within the building that ensure natural ventilation. The night-time cooling in summer also plays a key role, with solid, monolithic building materials, e.g. concrete, being "charged up" by the flow of cool air. The stored cooling effect is then released during the day and ensures a comfortable interior climate. Opening fanlights over the doors have been installed in those rooms bordered by a corridor on one side and these enable cross-ventilation via the staircase. Here the difference in height (the ventilation opening is at second floor level) promotes the "stack effect" (natural air pressure differential: pressure and suction effects).

HVAC concept after Waldhauser Haustechnik, Basel

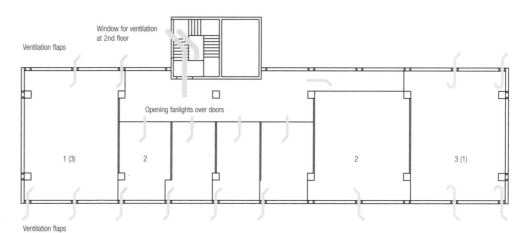

Fig. 20: Ventilation scheme
1) Movement of air (from facade to facade): by wind and/or temperature differences
2) Movement of air (from facade via corridor to staircase): by temperature differences/stack effect
3) Movement of air (at facade): thermal currents, different interior temperatures

Swiss School of Engineering for the Wood Industry, Biel
Marcel Meili, Markus Peter

Swiss School of Engineering for the Wood Industry, Biel, 1990–1999

This school, even before the new extension, already boasted a remarkable character. The site and the buildings form what is almost an island between residential districts and an industrial area, which stretches along the hard edge of the Jura Massif. The vocabulary of the ensemble of school buildings – a main building in the romantic, national style of the post-war years plus a single-storey workshop – seems to be anchored in the landscape and the breadth of the valley floor.

The new work changed these forms into a new overall figure, which, thanks to two different gestures, represents a further development of the relationship between the architecture and the open spaces. Firstly, the workshops at ground floor level with their pitched roofs now extend like an outstretched finger to almost touch the new teaching building. Secondly, this wing, a four-storey timber design, towers over the shallow silhouette of the timber workshops, its proximity achieving an almost dissonant proportional relationship with the more traditional architecture on the site.

The four-storey building is designed as a series of timber boxes assembled from prefabricated, storey-high frames. The gaps between the boxes create terraces and corridors which form a fluid link with the external spaces. Merely the central access cores are built of concrete to satisfy fire protection requirements.

The method of joining these room modules is allied to the technology of large timber spans. The floors consist of exposed, long-span box elements which render primary/secondary construction concepts superfluous. The bottom section of the loadbearing facade frames is a glued laminated timber beam matching the height of a spandrel panel. This serves as an upstand beam

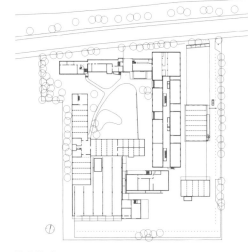

Fig. 3: Site plan

for the floor elements. This means it is possible to install large, subdivided windows whose proportions are no longer dictated by the close spacing of the timber studding, but instead by their relationship to the spacious rooms behind. Timber panels of untreated oak form the cladding to the facade. In this type of panel the joints between individual boards become invisible and allow the recessed joints between the elements to become more prominent.

The form of construction is therefore important in this project because only by overcoming timber engineering's own dimensional and divisional hierarchy was it possible to implement the three-dimensional concept. In this design the special qualities of traditional timber buildings abruptly encounter an approach that suppresses the additive character of the wood in favour of a more moulded, expansive and three-dimensional look.

Architects: Marcel Meili and Markus Peter, with Zeno Vogel, Zurich
Construction period: 1997–1999
Project manager: Zeno Vogel
Structural engineers: Conzett Bronzini Gartmann, Chur

Figs 1 and 2: The Swiss School of Engineering for the Wood Industry is a series of wooden boxes.

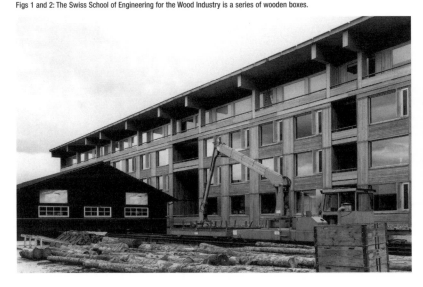

Planning phase
(reduced planning drawings, 1:200)

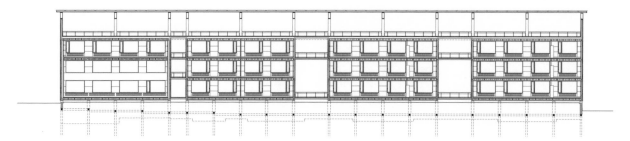

Fig. 4: Longitudinal section B-B

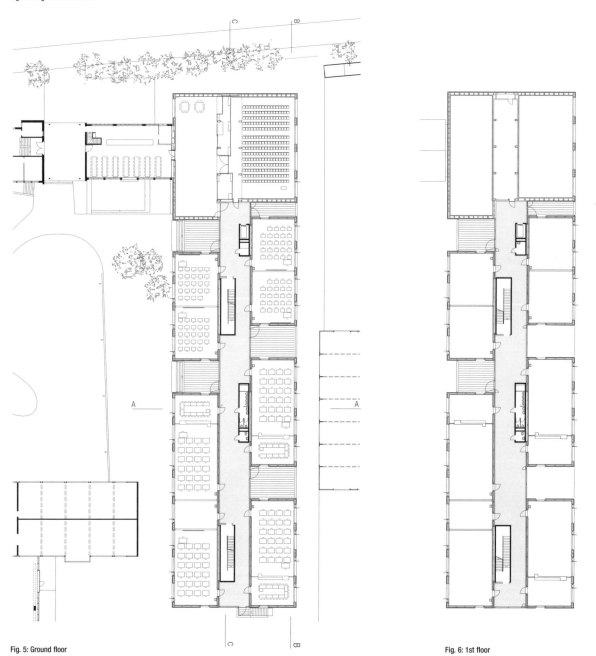

Fig. 5: Ground floor

Fig. 6: 1st floor

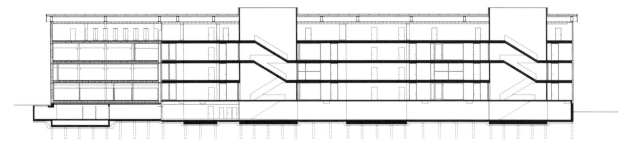

Fig. 7: Longitudinal section C-C

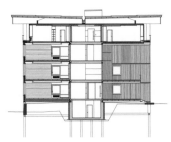

Fig. 8: Section A-A

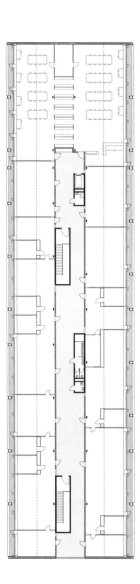

Fig. 9: 2nd floor   Fig. 10: 3rd floor

Jürg Conzett

Fig. 11: Model of concrete cores
Corridor access (fire-resistant escape routes), concrete towers for stability that accommodate stairs, lifts and sanitary facilities

Fig. 12: Concrete cores
Under construction, 1997; the concrete floors support only their own self-weight and therefore large spans and cantilevers are possible.

The structure – the engineer's report

The work of the engineer adhered to "contractor-like" virtues: the building should be simple, spacious and economic, should discover opportunities embodied in the architectural concept, exploit any regular components (also structurally) and thus essentially accomplish a harmonious relationship between the architectural and engineering goals.

With this in mind the foundation design for the new teaching building becomes particularly interesting. The heavy, solid central section rests on a concrete basement which in structural terms acts as a continuous box distributing the point loads from above in the longitudinal direction. The loads on the ground slab are distributed evenly into the subsoil; a longitudinal section through the central section reminds us of a floating ship. In contrast to this the loads of the lightweight seminar rooms under which there is no basement are transferred (as point loads corresponding with the loadbearing frame) to a loadbearing stratum via a ring of driven piles.

The normal spacing of the piles is 4.800 m, a dimension that matches the pile length well but also represents a sensible spacing for the main columns along the outer longitudinal wall. An 860 mm deep beam (in the spandrel panel) is just able to carry the floor loads over this span.

Above the windows, the floors are suspended from this beam and this leads to a very shallow lintel depth – an important aspect for the daylighting requirements of the interior.

In timber buildings it is less advisable to build non-loadbearing partitions to control the spread of sound and fire. Hence, the floors of the teaching units between rooms and corridors are hence supported on another timber frame. The concrete floors of the central section therefore do not have to carry vertical loads from the rooms, only their own weight, and consequently, they could be designed as prestressed flat slabs with long spans and cantilevers. The corridors do not have any auxiliary columns standing like piers against the walls and so the full width of the corridors is available to users.

The roof beams are likewise box elements, i.e. a top flange and a bottom flange in glued laminated timber linked by glued plywood and placed on top of the load-bearing columns. The roof consists of two large timber panels each 97 m long and 13 m wide. With a beam spacing of 9.6 m the box elements were able to be reduced to 220 mm thanks to the continuity effect – a concept that leaves plenty of scope for the interior layout of the topmost storey.

Fig. 13

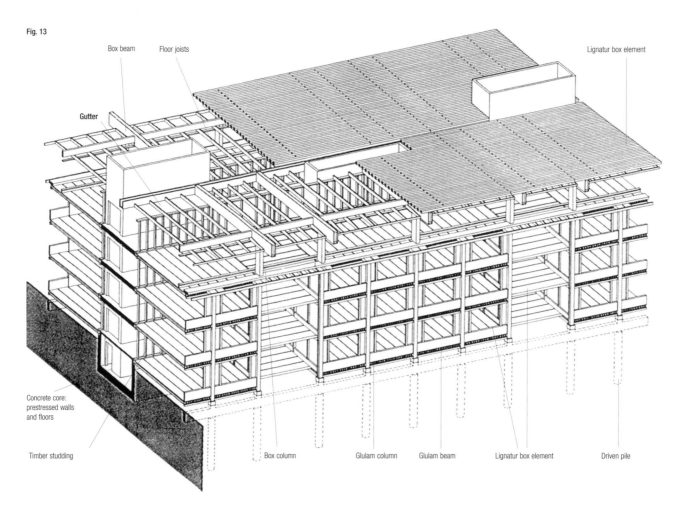

Box beam Floor joists

Lignatur box element

Gutter

Concrete core:
prestressed walls
and floors

Timber studding   Box column   Glulam column   Glulam beam   Lignatur box element   Driven pile

Fig. 14: Covered external zone
The covered external zone between the room boxes allows daylight to enter the corridor alternately from left and right, and – between the "boxes" – also ensures views of the site and the landscape beyond.

Fig. 15: Foyer
The three-storey foyer serves as a lobby for the adjoining assembly hall and the dining hall in the existing building.

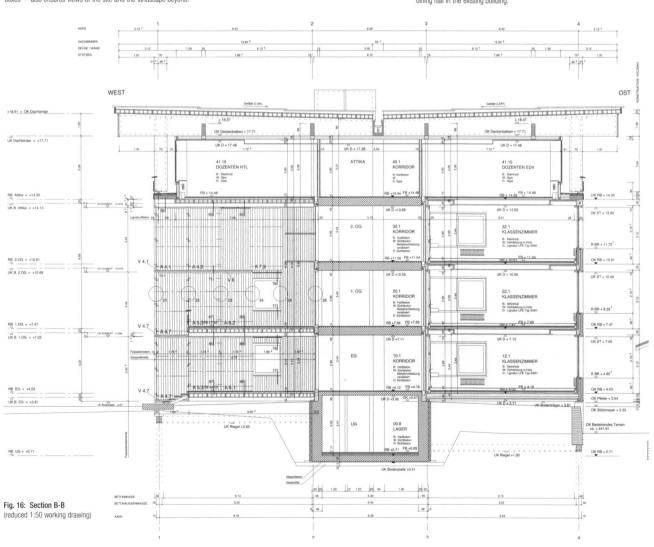

Fig. 16: Section B-B
(reduced 1:50 working drawing)

Detail design

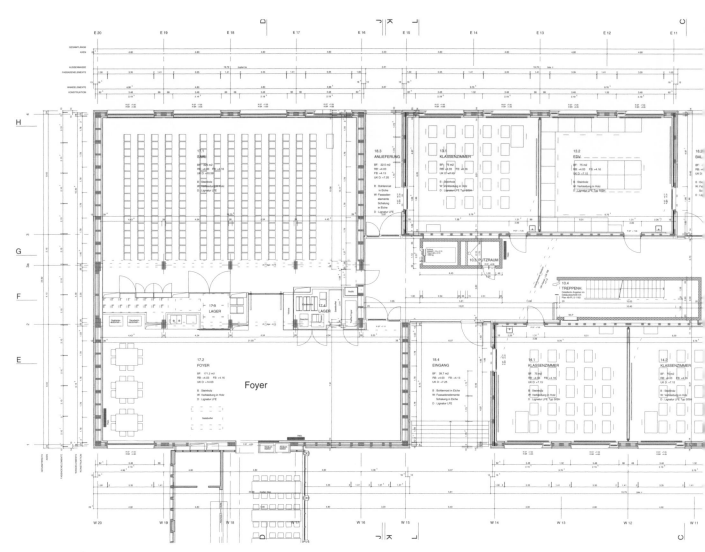

Foyer

Fig. 17 Plan of ground floor
(reduced 1:50 working drawing)

Fig. 18: Transition between concrete core and timber box
The timber and concrete parts are structurally independent systems. The timber
studding is covered on the corridor side with a cement fibreboard (Duripanel) for fire
protection purposes.

Fig. 19: Seminar room prior to fitting-out work
The ceiling comprises Lignatur box elements left exposed which present a
continuous soffit. This results in excellent flexibility for the positioning of partitions.

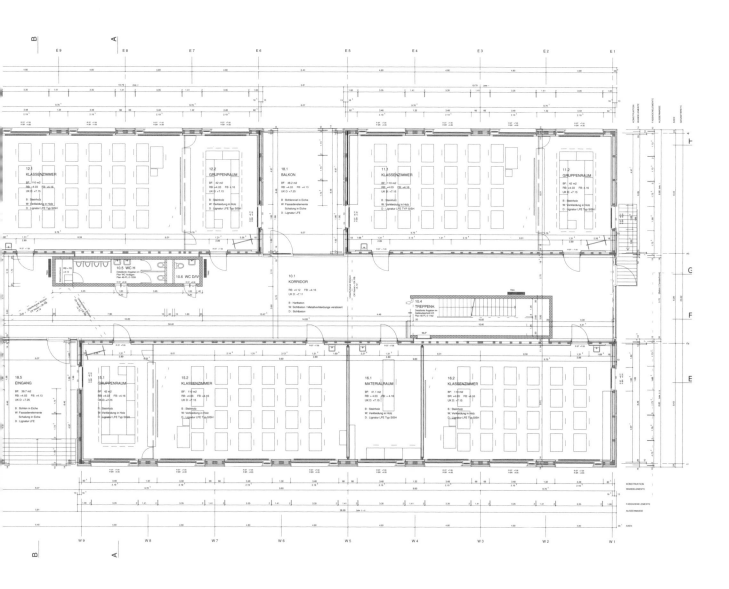

Fig. 20:
The two-storey assembly hall is located at one end of the building.

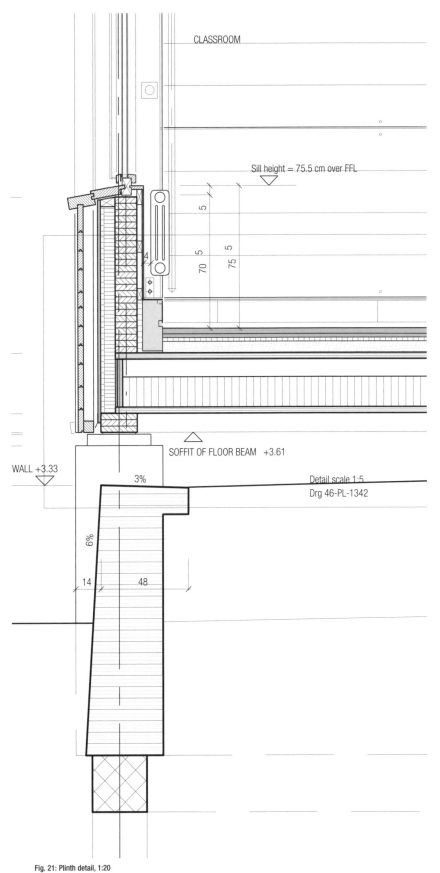

CLASSROOM

Sill height = 75.5 cm over FFL

Detail scale 1:5

Drg 46-PL-1342

SOFFIT OF FLOOR BEAM +3.61

WALL +3.33

3%

6%

14   48

Fig. 21: Plinth detail, 1:20

Fig. 22: Plinth

Fig. 23: Close-up of plinth
The columns that carry the prefabricated facade elements are supported by piles driven about 10 m into the ground. There is a ventilation gap beneath all parts of the timber construction.

Wall construction

Oak facade elements (frame and infill)	
Ventilated cavity	
Bitumen-impregnated wood fibre insulating board	
(Isolair NK)	16 mm
Mineral-fibre board	20 mm
Thermal insulation	80 mm
Upstand beam (in spandrel panel)	120 mm
Inner lining with multiplex boards,	
surface oiled with aluminium pigments	

Floor construction

Flooring cement, 2 layers (e.g. Euböolith)	30 mm
composite of gypsum and asphaltic cardboard	
Chipboard backing	21 mm
Impact sound insulation, PS81	20 mm
Battens laid out in a grid	65 x 50 mm
Sand or chippings as ballast	
(for structure-borne sound)	
Polyethylene sheet	
Lignatur LFE element, with 160 mm	
Homatherm insulation	1000 x 320 mm

Plinth

Tamped concrete with exposed aggregate	
finish, broken limestone aggregate	max. 63 mm

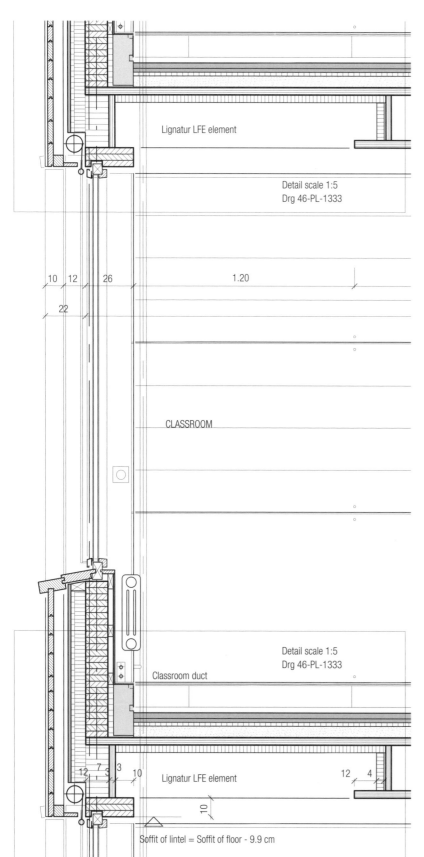

Lignatur LFE element

Detail scale 1:5
Drg 46-PL-1333

10 12   26   1.20

22

CLASSROOM

Detail scale 1:5
Drg 46-PL-1333

Classroom duct

12 7 3 10   Lignatur LFE element   12 4

10

Soffit of lintel = Soffit of floor - 9.9 cm

Fig. 24: Window detail, 1:20

Fig. 25: Window
The window is fitted directly into the structural frame. A narrow opening light for
ventilation has been included instead of just providing a large undivided glazed area.

Fig. 26: Sunshading
Sunshading in the form of an aluminium shutter in front of the ventilation light plus a
fabric awning in front of the fixed light

Wall construction

Oak facade elements (frame and infill)	
Ventilated cavity	
Bitumen-impregnated wood fibre insulating board	
(Isolair NK)	16 mm
Mineral-fibre board	20 mm
Thermal insulation	80 mm
Upstand beam (in spandrel panel)	120 mm
Inner lining	

Floor construction

Flooring cement, 2 layers (e.g. Euböolith)	30 mm
composite of gypsum and asphaltic cardboard	
Chipboard backing	21 mm
Impact sound insulation, PS81	20 mm
Battens laid out in a grid	65 x 50 mm
Sand or chippings as ballast (for structure-borne sound)	
Polyethylene sheet	
Lignatur LFE element, with	
160 mm Homatherm insulation	1000 x 320 mm

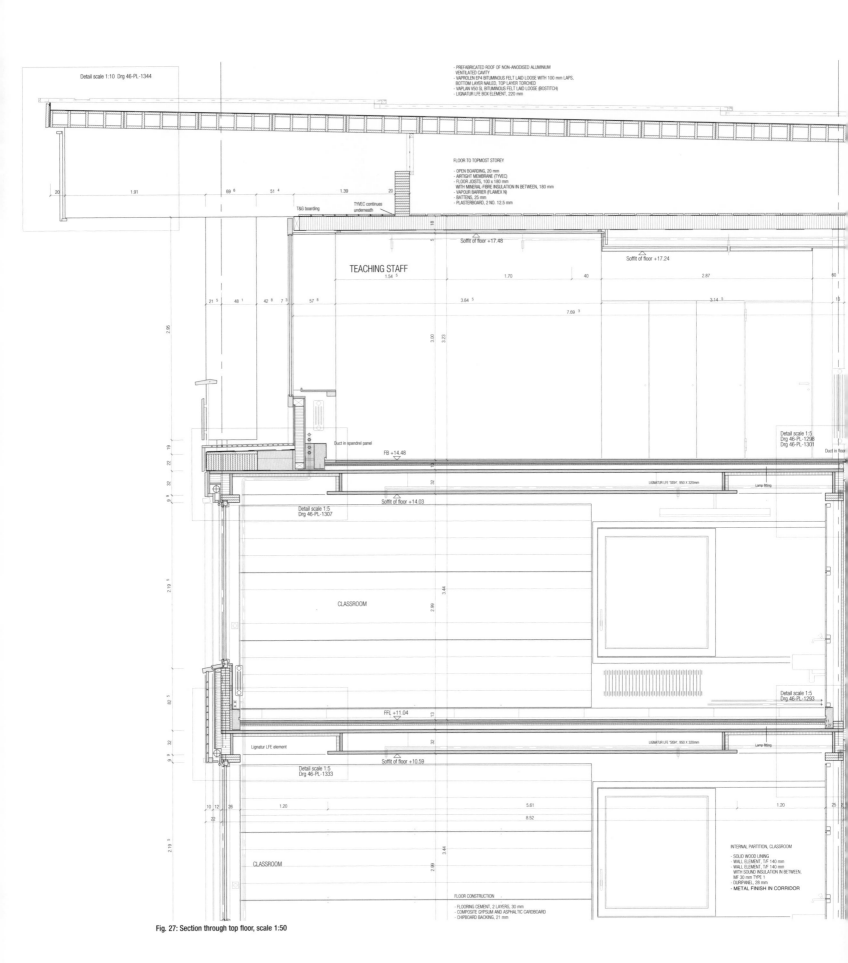

Detail scale 1:10 Drg 46-PL-1344

- PREFABRICATED ROOF OF NON-ANODISED ALUMINIUM
  VENTILATED CAVITY
- VAPROLEN EP4 BITUMINOUS FELT LAID LOOSE WITH 100 mm LAPS,
  BOTTOM LAYER NAILED, TOP LAYER TORCHED
- VAPLAM V50 SL BITUMINOUS FELT LAID LOOSE (BOSTITCH)
- LIGNATUR LFE BOX ELEMENT, 220 mm

FLOOR TO TOPMOST STOREY

- OPEN BOARDING, 20 mm
- AIRTIGHT MEMBRANE (TYVEC)
- FLOOR JOISTS, 100 x 180 mm
  WITH MINERAL-FIBRE INSULATION IN BETWEEN, 180 mm
- VAPOUR BARRIER (FLAMEX N)
- BATTENS, 25 mm
- PLASTERBOARD, 2 NO. 12.5 mm

T&G boarding

TYVEC continues
underneath

TEACHING STAFF

Soffit of floor +17.48

Soffit of floor +17.24

Duct in spandrel panel

Detail scale 1:5
Drg 46-PL-1298
Drg 46-PL-1301

FB +14.48

LIGNATUR LFE 'SIBH', 950 X 320mm

Lamp fitting

Soffit of floor +14.03

Detail scale 1:5
Drg 46-PL-1307

CLASSROOM

Detail scale 1:5
Drg 46-PL-1293

FFL +11.04

LIGNATUR LFE 'SIBH', 950 X 320mm

Lamp fitting

Lignatur LFE element

Soffit of floor +10.59

Detail scale 1:5
Drg 46-PL-1333

INTERNAL PARTITION, CLASSROOM

- SOLID WOOD LINING
- WALL ELEMENT, T/F 140 mm
- WALL ELEMENT, T/F 140 mm
  WITH SOUND INSULATION IN BETWEEN,
  MF 30 mm TYPE 1
- DURIPANEL, 28 mm
- METAL FINISH IN CORRIDOR

CLASSROOM

FLOOR CONSTRUCTION

- FLOORING CEMENT, 2 LAYERS, 30 mm
- COMPOSITE GYPSUM AND ASPHALTIC CARDBOARD
- CHIPBOARD BACKING, 21 mm

Fig. 27: Section through top floor, scale 1:50

Fig. 28: 3rd floor
Wholly in keeping with a *plan libre*, the column grid on the 3rd floor enables
complete freedom for the plan layout. Large box beams supporting the roof are
placed on top of the loadbearing box columns, and these together form a stiff
half-frame.

Fig. 29: Corridor on 3rd floor
The corridor on the 3rd floor is an enclosed space without references to the outside.
The dark, graphite-enriched oil paint finish on the walls seems to make the space
even narrower.

Fig. 30: General view
Together the monumental half-frames carry the roof with its generous overhangs.
The shadows cast on the set-back facade by these large surface areas reinforce the
visual effect of the column, beam and slab elements.

Section through topmost (3rd) storey, 1:50

(reduced 1:20 working drawing)

Roof construction

Prefabricated roof of anodised aluminium	
Ventilated cavity	
Secondary covering layer: bituminous felt	
(Vaprolen EP4) laid loose with 100 mm laps,	
bottom layer nailed,	
top layer torched	
Bituminous felt (Vaplan V50 SL) laid loose (Bostitch)	
Lignatur LFE box element	220 mm

Floor to topmost storey

Open boarding	20 mm
Airtight membrane (TYVEC)	
Floor joists, 100 x 180 mm	
with mineral-fibre insulation in between	
(suspended from beam)	180 mm
Vapour barrier (FLAMEX N)	
Battens	25 mm
Plasterboard (e.g. Rigips)	2 No. 12.5 mm

Floor construction

Flooring cement, 2 layers (e.g. Euböolith)	20 mm
Composite gypsum and asphaltic cardboard	
Chipboard backing	30 mm
Impact sound insulation, PS81	20 mm
Battens laid in a grid with sand or	
chippings in between as ballast	
(for airborne sound)	65 x 50 mm
Polyethylene sheet	
Lignatur LFE box element	320 mm

Private house, Sevgein
Bearth + Deplazes

Situation and theme

A small clearing on the edge of the village of Sevgein is the site for this house, a man-made wedge standing between the mountain ridge and the foothills. Starting at the carport next to the road, a narrow footpath leads down to the house itself, greeting us with beautiful views towards Flims and Vorderrhein in the distance. With its minimal footprint, this tower-like unit responds to the idiosyncrasies of the plot and exploits the tolerances of the building regulations (this is still classed as being in the village) while attempting to uphold the openness of the clearing. This building, for which several models were made first, stands as if it were itself a group of trees hugging the edge of forest and hence leaves the largest possible open space.

Designed with a split-level floor arrangement to make maximum use of the interior, the lowest level also follows the line of the terrain. The slope down from the road to the entrance door continues within the house in the stairs, which run down to the dining room.

Fig. 2: Site plan

Architects: Bearth + Deplazes, Chur
Construction period: 1998–1999
Assistant: Bettina Werner
Structural engineer: Jürg Buchli, Haldenstein

Fig. 1: View from north-east
The large expanse of glass – bordered by floor, ceiling and walls – reveals the extent of the living room.

Fig. 3: Stairs
Views into the adjacent rooms in both directions

Internal layout and loadbearing structure I

The split-level arrangement mentioned above permits visual links to the room at the next level above or below and, on the whole, helps to give the house a more spacious feeling. The rooms' arrangement falls into place thanks to the inclusion of a "spine" containing kitchen, bathrooms and utility room. Each level (provided with sliding doors) benefits from the lighting of its neighbour. The result is that, for example, the living room, which faces the valley and hence north, is supplied with daylight from the south via the gallery and the stairs. This theme of a vertical layout finds expression not only in a "helix of rooms" but also in the two-storey entrance hall. The timber platform frame facades and the timber stud walls of the central spine are loadbearing and are supported on the in situ concrete basement.

Fig. 5: Attic

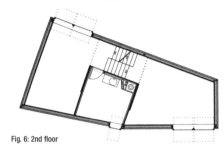

Fig. 6: 2nd floor

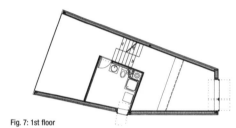

Fig. 7: 1st floor

Fig. 8: Ground floor

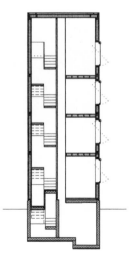

0 1   5 m

Fig. 4: Section

Light from south

Fig. 9: Longitudinal section

Internal layout and loadbearing structure II

A prefabricated timber structure was chosen because of the geographical location (mountain village with difficult access) and also to facilitate a high degree of self-installation by the owners themselves (facade planking with glaze finish and interior planking with paint finish). Critical factors for the overall architectural impression therefore lay not so much in the accurately conceived and drawn details, as in the working practices, e.g. the cladding used for the facade.

Three different plank widths were fixed vertically, with the only criterion being that the same size planks should be used above and below the window openings. This "automatically" resulted in an interesting, yet technically correct, effect with sections of the facade characterised by the joints between the planks. The dark grey facade minimises the wooden nature of the building and makes it clear that the prime intention here was not to build a "timber house".

Fig. 12: Timber platform frame elements waiting to be erected
The timber platform frame construction was erected in two days.

Fig. 13: Assembling the wall and floor elements
The floor elements are suspended between the walls on Z-sections.

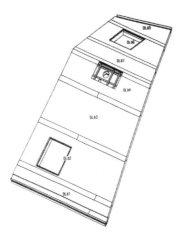

Fig. 10: Axonometric view of roof

Fig. 14: Installing a roof element
Prefabrication guarantees a good degree of accuracy.

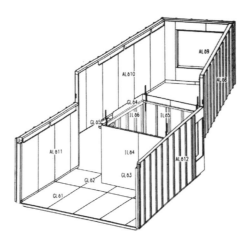

Fig. 11: Axonometric view of wall elements

Facade and roof construction

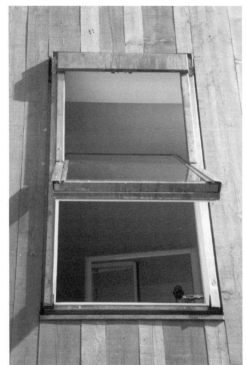

Fig. 17: Close-up of window
The ventilation flap and roller blind are behind the fascia panel at the top.

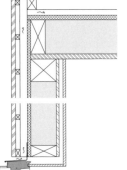

Standard VELUX roof window
type GGL 810/GGL 310

Roof construction

Copper roof with locked double welt seams	0.6 mm
Bitumen felt	
Timber boarding	24 mm
Ventilated cavity	100 mm
Bitumen-impregnated wood fibre	
insulating board	24 mm
Structural timber, spruce/fir	80 / 180 mm
with Isofloc thermal insulation between	
3-ply core plywood, spruce/fir	27 mm
Total	*355 mm*

Wall construction

Vertical planks with butt joints	22 mm
Battens laid in a grid	25 mm
Counter battens/ventilated cavity	40 mm
Softboard	18 mm
Timber studs/thermal insulation	140 mm
OSB 3-ply core plywood	15 mm
Battens laid in a grid	15 mm
Wood panelling	15 mm
Total	*290 mm*

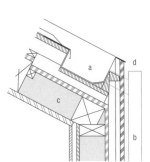

a) Gutter
b) Copper downpipe, d = 70 mm, top end left open
c) Roof construction thinner locally to accommodate gutter
d) Timber cladding up to underside of verge or eaves flashing,
   facade ventilation cavity continues beneath roof surface

Fig. 15: Detail of eaves with gutter, 1:20

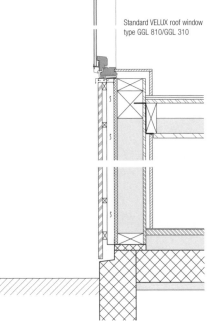

Fig. 16: Section through facade, 1:20

Openings and loadbearing structure

Principally, the timber platform frame construction does not dictate any specific approach to positioning the openings, but rather permits an almost random arrangement. Two types of window are used in this house: a large expanse of glazing for the living room, running from floor to ceiling and from wall to wall, and VELUX roof windows, used not only in the roof but also in the facade! The use of standard roof windows in the walls is unusual, but offers all the advantages of a conventional wood/metal window for the price of a wooden window and, furthermore, allows for ventilation regardless of the weather conditions. The ventilation flap fitted as standard to these windows is protected by the peripheral sheet copper flashing, which also accommodates a roller blind to cut out direct sunlight. Every window is positioned such that one reveal is aligned with one wall, which is therefore used to spread the incoming light throughout the room. The position of the windows also changes from floor to floor on a rotational basis; this highlights the detached nature of the building but also reflects the fluid internal layout. It follows logically that the vertical arrangement of the windows one atop the other in the central spine deviates from this since these rooms are not part of the spatial continuum.

Fig. 19: Internal view of window on 2nd floor
The reveal merges into the wall.

Fig. 20: Internal view of living room window
The frameless glazing seems to eliminate the physical separation.

Fig. 18: West facade
The linear arrangement of the windows identifies the position of the "static" rooms.

Fig. 21: Window in attic
A VELUX roof window used in the traditional way!

Leutschenbach School, Zurich
Christian Kerez

Felix Ackerknecht

Leutschenbach School is situated on the northern edge of the town, where the city of Zurich merges with the neighbouring communities and hence experiences enormous impetus. Numerous houses and apartments are being built in this, the largest development area of the city. Housing for families is a priority, and a school is therefore also required. The Leutschenbach district is burdened by infrastructure elements such as railway embankment, bus depot and waste incineration plant, which meant that the local authority demanded a considerable urban integration as well as pedagogic objectives.

Urban planning

In order to create an urban-planning highlight in this area with its large-scale built environment, the gymnasium, classrooms and auditorium are stacked one above the other and therefore form a tall, prominent structure. This vertical arrangement of functions that in schools are normally placed adjacent to each other enabled a large part of the site to be kept free for a public park with large recreation and relaxation zones, and a separate nursery pavilion. The generous external facilities serving the whole district link the school to the adjoining Andreaspark housing estate and round off the whole development.

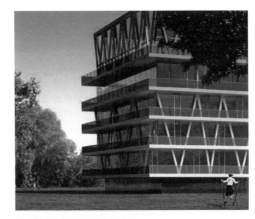

Fig. 1: Photomontage of model of school
Instead of designing a group of independent buildings with different functions, a compact and stimulating arrangement of functions was developed within a single building volume.

The free-standing, tall, cube-like structure attracts public interest; its stance is a reference back to the state schools of the late 19th century. However, the principle of the layering of functions is reminiscent of the "modern dream" formulated by Hilbersheimer and Le Corbusier, the difference here being that there is no repetition of identical storeys. Diagonal members have a monumental importance in this building and gives each storey an unmistakable identity.

Client:	Zurich Building Department
Architect:	Christian Kerez, Zurich
Construction:	May 2005 to April 2008
Assistants:	Christian Scheidegger (project manager), Lukas Camponovo, Andrea Casiraghi, Michael Eidenbenz
Site management:	BGS Architekten GmbH, Rapperswil
Structural engineers:	Dr. Schwartz Consulting AG, Zug (senior consultant, solid construction) dsp Ingenieure & Planer AG (structural steelwork, excavations, foundations)
Geology:	Gysi Leoni Mader, Zurich
Building physics:	BAKUS, Zurich; Martin Lienhard
HVAC engineers:	Waldhauser Haustechnik AG, Münchenstein
Electrical engineers:	Giovanoli + Tanner, Uster
External works:	4d AG, Bern

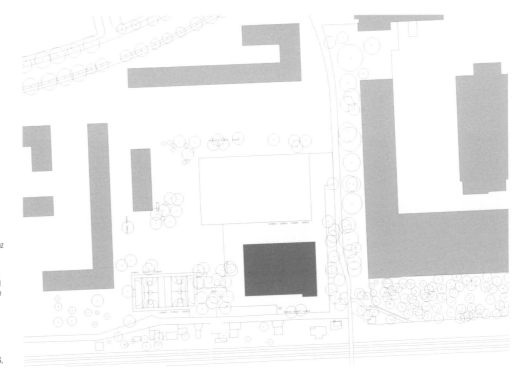

Fig. 2: Site plan, 1:2500

Organisation

The school serves both the primary and secondary education needs of the district. The two education levels each have their own, separate entrance areas on opposite sides of the building, surrounded by the canteen and the after-school club. A staircase in the centre of the building provides access as far as the fourth floor for both education levels. The single flights, kept separate for primary and secondary education pupils, link foyers around which the classrooms are arranged.

Escape routes from the classrooms lead to balconies on the outside of the building and separate escape stairs. The foyers within the building are therefore not subjected to the fire protection provisions for escape routes and may contain furniture and fittings. They can be used as communal areas and for teaching and hence can be counted as usable floor space. This ingenious arrangement of the plan area obviates the need for access corridors and hence reduces the overall volume of the building, which makes it easier to understand the elaborate, costly, steel-and-glass construction.

On the fourth floor, the two separate staircases for the two education levels meet in one large foyer, which is surrounded by common facilities such as the auditorium and the library. The three-part gymnasium crowns the whole school building. Together with the changing rooms and showers, this is the largest single usable space in the building and as such determines the plan area, the "footprint" of the cube.

Interior layout

The setting for the layering and hence the basic arrangement of the building is achieved by using substantially different storey heights. Starting with a seemingly compressed ground floor, the height of each storey increases as we go up the building. The staircases linking the storeys play a key role in this scene. The stairs are not housed in blank shafts, but combine on each floor with the outward-facing foyers.

Generally, any form of compartmentation is strictly avoided within the building. Apart from the concrete floor slabs, this unusually deep structure is not divided into compartments, but instead the different zones are subtly marked by internal partitions of translucent glass and doors of transparent glass that let the daylight through. Glass external walls maximise the spatial continuity between building and environment.

In order to unite the interior even more strongly with the exterior, the seamless, cast finish to the outdoor recreation area continues beneath the glazed envelope into the interior of the building. On the upper floors, the floor slabs cantilever out over the glazed envelope and extend the interior to the outside by means of balconies with glass safety barriers.

Fig. 3: Schematic diagram of classroom block
Primary and secondary education areas are reached separately via interconnected but offset foyers.

Fig. 4: Photo of model
5th floor: gymnasium

Fig. 5: Photo of model
4th floor: foyer

Fig. 6: Photo of model
2nd floor: access foyer

Fig. 7: Photo of model
Ground floor: entrance area

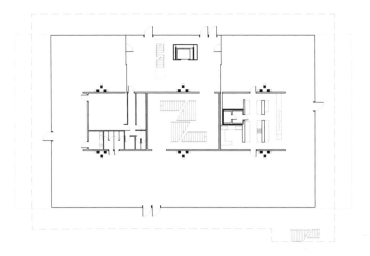

Fig. 8: Plan of ground floor, 1:600

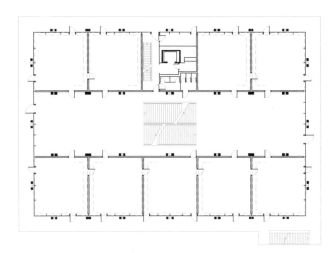

Dotted lines: curtains

Fig. 9: Plan of 1st floor, 1:600

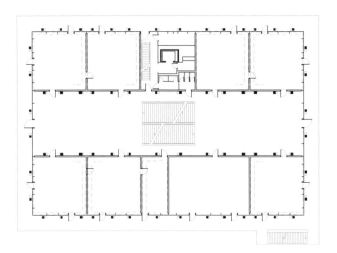

Dotted lines: curtains

Fig. 10: Plan of 2nd floor, 1:600

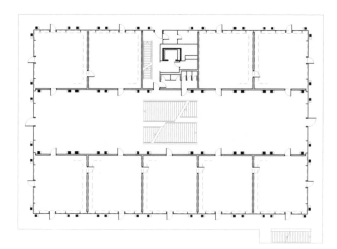

Dotted lines: curtains

Fig. 11: Plan of 3rd floor, 1:600

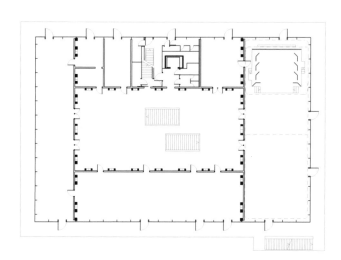

Dotted lines: curtains

Fig. 12: Plan of 4th floor, 1:600

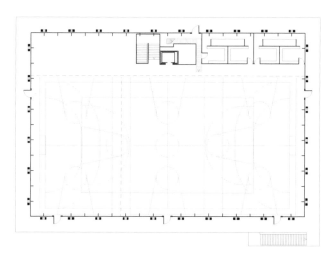

Dotted lines: movable play area dividers

Fig. 13: Plan of 5th floor, 1:600

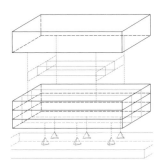

Fig. 14: Schematic diagram of vertical loading paths
Light grey: loadbearing structure within building envelope
Dark grey: loadbearing structure outside building envelope

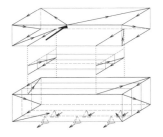

Fig. 15: Schematic diagram of horizontal loading paths
Arrows: flow of forces for horizontal load actions

Loadbearing structure

In order to avoid an enclosing effect as far as possible, the loadbearing structure has been essentially resolved into trussed steel girders. The only parts of the load-bearing structure that have not been thinned out are the reinforced concrete floor slabs.

All the common facilities such as canteen, after-school club, library and auditorium are located in those areas where the loadbearing structure is placed in the middle of the building, clear of the facade. So in these areas, ground floor and fourth floor, the view of the outside world is not obstructed by trussed girders.

In contrast, the classroom floors are enclosed by trussed girders. As these trussed girders are positioned outside the building envelope, they bear on pads made from high-tech plastic, which act as thermal breaks. The trussed girders that surround the three-storey classroom block are suspended from eight supports on the fourth floor. These supports are located at the ends of trussed girders that pass right through the building, two longitudinal and two transverse, one above the other. Further trussed girders, enclosing the gymnasium, are supported on the two upper, transverse trussed girders. The two longitudinal trussed girders below transfer the entire load of the building to six 3-leg

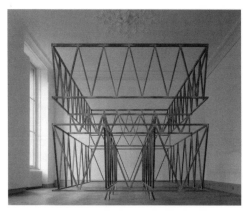

Fig. 17: Model of loadbearing structure

steel columns on the ground floor, which carry the loads through the basement to pile foundations and into the subsoil.

This concentration of the loads rules out damage that could be caused by differential settlement due to the poor subsoil. It also guarantees an entrance area unencumbered by loadbearing members below a slab cantilevering more than 10 m. Added to this is the fascinating effect that the building's substructure seems to bear no relation to its superstructure.

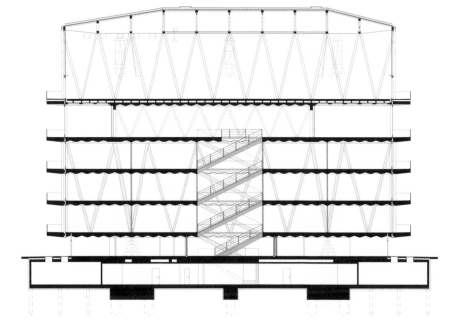

Fig. 16: 1st floor cantilevering over ground floor
Six 3-leg steel columns within the building carry all the loads of the upper floors.

Fig. 18: Longitudinal section, 1:500
Fire protection to the structural steelwork is in the form of a special coating and a sprinkler system.

Design

The polygonal, "wavy" soffits to the exposed concrete floor slabs result from an optimisation that takes into account loadbearing action, building services, room acoustics and architectural aspects. The profiled effect of the concrete floor slabs improves the loadbearing action of the one-way spanning suspended floor construction consisting of T-beam slab strips, similar to a beam-and-slab floor, but also provides ample space for the building services (electrics, ventilation, heating, fire protection), which are fully integrated into the floor slabs. Luminaires, loudspeakers and sensors are let into the deeper zones of the floor slabs, air outlets and sprinklers in the shallower zones. The shape of the ceiling, with its sloping surfaces, improves the room acoustics by diffusing the sound. A porous material has been fitted into recesses in these surfaces to improve sound attenuation. The furnishings and fittings also help to absorb sound.

In order to reduce the dead loads, lightweight concrete was used for the upper floors, cast on multiple-use formwork main from Bakelite-faced plywood panels. To spare resources, recycled-aggregate concrete was used for the basement.

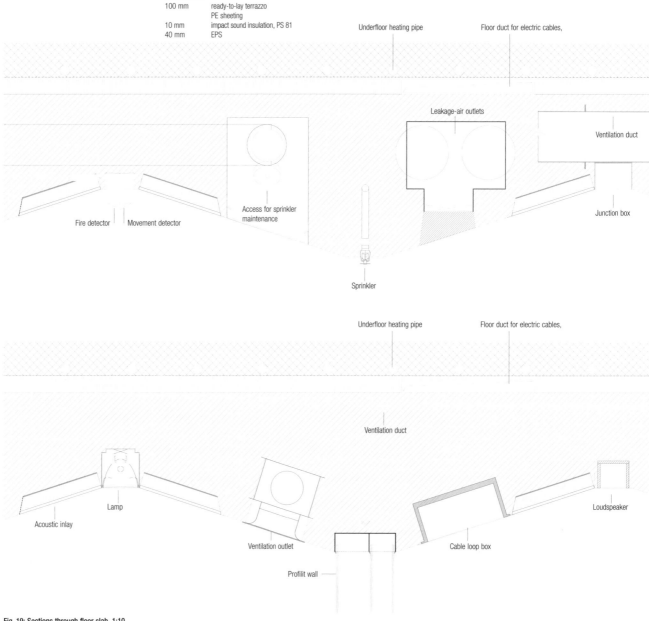

Floor finishes:
100 mm   ready-to-lay terrazzo
           PE sheeting
10 mm   impact sound insulation, PS 81
40 mm   EPS

Underfloor heating pipe

Floor duct for electric cables,

Leakage-air outlets

Ventilation duct

Fire detector   Movement detector

Access for sprinkler maintenance

Junction box

Sprinkler

Underfloor heating pipe

Floor duct for electric cables,

Ventilation duct

Lamp

Acoustic inlay

Ventilation outlet

Loudspeaker

Cable loop box

Profilit wall

Fig. 19: Sections through floor slab, 1:10

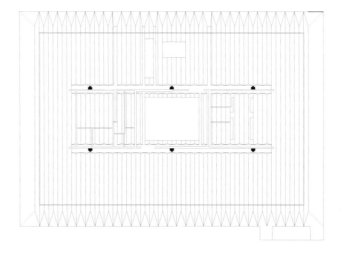

Fig. 20: View of soffit, ground floor, 1:600

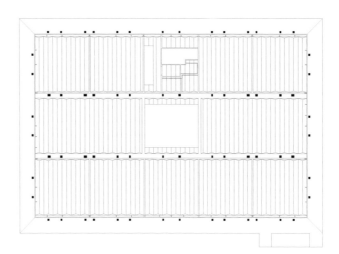

Fig. 21: View of soffit, 1st floor, 1:6000

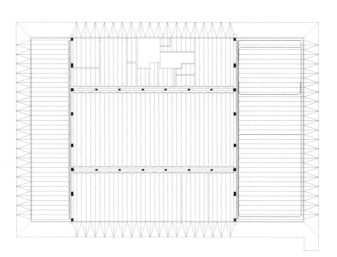

Fig. 22: View of soffit, 4th floor, 1:600

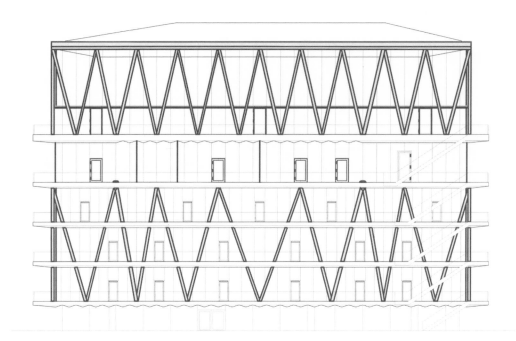

Fig. 23: Elevation of facade, 1:400

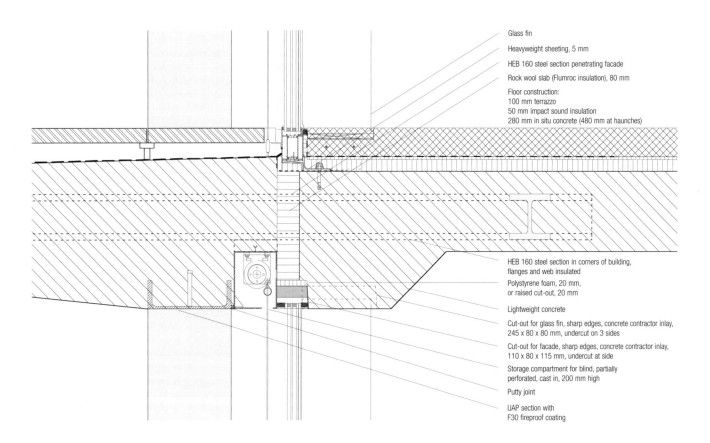

Glass fin

Heavyweight sheeting, 5 mm

HEB 160 steel section penetrating facade

Rock wool slab (Flumroc insulation), 80 mm

Floor construction:
100 mm terrazzo
50 mm impact sound insulation
280 mm in situ concrete (480 mm at haunches)

HEB 160 steel section in corners of building,
flanges and web insulated

Polystyrene foam, 20 mm,
or raised cut-out, 20 mm

Lightweight concrete

Cut-out for glass fin, sharp edges, concrete contractor inlay,
245 x 80 x 80 mm, undercut on 3 sides

Cut-out for facade, sharp edges, concrete contractor inlay,
110 x 80 x 115 mm, undercut at side

Storage compartment for blind, partially
perforated, cast in, 200 mm high

Putty joint

UAP section with
F30 fireproof coating

Fig. 24: Section through facade, 1:10

The loads and hence also the deformations of the structural steelwork's complex geometry gradually increased during the construction work as the concrete floors were added. Temporary steel props were periodically removed and later replaced in order that the ensuing deformations could take place in a controlled manner. As the complex geometry of the structural steelwork made it difficult to predict the deformations, the trussed girders were measured continuously during the work. This enabled the anticipated definitive deformations to be reliably predicted at the time of ordering the glass walls.

The building as a whole retains the essential characteristics of a structural carcass, like the reduction to just a few elements and abrupt changes of material. Both the internal and external glass walls are let directly into the floor and soffit without intervening frames.

The building envelope consists of frameless triple glazing with stiffening glass fins. Internal walls are made from translucent "Profilit" profiled glass units. All internal and external doors are mounted in steel frames, which are anchored to the floor only so that no load is transferred from the door to the glass wall.

The peripheral balconies protect the building against direct sunlight. In addition, the incoming sunlight can be regulated with blinds, which are recessed into the cantilevering floor slabs on the outside of the glass walls.

Although the trussed girders and cantilevering balcony slabs mean that some parts of the loadbearing structure penetrate the building envelope, Leutschenbach School still complies with the "Minergie" standard. The resulting heat losses are compensated for by the compactness of the building volume and the excellent insulating value of the triple glazing. However, in order to prevent damage, no water may be allowed to condense on those parts of the construction with above-average cooling rates (thermal bridges).

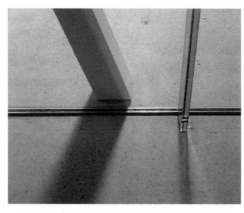

Fig. 27: Facade pattern

Building services

The heating energy is taken from the district heating network of the neighbouring waste incineration plant and distributed throughout the building by way of underfloor heating with a low flow temperature.

Fresh air is blown by fans into a central vertical shaft and distributed horizontally via ventilation ducts let into the concrete floors. On the upper floors, the fresh air enters the rooms via outlets mounted below the floor slabs, and on the ground floor by way of displacement ventilation through the floor.

The exhaust air flows through acoustically attenuated ducts in the walls ("leakage-air outlets") into the foyers and from there through the vertical shafts.

In summer, the fresh air can be cooled passively by humidifying the exhaust air in a heat exchanger ("adiabatic cooling"). In winter, the fresh air can be preheated by the exhaust air in a heat exchanger.

Air-treatment plant is housed in the basement and also between the steel members of the roof construction. This arrangement means the open ground floor could be kept free of vertical ventilation ducts.

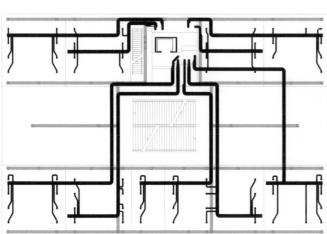

Fig. 25: Floor slab during construction
Installation of building services in floor slab, e.g. ventilation ducts

Fig. 26: Schematic diagram of horizontal distribution of media in concrete floor slabs
Dark grey: ventilation ducts; light grey: electric ducts

Fig. 28–29: Photos taken during construction

Above, from top to bottom: The external trussed girder surrounding the three-storey classrooms block is supported from eight elaborate bearings with thermal breaks.
The structural steelwork was prefabricated in large components limited only by the transport options and welded together in an on-site workshop.

Left, from top to bottom: The in situ concrete floor slabs were cast around the structural steelwork to achieve a composite action.
Six 3-leg steel columns carry the loads through the basement to pile foundations and into the subsoil.

Office building, Picassoplatz, Basel
Peter Märkli

Stephan Achermann

Architect:	Peter Märkli, Zurich
Project managers:	Jakob Frischknecht, Nathalie Herter
Competition:	2002
Construction	2003–2007
Structural engineers:	Ulmann & Kunz, Basel (excavation), Jauslin & Stebler Ingenieure AG, Basel
Building physics:	Gartenmann Engineering AG, Basel
Building services:	Bures & Voith Klima Planing AG, Basel
Facade:	Feroplan Engineering AG, Zurich

Urban planning, building

In terms of the urban planning, this office building, on the corner plot of a dominant perimeter block development, occupies a challenging, prominent position on Picassoplatz in Basel. The longer side of the plot faces Brunngässlein, the shorter side Picassoplatz itself, which owes its character to a number of imposing structures.

The exact volumetric formulation and positioning of "Businesscenter Picassoplatz" is a subtle response to the complex urban context here. Looked at from the street, the observer might at first think that two individual towers share a common ground-floor storey. However, a closer look reveals that the building indeed consists of a single volume that is simply set back from the first floor upwards. This concept results in a three-dimensional, courtyard-like widening of the little street Brunngässlein and also revitalises Picassoplatz by opening up the streetscape. The exact geometry of the building runs parallel to the municipal building lines. The taller part of the building rounds off the line of buildings along Dufourstrasse, and with its taller top storey forms a sort of end block facing Picassoplatz. The smaller part fits neatly into the streetscape

and the line of buildings along Brunngässlein. The setback part is orthogonal to the respective building lines, whereas the ground-floor storey traces the lines of the streets exactly and is not set back at any point. Differentiating the building in this way is the architect's direct answer to the dissimilar urban situations. The exact proportions and segmentation of the individual parts is based on a system of dimensions that divides a selected initial size into eighths, sixteenths, thirty-seconds etc.

Fig. 2: Sketch of urban situation by Peter Märkli

Fig. 1: View from Picassoplatz
The northern part of the building with its highly characteristic vertical facade segmentation

Fig. 3: View from 7th floor towards Picassoplatz

Architecture, typology

Office buildings must offer good flexibility of use. Consequently, an intelligent and flexible floor layout has to be designed together with the building envelope and the infrastructure. That layout has to provide space for a maximum number of good working positions with a link to the outside world and the best possible natural illumination. It must allow users to subdivide and adapt the floor areas to suit their needs.

Setting back the upper floors, necessary in this urban setting anyway, ensures optimum daylight conditions in the relatively deep office spaces. At the same time, this set-back arrangement divides each floor area into two zones, which – as the service cores can be accessed from both sides – means that different tenants can use the building independently. The subdivision of the facade into slender panels approx. 3.10 m wide makes the floors suitable for both open-plan and tiny cellular offices.

The building has two different service cores: a prestigious, principal core directly behind the glass facade, with spacious stairs and lifts, and a rather more functional core at the back of the building with a minimal staircase, ancillary rooms, and shafts for services. This positioning of the main vertical circulation route and the functional core leads to the internal constraints creating an interesting contrast with the open, brightly lit office areas – at least where open-plan layouts are used. In addition, placing the two vertical circulation routes here ensures compliance with fire safety regulations regarding gross floor areas, number of escape stairs and lengths of escape routes. The prominent situation of the principal stairs adjacent to the facade, the reddish slate floor covering and the smart olivewood handrails give the stairs a classy character; and the generous size means landings can also serve as reception and meeting zones. On the ground floor, panels of olivewood highlight the entrances in the facade of glass and steel. The connection between entrance and principal staircase forms the backbone to the building and the materials used here strengthen the prestigious nature of the architecture.

Fig. 4: Location plan, 1:2500

Fig. 5: The imposing main staircase directly behind the facade

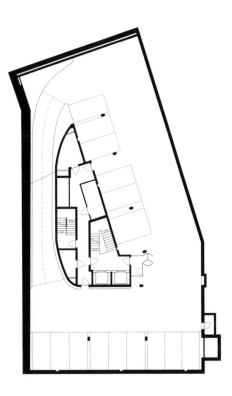

Fig. 6: Plan of basement levels 1–3, 1:500

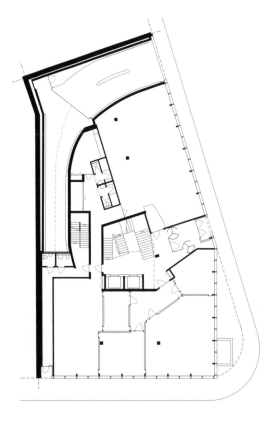

Fig. 7: Plan of ground floor, 1:500

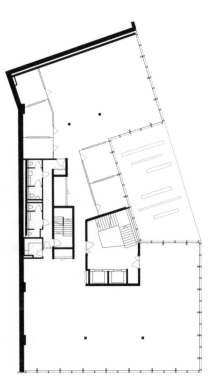

Fig. 8: Plan of 1st to 6th floors, 1:500

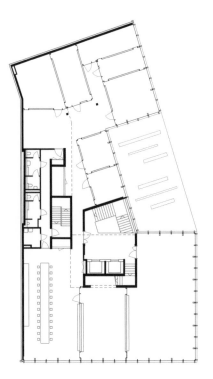

Fig. 9: Plan of 7th floor, 1:500

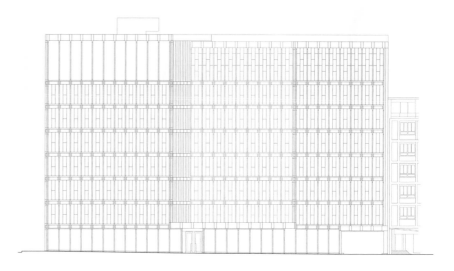

Fig. 10: North facade (facing Brunngässlein), 1:500

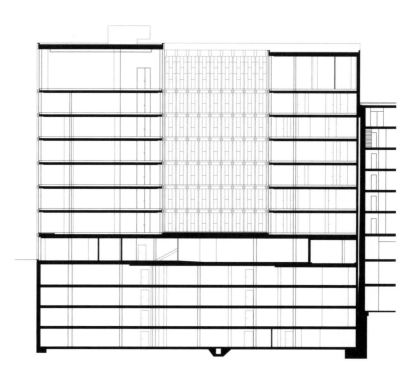

Fig. 11: Longitudinal section, 1:500

The design of "Businesscenter Picassoplatz" is based on the conventional concept of core and shell plus fitting-out at a later date by the tenants. In order to reinforce and consolidate the architectural expression and character of the building, special attention was given to the fixed formulation of facade, entrance area and vertical circulation at the draft design stage. Tenant fitting-out options in the office spaces – even in the case of different tenants at a later date – are limited to subdividing those spaces into smaller units and choosing the materials and colours of the finishes.

Facade

The design employs the classic three-part subdivision into ground-floor storey, middle part and in this case a taller topmost storey. Continuous vertical lesenes and horizontal bands with glass infilling for every storey define the uniform facade structure of this building. The arrangement of

Fig. 13: The relief in the facade
View from Brunngässlein

the two elements and the relief achieves a subtle sculpted effect and lend the facade of this office building a specific, refined expression without losing the human scale. On the office floors, further, delicate subdivision has been introduced to frame the opening lights. Subdividing the areas of glass in this way creates a greater degree of separation between interior and exterior, and prevents the two from simply merging, as is often the case with glass facades. Without this delicate subdivision of the glass on the ground-floor and top storeys there is a subtle differentiation in the facade. The public and semi-public parts of the building can be surmised from the street outside.

Steel, not aluminium, was chosen as the material for the sections and sheet metal of the facade; steel matches the urban and architectural language desired. The strength and fabrication of the material lends the building its compact, elegant character. Steel's higher strength enables delicate sections with fewer sharp edges to be used, and allows welding to create homogeneous elements. The facade from the first to the sixth floors is made up of prefabricated elements. The storey-high frames were factory-welded and finished with a fluoropolymer powder coating before the glass infill panels were installed. These prefabricated elements were transported to the building site and attached to the Halfen rails cast into the ends of the floor slabs. The factory-fabricated sheet metal cladding units, consisting of lesenes, facade nodes and sunblind housings, were added afterwards. The shapes of these cladding elements, the erection sequence on site

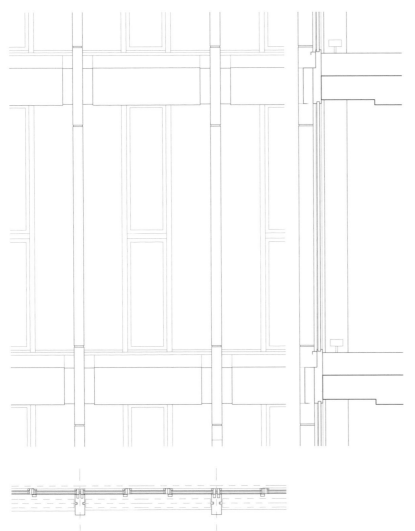

Fig. 12: Facade to standard floor
Elevation, horizontal and vertical sections

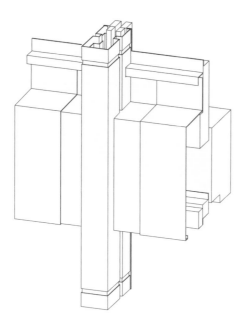

Fig. 14: Isometric view of facade node
Principle of overlapping sheet metal: node plate, lesene, sunblind housing

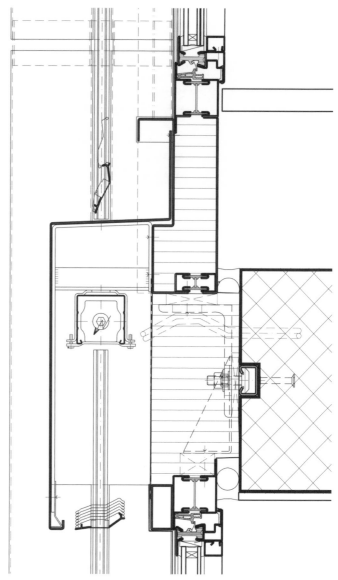

Fig. 15: Section through facade to standard floor, 1:5
Fixing of facade elements to end of floor slab

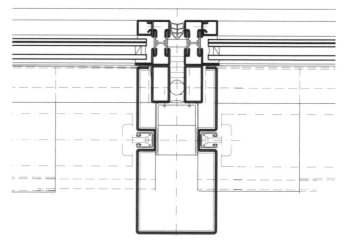

Fig. 16: Horizontal section through facade to standard floor, 1:5
Metal facade with steel cladding

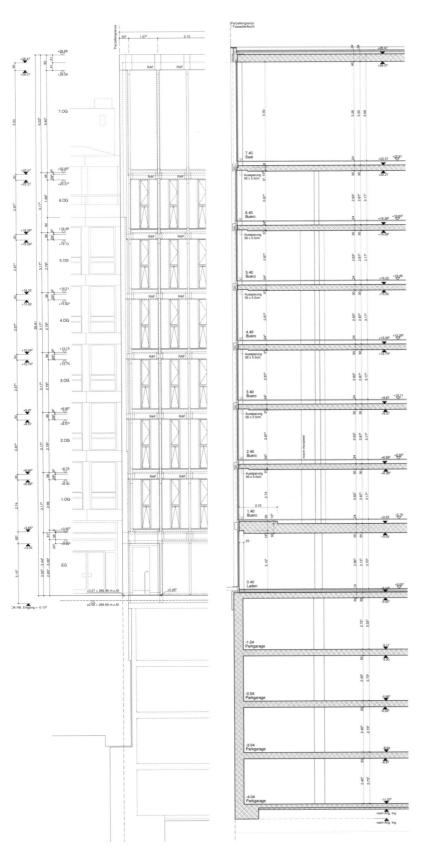

Fig. 17: East facade, elevation and section, 1:200
Reduced 1:50 working drawing

and the jointing principle for the individual parts resulted in the advantage that all sealing problems could be solved without the need for any sealing materials. Fixing holes in the sheet metal parts were factory-drilled prior to powder coating. Bolting the sheet metal directly on site would have damaged the powder coating and led to corrosion. By using fixed bolts on one side and suspension from an elongated hole, the sheet metal can expand and contract as temperatures change. The tracks for the sunblinds are fitted flush with the sides of the lesenes and the horizontal bands incorporate the external sunblind housings. The individual elements therefore have functional as well as aesthetic significance.

Structure, building services

In structural terms, "Businesscenter Picassoplatz" is a conventional column-and-slab design. To carry the vertical loads, the main reinforced concrete columns are supplemented by slender steel stanchions in the plane of the facade, matching the layout of the facade. Horizontal forces are resisted by the concrete service cores and rear walls (fire walls) that transfer the loads to the foundations and the subsoil.

Building services are routed vertically via two shafts in the functional core, and horizontally via raised access floors. Compared with routing services above suspended ceilings, which would have meant that a certain proportion of the soffit would have had to be left open to ensure the effectiveness of the thermoactive floor slabs, the chosen solution resulted in an extra approx. 20–30 cm of clear height. Another advantage is the flexible routing of services; it is relatively easy to adapt services to new interior layouts in the event of future changes of use/tenant. With 30 cm concrete floor slabs, a 24 cm raised access floor and a clear ceiling height of 2.63 m, the resulting storey height for standard floors is 3.17 m.

The incoming air for ventilation in the offices is routed horizontally through the raised access floor. Grilles in the floor release the fresh air into the rooms above. The exhaust air (from individual offices) is routed via sound-insulated leakage air grilles in the walls and then centrally via the vertical shafts. In addition to mechanical ventilation, the offices can also be ventilated naturally via the opening lights in the facade.

A district heating system covers space heating and hot water requirements. Thermoactive floor slabs and convectors along the facades meet the space heating requirements. The convectors can be controlled individually and prevent cold air downdraughts at the glass facade. The thermoactive floor slabs, backed up by a mechanical cooling system, are also used to cool the interior in summer. So that the thermoactive system can exploit its full potential, only parts of the soffit are covered by surface-mounted luminaires and acoustic panels.

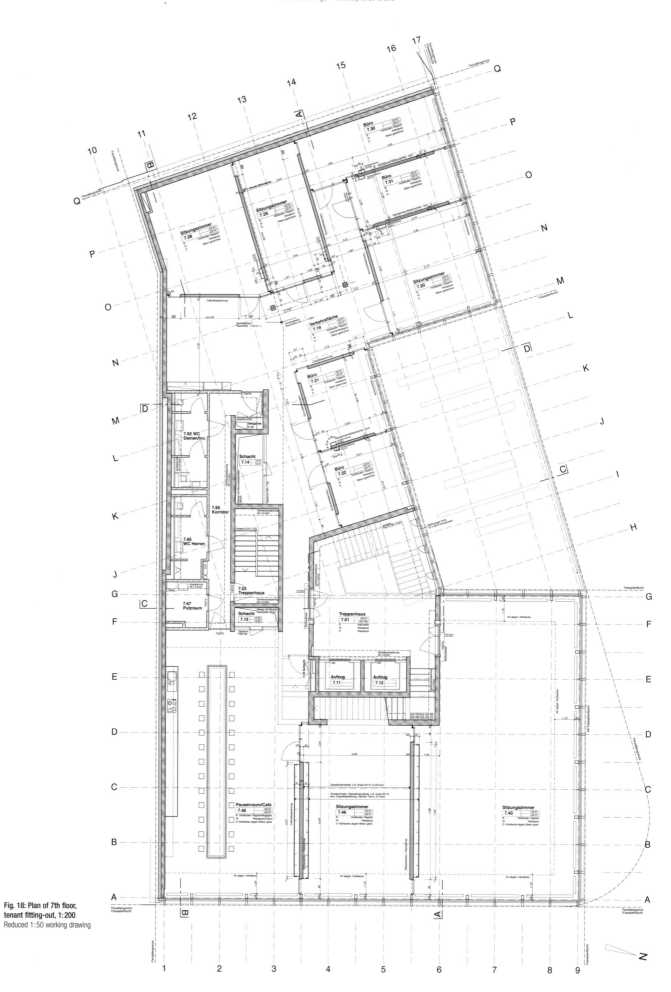

**Fig. 18: Plan of 7th floor,
tenant fitting-out, 1:200**
Reduced 1:50 working drawing

Drawings	Foundation – Plinth	Wall – Floor	Opening	Floor	Roof – Parapet
Preparation of drawings for buildings: Excerpt from Swiss standard SIA 400					
Presentation on drawings: Example: timber platform frame construction					
Symbols: Legend for the catalogue of components					
	Single-leaf masonry	Single-leaf masonry, rendered	Single-leaf masonry	Hollow clay block floor	Pitched roof – warm deck: Fibre-cement – external cladding, lightweight
	Double-leaf masonry, rendered	Double-leaf masonry, rendered	Double-leaf masonry, rendered	Hourdis-type hollow clay block floor	Pitched roof – warm deck, monopitch roof: Fibre-cement – facing masonry
	Facing masonry	Facing masonry	Facing masonry	Solid concrete slab	Pitched roof – cold deck: Roof tiles – masonry in brick-work bond
	Fair-face concrete with internal insulation	Fair-face concrete with internal insulation	Fair-face concrete with internal insulation	Ribbed concrete slab	Pitched roof – cold deck: Sheet metal – single-leaf masonry
	External insulation, rendered	External insulation, rendered	External cladding, lightweight	Concrete waffle slab	Flat roof – warm deck: Bitumen – double-leaf masonry, rendered
	External cladding, lightweight	External cladding, lightweight	External cladding, heavyweight	Hollow-core concrete slab	Flat roof – warm deck: Bitumen – fair-face concrete with internal insulation
	External cladding, heavyweight	External cladding, heavyweight	External insulation, rendered	Composite slab, profiled metal sheeting– concrete	Flat roof – warm deck: Plastics – external cladding, heavy-weight
	Timber platform frame construction	Non-loadbearing external wall	Non-loadbearing external wall	Solid timber floor	Flat roof – warm deck: Bitumen – non-loadbearing external wall
	Solid timber panel construction: Plinth – Roof	Timber platform frame construction	Timber platform frame construction	Timber joist floor	Flat roof – upside-down roof: Bitumen – external insulation, rendered
		Solid timber panel construction	Solid timber panel construction	Timber box element floor	Flat roof – cold deck, uncoated roof: Bitumen – timber platform frame construction
			Hinged door, external – wood	Steel floor	Flat roof – warm deck, suitable/unsuitable for foot traffic
			Hinged door, external – wood/glass		Flat roof – cold deck
			Sliding door, external – metal/glass		Flat roof – upside-down roof, with rooftop planting
			Hinged door, internal – wood		
			Sliding door, internal – wood		

Preparation of drawings for buildings
Excerpt from Swiss standard SIA 400:2000

B.1.4   Scales

All the scales used on a drawing are to be stated in the title block of the drawing.

The following scales are used in the building industry:

Scale	Generally used for the following	
1:10000	Location drawings, block plans	
1: 5000		
1: 2000		
1: 1000	Site plans, cadastral surveys	
1: 500		
1: 200	Urban site plans, competition drawings, preliminary scheme drawings	
1: 100	General arrangement (GA) drawings	
1: 50	Fabrication drawings	
1: 20		Working drawings
1: 10	Detail drawings	
1: 5		
1: 1		

Fig. 1: Standard scales for architectural drawings

Fig. 2: Example of a scale bar for a 1:20 drawing

Owing to the widespread use of reduction techniques it is recommended to include a scale bar on every drawing. This enables approximate dimensions to be taken from the drawing even after it has been reduced in size.

Reductions and enlargements must be indicated as such.

B.5   DIMENSIONS AND LEVELS

B.5.1   General

Dimensions have priority over the accuracy of the drawing. It is recommended to draw a line over dimensions that do not match the dimensions as drawn. This also applies to drawings produced with a CAD system.

B.5.2   Units of measurement

The units of measurement kilometre, metre, centimetre and millimetre shall be used for dimensions and levels, with the unit selected being indicated on the drawing.

Example: Dimensions in m

Decimal fractions shall be separated from the whole number by means of a decimal point.

Examples in m: 2.75
                      0.52

In accordance with modern usage in the Swiss building industry, components that are smaller than one metre – when the basic unit of measurement is the metre – may also be specified in centimetres. In this case millimetres – in conjunction with dimensions in centimetres – are written in superscript form.

Examples: $52 = 0.52$ m
                 $2^5 = 2.5$ cm
                 $0^5 = 0.5$ cm

Angles are specified in the old 360-degree format.

Examples: 24°   32.5°   45°

The term fall is used for drainage, incline for trafficable surfaces. Falls and inclines are given in per cent (%) or per thousand (‰). Falls are indicated by an arrow pointing downwards (e.g. draining a garage forecourt), inclines by an arrow pointing upwards (e.g. stairs or ramp).

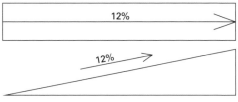

Fig. 3: Indicating an incline on plan and in section

B.5.3   Dimensions

Dimension lines and dimension projection lines should be drawn with the thinnest line used.

Marks indicating the extent of the dimension line should be twice as thick as the dimension line itself.

Dimension projection lines extend almost to the object being dimensioned. If possible, dimension projection lines should not cross one another.

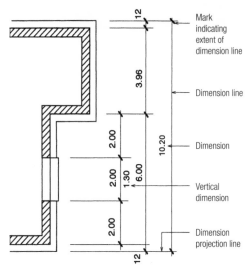

Fig. 4: Dimension lines and dimension projection lines on plan

Dimensions should be written a distance of about half the height of the lettering above the dimension line and such that they can be read from the bottom or the right-hand side of the drawing.

In the case of sloping dimension lines the dimensions should always be written above the dimension line – as seen from the bottom of the drawing.

Dimensions written below the dimension line are vertical dimensions measured from top of threshold or finished floor level (FFL) to underside of structural lintel or underside of structural floor. In the case of windows the dimension is measured from top of finished spandrel panel to underside of structural lintel (= structural opening).

Width and height dimensions (e.g. 30 x 1.80) shall be specified in the case of square/rectangular sections. The symbol for diameter shall be written in front of the dimension in the case of round sections (e.g. Ø 12).

Examples of how to specify dimensions are shown in figures 5 to 8.

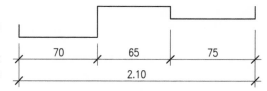

Fig. 5: String of dimensions with overall dimension

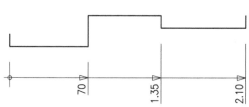

Fig. 6: Chain dimensions

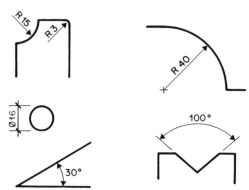

Fig. 7: Specifying radii, diameters and angles

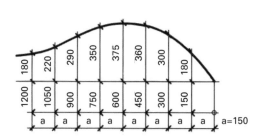

Fig. 8: Specifying an irregular curve

B.5.4   Levels

Levels must always be specified in metres.

Our starting point is the level ±0.00. This is frequently the finished floor level (FFL) of the ground floor. In exceptional cases a new ±0.00 level may be defined for every storey. If this is the case, this new datum should be defined exactly in the title block of the drawing.

Example: level ±0.00 for 2nd floor = 518.60 m above sea level

If a level is valid for the entire area of a plan, it may be stated once in the title block of the drawing.

 Finished level, topside

 Finished level, underside

 Structural level, topside

 Structural level, underside

±0.00
−0.10   Finished and structural levels, topside

Fig. 9: Specifying levels on sections

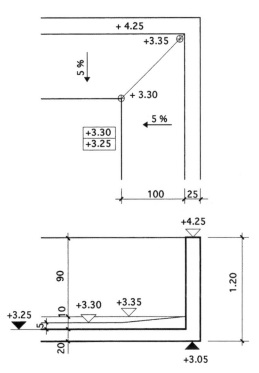

Fig. 10: Example: levels on plan and in section

B.7   PROJECTIONS

B.7.1   Principles of representation

All parts of the building are three-dimensional components which can be represented only in two dimensions on paper. The representation is carried out by projecting the component onto one plane, the drawing plane.

Figure 12 shows the three-dimensional object represented by the drawings given below.

B.7.2   Standard projection

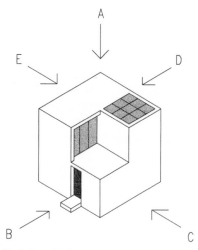

Fig. 12: Perspective view

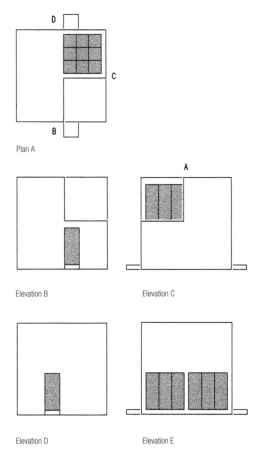

Plan A

Elevation B   Elevation C

Elevation D   Elevation E

Fig. 11: Standard projection
Representation of a non-sectioned object

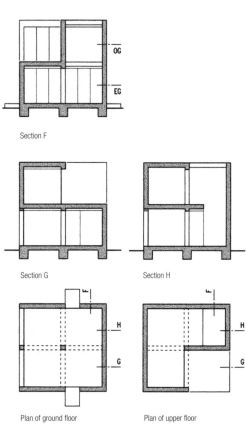

Section F

Section G   Section H

Plan of ground floor   Plan of upper floor

Fig. 13: Standard projection
Representation of a sectioned object

B.8.3 Building materials

B.8.3.1 Pictorial representation

Sectioned surfaces are usually shown enclosed by thick lines and, in addition, by the markings given below.

The density of the markings should be adjusted to suit the scale of the drawing.

Sectioned surfaces on drawings at a scale of 1:100 and smaller are often shown in black or by means of some other equivalent marking for all building materials

Material		Colour
Clay bricks		bright red
Steel (scale 1:1)		
Refractory bricks		dark red
Calcium silicate bricks		grey
Cement bricks		olive green
Plain and reinforced concrete		green
Reconstituted stone		blue-grey
Fair-face concrete	Type ____	green
Mortar, plaster, render		violet
Solid timber		yellow to brown
Solid timber/ glued laminated timber		yellow to brown
Wood-based products		light brown
Metal		light blue
Steel (in section)		black
Insulating materials		pink
Barriers (air, vapour, water)		black/white
Sealing compounds		yellow
Glass		dark green
Plastics		grey
Stone, general		blue

B.8.3.2 Abbreviations
(on Swiss German-language drawings)

Concrete	B
Lightweight concrete	LB
Portland cement	CEM I
Hydraulic lime	HL
White lime	CL
Masonry	M

Standard masonry without special properties made from:

– clay bricks	MB
– lightweight clay bricks	MBL
– cement bricks	MC
– lightweight cement bricks	MCL
– calcium silicate bricks	MK
– aerated concrete bricks	MP
– lightweight aerated concrete bricks	MPL

Masonry with special properties is additionally indicated by means of:

– built in masonry bond
– prefabricated
– with declared compressive strength
– external facing leaf masonry
– reinforced
– prestressed
– weathered facing masonry
– non-weathered facing masonry
– with increased fire resistance
– for sound insulation
– for thermal insulation
– with additional requirements for seismic regions

Glued laminated timber (glulam)	BSH

B.9.3   Stairs and ramps

On plans stairs are to be cut through at about two thirds of their height. In the case of multi-storey stairs the upper part of the lower and the lower part of the upper flight are to be shown.

A continuous arrow shows the upward direction of stairs and ramps.

If the stairs rise only one storey, the stairs above the cut line are represented by chain-dot lines.

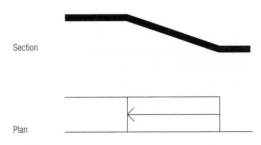

Section

Plan

Fig. 16: Ramp
Plan and section

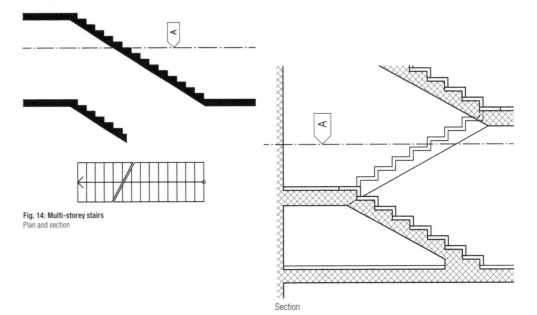

Fig. 14: Multi-storey stairs
Plan and section

Section

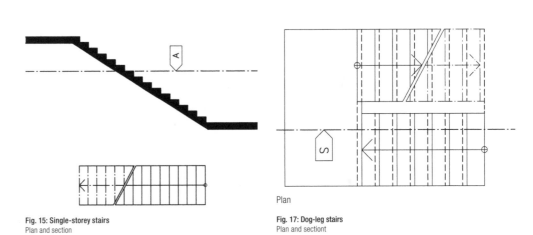

Fig. 15: Single-storey stairs
Plan and section

Plan

Fig. 17: Dog-leg stairs
Plan and sectiont

Presentation on drawings
Example: timber platform frame construction

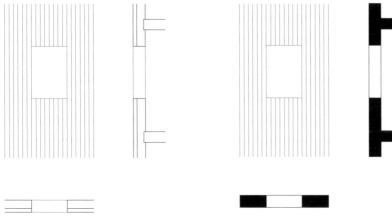

Plan, section, elevation, scale 1:100, outline or shown solid black

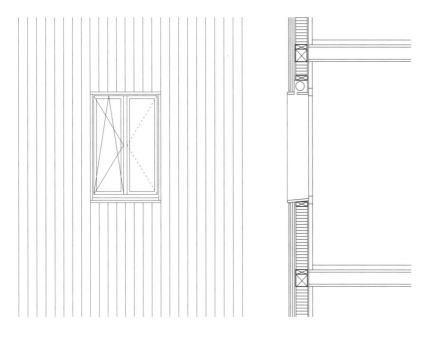

Plan, section, elevation, scale 1:50

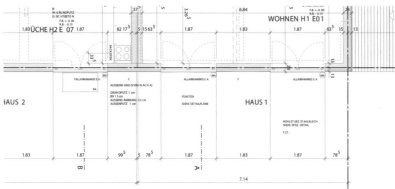

Example: dimensions on working drawings

General arrangement drawings, scale 1:100

The general arrangement (GA) drawings contain all the information required for a full understanding of the project. They are (principally) intended for the client and the building authorities.

– Plans, sections, elevations
– Boundaries, neighbouring buildings
– Existing terrain, new landscaping

The expression of size and space is conveyed graphically. Openings are shown as holes, strips etc. Windows, plinths, roof edges, facade surfaces, etc. are only drawn where they are relevant to the project.

The general arrangement drawings are used as the basis for the building approval drawings. In most cases the general arrangement drawings are equivalent to the building approval drawings. The local building authorities prescribe which additional information the building approval drawings must contain.

Working drawings, scale 1:50

The working drawings (and fabrication drawings) are essentially limited to the primary building components without finishes and show elements of the construction such as walls, floors, roofs, spandrel panels, lintels (with or without sunshading) and stairs. These drawings serve as a means of communication between the members of the design team and the contractor(s), and are used for actually carrying out the construction work on site. The layers (loadbearing, insulating, protective) are shown when they can be reasonably represented at this scale. The surface finishes are defined via legends (texts). The plinth–wall, wall–floor, wall–roof junction details plus openings etc. are shown schematically (continuity of layers). Thin layers such as plaster etc. are ignored. The windows may be shown simplified: frame and lights together as a box; where necessary, frame and lights are distinguished on elevations and the type of opening indicated.

Type of sunshading, internal or external.

Floor/roof construction described in text.

Dimensions on working drawings

Dimensions are arranged in a hierarchical form beginning with the principal dimensions furthest from the component, parts nearer to the component and details closest to the component. Dimension lines should not cross one another. The working drawings are usually dimensioned in metres rounded off to the nearest half a centimetre (e.g. 3.96⁵). All dimensions less than one metre are given in centimetres (e.g. 55). On detail drawings with higher accuracy requirements dimensions can also be specified in millimetres (e.g. metalwork drawings). It is important to ensure that the units of measurement remain the same throughout and a suitable note appears in the title block (e.g. all dimensions in mm).

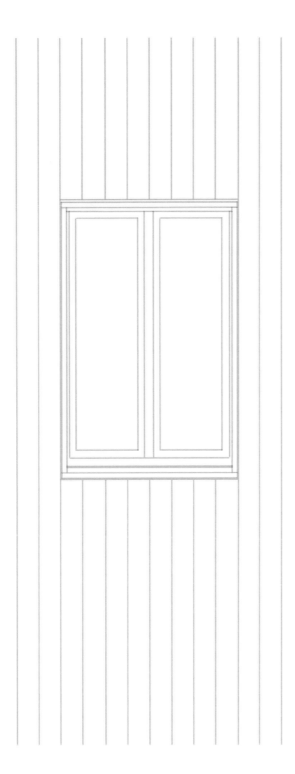

Plan, section, scale 1:20

Detail drawings, scale 1:20

The detail drawings should be regarded as supplementing the 1:50 working drawings. Every layer is shown and marked/hatched/shaded accordingly. Loadbearing parts of the construction are indicated by means of thicker lines. Junctions such as floor bearings are to be drawn and annotated in detail. Windows are shown schematically with frame and lights by means of individual boxes. All parts of construction such as sunshading with guide tracks, battens, window sills/boards etc. must be clearly identifiable.

The floor construction should be drawn showing all layers, including junctions and terminations. If special fittings are included (e.g. underfloor heating pipes), then these should be mentioned.

See to the following catalogue of building components for further examples of drawings. The building components are in some instances shown with too much detail. Freehand sketches may be more abstract. The layout of the drawing must always be considered first.
– Size of drawings, size of paper
– Alignment of plan, section, elevation

General remarks on representation in drawings

Many companies (e.g. window manufacturers) provide detail drawings in various data formats. These are highly detailed (1:1). They are included at this scale and are often too precise at the other scales involved. The abstract means of representation mentioned above are generally adequate.

The person producing the drawing should always consider for whom the drawing is intended and what information that person needs. Wherever possible, standard paper sizes are used:

Format	Dimensions in mm	
DIN A4	210 x	297
DIN A3	297 x	420
DIN A2	420 x	594
DIN A1	594 x	841
DIN A0	841 x	1189

Exchange of drawings between specialists and members of the design team can take place using various formats: DXF, DWG.

Drawing information included in title block:
– Client
– Person responsible for the drawing
– Content of the drawing
– Scale
– Scale bar for reduced drawings
– North arrow
– ±0.00 = metres above sea level

Symbols
Legend for the catalogue of components

	Vapour barrier/check
	Waterproofing, airtight membrane
	Separating layer
	Impact sound insulation
	Thermal insulation
	Thermal insulation, impervious to vapour
	Thermal insulation, waterproof
	Reconstituted stone
	In situ concrete
	Lean concrete
	Wood-based board
	Section solid timber

Plinth, single-leaf masonry
1:20

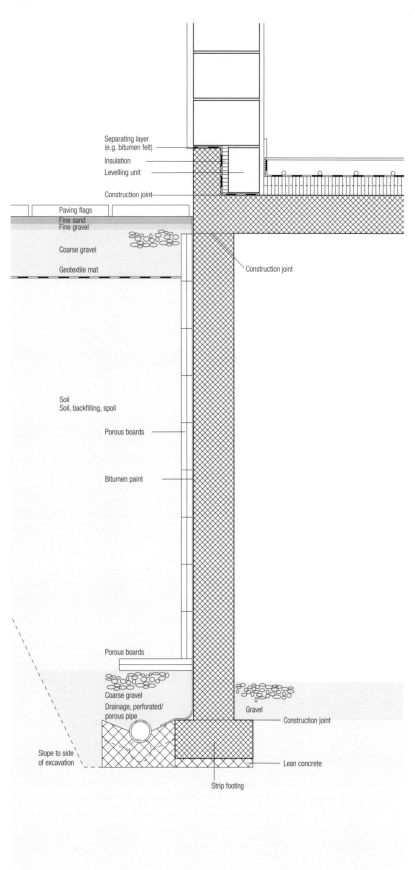

Separating layer
(e.g. bitumen felt)

Insulation

Levelling unit

Construction joint

Paving flags
Fine sand
Fine gravel

Coarse gravel

Geotextile mat

Construction joint

Soil
Soil, backfilling, spoil

Porous boards

Bitumen paint

Porous boards

Coarse gravel

Drainage, perforated/
porous pipe

Gravel

Construction joint

Slope to side
of excavation

Lean concrete

Strip footing

Wall construction
- Render	35 mm
- Single-leaf masonry, 36.5 x 24.8 x 23.8 cm	365 mm
- Plaster	25 mm
Total	*425 mm*

Floor construction
- Hard-fired floor tiles	10 mm
- Tile adhesive	5 mm
- Screed with underfloor heating	80 mm
- Separating layer (e.g. 1 mm plastic sheet)	
- Thermal insulation, vapourproof (e.g. cellular glass)	150–300 mm
- Concrete slab over basement	200 mm
Total	*445–595 mm*

Wall construction, damp basement
- Porous boards	60 mm
- Waterproofing (e.g. bitumen paint)	2 mm
- In situ concrete wall	220 mm
Total	*282 mm*

Floor construction, damp basement
- Layer of stones (e.g. rounded gravel)	200 mm

Plinth, double-leaf masonry, rendered
1:20

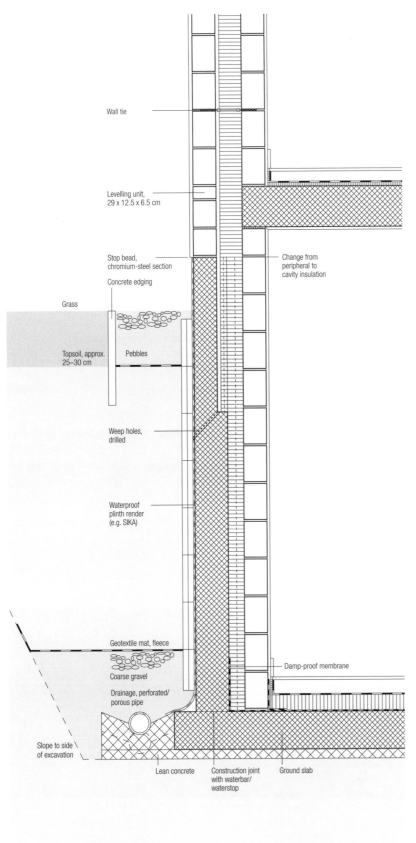

Wall tie

Levelling unit,
29 x 12.5 x 6.5 cm

Stop bead,
chromium-steel section

Concrete edging

Grass

Topsoil, approx.
25–30 cm

Pebbles

Weep holes,
drilled

Waterproof
plinth render
(e.g. SIKA)

Geotextile mat, fleece

Coarse gravel

Drainage, perforated/
porous pipe

Slope to side
of excavation

Change from
peripheral to
cavity insulation

Damp-proof membrane

Lean concrete   Construction joint   Ground slab
with waterbar/
waterstop

Wall construction
- Render	20 mm
- Clay masonry, B, 29 x 12.5 x 19 cm	125 mm
- Cavity (construction tolerance)	20 mm
- Thermal insulation (e.g. rockwool)	150–300 mm
- Clay masonry, B 0, 29 x 12.5 x 19 cm	125 mm
- Plaster	15 mm
Total	*455–605 mm*

Floor construction
- Ready-to-lay parquet flooring	15 mm
- Screed	60 mm
- Separating layer (e.g. 1 mm plastic sheet)	
- Impact sound insulation	20 mm
- Concrete slab over basement	210 mm
- Plaster to soffit	10 mm
Total	*315 mm*

Wall construction, heated basement
- Porous boards	60 mm
- Waterproof plinth render	10 mm
- In situ concrete wall	180 mm
- Thermal insulation (vapourproof)	150–300 mm
- Clay masonry, B, 25 x 12 x 14 cm	120 mm
- Plaster	10 mm
Total	*530–680 mm*

Floor construction, heated basement
- Ready-to-lay parquet flooring	15 mm
- Screed	80 mm
- Thermal insulation (e.g. cellular glass, expanded polystyrene)	150–300 mm
- Damp-proof membrane (e.g. Robit)	
- Concrete ground slab	200 mm
- Lean concrete	50 mm
Total	*495–645 mm*

Plinth, facing masonry
1:20

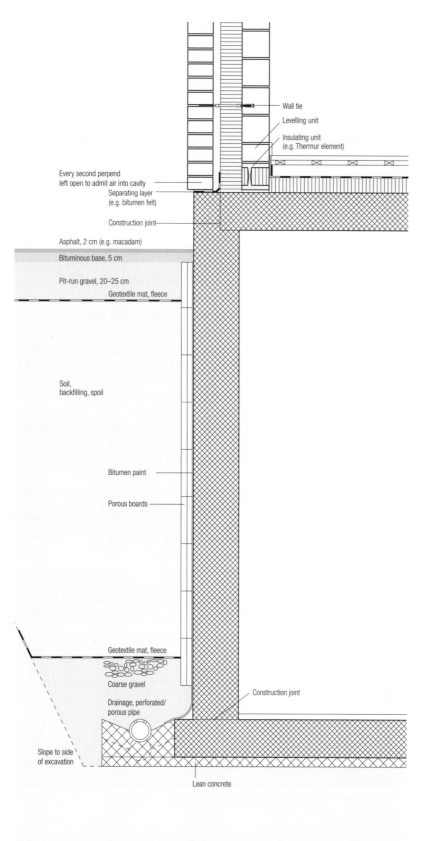

Wall tie
Levelling unit
Insulating unit
(e.g. Thermur element)

Every second perpend
left open to admit air into cavity
Separating layer
(e.g. bitumen felt)

Construction joint

Asphalt, 2 cm (e.g. macadam)

Bituminous base, 5 cm

Pit-run gravel, 20–25 cm
Geotextile mat, fleece

Soil,
backfilling, spoil

Bitumen paint

Porous boards

Geotextile mat, fleece

Coarse gravel

Drainage, perforated/
porous pipe

Construction joint

Slope to side
of excavation

Lean concrete

Wall construction
- Clay masonry, BS, course 1, 29 x 14 x 6.5 cm
  Clay masonry, BS, course 2, 14 x 14 x 6.5 cm
  (Variations: diverse facing masonry modules, pre-
  fabricated concrete bricks or elements etc.) 140 mm
- Ventilated cavity min.   40 mm
- Thermal insulation (e.g. rockwool)   150–300 mm
- Clay masonry, BS, 25 x 15 x 14 cm   150 mm
- *Total*   *480–630 mm*

Floor construction
- Wooden floorboards   24 mm
- Battens   30 mm
- Layer of felt   2 mm
- Screed   60 mm
- Separating layer (e.g. 1 mm plastic sheet)
- Thermal insulation, vapourproof   150–300 mm
- Concrete slab over basement   200 mm
- *Total*   *466–616 mm*

Wall construction, unheated basement
- Porous boards   60 mm
- Waterproofing (e.g. bitumen paint)   2 mm
- In situ concrete wall   240 mm
- *Total*   *302 mm*

Floor construction, unheated basement
- Screed   30 mm
- Concrete ground slab   200 mm
- Lean concrete   50 mm
- *Total*   *280 mm*

Plinth, fair-face concrete with internal insulation
1:20

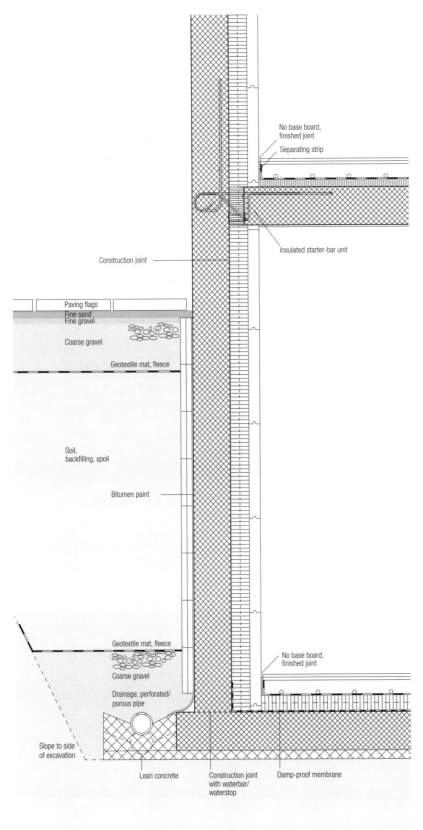

No base board,
finished joint

Separating strip

Insulated starter-bar unit

Construction joint

Paving flags
Fine sand
Fine gravel

Coarse gravel

Geotextile mat, fleece

Soil,
backfilling, spoil

Bitumen paint

Geotextile mat, fleece

Coarse gravel

Drainage, perforated/
porous pipe

No base board,
finished joint

Slope to side
of excavation

Lean concrete

Construction joint
with waterbar/
waterstop

Damp-proof membrane

Wall construction
- Fair-face concrete, coloured	220 mm
- Thermal insulation, vapourproof (e.g. cellular glass)	150–300 mm
- Gypsum boards, plaster skim/paint finish	60 mm
Total	*430–580 mm*

Floor construction
- Stone floor tiles	15 mm
- Mortar bed	15 mm
- Screed with underfloor heating	80 mm
- Separating layer (1 mm plastic sheet)	
- Impact sound insulation	40 mm
- Concrete slab over basement	200 mm
- Plaster to soffit	10 mm
Total	*360 mm*

Wall construction, heated basement
- Porous boards	60 mm
- Concrete with water-repelling admixture (e.g. Efa filler)	220 mm
- Thermal insulation, vapourproof (e.g. cellular glass)	150–300 mm
- Gypsum boards, plaster skim/paint finish	60 mm
Total	*490–640 mm*

Floor construction, heated basement
- Stone floor tiles	15 mm
- Mortar bed	15 mm
- Screed with underfloor heating	80 mm
- Thermal insulation, waterproof (e.g. cellular glass)	150–300 mm
- Damp-proof membrane (e.g. Robit)	
- Concrete ground slab	200 mm
- Lean concrete	50 mm
Total	*510–660 mm*

Plinth, external insulation, rendered
1:20

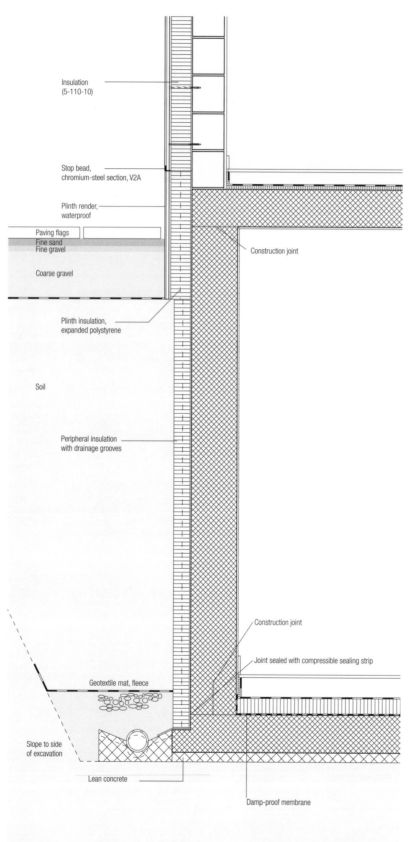

Insulation
(5-110-10)

Stop bead,
chromium-steel section, V2A

Plinth render,
waterproof

Paving flags
Fine sand
Fine gravel

Coarse gravel

Plinth insulation,
expanded polystyrene

Soil

Peripheral insulation
with drainage grooves

Geotextile mat, fleece

Slope to side
of excavation

Lean concrete

Construction joint

Construction joint

Joint sealed with compressible sealing strip

Damp-proof membrane

Wall construction
e.g. Wancor-Therm K

- Mineral render finish coat (coloured or painted)	2 mm
- Bonding render (with glass mat inlay over entire surface)	4 mm
- Mineral render undercoat	20 mm
- Insulation board (5-150-10 3-layer board), fixed with plastic fasteners	150–300 mm
- Clay masonry, B, 29 x 17.5 x 19 cm	175 mm
- Plaster	15 mm
Total	*366–516 mm*

Floor construction

- Magnesite flooring (seamless)	15 mm
- Screed	65 mm
- Separating layer (e.g. 1 mm plastic sheet)	
- Impact sound insulation	20 mm
- Concrete slab over basement	200 mm
- Plaster to soffit	10 mm
Total	*310 mm*

Wall construction, heated basement

- Mortar coat (waterproof)	3 mm
- Peripheral insulation with drainage grooves	100 mm
- Waterproofing (e.g. bitumen paint)	2 mm
- In situ concrete wall	240 mm
- Plaster	10 mm
Total	*355 mm*

Floor construction, heated basement

- Magnesite flooring	15 mm
- Screed	80 mm
- Separating layer (e.g. 1 mm plastic sheet)	
- Insulation (e.g. Floormate 200)	150–300 mm
- Damp-proof membrane (e.g. Robit)	
- Concrete ground slab	200 mm
- Lean concrete	50 mm
Total	*495–645 mm*

Plinth, external cladding, lightweight

1:20

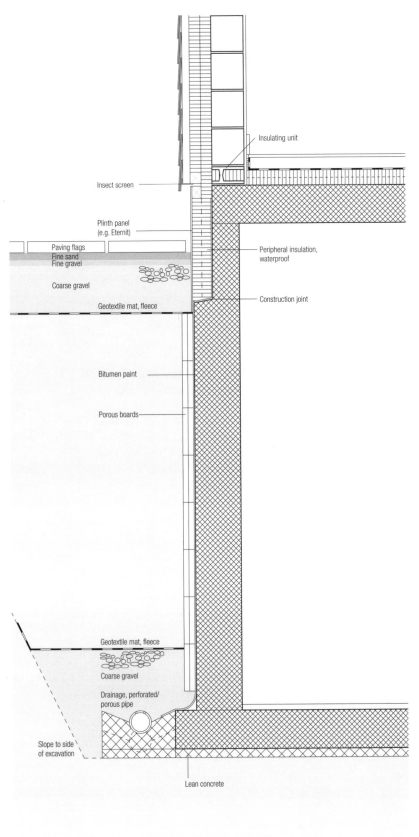

Insulating unit

Insect screen

Plinth panel
(e.g. Eternit)

Paving flags

Fine sand
Fine gravel

Coarse gravel

Geotextile mat, fleece

Peripheral insulation,
waterproof

Construction joint

Bitumen paint

Porous boards

Geotextile mat, fleece

Coarse gravel

Drainage, perforated/
porous pipe

Slope to side
of excavation

Lean concrete

Wall construction

- Cladding in medium and large format e.g. Eternit slates, rectangular double-lap arrangement, 300 x 600 mm	10 mm
- Ventilated cavity (40 x 70 mm vertical battens)	40 mm
- Thermal insulation (e.g. 1 layer 60 mm + 1 layer 90 mm, between grid of 60 x 90 mm battens)	150–300 mm
- Clay masonry, B, 29 x 17.5 x 19 cm	175 mm
- Plaster	15 mm
Total	*390–540 mm*

Floor construction

- Ready-to-lay parquet flooring	15 mm
- Screed	60 mm
- Separating layer (e.g. 1 mm plastic sheet)	
- Thermal insulation, vapourproof (e.g. expanded polystyrene)	150–300 mm
- Concrete slab over basement	200 mm
Total	*425–575 mm*

Wall construction, unheated basement

- Porous boards	60 mm
- Waterproofing (e.g. bitumen paint)	3 mm
- In situ concrete wall	260 mm
Total	*323 mm*

Floor construction, unheated basement

- Screed	30 mm
- Concrete ground slab, roughened	200 mm
- Lean concrete	50 mm
Total	*280 mm*

Plinth, external cladding, heavyweight
1:20

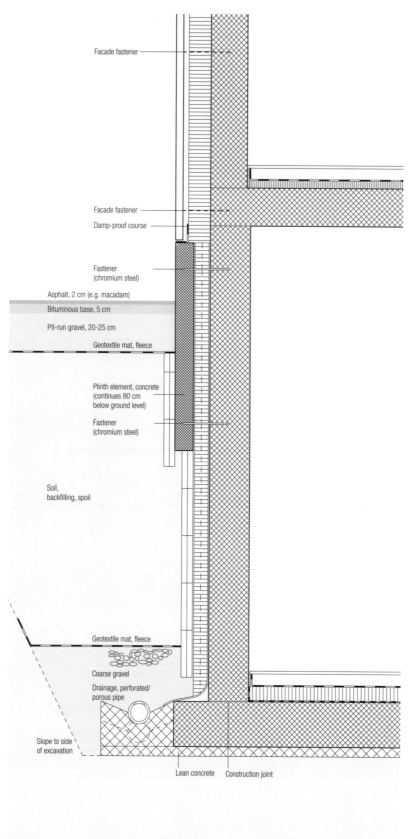

Facade fastener

Facade fastener

Damp-proof course

Fastener (chromium steel)

Asphalt, 2 cm (e.g. macadam)

Bituminous base, 5 cm

Pit-run gravel, 20-25 cm

Geotextile mat, fleece

Plinth element, concrete (continues 80 cm below ground level)

Fastener (chromium steel)

Soil, backfilling, spoil

Geotextile mat, fleece

Coarse gravel

Drainage, perforated/ porous pipe

Slope to side of excavation

Lean concrete   **Construction joint**

Wall construction
- Stone slabs (e.g. slate)	20–40 mm
- Ventilated cavity	30 mm
- Thermal insulation	150–300 mm
- Fair-face concrete internally	200 mm
Total	*400–570 mm*

Floor construction
- Ready-to-lay parquet flooring	15 mm
- Screed	80 mm
- Separating layer (e.g. 1 mm plastic sheet)	
- Impact sound insulation	40 mm
- Concrete slab over basement	200 mm
Total	*335 mm*

Wall construction, heated basement
- Plinth element (precast concrete)	100 mm
- Peripheral insulation	100 mm
- Waterproofing (e.g. bitumen paint)	2 mm
- In situ concrete wall	220 mm
Total	*422 mm*

Floor construction, heated basement
- Ready-to-lay parquet flooring	15 mm
- Screed	80 mm
- Separating layer (e.g. 1 mm plastic sheet)	
- Insulation (e.g. cellular glass)	150–300 mm
- Damp-proof membrane (e.g. Robit)	
- Concrete ground slab	240 mm
- Lean concrete	50 mm
Total	*535–685 mm*

Plinth, timber platform frame construction
1:20

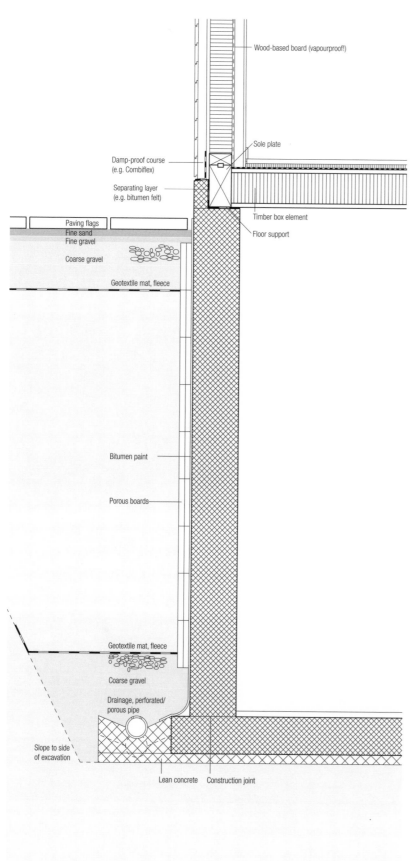

Wood-based board (vapourproof!)

Sole plate

Damp-proof course
(e.g. Combiflex)

Separating layer
(e.g. bitumen felt)

Timber box element

Floor support

Paving flags
Fine sand
Fine gravel

Coarse gravel

Geotextile mat, fleece

Bitumen paint

Porous boards

Geotextile mat, fleece

Coarse gravel

Drainage, perforated/
porous pipe

Slope to side
of excavation

Lean concrete   Construction joint

Wall construction
- Horizontal boards	24 mm
- Vertical battens (ventilated cavity)	40 mm
- Bitumen-impregnated softboard (airtight membrane)	18 mm
- Timber studding, insulation (e.g. Isofloc)	150–300 mm
- Wood-based board (plywood, vapourproof!)	12 mm
- Vertical battens (space for services)	50 mm
- Wood-cement particleboard (e.g. Fermacell) or fibre-reinforced plasterboard (e.g. Sasmox)	12 mm
Total	*306–456 mm*

Floor construction
- 3-ply core plywood, floating, tongue and groove	27 mm
- Impact sound insulation	20 mm
- Vapour barrier	
- Lignatur timber box element, soffit left exposed	220 mm
Total	*267 mm*

Wall construction, unheated basement
- Porous boards	60 mm
- Waterproofing (e.g. bitumen paint)	2 mm
- In situ concrete wall	240 mm
Total	*302 mm*

Floor construction, unheated basement
- Screed	30 mm
- Concrete ground slab	200 mm
- Lean concrete	50 mm
Total	*280 mm*

Solid timber panel construction: Plinth – Roof
1:20

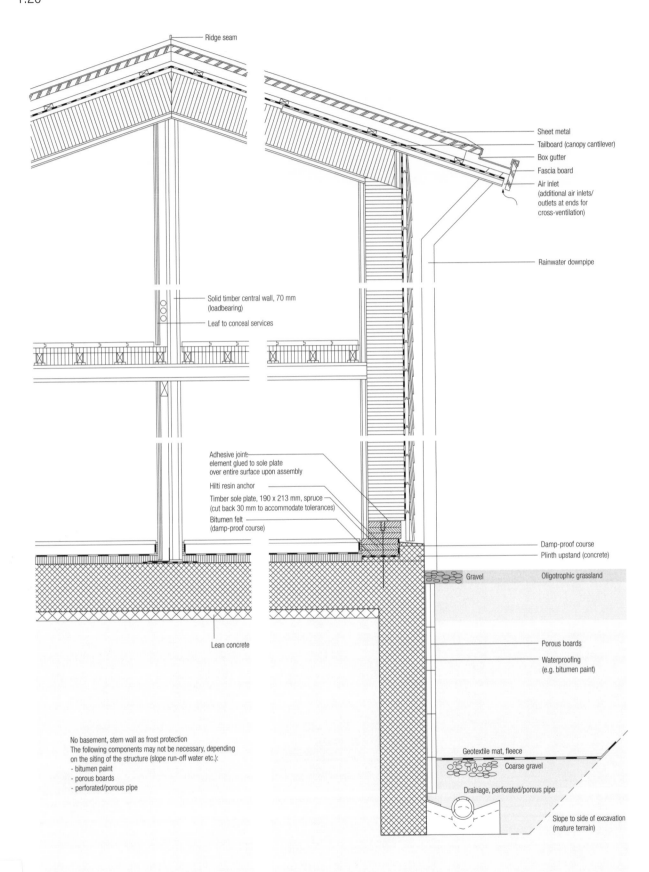

Ridge seam

Sheet metal

Tailboard (canopy cantilever)

Box gutter

Fascia board

Air inlet
(additional air inlets/
outlets at ends for
cross-ventilation)

Rainwater downpipe

Solid timber central wall, 70 mm
(loadbearing)

Leaf to conceal services

Adhesive joint:
element glued to sole plate
over entire surface upon assembly

Hilti resin anchor

Timber sole plate, 190 x 213 mm, spruce
(cut back 30 mm to accommodate tolerances)

Bitumen felt
(damp-proof course)

Damp-proof course

Plinth upstand (concrete)

Gravel　　　　Oligotrophic grassland

Lean concrete

Porous boards

Waterproofing
(e.g. bitumen paint)

Geotextile mat, fleece

Coarse gravel

Drainage, perforated/porous pipe

Slope to side of excavation
(mature terrain)

No basement, stem wall as frost protection
The following components may not be necessary, depending
on the siting of the structure (slope run-off water etc.):
- bitumen paint
- porous boards
- perforated/porous pipe

Figs 1 and 2: Solid timber panel construction, completed with shingle cladding (top);
erecting the panels (bottom)
Bearth & Deplazes: private house (Bearth-Candinas), Sumvitg (CH), 1998

Roof construction
- Sheet metal	0.6 mm
- Roof decking	30 mm
- Counter battens 50 x 80 mm (ventilated cavity)	80 mm
- Timber blocks for cross-ventilation, 30 x 50 mm	30 mm
- Secondary waterproofing/covering layer	3 mm
- Softboard	22 mm
- Solid timber ribs (e.g. 40 x 200 mm), with thermal insulation in between	150–300 mm
- Solid timber panel	35 mm
Total	*350–500 mm*

Floor construction, upper floors
- Solid timber floorboards (tongue and groove, concealed nailing)	24 mm
- Counter battens, 40 x 30 mm (with insulation in between)	30 mm
- Battens, 50 x 30 mm (with insulation in between)	50 mm
- Rubber strips as separating layer beneath battens (for impact sound insulation)	10 mm
- Solid timber panel (span: 3 m)	90 mm
Total	*204 mm*

Wall construction
- Larch shingles (without ventilated cavity), 3 layers	20 mm
- Spruce boards (tongue and groove), horizontal	20 mm
- Airtight membrane	
- Thermal insulation (around transverse ribs)	150–300 mm
- Solid timber panel (loadbearing, incl. vapour check function due to adhesive)	35 mm
Total	*225–375 mm*

Floor construction, ground floor
- Hard-fired floor tiles	30 mm
- Screed (with underfloor heating)	60 mm
- Separating layer (fleece)	2 mm
- Impact sound insulation	40 mm
- Reinforced concrete	250 mm
- Lean concrete	50 mm
Total	*432 mm*

Example:
Bearth & Deplazes: private house
(Bearth-Candinas), Sumvitg (CH), 1998

Single-leaf masonry, rendered
1:20

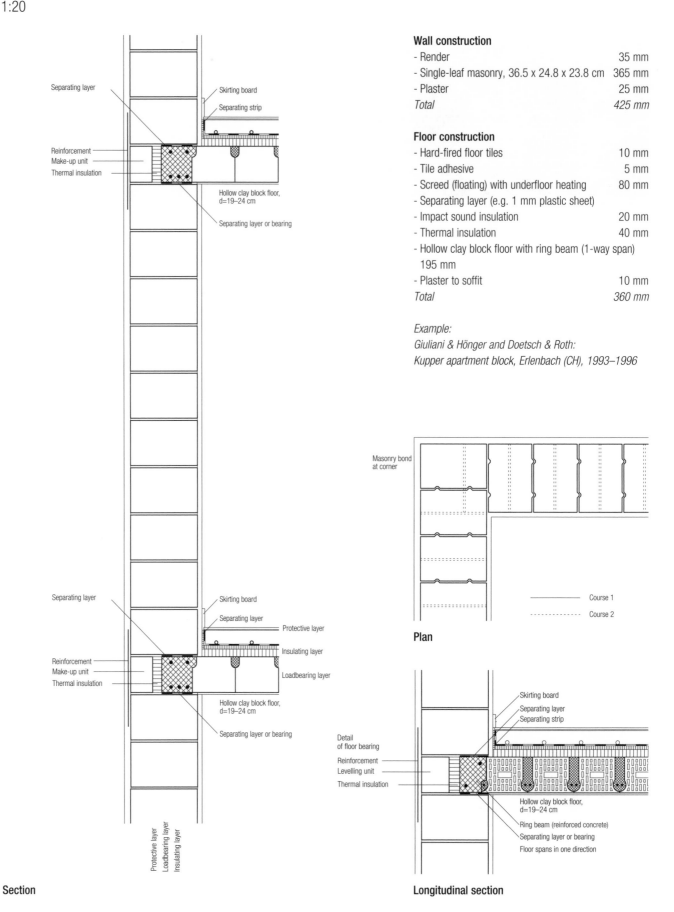

Section

Longitudinal section

Plan

Wall construction

- Render	35 mm
- Single-leaf masonry, 36.5 x 24.8 x 23.8 cm	365 mm
- Plaster	25 mm
Total	*425 mm*

Floor construction

- Hard-fired floor tiles	10 mm
- Tile adhesive	5 mm
- Screed (floating) with underfloor heating	80 mm
- Separating layer (e.g. 1 mm plastic sheet)	
- Impact sound insulation	20 mm
- Thermal insulation	40 mm
- Hollow clay block floor with ring beam (1-way span) 195 mm	
- Plaster to soffit	10 mm
Total	*360 mm*

Example:
Giuliani & Hönger and Doetsch & Roth:
Kupper apartment block, Erlenbach (CH), 1993–1996

Labels in drawing:

Separating layer
Skirting board
Separating strip
Reinforcement
Make-up unit
Thermal insulation
Hollow clay block floor, d=19–24 cm
Separating layer or bearing

Separating layer
Skirting board
Separating layer
Protective layer
Reinforcement
Make-up unit
Thermal insulation
Insulating layer
Loadbearing layer
Hollow clay block floor, d=19–24 cm
Separating layer or bearing

Protective layer
Loadbearing layer
Insulating layer

Masonry bond at corner
Course 1
Course 2

Detail of floor bearing
Reinforcement
Levelling unit
Thermal insulation
Skirting board
Separating layer
Separating strip
Hollow clay block floor, d=19–24 cm
Ring beam (reinforced concrete)
Separating layer or bearing
Floor spans in one direction

Double-leaf masonry, rendered
1:20

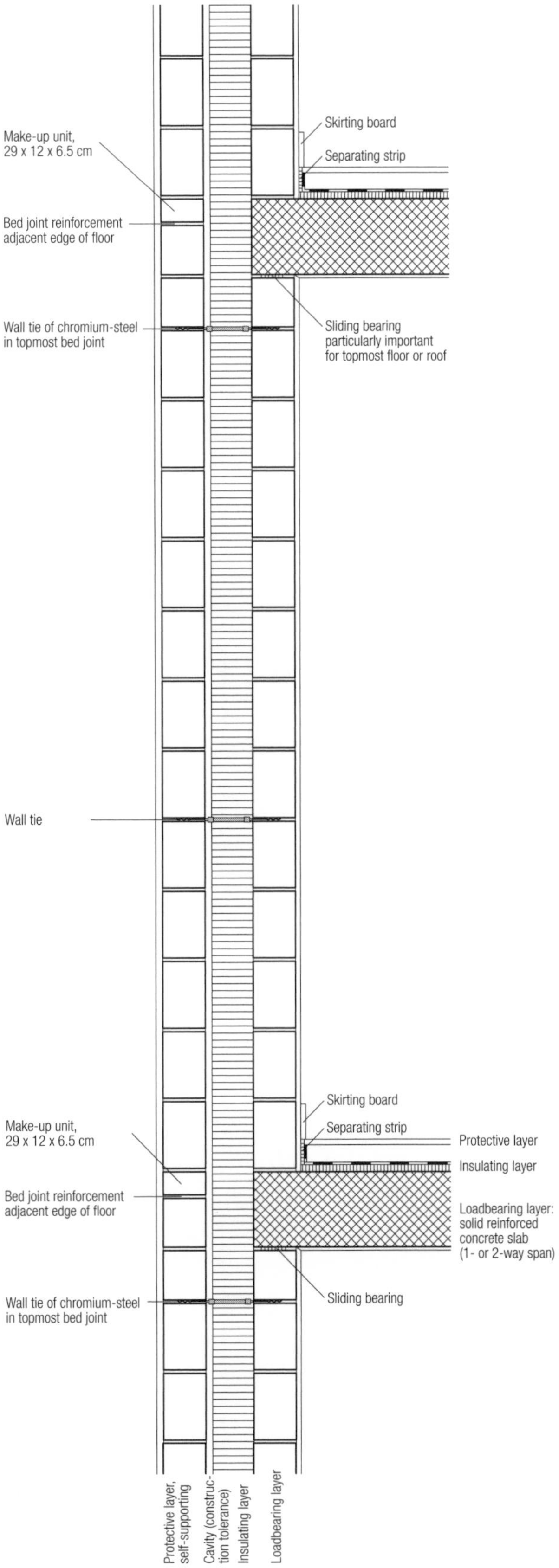
Make-up unit, 29 x 12 x 6.5 cm
Bed joint reinforcement adjacent edge of floor
Wall tie of chromium-steel in topmost bed joint
Skirting board
Separating strip
Sliding bearing particularly important for topmost floor or roof
Wall tie
Make-up unit, 29 x 12 x 6.5 cm
Bed joint reinforcement adjacent edge of floor
Wall tie of chromium-steel in topmost bed joint
Skirting board
Separating strip
Protective layer
Insulating layer
Loadbearing layer: solid reinforced concrete slab (1- or 2-way span)
Sliding bearing
Protective layer, self-supporting
Cavity (construction tolerance)
Insulating layer
Loadbearing layer

Section

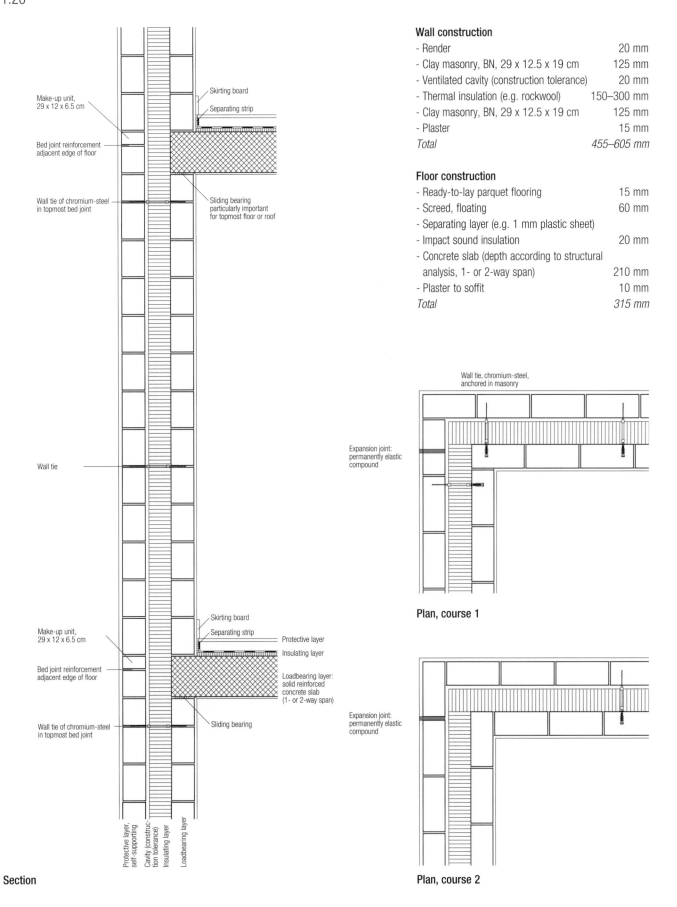

Wall construction

- Render	20 mm
- Clay masonry, BN, 29 x 12.5 x 19 cm	125 mm
- Ventilated cavity (construction tolerance)	20 mm
- Thermal insulation (e.g. rockwool)	150–300 mm
- Clay masonry, BN, 29 x 12.5 x 19 cm	125 mm
- Plaster	15 mm
Total	*455–605 mm*

Floor construction

- Ready-to-lay parquet flooring	15 mm
- Screed, floating	60 mm
- Separating layer (e.g. 1 mm plastic sheet)	
- Impact sound insulation	20 mm
- Concrete slab (depth according to structural analysis, 1- or 2-way span)	210 mm
- Plaster to soffit	10 mm
Total	*315 mm*

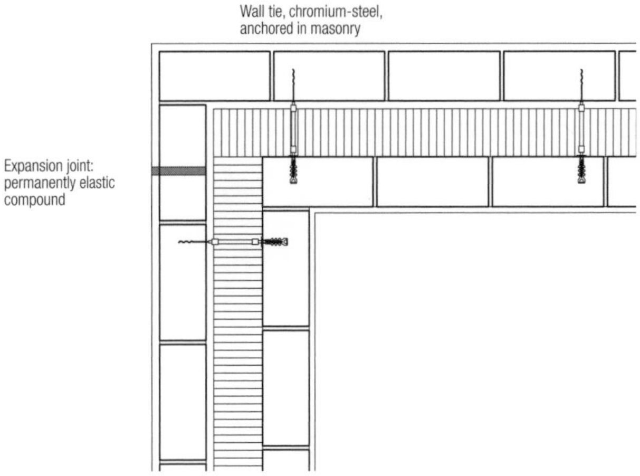
Wall tie, chromium-steel, anchored in masonry
Expansion joint: permanently elastic compound

Plan, course 1

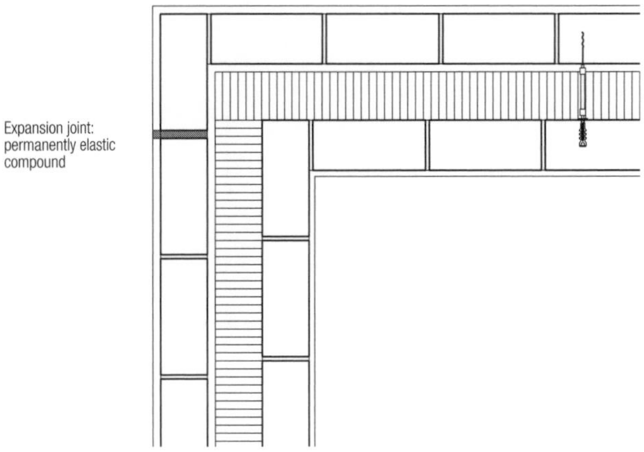
Expansion joint: permanently elastic compound

Plan, course 2

Facing masonry
1:20

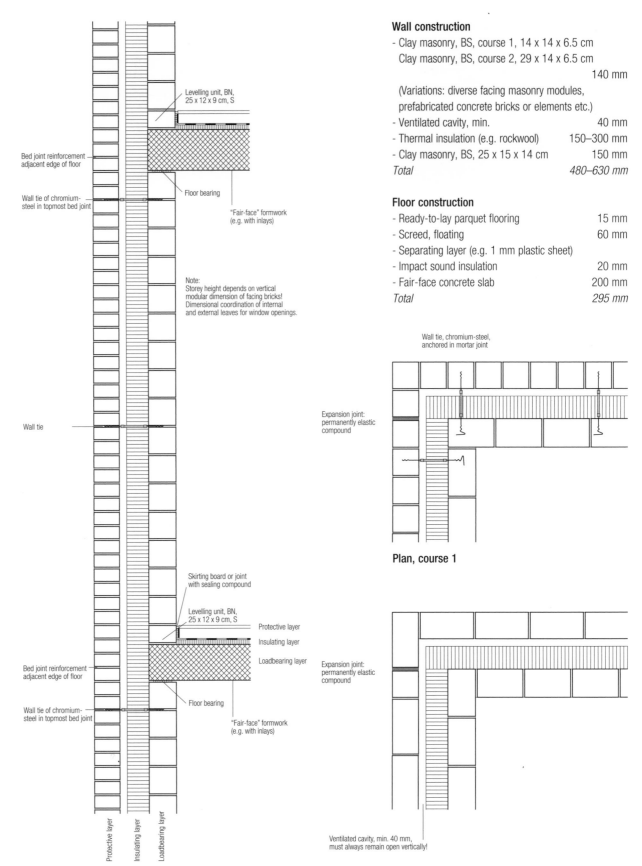

Wall construction
- Clay masonry, BS, course 1, 14 x 14 x 6.5 cm
  Clay masonry, BS, course 2, 29 x 14 x 6.5 cm
                                                          140 mm

  (Variations: diverse facing masonry modules,
  prefabricated concrete bricks or elements etc.)
- Ventilated cavity, min.   40 mm
- Thermal insulation (e.g. rockwool)   150–300 mm
- Clay masonry, BS, 25 x 15 x 14 cm   150 mm
- *Total*   *480–630 mm*

Floor construction
- Ready-to-lay parquet flooring   15 mm
- Screed, floating   60 mm
- Separating layer (e.g. 1 mm plastic sheet)
- Impact sound insulation   20 mm
- Fair-face concrete slab   200 mm
- *Total*   *295 mm*

Labels within the drawing:

Levelling unit, BN, 25 x 12 x 9 cm, S

Bed joint reinforcement adjacent edge of floor

Wall tie of chromium-steel in topmost bed joint

Floor bearing

"Fair-face" formwork (e.g. with inlays)

Note:
Storey height depends on vertical modular dimension of facing bricks! Dimensional coordination of internal and external leaves for window openings.

Wall tie

Skirting board or joint with sealing compound

Levelling unit, BN, 25 x 12 x 9 cm, S

Protective layer

Insulating layer

Loadbearing layer

Bed joint reinforcement adjacent edge of floor

Floor bearing

Wall tie of chromium-steel in topmost bed joint

"Fair-face" formwork (e.g. with inlays)

Protective layer | Insulating layer | Loadbearing layer

Wall tie, chromium-steel, anchored in mortar joint

Expansion joint: permanently elastic compound

Plan, course 1

Expansion joint: permanently elastic compound

Ventilated cavity, min. 40 mm, must always remain open vertically!

Plan, course 2

Fair-face concrete with internal insulation
1:20

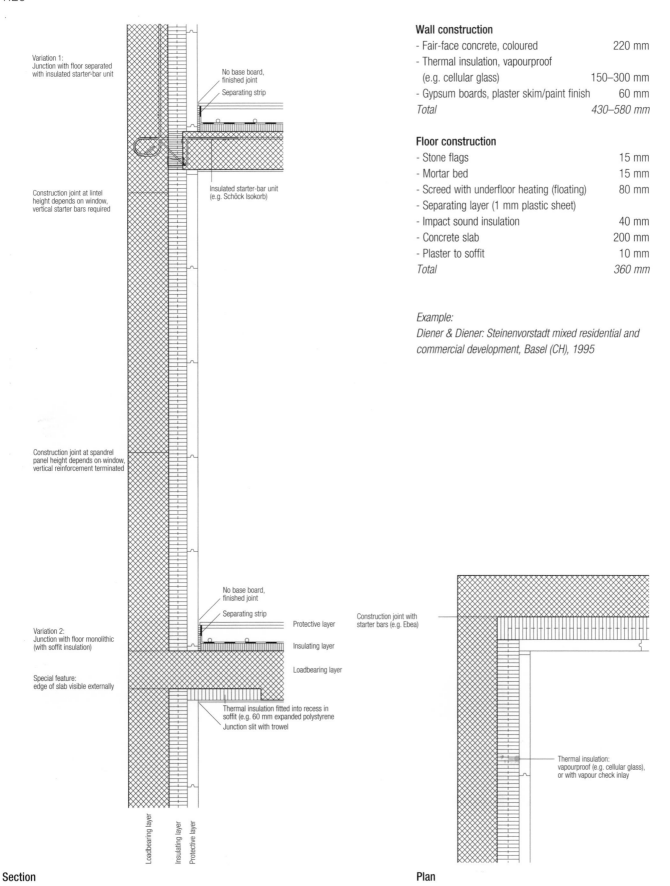

Wall construction
- Fair-face concrete, coloured — 220 mm
- Thermal insulation, vapourproof (e.g. cellular glass) — 150–300 mm
- Gypsum boards, plaster skim/paint finish — 60 mm
- Total — 430–580 mm

Floor construction
- Stone flags — 15 mm
- Mortar bed — 15 mm
- Screed with underfloor heating (floating) — 80 mm
- Separating layer (1 mm plastic sheet)
- Impact sound insulation — 40 mm
- Concrete slab — 200 mm
- Plaster to soffit — 10 mm
- Total — 360 mm

Example:
Diener & Diener: Steinenvorstadt mixed residential and commercial development, Basel (CH), 1995

Section

Plan

501

External insulation, rendered
1:20

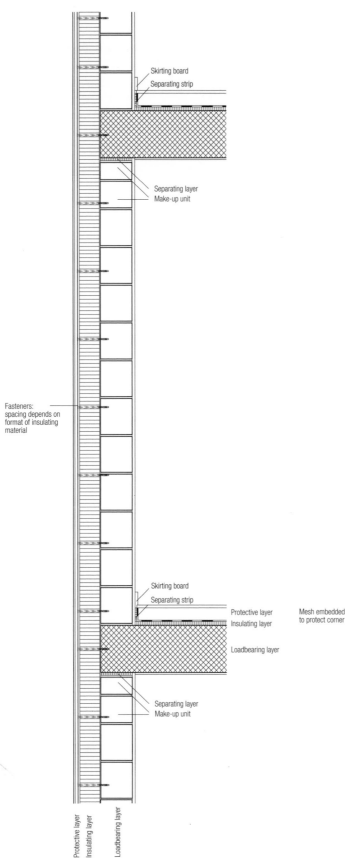

Skirting board

Separating strip

Separating layer
Make-up unit

Fasteners:
spacing depends on
format of insulating
material

Skirting board

Separating strip

Protective layer

Insulating layer

Loadbearing layer

Separating layer
Make-up unit

Protective layer
Insulating layer
Loadbearing layer

Section

Wall construction
e.g. Wancor-Therm K

Mineral render finish coat (coloured or painted)	2 mm
- Bonding render (with glass mat inlay over entire surface)	4 mm
- Mineral render undercoat	20 mm
- Insulation board (5-150-10 3-layer board), fixed with plastic fasteners	150–300 mm
- Clay masonry, B, 29 x 17.5 x 19 cm	175 mm
- Plaster	15 mm
Total	*366–516 mm*

Floor construction

- Magnesite flooring (seamless)	15 mm
- Screed	65 mm
- Separating layer (e.g. 1 mm plastic sheet)	
- Impact sound insulation	20 mm
- Concrete slab	200 mm
- Plaster to soffit	10 mm
Total	*310 mm*

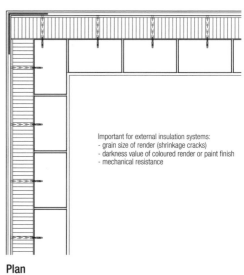

Mesh embedded
to protect corner

Important for external insulation systems:
- grain size of render (shrinkage cracks)
- darkness value of coloured render or paint finish
- mechanical resistance

Plan

External cladding, lightweight
1:20

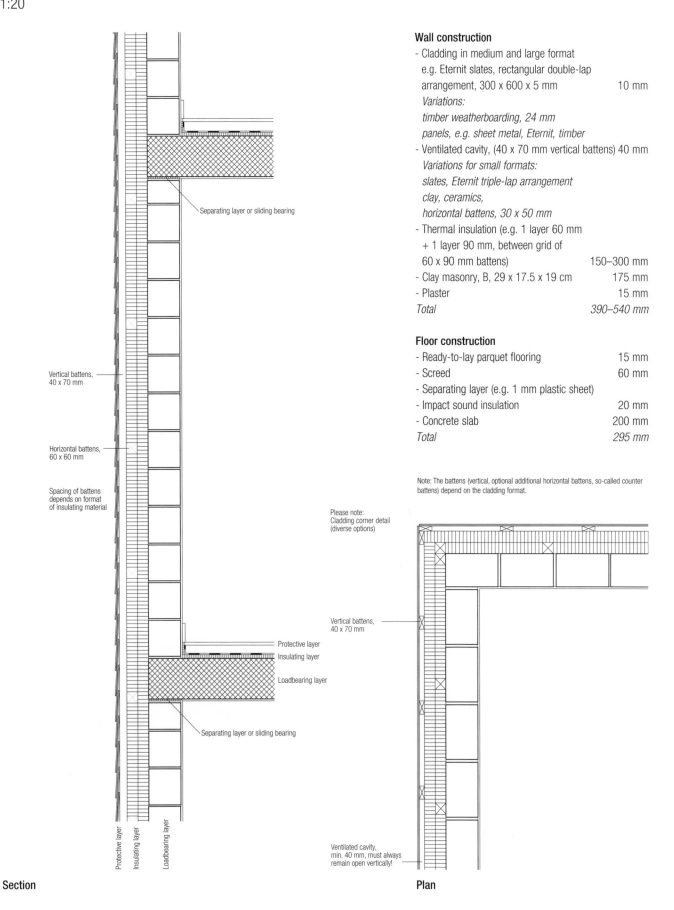

Wall construction
- Cladding in medium and large format
  e.g. Eternit slates, rectangular double-lap
  arrangement, 300 x 600 x 5 mm   10 mm
  Variations:
  timber weatherboarding, 24 mm
  panels, e.g. sheet metal, Eternit, timber
- Ventilated cavity, (40 x 70 mm vertical battens) 40 mm
  Variations for small formats:
  slates, Eternit triple-lap arrangement
  clay, ceramics,
  horizontal battens, 30 x 50 mm
- Thermal insulation (e.g. 1 layer 60 mm
  + 1 layer 90 mm, between grid of
  60 x 90 mm battens)   150–300 mm
- Clay masonry, B, 29 x 17.5 x 19 cm   175 mm
- Plaster   15 mm
Total   *390–540 mm*

Floor construction
- Ready-to-lay parquet flooring   15 mm
- Screed   60 mm
- Separating layer (e.g. 1 mm plastic sheet)
- Impact sound insulation   20 mm
- Concrete slab   200 mm
Total   *295 mm*

Note: The battens (vertical, optional additional horizontal battens, so-called counter battens) depend on the cladding format.

Please note:
Cladding corner detail
(diverse options)

Separating layer or sliding bearing

Vertical battens,
40 x 70 mm

Horizontal battens,
60 x 60 mm

Spacing of battens
depends on format
of insulating material

Protective layer
Insulating layer
Loadbearing layer

Separating layer or sliding bearing

Vertical battens,
40 x 70 mm

Ventilated cavity,
min. 40 mm, must always
remain open vertically!

Protective layer
Insulating layer
Loadbearing layer

Section

Plan

External cladding, heavyweight
1:20

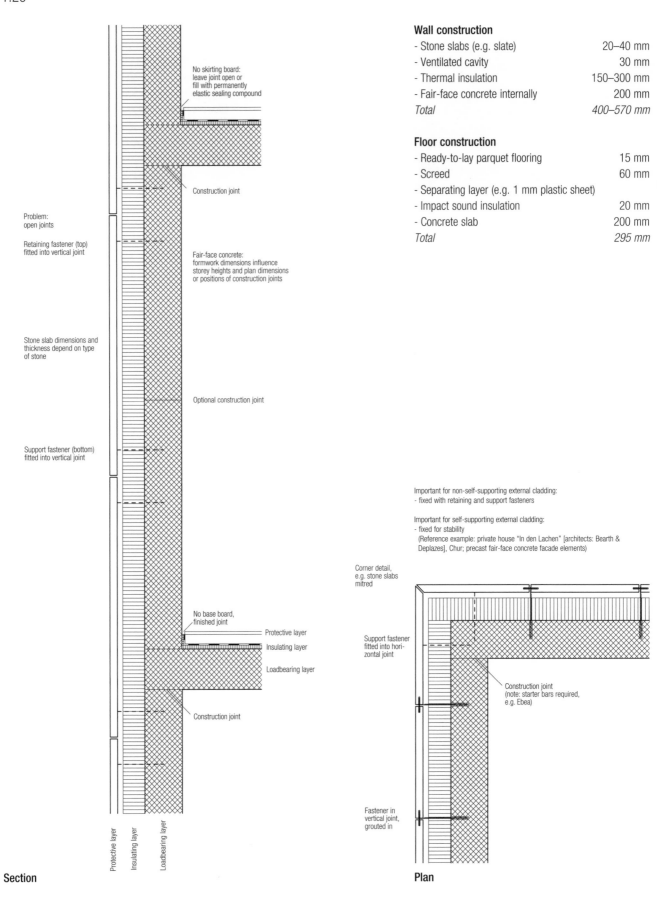

Wall construction

- Stone slabs (e.g. slate)	20–40 mm
- Ventilated cavity	30 mm
- Thermal insulation	150–300 mm
- Fair-face concrete internally	200 mm
Total	*400–570 mm*

Floor construction

- Ready-to-lay parquet flooring	15 mm
- Screed	60 mm
- Separating layer (e.g. 1 mm plastic sheet)	
- Impact sound insulation	20 mm
- Concrete slab	200 mm
Total	*295 mm*

Labels in section:

No skirting board:
leave joint open or
fill with permanently
elastic sealing compound

Construction joint

Problem:
open joints

Retaining fastener (top)
fitted into vertical joint

Fair-face concrete:
formwork dimensions influence
storey heights and plan dimensions
or positions of construction joints

Stone slab dimensions and
thickness depend on type
of stone

Optional construction joint

Support fastener (bottom)
fitted into vertical joint

No base board,
finished joint

Protective layer

Insulating layer

Loadbearing layer

Construction joint

Protective layer

Insulating layer

Loadbearing layer

Section

Important for non-self-supporting external cladding:
- fixed with retaining and support fasteners

Important for self-supporting external cladding:
- fixed for stability
(Reference example: private house "In den Lachen" [architects: Bearth &
Deplazes], Chur; precast fair-face concrete facade elements)

Corner detail,
e.g. stone slabs
mitred

Support fastener
fitted into hori-
zontal joint

Construction joint
(note: starter bars required,
e.g. Ebea)

Fastener in
vertical joint,
grouted in

Plan

Non-loadbearing external wall
1:20

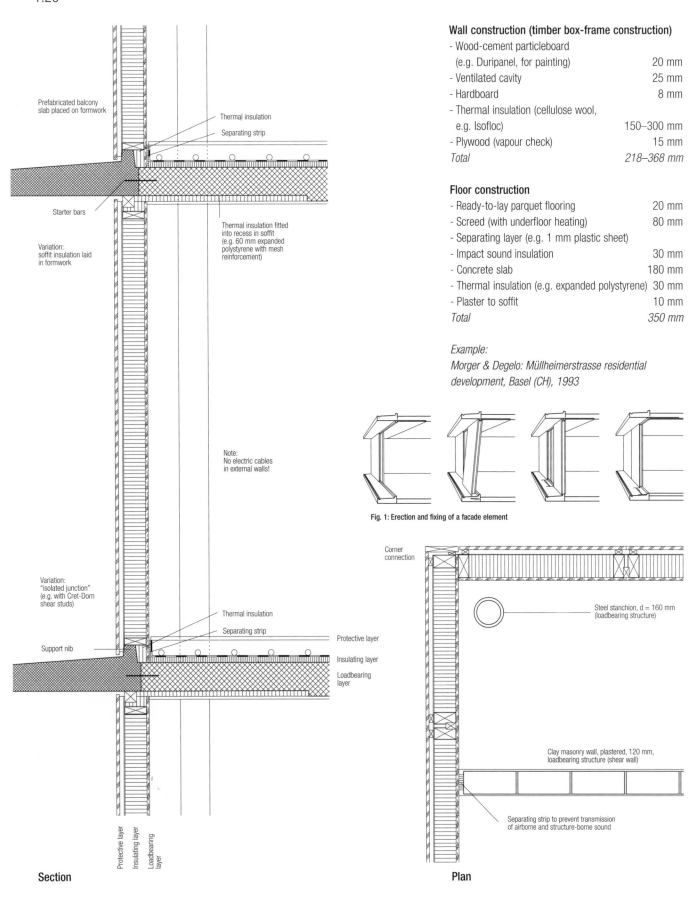

Prefabricated balcony
slab placed on formwork

Thermal insulation

Separating strip

Starter bars

Variation:
soffit insulation laid
in formwork

Thermal insulation fitted
into recess in soffit
(e.g. 60 mm expanded
polystyrene with mesh
reinforcement)

Note:
No electric cables
in external walls!

Variation:
"isolated junction"
(e.g. with Cret-Dorn
shear studs)

Thermal insulation

Separating strip

Support nib

Protective layer

Insulating layer

Loadbearing
layer

Protective layer
Insulating layer
Loadbearing layer

Section

Wall construction (timber box-frame construction)

- Wood-cement particleboard (e.g. Duripanel, for painting)	20 mm
- Ventilated cavity	25 mm
- Hardboard	8 mm
- Thermal insulation (cellulose wool, e.g. Isofloc)	150–300 mm
- Plywood (vapour check)	15 mm
Total	*218–368 mm*

Floor construction

- Ready-to-lay parquet flooring	20 mm
- Screed (with underfloor heating)	80 mm
- Separating layer (e.g. 1 mm plastic sheet)	
- Impact sound insulation	30 mm
- Concrete slab	180 mm
- Thermal insulation (e.g. expanded polystyrene)	30 mm
- Plaster to soffit	10 mm
Total	*350 mm*

Example:
Morger & Degelo: Müllheimerstrasse residential development, Basel (CH), 1993

Fig. 1: Erection and fixing of a facade element

Corner
connection

Steel stanchion, d = 160 mm
(loadbearing structure)

Clay masonry wall, plastered, 120 mm,
loadbearing structure (shear wall)

Separating strip to prevent transmission
of airborne and structure-borne sound

Plan

Timber platform frame construction
1:20

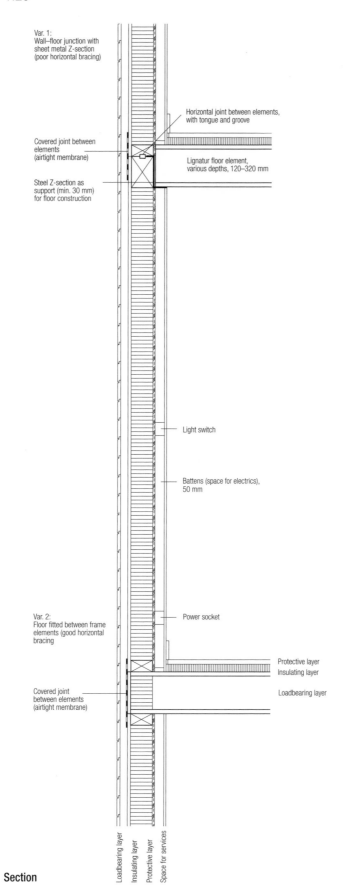

Var. 1:
Wall–floor junction with sheet metal Z-section (poor horizontal bracing)

Horizontal joint between elements, with tongue and groove

Covered joint between elements (airtight membrane)

Lignatur floor element, various depths, 120–320 mm

Steel Z-section as support (min. 30 mm) for floor construction

Light switch

Battens (space for electrics), 50 mm

Var. 2:
Floor fitted between frame elements (good horizontal bracing

Power socket

Protective layer
Insulating layer

Loadbearing layer

Covered joint between elements (airtight membrane)

Loadbearing layer
Insulating layer
Protective layer
Space for services

Section

Wall construction

- Horizontal boards	24 mm
- Vertical battens (ventilated cavity)	40 mm
- Bitumen-impregnated softboard (airtight membrane)	18 mm
- Timber studding, insulation (cellulose wool, e.g. Isofloc)	150–300 mm
- Wood-based board (plywood, vapourproof)	12 mm
- Vertical battens (space for services)	50 mm
- Wood-cement particleboard or fibre-reinforced plasterboard	12 mm
Total	*306–456 mm*

Floor construction

- 3-ply core plywood, floating, with tongue and groove	27 mm
- Impact sound insulation	40 mm
- Lignatur timber box element, soffit left exposed	220 mm
Total	*287 mm*

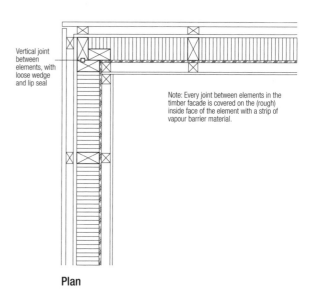

Vertical joint between elements, with loose wedge and lip seal

Note: Every joint between elements in the timber facade is covered on the (rough) inside face of the element with a strip of vapour barrier material.

Plan

Lignatur element, 100 cm wide, insulated or uninsulated, depth depends on span

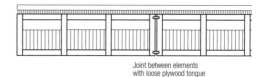

Joint between elements with loose plywood tongue

Schematic section

Solid timber panel construction
1:20

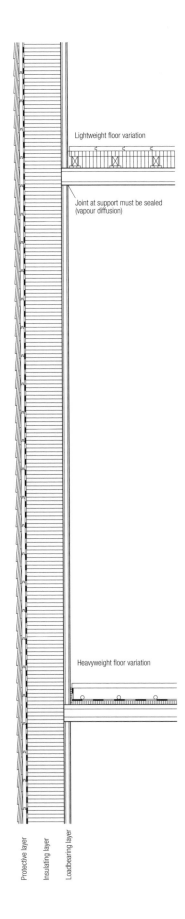

Lightweight floor variation

Joint at support must be sealed
(vapour diffusion)

Heavyweight floor variation

Protective layer   Insulating layer   Loadbearing layer

Section

Wall construction
- Larch shingles (without ventilated cavity), double-lap arrangement	20 mm
- Spruce boards (tongue and groove), horizontal	20 mm
- Airtight membrane	
- Thermal insulation (around the transverse ribs)	150–300 mm
- Solid timber panel (loadbearing, incl. vapour check function due to adhesive)	35 mm
Total	*225–375 mm*

Floor construction, "lightweight"
- Solid timber floorboards (tongue and groove, concealed nailing)	24 mm
- Counter battens, 40 x 30 mm (with insulation between)	30 mm
- Battens, 50 x 30 mm (with insulation in between)	50 mm
- Rubber strips as separating layer beneath battens (for impact sound insulation)	10 mm
- Solid timber panel (span: 3 m)	90 mm
Total	*204 mm*

Floor construction, "heavyweight"
- Hard-fired floor tiles	30 mm
- Screed (with underfloor heating)	60 mm
- Separating layer (fleece)	2 mm
- Impact sound insulation	40 mm
- Solid timber panel (span: 3 m)	90 mm
Total	*222 mm*

Example:
Bearth & Deplazes: private house (Bearth-Candinas),
Sumvitg (CH), 1998

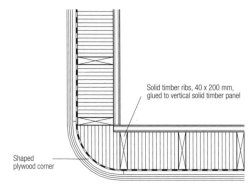

Solid timber ribs, 40 x 200 mm,
glued to vertical solid timber panel

Shaped
plywood corner

Plan

Opening, single-leaf masonry
1:20

External elevation

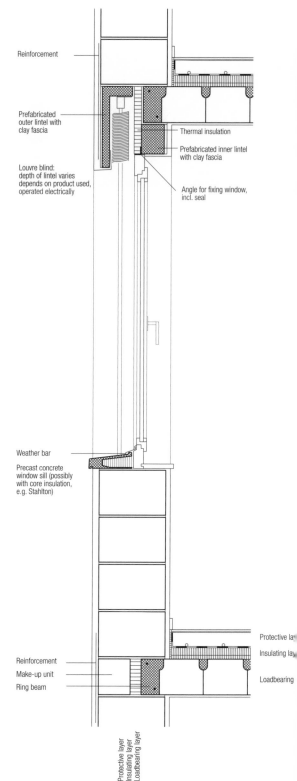

Reinforcement

Prefabricated
outer lintel with
clay fascia

Louvre blind:
depth of lintel varies
depends on product used,
operated electrically

Thermal insulation

Prefabricated inner lintel
with clay fascia

Angle for fixing window,
incl. seal

Weather bar

Precast concrete
window sill (possibly
with core insulation,
e.g. Stahlton)

Protective la~

Insulating la~

Reinforcement

Make-up unit

Ring beam

Loadbearing

Protective layer
Insulating layer
Loadbearing layer

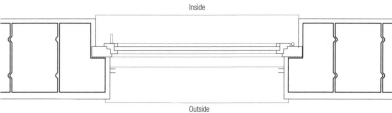

Inside

Outside

Plan of course 1

Wall construction

- Render	35 mm
- Single-leaf masonry, 36.5 x 24.8 x 23.8 cm	365 mm
- Plaster	25 mm
Total	*425 mm*

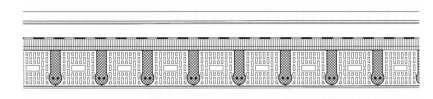

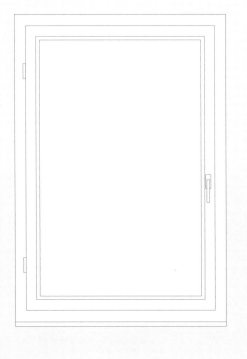

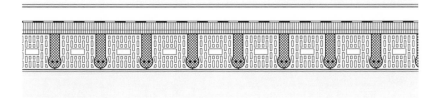

Internal elevation

Special reveal unit, specific dimensions of manufacturer

Guide track for louvre blind

Outside

Separating strip between masonry and window frame, incl. seal

Inside

Plan of course 2

Opening, double-leaf masonry, rendered
1:20

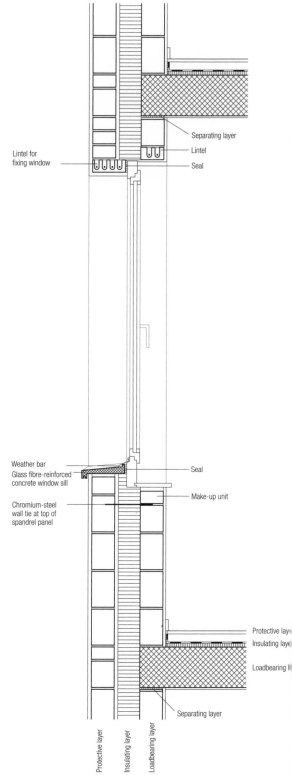

Lintel for
fixing window — Lintel

Separating layer

Seal

Weather bar
Glass fibre-reinforced
concrete window sill

Seal

Make-up unit

Chromium-steel
wall tie at top of
spandrel panel

Protective lay
Insulating laye

Loadbearing l

Separating layer

Protective layer

Insulating layer

Loadbearing layer

External elevation

Inside

Outside

Plan of course 1

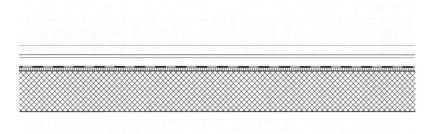

Wall construction

- Render	20 mm
- Clay masonry, BN, 29 x 12.5 x 19 cm	125 mm
- Cavity (construction tolerance)	20 mm
- Thermal insulation (e.g. rockwool)	150–300 mm
- Clay masonry, BN, 29 x 12.5 x 19 cm	125 mm
- Plaster	15 mm
Total	*455–605 mm*

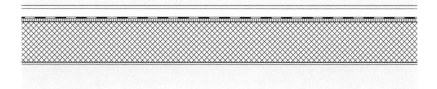

Internal elevation

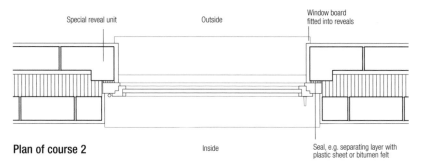

Special reveal unit   Outside   Window board fitted into reveals

Plan of course 2   Inside   Seal, e.g. separating layer with plastic sheet or bitumen felt

Opening, facing masonry
1:20

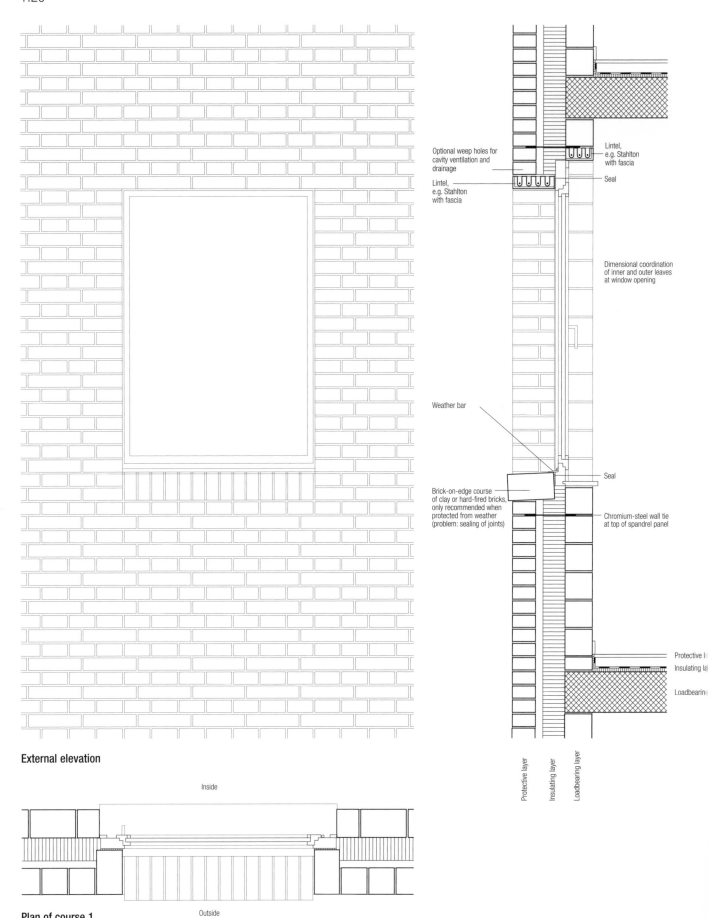

Optional weep holes for cavity ventilation and drainage

Lintel, e.g. Stahlton with fascia

Lintel, e.g. Stahlton with fascia

Seal

Dimensional coordination of inner and outer leaves at window opening

Weather bar

Brick-on-edge course of clay or hard-fired bricks, only recommended when protected from weather (problem: sealing of joints)

Seal

Chromium-steel wall tie at top of spandrel panel

Protective l

Insulating la

Loadbearin

Protective layer

Insulating layer

Loadbearing layer

External elevation

Inside

Plan of course 1   Outside

Wall construction
- Clay masonry, BS, course 1, 14 x 14 x 6.5 cm   140 mm
  Clay masonry, BS, course 2, 29 x 14 x 6.5 cm
  (Variations: diverse facing masonry modules,
  prefabricated concrete bricks or elements etc.)
- Ventilated cavity   min. 40 mm
- Thermal insulation (e.g. rockwool)   150–300 mm
- Clay masonry, BS, 25 x 15 x 14 cm   150 mm
Total   *480–630 mm*

Internal elevation

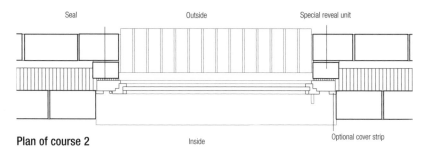

| Seal | Outside | Special reveal unit |

Plan of course 2   Inside   Optional cover strip

Opening, fair-face concrete with internal insulation
1:20

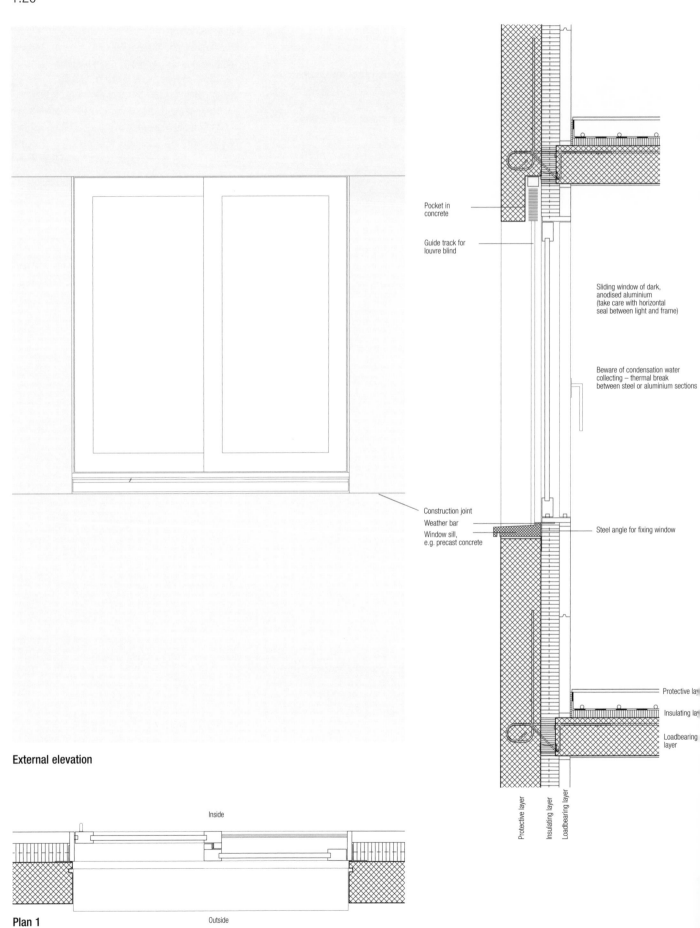

Pocket in concrete

Guide track for louvre blind

Sliding window of dark, anodised aluminium (take care with horizontal seal between light and frame)

Beware of condensation water collecting – thermal break between steel or aluminium sections

Construction joint
Weather bar
Window sill, e.g. precast concrete

Steel angle for fixing window

Protective layer

Insulating layer

Loadbearing layer

Protective layer   Insulating layer   Loadbearing layer

External elevation

Inside

Plan 1   Outside

Wall construction

- Fair-face concrete, coloured   220 mm
- Thermal insulation, vapourproof
  (e.g. cellular glass)   150–300 mm
- Gypsum boards, plaster skim/paint finish   60 mm
Total   *430–580 mm*

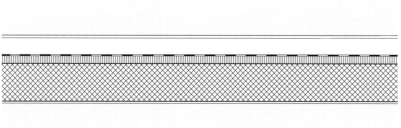

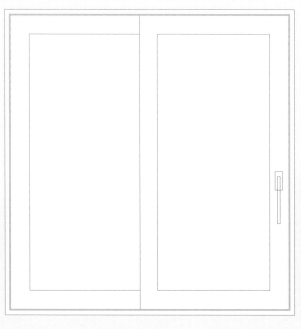

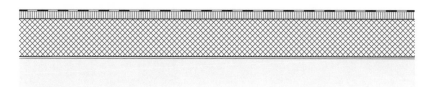

Internal elevation

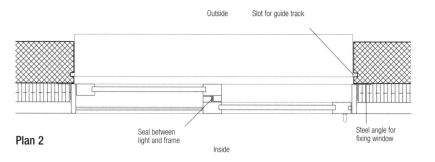

Plan 2

Opening, external cladding, lightweight
1:20

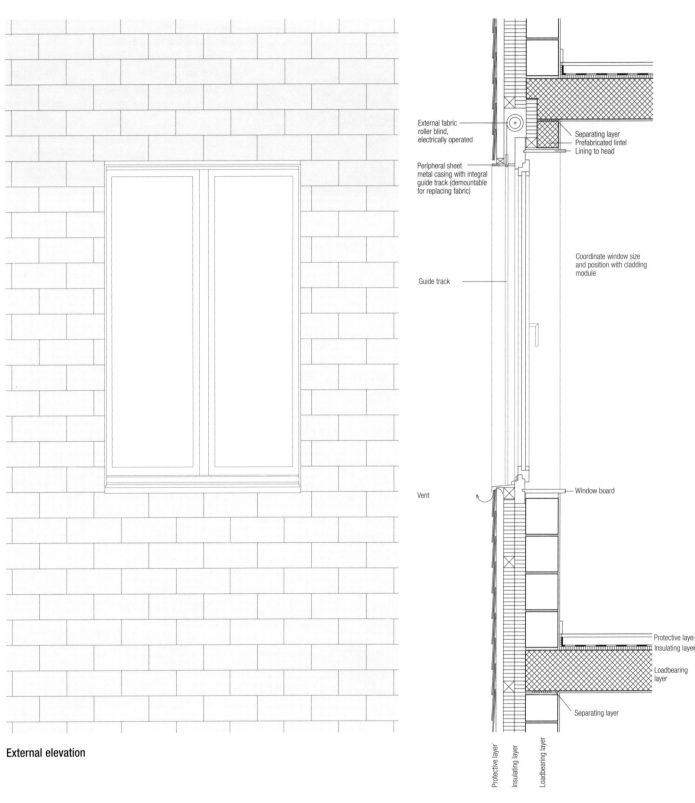

External fabric roller blind, electrically operated

Separating layer
Prefabricated lintel
Lining to head

Peripheral sheet metal casing with integral guide track (demountable for replacing fabric)

Coordinate window size and position with cladding module

Guide track

Vent

Window board

Protective layer
Insulating layer

Loadbearing layer

Separating layer

Protective layer
Insulating layer
Loadbearing layer

External elevation

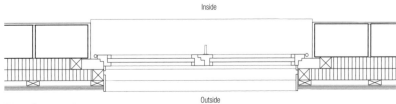

Inside

Outside

Plan of course 1

Wall construction

- Cladding in medium and large format
  e.g. Eternit slates, rectangular double-lap
  arrangement, 300 x 600 x 5 mm   10 mm
  Variations:
  timber weatherboarding, 24 mm
  panels, e.g. sheet metal, Eternit, timber
- Ventilated cavity (40 x 70 mm vertical battens) 40 mm
  Variations for small formats:
  slates,
  Eternit triple-lap arrangement,
  clay/ceramics,
  horizontal battens, 30 x 50 mm
- Thermal insulation (e.g. 1 layer 60 mm
  + 1 layer 90 mm, between grid of
  60 x 90 mm battens)   150–300 mm
- Clay masonry, B, 29 x 17.5 x 19 cm   175 mm
- Plaster   15 mm
Total   *390–540 mm*

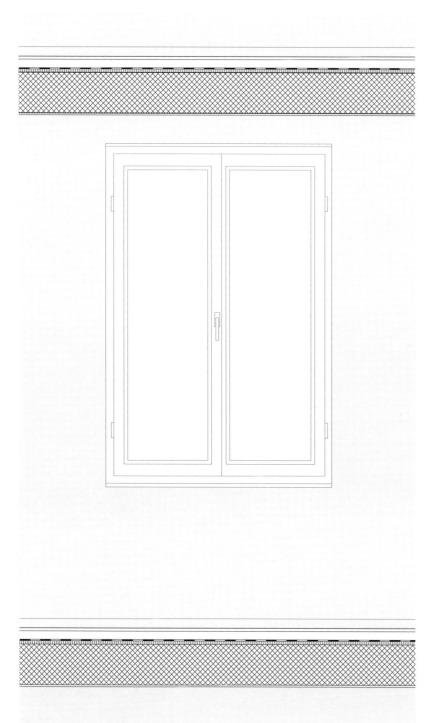

Internal elevation

Outside

Peripheral sheet metal casing
with integral guide track

Inside

Plan of course 2

Opening, external cladding, heavyweight
1:20

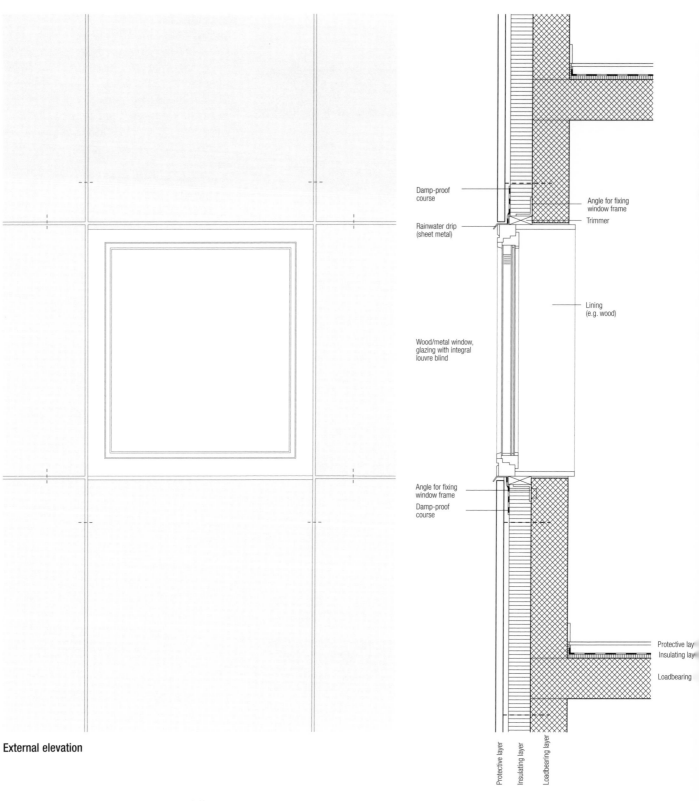

Damp-proof
course

Angle for fixing
window frame

Rainwater drip
(sheet metal)

Trimmer

Lining
(e.g. wood)

Wood/metal window,
glazing with integral
louvre blind

Angle for fixing
window frame

Damp-proof
course

Protective lay
Insulating lay

Loadbearing

Protective layer

Insulating layer

Loadbearing layer

External elevation

Inside

Plan 1

Outside

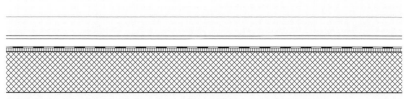

Wall construction

- Stone slabs (e.g. slates)	20–40 mm
- Ventilated cavity	30 mm
- Thermal insulation	150–300 mm
- Fair-face concrete internally	200 mm
Total	*400–570 mm*

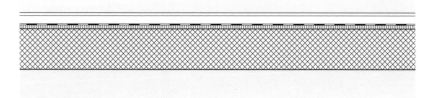

Internal elevation

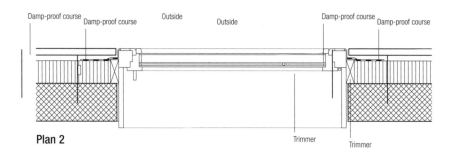

Plan 2

Opening, external insulation, rendered
1:20

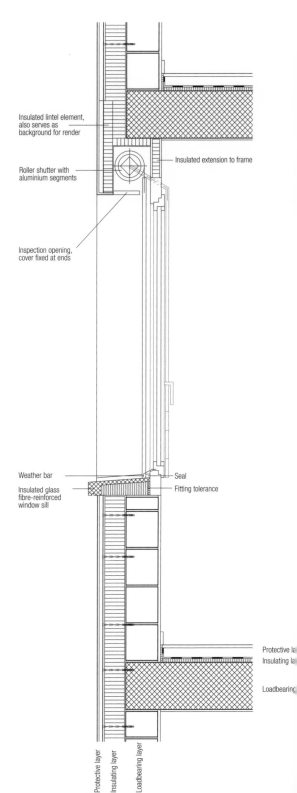

Insulated lintel element, also serves as background for render

Insulated extension to frame

Roller shutter with aluminium segments

Inspection opening, cover fixed at ends

Weather bar

Seal

Insulated glass fibre-reinforced window sill

Fitting tolerance

Protective la

Insulating la

Loadbearing

Protective layer

Insulating layer

Loadbearing layer

External elevation

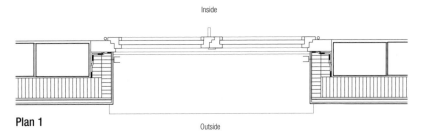

Inside

Plan 1　　　　Outside

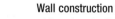

Wall construction
- Mineral render finish coat (coloured or painted)   2 mm
- Bonding render
  (with glass mat inlay over entire surface)   4 mm
- Mineral render undercoat   20 mm
- Insulation board (5-150-10 3-layer board),
  fixed with plastic fasteners   150–300 mm
- Clay masonry, B, 29 x 17.5 x 14 cm   175 mm
- Plaster   15 mm
Total   *366–516 mm*

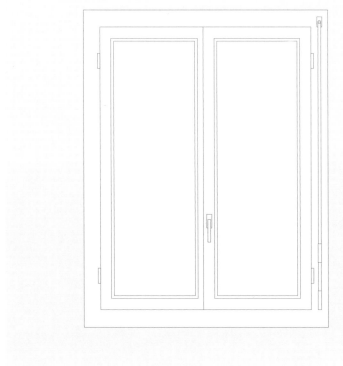

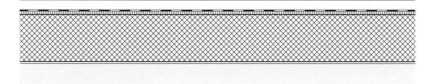

Internal elevation

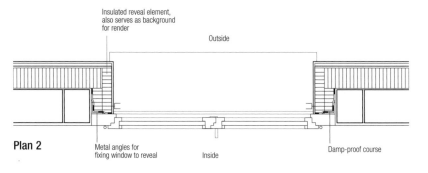

Insulated reveal element,
also serves as background
for render

Outside

Plan 2

Metal angles for
fixing window to reveal

Inside

Damp-proof course

Opening, non-loadbearing external wall
1:20

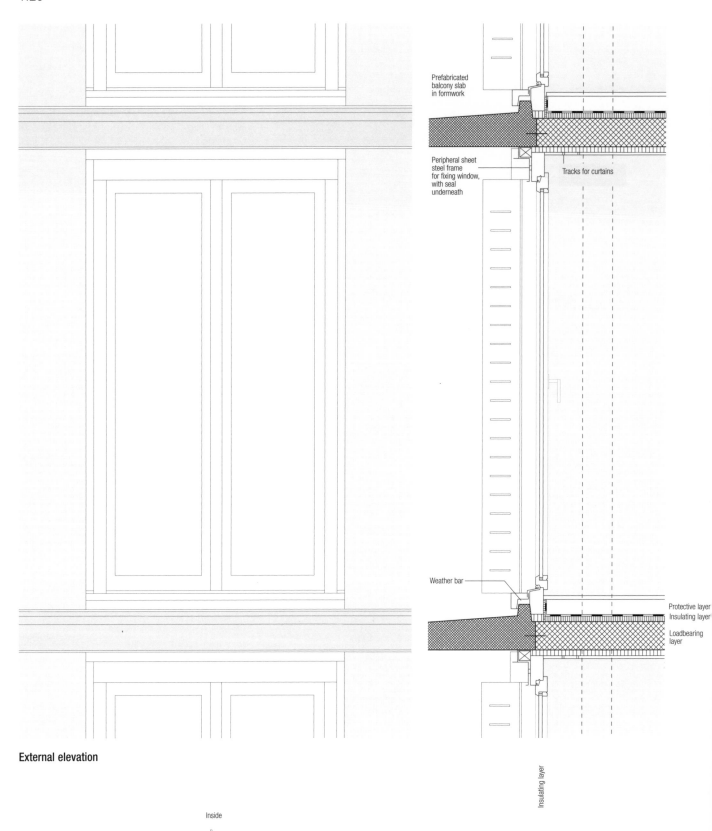

Prefabricated
balcony slab
in formwork

Peripheral sheet
steel frame
for fixing window,
with seal
underneath

Tracks for curtains

Weather bar

Protective layer
Insulating layer

Loadbearing
layer

Insulating layer

External elevation

Inside

Outside

Plan 1

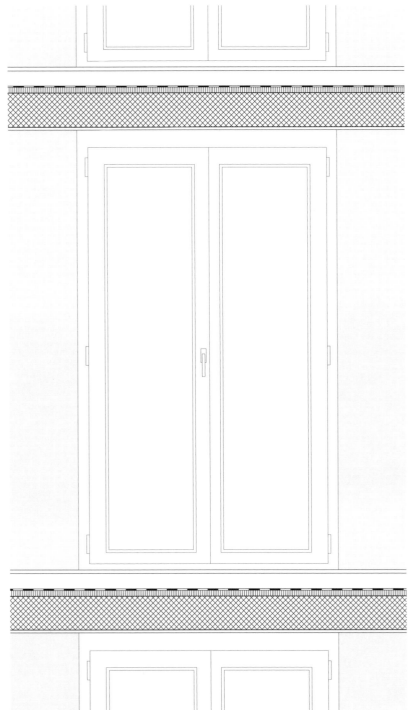

Wall construction (timber box-frame construction)

- Wood-cement particleboard (e.g. Duripanel, for painting)	20 mm
- Ventilated cavity	25 mm
- Hardboard	8 mm
- Thermal insulation (e.g. Isofloc)	150–300 mm
- Plywood (vapour check)	15 mm
Total	*188–368 mm*

Internal elevation

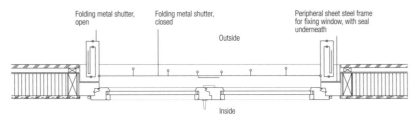

Folding metal shutter, open

Folding metal shutter, closed

Peripheral sheet steel frame for fixing window, with seal underneath

Outside

Inside

Plan 2

Opening, timber platform frame construction
1:20

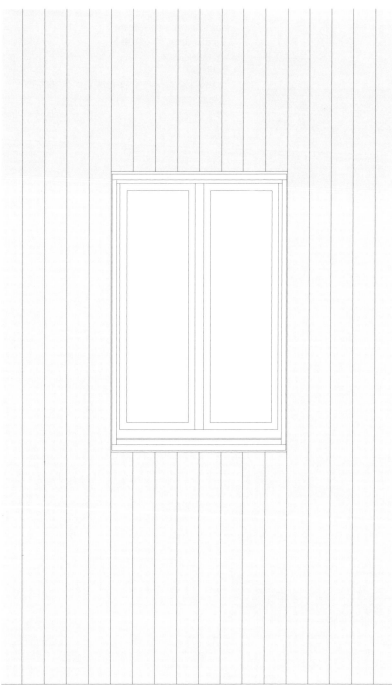

External elevation

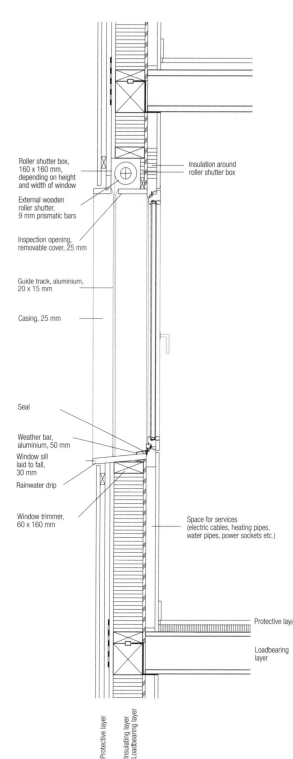

Roller shutter box,
160 x 160 mm,
depending on height
and width of window

External wooden
roller shutter,
9 mm prismatic bars

Inspection opening,
removable cover, 25 mm

Guide track, aluminium,
20 x 15 mm

Casing, 25 mm

Seal

Weather bar,
aluminium, 50 mm

Window sill
laid to fall,
30 mm

Rainwater drip

Window trimmer,
60 x 160 mm

Insulation around
roller shutter box

Space for services
(electric cables, heating pipes,
water pipes, power sockets etc.)

Protective layer

Loadbearing
layer

Protective layer

Insulating layer
Loadbearing layer

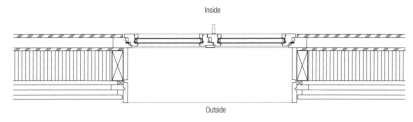

Inside

Outside

Plan 1

Wall construction

- Boards (e.g. untreated larch)	21 mm
- Battens, 27 x 50 mm, horizontal	27 mm
- Battens, 27 x 50 mm, vertical (ventilated cavity)	27 mm
- Bitumen-impregnated softboard	22 mm
- Timber studding with insulation in between	150–300 mm
- Wood-based board, OSB (vapour check)	15 mm
- Battens (space for services)	54 mm
- Wood-cement particleboard	18 mm
Total	*334–484 mm*

Internal elevation

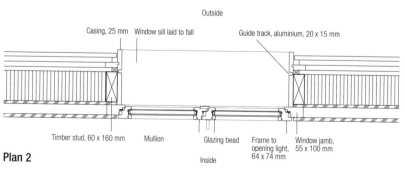

Outside

Casing, 25 mm   Window sill laid to fall   Guide track, aluminium, 20 x 15 mm

Timber stud, 60 x 160 mm   Mullion   Glazing bead   Frame to opening light, 64 x 74 mm   Window jamb, 55 x 100 mm

Plan 2   Inside

Opening, solid timber panel construction
1:20

External elevation

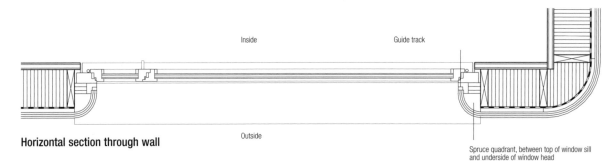

Horizontal section through wall

Inside

Guide track

Outside

Spruce quadrant, between top of window sill
and underside of window head

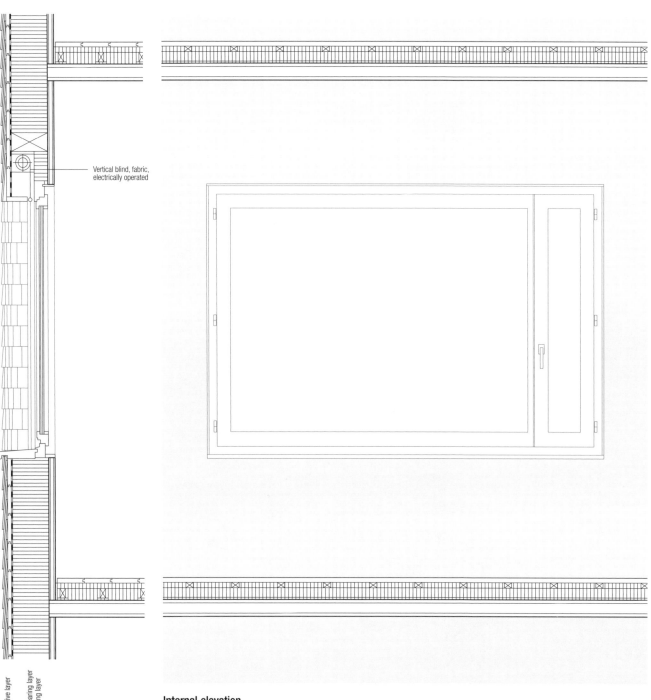

Vertical blind, fabric,
electrically operated

Protective layer

Loadbearing layer
Insulating layer

Internal elevation

Wall construction

- Larch shingles (without ventilated cavity),
  double-lap arrangement   20 mm
- Spruce boards (tongue and groove),
  horizontal (signature planks)   20 mm
- Airtight membrane
- Thermal insulation
  (around transverse ribs)   150–300 mm
- Solid timber panel (loadbearing,
  incl. vapour check function due to adhesive)   35 mm

Total   *225–375 mm*

Floor construction

- Floor covering   30 mm
- Screed   60 mm
- Separating layer
- Impact sound insulation   20 mm
- Solid timber panel (span: 3 m)   90 mm

Total   *200 mm*

Hinged door, external – wood
1:20

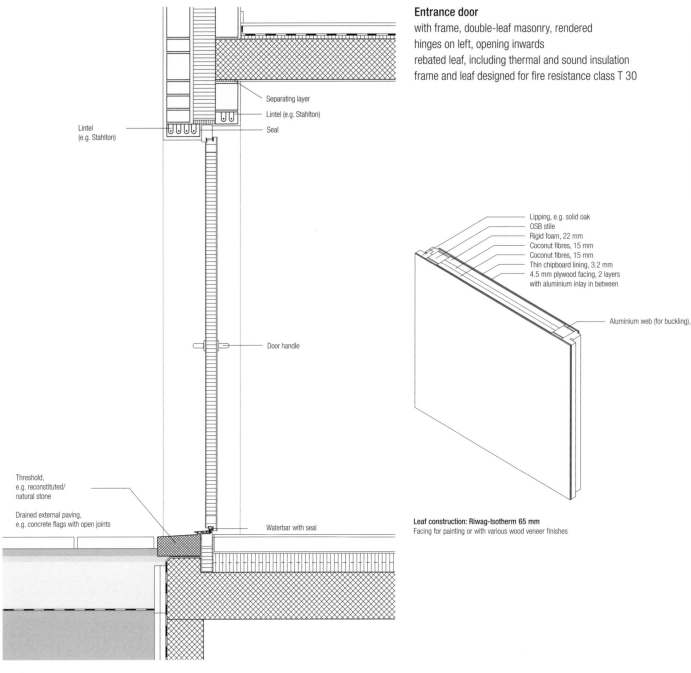

Entrance door
with frame, double-leaf masonry, rendered
hinges on left, opening inwards
rebated leaf, including thermal and sound insulation
frame and leaf designed for fire resistance class T 30

Separating layer

Lintel (e.g. Stahlton)

Lintel
(e.g. Stahlton)

Seal

Lipping, e.g. solid oak
OSB stile
Rigid foam, 22 mm
Coconut fibres, 15 mm
Coconut fibres, 15 mm
Thin chipboard lining, 3.2 mm
4.5 mm plywood facing, 2 layers
with aluminium inlay in between

Aluminium web (for buckling)

Door handle

Threshold,
e.g. reconstituted/
natural stone

Drained external paving,
e.g. concrete flags with open joints

Waterbar with seal

Leaf construction: Riwag-Isotherm 65 mm
Facing for painting or with various wood veneer finishes

Section

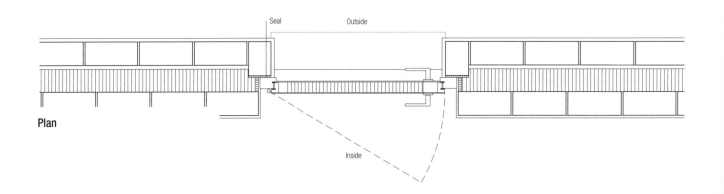

Seal   Outside

Plan

Inside

Hinged door, external – wood/glass
1:20

Entrance door

with frame, external cladding, lightweight
hinges on right, opening outwards
glazed leaf, rebated, fits flush with frame

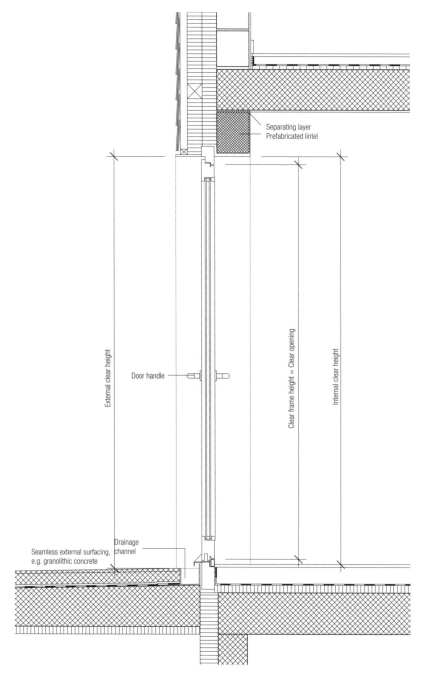

Separating layer
Prefabricated lintel

External clear height

Door handle

Clear frame height = Clear opening

Internal clear height

Drainage channel

Seamless external surfacing, e.g. granolithic concrete

Section

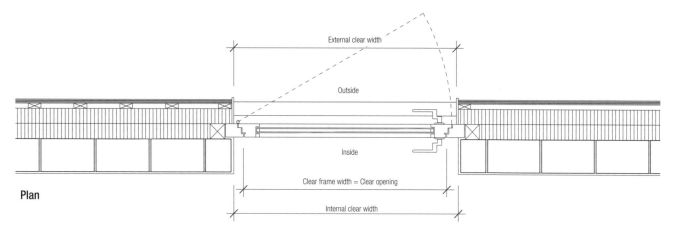

External clear width

Outside

Inside

Clear frame width = Clear opening

Internal clear width

Plan

Sliding door, external – metal/glass
1:20

Glazed patio door
Special design, brand: "sky-frame"
Double sliding aluminium door with thermal break

Glass elements attached to aluminium frame fitted into threshold, jambs and head. The sliding elements run on ball-bearing trolleys with little rolling resistance.

Fig. 1: Peter Kunz: private house, Winterthur (CH), 2003

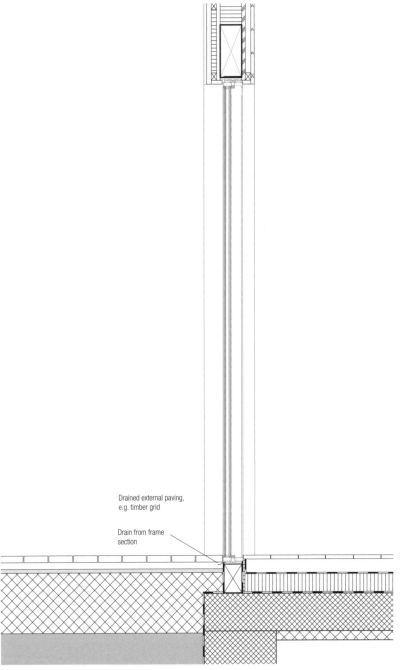

Drained external paving, e.g. timber grid

Drain from frame section

Section

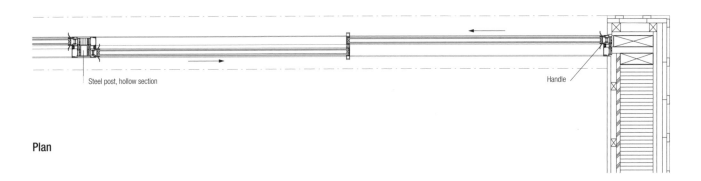

Steel post, hollow section

Handle

Plan

Hinged door, internal – wood
1:20

Internal door
with frame fitted in opening, facing brickwork
hinges on left
leaf fits flush with frame, rebated

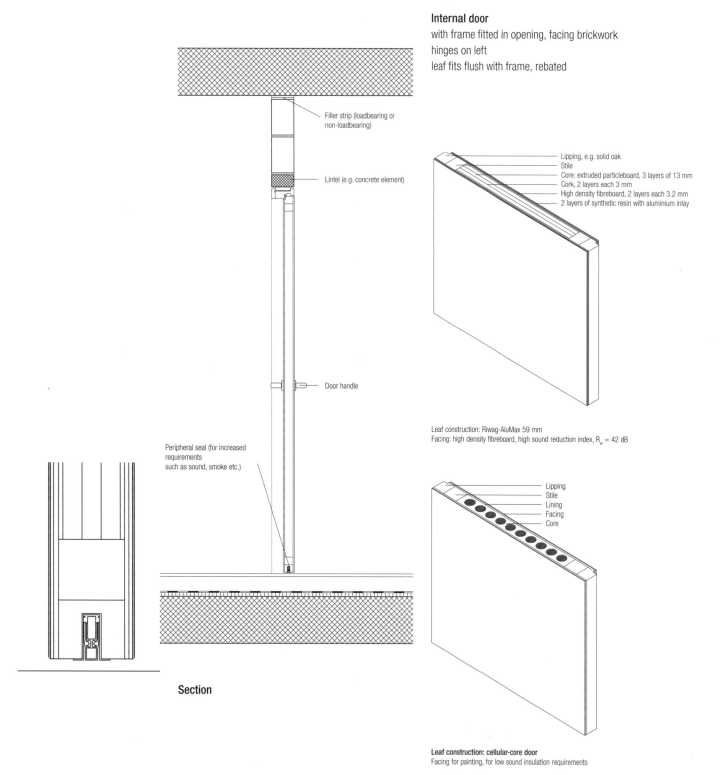

Filler strip (loadbearing or non-loadbearing)

Lintel (e.g. concrete element)

Door handle

Peripheral seal (for increased requirements
such as sound, smoke etc.)

Lipping, e.g. solid oak
Stile
Core: extruded particleboard, 3 layers of 13 mm
Cork, 2 layers each 3 mm
High density fibreboard, 2 layers each 3.2 mm
2 layers of synthetic resin with aluminium inlay

Leaf construction: Riwag-AluMax 59 mm
Facing: high density fibreboard, high sound reduction index, $R_w = 42$ dB

Lipping
Stile
Lining
Facing
Core

Leaf construction: cellular-core door
Facing for painting, for low sound insulation requirements

Section

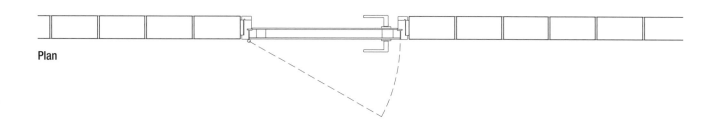

Plan

Sliding door, internal – wood
1:20

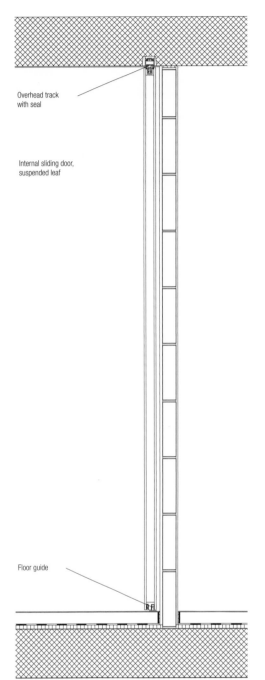

Overhead track
with seal

Internal sliding door,
suspended leaf

Floor guide

Section

Internal door
single leaf, fitted into a slot in the wall
for low sound insulation requirements

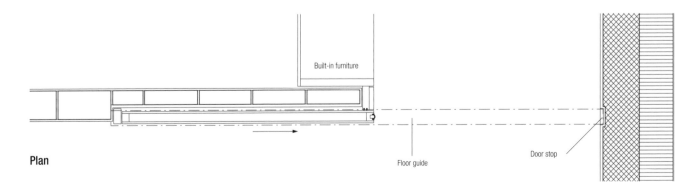

Built-in furniture

Plan

Door stop

Floor guide

Hollow clay block floor
1:20

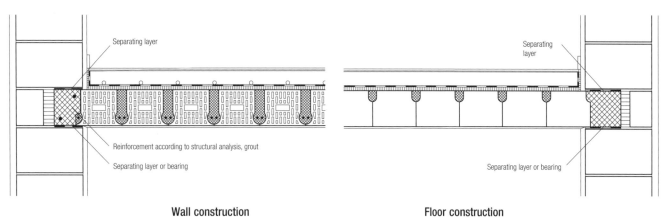

Wall construction

Single-leaf masonry

- Render	35 mm
- Single-leaf masonry, 36.5 x 24.8 x 23.8 cm	365 mm
- Plaster	25 mm

Floor construction

- Floor covering, e.g. plain clay tiles	10 mm
- Tile adhesive	1–2 mm
- Screed with underfloor heating	80 mm
- Separating layer (e.g. 1 mm plastic sheet)	
- Impact sound insulation	20 mm
- Hollow clay block floor	190–240 mm
- Plaster to soffit	10 mm

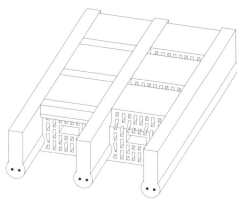

Structure

- 1-way span (2-way possible: waffle systems)
- Same material for the soffit
- No concrete topping required
- Cantilevers not possible
- Not suitable for point loads
- Elements up to 6.6 m long in widths from 1 to 2.5 m
  (e.g. Bricosol)

Features

- Adaptable flooring system
- No formwork
- Little propping needed
- Dry construction, can be installed any time of the year
- Can carry loads the next day

Fig. 1: Top: hollow clay blocks and reinforced concrete ribs;
bottom: erection of factory-prefabricated elements (here: Bricosol products)

Hourdis-type hollow clay block floor
1:20

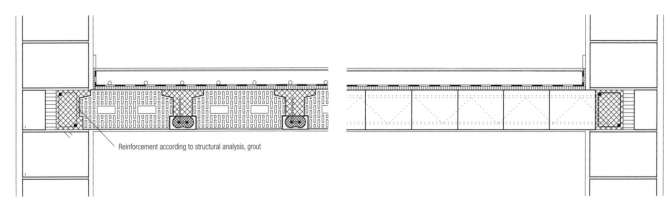

Reinforcement according to structural analysis, grout

Wall construction

Single-leaf masonry

- Render	35 mm
- Single-leaf masonry, 36.5 x 24.8 x 23.8 cm	365 mm
- Plaster	25 mm

Floor construction

- Floor covering, e.g. plain clay tiles	10 mm
- Tile adhesive	
- Screed with underfloor heating	80 mm
- Separating layer (e.g. 1 mm plastic sheet)	
- Impact sound insulation	20 mm
- Hourdis-type hollow clay block floor	210–250 mm
- Plaster to soffit	10 mm

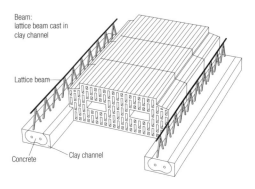

Beam:
lattice beam cast in
clay channel

Lattice beam

Concrete

Clay channel

Structure

- 1-way span (2-way possible: waffle systems)
- Same material for the soffit
- With or without concrete topping, depending on loads
- Cantilevers not possible
- Not suitable for point loads
- Span with in situ reinforcement: up to 7 m
- Span with prestressing: up to 7.5 m

Features

- In situ reinforcement: adaptable flooring system
- Prestressed: beams (tension chords) are prestressed; most systems fall into this category.
- No formwork
- Little propping needed

Fig. 2: Fitting the individual Hourdis-type elements between the reinforced concrete beams

Solid concrete slab
1:20

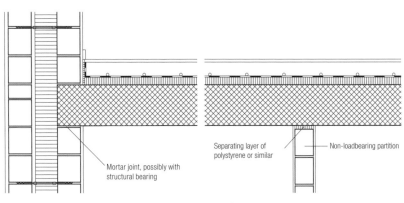

Mortar joint, possibly with structural bearing

Separating layer of polystyrene or similar

Non-loadbearing partition

Wall construction

Double-leaf masonry, rendered

- Render	20 mm
- Modular masonry units	125 mm
- Cavity (construction tolerance)	20 mm
- Thermal insulation	150–300 mm
- Modular masonry units	125 mm
- Plaster	15 mm

Floor construction

- Floor covering,	
e.g. ready-to-lay parquet flooring	15 mm
- Screed with underfloor heating	80 mm
- Separating layer (e.g. 1 mm plastic sheet)	
- Impact sound insulation	40 mm
- In situ solid concrete slab with glaze finish	
(depth of slab depends on span)	210 mm

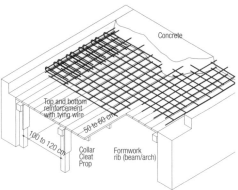

Concrete

Top and bottom reinforcement with tying wire

50 to 60 cm

100 to 120 cm

Collar Cleat Prop

Formwork rib (beam/arch)

Structure

- 1- or 2-way spans
- Economic spans:
  up to approx. 5 m simply supported
  up to approx. 7 m continuous
- Estimate of structural depth:
  $d/L = 1/30$ for rectangular slabs
  $d/L = 1/35$ for square slabs

Features

- High material consumption in relation to span
- Wet construction

Formwork

- In situ concrete: considerable propping and formwork requirements

Fig. 3: Prior to pouring the concrete: formwork, reinforcement and any services (electric cables, water pipes, ventilation ducts etc.) that are to be cast in

Ribbed concrete slab
1:20

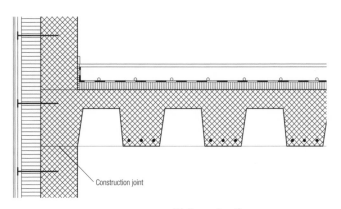

Construction joint

Construction joint

Wall construction
External insulation, rendered

- Mineral render finish coat	2 mm
- Bonding render	4 mm
- Mineral render undercoat	20 mm
- Insulation	150–300 mm
- Concrete (loadbearing layer)	200 mm
- Bonding coat	
- Plaster	15 mm

Floor construction

- Floor covering, e.g. stone tiles	15 mm
- Tile adhesive (thick- or thin-bed)	3–5 mm
- Screed with underfloor heating	80 mm
- Separating layer (1 mm plastic sheet)	
- Impact sound insulation	40 mm
- Ribbed concrete slab	
(depth of slab depends on span)	varies

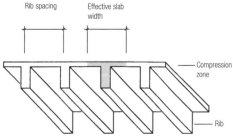

Rib spacing

Effective slab width

Compression zone

Rib

Structure
- 1-way span
- Weight-savings compared to a solid slab
- Spans:
  4–12 m simply supported
  5–20 m continuous
- Depths:
  slab 5 to 8 cm
  ribs 30 to max. 90 cm
- Services may be routed between the ribs

Performance
- Mass–surface area ratio is good for heat storage capacity

Features, formwork
- Extra formwork required in tension zone
- Prefabricated formwork:
  reusable formwork
  average formwork requirements
- In situ formwork: increased formwork requirements
- Prefabrication: lightweight "ribbed slab" elements constructed under factory conditions

Sound
- Large surface area (surface texture) improves internal acoustics

Fig. 4: Bearth & Deplazes: School with hall, Vella (CH), 1997

Concrete waffle slab
1:20

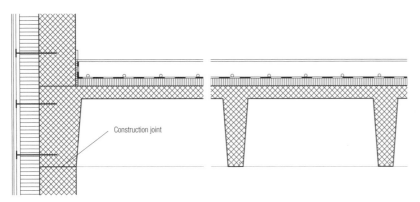
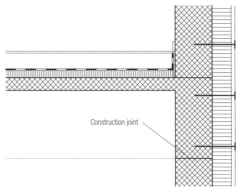

Construction joint

Construction joint

Wall construction

External insulation, rendered

- Mineral render finish coat	2 mm
- Bonding render	4 mm
- Mineral render undercoat	20 mm
- Insulation board (5-150-10 3-layer board), fixed with plastic fasteners	150–300 mm
- Concrete (loadbearing layer)	200 mm
- Bonding coat	
- Plaster	15 mm

Floor construction

- Floor covering, e.g. hard-fired floor tiles	15 mm
- Tile adhesive	3–5 mm
- Screed with underfloor heating	80 mm
- Separating layer (e.g. 1 mm plastic sheet)	
- Impact sound insulation	40 mm
- Concrete waffle slab	varies

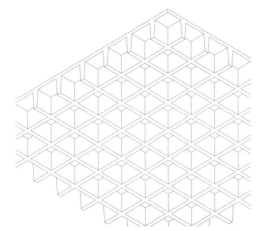

Structure
- 2-way span
- Modularity
- Appropriate choice of rib depth enables large spans

Features
- Low material consumption (in situ concrete)
- High formwork requirements when constructed in situ

Formwork variations
- Gypsum, timber, steel or plastic waffle formers on boarding
- Reusable prefabricated formwork elements
- Permanent formwork (e.g. Durisol), tapering waffle formers ease striking

Sound
- Large surface area (surface texture) improves internal acoustics

Fig. 5: Louis I. Kahn: Yale University Art Gallery, New Haven (USA), 1953

Hollow-core concrete slab
1:20

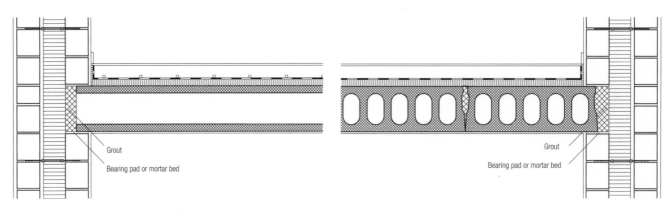

Grout

Bearing pad or mortar bed

Grout

Bearing pad or mortar bed

Wall construction

Double-leaf masonry, rendered

- Render	20 mm
- Modular masonry units	125 mm
- Cavity (construction tolerance)	20 mm
- Thermal insulation	150–300 mm
- Modular masonry units	125 mm
- Plaster	15 mm

Floor construction

- Floor covering, e.g. linoleum	5 mm
- Screed with underfloor heating	80 mm
- Separating layer (e.g. 1 mm plastic sheet)	
- Impact sound insulation	40 mm
- Hollow-core concrete unit	120–300 mm
- Bonding coat	
- Plaster to soffit	10 mm

Structure

- 1-way span, but not identifiable as such
- Spans up to 12 m
- Depths up to 300 mm

Features

- Prefabrication
- Short erection time
- Dry construction: short drying time
- Dry erection

Formwork

- No propping necessary
- Smooth soffit

Fig. 6: The concrete elements are lifted into position with a crane.

Composite slab, profiled metal sheeting–concrete
1:20

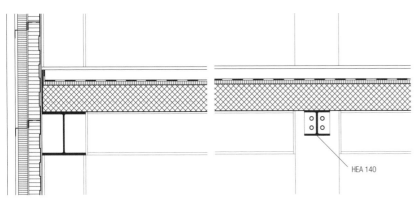

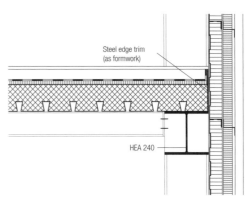

HEA 140

Steel edge trim
(as formwork)

HEA 240

Wall construction

External cladding, with ventilated cavity

- Corrugated metal sheeting, galvanised	varies
Ventilated cavity (vertical sheeting)	> 40 mm
- Thermal insulation	50 mm
- Thermal insulation in sheet steel trays (galvanised)	100–250 mm
- Steel colums, steel beams	varies

Floor construction

- Floor covering, e.g. magnesite	10 mm
- Screed	60 mm
- Separating layer (e.g. 1 mm plastic sheet)	
- Impact sound insulation	20 mm
- Reinforced concrete topping	130–180 mm
- Profiled metal sheeting	
- Steel primary/secondary beams (e.g. HEA or HEB sections)	varies

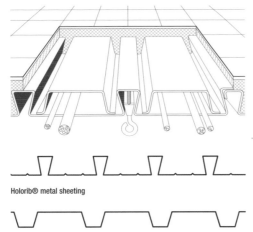

Structure

- 1-way span
- Profiled metal sheeting, reinforced concrete topping
- Relatively good fire resistance
- Provides ducting for services
- Span in direction of profiling without supporting construction (primary/secondary beams): up to 6 m
- Structural depth: 13–22 cm; concrete topping: 8–20 cm

Holorib® metal sheeting

Trapezoidal metal sheeting

Features

- Little propping needed
- Reduces the work on site

Formwork

- No formwork or main reinforcement
- Low handling weight

Sound

- Good airborne and impact sound insulation
- Beware of flanking transmissions!

Fig. 7: Top: soffit of profiled metal sheeting; bottom: profiled metal sheeting with concrete topping

Solid timber floor
1:20

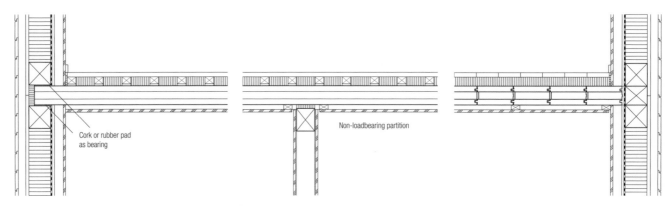

Cork or rubber pad
as bearing

Non-loadbearing partition

Wall construction

Platform frame construction

- Weatherboarding	24 mm
- Battens, ventilated cavity	40 mm
- Softboard (airtight membrane)	18 mm
- Thermal insulation, frame	150–300 mm
- Vapour check	
- Plain angled connections	
- Battens (space for services)	50 mm
- Wood-cement particleboard	12 mm

Floor construction

- Wooden floorboards	24 mm
- Impact sound insulation, counter battens	40 mm
- Rubber strips as separating layer beneath battens (for impact sound insulation)	
- Solid timber floor (depth depends on span)	80–120 mm
- Battens	24 mm
- Wood-cement particleboard	15 mm

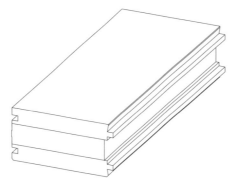

Structure

- 1-way span
- Rigid floor without vibration problems
- Spans of 4–5 m
- Depths of 80–120 mm, hollow elements over 120 mm
- Relatively large mass (good inertia)

Features

- Prefabricated glued individual solid timber elements
- Dry construction
- Simple assembly
- Fast assembly
- simultaneous planning and construction not possible!

Fig. 8: Staggered positioning of solid timber elements

Timber joist floor
1:20

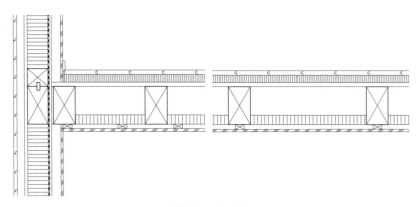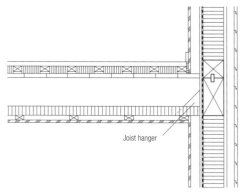

Joist hanger

Wall construction

Platform frame construction

- Weatherboarding   24 mm
- Battens, ventilated cavity   40 mm
- Softboard (airtight membrane)   18 mm
- Thermal insulation, frame   150–300 mm
- Vapour check
- Plain angled connections
- Battens (space for services)   50 mm
- Wood-cement particleboard   12 mm

Floor construction

- Wooden floorboards (tongue and groove)   24 mm
- Impact sound insulation, battens,
  rubber strips as separating layer beneath battens
  (for impact sound insulation)   40 mm
- Counter-floor (e.g. diagonal boarding with
  butt joints)   20 mm
- Joists (depth depends on span)
  120 x 200 mm   200 mm
- Sound insulation   50 mm
- Battens   24 mm
- Wood-cement particleboard   15 mm

Log construction   Timber-frame construction

Timber studding   Platform frame construction

Fig. 9: Various types of timber construction

Structure

- 1-way span
- Joist spacing: 50–80 cm
- Susceptible to vibration
- Greater load-carrying capacity when joist ends are
  built in
- Additional measures, e.g. diagonal boarding
  (counter-floor, soffit) required in order to achieve
  stiffening effect
- Spans: up to 5 m

Features

- Dry construction
- Simple assembly
- Fast assembly
- Labour-intensive

Sound

- Problematic ariborne and impact sound insulation

Fig. 10: Daniele Marques: private house (Ober-Riffig), Emmenbrücke (CH), 1993

Timber box element floor
1:20

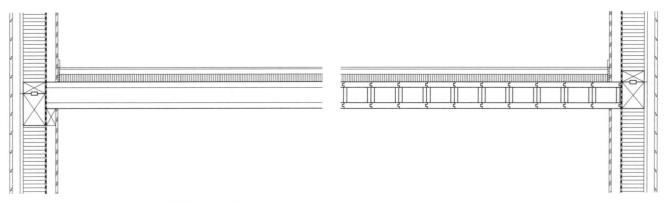

Wall construction

Platform frame construction

- Weatherboarding — 24 mm
- Battens, ventilated cavity — 40 mm
- Softboard (airtight membrane) — 18 mm
- Thermal insulation, frame — 150–300 mm
- Vapour check
- Battens (space for services) — 50 mm
- Wood-cement particleboard — 12 mm

Floor construction

- Floor covering, e.g. ready-to-lay
  parquet flooring — 10 mm
- 3-ply core plywood — 27 mm
- Impact sound insulation, 2 layers each 20 mm — 40 mm
- Timber box element floor on supporting members
  (structural depth depends on span) — 120–320 mm
- Glaze finish

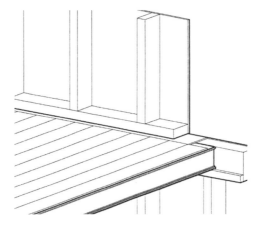

Structure

- Timber box elements made from solid planks
  (e.g. Lignatur)
- High loadbearing capacity coupled with low self-weight
- 1-way span
- Rigid floor without vibration problems
- Spans of 4–8 m
- Depths of 12–32 cm

Features

- Simple erection
- Dry construction
- Timber box elements prefabricated individually or in
  larger subassemblies
- Fast erection

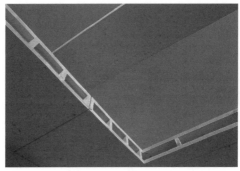

Fig. 11: Opening in timber box element floor, with voids not yet closed off

Steel floor
1:20

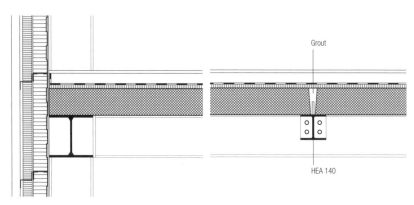
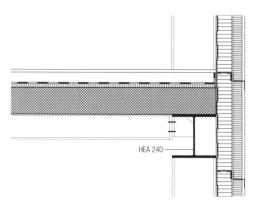

Wall construction

External cladding, with ventilated cavity

- Corrugated metal sheeting, galvanised	varies
- Ventilated cavity (vertical sheeting)	> 40 mm
- Thermal insulation	50 mm
- Thermal insulation in sheet steel trays	
(galvanised)	100–250 mm
- Steel colums, steel beams	varies

Floor construction

- Floor covering, e.g. magnesite	10 mm
- Screed	60 mm
- Separating layer (e.g. 1 mm plastic sheet)	
- Impact sound insulation	20 mm
- Concrete	150–300 mm
- Steel primary/secondary beams	
(e.g. HEA or HEB sections)	varies

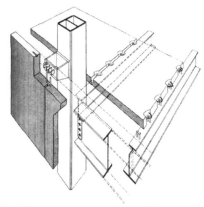

Structure

- 1-way span
- Modularity (for standard plate widths)
- Prefabrication
- Services can be routed along steel beams
- Low weight
- Steel beams limit fire resistance
- Spans of up to 6 m

Features

- Dry construction
- No formwork and no propping
- Fast assembly

Fig. 12: Primary structure of (solid) rolled sections, secondary structure of (open) lattice beams

Pitched roof – warm deck
Fibre-cement – external cladding, lightweight

Fig. 1: Bearth & Deplazes: private house
(Werner), Trin (CH), 1994

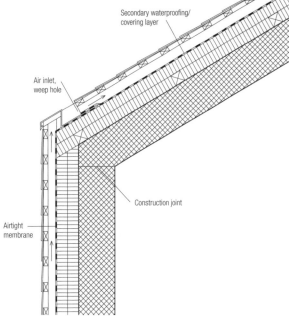

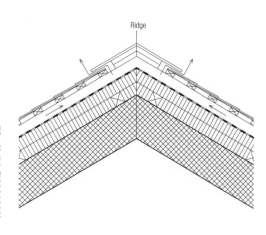

Secondary waterproofing/
covering layer

Air inlet,
weep hole

Construction joint

Airtight
membrane

Eaves

Ridge

Ridge

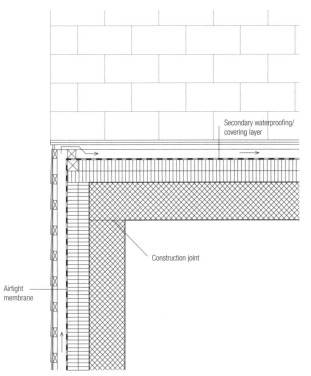

Secondary waterproofing/
covering layer

Construction joint

Airtight
membrane

Verge

Roof construction
- Slates (Eternit)	approx. 3.5 mm
- Battens, 24 x 48 mm	24 mm
- Counter battens, 48 x 48 mm, ventilated cavity	48 mm
- Secondary waterproofing/covering layer on battens	3 mm
- Thermal insulation and battens (in both directions)	150–300 mm
- Concrete roof	200 mm
Total	*approx. 430–580 mm*

Wall construction
- Slates	35 mm
- Battens	24 mm
- Counter battens, ventilated cavity	48 mm
- Airtight membrane	1 mm
- Thermal insulation and battens (in both directions)	150–300 mm
- Concrete wall	200 mm
Total	*458–608 mm*

Pitched roof – warm deck, monopitch roof
Fibre-cement – facing masonry

Fig. 2: Beat Rothen: private house (Leibundgut), Uhwiesen (CH), 1997

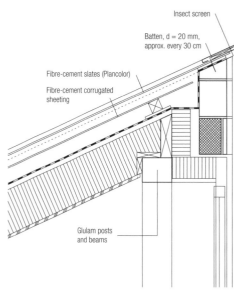

Insect screen

Batten, d = 20 mm, approx. every 30 cm

Fibre-cement slates (Plancolor)

Fibre-cement corrugated sheeting

Glulam posts and beams

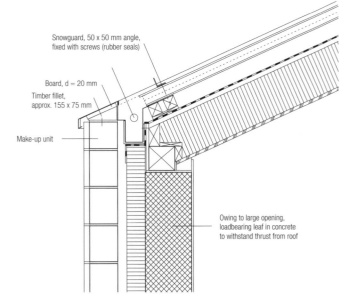

Snowguard, 50 x 50 mm angle, fixed with screws (rubber seals)

Board, d = 20 mm

Timber fillet, approx. 155 x 75 mm

Make-up unit

Owing to large opening, loadbearing leaf in concrete to withstand thrust from roof

Eaves

Ridge

Airtight membrane

The external cement bricks are open to diffusion. The (ventilated) cavity is only open at the base (weep holes) to water penetrating from outside.

Verge

Roof construction
- Roof covering: Eternit "Integraldach" system
- Fibre-cement slates (Plancolor)   7 mm
- Secondary waterproofing/covering layer of fibre-cement corrugated sheeting (Welleternit)   57 mm
- Horizontal battens, 60 x 60 mm   60 mm
- Birdsmouth rafter connection   20 mm
- Secondary waterproofing/covering layer (Pavatex)
- Rupli timber elements: Gutex softboard, structural timber members with Isofloc thermal insulation in between, 3-ply core plywood sprouce (vapourproof)   260 mm

Total   *404 mm*

Wall construction
- Facing masonry, cement bricks, 18 x 19 x 30 cm   180 mm
- Cavity   50 mm
- Thermal insulation   150–300 mm
- Clay masonry   150 mm
- Plaster   10 mm

Total   *540–690 mm*

Pitched roof – cold deck
Roof tiles – masonry in brickwork bond

Fig. 3: Gigon & Guyer: House C (CH), 1994

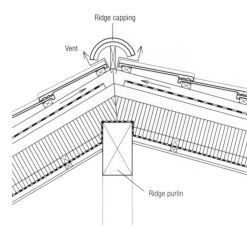

Ridge capping

Vent

Ridge purlin

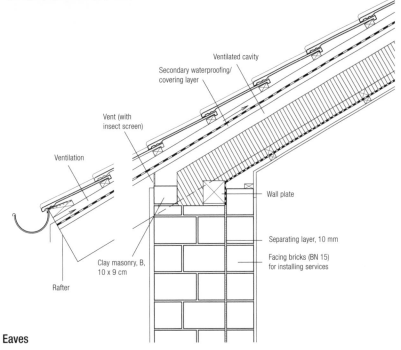

Ventilated cavity

Secondary waterproofing/
covering layer

Vent (with
insect screen)

Ventilation

Wall plate

Separating layer, 10 mm

Facing bricks (BN 15)
for installing services

Clay masonry, B,
10 x 9 cm

Rafter

Eaves   **Ridge**

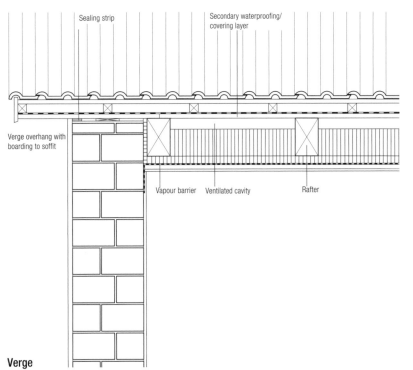

Sealing strip

Secondary waterproofing/
covering layer

Verge overhang with
boarding to soffit

Vapour barrier   Ventilated cavity   Rafter

Verge

Roof construction
- Concrete interlocking tiles	approx. 70 mm
- Tiling battens, 30 x 50 mm	30 mm
- Counter battens, 45 x 50 mm	45 mm
- Seamless secondary waterproofing/ covering layer on roof decking	22 mm
- Ventilated cavity	60 mm
- Thermal insulation, rockwool	140–260 mm
- Thermal insulation, rockwool	40 mm
- Vapour barrier	
- Battens, 24 x 48	24 mm
- Lining (plasterboard)	12.5 mm
Total	*approx. 440–560 mm*

Wall construction
- Render	25 mm
- Masonry in brickwork bond, Optitherm 15 and 23	390 mm
- Plaster	15 mm
Total	*430 mm*

Pitched roof – cold deck
Sheet metal – single-leaf masonry

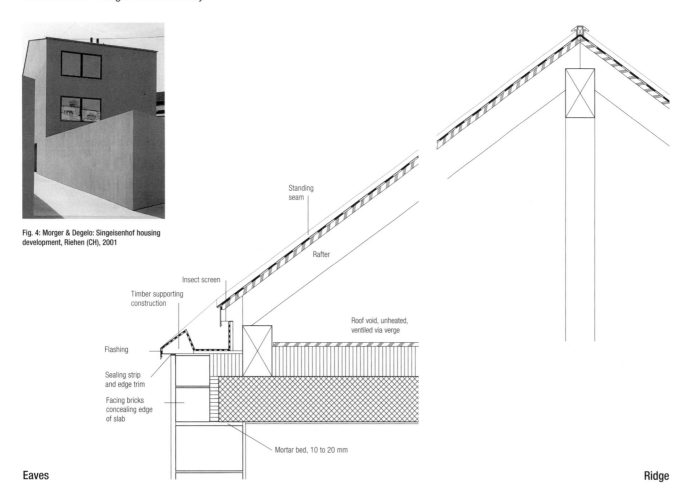

Fig. 4: Morger & Degelo: Singeisenhof housing
development, Riehen (CH), 2001

Standing seam

Rafter

Insect screen

Timber supporting construction

Flashing

Sealing strip and edge trim

Facing bricks concealing edge of slab

Roof void, unheated, ventiled via verge

Mortar bed, 10 to 20 mm

Eaves

Ridge

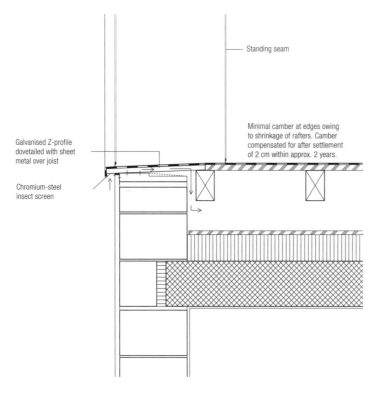

Standing seam

Galvanised Z-profile dovetailed with sheet metal over joist

Chromium-steel insect screen

Minimal camber at edges owing to shrinkage of rafters. Camber compensated for after settlement of 2 cm within approx. 2 years.

Verge

Roof construction (cold deck)
- Sheet copper, in bays with standing seams   0.6 mm
- Secondary waterproofing/covering layer, F3 film
- Roof decking   27 mm
- Rafters, 100 x 160 mm   160 mm

Total   *188 mm*

Floor construction (insulated)
- Chipboard   20 mm
- Insulation, rockwool   150–300 mm
- Concrete slab   240 mm
- Plaster   10 mm

Total   *420–570 mm*

Wall construction
- Render   25 mm
- Single-leaf masonry, ThermoCellit   365 mm
- Plaster   15 mm

Total   *405 mm*

Flat roof – warm deck
Bitumen – double-leaf masonry, rendered

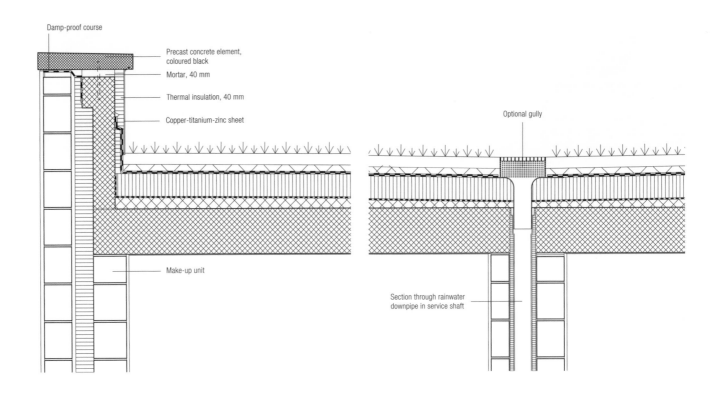

Damp-proof course

Precast concrete element, coloured black

Mortar, 40 mm

Thermal insulation, 40 mm

Copper-titanium-zinc sheet

Make-up unit

Optional gully

Section through rainwater downpipe in service shaft

Fig. 5: Ackermann & Friedli: Ackermättli School, Basel (CH), 1996

Roof construction

- Topsoil	60 mm
- Drainage/protection mat	35 mm
- Calendered polymeric roofing, 2 layers	
- Thermal insulation	150–300 mm
- Vapour barrier (Reasons: residual moisture in concrete, temporary roof during construction, protection, against vapour diffusion, especially at cracks and penetrations)	
- Screed laid to falls	30–60 mm
- Concrete slab	240 mm
- Plaster	5 mm
Total	*520–700 mm*

Wall construction

- Render	20 mm
- Clay masonry, B, 29 x 15 x 19 cm	150 mm
- Cavity (construction tolerance)	20 mm
- Thermal insulation	150–300 mm
- Clay masonry, B, 29 x 17.5 x 19 cm	175 mm
- Plaster	15 mm
Total	*530–680 mm*

Flat roof – warm deck
Bitumen – fair-face concrete with internal insulation

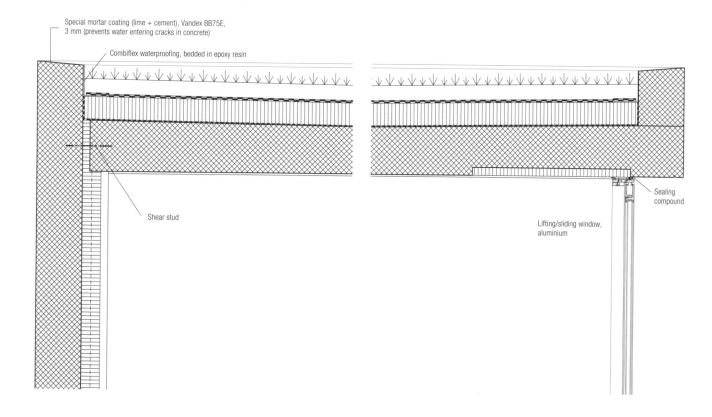

Special mortar coating (lime + cement), Vandex BB75E,
3 mm (prevents water entering cracks in concrete)

Combiflex waterproofing, bedded in epoxy resin

Shear stud

Sealing
compound

Lifting/sliding window,
aluminium

Fig. 6: Morger & Degelo: private house (Müller),
Staufen (CH), 1999

Roof construction
- Substrate for extensive planting	80 mm
- Bitumen roofing felt, 2 layers, EP3, EP4 (root-resistant)	7 mm
- Thermal insulation	150–300 mm
- Vapour barrier (Reasons: residual moisture in concrete, temporary roof during construction, protection, against vapour diffusion, especially at cracks and penetrations)	
- Concrete slab laid to falls	200–270 mm
- Plaster	5–10 mm
Total	*442–667 mm*

Wall construction
- Fair-face concrete	250 mm
- Internal insulation, extruded polystyrene	150–300 mm
- Plasterboard	40 mm
Total	*440–590 mm*

Flat roof – warm deck
Plastics – external cladding, heavyweight

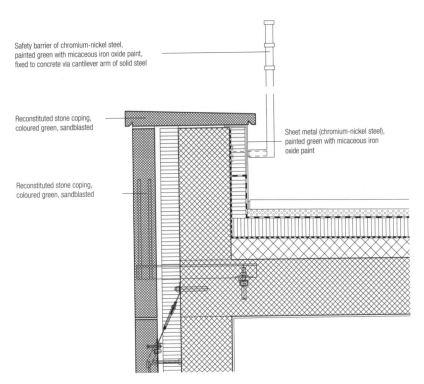

Safety barrier of chromium-nickel steel,
painted green with micaceous iron oxide paint,
fixed to concrete via cantilever arm of solid steel

Reconstituted stone coping,
coloured green, sandblasted

Reconstituted stone coping,
coloured green, sandblasted

Sheet metal (chromium-nickel steel),
painted green with micaceous iron
oxide paint

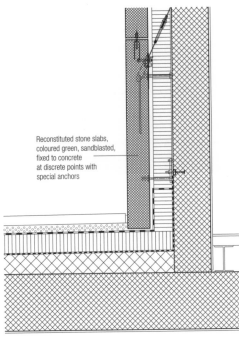

Reconstituted stone slabs,
coloured green, sandblasted,
fixed to concrete
at discrete points with
special anchors

Fig. 7: Diener & Diener: Warteckhof mixed
residential and commercial development, Basel
(CH), 1996

Roof construction
- Concrete flags	50 mm
- Gravel	40 mm
- Synthetic roofing felt	
- Thermal insulation	150–300 mm
- Vapour barrier	
- Screed laid to falls	20–80 mm
- Concrete slab	300 mm
- Plaster	5–10 mm
Total	*565–780 mm*

Wall construction
- Reconstituted stone slabs, coloured green, sandblasted	120 mm
- Cavity (construction tolerance)	30 mm
- Thermal insulation	150–300 mm
- Concrete wall	200 mm
- Plaster	10 mm
Total	*510–660 mm*

Flat roof – warm deck
Bitumen – non-loadbearing external wall

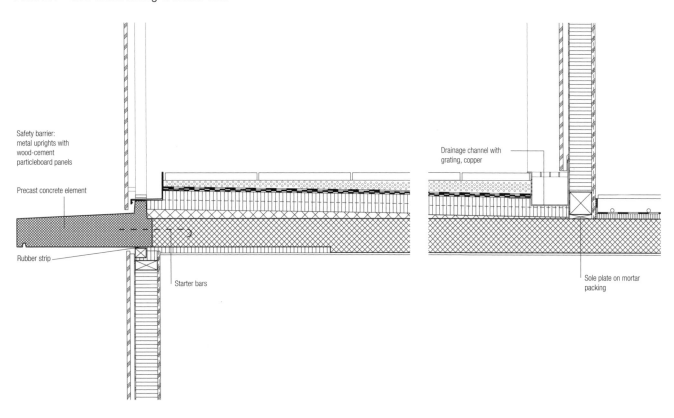

Safety barrier:
metal uprights with
wood-cement
particleboard panels

Precast concrete element

Rubber strip

Starter bars

Drainage channel with
grating, copper

Sole plate on mortar
packing

Fig. 8: Morger & Degelo: publicly assisted
housing, Basel (CH), 1993

Terrace construction

- Concrete flags laid horizontally	40 mm
- Chippings (to compensate for falls)	min. 30 mm
- Protective fleece	
- Waterproofing, 2 layers, bituminous, fully bonded	
- Cellular glass laid in hot bitumen	150 mm
- Screed laid to falls, 1.5%	20–60 mm
- Concrete slab	180 mm
- Plaster	10 mm
Total	*430–470 mm*

Wall construction

- Wood-cement particleboard	18 mm
- Ventilated cavity	23 mm
- Hardboard	5 mm
- Thermal insulation	150–300 mm
- Plywood	15 mm
Total	*211–361 mm*

Flat roof – upside-down roof
Bitumen – external insulation, rendered

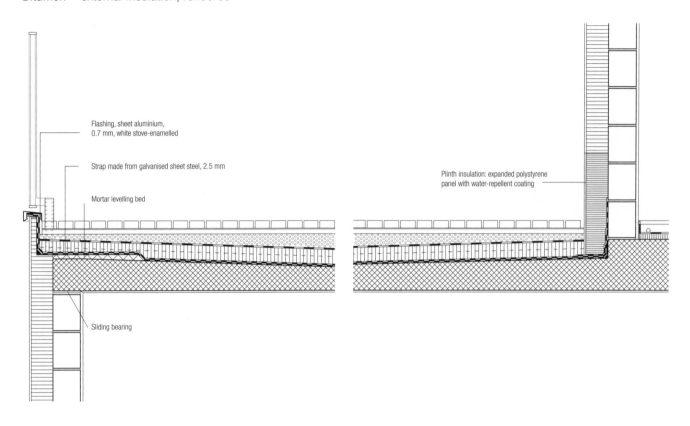

Flashing, sheet aluminium,
0.7 mm, white stove-enamelled

Strap made from galvanised sheet steel, 2.5 mm

Mortar levelling bed

Plinth insulation: expanded polystyrene
panel with water-repellent coating

Sliding bearing

**Fig. 9: Oliver Schwarz architectural practice:
Peter apartment block, Rüschlikon (CH), 1997**

Roof construction
- Okoume battens	40 mm
- Okoume supporting battens	30 mm
- Fine chippings, bonded	40–90 mm
- Protective fleece	
- Thermal insulation, extruded polystyrene	150–300 mm
- Calendered polymeric roofing, 2 layers	
- Concrete slab laid to falls	120–170 mm
- Plaster	5–10 mm
Total	*385–640 mm*

Wall construction
- Render (depends on system)	5 mm
- External insulation, extruded polystyrene	150–300 mm
- Clay masonry	150 mm
- Plaster	15 mm
Total	*320–470 mm*

Flat roof – cold deck, uncoated roof
Bitumen – timber platform frame construction

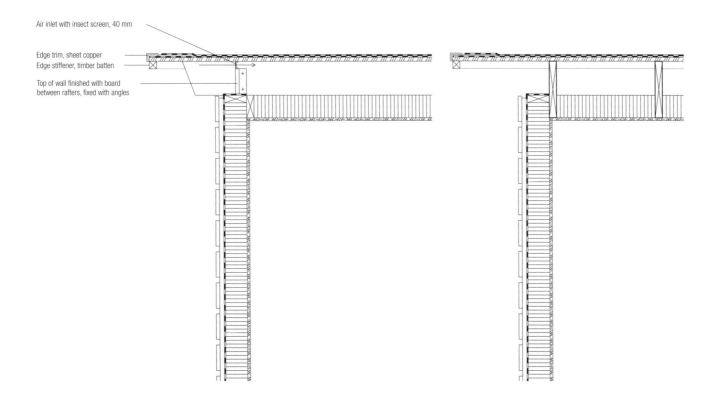

Air inlet with insect screen, 40 mm

Edge trim, sheet copper
Edge stiffener, timber batten

Top of wall finished with board
between rafters, fixed with angles

Fig. 10: Morger & Degelo: temporary nursery
school, Basel (CH), 1993

Roof construction
- Granule-surfaced bitumen felt, 2 layers
- Plywood   21 mm
- Timber joists, 40 x 300 mm   300–450 mm
  with 150 mm cavity,
  and 150–300 mm thermal insulation in between
- Plywood (airtight membrane)   15 mm

Total   *336–486 mm*

Wall construction
- Horizontal boarding externally, rough finish   21 mm
- Vertical boarding with ventilated cavity   24 mm
- Protective layer to thermal insulation
- Timber frame,
  with thermal insulation in between   150–300 mm
- Plywood (airtight membrane)   15 mm

Total   *210–360 mm*

Flat roof – warm deck
suitable/unsuitable for foot traffic

Fig. 11: Bearth & Deplazes: private house
"In den Lachen", Chur (CH), 1997

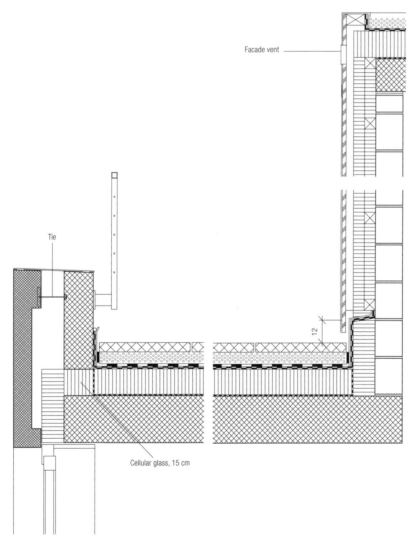

**Warm deck,
unsuitable for foot traffic
Verge**

Facade vent

Tie

Cellular glass, 15 cm

12

**Warm deck, suitable for foot traffic,
parapet; longitudinal section**

**Warm deck, suitable for foot traffic
Junction with rooftop structure**

Roof construction
- Drainage mat	50 mm
- Protective mat	13 mm
- Waterproofing	
- Thermal insulation	150–300 mm
- Vapour barrier	
- Reinforced concrete slab	180 mm

Wall construction
- Sheet aluminium	
- Open boarding or backing panel	22 mm
- Ventilated cavity (vertical battens)	40 mm
- Thermal insulation, laid cross-wise,	
2 layers	150–300 mm
- Clay brickwork type B	150 mm

Roof construction, adjacent to parapet
- Concrete flags, 50 x 50 cm	50 mm
- Chippings (drainage layer)	60 mm
- Rubber mat	13 mm
- Waterproofing (Sarnafil TG 63 – 13)	
- Thermal insulation	150–300 mm
- Vapour barrier	
- Calendered polymeric roofing laid in hot bitumen	
- Reinforced concrete slab (fall: 0.5 %)	200–500 mm

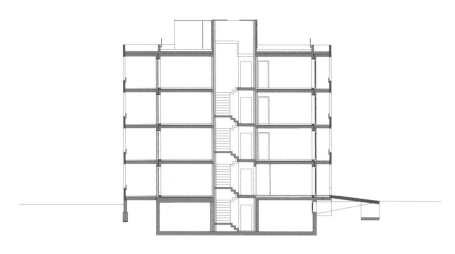

Section

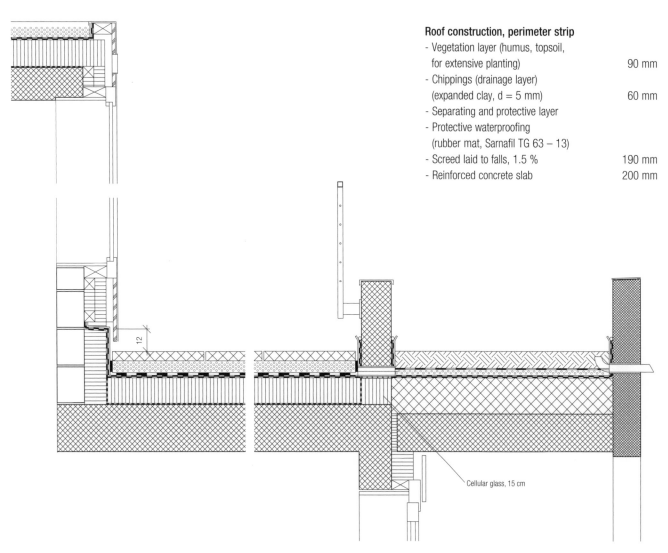

Roof construction, perimeter strip
- Vegetation layer (humus, topsoil,
  for extensive planting)   90 mm
- Chippings (drainage layer)
  (expanded clay, d = 5 mm)   60 mm
- Separating and protective layer
- Protective waterproofing
  (rubber mat, Sarnafil TG 63 – 13)
- Screed laid to falls, 1.5 %   190 mm
- Reinforced concrete slab   200 mm

12

Cellular glass, 15 cm

Warm deck, suitable for foot traffic,
terrace

Roof, perimeter strip, with planting
Section

Flat roof – cold deck

Fig. 12: Gigon & Guyer: Kirchner Museum,
Davos (CH), 1992

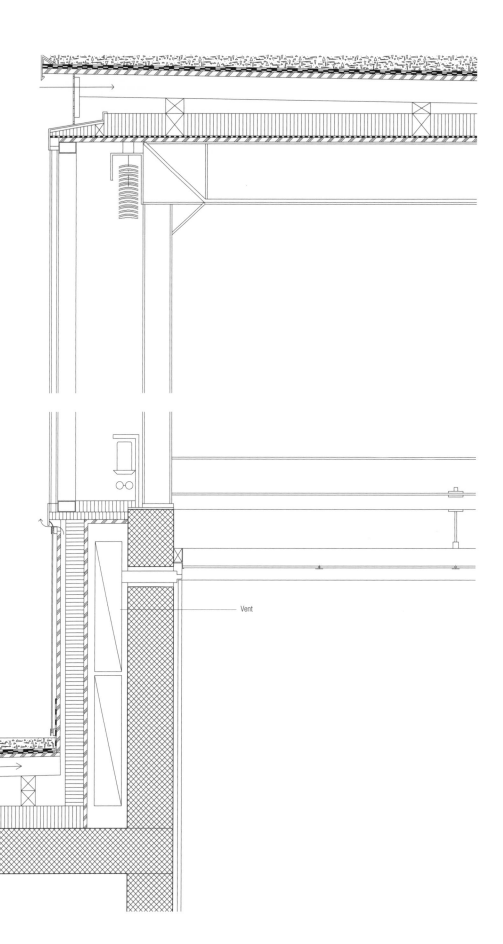

Vent

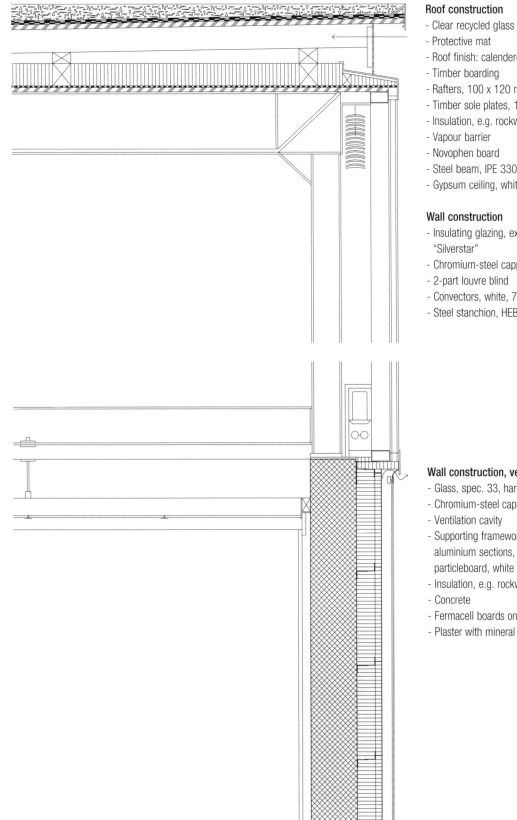

Roof construction

- Clear recycled glass   60 mm
- Protective mat   10 mm
- Roof finish: calendered polymeric roofing, 2 layers
- Timber boarding   27 mm
- Rafters, 100 x 120 mm   120 mm
- Timber sole plates, 100 x 120 mm   120 mm
- Insulation, e.g. rockwool   150–300 mm
- Vapour barrier
- Novophen board   25 mm
- Steel beam, IPE 330   330 mm
- Gypsum ceiling, white   15 mm

Wall construction

- Insulating glazing, extra-clear, acid-etched, "Silverstar"   2 x 6 mm
- Chromium-steel capping
- 2-part louvre blind
- Convectors, white, 70 x 100 mm   100 mm
- Steel stanchion, HEB 160   160 mm

Wall construction, ventilated facade

- Glass, spec. 33, hardened, acid-etched   6 mm
- Chromium-steel capping
- Ventilation cavity
- Supporting framework:
  aluminium sections, white, wood cement
  particleboard, white   35 mm
- Insulation, e.g. rockwool   150–300 mm
- Concrete   250 mm
- Fermacell boards on battens   15 mm
- Plaster with mineral paint finish

Flat roof – upside-down roof
with rooftop planting

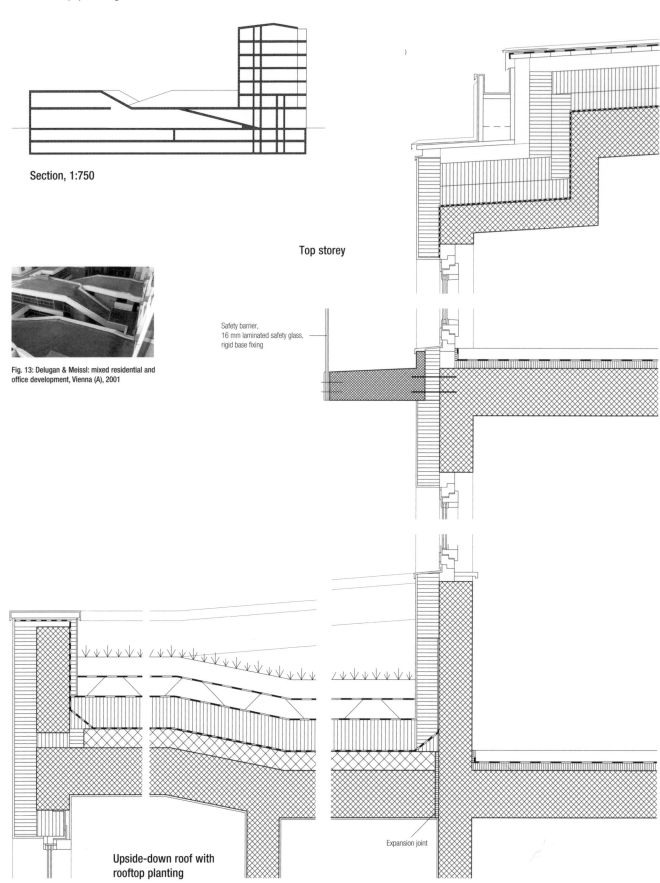

Section, 1:750

Fig. 13: Delugan & Meissl: mixed residential and office development, Vienna (A), 2001

Top storey

Safety barrier,
16 mm laminated safety glass,
rigid base fixing

Expansion joint

Upside-down roof with rooftop planting

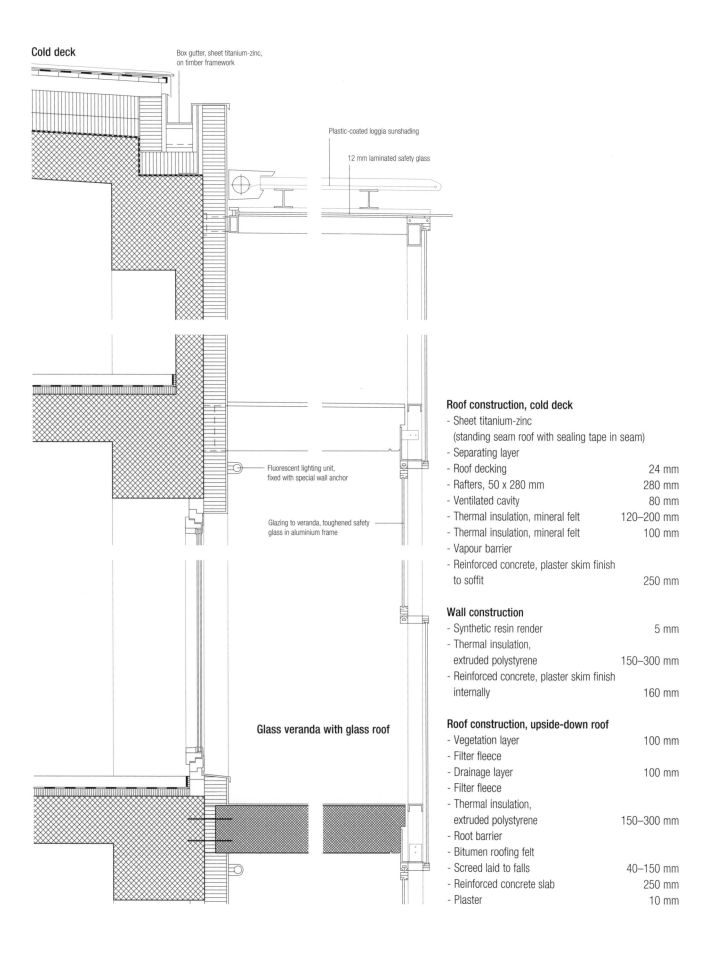

Cold deck

Box gutter, sheet titanium-zinc,
on timber framework

Plastic-coated loggia sunshading

12 mm laminated safety glass

Fluorescent lighting unit,
fixed with special wall anchor

Glazing to veranda, toughened safety
glass in aluminium frame

Glass veranda with glass roof

Roof construction, cold deck
- Sheet titanium-zinc
  (standing seam roof with sealing tape in seam)
- Separating layer
- Roof decking   24 mm
- Rafters, 50 x 280 mm   280 mm
- Ventilated cavity   80 mm
- Thermal insulation, mineral felt   120–200 mm
- Thermal insulation, mineral felt   100 mm
- Vapour barrier
- Reinforced concrete, plaster skim finish
  to soffit   250 mm

Wall construction
- Synthetic resin render   5 mm
- Thermal insulation,
  extruded polystyrene   150–300 mm
- Reinforced concrete, plaster skim finish
  internally   160 mm

Roof construction, upside-down roof
- Vegetation layer   100 mm
- Filter fleece
- Drainage layer   100 mm
- Filter fleece
- Thermal insulation,
  extruded polystyrene   150–300 mm
- Root barrier
- Bitumen roofing felt
- Screed laid to falls   40–150 mm
- Reinforced concrete slab   250 mm
- Plaster   10 mm

APPENDIX

Further reading

I. Theory and history of design

Centre Georges Pompidou (pub.): *L'art de l'ingénieur: constructeur, entrepreneur, inventeur*, Paris, 1997

Edward R. Ford: *The Details of Modern Architecture I & II*, Cambridge, Mass., 1990; Basel, Boston, Berlin, 1994

Kenneth Frampton: *Studies in Tectonic Culture*, Harvard, 1985

Rainer Graefe (ed.): *Zur Geschichte des Konstruierens*, Stuttgart, 1989

Hans Kollhoff (ed.): *Über Tektonik in der Baukunst*, Braunschweig, Wiesbaden, 1993

Miron Mislin: *Geschichte der Baukonstruktion und Bautechnik*, vol. 1: *Antike bis Renaissance*, vol. 2: *Barock bis Neuzeit*, Düsseldorf, 1997

Christian Norberg-Schulz: *Logik der Baukunst*, Bauwelt Fundamente, vol. 15, Berlin, 1965

Gottfried Semper: *Style: Style in the Technical and Tectonic Arts; Or, Practical Aesthetics*, Harry Francis Mallgrave (ed.), Los Angeles, 2004

Konrad Wachsmann: *The Turning Point in Building*, Stuttgart, 1989

II. General design textbooks

Oskar Büttner, Erhard Hampe: *Bauwerk Tragwerk Tragstruktur*, Berlin, 1985

Heino Engel: *Tragsysteme*, Ostfildern-Ruit, 1997

Ruedi Hungerbühler: *Konstruktion im Hochbau. Rohbauelemente, Montagebau, Aufbau*, Zurich, Dietikon, 1983

Interkantonales Lehrmittel Kollegium: *Konstruktionslehre Hochbau*, vol. 1 and vol. 2, Zurich, 2001

Pier Luigi Nervi: *Neue Strukturen*, Stuttgart, 1963

Ernst Neufert: *Bauentwurfslehre*, Braunschweig, Wiesbaden, 2002

Dietrich Neumann, Ulrich Weinbrenner: *Frick/Knöll/Baukonstruktionslehre*, vol. 1, Stuttgart, Leipzig, Wiesbaden, 2002

Dietrich Neumann, Ulrich Weinbrenner, Ulf Hestermann, Ludwig Rongen: *Frick/Knöll/Baukonstruktionslehre*, vol. 2, Stuttgart, Leipzig, Wiesbaden, 2003

Heinz Ronner: *Baukonstruktion im Kontext des architektonischen Entwerfens. Decke, Boden*, Basel, 1991

Heinz Ronner: *Baukonstruktion im Kontext des architektonischen Entwerfens. Haus, Dächer*, Basel, 1991

Heinz Ronner: *Baukonstruktion im Kontext des architektonischen Entwerfens. Haus, Sockel*, Basel, 1991

Heinz Ronner: *Baukonstruktion im Kontext des architektonischen Entwerfens. Öffnungen*, Basel, 1991

Heinz Ronner: *Baukonstruktion im Kontext des architektonischen Entwerfens. Wand, Mauer*, Basel, 1991

Heinz Ronner, Fredi Kölliker, Emil Rysler: *Baukonstruktion im Kontext des architektonischen Entwerfens. Zirkulation, Baustruktur, Zahn der Zeit*, Basel, 1994

Arthur Rüegg, Swiss Federal Institute of Technology Chair of Architecture and Technology III+IV, current lecture manuscripts

Heinrich Schmitt, Andreas Heene: *Hochbaukonstruktion. Die Bauteile und das Baugefüge, Grundlagen des heutigen Bauens*, Wiesbaden, 2001

René Vittone: *Bâtir – Manuel de la construction*, Lausanne, 1996

Pierre Zoelly: *Terratektur – Einstieg in die unterirdische Architektur*, Basel, 1989

III. Construction methods

Joachim Achtziger, Günter Pfeifer, Rolf Ramcke, Konrad Zilch: *Masonry Construction Manual*, Basel, 2001

David P. Billington: *Robert Maillart and the Art of Reinforced Concrete*, Cambridge, Mass., 1991

Tanja Brotrück: *Basics Roof Construction*, Basel, 2006

Hans Busso von Busse, Nils Valerian Waubke, Rudolf Grimme, Jürgen Mertins: *Atlas Flache Dächer, Nutzbare Flächen*, Basel, 2000

Cleo Baldon, Ib Melchior: *Steps & Stairways*, New York, 1989

Gert Chesi: *Architektur und Mythos – Lehmbauten in Afrika*, Innsbruck, 1995

August Ferdinand Fleischinger, W. A. Becker: *Die Mauer-Verbände. Klassische Vorlagenbücher für den Praktiker*, vol. 6, Hanover, 1993

Wolfram Graubner: *Holzverbindungen – Gegenüberstellungen japanischer und europäischer Lösungen*, Stuttgart, 1986

Friedrich Grimm: *Konstruieren mit Walzprofilen*, Berlin, 2003

Herbert and Astrid Gruber: *Bauen mit Stroh*, Staufen i. Brsg., 2000

Franz Hart, Walter Henn, Hansjürgen Sontag: *Stahlbau Atlas: Geschossbauten*, Munich, 1982

Manfred Hegger, Volker Auch-Schwelk, Matthias Fuchs, Thorsten Rosenkranz: *Construction Materials Manual*, Basel, 2006

Manfred Hegger, Matthias Fuchs, Thomas Stark, Martin Zeumer: *Energy Manual*, Basel, 2008

Thomas Herzog, Roland Krippner, Werner Lang: *Facade Construction Manual*, Basel, 2004

Friedbert Kind-Barkauskas, Bruno Kauhsen, Stefan Polónyi, Jörg Brandt: *Concrete Construction Manual*, Basel, 2002

Ulrich Knaack: *Konstruktiver Glasbau*, Cologne, 1998

Josef Kolb: *Systembau mit Holz*, Zurich, 1992

Heinz W. Krewinkel: *Glass Buildings – Material, Structure and Detail*, Basel, 1998

Nils Kummer: *Basics Masonry Construction*, Basel, 2007

Alfred Meistermann: *Basics Loadbearing Systems*, Basel, 2007

Florian Musso, Roland Krippner: *Basics Facade Apertures*, Basel, 2008

Julius Natterer, Thomas Herzog, Michael Volz, Wolfgang Winter: *Timber Construction Manual*, Basel, 2003

Günter Pfeifer, Antje Liebers, Holger Reiners: *Der neue Holzbau*, Munich, 1998

Andrew Plumridge, Wim Meulenkamp: *Brickwork: Architecture & Design*, New York, 1993

Eckhard Reyer, Kai Schild, Stefan Völkner: *Kompendium der Dämmstoffe*, Stuttgart, 2002

Christian Schittich, Dieter Balkow, Gerald Staib, Matthias Schuler, Werner Sobek: *Glass Construction Manual*, Basel, 2006

Fritz Schumacher: *Das Wesen des neuzeitlichen Backsteinbaues*, Munich, 1985

Helmut C. Schulitz, Werner Sobek, Karl Habermann: *Steel Construction Manual*, Basel, 2001

Eberhard Schunck, Hans Jochen Oster, Rainer Barthel, Kurt Kiessl: *Roof Construction Manual – Pitched Roofs*, Basel, 2002

Swiss School of Engineering for the Wood Industry: *Mehrgeschossiger Holzhausbau*, Biel, 1997

Ludwig Steiger: *Basics Timber Construction*, Basel, 2007

John A. Templer: *The Staircase: Studies of Hazards, Falls, and Safer Design*, Cambridge, 1992

René Walther: *Bauen mit Beton – Einführung für Architekten und Bauingenieure*, Berlin, 1997

Michael Wigginton: *Glass in Architecture*, London, 2002

Jan Wurm: *Glass Structures: Design and Construction of Self-supporting Skins*, Basel, 2007

Klaus Zwerger: *Wood and Wood Joints*, Basel, 1997

Picture credits

How to use this book

10.1: Prof. Deplazes, based on a statement by Kenneth Frampton.

12.2: Wolfgang Lauber (ed.): *Architektur der Dogon – Traditioneller Lehmbau und Kunst der Mali*, Prestel Verlag. Munich, 1998, p. 58. Photo: Wolfgang Lauber.

12.3: Joachim Achtziger, Günter Pfeifer, Rolf Ramcke, Konrad Zilch: *Masonry Construction Manual*, Birkhäuser Publishers. Basel, 2001, p. 30. Photo: Ulrike Enders.

12.4: Source unknown

12.5: Source unknown

12.6: Annegret Burg: Kollhoff – *Architekten Kollhoff und Timmermann*, Birkhäuser Publishers. Basel, 1998, p. 63. Photo: Schwendinger & Büttner.

MATERIALS – MODULES

Masonry

22.1: Ekkehard Mai (ed.): *Das Capriccio als Kunstprinzip*, SKIRA Verlag. Milan, 1996.

23.2–5: Photo: Ákos Moravánszky.

24.6: *Detail*, No. 1/2. Munich, 2002, p. 30.

24.7–25.11: Photo: Ákos Moravánszky.

26.12: *SITE*: Architecture as Art, Academy Editions. London, 1980, p. 36. Photo: SITE, courtesy Ronald Feldman Fine Arts, New York.

26.13: Photo: Ákos Moravánszky.

26.14: John Wilton-Ely: *Giovanni Battista Piranesi – Vision und Werk*, Hirmer Verlag. Munich, 1978, p. 62.

26.15: Photo: Ákos Moravánszky.

27.16: Werner Lindner, Friedrich Tamms: *Mauerwerk*, Alfred Metzner Verlag. Berlin, 1938, p. 132.

27.17–29.21: Photo: Ákos Moravánszky.

29.22: *Detail*, No. 1/2. Munich, 2002, p. 38.

29.23: Photo: Ákos Moravánszky.

29.24: Eladio Dieste: *La Estructura Ceramica*. Bogotá, 1987, p. 132, Fig. 14.

30.25–26: Photo: Ákos Moravánszky.

31.27: Source unknown

31.28–30: Photo: Stahlton AG, Zurich.

32.31: Andrew Plumridge, Wim Meulenkamp: *Brickwork: Architecture & Design*, New York, 1993, p. 83.

32.32: Joachim Achtziger, Günter Pfeifer, Rolf Ramcke, Konrad Zilch: *Masonry Construction Manual*, Birkhäuser Publishers. Basel, 2001, p. 79.

33.33–34: Prof. Deplazes. Graphic: Maud Châtelet.

35.35: Werner Blaser: *Mies van der Rohe – Die Kunst der Struktur*, Artemis Verlag. Zurich, 1996, p. 20/21. Fig.: © 2013, ProLitteris, Zurich.

36.36–37.42: Prof. Deplazes. Graphic: Barbara Wiskemann.

37.43: Andrew Plumridge, Wim Meulenkamp: *Brickwork: Architecture & Design*, New York, 1993, p. 81.

37.44: Annegret Burg: Kollhoff – *Architekten Kollhoff und Timmermann*, Birkhäuser Publishers. Basel, 1998, p. 92.

37.45: Prof. Deplazes.

37.46: Joachim Achtziger, Günter Pfeifer, Rolf Ramcke, Konrad Zilch: *Masonry Construction Manual*, Birkhäuser Publishers. Basel, 2001, p. 39. Photo: Rolf Ramcke.

38.47–49: Prof. Deplazes. Graphic: Barbara Wiskemann.

38.50: Andrew Plumridge, Wim Meulenkamp: *Brickwork: Architecture & Design*, New York, 1993, p. 86.

38.51: August Ferdinand Fleischinger, W. A. Becker: *Die Mauer-Verbände. Klassische Vorlagenbücher für den Praktiker*, vol. 6, Verlag Th. Schäfer. Hannover, 1993, pl. 2. Photo: August Ferdinand Fleischinger, W. A. Becker.

38.52–53: Joachim Achtziger, Günter Pfeifer, Rolf Ramcke, Konrad Zilch: *Masonry Construction Manual*, Birkhäuser Publishers. Basel, 2001, p. 101, p. 35.

39.54–56: Keller AG brickworks, catalogue: *Wall ties*, 9/98. Pfungen, 1998, p. 6 and p. 1.

39.57 left and right: Keller AG brickworks, catalogue: *Wall ties*, 9/99. Pfungen, 1999, p. 1.

40.58: Source unknown

40.59: Source unknown

41.60: Maija Holma, Markku Lahti: *Alvar Aalto – eine sensiblere Struktur für das Leben*, Rakennustieto Oy. Helsinki, 1996, p. 85. Photo: Maija Holma.

42.61: Fritz Schumacher: *Das Wesen des neuzeitlichen Backsteinbaues*, Callwey Verlag. Munich, 1985, p. 103.

42.62: Photo: Hild und K Architekten, Munich.

43.63: Piergiacomo Bucciarelli: *Fritz Höger: hanseatischer Baumeister*, 1877–1949, Vice Versa Verlag. Berlin, 1992, p. 41.

43.64: Wilfried Wang: *Architect Sigurd Lewerentz*, Arkitekturmuseet Archivet Stockholm. Buggförlaget, 1997, vol. 1, photos of the work, p. 168. Photo: Fabio Galli.

44.65: Heinz Ronner: *Wand, Mauer*, Birkhäuser Publishers. Basel, 1991, p. 49.

44.66: Wolfgang Voigt (ed.): *Heinz Bienefeld, 1926–1995*, vol. 3, Deutsches Architektur Museum, exhibition catalogue. Frankfurt a. M., 1999, p. 100. Photo: Lukas Roth.

45.67: Photo: Ralph Feiner.

45.68: Annegret Burg: *Kollhoff – Architekten Kollhoff und Timmermann*, Birkhäuser Publishers. Basel, 1998, p. 82. Photo: Heinrich Helfenstein.

45.69: Alejandro de la Sota: *Alejandro de la Sota Architect*, Ediciones Pronaos. Madrid, 1989, p. 35. Photo: Alejandro de la Sota.

46.70 left and right: Benedetto Gravagnuolo: *Adolf Loos – Theory and Works*, Löcker Verlag. Vienna, 1982, p. 195. Fig.: © 2013, ProLitteris, Zurich.

46.71 top: H. Allen Brooks: *The Le Corbusier Archive: Le Corbusier*. Ahmedabad, 1953–1960, Le Corbusier Foundation. Paris, 1983, p. 118. Fig.: © FLC / 2013, ProLitteris, Zurich.

46.71 bottom: Willy Boesiger: *Le Corbusier + Son Atelier Rue De Sevres 35 – Œuvre Complète*, 1952–57, Editions Girsberger. Zurich, 1957, p. 116. Fig.: © FLC / 2013, ProLitteris, Zurich.

47.72: Joachim Driller: *Marcel Breuer: Die Wohnhäuser 1923–1973*, Deutsche Verlags-Anstalt. Munich, 1998, p. 155.

47.73: David Masello: *Marcel Breuer & Herbert Beckhard – Die Landhäuser, 1945–1984*, Birkhäuser Publishers. Basel, 1996, p. 14. Photo: Museum of Modern Art, N.Y.

48.74 left and right: Jonas Geist: *Karl Friedrich Schinkel – Die Bauakademie. Eine Vergegenwärtigung*, S. Fischer Verlag. Frankfurt a. M., 1993, p. 53 and p. 40.

49.75–76: Keller AG brickworks, Pfungen, catalogue: *preton-Wandelemente*, Merkur Druck. Langental, 2000.

50.77: Burkard Meyer Architekten, Baden. Photo: Reinhard Zimmermann.

50.78–79: Burkard Meyer Architekten, Baden.

50.80: Burkard Meyer Architekten, Baden. Graphic: preton, Wandelemente.

51.81–82: Hans Kollhoff.

52.83–84: Chair of Architecture & Digital Fabrication, D_ARCH, Swiss Federal Institute of Technology, Zurich.

53.85: Gramazio & Kohler Architekten.

53.86: Margarete Kühn (ed.): *Karl Friedrich Schinkel, Lebenswerk. Die Reise nach Frankreich und England im Jahre 1826*, Dt. Kunstverlag. Munich, Berlin 1990, p. 84.

53.87–88: Bearth & Deplazes Architekten.

54.89: Peter Nigst (ed.): *Rafael Moneo. Bauen für die Stadt*, Gerd Hatje Verlag. Stuttgart 1993, p. 51. Photo: Rafael Moneo.

54.90: Photo: Rafael Moneo.

54.91 left: *El Croquis*, Nos 19–22, El Croquis Editorial. Madrid 1985, p. 108.

54.91 right: Luis Fernandez-Galiano (ed.): *A&V Monografias de Architectura y Vivienda*, No. 36. Madrid 1992, p. 9.

55.92–96: Rossbauer, Brnic, Graf Architekten / Swiss Federal Institute of Technology, Zurich.

Concrete

56.1: James Gilchrist Wilson: *Sichtflächen des Betons*, Bauverlag. Wiesbaden-Berlin, 1967, p. 41.

57.2: Philip Jodidio: *Tadao Ando*, Taschen-Verlag. Cologne, 1997, p. 68. Photo: Tomio Ohashi.

58.3: Thomas Boga: *Die Architektur von Rudolf Olgiati*, gta Verlag. Zurich, 1977, p. 181.

58.4: Centre Georges Pompidou (ed.): *L'art de l'ingénieur: constructeur, entrepreneur, inventeur*, Editions du Centre Georges Pompidou. Paris, 1997, p. 80.

59.5: Hazan Institut Français d'Architecture: *Le Béton en représentation*, Editions Hazan. Paris, 1993, p. 136. Photo: A. Jesta, Gênes, épreuve 28 x 23 cm. © Fonds Perret (535 AP) et Hennebique (761fa).

59.6: Potsdam Astrophysical Institute: *Der Einsteinturm in Potsdam – Architektur und Astrophysik*. Ars Nicolai. Berlin, 1995, p. 101.

60.7: W. Schrämli: *Beton-Praxis: der Weg zum dauerhaften Beton*, HOLCIM (Schweiz) AG. Zurich, 1997, p. 24.

61.8–11: loc. cit., p. 14.

62.12: *Betonpraxis. Der Weg zum dauerhaften Beton*, Holcim (Switzerland) AG. Zurich, 2003, p. 19.

63.13: René Walther: *Bauen mit Beton – Einführung für Architekten und Bauingenieure*, Ernst und Sohn Verlag. Berlin, 1997, p. 125.

63.14: Photo: Holzco-Doka Schalungstechnik, Niderhasli.

63.15: René Walther: Loco citato, p. 121.

64.16–17: Roland Schmitt: *Die Schalungstechnik – Systeme, Einsatz und Logistik*, Ernst und Sohn Verlag. Berlin, 2001, p. 266, 512.

65.18: W. Schrämli: *Beton-Praxis: der Weg zum dauerhaften Beton*, HOLCIM (Schweiz) AG. Zurich, 1997, p. 47.

65.19–20: Prof. Deplazes. Graphic: Maud Châtelet.

66.21: Technical Research & Advice Centre of the Swiss Cement Industry: *Cement Bulletin*, No. 16. Wildegg, 1987.

67.22: Rudolf Olgiati: *Eine Streitschrift*, Verlag Magazin + Buch. Stuttgart, 1994, p. 26. Photo: Judith M. Gieshuber.

67.23: Friedbert Kind-Barkauskas, Bruno Kauhsen, Stefan Polónyi, Jörg Brandt: *Concrete Construction Manual*, Birkhäuser Publishers. Basel, 2002, p. 193. Photo: Christian Schittich.

68.24–25: James G. Wilson: *Sichtflächen des Betons*, Bauverlag. Wiesbaden-Berlin, 1967, p. 45.

68.26: David Bruce Brownlee, David G. De Long: *Louis I. Kahn – In the Realm of Architecture*, The Museum of Contemporary Art. Los Angeles, 1991, pp. 182–83. Photo: Grant Mudford.

68.27: Günter Rapp: *Technik des Sichtbetons*, Beton-Verlag. Düsseldorf, 1969, p. 21. © Verlag Bau und Technik.

68.28: Loco citato, p. 216.

68.29: Loco citato, p. 226.

69.30: Prof. Keller, Faculty of Building Physics, Swiss Federal Institute of Technology, Zurich.

69.31: Graphic: Aschwanden AG, Lyss.

69.32: Prof. Deplazes. Photo: Thomas Melliger.

69.33: Prof. Keller, Faculty of Building of Building Physics, Swiss Federal Institute of Technology, Zurich.

69.34: Prof. Deplazes. Graphic: Thomas Melliger.

69.35: Photo: Schöck-ebea AG, Aarau.

69.36: Graphic: Aschwanden AG, Lyss.

69.37: Prof. Keller, Faculty of Building of Building Physics, Swiss Federal Institute of Technology, Zurich.

69.38–70.40: Prof. Deplazes. Graphic: Thomas Melliger.

70.41–42: Graphic: Halfen Deha, Dällikon.

70.43 Photos: Elemente AG, Veltheim.

71.44–47: Prof. Deplazes. Graphic: Thomas Melliger.

71.48: Graphic: Halfen Deha, Dällikon.

71.49: Prof. Deplazes. Photos: Thomas Melliger.

72.50: Prof. Deplazes.

73.51: René Walther: *Bauen mit Beton – Einführung für Architekten und Bauingenieure*, Ernst und Sohn Verlag. Berlin, 1997, p. 140.

73.52: Friedbert Kind-Barkauskas, Bruno Kauhsen, Stefan Polónyi, Jörg Brandt: *Concrete Construction Manual*, Birkhäuser Publishers, 2002, p. 271.

73.53: Loco citato, p. 60.

73.54: Loco citato, p. 206.

74.55: René Walther: *Bauen mit Beton – Einführung für Architekten und Bauingenieure*, Ernst und Sohn Verlag. Berlin, 1997, p. 309.

74.56: Loco citato, p. 181.

74.57: Institut Français D'Architecture (ed.): *Les Frères Perret*, Editions Norma. Paris, 2000, p. 94. © Auguste Perret, UFSE, SAIF, 2004.

74.58: Herman Hertzberger: *Lessons for Students in Architecture*, 010 Publishers. Rotterdam, 1998, p. 128. Photo: Jan Versnel.

75.59–61: Heino Engel: *Tragsysteme*, Hatje Verlag. Ostfildern-Ruit, 1997, p. 207.

75.62: Otto Künzle: *Tragkonstruktionen IV. Sommersemester 2. Jahreskurs – Stahlbeton*, Faculty of Architecture, Swiss Federal Institute of Technology, Zurich, p. 138.

75.63: Friedbert Kind-Barkauskas, Bruno Kauhsen, Stefan Polónyi, Jörg Brandt: *Concrete Construction Manual*, Birkhäuser Publishers. Basel 2002, p. 21.

75.64: Johann Christoph Bürkle: *Morger & Degelo Architekten*, Niggli Verlag. Sulgen, 2000, p. 141. Photo: Michael Fontana.

76.65–66: René Walther: *Bauen mit Beton – Einführung für Architekten und Bauingenieure*, Ernst und Sohn Verlag. Berlin, 1997, p. 251.

76.67: Loco citato, p. 253.

76.68: Christoph Luchsinger: *Hans Hofmann – vom Neuen Bauen zur neuen Baukunst*, gta Verlag. Zurich, 1985, p. 112.

76.69: David P. Billington: *Robert Maillart and the Art of Reinforced Concrete*, Cambridge, Mass., 1991, p. 105.

76.70: Ekkehard Ramm, E. Schunck, (eds.): *Heinz Isler – Schalen*. Exhibition Catalogue, Gesellschaft für Ingenieurbaukunst, Swiss Federal Institute of Technology, Zurich, 2002, p. 61. © Gesellschaft für Ingenieurbaukunst.

76.71: René Walther: Loco citato, p. 262.

Timber

78.1, 79.2: Bearth + Deplazes. Photo: Timo Allemann.
80.3: Josef Kolb: *Systembau mit Holz*, Baufachverlag. Zurich, 1992, p. 23.
81.4–5: Bearth + Deplazes.
82.6: Lignum, Swiss Timber Study Group, Zurich.
83.7: Prof. Deplazes. Graphic: Maud Châtelet.
83.8: Prof. Deplazes.
83.9: Prof. Deplazes. Graphic: Maud Châtelet.
83.10–11: Swiss standard SIA 265/1: Holzbau: Schnittarten. 4.2262 Kantholz und Latten, Schweizer Ingenieur- und Architektenverein. Zurich, p. 52.
84.12: Photos: Lignum, Swiss Timber Study Group, catalogue: *Lignatec 10/2000. Holzfaserprodukte*. Zurich, 2000, p. 4.
85.13: Karl-Heinz Götz, Dieter Hoor: *Holzbau Atlas*, Institut für internationale Architektur-Dokumentation. Munich, 1978, p. 21.
85.14: Prof. Deplazes. Graphic: Daniel Gut.
85.15: Karl-Heinz Götz, Dieter Hoor, Loco citato.
86.16: Günter Pfeifer, Antje Liebers, Holger Reiners: *Der neue Holzbau*, Callwey Verlag. Munich, 1998, p. 15.
86.17: Prof. Deplazes. Graphic: Maud Châtelet.
86.18: Günter Pfeifer, Antje Liebers, Holger Reiners: *Der neue Holzbau*, Callwey Verlag. Munich, 1998, p. 19.
86.19: *Detail*, No. 1. Munich, 2001, p. 94.
87.20 top: Günter Pfeifer, Antje Liebers, Holger Reiners: *Der neue Holzbau*, Callwey Verlag. Munich, 1998, p. 24.
87.20 bottom: Photo: Borimir Radovic.
87.21–22: *Detail*, No. 1. Munich, 2001, p. 97. Photo: Borimir Radovic.
88.23: Günter Pfeifer, Antje Liebers, Holger Reiners: *Der neue Holzbau*, Callwey Verlag. Munich, 1998, p. 26.
88.24: Pavatex Gmbh, Leutkirch.
88.25: Günter Pfeifer, Antje Liebers, Holger Reiners: *Der neue Holzbau*, Callwey Verlag. Munich, 1998, p. 26.
89.26: Prof. Deplazes. Graphic: Maud Châtelet.
89.27: Finnforest Merk Dickholz GmbH, catalogue: *LenoTec-Massivbau*. Aichach, 2001, p. 15.
90.28: Pius Schuler AG, Rothenturm: *Wood Industry Catalogue*, p. 159.
90.29–30: Tschopp Holzbau: *BRESTA catalogue*. Hochdorf.
91.31: Prof. Deplazes. Graphic: Maud Châtelet.
91.32: Ligu, Das Holzbauelement, Kirchlinteln.
92.33–34: Lignatur AG, Waldstatt.
93.35: STEKO Holzbausysteme AG, Uttwil, Catalogue: *STEKO – Systembeschrieb, Planung, Konstruktion*, Kesswil.
94.36: Finnforest Merk Dickholz GmbH, Catalogue: *LenoTec-Bausystem*, Aichach, 2001, p. 12.
94.37: Woodwelding SA, Zurich.
95.38: Prof. Deplazes. Graphic: Daniel Gut.
95.39: Source unknown
95.40: Matej Draslar and Andreas Lochmatter, Archive Prof. Deplazes, 2007.
96.41–97.43: Josef Kolb: *Systembau mit Holz*, Baufachverlag. Zurich, 1992, p. 15.
97.44: Prof. Deplazes. Graphic: Daniel Gut.
98.45–46: Josef Kolb: Loco citato, p. 15.
99.47: Bearth + Deplazes.
99.48: Josef Kolb: Loco citato, p. 80.
99.49: Bearth + Deplazes.
100.50: Holzforum, Bern.
100.51–101.52: Prof. Deplazes. Graphic: Daniel Gut.
102.53: Bearth + Deplazes.
103.54: Prof. Deplazes.
104.55–105.60: Christoph Henrichsen: "Die Werkstätten am Grossschrein von Ise", in: *Detail*, No. 10. Munich, 2002, p. 1285, 1288.

106.61: Reyner Banham, Hiroyuki Suzuki: *Modernes Bauen in Japan*, Deutsche Verlags-Anstalt. Stuttgart, 1987, p. 109.
106.62: Photo: Website. No longer available.
107.63: Reyner Banham, Hiroyuki Suzuki: *Modernes Bauen in Japan*, Deutsche Verlags-Anstalt. Stuttgart, 1987, p. 109.
107.64 top and bottom: Arthur Drexler: *The Architecture of Japan*, The Museum of Modern Art. New York, 1944, p. 18.
108.65: Urs Meister: "Die Fäden des Netzes", in: *tec21*, No. 21. Zurich, 2001, p. 19. Photo: Urs Meister.
108.66–67: Wolfram Graubner: *Holzverbindungen – Gegenüberstellungen japanischer und europäischer Lösungen*, Deutsche Verlags-Anstalt. Stuttgart, 1984, p. 71, 43.
109.68: Urs Meister: "Die Fäden des Netzes", in: *tec21*, No. 21. Zurich, 2001, p. 24. Photo: Urs Meister.
109.69: Arthur Drexler: *The Architecture of Japan*, The Museum of Modern Art. New York, 1944, p. 84.
109.70: Klaus Zwerger: *Wood and Wood Joints*, Birkhäuser Publishers. Basel, 1997, p. 146. Photo: Bunhazai Kenzo, Butsu Hozon Gi, Jiutsu Kyshai.
110.71: Reyner Banham, Hiroyuki Suzuki: *Modernes Bauen in Japan*, Deutsche Verlags-Anstalt. Stuttgart, 1987, p. 108.
110.72: Arthur Drexler: *The Architecture of Japan*, The Museum of Modern Art. New York, 1944, p. 67.
110.73: Urs Meister: "Die Fäden des Netzes", in: *tec21*, No. 21. Zurich, 2001, p. 25.
111.74: Loco citato, p. 23. Photo: Urs Meister.
111.75: Arthur Drexler: *The Architecture of Japan*, The Museum of Modern Art. New York, 1944, p. 149.
111.76: Leaflet from the Schaffhausen New Art Gallery, Raussmüller Collection. Basel. Setting: Carl André: Shiloh, 1980, 91 x 563 x 563 cm, courtesy Raussmüller Collection.
112.77–78: Photo: Urs Meister.

Steel

113.1: *tec21*, No. 23. Zurich, 2003, p. 14. Photo: Georg Aerni.
113.2: *Archithese*, No. 6, Niggli Verlag. Sulgen, 1994, p. 70. Photo: Hans Ruedi Disch.
114.3: Helmut C. Schulitz, Werner Sobek, Karl Habermann: *Steel Construction Manual*, Birkhäuser Publishers. Basel, 2001, p. 47. Photo: Deutsches Museum, Munich.
114.4: Loco citato, p. 27. Photo: Bavaria State Library, Munich.
114.5: Roland Rohn, Swiss Steel Association (ed.): *Bauen in Stahl*, Swiss Steel Association. Zurich, 1956, p. 200.
115.6: Hans Frei: *Louis Henry Sullivan*, Artemis Verlag. Zurich, 1992, p. 127.
115.7: Cocoon Vision AG, Basel.
115.8: Manfred Sack: *Richard Neutra*, Studio Paperback. Birkhäuser Publishers, 1994, p. 38.
116.9: Johann Christoph Bürkle: *Wohnhäuser der klassischen Moderne*, Deutsche Verlags-Anstalt. Stuttgart, 1994, p. 100.
116.10: Loco citato, p. 101.
116.11: Anatxu Zabalbeascoa: *Houses of the Century*, Editorial Gustavo Gili. Barcelona, 1998, p. 100. Photo: Scot Frances. © 2013, ProLitteris, Zurich.
116.12: Maurice Besset: *Le Corbusier*, Skira Verlag. Geneva, 1987, p. 155.
117.13: Swiss Steel Association (ed.): *Bauen in Stahl*, Swiss Steel Building Centre. Zurich, 1956, p. 291.

117.14–15: Laurence Allégret, V. Vaudou: *Jean Prouvé et Paris*, Editions du Pavillion de l'Arsenal. Paris, 2001, p. 282, 283.

117.16: Helmut C. Schulitz, Werner Sobek, Karl J. Habermann: *Steel Construction Manual*, Birkhäuser Publishers. Basel, 2001, p. 269. (Original: Solothurn Art Society [ed.]: *Fritz Haller – Bauen und Forschen*. Solothurn, 1988). Photo: Christian Moser.

118.17–18: Coosje van Bruggen, Frank O. Gehry: *Guggenheim Museum Bilbao*, Guggenheim Museum Publications. New York, 2000, title page and p. 159.

119.19–20: Photo: Christian Richters.

119.21: Bell-Pottinger, London. Photo: Nigel Young.

120.22: Friedrich Grimm: *Konstruieren mit Walzprofilen*, Ernst und Sohn Verlag. Berlin, 2003, p. 9.

121.23–122.30: Prof. Deplazes. Graphic: Alois Diethelm.

123.31: Swiss Central Office for Structural Steelwork (SZS), *Steeldoc* March 2006.

124.32: Prof. Deplazes. Graphic: Alois Diethelm.

125.33–34: Swiss Central Office for Structural Steelwork (SZS), *Steeldoc* 01/06. Zurich, 2006.

126.35–36: Prof. Deplazes. Graphic: Alois Diethelm.

127.37: Tuchschmid Engineering AG, Nüssli Special Events AG, JAKEM AG (ed.), brochure: *Monolith – Augenblick und Ewigkeit*, 2002.

127.38: Franz Hart, Walter Henn, Hansjürgen Sontag: *Stahlbau Atlas: Geschossbauten*. Institut für internationale Architektur-Dokumentation. Munich, 1982, p. 274, 276.

128.39–40: Prof. Deplazes. Graphic: Alois Diethelm.

129.41–44: Friedrich Grimm: *Konstruieren mit Walzprofilen*. Ernst und Sohn Verlag. Berlin, 2003, p. 55, 86.

130.45–46: Prof. Deplazes. Graphic: Alois Diethelm.

131.47: Friedrich Grimm: *Konstruieren mit Walzprofilen*, Ernst und Sohn Verlag. Berlin, 2003, p. 84.

131.48–49: Loco citato, p. 81.

131.50: Loco citato, p. 80.

132.51: Prof. Deplazes.

133.52: *Detail*, No. 4. Munich, 1999, p. 626.

133.53–55: Laurence Allégret, V. Vaudou: *Jean Prouvé et Paris*, Editions du Pavillion de l'Arsenal. Paris, 2001, p. 195, 262. Photo: Centre Pompidou.

133.56: Loco citato, p. 153.

134.57–58: *Werk, Bauen + Wohnen*, No. 11. Zurich, 2000, p. 32.

134.59: *Architektur Aktuell*, 230/231. Springer Verlag. Vienna, 1999, p. 124. Photo: Georg Marterer.

134.60: Loco citato, p. 56. Photo: Philippe Ruault.

135.61: Esther McCoy, Peter J. Blake: *Craig Ellwood*, Hennessey & Ingalls. Santa Monica, 1997, p. 99, 101.

135.62: Gerhard Mack: *Herzog & de Meuron, 1989–1991*, vol. 2, Birkhäuser Publishers. Basel, 1991, p. 25.

135.63: Richard Levene, Fernando Márquez Cecilia: *El Croquis 86*, El Croquis Editorial. Madrid, 1998, p. 87.

135.64: Esther McCoy, Peter J. Blake: *Craig Ellwood*, Hennessey & Ingalls. Santa Monica, 1997, p. 99, 101.

135.65: Gerhard Mack: *Herzog & de Meuron, 1989–1991*, vol. 2, Birkhäuser Publishers. Basel, 1991, p. 16.

135.66: Richard Levene, Fernando Márquez Cecilia: *El Croquis 86*, El Croquis Editorial. Madrid, 1998, p. 75. Photo: Hisao Suzuki.

136.67: Helmut C. Schulitz, Werner Sobek, Karl J. Habermann: *Steel Construction Manual*, Birkhäuser Publishers. Basel, 2001, p. 129.

136.68–69: Deyan Sudjic: *Norman Foster, Richard Rogers, James Stirling*, Thames and Hudson. London, 1986, p. 100, 101. Photo: Richard Bryant.

136.70: Heinz W. Krewinkel: *Glass Buildings – Material, Structure and Detail*, Birkhäuser Publishers. Basel, 1998, p. 27.

136.71: Oskar Büttner, Erhard Hampe: *Bauwerk, Tragwerk, Tragstruktur*, Ernst und Sohn Verlag. Berlin, 1985, p. 263.

137.72 a and b: *Detail*, No. 7. Munich, 2001, p. 1267, 1277.

137.73: Internet: Source no longer available.

137.74: Norman Foster: *Foster Catalogue*, 2001, Prestel Verlag. Munich, 2001, p. 96.

137.75: Rainer Graefe (ed.): *Vladimir G. Suchov, 1853–1939. Die Kunst der sparsamen Konstruktion*, Deutsche Verlags-Anstalt. Stuttgart, 1990, p. 97.

138.76 a: "Pier Luigi Nervi" in: *Process Architecture*, No. 23. Tokyo, 1981, p. 100.

138.76 b: Loco citato, p. 103.

138.77: Helmut C. Schulitz, Werner Sobek, Karl J. Habermann: *Steel Construction Manual*, Birkhäuser Publishers. Basel, 2001, p. 326. Photo: Richard Bryant.

138.78: *A&V Monografias de Arquitectura y Vivienda*, No. 36. Madrid, 1992, p. 44.

138.79: Kenneth Powell: *Stansted – Norman Foster & the Architecture of Flight*, A Blueprint Monograph, Fourth Estate. London, 1992, p. 76, 77. Photo: Richard Bryant, Philip Sayer.

138.80: *A&V Monografias de Arquitectura y Vivienda*, No. 36. Madrid, 1992, p. 48.

Insulation

139.1: Prof. Deplazes.

139.2 top and bottom: Lucerne Architecture Gallery; Toni Haefliger, Heinz Huesler, Heinz Wirz: *Herzog & de Meuron – Das neue Suva-Haus in Basel, 1988–1993*, Edition Architekturgalerie. Lucerne, 1994, p. 32, 33 and 47. Photo: Toni Haefliger. Courtesy 2004 Architekturgalerie Luzern.

140.3: Prof. Deplazes. Graphic: Eva Geering.

141.4: Jeffrey Kipnis: *Philip Johnson – Recent Work*, Academy Editions. London, 1996, p. 30.

142.5: Atelier Werner Schmidt, Areal Fabrica, Trun.

142.6: Herbert & Astrid Gruber: *Bauen mit Stroh*, Oekobuch. Staufen i. Brsg., 2000, p. 11.

143.7: Photo: Dietrich Schwarz.

143.8: Prof. Deplazes. Graphic: Maud Châtelet.

143.9: Ernst Schweizer AG, Hedingen.

143.10–11: Prof. Deplazes.

143.12: Prof. Deplazes. Graphic: Maud Châtelet.

144.13: Saint-Gobain Isover Austria AG, Stockerau.

144.14: Deutsche Foamglas GmbH, Haan.

144.15: Styrofoam, Berlin.

144.16: Pavatex Gmbh, Leutkirch.

144.17: Deutsche Rockwool, Gladbeck.

144.18: Styropor (BASF), Ludwigshafen.

144.19: Swisspoor AG, Steinhausen.

144.20: Isofloc AG, Bütschwil.

144–145.21: Eckhard Reyer, Kai Schild, Stefan Völkner: *Kompendium der Dämmstoffe*, Fraunhofer IRB Verlag. Stuttgart, 2002.

146.22–23: Prof. Deplazes.

Glass or plastic

147.1–2: Sigmar Spauszus, Jürgen D. Schnapp: *Glas allgemeinverständlich – eine Einführung in Theorie und Praxis*, VEB Fachbuchverlag. Leipzig, 1977.

148.3: Bregenz Art Gallery (ed.): *Nachtwallfahrtskapelle Locherboden*, Hatje Cantz Verlag. Stuttgart, 1997, p. 67. Fig.: © 2013, ProLitteris, Zurich.

148.4: Michael Wigginton: *Glass in Architecture*, London, 2002, p. 53.

148.5: Rolf Toman (ed.): *Die Kunst der Gotik*, Könemann Verlag. Cologne, 1998, p. 85. Photo: Achim Bednorz.

149.6: Ulrich Knaack: *Konstruktiver Glasbau*, Rudolf Müller Verlag. Cologne, 1998, p. 51.

149.7: Jeannine Fiedler, Peter Feierabend: *Bauhaus*, Könemann Verlag. Cologne, 1999, p. 222. Photo: Markus Hawlik/Bauhaus Archive Berlin.

149.8: Thomas L. Schumacher: *Il Danteum di Terragni*,Officina Edizioni. Rome, 1980.

149.9: Ulrich Knaack: *Konstruktiver Glasbau*, Rudolf Müller Verlag. Cologne, 1998, p. 20.

151.10: Christoph Elsener, Prof. Deplazes.

151.11: Louis K. Meisel: *Richard Estes, The Complete Paintings 1966-1985*, Harry N. Abrams. New York 1986, p. 79. Painting: Private Collection, New Orleans. Courtesy Louis K. Meisel Gallery, © Richard Estes.

152.12: Photo: © 2008. Digital image, The Museum of Modern Art, New York / Scala, Florence. Fig.: © 2013, ProLitteris, Zurich.

152.13: Fritz Neumeyer (ed.): *Ludwig Mies van der Rohe, Hochhaus am Bahnhof Friedrichstrasse*, Ernst Wasmuth Verlag. Tübingen, Berlin, 1993, p. 43. Fig.: © 2013, ProLitteris, Zurich.

152.14: Terence Riley, Barry Bergdoll (ed.): *Mies in Berlin. Ludwig Mies van der Rohe, die Berliner Jahre, 1907-1938*, Prestel Verlag. Munich 2002, p. 189. Photo: © 2008. Digital image, The Museum of Modern Art, New York / Scala, Florence. Fig.: © 2013, ProLitteris, Zurich.

152.15: Photo: Ezra Stoller © Esto.

153.16: Walter Müller-Wulckow: *Architektur der Zwanziger Jahre in Deutschland, vol. Bauten der Gemeinschaft*, new edition 1975, Karl Robert Langewiesche Nachfolger, Hans Köster Königstein im Taunus, p. 86. Photo: © 2013, ProLitteris, Zurich.

153.17: Ulrich Pfammatter: *In die Zukunft gebaut*, Prestel-Verlag. Munich 2005, p. 187.

153.18: Martin Pawley: *Norman Foster, A Global Architecture*, Thames & Hudson. London 1999, p. 52. Photo: Tim Street-Porter.

153.19: Christian Schittich, Gerald Staib, Dieter Balkow, Matthias Schuler, Werner Sobek: *Glass Construction Manual*, Birkhäuser Publishers. Basel 1999, p. 50. Photo: Ken Kirkwood.

154.20: From the film "Lost in Translation", Focus Features, 2003.

154.21: Christoph Elsener, Prof. Deplazes.

155.22: Christoph Elsener, Prof. Deplazes.

155.23: Félix Solaguren-Beascoa (ed.): *Arne Jacobsen, Edificios Públicos, Public Buildings*, GG Editorial Gustavo Gili S.A. Barcelona 2005, p. 53. Photo: © Strüwing.

156.24: Michael Wigginton: *Glas in der Architektur*, DVA. Stuttgart 1996, p. 136.

156.25: *Architektur Aktuell* 7/8, Springer Verlag. Vienna 2007, p. 57. Photo: Christian Richters.

156.26: Loco citato, p. 65. Photo: Christian Richters.

157.27: From the film "Philadelphia", Clinica Estetico, Tristar Pictures, 1993.

158.28: *El Croquis* 32/33, El Croquis Editorial. Madrid 1988, p. 92.

158.29: Loco citato, p. 96. Photo: Hisao Suzuki.

158.30: Loco citato, p. 97. Photo: Hisao Suzuki.

159.31: Lloyd Kahn: *Shelter II*, Shelter Publications. Bolinas, CA, 1978, p. 203. Photo: Doug Lehman.

159.32: Elke Genzel, Pamela Voigt: *Kunststoffbauten Teil1, Die Pioniere*, Bauhaus-Universität Weimar, Universitätsverlag. Weimar, 2005, p. 41. Photo: © Monsanto Chemical Company.

159.33: James Ward (ed.): *The Artifacts of R. Buckminster Fuller, A Comprehensive Collection of His Designs and Drawings in Four Volumes*, Garland. New York / London, 1985, p. 217. Photo: Courtesy, The Estate of R. Buckminster Fuller.

159.34: Elke Genzel, Pamela Voigt: *Kunststoffbauten Teil1, Die Pioniere*, Bauhaus-Universität Weimar, Universitätsverlag. Weimar, 2005, p. 111, Fig. 7. Photo: Paul Kramer.

160.35: *db 4* „Kunststoff-Konstrukte", Konradin Medien GmbH. Leinfelden-Echterdingen, 2006, title page. Photo: © Stefan Pangritz.

160.36: Faserplast AG, Rickenbach-Wil. Photo: Katharina Stehrenberger.

160.37: *Pausendach Innenhof der Daniel-Staub Realschule von Heinz Isler*, student project in course module FVK 06/07, Zurich University of Applied Sciences.

161.38: Elke Genzel, Pamela Voigt: *Kunststoffbauten Teil1, Die Pioniere*, Bauhaus-Universität Weimar, Universitätsverlag. Weimar, 2005, p. 240. Photo: © Studio Piano, Architects. Contractor: Impresa E. Piano.

161.39: Elke Genzel, Pamela Voigt: *Kunststoffbauten Teil1, Die Pioniere*, Bauhaus-Universität Weimar, Universitätsverlag. Weimar, 2005, p. V ff. Photo: © Heinz Isler.

162.40: Loco citato. Photo: Heinz Hossdorf.

162.41: Loco citato. Photo: Heinz Hossdorf.

162.42: Loco citato. Photo: © Heinz Isler.

163.43: Loco citato. Photo: © Heinz Isler.

163.44: Schweizerische Zentralstelle für Stahlbau: *Bauen in Stahl 11*. Zurich, 1979, p. 63. Photo: © Stahlbau Zentrum Schweiz.

163.45: Dieter Bogner, Kunsthaus Graz AG (ed.): A *friendly Alien – Ein Kunsthaus für Graz*, Hatje Cantz Verlag. Ostfildern-Ruit, 2004, p. 90. © ARGE Kunsthaus, Graz.

163.46: Loco citato, p. 153. Photo: Paul Ott.

164.47: Frei Otto, Winfried Nerdinger: *Frei Otto, Das Gesamtwerk*, Birkhäuser Verlag. Basel, 2005, p. 266. Photo: Eberhard Möller, Munich.

164.48: Ulrich Pfammatter: *In die Zukunft gebaut*, Prestel Verlag. Munich, 2005, p. 86. Photo: Ulrich Pfammatter.

164.49: Horst Berger: *Light Structures*, Birkhäuser Verlag. Basel, 1996, p. 15.

165.50: © R+R Fuchs Ingenieurbüro für Fassadentechnik GmbH, Munich and Herzog & de Meuron, Basel.

165.51: *Detail*, No. 9, „Stadien", Institut für internationale Architektur-Dokumentation GmbH & Co. KG. Munich, 2005, p. 975. Photo: Allianz Arena / B. Ducke.

165.52: *Detail*, No. 9, „Stadien", Institut für internationale Architektur-Dokumentation GmbH & Co. KG, Munich, 2005, p. 975. Photo: Hubertus Hamm.

166.53: Gyorgy Kepes: *Struktur in Kunst und Wissenschaft*, La Connaissance. Brussels, 1967, p. 32.

166.54: INOUTIC, *Magalog für Architekten*, No. 1, „Kunststoffwelten", Inoutic / Deceuninck. Munich, 2007, p. 23.

ELEMENTS

Foundation – Plinth

169.1: From the James Bond 007 film "You only live twice", Eon Productions, Pinewood Studios, Buckinghamshire, UK, 1967.

169.2: Werner Cords-Parchim: *Das Handbuch des Landbaumeisters*, Neumann Verlag. Radebeul, 1969, p. 148.
169.3–4: Prof. Deplazes. Graphic: Alois Diethelm.
170.5: GA architect, No. 16, "Tadao Ando, Vol. 3., 1994–2000", Tokyo, 2000, p. 27.
170.6: Prof. Deplazes. Graphic: Alois Diethelm.
170.7: Pierre Zoelly: *Terratektur – Einstieg in die unterirdische Architektur*, Birkhäuser Publishers. Basel, 1981, p. 123.
170.8: *El Croquis*, "Tadao Ando 1983–2000", El Croquis Editorial. Madrid, 2000, p. 108. Photo: Hiroshi Ueda.
171.9: Henri Stierlin (ed.): *Architektur der Welt: Griechenland*, Taschen Verlag. Cologne, 1980. p. 159.
Photo: Henri Stierlin.
171.10: *Der Architekt*, No. 11, Bonn, 1991, p. 554.
171.11: Peter Meili: *Manuscripts for lecture on building underground*, Inst. für Strassen- & Untertagebau, Swiss Federal Institute of Technology, Zurich, 1975, p. 92, 93.
171.12: Martin Hervé: *Guide de l'architecture moderne à Paris*, Editions Alternatives. Paris, 1990, p. 63.
172.13: *Werk*, No. 1. Zurich, 1962, p. 45.
Photo: Alfred Hablützel.
172.14: Birgit Abrecht: *Architekturführer Island*, Deutsche Verlags-Anstalt. Munich, 2000, p. 14.
172.15–16: *Archithese*, No. 1, Niggli Verlag. Sulgen, 2001, p. 12.
172.17: Photo: Adrian Kramp.
173.18: Oscar Riera Ojeda (ed.): *Ten Houses – Eduardo Souto de Moura*, Rockport Publishers. Gloucester, 1998, p. 84. Photo: Luis Ferreira Alves.
173.19: *Werk, Bauen + Wohnen*, No. 10, Zurich, 1975, p. 882. Photo: Henri Stierlin.
173.20 left and right: Vincenzo Albertini, Antonio Baldi, Clemente Esposito: *Naples, the Rediscovered City*, Associazione Napoli Sotterranea. Naples, 1996, p. 41, 133.
173.21: Prof. Deplazes. Graphic: Alois Diethelm.
174.22–23: Georg Gerster: *Kirchen im Fels*, Atlantis Verlag. Zurich, 1972, p. 13, 104.
Graphic: Albert Gerster.
174.24: John Carmody, Raymond Sterling: *Earth Sheltered Housing Design*, New York, 1985, p. 139.
174.25: Jean-Paul Loubes: *Maisons creusées du fleuve jaune*, Ed. Créaphis. Paris, 1988, p. 108.
174.26: John Carmody, Raymond Sterling: Loco citato, p. 139.
175.27: *Werk, Bauen + Wohnen*, No. 10, Zurich, 1975, p. 888, revised by the editor.
175.28: Pierre Zoelly: *Terratektur – Einstieg in die unterirdische Architektur*, Birkhäuser Publishers. Basel, 1989, p. 98.
175.29: Prof. Deplazes. Graphic: Alois Diethelm.
175.30: Photo and graphic: Christian Kerez.
176.31: Rolf H. Ruebener: *Grundbautechnik für Architekten*, Werner-Verlag. Düsseldorf, 1985, p. 122.
176.32 top and bottom: *Daidalos*, issue 48, "Sous Terrain", Bertelsmann. Berlin, 1993, p. 63, 65.
177.33: Prof. Deplazes. Photo: Janet Schacke.
177.34: IPG Keller AG, Kreuzlingen. Graphic: Rainer Keller.
177.35–178.43: Prof. Deplazes. Graphic/Photo: Thomas Melliger.
179.44: Heinz Ronner: *Baukonstruktion im Kontext des architektonischen Entwerfens. Haus – Sockel*, Birkhäuser Publishers. Basel, 1991, p. 45. Graphic: Heinz Ronner.
179.45: Prof. Deplazes.
179.46– 47: Graphic: Heinz Ronner.

179.48: Heinz Ronner: *Baukonstruktion im Kontext des architektonischen Entwerfens. Haus – Sockel*, Birkhäuser Publishers. Basel, 1991, p. 46. Graphic: Heinz Ronner.
180.49–181.54: Prof. Deplazes. Graphic: Thomas Wirz.
182.55: Source unknown
182.56: Prof. Deplazes. Graphic: Alois Diethelm.
182.57: Peter Blake: *Philip Johnson*, Studio Paperback, Birkhäuser Publishers. Basel, 1996, p. 59.
182.58: Jean-Marie Pérouse de Montclos: *Histoire de l'architecture française – De la Rennaissance à la Révolution*, Edition Mengès. Paris, 1995, p. 301. Photo: Caroline Rose.
182.59: Diener & Diener, Basel. Photo: Hans Ruedi Disch.
183.60–61: Professur Deplazes. Photo: Alois Diethelm.
183.62: Werner Oechslin (ed.): *Daniele Marques*, gta Verlag. Zurich, 2003, p. 55.
Photo: Christian Kerez.
183.63: Loco citato, p. 54. Photo: Christian Kerez.
183.64: Friedbert Kind-Barkauskas, Bruno Kauhsen, Stefan Polónyi, Jörg Brandt: *Concrete Construction Manual*, Birkhäuser Publishers. Basel, 2002, p. 217. Photo: Heinrich Helfenstein.
184.65: Photo: Gion A. Caminada.
184.66: Dolf Schnebli, Tobias Amman, Flora Ruchat-Roncati: *Werkverzeichnis, 1984–1990*. Zurich, Agno, Verscio, 1991, p. 97. Photo: Heinrich Helfenstein.
184.67: Prof. Deplazes. Photo: Alois Diethelm.
184.68: Peter Zumthor: *Peter Zumthor Häuser, 1979 –1997*, Birkhäuser Publishers. Basel, 1999, p. 108.
Photo: Hélène Binet.
184.69: Prof. Deplazes. Graphic: Alois Diethelm.
185.70: Prof. Deplazes.

Facade
186.1: Biblioteca Nazionale Centrale, reprod. with kind permission of the Ministero per i Beni e le Attività Culterali, Italy.
186.2: Winfried Nerdinger: *Gottfried Semper, 1803–1879. Architektur und Wissenschaft*, Prestel Verlag/gta. Munich, Zurich, 2003, p. 112.
187.3: © Staatliche Museen zu Berlin, Kupferstichkabinett; Karl Friedrich Schinkel, Collection of Architectural Designs.
187.4: Eugène Emmanuel Viollet-le-Duc: *Entretiens sur l'architecture*, Morel et Cie Editeurs. Paris, 1864–1872, Atlas, pl. XXXVI.
187.5: Robert Gargiani: *August Perret*, Gallimard/Electa. Milan, 1993, p. 76. Photo: Robert Gargiani.
188.6: Loco citato, p. 77. Photo: Robert Gargiani.
188.7: Loco citato, p. 62. Photo: Robert Gargiani.
188.8: Chup Friemert: *Die gläserne Arche. Kristallpalast London, 1851 & 1854*, Prestel Verlag. Munich, 1984, p. 134.
188.9: Winfried Nerdinger: *Der Architekt Walter Gropius*, Gebr. Mann Verlag. Berlin, 1996, p. 35. Photo: Albert Renger-Patzsch; © Albert Renger Patzsch Archive/Ann und Jürgen Wilde, Cologne / 2013, ProLitteris, Zurich.
189.10: Theo van Doesburg: *Theo van Doesburg. Peintre et architecte*, Gallimard/Electa. Paris, 1993, p. 119.
189.11: Carsten-Peter Warncke: *De Stijl, 1917–1931*, Benedikt Taschen Verlag. Cologne, 1990, p. 136. Photo: Frank van den Oudsten/Lenneke Büller, Amsterdam.
190.12: Jonathan M. Woodham: *Twentieth-century ornament*, Rizzoli. New York, 1990, p. 11.
190.13: Alexander Koch: *Die deutsche Kunst und Dekoration*, vol. 10, Koch Verlag. Darmstadt, 1902. Fig.: © 2013, ProLitteris, Zurich.

190.14: Stanislaus von Moos: *Venturi, Rauch & Scott Brown*, Verlag Schirmer Mosel. Munich, 1987, p. 203

191.15: Gordon Matta-Clark: *You Are the Measure*, The Whitney Museum of American Art. New York, 2007, p. 117. Fig.: © 2013 ProLitteris, Zurich.

194.16: *Werk, Bauen + Wohnen*, No. 4, Verlag Werk AG. Zurich, 1999, p. 21. Photo: Scagliola / Brakkee, Rotterdam.

194.17: Peter Zumthor: *Peter Zumthor Works, Buildings and Projects 1979-1997*, Lars Müller Publishers. Baden, 1998, p. 206. Photo: Hélène Binet.

195.18: *Miguel Fisac, Medalla de Oro de la Arquitectura 1994*, Edición al cuidado de Andrés Cánovas. Madrid, 1997.

196.19: Gerhard Mack: *Herzog & de Meuron, Das Gesamtwerk, Bd. 1 1978-1988*, Birkhäuser Publishers. Basel, 1997, p. 160. Photo: Margherita Spiluttini.

196.20: J. Christoph Bürkle (ed.): *Gigon Guyer Architekten, Arbeiten 1989 bis 2000*, Verlag Niggli AG. Sulgen / Zurich, 2000, p. 176.

197.21: Peter Zumthor: *Peter Zumthor Works, Buildings and Projects 1979-1997*, Lars Müller Publishers. Baden, 1998, p. 109. Photo: Hélène Binet.

198.22: *Werk, Bauen + Wohnen*, No. 5, Verlag Werk AG. Zurich, 2006, p. 35. Photo: Gerry Johansson.

198.23: *Werk, Bauen + Wohnen*, No. 6, Verlag Werk AG. Zurich, 2002, p. 29. Photo: Rob t'Hart.

199.24: von Ballmoos Krucker Architekten: *Register Kommentare*, gta Verlag. Zurich, 2007, p. 56.

Opening

200.1: *Daidalos*, issue No. 13, Bertelsmann Fachzeitschriften. Berlin, 1984, p. 64. Fig.: Franz Louis Catel: "Schinkel in Neapel" (1824).

201.2: Loco citato, p. 66. Photo: Le Corbusier Foundation, Paris. © FLC / 2013, ProLitteris, Zurich.

201.3: Loco citato, p. 66. Fig.: © Succession Marcel Duchamp / 2013, ProLitteris, Zurich.

202.4: Le Corbusier: *Almanach D'Architecture Moderne*, Crés. Paris, 1926, p. 92. Photo: Le Corbusier/ Le Corbusier Foundation, Paris.

203.5: *Daidalos*, issue No. 13, Bertelsmann Fachzeitschriften. Berlin, 1984, p. 68. Fig.: Le Corbusier, Richter & Gut Collection, Lausanne. © FLC / 2013, ProLitteris, Zurich.

203.6: Loco citato, p. 68. Sketch: Le Corbusier. © FLC / 2013, ProLitteris, Zurich.

203.7: Loco citato, p. 68. Fig.: Le Corbusier Foundation, Paris. © FLC / 2013, ProLitteris, Zurich.

204.8: Loco citato, p. 69. Fig.: Le Corbusier Foundation, Paris. © FLC / 2013, ProLitteris, Zurich.

205.9: Loco citato, p. 71. Fig.: Le Corbusier Foundation, Paris. © FLC / 2013, ProLitteris, Zurich. (Original: Le Corbusier: *Almanach D'Architecture Moderne*. Paris, 1925, p. 95).

205.10–11: Loco citato, p. 70. Sketch: Le Corbusier. © FLC / 2013, ProLitteris, Zurich. (original: *Une petite Maison*, 1923, Les Carnets de la recherche patiente, Editions Girsberger. Zurich, 1954).

206.12: Loco citato, p. 72. Fig.: Le Corbusier Foundation, Paris. (Original: Le Corbusier: *Almanach D'Architecture Moderne*. Paris, 1925, p. 94).

206.13: Loco citato, p. 73. Photo: Bruno Reichlin. © FLC / 2013, ProLitteris, Zurich.

206.14–15: Loco citato, p. 72, 78. Sketch: Le Corbusier. © FLC / 2013, ProLitteris, Zurich. (Original: Une petite Maison, 1923, Les Carnets de la recherche patiente, Editions Girsberger. Zurich, 1954).

207.16: Loco citato, p. 74. Fig.: Caspar David Friedrich.

207.17: Loco citato, p. 74. Fig.: Henri Matisse. © Succession H. Matisse / 2013, ProLitteris, Zurich.

207.18: Loco citato, p. 74. Fig.: Robert Delaunay.

207.19: Loco citato, p. 77. Fig.: Max Beckmann. © 2013, ProLitteris, Zurich.

208.20: Loco citato, p. 75. Fig.: Paul Klee.

208.21: Loco citato, p. 75. Fig.: Henri Matisse. © Succession H. Matisse / 2013, ProLitteris, Zurich.

208.22: Loco citato, p. 75. Fig.: Joseph Albers. © The Josef and Anni Albers Foundation / 2013, ProLitteris, Zurich.

209.23–216.30: Prof. Deplazes.

217.31–32: Prof. Deplazes. Photo: Christoph Elsener.

217.33: Thomas Boga: *Die Architektur von Rudolf Olgiati*, gta Verlag. Zurich, 1977, p. 172.

217.34: Alejandro de la Sota: *Alejandro de la Sota Architect*, Ediciones Pronaos. Madrid, 1989, p. 85. Photo: Alejandro de la Sota.

217.35: Thomas Boga: *Die Architektur von Rudolf Olgiati*, gta Verlag. Zurich, 1977, p. 172.

218.36: Franceso Català-Roca, Xavier Monteys: *La Arquitectura de los años cincuenta en Barcelona*, Secretaria General Técnica, Centro de Publicationes. Madrid, 1987, p. 78. Photo: Franceso Català-Roca.

218.37: Source unknown

218.38: Gerhard Mack: *Herzog & de Meuron – The Complete Works Volume 1:, 1978–1988*, Birkhäuser Publishers. Basel, 1997, p. 67. Photo: Margherita Spiluttini.

218.39: Loco citato, p. 62.

218.40: Hans Helbling: *Otto Rudolf Salvisberg, 1882– 1940*, "Estratto dal fascicolo No. 17 della rivista Architetti". Florence, 1953, p. 12. © Institut für Geschichte und Theorie der Architektur (gta) – ETH Zürich.

219.41: *Process Architecture*, No. 11: "Harry Weese", Process Architecture Publishing. Tokyo, 1979, p. 107.

219.42–43: *Werk, Bauen + Wohnen*, No. 1/2, Zurich, 2001, p. 166. Photo: Hans Ruedi Disch.

219.44: Centre Georges Pompidou (ed.): *Louis I. Kahn – Le monde de l'architecte*, Editions du Centre Georges Pompidou. Paris, 1992, p. 129.

220.45–46: Raul Rispa (ed.): *Barragan – Das Gesamtwerk*, Birkhäuser Publishers. Basel, 1996, p. 142. © Barragan Foundation / 2013, ProLitteris, Zurich.

220.47–48: Bo & Wohlert. 220.48: Sculptures in fig.: Alberto Giacometti: L'homme qui marche. © Succession Alberto Giacometti / 2013, ProLitteris, Zurich.

220.49: Oscar Riera Ojeda (ed.): *Ten Houses – Eduardo Souto de Moura*, Rockport Publishers. Gloucester, 1998, p. 38. Photo: Luis Ferreira Alves.

221.50: Arthur Rüegg: "Farbkonzepte und Farbskalen in der Moderne", in: *Daidalos*. Architektur – Kunst – Kultur: "In Farbe", No. 51, Bertelsmann. Berlin, 1994, p. 74. Photo: Arthur Rüegg.

221.51: Edoardo Gellner: *Alte Bauernhäuser in den Dolomiten. Die ländliche Architektur der venetianischen Alpen*, Callwey Munich, 1989 (1st ed.: Edizioni Dolomiti, 1988), p. 252. IUAV – Archivio Progetti, Fondo Edoardo Gellner.

221.52: Catherine Donzel, Alexis Gregory, Marc Walter: *Grand American Hotels*, The Vendom Press. New York, 1989, p. 176.

221.53: Annegret Burg: *Kollhoff – Architekten Kollhoff und Timmermann*, Birkhäuser Publishers. Basel, 1998, p. 67. Photo: Heinrich Helfenstein.

222.54: Prof. Deplazes. Graphic: Christine Enzmann.

222.55–60: Prof. Deplazes. Graphic: Thomas Melliger.

223.61–70: Prof. Deplazes. Graphic: Christine Enzmann.

224.71: Hermann Forster Rohr- & Profiltechnik AG, Arbon.

224.72: Opo Oeschger AG, Kloten. Hermann Forster
Rohr- & Profiltechnik AG, Arbon.

225.73: Prof. Deplazes.

226.74–75: Prof. Deplazes. Graphics: Patric Allemann.

226.76: Willy Boesiger, Hans Girsberger: *Le Corbusier,
1910–65*, Birkhäuser Publishers. Basel, 1967, p. 143.
Fig.: © FLC / 2013, ProLitteris, Zurich.

227.77: *El Croquis*, No. 102: "Annette Gigon/Mike Guyer,
1989–2000", El Croquis Editorial. Madrid, 2000, p. 180.

227.78–82: Prof. Deplazes. Graphic: Patric Allemann.

227.83: Johann Christoph Bürkle, Ruggero Tropeano:
*Ein Prototyp des neuen Bauens in Zürich –
die Rotach-Häuser*, gta Verlag, exhibition catalogue.
Zurich, 1994, p. 75. Photo: M. Grasser, C. Eckert.

228.84: *Werk, Bauen + Wohnen*, No. 10, Zurich, 1997, p. 51.

228.85: Lisbeth Waechter-Böhm: *Baumschlager & Eberle:
Bauten und Projekte, 1996–2002*, Springer
Verlag. Vienna, 2003, p. 135. Photo: Eduard Huber.

228.86: Photo: Ernst Gisel.

229.87: *Archithese*, No. 2, Niggli Verlag. Sulgen, 2000,
p. 15. Photo: Mechthild Heuser.

229.88: Markku Lahti: *Alvar Aalto – elämälle herkempi
rakenne*, Rakennustieto Oy. Helsinki, 1996, p. 71. Photo:
Maija Holma.

Floor

230.1: Gesellschaft für Ingenieurbaukunst: *Robert Maillart:
Betonvirtuose*, Vdf Verlag. Zurich, 1996, p. 48. Photo:
Robert Maillart.

231.2: Pier Luigi Nervi: *Gestalten in Beton, Zum Werk von Pier
Luigi Nervi*, Rudolf Müller Verlag. Cologne, 1989.

231.3: Jürgen Joedike: *Bürobauten*, Verlag Arthur Niggli.
Teufen, 1959, p. 58.

231.4: Otto Frei, Bodo Rasch: *Gestalt finden*, Edition Axel
Menges. Munich, 1992, p. 209. Photo: Otto Frei,
Bodo Rasch.

231.5–6: Exhibition catalogue: *Alvar Aalto in seven buildings*,
Museum of Finish Architecture. Helsinki, 1998, p. 39, 28.

232.7: Jürgen Joedike: *Bürobauten*, Verlag Arthur Niggli. Teufen, 1959, p. 66. Photo: Aero Saarinen.

232.8–9: Pier Luigi Nervi: *Neue Strukturen*, Hatje Verlag.
Stuttgart, 1963, p. 24, 25. Photo: Pier Luigi Nervi.

232.10: Renzo Piano: *Carnet de travail*, Editions du Seuil.
Paris, 1997, p. 41. Fig.: Renzo Piano, Richard Rogers.

233.11: Michel Ragon: *Goldberg dans la ville*, Paris Art Center. Paris, 1985, p. 31.

233.12: Jürgen Joedike: *Bürobauten*, Verlag Arthur Niggli.
Teufen, 1959, p. 198. Photo: Hideo Kosaka.

233.13: Rem Koolhaas: *Delirious New York*,
010 Publishers. Rotterdam, 1994, p. 83.

234.14: *El Croquis*, No. 111, El Croquis Editorial. Madrid,
2002, p. 47.

234.15: Doris Weigel: *Die Einraumwohnung als räumliches
Manifest der Moderne*, Edition Argus. Schliengen, 1996,
p. 75, © Albertina Vienna. Photo: Adolf Loos, © 2013,
ProLitteris, Zurich.

235.16: Claude Parent: *Entrelacs de l' oblique*, in the series:
Collections Architecture "Les Hommes", Editions du
moniteur. Paris, 1981, p. 52. Fig.: Claude Parent, Paul
Virilio. © 2013, ProLitteris, Zurich.

235.17: Loco citato, p. 146.

235.18: Source unknown

235.19: *a+u*, No. 342, Tokyo, 1999/03, pp. 111/113.
Photo: Christian Richters.

235.20: *2G – revista internacional de architectura*, No. 16,
Editorial Gustavo Gili. Barcelona, 2000, p. 51.

Roof

238.1–3: Prof. Deplazes. Graphic: Thomas Wirz.

239. 4–243.16: Prof. Deplazes. Graphic: Daniel Gut.

244.17: Gerda Wangerin, Gerhard Weiss: *Heinrich Tessenow,
Ein Baumeister, 1876–1950, Leben – Lehre – Werk*,
Verlag Richard Bacht. Essen, 1976, p. 212.

244.18: Conradin Clavuot.

244.19: Inge Beckel, Annemarie Bucher, Christoph Kübler:
Hans Leuzinger, 1887–1971 – pragmatisch modern,
gta Verlag. Zurich, 1993, p. 55.

244.20: Conradin Clavuot, Chur.

245.21–22: Prof. Deplazes. Photo: Christoph Elsener.

245.23: Fig.: © FLC / 2013, ProLitteris, Zurich.

245.24: Source unknown

245.25: Wilfried Wang: *Herzog & de Meuron*, Studio
Paperback, Birkhäuser Publishers. Basel, 1998, p. 67.

245.26: Terence Riley, Barry Bergdoll: *Mies in Berlin,
1907–1938*, Prestel Verlag. Munich, 2001, p. 359. Photo:
David Hirsch.

246.27–29: Johann Christoph Bürkle: *Gigon Guyer
Architekten – Arbeiten, 1989–2000*, Niggli. Sulgen,
Zurich, 2000, p. 90, 85 and 186.

246.30–31: Photo: Ralph Feiner.

247.32: *Architecture*, No. 3: "Twentieth-Century
Museums 1", Kimbell Art Museum. Forth Worth, 1999.
Photo: Michael Badycomb.

247.33: David Bruce Brownlee, Grant Mudford, David
G. De Long: *Louis I. Kahn – In the Realm of Architecture*,
The Museum of Contemporary Art. Los Angeles, 1991,
p. 397.

247.34: Philip Drew: "Sydney Opera House – Jørn Utzon",
in: *Architecture In Detail*, Phaidon Press. London, 1995,
p. 22. Fig.: Lindy Atkin.

247.35 top: *Archithese*, No. 5, Niggli Verlag. Sulgen, 2002,
p. 33.

247.36 bottom: Allan Temko: *Eero Saarinen*, Georg Braziller
Press. New York, 1962, fig. 101. Photo: Ezra Stoller.

247.37: Philip Drew: "Sydney Opera House – Jørn Utzon", in:
Architecture In Detail, Phaidon Press. London, 1995,
p. 18. Photo: Anthony Browell.

248.38–43: Prof. Deplazes. Graphic: Barbara Wiskemann.

248.44: Prof. Deplazes.

249.45–46: Prof. Deplazes. Graphic: Barbara Wiskemann.

Stairs, lifts

250.1: John Wilton-Ely: *Giovanni Battista Piranesi –
Vision und Werk*, Hirmer Verlag. Munich, 1978, p. VIII.

250.2: Heinrich Klotz (ed.): *Haus-Rucker-Co, 1967 bis 1983*,
Vieweg & Sohn Verlag. Braunschweig, Wiesbaden, 1984,
p. 122.

250.3: Cleo Baldon, Ib Melchior: *Steps & Stairways*, Rizzoli
International Publications. New York, 1989, p. 212. Photo:
Eadweard Muybridge.

251.4: Jacques Sbriglio: *Immeuble 24 N.C. et apartement Le
Corbusier*, Birkhäuser Publishers. Basel, 1996, title page.
Photo: Le Corbusier Paris, Immeuble 24 rue Nungesser et
Coli, appartement de Le Corbusier, 1931, © FLC / 2013,
ProLitteris, Zurich.

251.5: Source unknown

251.6: Prof. Deplazes. Photos: Christoph Elsener.

251.7: Gerhard Mack: *Herzog & de Meuron –
The Complete Works*, Volume 3:, 1992–1996,
Birkhäuser Publishers. Basel, 1996, p. 202.

252.8: John A. Templer: *The Staircase: Studies of Hazards, Falls, and Safer Design*, The MIT Press. Cambridge, Mass., 1992, p. 87.

252.9: *El Croquis*, No. 68/69, "Alvaro Siza, 1958–1994", El Croquis Editorial. Madrid, 1997, p. 92. Photo: Roberto Collova.

252.10: John A. Templer: *The Staircase: history and theories*, The MIT Press. Cambridge, Mass. 1992, p. 141.

252.11: Frederick Gutheim: *Alvar Aalto*, George Braziller Press. New York, 1960, p. 34.

253.12: Fulvio Irace: *Gio Ponti – La casa all' italiana*, Electa. Milano, 1988, p. 164.

253.13: Richard Bösel, Christoph C. Frommel (ed.): *Borromini e l'Universo Barocco Documenti di Architettura*, Electa. Milano, 2000, p. 103.

253.14: Kurt Lustenberger: *Adolf Loos*, Zanichelli Editore. Bologna, 1998, p. 160. Fig.: © 2013, ProLitteris, Zurich.

253.15: *El Croquis*, "OMA – Rem Koolhaas, 1987–1998", El Croquis Editorial. Madrid, 1998, p. 128.

254.16: Source unknown

254.17: Ivo Kranzfelder: *Edward Hopper, 1882–1967 – Vision de la réalité*, Taschen Verlag. Cologne, 1998, p. 129. Photo: VG Bild-Kunst, Bonn.

254.18: Peter Testa: *Alvaro Siza*, Studio Paperback, Birkhäuser Publishers. Basel, 1996, p. 50.

254.19: Henri Stierlin (ed.): *Architektur der Welt: Griechenland*, Taschen Verlag. Cologne, 1980, p. 150. Photo: Henri Stierlin.

255.20–256.21: Ernst Neufert: *Bauentwurfslehre*, Verlag Vieweg & Sohn. Braunschweig/Wiesbaden, 2002, p. 197, 196.

257.22: Prof. Deplazes. Graphic: Daniel Gut.

258.23–25: Swiss standard SIA 358, 1996 ed.

259.26: *2G – revista internacional de architectura,* No. 3: "Søllerød Town Hall", Editorial Gustavo Gili. Barcelona 1997, p. 41. Photo: Bernardo Jordi.

259.27: Schindler Aufzüge AG.

260.28: Source unknown

260.60–262.35: Schindler Aufzüge AG.

263.36–41: Burkard Meyer Architekten, Baden.

264.42: Luis Fernandez-Galiano (ed.): *A&V Monografias de Architectura y Vivienda*, No. 77, "Herzog & de Meuron, 1980–2000". Madrid, 1992, p. 9.

264.43–45: Source unknown

265.46–49: Otto Rudolf Salvisberg: *Architekt Professor O. R. Salvisberg, Zürich: Krankenhäuser in St Immer und Pruntrut, Fernheizkraftwerk und Maschinenlaboratorium der ETH.* Zurich, Hoffmann Verlag. Stuttgart, 1936, vol. 1. Photos: Otto Rudolf Salvisberg.

265.50: Claude Lichtenstein: *O. R. Salvisberg – Die andere Moderne*, gta Verlag. Zurich, 1995, p. 86.

266.51–52: *Archithese*, No. 6, Niggli. Sulgen, 1998, p. 60.

266.53–55: Conradin Clavuot, Chur.

STRUCTURES

Forms of construction

269.1: Prof. Deplazes, ETH Zurich.

269.2: Rovira, Josep M.: *José Luis Sert,* 1901–1983, Electa Verlag, p. 256.

269.3: Picture archive Prof. Andrea Deplazes.

270.4–6: Prof. Deplazes, ETH Zurich.

270.7–277.9: Source unknown

271.10: Prof. Deplazes, ETH Zurich.

271.11: *Donald Judd – Architektur*, Westfälischer Kunstverein, Münster 1989, p. 35. Fig.: © 2013, ProLitteris, Zurich.

272.12: Source unknown

272.13: Prof. Deplazes, ETH Zurich.

272.14: Bianca, Stefano: *Urban form in the Arab world: past and present,* vdf Hochschulverlag, Zurich 2000, p. 136.

272.15: Prof. Deplazes, ETH Zurich.

272.16: Rolf Gerber: *Louis I. Kahns Interesse an schottischen Burgen*, grant from the E. Degen Foundation/ Rolf Gerber. ETH Zurich 2000 (orig.: Royal Commission on the Ancient and Historical Monuments of Scotland, Archive).

273.17: StudioPaperback: *Le Corbusier*, Artemis Verlag, Zurich 1972, p. 14. Fig.: © FLC / 2013, ProLitteris, Zurich.

273.18: Dirk van der Heuvel, Max Risselada: *Team 10: In search of Utopia of the Present 1953–81,* Nai Publishers, Rotterdam 2005, p. 29.

273.19: Prof. Deplazes, ETH Zurich.

273.20: Source unknown

274.21: Source unknown

274.22: Bianca, Stefano: *Urban form in the Arab world: past and present,* vdf Hochschulverlag, Zurich 2000, p. 39.

274.23: Source unknown

275.24: Prof. Deplazes, ETH Zurich.

276.25: Josip Andracic – antonov

276.26–27: Source unknown

278.28: Werner Blaser: *Elementare Bauformen*, Beton-Verlag. Düsseldorf, 1982, p. 43.

278.29: Uwe Albrecht: *Der Adelssitz im Mittelalter. Studien zum Verhältnis von Architektur und Lebensform in Nord- und Westeuropa*, Deutscher Kunstverlag. Munich / Berlin, 1995, p. 11.

279.30: ETH Library, Zurich, Section Rara.

279.31: Source unknown

279.32: Helmut C. Schulitz, Werner Sobek, Karl Habermann: *Stahlbau Atlas*, Birkhäuser Verlag. Basel, 2001, p. 72. Photo: Harry Callahan.

279.33: Stefan Grundmann: *Architekturführer Rom*, Edition Axel Menges. Stuttgart, 1997, p. 68.

280.34: Peter Nabokov, Robert Easton: *Native American Architecture*, Oxford University Press. New York, 1989, p. 194. © Richard Harrington / Library and Archives Canada / PA-114724.

280.35: William L. McDonald, John A. Pinto: *Hadrian's villa and its legacy*, Yale University Press. New Haven, 1995, p. 90. Illustration: Michael Lawrence.

280.36: Kenneth Frampton: *Grundlagen der Architektur*, Oktagon Verlag. München / Stuttgart, 1993, p. 177. Fig.: © 2013, ProLitteris, Zurich.

280.37: Vincent Ligtelijn: *Aldo van Eyck – Werke*, Birkhäuser Verlag. Basel, 1989, p. 91.

281.38: Loco citato, p. 117.

281.39: Kenneth Frampton: *Grundlagen der Architektur*, Oktagon Verlag. Munich / Stuttgart, 1993, p. 71.

281.40: Loco citato, p. 260.

281.41: Professur Deplazes. Photo: Christoph Wieser.

282.42: *Andrea Palladio. La Rotonda*, Electa. Milan, 2nd Edition 1990, p. 48.

282.43: Heinz Studer: B*austilkunde. Entwicklung der Baustile vom alten ägyptischen Reich bis Ende 20. Jahrhundert*, Schweizer Baudokumentation. Blauen, 3rd Edition 1987, p. 92.

282.44: Gideon S. Golany: *Chinese Earth-Sheltered Dwellings. Ingenious Lessons for Modern Urban Design*, University of Hawaii Press. Honolulu, 1992, p. 103.

282.45: Paul Frankl: *Entwicklungsphasen der neueren Baukunst*, B.G. Teubner. Leipzig / Berlin, 1914, p. 25.

283.46: Professur Deplazes. Photo: Christoph Wieser.

283.47: Giuliani Hönger, Zurich, Dirk Hebel.

283.48: *Scottish Towerhouses*, ETH Zurich. Zurich, 2005, p. 30.

283.49: Professur Deplazes.

284.50: Christopher Hobhouse: *1851 and the Crystal Palace*, John Murray. London, 1950, p. 48.

284.51: *Werk, Bauen + Wohnen*, «Fritz Haller», 7/8-1992, p. 14. © fritz haller bauen und forschen GmbH. Photo: Christian Moser, Bern.

284.52: Kurt Lustenberger: *Adolf Loos*. Studio Paperback, Birkhäuser Verlag. Basel, 1994, p. 119. Fig.: © 2013, ProLitteris, Zurich.

284.53: Loco citato, p. 118. © Albertina, Vienna. Fig.: © 2013, ProLitteris, Zurich.

285.54: Heinrich Kulka: *Adolf Loos – Bauen in der Welt*, Verlag Anton Schroll & Co. Vienna, 1931, Ill. 266. Fig.: © 2013, ProLitteris, Zurich.

285.55: Kurt Lustenberger: *Adolf Loos*. Studio Paperback. Birkhäuser Verlag. Basel, 1994, p. 161. Fig.: © 2013, ProLitteris, Zurich.

285.56: Jacques Lucan: *OMA – Rem Koolhaas*, Artemis Verlag. Zurich / Munich, 1991, p. 129.

285.57: Jennifer Sigler (Hrsg.): *S, M, L, XL. OMA Rem Koolhaas and Bruce Mau*, 010 Publishers. Rotterdam, 1995, p. 1313.

285.58: Colin Rowe: *Die Mathematik der idealen Villa*, Birkhäuser Verlag. Basel, 1996, p. 25. Fig.: © FLC / 2013, ProLitteris, Zurich.

286.59: Uwe Albrecht: *Der Adelssitz im Mittelalter. Studien zum Verhältnis von Architektur und Lebensform in Nord- und Westeuropa*, Deutscher Kunstverlag. Munich / Berlin, 1995, p. 24.

286.60: Staufer & Hasler Architekten, *Kantonsschule Wil – ein Holzbauwerk*, Niggli. Sulgen, 2004, p. 18.

286.61: © Staufer & Hasler Architekten, Frauenfeld. Photo: Heinrich Helfenstein, Zurich.

287.62: Willy Boesiger (Hrsg.): *Le Corbusier*. Studio Paperback. Artemis Verlag. Zurich, 1990, p. 192, 193. © FLC / 2013, ProLitteris, Zurich.

287.63: Giuliani Hönger, Zurich, Dirk Hebel.

287.64: Christian Kerez, Zurich, Photo: Walter Mair.

288.65: Stewart Brand, *How Buildings Learn,* New York: Penguin, 3rd ed., 1995, p. 13.

288.66: Rolf Toman (ed.), *Die Kunst des Barock,* Cologne: Könemann 1997, p. 217.

289.67: Daniel Schwarz, *Metamorphoses,* London: Thames and Hudson 1986, p. 61.

289.68: Christoph Wieser; Max Dudler, *IBM Schweiz,* Sulgen: Niggli 2005, p. 18 (Photo: René Dürr).

290.69–70: Winfried Nerdinger and Werner Oechslin (eds), *Gottfried Semper 1803–1879,* Zurich, Munich: gta Prestel 2003, p. 26 (Photo: Klaus Kinold), p. 350.

290.71–74: Stewart Brand, *How Buildings Learn,* New York: Penguin, 3rd ed., 1995.

290.75–76: Hannes Henz, Zurich.

291.77–80: Stewart Brand, *How Buildings Learn,* New York: Penguin, 3rd ed., 1995, pp. 36/37.

291.81–82: *E2A,* Lucerne: Quart Verlag 2007, pp. 47 and 48.

292.83–85: Andres Lepik, *Skyscrapers,* Munich: Prestel 2004, pp. 60 and 61.

292.86–89: Ruedi Walti and Christoph Wieser (1–4).

293.90: Christoph Wieser.

293.91–94: Plan from: Claes Caldenby (et al.), *Guide till Göteborgs Arkitektur,* Stockholm: Arkitektur Förlag 2006, p. 234; Photos: Christoph Wieser.

293.95: Christian Helmle, *Weisse Elefanten,* Berlin: Jovis 2007, p. 78.

293.96: Birgit Verwiebe (ed.), *Caspar David Friedrich. Der Watzmann,* Cologne: DuMont 2004, p. 133.

293.97: Thomas Kellein, *Caspar David Friedrich,* Munich: Prestel 1998, p. 69.

294.98: Christoph Wieser.

294.99: Valerio Olgiati, *2G,* No. 37, p. 90.

294.100–101: *Werk, Bauen + Wohnen,* 3-2005, pp. 26 and 29.

294.102: Photo archive Büro Olgiati © Büro Olgiati.

294.103: Andreas Kohne.

295.104–106: *Casabella,* 758, October 2007.

296.107: *tec21,* No. 25, Zurich, 2002, p. 21. Photo: Ruedi Weidmann/tec 21.

297.108: Jürgen Joedicke: *Architekturgeschichte des 20. Jahrhunderts,* Karl Krämer Verlag. Stuttgart, 1990, p. 151.

297.109: Burkard Meyer Architekten, Baden.

297.110: Burkard, Meyer Architekten, Baden. Photo: Reinhard Zimmermann.

297.111: François Wehrlin (ed.): *Kenzo Tange: 40 ans d'urbanisme et d'architecture,* Process Architecture Publishing. Tokyo, 1987, p. 101. Photo: Osamu Murai.

298.112: Bearth + Deplazes.

298.113–115: Prof. Deplazes. Graphic: Alois Diethelm.

298.116: Hans Wichmann: *System-Design Fritz Haller,* Birkhäuser Publishers. Basel, 1989, p. 132. Photo: Therese Beyeler.

299.117: Romaldo Giurgola, Jaimini Mehta: *Louis I. Kahn,* Artemis Verlag. Zurich, 1989, p. 61.

299.118: *Architectural Record,* McGraw-Hill. New York, Februar, 1947, p. 95.

299.119: Verein Deutscher Ingenieure (ed.): *Heizungsanlagen – Anleitung für Betrieb, Überwachung und Wartung,* VDI-Verlag. Düsseldorf, 1974, p. 3. Reproduced with kind permission of the publisher.

300.120–121: Johann Christoph Bürkle: *Wohnhäuser der klassischen Moderne,* Deutsche Verlags-Anstalt. Stuttgart, 1994, p. 100.

300.122: Loco citato, p. 128.

300.123: Paul Wijdeveld: *Ludwig Wittgenstein, Architekt,* Wiese Verlag. Basel, 1994, p. 124.

301.124–126: *Architectural Record,* McGraw-Hill. New York, December, 1960, p. 112, 114.

301.127: *Arch+,* No. 93, archplus Verlag. Aachen, 1988, p. 79. Photo: Rayner Banham.

301.128: Source unknown

301.129: *Architectural Record,* McGraw-Hill. New York, February, 1960. Cover picture.

302.130: *The Progressive Architecture Library,* Reinold. New York, February, 1966, p. 145, 148 and 151.

302.131: *Architectural Form.* Tokyo, May, 1963, p. 129.

302.132: *The progressive architecture library,* Reinold. New York, February, 1966, p. 145, 148 and 151.

302.133: Abby Bussel: *SOM Evolutions,* Birkhäuser Publishers. Basel, 2000, p. 50, 51. Photo: Ezra Stoller.

302.134: *Schweizerische Bauzeitung,* Zurich, 16 December, 1965, p. 920.

303.135: *Werk, Bauen + Wohnen,* No. 12, Zurich, 1964, p. 425.

303.136–137: *Schweizerische Bauzeitung*, Zurich, 16 December, 1965, p. 914.

303.138: *Archithese*, No. 1, Niggli Verlag. Sulgen, 2001, p. 53.

303.139: Istituto Lina Bo e P. M. Bardi (ed.): *Lina Bo Bardi*, Edizioni Charta. Milan, 1994, p. 104.

303.140: Herdeg Klaus: *Formal Structure in Indian Achitecture*, Rizzoli Press. New York, 1990, p. 19, revised.

304.141–143: Prof. Deplazes. Graphic: Alois Diethelm.

304.144: Prof. Deplazes.

304.145: dtv-Merian-Reiseführer: *Peking-Nordchina*, Deutscher Taschenbuch Verlag. Munich, 1990, p. 229.

304.146: Angelo Ambrosi, E. Degano, C. A. Zaccaria: *Architettura in pietra a secco*, Schena Editore. Fasano, 1990, p. 235.

305.147: Prof. Deplazes.

305.148: Gert Chesi: *Architektur und Mythos – Lehmbauten in Afrika*, Haymon-Verlag. Innsbruck, 1995, p. 202. Photo: Gert Chesi.

305.149 left: Prof. Deplazes. Graphic: Alois Diethelm.

305.149 right: Rainer Graefe (ed.): *Zur Geschichte des Konstruierens*, Fourier Verlag. Wiesbaden, 2000, p. 38. Revised by Prof. Deplazes.

305.150: Source unknown

305.151: Martin Grassnick (ed.): *Materialien zur Baugeschichte – Die Architektur des Mittelalters*, Vieweg Verlag. Braunschweig, Wiesbaden, 1990, MA 161.

305.152: Association of Swiss Cement, Lime & Gypsum Producers (ed.): *Bauen in Beton*, 1990/91. Zurich, 1991, p. 30. Photo: Atelier Kinold.

305.153: Prof. Deplazes. Graphic: Alois Diethelm.

306.154: Source unknown

306.155: Prof. Deplazes. Graphic: Alois Diethelm.

306.156: Centre Georges Pompidou (ed.): *Louis I. Kahn – Le Monde de l'architecte*, Editions du Centre Georges Pompidou. Paris, 1992, p. 245, © Kathleen James.

306.157: Willy Boesiger (ed.): *Le Corbusier – Oeuvre Complète*, 1952–1957, Birkhäuser Publishers. Basel, 1991, p. 213. Fig.: © FLC / 2013, ProLitteris, Zurich.

306.158: Prof. Deplazes. Graphic: Alois Diethelm.

307.159: Architettura Viva: *Pier Luigi Nervi, una scienza per l'architettura*, Istituto Mides. Rome, 1982, Project 13.

307.160: Prof. Deplazes. Graphic: Alois Diethelm.

307.161–163: Erwin Heinle, Jörg Schleich: *Kuppeln aller Zeiten – aller Kulturen*, Deutsche Verlags-Anstalt. Stuttgart, 1996, p. 224, 181 and 226.

308.164–165: *Archithese*, No. 5, Niggli Verlag. Sulgen, 1996, p. 6.

309.166: Jakob Hunziker: *Das Schweizerhaus*, vol. 2: "Das Tessin, Aarau", Verlag Sauerländer & Co.. Aarau, 1902, p. 25.

309.167: Photo: Christian Kerez.

310.168: Ateliers Jean Nouvel, Paris. Illustration: Vincent Lafont.

310.169: Paul Virilio: *Bunker-Archäologie*, Carl Hanser Verlag. Munich, 1992, p. 178.

310.170: Katharina Bürgin: *Objekte, 1992–1994*, Museum zu Allerheiligen. Schaffhausen, 1995, exhibition. Photo: Rolf Wessendorf.

311.171: Prof. Deplazes. Photo: L. Felder, M. Hauser, N. Di Iorio, M. Pausa.

311.172: Internet: Source unknown

311.173: Prof. Deplazes. Photo: L. Felder, M. Hauser, N. Di Iorio, M. Pausa.

311.174–175: Prof. Deplazes. Photo: Urs Meister.

312.176–314.188: Prof. Deplazes. Graphic/Photo: L. Felder, M. Hauser, N. Di Iorio, M. Pausa.

315.189: Anne and Keith McLachlan: *Tunisia Handbook*. Bath, Baufachverlag. Gütersloh, 1997. Graphic: Bath: Footprint Handbooks, 1997. Fig.: Bath: Footprint Handbooks.

316.190: Prof. Deplazes. Photo: Nik Biedermann.

316.191: Source unknown

316.192: David MacGibbon, Thomas Ross: *The castellated and domestic architecture of Scotland: from the twelfth to the eighteenth Century*, Davin Douglas Press. Edinburgh, 1887, Volume 1, p. 344.

316.193: Joachim Zeune: *Der schottische Burgenbau vom 15. bis 17. Jahrhundert*, Deutsches Burgeninstitut. Marksburg über Braubach, 1989, fig. 116. Graphic: C. J. Tabraham.

317.194: Sigrid Barten: *Eduardo Chillida. Skulpturen aus Ton*, Museum Bellerive, exhibition catalogue. Zurich, 1996, p. 66. Photo: Marlen Perez, © 2013, ProLitteris, Zurich.

317.195: Rolf Toman (ed.): *Die Kunst des Barock: Architektur, Skulptur, Malerei*, Könemann Verlagsgesellschaft. Cologne, 1997, p. 23.

317.196: Richard Fawcett: *Scottish Architecture from the Accession of the Stewarts to the Reformation 1371–1560*, Edinburgh University Press. Edinburgh, 1994, p. 240. Graphic: Richard Fawcett.

317.197: Rolf Gerber: *Louis I. Kahn's Interesse an schottischen Burgen*, E. Degen Foundation/Rolf Gerber. Swiss Federal Institute of Technology, Zurich, 2000, p. 51. Photo: Rolf Gerber.

318.198–201: Loco citato, p. 240. Graphic: Richard Fawcett.

318.202: Hermann Muthesius: *Das Englische Haus, Entwicklung, Bedingungen, Anlage, Aufbau, Einrichtung und Innenraum*, Ernst Wasmuth. Berlin, 1908, p. 78.

319.203: Rolf Gerber: *Louis I. Kahn's Interesse an schottischen Burgen*, E. Degen Foundation/Rolf Gerber. Swiss Federal Institute of Technology, Zurich, 2000. p. 64–66. Original: Royal Commission on the Ancient and Historical Monuments of Scotland, archives.

319.204–206: Prof. Deplazes. Graphic: Nik Biedermann.

320.207: David MacGibbon, Thomas Ross: *The castellated and domestic architecture of Scotland: from the twelfth to the eighteenth century*, Davin Douglas Press. Edinburgh, 1887, Volume 2, p. 116.

320.208: Loco citato, Volume 1, p. 189.

320.209: Prof. Deplazes. Fig.: © 2013, ProLitteris, Zurich.

320.210 top: Heinrich Kulka (ed.): *Adolf Loos – Das Werk des Architekten*, Verlag Anton Schroll & Co.. Vienna, 1931, fig. 229. © 2013, ProLitteris, Zurich.

320.210 bottom: Loco citato, fig. 225. © 2013, ProLitteris, Zurich.

321.211 top: Joseph Rykwert: *Louis I. Kahn*, H. N. Abrams. New York, 2001, p. 118, 119. Photo: Roberto Schezen.

321.211 centre: David Bruce Brownlee, Grant Mudford, David. G. De Long: *Louis I. Kahn – In the Realm of Architecture*, The Museum of Contemporary Art. Los Angeles, 1991, p. 260. Photo Grant Mudford.

321.211 bottom: Joseph Rykwert: *Louis I. Kahn*, H. N. Abrams. New York, 2001, p. 116.

321.212: Loco citato, p. 121.

322.213–216: Hannes Rössler (ed.): *Minihäuser in Japan*, Verlag Anton Pustet. Salzburg, 2000. Figs: Kei Sugino.

323.217–220: Prof. Deplazes. Figs: Catherine Gay.

326.221: Botond Bognar: *World Cities Tokyo*, Academy Editions. Tottenham, 1996, p. 91. Graphic: Kisho Kurokawa.

326.222–223: Dominique Deshoulières: *Rob Mallet-*

Stevens – Architecte, Archives d'Architecture Moderne. Brussels, 1980, p. 267, 268.

326.224: Kisho Kurokawa: *Kisho Kurokawa*, CEP Edition. Paris, 1982, p. 21. Photo: Kisho Kurokawa.

327.225: Atelier 5, Bern.

327.226: Henri Stierlin: *Islam – Frühe Bauwerke von Bagdad bis Córdoba*, Taschen Verlag. Cologne, 1996, p. 152. Photo: Berengo Gardin.

327.227: Atelier 5, Bern. Photo: Leonardo Bezzola.

327.228: Henri Stierlin: *Islam – Frühe Bauwerke von Bagdad bis Córdoba*, Taschen Verlag. Cologne, 1996, p. 155.

328.229: Esther McCoy, Peter J. Blake: *Craig Ellwood*, Hennessey & Ingalls. Santa Monica, 1997, p. 35.

328.230: Patrik Gmür: *Artaria & Schmidt – Wohnhaus Schaeffer Riehen/Basel*, 1927/28, gta Verlag. Zurich, 1993, p. 16.

328.231: Hans Wichmann: *System-Design Fritz Haller*, Birkhäuser Publishers. Basel, 1989, p. 49.

328.232: Patrik Gmür: *Artaria & Schmidt – Wohnhaus Schaeffer Riehen/Basel*, 1927/28, gta Verlag. Zurich, 1993, p. 20.

329.233: Colin Rowe: *The Mathematics of the Ideal Villa*, Cambridge, Mass., 1982, p. 25. Fig.: © FLC / 2013, ProLitteris, Zurich.

329.234: Laura Miotto, Savina Nicolino: *Lina Bo Bardi, aprirsi all'accadimento*, Testo & Immagine. Torino, 1998, p. 7.

329.235: Werner Blaser: *Mies van der Rohe – Die Kunst der Struktur*, Artemis Verlag. Zurich, 1965, p. 155. Fig.: © 2013, ProLitteris, Zurich.

330.236: Hans Wichmann: *System-Design Fritz Haller*, Birkhäuser Publishers. Basel, 1989, p. 96, 97. Photo: Therese Beyeler.

330.237: Loco citato, p. 70.

330.238: Source unknown

330.239: Source unknown

331.240–241: Prof. Deplazes. Graphic: Alois Diethelm.

331.242: Franz Carl Weber AG, Spreitenbach.

332.243: *Arch+*, No. 100/101, archplus Verlag. Aachen, 1989, p. 56.

332.244: *Detail*, No. 4, Munich, 2001, p. 660.

333.245 left: *Detail*, No. 4, Munich, 2001, p. 665, 667.

333.245 right: *Detail*, No. 4, Munich, 2001, p. 667.

333.246 top: Kathryn Smith: *Schindler House*. Harry N. Abrams. New York, 2001, p. 31.

333.246 bottom: Source unknown

333.247: A. Schwabe: "Der heutige Stand des Raumzellenbaues", in: *Der Architekt*, Bonn, 1968, fig. 14. Photo: Werkfoto Bayer.

334.248: Prof. Deplazes. Graphic: Alois Diethelm.

334.249: James Stirling: *James Stirling – Buildings and Projects, 1950–1974*, New York, 1975, p. 147. Photo: Brecht-Einzig, London.

334.250: Blake Gopnick, Michael Sorkin: *Moshe Safdie – Habitat '67*, Montreal, Testo & Immagine. Torino, 1998, p. 82.

334.251: Loco citato, p. 10, 11.

334.252: James Stirling: *James Stirling – Buildings and Projects, 1950–1974*, New York, 1975, p. 154.

334.253: Blake Gopnick, Michael Sorkin: *Moshe Safdie – Habitat '67*, Montreal, Testo & Immagine. Torino, 1998, p. 76.

Building performance, energy

335.1: Hans Kollhoff: *Hans Kollhoff – Architektur*, Prestel Verlag. Munich, 2002, p. 41. Photo: Ivan Nemec.

335.2: Source unknown

335.3: Gert Chesi: *Architektur und Mythos – Lehmbauten in Afrika*, Haymon-Verlag. Innsbruck, 1995, p. 14. Photo: Gert Chesi.

335.4: Loco citato, photo: Gert Chesi.

336.5: Source unknown

336.6: Karl Fritz Stöhr: *Die amerikanischen Turmbauten, die Gründe ihrer Entstehung, ihre Finanzierung, Konstruktion und Rentabilität*, Verlag R. Oldenbourg. Munich, Berlin, 1921, fig. 17. Photo: Karl Fritz Stöhr.

336.7: Source unknown

337.8: Richard Fawcett: *Scottish Achitecture from the Accession of the Stewarts to the Reformation 1371–1560*, Edinburgh University Press. Edinburgh, 1994, p. 240.

337.9: Source unknown, revised by Prof. Deplazes. Fig.: © FLC / 2013, ProLitteris, Zurich.

338.10: Bearth + Deplazes. Photo: Ralph Feiner.

338.11: Bearth + Deplazes. Photo: Ralph Feiner.

338.12: Prof. Deplazes.

340.13–315.14: Prof. Deplazes. Graphic: Thomas Wirz.

341.15–16: Prof. Deplazes.

342.17: Prof. Deplazes. Graphic: Thomas Wirz.

342.18–19: Prof. Deplazes.

344.20–21: Bearth + Deplazes. Photo: Ralph Feiner.

345.22–23: Bearth + Deplazes.

BUILDINGS

Selected projects

349.1: Burkard Meyer Architekten, Baden. Photo: Reinhard Zimmermann.

349.2–350.6: Burkard Meyer Architekten, Baden.

351.7–8: Burkard Meyer Architekten, Baden. Photos: Reinhard Zimmermann. In fig. 351.7: Le Corbusier: Fauteuil Grand Confort LC2, © FLC / 2013, ProLitteris, Zurich.

351.9–10: Burkard Meyer Architekten, Baden.

352.11: Burkard Meyer Architekten, Baden. Photo: Reinhard Zimmermann.

352.12–13: Burkard Meyer Architekten, Baden.

353.14–15: Prof. Deplazes. Photos: Alois Diethelm.

354.16–355.20: Prof. Deplazes. Photo/Graphic: Alois Diethelm.

355.21: Burkard Meyer Architekten, Baden. Photo: Reinhard Zimmermann.

356. 22–357.26: Prof. Deplazes. Graphic: Alois Diethelm.

357.27–28: Burkard Meyer Architekten, Baden. Photos: Reinhard Zimmermann.

358.29–30: Prof. Deplazes. Graphic: Alois Diethelm.

359.1: Photo: Ralph Feiner.

359.2: *Detail*, No. 1/2, Munich, 2002, p. 63. Photo: Ralph Feiner.

359.3: Prof. Deplazes.

359.4: Photo: Ralph Feiner.

360.5–361.7: Prof. Deplazes.

361.8: Bearth + Deplazes.

362.9–10: Prof. Deplazes.

363.11: Photo: Ralph Feiner.

363.12: Prof. Deplazes.

364.13: Photo: Ralph Feiner.

364.14: Prof. Deplazes.

364.15: *Detail*, No. 1/2, Munich, 2002, p. 67. Photo: Ralph Feiner.

364.16: Prof. Deplazes.

365.17: Photo: Ralph Feiner.

365.18: Prof. Deplazes.

365.19: Photo: Ralph Feiner.
366.20–21: Photos: Bearth + Deplazes.
366.22: Prof. Deplazes.
367.23: Photo: Ralph Feiner.
367.24: Prof. Deplazes.
367.25: Gustav Fusch: *Über Hypokausten – Heizungen und mittelalterliche Heizungsanlagen*, Pfriemer Bauverlag. Wiesbaden, 1986, p. 13. Reprint of 1st edition, Jänecke Verlag, Hannover, 1910.
367.26: Loco citato, p. 21.
368.1–3: Peter Märkli, Zurich.
369.4–6: Prof. Deplazes.
370.7–10: Peter Märkli, Zurich.
371.11: Peter Märkli, Zurich. Revised by Prof. Deplazes.
371.12: Prof. Deplazes.
372.13–373.15: Peter Märkli, Zurich. Revised by Prof. Deplazes.
373.16: Peter Märkli, Zurich.
373.17–374.19: Peter Märkli, Zurich. Revised by Prof. Deplazes.
375.20–376.24: Prof. Deplazes.
376.25: Peter Märkli, Zurich. Revised by Prof. Deplazes.
376.26–377.29: Prof. Deplazes.
377.30: Peter Märkli, Zurich. Revised by Prof. Deplazes.
377.31–32: Prof. Deplazes.
378.1: Alberto Dell'Antonio: *Paspels, Valerio Olgiati*, Edition Dino Simonett. Zurich, 1998, p. 45. Photos: Heinrich Helfenstein, Valerio Olgiati, Mira Blau Architekten.
378.2: *Archithese*, No. 2, Niggli Verlag. Sulgen, 1997, p. 36. Graphic: Valerio Olgiatti.
379.3: *Archithese*, No. 3, Niggli Verlag. Sulgen, 1998, p. 66.
379.4: Valerio Olgiati, Zurich.
379.5: *Archithese*, No. 2, Niggli Verlag. Sulgen, 1997, p. 37.
379.6–7: *Archithese*, No. 3, Niggli Verlag. Sulgen, 1998, p. 66, 67.
379.8–11: Valerio Olgiati, Zurich. Revised by Prof. Deplazes.
380.12–14: Gebhard Decasper, Ingenieur, Chur. Photos: Dickelmann.
381.15: Alberto Dell'Antonio: *Paspels, Valerio Olgiati*, Edition Dino Simonett. Zurich, 1998, p. 22, 23. Photos: Heinrich Helfenstein, Valerio Olgiati, Mira Blau Architekten.
381.16: Valerio Olgiati, Zurich.
381.17: Valerio Olgiati, Zurich. Revised by Prof. Deplazes.
382.18–19: Valerio Olgiati, Zurich.
382.20–366.23: Valerio Olgiati, Zurich. Revised by Prof. Deplazes.
384.24: Valerio Olgiati, Zurich.
385.25: Valerio Olgiati, Zurich. Revised by Prof. Deplazes.
385.26–27: Valerio Olgiati, Zurich.
386.28: Valerio Olgiati, Zurich. Revised by Prof. Deplazes.
386.29–30: Valerio Olgiati, Zurich.
387.1: *Archithese*, No. 1, Niggli Verlag. Sulgen, 2001, p. 50.
387.2: Loco citato, p. 53.
388.3: Loco citato, p. 52.
388.4: Loco citato, p. 51.
389.5–8: Loco citato, p. 53.
390.9–374.15: Miller & Maranta, Basel. Revised by Prof. Deplazes.
393.16–395.23: *Werk, Bauen + Wohnen*, No. 9, Zurich, 1997.
396.1: Giuliani Hönger, Zurich. Photo: Walter Mair.
396.2: Giuliani Hönger, Zurich.

397.3–401.17: Giuliani Hönger, Zurich. Photos: Walter Mair.
402/403.18: Giuliani Hönger, Zurich.
404.19: Giuliani Hönger, Zurich.
404.20: Giuliani Hönger, Zurich. Photo: Walter Mair.
405.21–406.22: Giuliani Hönger, Zurich.
407.1: Walter Mair.
407.2: Durisch + Nolli Architekten.
408.3–6: Durisch + Nolli Architekten.
409.7–10: Durisch + Nolli Architekten.
410.11: Tonatiuh Ambrosetti.
410.12: Durisch + Nolli Architekten.
411.13: Durisch + Nolli Architekten.
412.14: Durisch + Nolli Architekten.
412.15: Montana Bausysteme AG.
413.16–17: Tonatiuh Ambrosetti.
414.1–2: Tonatiuh Ambrosetti.
415.3–5: ETH Studio Monte Rosa.
415.6–7: ETH Studio Monte Rosa.
416.8–9: Tonatiuh Ambrosetti.
417.10–419.15: ETH Studio Monte Rosa.
420.16–421.20: ETH Studio Monte Rosa.
421.21–22: Tonatiuh Ambrosetti.
422.23: Tonatiuh Ambrosetti.
422.24–25: ETH Studio Monte Rosa.
423.26: Tonatiuh Ambrosetti.
423.27–28: ETH Studio Monte Rosa.
424.29: ETH Studio Monte Rosa.
424.30: Tonatiuh Ambrosetti.
425.31–33: Lauber IWISA AG.
426.1: Photo: Roger Frei, Zurich.
426.2: Burkard Meyer Architekten, Baden.
426.3: Photo: © ABB Switzerland Historical Archives.
427.4: Photo: Roger Frei, Zurich.
427.5: Photo: Burkard Meyer Architekten, Baden.
427.6–7: Photo: Roger Frei, Zurich.
428.8–405.12: Burkard Meyer Architekten, Baden.
429.13: Photo: Roger Frei, Zurich.
430.14–20: Burkard Meyer Architekten, Baden.
431.21–22: Photo: Thomas Schwendener, Prof. Deplazes.
431.23: Photo: Roger Frei, Zurich.
431.24: Burkard Meyer Architekten, Baden.
432.25–26: Mebatech AG, Baden.
432.27: Photo: Roger Frei, Zurich.
432.28: Mebatech AG, Baden.
432.29–30: Photo: Roger Frei, Zurich.
433.31: Burkard Meyer Architekten, Baden.
434.1: Photo: Ralph Feiner.
434.2: Prof. Deplazes.
435.3–4: Prof. Deplazes.
436.5–6: Photo: Ralph Feiner.
436.7: Prof. Deplazes.
437.8: Photo: Ralph Feiner.
437.9–10.276: Prof. Deplazes.
438.11: Photo: Ralph Feiner.
439.12: Prof. Deplazes.
440.13: Photo: Ralph Feiner.
440.14–15: *Detail*, No. 3, Munich, 2000, p. 384.
441.16: Photo: Ralph Feiner.
441.17: Prof. Deplazes.
441.18: Photo: Ralph Feiner.
442.19: *Glas und Praxis*, Glas Troesch AG Bützberg, 2000.
442.20: Prof. Deplazes.
443.1–2: Meili & Peter, Zurich. Photos: Georg Aerni.
443.3: Meili & Peter, Zurich. Revised by Prof. Deplazes.

444.4–421.10: Meili & Peter, Zurich. Revised by
  Prof. Deplazes.
446.11–12: Meili & Peter, Zurich.
446.13: Jürg Conzett, Chur.
447.14–15: Meili & Peter, Zurich. Photo: Georg Aerni.
447.16: Meili & Peter, Zurich. Revised by Prof. Deplazes.
448.17: Meili & Peter, Zurich. Revised by Prof. Deplazes.
448.18: Meili & Peter, Zurich.
448.19: Photo: Heinrich Helfenstein.
449.20: Photo: Georg Aerni.
450.21–428.27: Meili & Peter, Zurich.
453.28: Meili & Peter, Zurich.
  Photo: Andreas Schmidt.
453.29: Photo: Georg Aerni.
453.30: Meili & Peter, Zurich.
454.1: Photo: Ralph Feiner.
454.2: Prof. Deplazes.
455.3: Photo: Ralph Feiner.
455.4–9: Bearth + Deplazes.
456.10–11: Bearth + Deplazes.
  Graphic: Winterthur Holzbau.
456.12–14: Bearth + Deplazes.
457.15–16: Deplazes, Chair of Architecture.
457.17: Bearth + Deplazes. Photo: Ralph Feiner.
458.18–21: Photo: Ralph Feiner.
459.1–2: Christian Kerez, Zurich.
460.3: Felix Ackerknecht.
460.4–438.13: Christian Kerez, Zurich.
463.14–15: Dr. Ing. Mario Monotti (Büro dsp Ingenieure &
  Planer AG, Greifensee).
463.16: Photo: Walter Mair.
463.17–442.24 Christian Kerez, Zurich.
467.25: Photo: Fredy Küng / BGS Architekten.
467.26: Felix Ackerknecht.
467.27: Photo: Christian Kerez, Zurich.
468.28 top left: Photo: Marc Lendorff, huberlendorff Foto-
  grafie.
468.28 centre left: Photo: Dominique Marc Wehrli.
468.28 bottom left: Photo: Fredy Küng / BGS Architekten.
468.29 top right: Photo: Christian Kerez, Zurich.
468.29 centre right: Photo: Dominique Marc Wehrli.
468.29 bottom right: Photo: Dr. Schwartz Consulting AG, Zug.
469.1: Walter Mair.
469.2: Peter Märkli Architekten.
470.3: Walter Mair.
470.4: Peter Märkli Architekten.
470.5: Walter Mair.
471.6–473.13: Peter Märkli Architekten.
474.14: Peter Märkli Architekten.
474.15–16: Feroplan Engineering AG.
475.17–476.18: Peter Märkli Architekten.

CATALOGUE OF COMPONENTS

Unnumbered figures: Prof. Deplazes.

Drawings
479–484: All figures: Prof. Deplazes.

Foundation – Plinth
497.1: Bearth + Deplazes.
497.2: Photo: Ralph Feiner.

Wall – Floor
505.1: Prof. Deplazes. Graphic: Maud Châtelet.

Opening
530.1: Internet: www.sky-frame.ch. Photo: Peter Kunz.

Floor
533.1: Bricosol AG, Zurich.
534.2: Poropor. Hagapart AG, Zug. Catalogue.
535.3: Prof. Deplazes. Photo: Thomas Melliger.
536.4: Photo: Ralph Feiner.
537.5: Louis I. Kahn Collection.
538.6: Elementwerk Brun AG, Emmen.
539.7: Montana Bausysteme AG, Villmergen.
540.8: Lignatur AG, Waldstatt.
541.9: Valerio Olgiati, Zurich.
541.10: Werner Oechslin (ed.): *Daniele Marques*,
  gta Verlag. Zurich, 2003, p. 57.
542.11: Lignatur AG, Waldstatt.
543.12: Source unknown

Roof – Parapet
544.1: Photo: Ralph Feiner.
545.2: *Archithese*, No. 3, "Niederlande heute",
  Niggli Verlag. Sulgen, 1997, p. 65.
546.3: Johann Christoph Bürkle (ed.):
  Gigon Guyer Architekten – Arbeiten, 1989–2000,
  Niggli Verlag. Sulgen, Zurich, 2000, p. 73.
547.4: Morger & Degelo, Basel.
548.5: Photo: Heinrich Helfenstein.
549.6: Morger & Degelo, Basel. Photo: Ruedi Walti.
550.7: Diener & Diener, Basel. Photo: Hans Ruedi Disch.
551.8: Photo: Ruedi Walti.
552.9: Oliver Schwarz, Zurich.
553.10: Johann Christoph Bürkle: *Morger & Degelo
  Architekten*, Niggli Verlag. Sulgen, 2000, p. 19.
  Photo: Ruedi Walti.
554.11: Photo: Ralph Feiner.
556.12: Johann Christoph Bürkle (ed.):
  Gigon Guyer Architekten – Arbeiten, 1989–2000,
  Niggli Verlag. Sulgen, Zurich, 2000, p. 26/27.
558.13: *Detail*, No. 7/8, Munich, 2002, p. 931.

Index

With kind support of:

Schindler Aufzüge AG
Zugerstrasse 13
CH-6030 Ebikon
www.schindler.ch

Glas Trösch Holding AG
Industriestrasse 29
CH-4922 Bützberg
www.glastroesch.ch